Douglas Melendez

Special Edition

USING
Netscape 2

1-2-3: DOWNLOAD NETSCAPE SOFTWARE

First, tell us which operating system you use.

Windows 3.1

Windows 95 or NT

Mac OS

Unix

To purchase the latest fully supported version, you can go to the Netscape General Store.

Welcome to Netscape Personal Edition. Click the OK button to set up your Internet account.

Create Link

Anchor object

Selelected text will be used for a new link:

Netscape.

OK

Cancel

Unlink

Link to

Type URL address, or select from: Local Files...

http://www.netscape.com/

que®

PLUG YOURSELF INTO...

THE MACMILLAN INFORMATION SUPERLIBRARY™

Free information and vast computer resources from the world's leading computer book publisher—online!

FIND THE BOOKS THAT ARE RIGHT FOR YOU!

A complete online catalog, plus sample chapters and tables of contents give you an in-depth look at *all* of our books, including hard-to-find titles. It's the best way to find the books you need!

- ● STAY INFORMED with the latest computer industry news through our online newsletter, press releases, and customized Information SuperLibrary Reports.

- ● GET FAST ANSWERS to your questions about MCP books and software.

- ● VISIT our online bookstore for the latest information and editions!

- ● COMMUNICATE with our expert authors through e-mail and conferences.

- ● DOWNLOAD SOFTWARE from the immense MCP library:
    - Source code and files from MCP books
    - The best shareware, freeware, and demos

- ● DISCOVER HOT SPOTS on other parts of the Internet.

- ● WIN BOOKS in ongoing contests and giveaways!

TO PLUG INTO MCP: ➡

GOPHER: gopher.mcp.com

FTP: ftp.mcp.com

WORLD WIDE WEB: **http://www.mcp.com**

Special Edition
USING
Netscape 2

Mark Brown

with

Steven Forrest Burnett	*Margaret J. Larson*
Tim Evans	*Bill Nadeau*
Heather Fleming	*Paul Robichaux*
Galen Grimes	*Oran J. Sands III*
Raymond C. Gronberg	*Andrew Bryce Shafran*
David Gunter	*Todd Stauffer*
Derek H. Hamner	*Ian Stokell*
Jerry Hunnicutt	*Michael Thomas*
John Jung	*Sarah G.E. Tourville*
William Kirkner	*Paul Wallace*
Greg Knauss	*John Williams*

que®

Special Edition Using Netscape 2

Copyright© 1995 by Que® Corporation.

Library of Congress Catalog No.: 95-71751

ISBN: 0-7897-0612-1

96   6 5 4 3 2

Interpretation of the printing code: the rightmost double-digit number is the year of the book's printing; the rightmost single-digit number, the number of the book's printing. For example, a printing code of 96-1 shows that the first printing of the book occurred in 1996.

Screen reproductions in this book were created using Collage Plus from Inner Media, Inc., Hollis, NH.

Composed in *Stone Serif* and *MCP Digital* by Que Corporation.

Credits

For my parents, Robert and Margaret Brown, who brought me up right.

About the Author

Mark R. Brown has been writing computer magazine articles, books, and manuals for over 13 years. He was Managing Editor of *.info* magazine when it was named one of the six Best Computer Magazines of 1991 by the Computer Press Association, and was nominated by the Software Publisher's Association for the 1988 Software Reviewer of the Year award. He is currently the Manager of Technical Publications for Neural Applications Corporation, a major player in applying cutting-edge artificial intelligence techniques to industrial control applications, such as steel making and food processing. A bona fide personal computing pioneer, he hand-built his first PC in 1977, taught himself to program it in hexadecimal, and has since dabbled in dozens of different programming languages. He has been telecomputing since 1983, and is currently Webmaster of two World Wide Web sites: **http://www.neural.com**, and a personal Web site on the topic of airships, which will have moved to a new URL by the time this is published.

Mark is a life-long resident of Iowa, and offers of magazine editing jobs in California and New York City have not appealed to him in the least. He enjoys reading and writing, gaming, Iowa Hawkeye Big 10 football, walks in the park with his dog Bosco, and day trips through the Iowa countryside with his wife, Carol. (Chapters 11, 16, 17, 18, 22)

Steven Forrest Burnett is a technical writer, editor, and teacher of artificial linguistics, with a Master of Science in Technical Communication from North Carolina State University. Having dealt with Internet issues for several years, Steve also contributed to the book *Programming Client/Server Applications with RPC and DCE*. (Chapters 4, 12, 16, 20)

Tim Evans is a UNIX system administration and network security consultant. Employed by Taratec Development Corporation, his full-time contract assignment for the past three years has been at the DuPont Company's Experimental Station in Wilmington, Delaware. Tim pioneered development of DuPont's own World Wide Web, known as DuPont-Wide Web, widely used within the company for information sharing via its world-wide network. Previously, Tim worked for the U.S. Social Security Administration in various staff jobs for more than 20 years. In 1991, before the Internet got hot, he brought that government agency onto the Internet. At both DuPont and SSA, he provided support for large numbers of UNIX users, running UNIX on a variety of computer systems ranging from PC's to workstations to mini-computers.

A native of Missouri, Tim is a former Carny (he had his own merry-go-round to operate at age 14), auto assembly line worker, janitor, and bartender. His degrees in History show a Liberal Arts education can qualify you for almost any job, depending on what you do afterward. Tim also is a produced play-wright with an extensive background in community theatre, both on- and off-stage. He lives with his wife and best friend, Carol, and their Irish Setter, Judy! Judy! Judy!, in Delaware, just three hours from their vacation home in Chincoteague, Virginia. He can be reached via Internet e-mail at **tkevans@dupont.com.** (Chapters 5 and 16)

Heather A. Fleming received her first lessons on a computer when she was given an Apple IIe for a Christmas present at the age of 12. Working her way to a Stephens College graduation with a BA in Mathematics and Computer Science, she landed a job working at a lumber mill in Oregon, where, besides pulling green chain, she studied machinery automation. The next year spent studying Human and Computer Interaction at the University of Nebraska—Lincoln, University of Missouri—Columbia, and Stephens College set her on a career path that has kept her in Mid-Missouri writing training manuals for Datastorm Technologies, Inc. ever since. (Chapters 3 and 6)

Galen Grimes lives in a quiet, heavily wooded section of Monroeville, Pennsylvania, a suburb of Pittsburgh, with his wife Joanne, and an assort-ment of deer, raccoons, squirrels, possums, and birds, which are all fed from their backdoor. Galen is also the author of several other Macmillan Computer Publishing books, including Sams' *First Book of DR DOS 6*, Que's *10 Minute Guide to NetWare* and *10 Minute Guide to Lotus Improv*, and Que's *Windows 3.1 HyperGuide*. Galen has a Masters degree in Information Science from the Uni-versity of Pittsburgh, and by trade, is a project manager and NetWare LAN administrator for a large international bank and financial institution. (Chap-ters 1, 10, and 23)

Ray Gronberg is a journalist in Chapel Hill, North Carolina, where he spe-cializes in government and public affairs reporting. He has an MA in journal-ism from the University of North Carolina and a BA in political science from the University of North Carolina at Charlotte. His practical experience with computers, as a hobbyist, dates from the late 1970s and early 1980s, when the gee-whiz operating system was CP/M and "mass storage" was a cassette deck. He uses Internet Web and e-mail services heavily in the course of his daily reporting. Ray can be reached via e-mail at **gronberg@nando.net.** (Chapters 13 and 14)

David Gunter is a consultant and computer author based in Cary, North Carolina. His areas of interest include UNIX systems management and network and systems programming. David holds a Masters degree in computer science from the University of Tennessee. During his free time, David enjoys traveling, reading, and spending as much time as possible with his wonderful wife. (Chapters 2 and 34)

Derek Hamner is a senior in Computer Science at the University of North Carolina at Chapel Hill. He is currently the Webmaster at UNC—General Administration, performing Web site development and maintenance. His duties also include designing Web-based applications for automating general office activities. In his spare time, Derek provides consulting services to commercial Web sites, and is working on several large networked applications in Java.

Derek can be contacted via e-mail at **hamner@sunsite.unc.edu**. See **http://sunsite.unc.edu/hamner/** for more information. (Chapter 33)

Jerry Honeycutt is a business oriented, technical manager with broad experience in software development. He has served companies such as The Travelers, IBM, Nielsen North America, and most recently Information Retrieval Methods as Director of Windows Application Development. Jerry has participated in the industry since before the days of Microsoft Windows 1.0, and believes that everyone must eventually learn to use the Internet to stay in touch with the world.

Jerry wrote *Using Microsoft Plus!* and was a contributing author on *Special Edition Using Windows 95* for Que. He has also been printed in *Computer Language Magazine* and is a regular speaker at the Windows World and Comdex trade shows on topics related to software development and corporate solutions for Windows 95.

Jerry graduated from the University of Texas at Dallas in 1992 with a BS degree in Computer Science. He currently lives in the Dallas suburb of Frisco, Texas, with Becky, two Westies, Corky and Turbo, and two cats, Scratches and Chew-Chew. Please feel free to contact Jerry on the Internet at **jerry@honeycutt.com**, on CompuServe at **76477,2751**, or on the Microsoft Network at **Honeycutt**. (Chapters 7 and 15)

John Jung is an alumni from the University of Southern California with a
degree in Computer Science. He became interested in computers over 16
years ago and has been on the Net for over eight years. He wastes his time
watching TV, surfing the Net, and playing video games. John can be reached
at **jjung@netcom.com**. (Chapters 28 and 31)

Bill Kirkner (70742,312) started using CompuServe while he was a student
at Loyola College in Maryland, almost 10 years ago. It was around the same
time that he first started using the Internet, and he's been a member of the
Internet community ever since. In 1992, Bill earned his J.D. from the
Georgetown University Law Center, and now leads a team of World Wide
Web site designers, Internet trainers, and consultants specializing in marketing through online systems at Walcoff & Associates, Inc. in Fairfax, Virginia.
Bill currently lives in the Dupont Circle neighborhood of Washington, D.C.,
and can be reached on the Internet at **bk@access.digex.net**. (Chapter 32)

Greg Knauss lives in Los Angeles with his wife, Joeanne, and works as a
UNIX and Windows programmer. He graduated from the University of California, San Diego with a degree in Political Science, but has been programming and writing about computers for over 15 years. He has previously
worked on *Using HTML* for Que. (Chapter 30)

Margaret Larson is a founding partner of Wintergreen Associates, located
in Western Massachusetts. She has worked as a computer programmer and
software designer for 15 years. Originally from Ohio, Peg (as she is commonly
called) got her BA in Economics from UMass/Amherst and spent 5 years in
graduate school focusing on computerized economic forecasting and simula-
tion models. Her work has involved software design, testing, documentation,
technical writing, statistics, and data analysis.

In late 1994, when the company for which she worked was sold and moved
to Boston, she and her husband, Bill Nadeau, reorganized their consulting
business and founded Wintergreen Associates. They specialize in design and
maintenance of commercial Web sites with a focus on forms/CGI programming, management and analysis of large databases, and market research. You
can find a link to Peg's resume at Wintergreen's Web site—**http://
www.wintergreen.com/**. (Chapter 11)

Paul Robichaux, who has been an Internet user since 1986 and a software developer since 1983, is currently a software consultant for Intergraph Corporation, where he writes Windows NT and Windows 95 applications. In his spare time, he writes books and Macintosh applications; he still manages to spend plenty of time with his wife and young son. He can be reached via e-mail at **perobich@ingr.com**. (Chapter 35)

Oran J. Sands III (better known as 3.0) is a freelance writer, television producer, and—more importantly to his creditors—works for Que as a Product Development Specialist. A former Amiga desktop video guru, he now uses any computer put in front of him exclusively. He finds the Web even more distracting than reading his e-mail, and gets little done because of it. Schooled as an electrical engineer at Purdue University, he enjoys writing HTML code and making computer graphics (which explains a lot). He has a loving wife, three kids, a cat, a mortgage, and not enough time to enjoy them all. (Appendix A)

Andrew Bryce Shafran is a full-time writer and computer consultant living in Columbus, Ohio. He is a student at The Ohio State University, and might actually graduate some year. He loves writing books and magazine articles, especially about CompuServe and the WWW. His other Que books include *Creating Your Own Netscape Home Page* and *The Complete Idiot's Guide to CompuServe*, just to name a few.

You can visit his home page at **http://www.cis.ohio-state.edu/ ~shafran**. (Chapters 25 and 26)

Todd Stauffer has been writing nonstop about computers and the computer industry since he graduated from Texas A&M University, where he studied a bizarre combination of English literature, Managment Information Systems, and entirely too much golf. A die-hard fan of the Macintosh, Todd is author of *Using Your Mac, Easy America Online,* and co-author of *Special Edition Using the Internet With Your Macintosh*—all Que publications.

Todd has recently finished a stint as editor of *Texas Computing Magazine* and is currently a freelance writer and author, having a heck of a time deciding whether to live in Dallas, Texas or Colorado Springs, Colorado. He has worked previously as an advertising, technical, and magazine writer—all in the computer industry. He can be reached by Internet e-mail at **TStauffer@aol.com**. (Chapters 8, 24, 29)

Michael D. Thomas, Mary Jo's boy, graduated from the University of North Carolina in December 1995 with a concentration in Computer Science. Since August 1994, he has worked extensively with the World Wide Web. While a student, he acted as UNIX System Administrator on a campus Web server. In addition to running Web servers, he also has done extensive writing of CGI programs and formatting of Web pages. In May 1995, he added Java to a repertoire of programming languages, which also includes Perl, C, and C++. Michael's home page, which includes current links to Java information, can be found at **http://sunsite.unc.edu/mdthomas/**. (Chapter 33)

Sarah G.E. Tourville is Founder, President, and CEO of SAGRELTO Enterprises, Inc., 5107 Inverness Drive, Durham, NC 27712-1813, **sagrelto@sagrelto.com**, Web Site: **http://www.sagrelto.com/ sagrelto/sget/home.htm & home.sgm**.

SAGRELTO Enterprises, Inc. is a company dedicated to solving the problems of infoglut and assisting users and providers of information for the highways. SAGRELTO, one of the first companies to focus on preparing information for SGML on the Web, provides consulting, training, information preparation, server management, and software development services related to SGML, HTML, Internet, and the World Wide Web. Ms. Tourville's worked with SGML since 1990. (Chapter 21)

Paul Wallace lives in Knoxville, Tennessee, where he is pursuing a Ph.D. in Instructional Technology at the University of Tennessee. He is an Internet consultant specializing in content development, interface design, and interactive programming for the World Wide Web. In his diminishing free time, Paul can be found relaxing with friends in one of Knoxville's coffee shops, visiting the animal shelter, swimming laps, or patiently awaiting the next Dinosaur Jr. album. Paul is an accomplished surfer who has traveled to many of the world's best point breaks and hopes to visit the coast of South Africa. Paul can best be reached via his homepage at **http://www.clever.net/ wallace**. (Chapters 27, 28, and 31)

Ian Stokell is a freelance writer and editor living in the Sierra Foothills of northern California with his wife and three young children. He is also Managing Editor of *Newsbytes News Network*, an international daily newswire covering the computer and telecommunications industries. His writing career began with a 1981 article published in the UK's New Statesman and has since encompassed over 1,500 articles in a variety of computing and non-computing publications. He wrote the Networking chapter of Que's *Using the Macintosh, Special Edition*, and has also written on assignment for such magazines as *PC World* and *MacWeek*. He is currently seeking representation for two completed novels and a screenplay. (Chapter 9)

Bill Nadeau is a founding partner of Wintergreen Associates, and develops Web sites with his wife and partner, Peg Larson. Bill is a designer, writer, and programmer, and has worked as a consultant and contractor on a variety of projects with over 15 years experience in the field. Peg and Bill co-authored the *FreeThink Users Guide* and developed tutorials in multi-dimensional data modelling for clients such as The World Bank while working at Power Thinking Tools before FreeThink was purchased by Praxis International in late 1994. Bill has a BS in regional planning & environmental design, and some graduate training in architecture, as well as some schooling in music and visual arts. His is currently enmeshed in developing multimedia/CGI applications. (Chapter 11)

John F. Williams began his work with multimedia and personal computers after purchasing Director's predecessor, VideoWorks. At about the same time, he created one of the first commercial programs demonstrated for HyperCard's release in 1987. John continued to work in the infant multimedia industry, founding the startup development company Midnight Design in 1989, speaking at universities and conferences on multimedia, and honing his skills while working with some of the best multimedia design firms in the business. Since then, he has gone on to help create dozens of commercial and private CD-ROMs, as well as over 30 interactive demo disks for various companies (most recently the Director 4.0 Guided Tour for Macromedia). Today John is working on a variety of next-generation CD-ROM "titles" that Apple Computer, and some as-yet-to-be-found companies, will publish for Midnight Design. (Chapter 36)

Acknowledgments

It takes a lot of hard work to put together a book of this size and scope in such a short time.

All the writers associated with this project put forth a tremendous effort and deserve all the laurels we can heap upon them. The editors and staff at Que books certainly earned their kudos as well; special thanks go to Cheryl Willoughby, Ruth Slates, Mark Cierzniak, and Benjamin Milstead for their invaluable assistance and infallible guidance. And I'd like to add a special "thank you" to Oran J. Sands at Que for bringing me into this project.

Of course, we wouldn't have a book at all if it weren't for the excellent product produced by the programmers, planners, and management of Netscape Corporation. And the authors and developers of all the Netscape support programs mentioned in this book deserve our thanks, as well.

Then there are "all those wonderful people out there in the dark" who make up the World Wide Web. Certainly, to the people at CERN in Switzerland who first conceived and implemented the Web, our thanks. But the Web is made up of the efforts of literally millions of people, many of whom selflessly contribute the thoughts, ideas, articles, stories, graphics, movies, sound clips, and all the other elements that make up the multinational, multilingual, multimedia stew that is the World Wide Web. To all of them, our thanks for making Web surfing such an entertaining, enlightening, and engaging activity!

Finally, I'd like to thank my friends and family for their patient understanding of all the hours I had to spend away from them while working on this book. A special thanks goes to my wife, Carol, who has supported me whole-heartedly in this and all my other writing projects, with more patience than anyone could ever ask for or expect from another human being.

Mark R. Brown

We'd Like to Hear from You!

As part of our continuing effort to produce books of the highest possible quality, Que would like to hear your comments. To stay competitive, we *really* want you, as a computer book reader and user, to let us know what you like or dislike most about this book or other Que products.

You can mail comments, ideas, or suggestions for improving future editions to the address below, or send us a fax at (317) 581-4663. For the online inclined, Macmillan Computer Publishing has a forum on CompuServe (type **GO QUEBOOKS** at any prompt) through which our staff and authors are available for questions and comments. The address of our Internet site is **http://www.mcp.com** (World Wide Web).

In addition to exploring our forum, please feel free to contact me personally to discuss your opinions of this book: I'm **76245,476** on CompuServe, and I'm **mcierzniak@que.mcp.com** on the Internet.

Thanks in advance—your comments will help us to continue publishing the best books available on computer topics in today's market.

Mark Cierzniak
Product Development Specialist
Que Corporation
201 W. 103rd Street
Indianapolis, Indiana 46290
USA

Contents at a Glance

Building Sites and Servers

Netscape Customization

Contents

6 Loading and Configuring Netscape Personal Edition   121

7 Moving Around the Web   145

8 Finding Information on the Web 167

11 Forms and Transaction Security   253

II Using Helper Applications   393

16 Configuring Helper Applications   395

22 Adobe Acrobat and Other Portable Document Formats   551

25 HTML Primer   **617**

V Building World-Class Web Sites and Servers for Netscape   775

31 Creating a World-Class Web Site for Netscape   777

VI Advanced Netscape Customization   843

36 Netscape Plug-Ins 933

Appendix 949

Introduction

Everywhere you turn you find people talking about the World Wide Web. Corporations now include Web addresses in their TV commercials. Television show and movie debuts are accompanied by the launch of promotional pages on the Web. Newspapers and magazines supplement their readership with an online presence. Celebrity fan clubs set up houses of worship on the Net. TV news shows blare excited warnings about kids accessing pornography on the Web.

In just a few short years, the World Wide Web has become a part of daily life. Every day, millions of people all over the world browse the Web for news, product information, entertainment, and even good, hard data. And the browser of choice for the majority of them is Netscape Navigator.

People have always liked Netscape for its solid reliability, generous allotment of features, and free preview offer. And now, with the release of version 2.0, Netscape is even more useful and powerful than before.

Of course, there's more to learn, too—like JavaScript, the new Netscape scripting language and plug-ins, which allow multimedia files to display right in the Netscape window without launching helper applications.

That's why we're here. *Special Edition Using Netscape 2* gently guides you through all the steps to get Netscape set up and working to its full potential on your machine.

Who Should Use This Book?

This book is intended for anyone and everyone who wants to get the most out of Netscape and the World Wide Web.

Novices will find information on how to obtain, install, and configure Netscape. Intermediate users will discover tips, tricks, and techniques to make Netscape even more fun and useful. And advanced users will learn the nuts and bolts of Netscape operation, including how to use powerful new Netscape 2.0 features like plug-ins and the JavaScript scripting language.

How This Book Is Organized

Special Edition Using Netscape 2 is organized into six logical sections.

Part I, "Internet Fundamentals," explains what the Internet and World Wide Web are, and what they are likely to become in the future. It explains how the Web is organized and how it works. This section also presents an overview of what's new in Netscape 2.0.

Part II, "Mastering Netscape," talks you through loading and configuring Netscape for Windows, Windows 95, Macintosh, and UNIX. Both Netscape 2.0 and Netscape Personal Edition are covered. This section also tells you how to navigate on the Web using links, online search engines and indexes, bookmarks, and Netscape's new SmartMarks program. You'll also find information on how to use online forms, including a discussion of security. The section wraps up with information on using Netscape to access Internet services other than the World Wide Web, like e-mail, FTP, Gopher, and UseNet news.

Part III, "Using Helper Applications," guides you through the process of finding and configuring Netscape helper applications for audio, graphics, and video. You'll also be introduced to VRML (Virtual Reality Modeling Language) and SGML (Standard Generalized Markup Language), learn how they fit into the Web, and how to view them using Netscape helper applications. Adobe Acrobat and other portable document formats are also covered, as are compressed files and how to deal with them.

Part IV, "Building World Class Home Pages for Netscape," gets you started with HTML (HyperText Markup Language), the language used to create Web pages. You'll learn how to create links and use advanced graphics techniques like imagemaps to make your Web pages dynamic. You'll even learn about Netscape-specific and proposed future HTML commands. Finally, you'll discover how to work with the Web's most advanced page development tools, forms, and CGI-BIN scripts.

Part V, "Building World Class Web Sites and Servers for Netscape," builds on the knowledge you gained in part IV, tying together Web page creation techniques to help you build an excellent Web site. Then you'll ride along on a test-drive of the Netscape Commerce server, the software for the "other end" of the Web that delivers Web pages to users.

Part VI, "Advanced Netscape Customization," delves into the depths of Netscape 2.0's most powerful new features, with chapters on Sun's Java language for C, C++, and JavaScript customization of Netscape. This section finishes with a discussion of plug-ins, Netscape 2.0's exciting new feature that allows inline viewing of multimedia.

An appendix finishes out the book with information on what you'll find on the book's CD-ROM.

The Book's CD-ROM

Inside the back cover of this book you'll find a CD-ROM containing multi-megabytes of helper applications, links, tips, and programs that will help you get the most out of Netscape.

Whenever we mention a program in this book that is included on the book's CD, you'll see the icon at the right. Keep an eye out for it.

On the CD

Conventions Used in This Book

This book uses various stylistic and typographic conventions to make it easier to use.

Keyboard shortcut key combinations are joined by + signs; for example, Ctrl+X means to hold down the Ctrl key, press the X key, then release both.

Menu items and dialog box selections often have a mnemonic key associated with them. This key is indicated by an underline on the item on screen. To use these mnemonic keys, you press the Alt key, then the shortcut key. In this book, mnemonic keys are underlined, like this: <u>F</u>ile.

This book uses the following typeface conventions:

Typeface	Meaning
Italic	Variables in commands or addresses, or terms used for the first time
Bold	Text you type in, as well as addresses of Internet sites, newsgroups, mailing lists, and Web sites
Computer type	Commands, HTML tags

Note

Notes provide additional information related to the topic at hand.

Tip

Tips provide quick and helpful information to assist you along the way.

Caution

Cautions alert you to potential pitfalls or dangers in the operations discussed.

Troubleshooting

Troubleshooting boxes address problems that you might encounter while following the procedures in this book.

▶ See "Using
Compressed/
Encoded Files,"
pg. 571

Special Edition Using Netscape 2 uses marginal references like this one to point you to other places in the book with additional information relevant to the topic. Right-pointing arrows guide you forward, left-pointing arrows guide you to previous chapters.

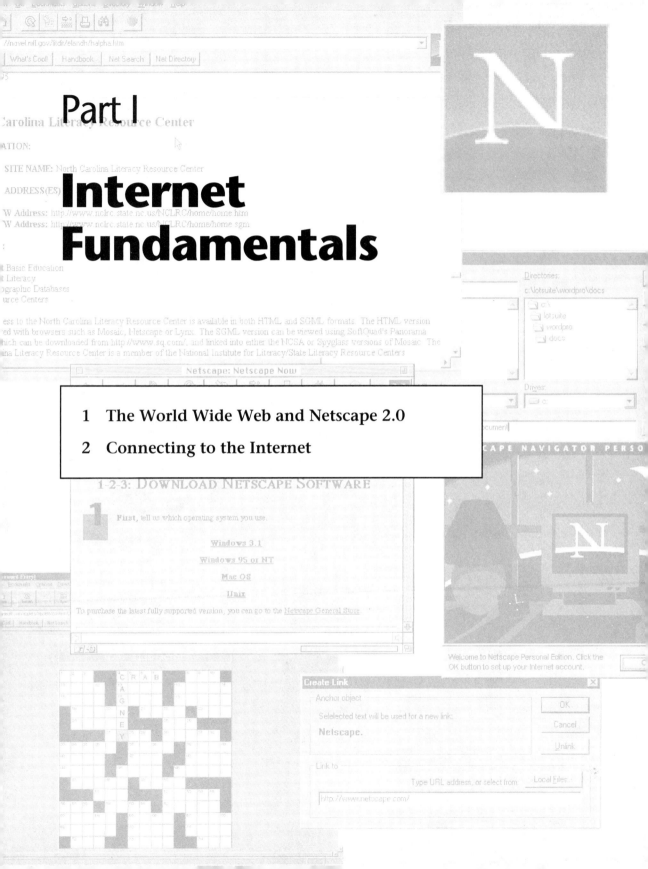

Part I

Internet Fundamentals

1 The World Wide Web and Netscape 2.0

2   Connecting to the Internet

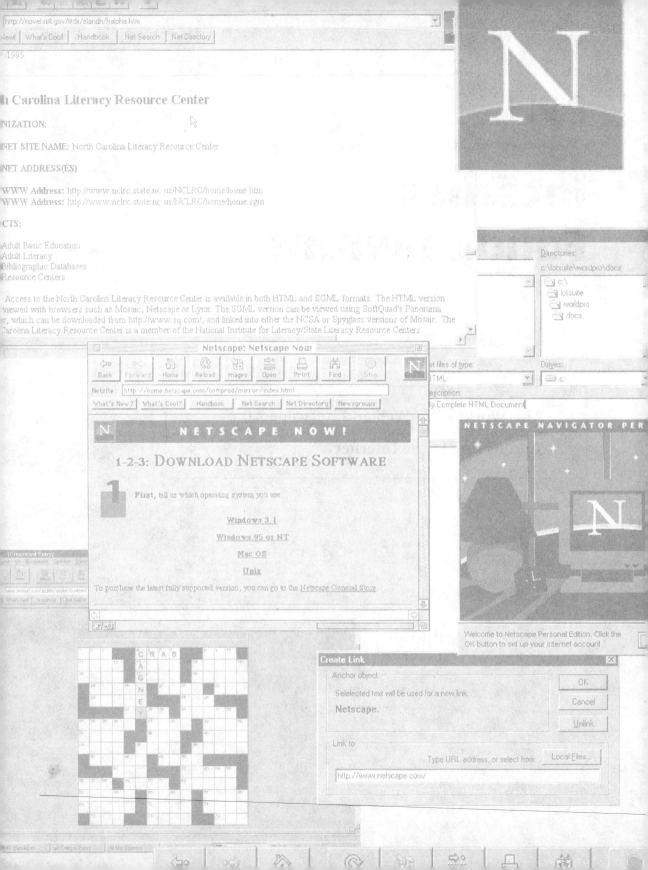

http://novel.nifl.gov/litdir/elandh/halpha.htm

Newt | What's Cool | Handbook | Net Search | Net Directory

-1995

h Carolina Literacy Resource Center

NIZATION:

NET SITE NAME: North Carolina Literacy Resource Center

NET ADDRESS(ES)

WWW Address: http://www.nclrc.state.nc.us/NCLRC/home/home.htm
WWW Address: http://www.nclrc.state.nc.us/NCLRC/home/home.sgm

CTS:

Adult Basic Education
Adult Literacy
Bibliographic Databases
Resource Centers

Access to the North Carolina Literacy Resource Center is available in both HTML and SGML formats. The HTML version
viewed with browsers such as Mosaic, Netscape or Lynx. The SGML version can be viewed using SoftQuad's Panorama
r, which can be downloaded from http://www.sq.com/, and linked into either the NCSA or Spyglass versions of Mosaic. The
Carolina Literacy Resource Center is a member of the National Institute for Literacy/State Literacy Resource Centers

Directories:
c:\lotsuite\wordpro\docs
c:\
lotsuite
wordpro
docs

Netscape: Netscape Now

Back | Forward | Home | Reload | Images | Open | Print | Find | Stop

Netsite: http://home.netscape.com/comprod/mirror/index.html

What's New? | What's Cool? | Handbook | Net Search | Net Directory | Newsgroups

st files of type:
TML

Drives:
c:

escription:
y Complete HTML Document

NETSCAPE NOW!

1-2-3: DOWNLOAD NETSCAPE SOFTWARE

1 First, tell us which operating system you use.

Windows 3.1

Windows 95 or NT

Mac OS

Unix

To purchase the latest fully supported version, you can go to the Netscape General Store.

NETSCAPE NAVIGATOR PER

Welcome to Netscape Personal Edition. Click the
OK button to set up your Internet account.

Crossword Entry

What's Cool | Handbook | Net Sea

C R A B
A
G
N
E
Y

Create Link

Anchor object

Selelected text will be used for a new link.

Netscape.

OK
Cancel
Unlink

Link to

Type URL address, or select from: Local Files...

http://www.netscape.com/

## CHAPTER 1

The World Wide Web and Netscape 2.0

The explosive proliferation of Internet usage and Web browsing have led many new users to freely exchange the terms *Internet* and *World Wide Web*, as if they are the same entity. Well, let's begin by setting the record straight—the Internet and the World Wide Web are not the same!

Internet is a collective term used to describe an interconnection of world-wide computer networks. Operating on the Internet are a variety of computer services such as e-mail, UseNet newsgroups, FTP, Telnet, Gopher, and the World Wide Web.

Even though the World Wide Web (most often referred to simply as the Web or WWW) has only been around since 1992 (the first Web server prototype was developed in 1990 at CERN, the European Laboratory for Particle Physics in Geneva, Switzerland), its growth on the Internet has been nothing short of phenomenal. In 1993, when the alpha version of Mosaic—the first graphic Web browser—was initially released, there were a total of 130 Web servers. By the end of 1995 it is estimated that there will be more than 13,000 Web servers worldwide, displaying more than 10 million Web pages!

The release of a version of Mosaic for Windows in late 1993 was one of the milestones that spurred Internet and Web activity. Netscape, a second generation Web browser, appeared on the scene not long after the PC version of Mosaic. Netscape forced open the door that Mosaic had been knocking on. Netscape's improved performance and added features helped create the near stampede to the Internet that has occurred in the last year or two.

Before diving into Netscape 2.0, to help give you an overall better idea of how we've gotten this far and what's going on behind the scenes, this chapter covers the history and operation of the Internet and the World Wide Web in addition to the following topics:

- Understanding the evolution, structure, and operation of the Internet
- What URLs are and how they are used to locate Internet resources
- How the World Wide Web works
- What future projects are being planned for the Web
- What's new in Netscape 2.0

Note

Throughout this chapter you will see references to certain publications such as RFC-1738 or RFC-1173. *RFCs* (Request For Comment) are informational documents that describe policies, procedures, and protocols on the Internet. If you're interested in reading the in-depth discussions that have taken place on various aspects of the Internet (from "soup-to-nuts" as the saying goes), this is your ticket. RFCs can be referenced from various locations on the Internet, but to save you the time of locating them, here's one reference point: **http://www.uwaterloo.ca/uw_infoserv/ rfc.html**.

Who Uses the World Wide Web

The World Wide Web is one of the most accessible places because it is accessible to virtually anyone worldwide who has access to a computer and a modem. For this reason, the Web has literally become "the kiosk for the entire planet." Because of the potential for getting a message to a very large and diverse audience, it's no wonder that there are now more than 10 million Web pages available for your viewing, all posted on the Web in just the last three years.

As I stated earlier, the initial release of Mosaic for Windows was one of the keys to the success of the Web because Mosaic on the "common" PC made the Web accessible to the masses of ordinary PC users.

So who are these masses of ordinary PC users who have posted those 10 million Web pages? The answer is literally anyone and everyone. Major corporations, small businesses, government agencies, politicians, social organizations, historical societies, and a burgeoning industry of would-be Web authors are among those who have Web pages they are trying to get you to view.

Many Web authors are simply trying to supply information over the Web, but more often you will see businesses either advertising their presence and products, advertising their services, or directly trying to sell you their wares.

When you look out on the Web, you will see Coca-Cola, IBM, CNN, the National Football League, the World History Archives, and the Virtual Quilt home page, just as an example of some of the diversity you'll find (see figs. 1.1, 1.2, 1.3, 1.4, 1.5, 1.6).

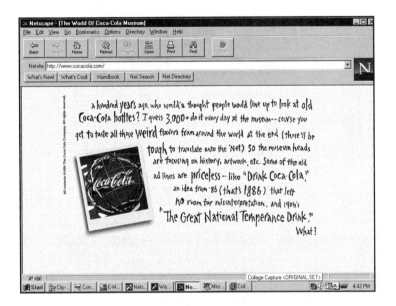

Fig. 1.1
The Coca-Cola home page.

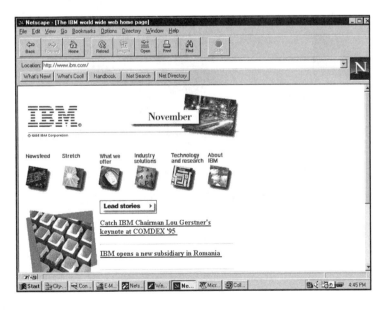

Fig. 1.2
The IBM home page.

Fig. 1.3
The CNN
Interactive home
page.

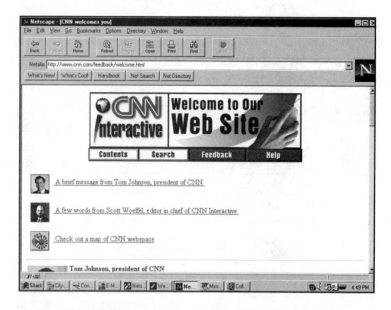

Fig. 1.4
The NFL home
page.

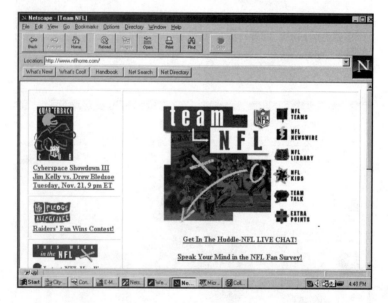

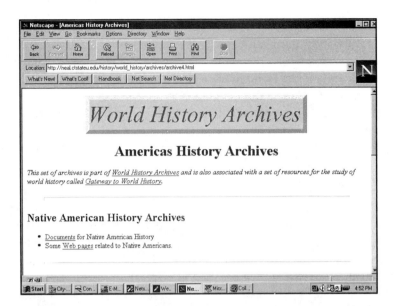

Fig. 1.5
The World History
Archives home
page.

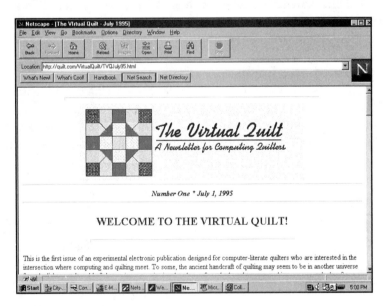

Fig. 1.6
The Virtual Quilt
home page.

Understanding the Evolution of the Internet

To understand how the Internet functions, you need to know something of
its history.

In the 1960s following the Cuban Missile Crisis, the RAND Corporation, America's foremost think tank, first proposed the idea of a decentralized computer network spanning this country. The proposal envisioned linking together military and academic computers in a network that could survive a nuclear attack. The key to this design was to decentralize the control and authority of this network, so that failure or destruction of one or more segments of the network would not result in the network's collapse. This design could only be accomplished if multiple pathways existed between each computer (*node*) on the network.

The original proposal, released in 1964 by RAND staffer Paul Baran, simply stated that each node in the network would be equal in status to all other nodes. Each node would have the authority to originate, pass, and receive messages from any other node. The messages would be broken down into smaller, standardized units for transmission called *packets*. Packets would be individually addressed to their destination node, and because each node would be capable of passing or forwarding (or *routing*) packets along the network to the designated address, each message was guaranteed to reach its destination. The network's multiple pathway design ensured that there would always be one or more pathways available for message transmission.

Creation of the Early ARPANET

In the late 1960s, the RAND Corporation, MIT, and UCLA experimented with the concept of a decentralized, packet-switching computer network, as did the National Physical Laboratory in Great Britain. In 1968, the Pentagon's Advanced Research Projects Agency (ARPA) began funding a project in the U.S. By the fall of 1969, the infant ARPANET came into being with its first four nodes:

- An SDS SIGMA 7 at UCLA
- An SDS940 at the Stanford Research Institute
- An IBM 360 at the University of California at Santa Barbara
- A DEC PDP-10 at the University of Utah

The early tests conducted on ARPANET proved highly successful. Scientists at the test institutions were able to transfer data and share computer facilities remotely. By 1971, ARPANET expanded to 15 nodes, and included links to MIT, RAND, Harvard, CMU in Pittsburgh, Case Western Reserve, and NASA/Ames. By 1972, there were a total of 37 nodes on ARPANET. In 1973, the first international connection to ARPANET was made to the University College of London and to the Royal Radar Establishment in Norway.

Despite the fact that the early makeup of ARPANET consisted of connections between this country's most prestigious research institutions, and that the earliest proposals for ARPANET stressed its importance as a means of allowing remote computing, the main traffic on ARPANET in its early days did not fit its intended role. At first scientists were using it to collaborate on research projects and exchange notes on work. But very quickly it became the equivalent of a high-speed, computerized "party-line." Many of its users were sending personal messages and gossip, and eventually using it mainly to just "schmooze."

Growth and Change of ARPANET in the '70s

Nevertheless, despite what it was being used for, ARPANET and the concept of a packet-switching, decentralized network were a huge success. During the 1970s, this decentralized structure made expansion easy and resulted in tremendous growth. Its decentralized structure, vastly different from corporate computer networks at the time, allowed connection of virtually any type of computer as long as it could communicate using the packet-switching protocol NCP, *Network Control Protocol* (the forerunner to TCP/IP, *Transmission Control Protocol/Internet Protocol*).

As early as 1974, Vint Cerf and Bob Kahn, both of NSF, published their first specifications for a *transmission control protocol*, which was being used by other networks to attach to the ARPAnet by 1977.

TCP/IP, released into public domain, differed from NCP in that it converted messages into packets at the source, and then reassembled them back into messages at the destination. IP, or *Internet protocol*, was used to establish the addressing for the packet, and was able to ensure that packet addressing guided packets through multiple nodes and, more importantly, across multiple networks even if the standards differed from ARPANET's early NCP standard. TCP/IP was the impetus in the late 1970s and early 1980s that led to further expansion of ARPANET, because it was fairly easy to implement on most any computer and allowed easy expansion from any existing node.

By 1983, ARPANET (which by then was commonly referred to as the Internet because of the vast array of interconnected computers and networks) officially dropped NCP and replaced it with the more advanced and more widespread TCP/IP, which had been officially adopted by the Department of Defense (DOD) the year before.

Expansion in the '80s and '90s

The 1980s was a period of tremendous growth for the Internet. The pattern established in the U.S. of interconnecting remote computer systems via a decentralized network was spreading worldwide, and many of those foreign computer networks wanted to become connected to the U.S. network. The Internet's reach broadened by the inclusion of:

- EUnet—the European UNIX Network in 1982
- EARN—the European Academic and Research Network in 1983
- JUNET—the Japanese UNIX Network in 1984
- JANET—the Joint Academic Network in the United Kingdom in 1984

It was also during the 1980s that the major players in this country, through funding from the National Science Foundation, established the NSFNET—five supercomputing centers at Princeton, CMU, UCSB, UIUC, and Cornell that loosely became known as the "Internet backbone in the U.S." The original speed of NSFNET in 1986 was a blazing 56 KBps. In less than two years the continued expansion of the Internet and demand for computing services led to an upgrade of the NSFNET backbone in 1988 to T1 speed (1.544 MBps). In 1987, there were more than 10,000 host computers interconnected on the Internet. By 1989, the number of hosts reached 100,000.

The 1990s and the Coming of the Web

The 1990s saw continued expansion of the Internet along with the invention of several Internet services and programs. In 1990, Archie was released by Bill Heelan, Alan Emtage, and Peter Deutsch. In 1991, the NSFNET backbone was upgraded to T3 status (44.736 MBps), and Brewster Kahle invented WAIS. Also in 1991, Paul Lindner and Mark McCahill of the University of Minnesota released Gopher, followed in 1992 by the release of Veronica from the University of Nevada. 1992 was also the year that the number of host computers on the Internet broke the one million mark.

But by far the greatest advancement to the Internet in the 1990s (some might even say in its entire existence) was the creation of the World Wide Web. In November of 1990, Tim Berners-Lee of CERN created the first Web server prototype using a NeXT computer. The Web as an actual functioning system did not go online until 1992. In February of 1993, the alpha version of Mosaic was released by NCSA. By September 1993, the first working version of Mosaic was released and WWW traffic was already 1% of NFSNET. By October 1993, there were already 200 Web servers in operation.

In the years following, Internet and Web expansion continued at even greater levels. Actual statistics on the number of host computers and Web servers are hard to measure because they change almost daily. A good guess on the number of host computers on the Internet (averaged from several sources) as of

June 1995 would be about 6.5 million, with the largest concentration, as you might expect, to be in the United States.

Internet Administration

The Internet, despite its initial development, support, and funding by ARPA and NSF, does not really belong to anyone, even though it has had a number of agencies and groups "overseeing" its operation. In 1979, ARPA first established the ICCB (Internetwork Configuration and Control Board). The ICCB was replaced in 1983 by the IAB (Internet Activities Board). In 1987, the NSF contracted with Merit Network, Inc. to manage the NSFNET backbone. Ordinarily, the management of the Internet would not warrant much mention, except that in 1993 NFS began laying the plans for a new U.S. Internet backbone as a total replacement for NSFNET. The new backbone went into operation in 1995 as Internet traffic was transitioned from the NSFNET, which ceased backbone operations on April 30, 1995. The new backbone is composed of the following:

- A very high speed Backbone Network Service (vBNS) OC3 line (155 MBps) funded by NSF; its use is restricted to organizations requiring high speeds for scientific calculations or visualizations

- Four regional Network Access Points, NAPs (located in San Francisco, Chicago, New York City, and Washington, D.C.) that interconnect the vBNS, other backbone networks, both domestic and foreign, and network service providers

- A routing arbiter (also funded by NSF) that arbitrates high speed and low speed bandwidth requests

Hypertext and Hypermedia Concepts

With an understanding of how the Internet has grown and evolved to its present state, understanding what URLs (*Uniform Resource Locators*) are and how they function is key to understanding how the Internet and the Web function and how Internet resources are located and accessed.

URLs are a very convenient method of identifying the location of devices and resources on the Internet. As defined in RFC-1738, all URLs follow this format:

    <scheme>:<scheme-dependent-information>

Some examples of <scheme> are http, FTP, and Gopher. This scheme tells you the application you are using:

- What type of resource you are trying to locate (for example, a Web page, a file, or a Gopher menu or Gopher document)
- What mechanism you need to access the resource (for example, a Web browser, an FTP utility to download the file, or a Gopher client)

The <scheme-dependent-information> usually indicates:

- The Internet host making the file available
- The full path to the file

A more recognizable pattern for most users is:

scheme://machine.domain/full-pathname-of-file

Here we see the scheme describing the type of resource separated from the computer and its Internet address by two slashes (//) and then the Internet address separated from the path and file name by one slash (/). URLs for http, FTP, and Gophers generally fit this pattern.

To make this example a bit clearer, let's use a real-world URL as an example. Here is the URL for my home page:

http://www.city-net.com/~gagrimes/galen1.html

Figure 1.7 shows you how my home page appears.

Fig. 1.7
The Galen Grimes
Most Excellent
Home Page.

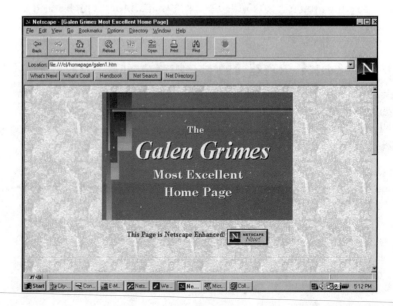

Here's the scheme for this URL broken down into its component parts:

- **http:**—indicates that you are using the HyperText Transfer Protocol to access the resource, which usually means you want to use your Web browser

- **www.city-net.com**—identifies the host computer and its Internet address (its domain name to be precise)

- **/~gagrimes/galen1.html**—identifies the path and file name on the host computer for the desired resource

Most Web pages follow this scheme. You may have noticed that when accessing http, FTP, or Gopher URLs, the "full pathname" sometimes ends in a single slash (/). This is used to point the URL to a specific directory instead of to a specific file. In this case the host computer will usually return what is called the *default index* for that directory. In http the default index file is usually named **index.html**, but can also be named **home.html**, **homepage.html**, **welcome.html**, or **default.html**.

So, let's say you're sitting in front of your PC in Phoenix (or anywhere for that matter) and decide to visit my Web page. You start Netscape, and enter **http://www.city-net.com/~gagrimes/galen1.html** in the location window, press Enter, and in a few seconds my home page appears.

How the Domain Name Service Works

One of the key components responsible for helping Netscape run on your computer and locate my home page file, galen1.html (which is stored on the Web server of my service provider, City-Net) is a program, or more precisely, a series of programs called the *domain name service*.

Here's how the domain name service, or DNS for short, works its magic. When you initially set up your connection to your Internet Service Provider (if you used Microsoft Plus! you did it using the Internet Setup Wizard) you were asked to enter the IP address of your DNS Server. The IP address you entered, which your service provider supplied you with, looked something like the IP address shown in figure 1.8.

Fig. 1.8
Entering IP
address of DNS
Server in Microsoft
Plus! Internet
Setup wizard.

> **Note**
>
> An IP address is a unique number, in the format *nnn.nnn.nnn.nnn* (where *nnn* is a
> number between 0 and 255) that is assigned to every physical device on the Internet.
> Your service provider is assigned a block of IP addresses (by the InterNIC Registration
> Services) that are in turn assigned to each user who is provided access to the
> Internet. Your provider either assigns you a permanent IP address that doesn't
> change, or each time you login to your provider, you are assigned a dynamic IP
> address, which could be any number in your provider's assigned block of IP address
> numbers.

When you enter the URL for my home page, **http://www.city-net.com/
~gagrimes/galen1.html**, Netscape parses the domain name from this URL
according to the URL scheme explained previously. The domain name
Netscape gets from this URL is **city-net.com**. Netscape, working in conjunction with Windows and your TCP/IP protocol stack, passes the domain name,
city-net.com, to your domain name service.

> **Note**
>
> You may have noticed that domain names often end in .com, .edu, or .org. These
> identifiers are used with the domain name to help identify the type of domain. The
> most common identifiers are shown here, along with examples of each:
>
> ■ *.com* for commercial organizations, for example, **netscape.com**, **ibm.com**,
>   **fedex.com**
>
> ■ *.edu* for educational institutions, for example, **psu.edu** for Penn State Univ.,
>   **cmu.edu** for Carnegie-Mellon Univ., **mit.edu** for the Massachusetts Institute
>   of Technology
>
> ■ *.gov* for government agencies, for example, **whitehouse.gov** for the White
>   House, **fbi.gov** for the FBI

- *.mil* for the military, for example, **army.mil** for the Army, **navy.mil** for the Navy
- *.org* for nonprofit organizations, for example, **red-cross.org** for the American Red Cross, **oneworld.org** for Save the Children Fund
- *.net* for network service providers, for example, **internic.net** for InterNIC, **si.net** for Sprint International

There are also identifiers for countries:

- *.uk* for United Kingdom
- *.ca* for Canada
- *.ch* for Switzerland (Confoederatio Helvetica); you may have noticed that the domain name for CERN is cern.ch
- *.li* for Liechtenstein
- *.cn* for China
- *.jp* for Japan
- *.br* for Brazil

The lack of a country identifier usually indicates the domain is in the United States.

Your domain name service in one sense is a very large database program running on one of your service provider's computers (other computers are running other services such as mail service, news service, and FTP to name a few). When the domain name is passed to the domain name service, the DNS returns the corresponding IP address.

Note

If by some chance your DNS does not contain the domain name, your DNS will attempt to locate the IP address by requesting the domain name from another DNS, in this case a centralized DNS containing .com domain names. If the domain name is still not located, the DNS will finally return an error message indicating the requested domain name does not exist.

In the previous example using my home page, the domain name **city-net.com** is passed to your DNS, and your DNS should return 199.234.118.2. The IP address is not only used for identification, it is also used to route the request to the appropriate host computer. The starting sequence of this IP address, 199., routes the request to North America. Additional routers connecting various Internet segments in North America, and containing routing tables for the segments they connect, eventually route the request to Pittsburgh and to City-Net. Once the request arrives at the domain **city-net.com**, it is routed to the appropriate host computer and finally to the appropriate directory path until the file **galen1.html** is located.

Because the request for **galen1.html** was made using http, the host computer, a Web server, returns the requested file for display by the requesting client, which in this case is Netscape, a Web browser.

The Web Metaphor: Hypertext Links

Now you have an understanding of how URLs work, and how URLs are used to help route files to the computers that request them. Figure 1.9 does a good job of illustrating Internet connections in the U.S. and how requests to various host computers could possibly be routed over the various interconnected Internet segments.

Fig. 1.9
Map of the U.S. illustrating how Internet network segments are interconnected.

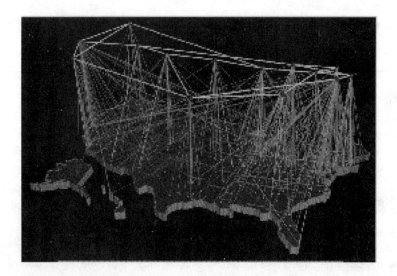

The World Wide Web is a means of supporting hypertext across the Internet. Hypertext is simply text that contains links, and these links provide additional information about certain keywords or phrases. Links are just what they sound like, and on Web pages, these links are used to connect one page (or file) to another page. We can use my home page as an example of Web page hypertext links. Figure 1.10 shows three links on my home page. These links are references to three additional Web pages, which also happen to be located on the same computer as my home page, which is the Web server of my service provider, City-Net.

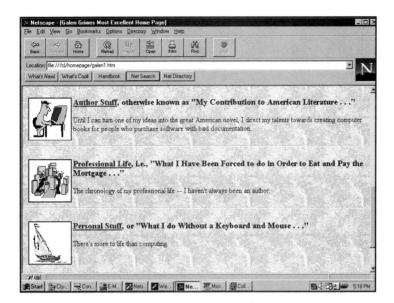

Fig. 1.10
Galen's home
page links.

Note

You can easily identify links when using Netscape because links will appear as either blue or magenta, underlined text.

Selecting the link Author Stuff will send another request from your PC across the interconnected segments of the Internet to the City-Net Web server, requesting the file **galen-a.htm**, which is the file name of the Author Stuff Web page. The URL for the Author Stuff page is included in this link. In a few seconds the page shown in figure 1.11 appears.

Scroll down this page and you will see additional links to more Web pages. These links, however, are to Web pages on the Web server operated by Macmillan Computer Publishing, the owner of Que, and this Web server is located in Indianapolis.

Selecting any of these links will send a request from your PC across the interconnected segments of the Internet to the Macmillan Web server in Indianapolis, requesting the file referenced in the URL in this link.

Fig. 1.11
Author Stuff page
link from Galen's
home page.

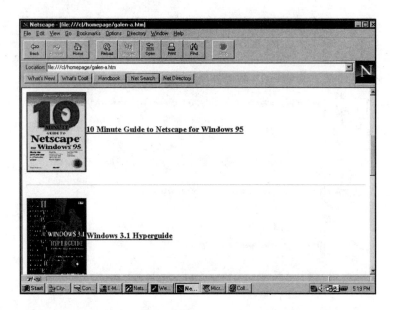

> **Note**
>
> Netscape will let you see the URLs in links even before you select the link. Use your mouse and place the pointing finger Netscape cursor on the link without clicking your mouse. Look down at the status bar and you'll see the URL for that link.

You should have a much better understanding now of how the hypertext metaphor applies to the Web and to Web pages. You can see that the World Wide Web resembles a spider's web with connections from any one point or Web page, branching outward to various other connection points, or other Web pages, which in turn can also contain connections to even more Web pages.

Other Internet Services Accessed Through the Web

In the past year or so, many Web browsers have exceeded their original purpose of simply displaying HTML pages. Many Web browsers are becoming all-purpose Internet tools that can also be used for accessing non-Web Internet services such as FTP, e-mail, newsgroups, and Gophers.

FTP

FTP, short for *file transfer protocol*, is an Internet protocol that allows you to upload or download text or binary files. FTP is most often used to download files from an archival storage site. In the past few years, numerous FTP sites have sprung up all over the Internet as repositories for shareware, freeware, and general PC utilities and various support files.

It has also become fairly common for computer hardware and software manufacturers to set up FTP sites for customer support. These FTP sites are stocked with software updates and hardware support drivers, which are free for customers to download.

FTP sites that are used for hardware and software support are usually advertised so users who need access to their contents can easily find the sites and the files they store. Unfortunately, many FTP sites do not fall in this category and largely remain unknown, except when passed from user to user, or when these sites are included in a list of FTP sites in books like this. Fortunately, there is another way to locate files on FTP sites. In 1990 Peter Deutsch, Alan Emtage, and Bill Heelan created a program they called Archie, which can be used to locate files stored (or archived, hence the name Archie) on FTP sites. A listing of Archie servers can be found at **http://pubweb.nexor.co.uk/ public/archie/servers.html** (see fig. 1.12).

Fig. 1.12
NEXOR List of
Archie Servers.

Until you become more familiar with using Archie servers, go to this Web site for a listing of FTP sites you might find helpful: **http://hoohoo.ncsa.uiuc.edu/ftp/** (see fig. 1.13).

Fig. 1.13
The Monster FTP
Sites List.

For more information on FTP and how to use this protocol, especially in Web browsers, see chapter 12, "Accessing Other Internet Services with Netscape."

▶ See "Accessing
Other Internet
Services with
Netscape,"
pg. 301

E-mail and UseNet Newsgroups

E-mail, short for electronic mail, is a simple system designed to allow the sending and receiving of messages across a network. For most of its history on the Internet, e-mail has been used primarily by businesses and academicians, but in the past few years a large percentage of e-mail messages have been created and read by individuals.

E-mail access is another traditional non-Web service that Web browsers are starting to encroach on. E-mail was one of the earliest services available on the Internet, having been invented in 1972 by Ray Tomlinson to send messages across the early distributed networks. E-mail today, probably the widest used of all Internet services, is still used primarily for sending messages, but an increasing percentage of e-mail messages now include some sort of file attachment.

UseNet newsgroups are strikingly similar in operation to e-mail, since both involve sending messages that often have file attachments, and like e-mail, newsgroup functionality is also starting to turn up in Web browsers. The first

UseNet newsgroup was set up in 1979 by Tom Truscott and Steve Bellovin using UUCP (UNIX-to-UNIX Communication Protocol) between Duke University and the University of North Carolina.

▶ See "E-mail with Netscape," pg. 321

E-mail and UseNet both suffered early on from the same problem—how to attach a non-text file to a text-based message. This chapter explains how the problems were solved in UseNet. (To understand how files are attached in e-mail, see chapter 13, "E-mail with Netscape.")

Gophers

Accessing Gopher servers is another non-Web function being taken over by Web browsers. Gopher servers, or simply Gophers, first appeared on the Internet in 1991, and were originally created and released by the University of Minnesota by Paul Lindner and Mark P. McCahill (Gophers were named after the UM mascot, the Golden Gopher).

Gophers are similar in operation to FTP sites in that they are established as repositories for files. Gopher files, however, are largely academic and informational text documents, and are meticulously arranged by subject under a hierarchical menu structure. Accessing a Gopher server to search for documents by subject is similar to using a Web search engine such as Lycos or WebCrawler. The only problem is that Gophers differ in the subjects they contain documents for. To solve this problem, developers at the University of Nevada in 1992 devised a Gopher database search program, which they dubbed Veronica. Veronica works to create its database of Gopher documents and menus like the robot search tools used in many Web search engines. It continuously scans Gopher servers to see what menus and documents are being stored.

If you want to see how gophers and Veronica work, point your (Gopher-functioning) Web browser to **gopher://veronica.scs.unr.edu/11/veronica**.

▶ See "Accessing Other Internet Services with Netscape," pg. 301

You can also get more information on gophers in chapter 12, "Accessing Other Internet Services with Netscape."

The Future of the Web

The Web, just like the Internet, is still growing, and more importantly, still evolving. As you might expect, numerous groups and organizations are developing new projects to assist in the evolution of the Web, most notably, the World Wide Web Consortium, or W3C for short, at CERN in Geneva, Switzerland. The W3C has posted on its Web server a list of some of the projects it currently has under development. If you want more information on these projects, go to **http://www.w3.org/hypertext/WWW/Bugs.html** to see the entire listing. The following sections are a sampling of some of the projects.

HTML Style Sheets

Most high-end word processors have some sort of style sheet capability, as do some HTML editors, but there is no HTML standard for style sheets. There are several proposals for how to implement HTML style sheets along with examples from some of the W3C members. This is a very active discussion forum, and much of the information and proposals can be found at **http://www.w3.org/hypertext/WWW/Style/Welcome.html**.

SGML and the Web

SGML, Standard Generalized Markup Language, is another HTML discussion hot button at W3C. The focus of the discussion is on extending HTML to encompass more of the SGML standard language. (For more information on SGML, see chapter 21, "Working with SGML.")

▶ See "Working with SGML," pg. 507

To get more information on this discussion and project:

http://www.w3.org/hypertext/WWW/MarkUp/SGML/

Internationalization of Character Sets

This will likely be one of the hot areas to watch for future HTML and Web development. Everyone agrees now that the Web has a severe bias toward English and the western-European/Latin writing system. There are several factors that have contributed to this bias, primarily 7-bit ASCII.

Note

ASCII is the American Standard Code for Information Interchange. The 7-bit ASCII code, which most computer manufacturers recognize, allows for the creation of only 128 characters and symbols, which does not include foreign or non-Latin-based characters. There are several 8-bit character sets that allow for 256 characters, but not an agreement on which one will be universally accepted.

Currently the greatest concentrations of Internet computers and domains are in the U.S. and Western Europe (see fig. 1.14).

With the Internet spreading into more countries that do not use the ISO-8859 Latin-1 character set (an 8-bit character set), there is pressure to approve a 16-bit character set (which would permit a total of 65,536 characters) standard, which will provide character sets for Eastern Europe, Asia, and the Pacific rim.

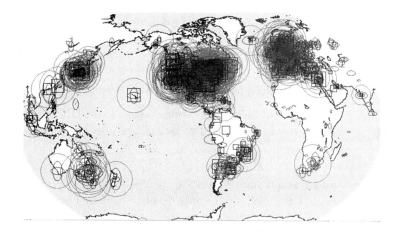

Fig. 1.14
Internet domain
concentrations
worldwide.

For more on this discussion see **http://www.w3.org/hypertext/WWW/
International/**.

Virtual Reality

This is a hot topic, not just at W3C, but all over the Web. Virtual reality is
considered the next step for multimedia on the Web, and there are several
proposals for how best to handle 3D VR graphics. Much of the discussion extends to how best to implement VR on the Web—should it be through
VRML, Virtual Reality Markup Language; should it be through PostScript extensions; or should a new VR platform be done "from the ground up." The
discussion in W3C can be found at **http://www.w3.org/hypertext/
WWW/Bugs/GraphicalComposition.html**.

(For more information on VRML and how VRML is implemented, see chapter
20, "Using VRML.")

▶ See "Using
VRML," pg. 491

Emerging Technologies

Several emerging technologies that could have an impact on the Web and the
Internet in the next few years are just on the horizon—specifically *ISDN* and
cable modems.

ISDN

ISDN, Integrated Services Digital Network, simply stated is digital telephone.
ISDN's main advantage over the current analog telephone system is speed.
With ISDN your connection to the Internet will be 4 1/2 times faster (128
Kbps) than the current top speed using analog telephone lines and 28.8 Kbps
modems.

ISDN's main drawbacks now are availability and cost. As of November 1995, ISDN was available to only about 70 percent of available telephone service areas in the U.S., with the heaviest concentrations in the northeast. Also, many Internet service providers are not set up to provide ISDN connections to their subscribers but are scrambling to offer ISDN connection.

The other drawback is cost. Each of the Regional Bells in the U.S. has established a separate pricing scheme for ISDN service. Through Bell Atlantic, there is a one-time installation charge of only $169.00, but there is a monthly charge of $39.00, plus an online charge of $0.02 per minute per channel ($0.04 per minute if you're multiplexing the two 64 Kbps channels into one 128 Kbps channel). Other Bell service providers have dropped the online charge but charge upwards of $500-700 for installation.

The other cost for ISDN is in the equipment. Equipment prices are dropping as more companies begin offering ISDN equipment, but costs for an NT-1 terminal adapter are still in the $300-500 range.

Cable Modems

The other emerging technology, which many experts feel is still several years away, is what is being called cable modems. Cable modems are in effect 2-way digital communications lines tied in over the same line used for cable TV. With many cable TV operators upgrading their service line to fiber optic, the potential here is for communications connections to the Internet in the 1-10 Mbps range. Cost will be another factor driving this technology as well, both for the user and the provider. Early speculation for cable modems estimate prices in the $500-700 range. Also, cable operators will have to install fiber optic hubs and routers at an estimated cost of $2,000-5,000 for every 30-50 users.

Obviously there are problems associated with both of these technologies, but once these are solved and either (or both) of these technologies is more widespread, the Internet backbone could begin to face serious bandwidth constraints. Apparently, this concern is being addressed. In April 1995 the NFSNET backbone was phased out and replaced with a new "very high speed Backbone Network Service" (vBNS). The vBNS is currently running at 155 MBps. In 1996, it is scheduled to be upgraded to operate at 622 MBps. While no mention is made of upgrading other segments of the Internet backbone in this country, this example clearly shows that bandwidth concerns remain a high priority.

Exploring the WWW with Netscape 2.0

Netscape has managed to remain the leader of the pack among Web browsers due in large part to the fact that Netscape has most often been the first Web browser to incorporate new features and new extensions to HTML. Netscape is also offering two versions of its 2.0 product—Netscape Navigator 2.0, intended primarily for the end-user, and Netscape Navigator Gold 2.0, which has all the same features as the standard 2.0 version but with integrated HTML document creation tools targeted at developers.

Version 2.0 pushes the limits of a Web browser even further by incorporating new features both for end-users who will use Netscape primarily as a Web browser, and for HTML authors and developers who will be incorporating many of the proposed HTML 3.0 features into their Web sites.

The following gives a cursory overview of some of the new features you'll be seeing in Netscape 2.0. All of these features are explained in greater detail in later chapters.

Improved Browsing Performance

In addition to the other new features Netscape is adding to its Web browser, users will also notice improvements in speed and performance. Netscape has made improvements to speed up multiple, simultaneous loading of text, images, and files. Caching, including caching from CD-ROM-based media, is quicker. And most importantly, to prepare for more widespread use of multimedia on the Web, Netscape has also created a new level of support for audio and video types utilizing dynamic code modules called *plug-ins,* which will integrate better with the core browser application than previously with helper applications.

Enhanced Security

Netscape took quite a beating by the trade press when a team of graduate students using some high-powered computing muscle managed to decrypt one Netscape message. Even though the means used to decrypt that one message were well beyond the efforts of most would-be hackers, it nevertheless exposed a small chink in Netscape's armor. Netscape 2.0 security is even tighter and ensures that e-mail and newsgroup messages as well as financial transactions can be transmitted with near absolute certainty that what you send is secure and will only be seen by the intended recipient.

Netscape 2.0 now uses the Secure Courier open protocol, which creates a secure digital envelope when transmitting financial information over the Net.

This same secure MIME open protocol will also encrypt e-mail you send and receive as well as newsgroup messages you post.

▶ See "Forms and Transaction Security," pg. 253

Netscape also has made arrangements with VeriSign to allow Netscape users the ability to create their own digital identities by getting an online Digital ID from VeriSign (**http://www.verisign.com**). (Netscape's new security features are presented in-depth in chapter 11, "Forms and Transaction Security.")

Integrated E-mail

In previous versions of Netscape you could send e-mail, but you had to utilize another e-mail application to read and manage your incoming e-mail. Netscape 2.0 now has a fully integrated e-mail system (see fig. 1.15).

Fig. 1.15
Netscape Mail's new interface.

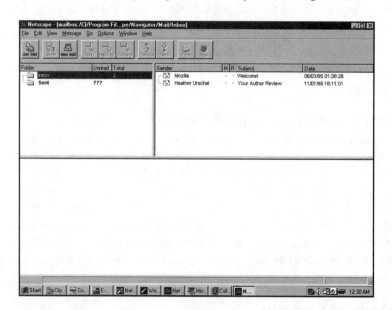

Netscape's new e-mail system:

- Allows you to archive messages in a hierarchical folder structure, which includes drag-and-drop capabilities
- Permits you to maintain a personal address book with mailing lists
- Provides for offline reading and creation of e-mail messages

▶ See "E-mail with Netscape," pg. 321

Netscape's newly improved security features are also included within its expanded e-mail functionality to ensure the highest level of security possible for e-mail messages. (Chapter 13, "E-mail with Netscape," covers usage of Netscape mail in detail.)

Enhanced Newsgroup Capabilities

Netscape 2.0 has expanded its newsgroup functionality to allow you to read, sort, and post newsgroup messages using a fully threaded, MIME-compliant newsreader. Netscape has designed its news reader to share the same interface with Netscape mail (see fig. 1.16).

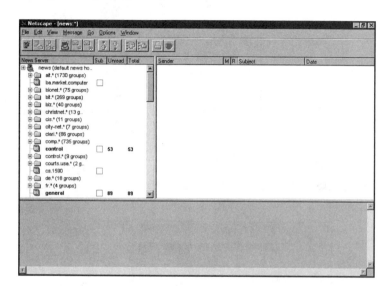

Fig. 1.16
Netscape news reader interface is the same as Netscape Mail.

As a MIME-compliant news reader, Netscape 2.0 now allows you to embed live objects, URLs, HTML pages, or images in your postings. The newsreader also supports multiple news servers. (Netscape's expanded newsgroup support is covered in chapter 15, "Reading UseNet Newsgroups with Netscape.")

▶ See "Reading UseNet Newsgroups with Netscape," pg. 371

Enhanced Bookmarks

Netscape has always had the best and easiest Web bookmark capabilities of any Web browser, but now bookmarking has gotten better. Netscape 2.0 includes an add-on bookmarking application called SmartMarks, which not only gives you more control and flexibility in managing your Web bookmarks, but now also allows you to manage your bookmarks within a true, hierarchical menu/folder system (see fig. 1.17).

SmartMarks also incorporates a new HTML feature tag called BULLETINS, which allows Web authors to post messages to SmartMarks that you can receive without actually visiting the Web site (see fig. 1.18).

I

Internet Fundamentals

Fig. 1.17
SmartMarks
hierarchical
menu/folder
system and Web
page monitor.

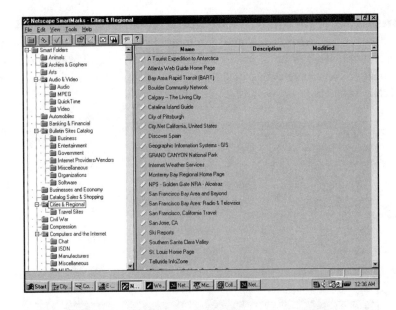

Fig. 1.18
BULLETIN tag
message from
monitored Web
page.

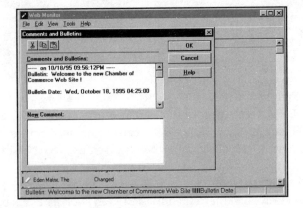

▶ See "Using
SmartMarks,"
pg. 229
SmartMarks can also be set to periodically monitor Web pages, again without intervention on your part, or without you having to visit the Web site, and alert you to changes in Web page content or links. (The new SmartMarks add-on is explained in detail in chapter 10, "Using SmartMarks.")

Java

Netscape 2.0 also incorporates support for Sun's Java object-oriented programming language. If you haven't encountered Java applets (small applications) on the Web, chances are you will as more and more Web site administrators are turning to Java to produce small, portable Web applications. Java is well suited for use on the Web because Java applets are platform independent, meaning that the same Java application will work with your Netscape browser regardless of whether you are running Netscape on a PC under Windows 95, on an Apple Macintosh, or on a Sun Sparc workstation running UNIX. If you're curious about Java and how it is being used on the Web, or how Sun is promoting its new programming language, Sun has set up an informational site at **http://www.javasoft.com/about.html**. (Netscape's support for the Java programming language is presented in detail in chapter 33, "Sun's Java and the Netscape Browser," and chapter 34, "Java for C++ Programmers.")

Frames

Netscape 2.0 permits the Web page author the ability to split the screen into two or more independent dynamic or static frames. This permits the developer to place a static Web page element in one frame, such as a toolbar, title screen, or copyright notice, while at the same time allowing the user to browse the page using the dynamic frame. Users who are familiar with spreadsheet programs that allow you to split a worksheet into multiple windows will immediately understand and appreciate the concept and functionality that frames will add to Web pages. Figure 1.19 illustrates a Web page utilizing Netscape 2.0's new frames feature.

Fig. 1.19
Web page displayed in a static and dynamic frame.

Targets

▶ See "Netscape-
Specific and
Future HTML
Commands,"
pg. 721

Targets work in conjunction with frames to allow you to assign a name to a particular frame and then target that named frame with a URL. Simply stated, this means that you can designate a link on a Web page to open into a designated frame. The designated frame can open as an additional frame or can open full-screen and cover any existing frames. (Using frames and targets in Netscape-enhanced Web pages is covered in detail in chapter 29, "Netscape Specific and Future HTML Commands.")

Netscape Scripting Language

▶ See
"JavaScript,"
pg. 895

Another new feature Netscape has included in version 2.0 for developers is its own scripting language. Netscape's scripting language, *JavaScript*, is a programmable API that gives developers the ability to script certain events, actions, and objects across the multiple platforms supported by Netscape. (It is based on the Java programming language developed by Sun and is presented in greater detail in chapter 35, "JavaScript.")

Developer Editing Tool

One problem that has plagued Web page developers almost since the invention of the Web has been finding a suitable HTML editor. While there are numerous editors on the market, Web authors can be as particular about HTML editors as programmers are about which editor they are most comfortable with. Netscape has either made it easier for editors or complicated matters by including its own set of editing tools in its Netscape Navigator Gold 2.0 version.

(Using Netscape's new document creation capabilities are covered in chapters 29, "Netscape Specific and Future HTML Commands," and 30, "Netscape Forms and CGI-BIN Scripts.")

Inline Plug-Ins

In previous versions of Netscape, if you encountered a data or file type that was not native to Netscape, such as an MPEG or QuickTime full-motion video file, or a RealAudio or MIDI sound file, Netscape would only be able to display or play this file if you had installed a helper app, an application known to Netscape and configured into Netscape to handle a non-native file type. In Netscape 2.0, the functionality of helper apps is extended into what are now called inline plug-ins. Inline plug-ins function similar to helper apps in that they extend Netscape's ability to use and display a wider range of file types. Plug-ins can be utilized by Netscape in one of three forms:

- An embedded plug-in can be embedded into a Web page the same as you would embed a .GIF or .JPEG image using the EMBED tag. This would be one way of ensuring users that any plug-in they need to display as a part of an HTML document would always be available.

- A full-screen plug-in that would behave similar to most helper apps in previous versions of Netscape. When you encounter a data type that needs the plug-in it would appear and fill the Netscape viewing window. Distribution of this type of plug-in would be the responsibility of the manufacturer and user since it would require some effort on the part of the user to at least ensure that plug-ins are copied into the appropriate folders.

- A hidden plug-in is one that would function in the background with no visible display such as a MIDI or other type of sound player.

As you can probably guess, plug-ins are designed to allow for a more seamless integration into Netscape (at least more seamless than helper apps) while at the same time extending the operation of the core program. (Using plug-ins with Netscape is presented in greater detail in chapter 36, "Netscape Plug-Ins.")

▶ See "Netscape Plug-Ins," pg. 933

## CHAPTER 2

Connecting to the Internet

Getting a connection to the Internet can seem to be an overwhelming problem. There are literally hundreds of Internet service providers (ISPs), many different types of connections, different levels of support, and different pricing plans. How are you supposed to sort through all of it so that it makes sense?

In this chapter, we tackle the major issues related to getting connected to the Internet and show you how to evaluate the various considerations. In particular, we look at:

- Determining the type of Internet connection you need
- Pricing and services
- How to choose an Internet service provider
- Setting up Windows 95 for PPP

TCP/IP Basics

Before we dive into the details of setting up an Internet connection, we need to talk about a few details of the protocols that make the Internet work. In order to understand all the issues involved with an Internet connection, you need to understand the basics of TCP/IP, domain names, and IP addresses.

The History of TCP/IP

The suite of widely used protocols known as *Transmission Control Protocol/Internet Protocol (TCP/IP)* has become increasingly important as national networks such as the Internet depend on it for their communications.

In the mid-1970s, the U.S. Department of Defense (DOD) recognized an electronic communication problem developing within its organization. Communicating the ever-increasing volume of electronic information among DOD staff, research labs, universities, and contractors had hit a major obstacle. The various entities had computer systems from different computer manufacturers, running different operating systems, and using different networking topologies and protocols. How could information be shared between all of them?

The Advanced Research Projects Agency (ARPA) was assigned to resolve the problem of dealing with different networking equipment and topologies. ARPA formed an alliance with universities and computer manufacturers to develop communication standards. This alliance specified and built a four-node network that is the foundation of today's Internet. During the 1970s, this network migrated to a new, core protocol design that became the basis for TCP/IP.

No matter what version of Netscape you are running, they all require a TCP/IP protocol stack to be present in order to communicate with the Internet. TCP/IP is the "language" that computers on the Internet use to speak to each other.

Domain Names

With millions of computers on the Internet, how do you specify the one that you want to interact with? You must know the name of the computer, just as you must know the name of someone you want to send a letter to. These names are specified by a convention called the *domain name service (DNS)*.

A domain name typically gives a hierarchical structure for a computer or group within an organization. The portion of the name to the far right, the *domain field*, provides the most general category. The United States has eight domain fields, which are listed in table 2.1.

Table 2.1 Listing of U.S. Domains	
Domain	**Description**
arpa	ARPANET members (obsolete)
com	Commercial and industrial organizations
edu	Universities and educational institutions
gov	Non-military government organizations
mil	Military
net	Network operation organizations
org	Other organizations
us	United States ISO domain

When you hook up to the Internet, you are a part of some domain, whether it is your own domain or that of your company or service provider. You also give your computer a name to identify it as part of your domain. For dial-up accounts with an Internet service provider, you can usually pick the host name for your computer yourself.

Let's look at an example. Assume that you have a personal account through a fictional Internet service provider named SpiffyNet. SpiffyNet's domain name is *spiffy.net*. SpiffyNet allows you to pick the name for your computer, so in a fit of creativity, you choose to call your computer *viper*. Thus, the full host and domain name of your computer would be *viper.spiffy.net*.

IP Addresses

Just as you have a name to identify a computer, your computer also has a number that uniquely identifies it to the rest of the world. This number is known as the *IP address* of your computer. Let's look a little closer at how IP addresses work.

An IP address is a 32-bit value that is divided into four 8-bit fields, each separated by a period. This means that the address would look something like 192.1.5.1. Each computer has exactly one IP address for each physical interface that it has connected to a network.

> **Note**
>
> In networking terminology, an 8-bit field is known as an *octet*.

The IP address of a computer is divided into two parts: a network section, which specifies a particular network, and a host portion, which identifies a particular machine on the network. There now are five categories of IP addresses based on the type of network address. These are referred to as *Class A* through *Class E*.

In a Class A address, the first octet has a value between 1 and 126, and the network portion consists of the first octet. This obviously limits the number of Class A networks to 126; however, each network can have more than 16 million computers. Class A networks are limited to major corporations and network providers.

Class B networks use the first two octets to specify the network portion and have the first octet in the range of 128 to 191. This leaves the last two octets free for the host ID. The Class B network space provides for 16,382 network ID numbers, each with 65,534 host IDs. Large companies and organizations such as universities are typically assigned Class B addresses.

Class C addresses use three octets to specify the network portion, with the first octet in the range from 192 to 223. This provides for more than 2 million different Class C networks, but only 254 hosts per network. Class C networks are usually assigned to small businesses or organizations.

In Class D addresses, the first octet is in the range from 224 to 239 and is used for multicast transmissions.

Class E addresses, with the first octet in the range of 240 to 247, are reserved for future use.

When computers communicate using TCP/IP, they use the numeric IP address. DNS names are simply a device that helps us humans remember which host is which and what network it's connected to. Originally, when the Internet was first formed, the number of hosts on the Net was very small. As a result, each host had a complete list of all host names and addresses in a local file. For obvious reasons, this system quickly became unwieldy. When a new host was added, it was necessary to update every host file on every computer. With the explosive growth of the Internet, the host files also grew quite large. The mapping of DNS names to IP addresses is now accomplished via a distributed database and specific software that performs the lookup.

Static Versus Dynamic IP Addresses

As you've probably figured out by now, your computer has to have an IP address to communicate on the Internet. How does it get it? Well, in most cases it is assigned by your ISP when you set up your account. Even if you are setting up a whole network of computers, your ISP will probably handle everything for you.

For direct Internet connections, the IP address of your computer is permanently assigned to you. It never changes. These are known as *static* IP addresses. Most Internet service providers, however, use a scheme known as *dynamic* IP addressing.

Because most ISPs typically have many more dial-up customers than they do modems, only a fraction of their dial-up customers can be online at any given moment. This usually isn't a problem, unless you want to sit in front of your computer and run Netscape 24 hours a day! In short, this means that an ISP can "recycle" IP addresses by only assigning them when your system dials up to connect to the service. This allows ISPs to get by with far fewer IP addresses than if they were statically assigned.

How does this affect you, the network user? First, you have to configure your networking software differently depending on whether you have a static or dynamic IP address. Second, there are a few things that you just can't do if you have a dynamic IP address. Specifically, because your IP address is dynamic—it changes every time you login—your host name can be registered in a domain name service database along with your IP address. Basically, this prevents anyone out on the Internet from being able to initiate contact with your computer. You won't be able to run an FTP server or a Web server if your computer has a dynamic IP address. Similarly, some commercial database services limit access to specific IP addresses based on subscription. Obviously, if your IP address is changing all the time, this scheme won't work.

While these limitations don't really affect a lot of people, they can be a real problem if you really want to run an FTP or Web server. Some ISPs charge extra for static IP addresses—sometimes a lot extra! If having a static IP address is a real issue for you, make sure you check with your ISP before signing a service contract.

Types of Internet Connections

Depending on how much money you want to spend, you can get many different levels of connection to the Internet. These connection levels primarily differ in the amount of data you can transfer over a given period of time. We refer to the rate at which data can be transferred as the *bandwidth* of the connection.

There are two categories of Internet connections: dial-up and direct connections. A *dial-up connection* uses a modem to dial another modem at an Internet service provider, perform some connection sequence, and bring up the TCP/IP network. A *direct connection* uses a dedicated, data-grade telephone circuit as the connection path to the Internet. Let's look at these in a bit more detail.

Dial-Up Connections

When you sign up for a dial-up Internet account, you use a modem to dial a telephone number for an Internet service provider. After the modems connect, your computer performs some type of login sequence and the computers start to communicate via TCP/IP.

Note

For Netscape to be usable with a dial-up connection, you need, at a minimum, a 14.4KBps modem. A faster modem, such as a 28.8KBps model, is recommended.

The login sequence that your system performs depends on the requirements of your particular ISP. Most of the time, these login sequences are automated by using a script file. (For more information on script files, see "Setting Up Windows 95 for PPP" later in this chapter.)

We use a bit of smoke and mirrors when we refer to "starting TCP/IP networking." What this really means is telling the remote system that you want to start communicating via TCP/IP instead of just via ASCII terminal emulation. The way this is accomplished via a dial-up connection is by using a protocol such as *PPP*.

PPP, the *Point to Point Protocol*, and SLIP, the *Serial Line Internet Protocol*, allow you to use TCP/IP communications over a dial-up connection. While either of these protocols works for serial TCP/IP, most ISPs are migrating to PPP, as it is newer and has more robust features. For this discussion, we are assuming you use PPP.

The way you start PPP varies depending on your ISP. In some cases, it starts automatically for you when you login. In other cases, you may have to execute a command from a login shell on the ISP. Still another way is to make a selection from an interactive menu. It really depends on your ISP.

Direct Connections

The other major way of connecting to the Internet is through a *direct connection*. This method is typically used by large offices and companies to tie their internal networks into the Internet. Quite simply, it requires a lot of money.

A direct connection consists of a dedicated, data-grade telephone line that runs between your location and your service provider. Depending on the bandwidth of this line, the charges from your phone company can be several thousand dollars per month! In addition to this charge, you also have the recurring monthly charge from your ISP, which can also be very expensive. Add to that the cost of the network hardware required, and this option quickly prices itself out of reach of individuals and small companies.

But let's assume for a second that you have the money to set up a direct Internet connection. How do you do it and what does it buy you? Well, the main things that it gives you are the ability to have a large pipe into the Internet through which to pump data, the ability to assign IP addresses to a whole network of computers, and static IP addressing. As for setting up the connection, most established ISPs have a setup package where they order your phone line, provide the hardware, register your domain name, and get your IP addresses for you—all for a flat fee. It's best to check with the ISP of your choice for more information.

Types of Services

Now that we've gotten the basics out of the way, let's look at what services you can get from an ISP. Most ISPs provide dial-up and direct connect services, with a whole menu of services that you can select from.

Dial-Up IP

For most ISPs, the basic level of dial-up IP gives you PPP-based, dynamic IP addressing on a public dial-up number. This number is connected to a modem bank, and rotates to the next available modem when you dial in—if there is a modem available. For most ISPs, busy signals are a common problem, especially during the prime evening and weekend hours.

Some ISPs provide a couple of levels of service above the basic dial-up PPP account. For example, you may be able to pay an additional fee to dial into a restricted number that has a better user-to-modem ratio. For even more money, the ISP may provide you with a dedicated dial-up line—a phone line that only you can dial in on. It's important to decide what type of dial-up account you are going to need, as this is one of the primary factors that affects the cost of your Internet service.

E-mail

If you've managed to get this far and set up an Internet connection, you probably want e-mail, right? By using a dial-up PPP account, you can read and send e-mail via the *Post Office Protocol* (*POP*). To do this, you get an e-mail client program, such as Eudora, for your PC and configure it with your e-mail account information and the IP address of your network mail server. If you have a dial-up account, your network mail server is a computer located at your ISP's offices.

> **Note**
>
> E-mail is transferred between systems on the Internet using a protocol known as the *Simple Mail Transport Protocol,* or SMTP. POP is the protocol that a local e-mail client program uses to retrieve mail from a mail server.

Most personal dial-up accounts provide you with at least one e-mail address. Some ISPs even provide as many as five different addresses for personal or family accounts. Other ISPs make you pay an additional monthly charge for extra e-mail IDs. Business accounts usually have a fixed number as well. If you have more than one person who will be using e-mail from your system, you might want to shop around to see what the ISP policies on multiple e-mail addresses are in your area.

News

Just as with e-mail, if your Internet service provider gives you access to
UseNet news, you can probably read and post news from your PC by using a
newsreader, such as Netscape, that supports the *Network News Transport Protocol (NNTP)*. To do this, you simply configure your newsreader with the names
or addresses of your mail and news hosts—the computers that you exchange
e-mail and news with. Most ISPs provide UseNet news as part of the basic
dial-up PPP account service.

Shell Access

Another service that is often available with a dial-up account is *shell access*.
This refers to the ability to access a command-line processor on the remote
ISP system.

Note

Because most ISPs use a UNIX system to provide Internet access, and UNIX command-line processors are known as *shells*, the term shell access has become rather
common.

Your ISP may or may not provide shell access as part of your basic network
package. Most people can get by fine without having shell access. It is useful
for accessing your account over the Internet, via Telnet or FTP from another
location, as well as doing things like compiling C code. But if you are just
running Netscape from home, you can probably survive without it.

Note

Be aware that some ISPs sell a "shell-access-only" account as a dial-up account.
Typically you cannot run PPP or SLIP from this type of account. Because Netscape
needs TCP/IP to run, you need to make sure that you get the right type of service
from your ISP.

Web Servers

The Web is a hot item—obviously, or you wouldn't be reading a book about
Netscape! Another service that is provided by many ISPs is access to a Web
server. Web servers allow you to put home pages on the Web so they can be
accessed by people with Web browsers like Netscape. Figure 2.1 shows an example of a Web page.

Fig. 2.1
The home Web
page for Mac-
millan Computer
Publishing.

Note

Don't confuse Netscape with a Web server—you can still surf the Net with Netscape
even if you don't have Web server access.

Having access to a Web server means that you can write Web pages in HTML
and make them available on the Web. Many ISPs provide their personal account customers the ability to create personal Web pages. Businesses usually
have to pay an additional fee for the service.

Note

Companies that have a direct connection to the Internet can simply set up their own
Web server on one of their own machines.

If your ISP doesn't provide Web server access, don't give up hope. There are
many companies that provide Web services alone, without providing any
type of interactive access to the Internet. Basically, you pay a monthly fee to
have the Web provider's site place your pages in the World Wide Web. These
Web service providers also typically offer consulting and design services to
help you create effective Web pages.

Virtual Domains

If you are setting up a business account, you may want to use your own domain name, instead of simply using the name of your ISP. A domain name that is actually a directory on an ISP's server is commonly referred to as a *virtual domain.*

In order to set up a virtual domain, you must register your domain name with the Network Information Center (NIC). The NIC acts as the clearinghouse for all Internet domain names. You can reach the NIC by Telnet at **rs.internic.net**, on the Web at **http://rs.internic.net**, by e-mail at **question@internic.net**, or by telephone at 1-703-742-4777. You must fill out a domain name registration template and submit it to the NIC. Currently, the NIC charges a fee of $100 to register a domain, and $50 per year to use the domain. The $100 fee covers the first two years.

As part of the registration process, you must provide information about which network name servers advertise your domain name. In short, this means that you have to find an ISP that provides virtual domains, and have it enter your domain name in its name server.

As with everything else, most ISPs charge an additional fee for supporting virtual domains. If this is a service that you require, make sure you shop around and ask questions.

Finding an Internet Service Provider

With the explosive growth of the Internet, there are now lots of ISPs to choose from. The services, cost, and customer satisfaction of ISPs vary widely. Some are terrible—a few are wonderful—most fall somewhere in the middle.

National Providers

You can divide ISPs into categories based on whether or not they have a national presence or they are mainly a local company. If you think about it, any ISP has a national presence in the sense that it is connected to the Internet and can be reached from anywhere. What we are referring to is the ability to contact the ISP via a local telephone call. Several of the larger ISPs have local dial access in many different locations, effectively making them national providers.

There are pros and cons to using a national provider. The company is usually larger—not a basement operation—and it usually has competent technical support people working for it. Also, national providers usually have a better uptime percentage than local providers and also have a better price structure.

On the other hand, because national ISPs tend to be larger, it may be harder to reach a technical support person when you have a problem. You may find that their policies are less flexible than local providers, and that they are less willing to make exceptions and work with you. If you are setting up a business connection, your ISP's office may be hundreds or thousands of miles away. If you are the kind of person that values working with a local company, this could present a problem for you.

Regional and Local Providers

Local and regional providers are ISPs that serve a regional market, instead of having a national presence. Like national providers, there are pros and cons here, too. You will probably find that local providers are more flexible on their services and policies. For business, you are usually able to meet face to face with someone in the office to discuss your Internet needs. On the down side, the service quality of local ISPs tends to be less reliable. Sometimes these companies are very small operations, with limited hardware and technical support. You may find that it is difficult to connect due to busy signals during certain times of the day.

Local and regional ISPs are notorious for expanding their customer base faster than their hardware will support. When their servers get overloaded, response creeps to a crawl and uptime suffers. Phone lines are continually busy. If this happens to an ISP, it has to respond immediately or its systems will become unusable.

A Word About Private Information Services

Most people are aware of private national information services like CompuServe or America Online. While these services do provide Internet access, including Web access, they do not, when this book was written, provide routed IP access to the Internet. In short, this means that you have to use their tools and interfaces to access the Net. Because you will not have a routed IP connection, you cannot use the network tools of your choice, such as Netscape, via one of these services.

Service Levels and Cost

As you have seen, there are a lot of things to consider when selecting an ISP. The level of service you need is probably the main thing that affects the cost of your connection. Dial-up modem connections in the general public modem pool are usually cheapest. A restricted modem group is more expensive. A dedicated dial-up line costs even more. Direct connections via leased lines are among the most expensive.

In addition to service level, many ISPs offer different connection pricing plans. Some plans give you a fixed number of connect hours per month and charge you for extra hours. Other plans may give you unlimited hours during a certain time period, and charge you for hours outside of that window. Still other plans give you unlimited connect time for your fee.

Before choosing an ISP, take time to evaluate how you are going to use the service and what level of service you need. Check with computer users in your area to see if they can recommend a local service or a national service that works well.

Netscape and Windows 95

There are several different ways that you can use Netscape to connect to the Internet. You can connect over Microsoft's TCP/IP, a third-party TCP/IP package, or you can purchase one of the bundled starter kits, such as the Earthlink Netscape Total Access package. In this section, we look at how to set up Netscape to run under Windows 95.

Setting Up Windows 95 for PPP

If you're using Netscape under Windows 95, you're in luck. Windows 95 includes support for PPP, which is what enables Netscape to access the Internet. Assuming that you have an account already set up with an Internet service provider, it's not too difficult to configure Windows 95 so that it provides you dial-up PPP support.

There are several bits of information that you need to correctly configure PPP for Windows 95. Your ISP should provide all this information when you set up your account. If you don't know some of these items, contact your ISP for help. You need to know:

- The username that you use to login to your ISP
- The password for your ISP account
- The telephone number for your ISP
- The host name for your computer
- The network domain name for your ISP
- The IP address of your ISP's default gateway or router
- The IP subnet mask of your ISP's network

- The IP address of your ISP's DNS name server
- Whether you have a static or dynamic IP address
- The IP address of your computer, if you have a static address

After you gather all the above information, you're ready to start installing PPP for Windows 95. You probably didn't install all the components for PPP when you installed Windows 95, so we need to check to see what's already there and install the ones that are missing.

Dial-Up Networking, the Dial-Up Adapter, and TCP/IP

The dial-up networking and dial-up adapter items are necessary to set up a dial-up account to the Internet. Make sure you have your installation media handy throughout this process. For simplicity, I'll assume that you are installing from a CD-ROM. To check and see if dial-up networking is installed:

1. Click the Start button, and choose Settings, Control Panel.

2. Double-click the Add/Remove Programs icon.

3. Select the Windows Setup tab. This brings up the section of the Add/Remove Programs dialog box that allows you to install or change various components of Windows 95.

4. Select the Communications option.

5. Click the Details button. This brings up the Communications dialog box showing current configuration of your Windows 95 communications system.

6. Make sure the Dial-Up Networking entry is selected. If it is not selected, select it and click OK.

Now that the dial-up networking package is installed, you need to check for the dial-up adapter. Basically, this program allows Windows 95 to use your telephone to make a network connection. To check and see if the dial-up adapter is installed:

1. Click the Start button, and choose Settings, Control Panel.

2. Double-click the Network icon. This brings up the Network control panel, which allows you to configure your network setup.

3. Select the Configuration tab. This portion of the Network dialog box allows you to add new network protocols and adapters to your Windows 95 environment. Figure 2.2 shows the Network dialog box.

4. Look for TCP/IP and Dial-up Adapter in the list.

Fig. 2.2
The Network
dialog box for
configuring your
network environ-
ment.

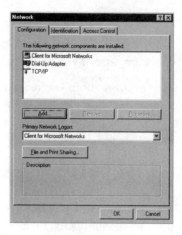

If you don't see the Dial-Up Adapter in the Network dialog box:

1. Click the Add button. This brings up the Select Network Component Type dialog box, which is where you tell Windows 95 what sort of net-working item you want to add to your computer.

2. Double-click Adapter. This brings up the Select Network adapters dialog box. We want to add the Dial-Up Adapter so that we can use dial-up networking.

3. The lefthand scroll box is labeled Select Network Component Type. Scroll this box until you see the Microsoft entry.

4. Select Microsoft from the Select Network Component Type scroll box. Choose Dial-Up Adapter from the righthand scroll box labeled Network Adapters.

5. Click OK.

If you don't see TCP/IP in the Network dialog box:

1. Click the Add button to add the protocol to your computer.

2. Double-click Protocol. TCP/IP is a networking protocol and that is what we need to add. This brings up the Select Network Protocol dialog box.

3. Scroll the left scroll box, labeled Manufacturers, until you see the Microsoft entry.

4. Select Microsoft in the left scroll box and then choose TCP/IP in the right scroll box, labeled Network Protocols.

5. Click OK.

At this point, you should see both TCP/IP and the dial-up adapter in the Network dialog box. Click Properties, and then Bindings and verify that the TCP/IP box is selected.

Dial-Up Scripting

You will probably want to create a script that handles logging you in to your ISP's system. This way, you can just double-click an icon and have Windows 95 dial your ISP, log you in automatically, and start PPP. We'll come back to scripting in a bit, but first you need to verify that the Dial-Up Scripting program has been installed.

1. Click Start and choose Programs, Accessories.

2. Look for an entry for the Dial-Up Scripting Tool.

If the Dial-up Scripting Tool isn't installed:

1. Click the Start button, and choose Settings, Control Panel.

2. Double-click the Add/Remove Programs icon.

3. Select the Windows Setup tab. Remember, this is where you add components to your Windows 95 system. We need to install the Dial-Up Scripting Tool from your Windows 95 CD.

4. Click the Have Disk button. This tells Windows 95 that you need to install something from the CD.

5. You will need to enter the path to the dial-up scripting program on your Windows 95 CD. For example, if your CD is drive G:, you would enter **G:\admin\apptools\dscript**.

6. Click the OK button.

Entering the Address Information

Okay, at this point you should have all the drivers and other programs installed so that you can configure TCP/IP with your network information. A couple of steps in this section depend in whether you have a static or dynamic IP address, so pay attention!

1. Click the Start button, and choose Settings, Control Panel.

2. Double-click the Network icon, and select the TCP/IP Protocol entry.

3. Click the Properties button.

4. If you have a static IP address, select the option labeled Specify an IP Address, type your IP address into the box, and fill in the Subnet Mask box with your subnet mask.

5. If you have a dynamic IP address, choose the Obtain an IP Address Automatically option.

6. Select Disable WINS Resolution.

7. In the section marked Gateway, type the IP address for your ISP's gateway or router, and then click the Add button.

8. Select the Enable DNS option.

9. Type the host name of your computer in the Host box.

10. Enter the domain name of your ISP in the Domain box.

11. In the DNS Server Search Order section, enter the IP address of your ISP's DNS server.

12. Type the domain name for your ISP in the Domain Suffix Search Order section, and then click the Add button.

13. Double-check all your entries, and then click OK.

14. At this point, Windows 95 asks you to reboot your computer. Click Yes.

At this point, your Windows 95 environment should have support for Dial-up Networking, TCP/IP, and the Dial-up Scripting Tool. Hopefully, you were able to successfully add any of those components that were not already installed.

Setting Up a Connection Icon

Now we're almost ready to log on. The connection icon is the icon that you use to initiate your PPP connection. To start configuring it, double-click the My Computer icon on your desktop. Next, double-click the Dial-Up Networking icon, and then double-click the Make New Connection icon. This brings up a wizard box that helps you set up a new connection entry. Simply follow these steps:

1. Enter the connection name that you want to use into the dialog box.

2. Click the Configure button, and then select the General tab.

3. In the Maximum Speed box, set the port speed for your modem. In general, 57600 is a good setting.

4. Make sure that the box marked Only Connect at This Speed is *not* checked.

5. If you are not going to use a script to automate your login process, select the Options tab. From here, you can have PPP open a login window for you so that you can manually login to your server.

6. Click OK, and then press Next in the wizard dialog box.

7. Enter the area code and phone number of your ISP in the dialog box and click Next.

8. Click Finish

At this point, you should see a new connection icon, with the name that you specified, on your system. There are just a couple of more things to do before it's ready to use.

1. Click the right mouse button on your connection icon. This brings up a pop-up menu for the connection icon.

2. Choose Properties from the pop-up menu.

3. Click the Server Type button, and then PPP from the list box.

4. Verify that the TCP/IP box in the Allowed Network Protocols section is checked, and make sure that the Log on to Network box is not selected.

5. Click OK.

6. Click OK again.

We're done configuring TCP/IP! If you want to set your modem to automatically redial, you can do so from the Settings option on the Connections menu in the Dial-Up Networking folder.

Basic Scripting

As we mentioned earlier, using a script to automate your login process makes things a lot easier. You can start your connection session and run to the fridge while Windows 95 retries your ISP dial-up line and logs you in! Also, scripting is very easy. You can think of a script as telling Windows 95 what to look for from the ISP server. Just as you might look for a login: prompt to type your username, you can have your script do the same thing. The Dial-Up Scripting Tool is the way you create scripts to control your dial-up network session. Figure 2.3 shows the Dial-Up Scripting Tool.

Fig. 2.3
The Windows 95 Dial-Up Scripting Tool.

To make a script, follow these steps:

1. Click the Start button; select Programs, and then Accessories.

2. Select the Dial-Up Scripting Tool.

3. Click the Edit button to start editing a script.

All scripts start with the line

```
proc main
```

and end with the line

```
endproc
```

Between these two statements, you enter the commands that tell Windows 95 what to transmit and what to wait for. There are three basic commands that you need to know in order to write a script: transmit, waitfor, and delay.

The *delay* statement causes your script to wait for a specified number of seconds. For example:

```
delay 3
```

causes the script to pause for three seconds.

The *waitfor* statement makes the script wait until the specified string is received. For example:

```
waitfor "ssword"
```

waits for the string "ssword" to be received by your system.

The third statement, *transmit*, transmits a string to the remote system. It does not automatically send a carriage return at the end of the string. To send a carriage return, you need to transmit the string "^M" to the remote system. Here is an example of a script:

```
proc main
delay 1
transmit "^M"
delay 1
transmit "^M"
delay 1
transmit "^M"
waitfor "name>"
transmit $USERID
transmit "^M"
waitfor "ssword>"
transmit $PASSWORD
transmit "^M"
```

```
waitfor "enu:"
transmit "3"
transmit "^M"
endproc
```

> **Note**
>
> It is usually a good idea to only use the last part of a string in a *waitfor* statement, in case the first character or two gets garbled by the network. For example, you should use `waitfor "ssword>"` instead of `waitfor "password>"`.

The above script waits for 1 second and then sends a carriage return to the remote system. It then repeats this sequence two more times. The script then waits for the string *name>* from the remote system. It sends the contents of the special variable $USERID, which contains the user ID that you enter when you start the network connection program. It follows the user ID with a carriage return.

The script then waits for the *ssword>* prompt from the remote system and sends the contents of the $PASSWORD variable. This variable contains the password that you enter when you start the network connection program. It follows the password with a carriage return. It then waits for the string *enu:*, and sends the number 5 and a carriage return. That's all there is to it!

Once you have written your script, save it with a .SCP extension. Then, in the Dial-Up Scripting Tool, select the network connection that you want to attach the script to and click Apply. Your script is now associated with that network connection and will be executed automatically any time you run that particular network connection.

You can also select the Step through Script box to be able to step through the script one line at a time to debug it. By selecting the Start Terminal Screen Minimized box, you will see no terminal box displaying the progress of your script. Uncheck this box if you want to watch your script execute as it runs.

Netscape and Earthlink

An Internet service provider, Earthlink, has teamed up with Netscape to provide an Internet access package that is easy to set up. The Earthlink Total Access software package comes with an automatic setup program, and also provides Netscape and the Eudora electronic mail program.

To obtain Total Access for Windows 95, you can download it from a variety of sites. It is available via anonymous FTP from **www.earthlink.net**, or you can contact Earthlink directly at 1-800-395-8425.

Once you have the software, it is easy to install. Just run the setup program that comes with the installation kit. For example, if Total Access were in drive A:, you would type:

a:\setup

This brings up an installation wizard that guides you through the installation process. When the installation wizard prompts you for the installation directory, enter the name of the directory where you want Total Access installed. Total Access is installed in the specified directory, and a program group is added to Windows 95.

After you complete the installation process, registration with Earthlink is very straightforward. You are prompted to create a new account or use an existing account, fill out a form with your name and address, and choose a username and password. You then get a choice of a couple of different connection pricing plans, and you enter your credit card number for billing purposes. Total Access then dials out to Earthlink via your modem and creates your account for you. Once your account is created, you are ready to take your virtual surfboard in hand and join your fellow Net citizens on the Internet.

Part II

Mastering Netscape

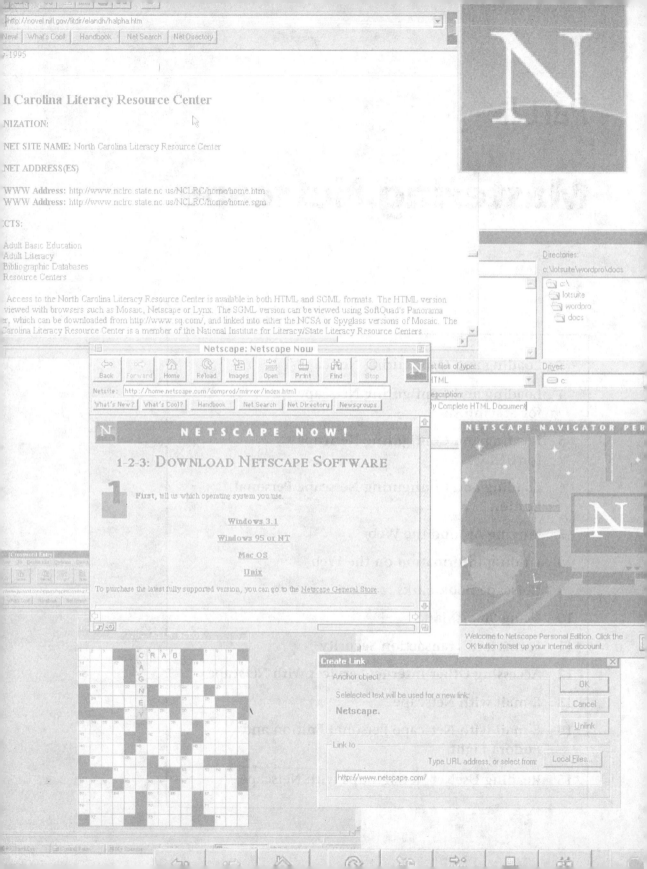

## CHAPTER 3

Loading and Configuring Netscape

In chapter 1 we discussed the history of the World Wide Web, its uses, and the direction in which it is developing. But we have yet to access the Web's bounty of information. The Web has become one of the most common methods of finding specific information about any topic under the sun. In fact, Netscape, the most popular World Wide Web browser, is used by almost 80 percent of all households and businesses connected to the Internet. That number is pretty amazing when you consider the abundant number of World Wide Web browsers available, many of which are free.

When considering the purchase of any product, you try to look at all the options available so you can get the best value for your money. The fact that Netscape is so widely used may assist you in making the decision to purchase Netscape Navigator.

Other World Wide Web browsers have some very nice features, or may cost less, but none offer the diversity and power of Netscape. When you are using Netscape the hard part is figuring out where you want to go.

In this chapter, you learn how to:

- Load Netscape from the CD
- Download Netscape from the Internet
- Get on the Web for the first time
- Get help with Netscape products

Downloading Netscape from the Internet

Netscape Navigator version 2.0 is available on the Internet, and there are several ways that you can access this file. Netscape is not freeware; the license allows a 90-day evaluation period for the software before you register. Licensing is not hard, though. Netscape allows you to register through its World Wide Web site, over the phone, or through standard U.S. Postal Service mail. Remember, you cannot receive technical support for Netscape products unless you register the version you use.

Using File Transfer Protocol

FTP, *File Transfer Protocol*, is the standard method used to upload and download files from Internet sites. Many of these sites allow *anonymous logins*, which means you do not have to have an account on the system to use the file resources.

Tip

Many FTP sites *mirror* other FTP sites. Mirroring involves copying files from the original location (often a busy site) to a matching location on another computer. FTP mirror sites make it much easier to get important information when you need it by making the software more accessible by more people.

Finding and Downloading the File

On the CD that comes with this book, you will find a copy of WS_FTP32.EXE. This is a 32-bit FTP program designed to run under a 32-bit operating system such as Windows 95. After you install the software, as shown in appendix A, go to a Netscape mirror site, or one of the sites listed by Archie, and transfer a copy of Netscape to your computer.

In this example, we use the following address from one of the Netscape corporate FTP sites: **ftp://ftp7.netscape.com/2.0beta/windows/ n32e20b1j.exe**.

II

Mastering Netscape

> **Tip**
>
> The first portion of this address, *ftp://*, shows you the type of *URL* (*Uniform Resource Locator*) being used. A URL is a single address in an expanded network addressing system. Not only does it tell you the name of the computer on which a file is located, but it also tells you specifically where the file is and how to view it. The second portion of the address, *ftp7.netscape.com*, is the Internet address of the computer with the Netscape files you are looking for. The third part of the address, */2.0beta/windows/*, is the path to the Netscape program. The last part of the address, *n32e20b1j.exe*, is the name of the specific file.

1. To transfer the file to your computer, you must first start WS_FTP32. Open the Start menu and select the WS_FTP32 icon.

2. Click the Connect button at the bottom of this screen.

3. In the Name: field on the Host dialog box, type **Netscape**.

4. In the Host: field, enter the address for Netscape's FTP site: **ftp.netscape.com**.

5. Select the Anonymous Login check box. Netiquette tells us to use our full e-mail address as a password when anonymously logging into any FTP server. Please type your e-mail address in the Password field if it is not already showing.

6. In the Initial Directory field, type **/2.0beta/windows/**. When you have completed these steps, your screen should look similar to figure 3.1.

Fig. 3.1
A completed Host entry for an FTP client.

7. Click the Save button to save your Netscape entry. Saving allows you to use this entry in the future without having to re-type it.

8. To connect to Netscape Communications Corporation, click OK. Once you connect, you are automatically placed in the correct directory to find and download Netscape 2.0.

9. The right side of your screen shows the remote host information. In this list you should see a file named n32e20b1j.exe. This is the file you

want. Highlight this file, and click the download button, shown in the margin, located between the two halves of the window. WS_FTP32 moves n32e20b1j.exe into the directory shown on the left half of your screen.

Fig. 3.2
The File Transfer button—used in WS_FTP32 to download files to your local machine.

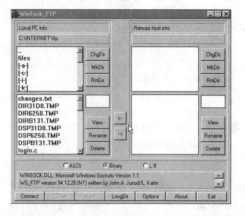

Tip

It is always best to download files into a temporary directory. By creating a temporary directory to receive your download, you can extract the compressed file into that directory without moving it. Using a temporary directory also makes clean-up a snap. All you have to do is delete the temporary directory and you are done.

Once the transfer is complete, click the Close button to disconnect from the Netscape host machine, and then choose Exit to shut down WS_FTP32.

Note

The steps for downloading this Netscape file work for any other file on any other system. You simply need to create a host entry for that other computer, as we did for Netscape.

The copy of Netscape that you just downloaded is in a *self-extracting executable file*. Double-click it from Windows Explorer, or run it from a DOS window. This extracts the installation and setup files. At this point, you can install Netscape in the same way as shown in the section "Installing the Netscape Browser." Remember to look at your temporary download directory, rather than the CD, when you are looking for the setup program to start the installation.

Creating an Archie Search

Archie is a file searching utility that searches a large list of sites and shows you all the files, articles, or UseNet newsgroups that discuss the topic you want to find. You can run an Archie search in several ways:

- Through e-mail
- Through Telnet
- Through an Archie client
- Through the World Wide Web

Install WS Archie as specified in appendix A, "What's on the CD," and then follow these steps to use Archie to search for Netscape at the various FTP sites.

▶ See "FTP/ Archie," pg. 951

1. Open the Start menu and run WS Archie.

2. In the Search For: field, type **Netscape**.

3. Select an Archie server from the Archie Server drop-down list shown in figure 3.3.

On the CD

archie.doc.ic.ac.uk	United Kingdom
archie.doc.ic.ac.uk	United Kingdom
archie.hensa.ac.uk	United Kingdom
archie.au	Australia
archie.edvz.uni-linz.ac.at	Austria
archie.univie.ac.at	Austria
archie.uqam.ca	Canada

Fig. 3.3
The list of available Archie servers provided with WS Archie.

Note

Netiquette asks all anonymous users to select the Archie server closest to your home to minimize the impact of multiple outside users using the site. Often Archie servers serve more than one function; they often provide a file storage area for the company that owns the machine. If everyone in the United States were to use the same Archie server, it would quickly become overrun, and neither the computer's owner nor the remainder of the Internet public could get access to information they need. It is much easier for all the users of the Internet if everyone from Ohio uses an Archie server in Ohio. In this way, each area of the globe has a better chance of getting the information it needs, when it needs it.

II

Mastering Netscape

4. Click the Search button. You see a screen similar to that shown in figure 3.4.

Fig. 3.4
An Archie search provides you with a listing of every instance in which it finds a reference to the search keyword.

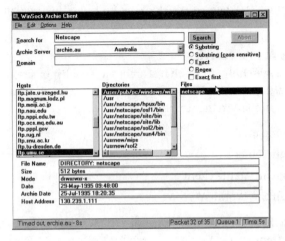

You now have two options. If you have already installed WS_FTP32, Archie uses it to download a file from its site list. Otherwise, write down the address showing the location of the Netscape files, and then use the FTP program to download the file at a later time.

Using the World Wide Web

The World Wide Web is one of the best places to find information on any subject. If you are currently using another Web browser to access the Internet, you might be able to download Netscape 2.0 from the Netscape home page located at **http://home.netscape.com**.

Note

Check to see if your current World Wide Web browser supports FTP. Generally, you find this listed as a feature in the Help file that comes with the browser.

---

1. With your current Web browser, go to the Netscape home page at **http://home.netscape.com**. If your browser allows you to manually enter a URL, you can go directly to **http://home.netscape.com/ comprod/mirror/index.html** and skip step number two. This is the address of the opening page for downloading Netscape.

2. Scroll through the document shown in figure 3.5 until you find the Netscape Now button located on that screen (see fig. 3.6).

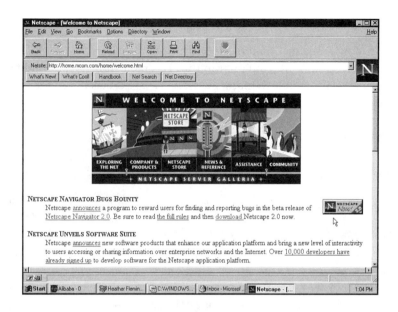

Fig. 3.5
The Netscape
Communications
Corporation's
World Wide Web
home page.

Fig. 3.6
The Netscape Now
button.

3. Netscape asks for the name of the operating system you use. Click the
   Windows 95 or NT option.

4. The Download Netscape Software step 2 screen requests the name of the
   product you want to download. Some of your options are

   - Netscape 2.0 beta with Java

   - Netscape 2.0 beta without Java

   - Netscape Navigator 1.22 Security Update

   - Netscape SmartMarks

   - Netscape Chat

   You need to select Netscape 2.0 beta with Java if you are planning to
   use the new Java support that is provided or if you want to include any
   Java programs in your documents. If you are not currently interested in
   Java, you can select Netscape 2.0 beta without Java.

5. A list of locations from which you can download Netscape appears. This
   list includes the majority of the mirror sites listed in the section titled
   "The Netscape Mirror Site List." Choose the site closest to your current
   computer location.

6. Once you have downloaded Netscape, close your Web browser.

Because most of the sites holding Netscape store the program as a self-extracting executable file, you can run the executable from a DOS window, or by double-clicking it in Windows Explorer. This extracts the compressed files and allows you to install Netscape. From this point, you can follow the instructions in the section entitled "Installing the Netscape Browser" to install it.

Note

Time is always of the essence in today's hurried society. We constantly rush to get to work on time, pick up the kids after school, fix and eat dinner, and, hopefully, catch up on weekend projects looming over our heads on Wednesday.

It is always nice to start a new project with some idea about the amount of time that it is going to involve. The following table shows the average download time I experienced when transferring this file several times while preparing this book. These times should be close to what you will experience, although you should not worry if your times are a bit longer or shorter.

Connection Type	Total Transfer Time
14,400 modem	20 minutes
28,800 modem (at least a 24000 baud carrier)	9 minutes
57,600 network	6 minutes
T1 cable	3 minutes

The Netscape Mirror Site List

Netscape allows only a few sites to mirror its information. The following list shows you all the official sites from North America, and many major sites from other areas of the globe. Of course, you can always download a copy of Netscape from the Netscape Communications Corporation site, listed in the North American section, from anywhere in the world.

Since the most logical place to get a program is from the company that makes it, especially if it is not available mail order, it would stand to reason that this corporation would have the busiest file servers. This reasoning holds true for the Netscape FTP sites. You will often find that the main Netscape site is busy, even though they have seven servers available from which you can download programs. The solution to this information bottleneck lies in the development of mirror sites. Mirror sites provide easy access to information by having copies of files from other computers that could be located across the continent, or on the other side of the globe. Mirror sites draw away from the pool of people that are waiting to get onto the main file server.

North America

- Massachusetts Institute of Technology, Cambridge—**ftp:// ftp.lcs.mit.edu/pub/netscape/2.0beta/windows/ n32e20b2.exe**

- Netscape Communications Corp.—

  ftp://ftp2.netscape.com/2.0beta/windows/n32e20b2.exe

  ftp://ftp3.netscape.com/2.0beta/windows/n32e20b2.exe

  ftp://ftp4.netscape.com/2.0beta/windows/n32e20b2.exe

  ftp://ftp5.netscape.com/2.0beta/windows/n32e20b2.exe

  ftp://ftp6.netscape.com/2.0beta/windows/n32e20b2.exe

  ftp://ftp7.netscape.com/2.0beta/windows/n32e20b2.exe

- University of Nebraska, Omaha—**ftp://unicron.unomaha.edu/ pub/netscape/2.0beta/windows/n32e20b2.exe**

- New York University, New York—**ftp://found.nyu.edu/pub/ netscape/2.0beta/windows/n32e20b2.exe**

- University of Illinois School of Life Sciences —**ftp:// ftp.life.uiuc.edu/pub/netscape/2.0beta/windows/ n32e20b2.exe**

- University of North Carolina at Chapel Hill—**ftp:// sunSITE.unc.edu/pub/packages/infosystes/WWW/clients/ netscape/2.0beta/windows/n32e20b2.exe**

- Washington University, St. Louis—**ftp://wuarchive.wustl.edu/ packages/www/Netscape/2.0beta/windows/n32e20b2.exe**

- University of Oregon, Eugene—**ftp://ftp.uoregon.edu/Netscape/ 2.0beta/windows/n32e20b2.exe**

South America

There are currently no mirror sites available in South America. You will need to use the North American sites when downloading Netscape.

Europe

There are no sites mirroring Netscape within Europe. You must use the Netscape Communications Corporation sites shown in the North America listing or the next closest site to your location.

Asia

- Keio University, Japan—**ftp://bash.cc.keio.ac.jp/pub/ netscape/ 2.0beta/windows/n32e20b2.exe**
- Radiation Lab/Accelerator Research Facility, Japan—**ftp:// ftp.riken.go.jp/pub/ WWW/netscape2.0b/windows/ n32e20b2.exe**
- Institute of Physical and Chemical Research (RIKEN), Japan—**ftp:// ftp.riken.go.jp/pub/ WWW/netscape2.0b/windows/ n32e20b2.exe**
- Hebrew University of Jerusalem, Israel—**ftp://sunsite.huji.ac.il/ pub/ Netscape/2.0beta/windows/n32e20b2.exe**

Africa

There are no sites mirroring Netscape within the continent of Africa. You must use the Netscape Communications Corporation sites shown in the North America listing or the next closest site to your location.

Australia

- University of Adelaide—**ftp://ftp.adelaide.edu.au/pub/WWW/ Netscape/2.0beta/windows/n32e20b2.exe**

Loading Netscape

Of course, you have to install the program before you can catch that first wave. But don't worry; Netscape has included a wizard that guides you through the entire installation process. Netscape has a few system requirements that you must have to complete the installation and run the program effectively.

Installation Requirements

The following list shows all the requirements for installing and running Netscape Navigator v.2.0.

- Mouse
- Windows 95

- 386SX or compatible machine
- 2MB of hard drive space
- 4MB of memory (8MB recommended)
- LAN or a SLIP/PPP connection to the Internet

Caution

These are just the minimum requirements to run Netscape 2.0 under Windows 95. Keep in mind that you need more hard drive space if you keep a large list of sites you have visited or if you download lots of images and other files.

The minimum requirements only take into consideration the amount of hard drive space and memory that is required to load and run the program in most situations. When you visit a Web site that has an extraordinary amount of graphics on it, the page takes a long time to load if you only have the "minimum" amount of RAM.

Installing the Netscape Browser

The installation process is relatively quick and painless. Because Netscape uses a wizard to walk you through the installation, most of your questions are answered right on the screen. If you experience problems during the installation, call one of the phone numbers listed in the section titled "Using Netscape Phone Support" later in this chapter.

1. Close any Windows or DOS programs that are running. Sometimes other programs use files or memory that Netscape needs to use during the install process.

2. Place the CD in your CD-ROM drive. Click the Start button or press Ctrl+Esc and select Run.

3. Type **c:\temp\setup** in the Open: field of the Run dialog box (replace "temp" with the path to the setup program on your hard drive).

Fig. 3.7
The Windows 95 Run dialog box from which you start the installation of Netscape.

4. Click OK to start the installation of Netscape 2.0. First, the setup wizard (which guides you through the installation process) is installed. Once the wizard's initialization is complete, an introduction and a warning on Netscape appear. Click Next.

5. Netscape requires a specific destination directory, as shown in figure 3.8. This is the directory that stores the main portion of Netscape. You can either use the default directory, or you can enter your own directory name.

Fig. 3.8
The default installation directory for Netscape 2.0 is C:\Program Files\Netscape \Navigator\.

To specify your own directory, click Browse. You see a list showing your current directory structure, as shown in figure 3.9. Select the directory you want to place Netscape into, or type the name of a new directory, and click OK.

Fig. 3.9
You can easily select an alternative directory from this Choose Directory dialog box.

Note

The examples in this book use the default path. If you install Netscape in another directory, please go to that location when you see a reference to *c:\Program Files\Netscape.*

Whether you choose to create your own directory or use the predefined directory structure, you need to click Next to continue.

6. Netscape now copies the files from the CD to your hard drive. The scales shown in figure 3.10 enable you to keep track of the installation process. When it is done, the wizard creates a program group folder and shortcut icons that allow you to run Netscape directly from your Start menu.

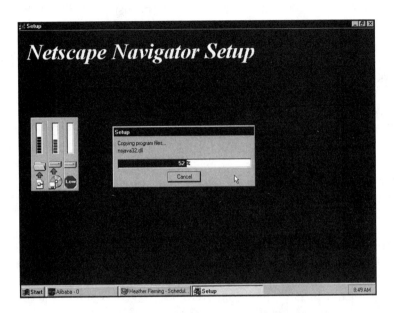

Fig. 3.10
Netscape makes it easy to see how your installation is progressing by providing a setup status bar and checks on your available disk space.

7. When you see the short message letting you know that the installation was successful, click OK. A prompt asking you to read the README.TXT file should appear. Choose Yes or No.

Note

The README.TXT file is full of useful information. It guides you through setting up Netscape to deal with Win32s, and lets you know how to procure and load the appropriate WINSOCK.DLL file. The README.TXT file also gives some basic pointers on where to get more information if you encounter problems using Netscape. Although it does not provide very much helpful information for individuals that are first-time users of Netscape, it may assist some old pros fix a new problem.

Now you have Netscape installed. Because this is the latest version that is available, you should not have to go anywhere soon to get a newer version.

Getting on the Web for the First Time

◀ See "Connect-
ing to the
Internet,"
pg. 37

The World Wide Web is considered one of the best places to get information on any subject, at any time. To reach this large body of information, you first need to connect to the network of computer systems that makes up the Internet. Use the information in the following sections to connect to your Internet service provider or to your company's network. If you have problems attaining these connections, chapter 2 provides you with more detailed information.

Connecting to Your Service Provider

Although the term service provider usually refers to a dial-up SLIP or PPP connection, you can also use a standard TCP/IP LAN connection. There are specific details in chapter 2, "Connecting to the Internet," that discuss how to set up a working Internet connection for all the operating systems used by Netscape products. The following section covers only the basic steps in the setup process for Windows 95.

Making a LAN Connection

When using a *Local Area Network* (*LAN*) to connect to the Internet, you must make sure that your computer is correctly configured to use the specific type of network to which it is physically attached. You have to know the specific type of network card that your computer uses and the names of the drivers that are required to run your card. Once you have this information, you must load those drivers, or tell your computer to do it automatically for you each time it starts, before you can connect to the network. The following steps guide you through the process of getting these drivers loaded and running properly.

1. Open the Control Panel and select the Networks icon.

2. On your Network Properties screen, make sure that you have a TCP/IP protocol loaded for your network card.

> **Note**
>
> This protocol needs to be configured with the following information:
>
> ■ Your network IP address
>
> ■ The address of your Internet gateway
>
> ■ The address of the Domain Name Servers (DNS) used by your facility

Complete the configuration by choosing Properties and filling out the forms on the tab dialog box that appears. See chapter 2 for detailed information on how to configure these settings.

◀ See "Direct Connections," pg. 42

3. Choose the OK button to exit this screen once you have ensured that the proper drivers are loaded.

4. Double-click the Netscape Navigator icon on your desktop. If you do not find this icon, you can open the Start menu, select Programs, and then the Netscape folder and choose the Netscape icon located on this menu to start the program.

Netscape finds your network and travels through it and out onto the Internet to find Netscape's home page. Once you are there you can travel across the Net to anywhere.

▶ See "Finding Information on the Web," pg. 167

Troubleshooting

Every time I open Netscape I get an error message telling me that I have a Winsock error.

Generally, you get this error when you do not have your TCP/IP protocol properly loaded. Go back to the Control Panel's Network Properties dialog box and ensure that the appropriate TCP/IP and network drivers for your network card are loaded. If you have selected the wrong network card, you will load inappropriate drivers and receive this message. If you just installed your network drivers, you must restart your computer for them to load. Windows 95 does not automatically load the drivers into your computer's memory after you install them.

Making a SLIP/PPP Connection

Very few home users and relatively few businesses have a direct connection to the Internet, which leaves the majority of the world connecting to the Internet through a SLIP or PPP connection and a modem. Because Netscape does not provide you with a dialing program, you have to use the one that comes with Windows 95, or another third-party dial-up connector. Before you attempt to use Netscape the first time, check your dial-up program. It will save you time in the long run.

1. Open the Control Panel and select the Networks icon.

2. Check to ensure that you have the dial-up adapter and a TCP/IP protocol loaded for that adapter.

II

Mastering Netscape

3. Open the Start menu and choose the Programs option, and then choose the Accessories option. This opens the Accessories pop-up menu on which you will find an icon labeled Dial-Up Networking. This is the utility that dials your phone connection for you.

4. Open the Start menu, select the Programs option, and then choose the Netscape Navigator group option.

5. Choose the Netscape Navigator option from the resulting menu.

Netscape automatically starts the dial-up networking client, which calls your service provider and establishes a connection. Depending on how you have installed the dial-up client, you might have to manually enter your name and password. When you establish your connection, all the features of Netscape are available.

Selecting a Home Page

▶ See "The Home
Page Button,"
pg. 169

We have all heard about creating personal home pages that reflect our hobbies and interests. Netscape also uses the term "home page" to designate its point of entry onto the Web when the program is first started. When you first run Netscape, you see Netscape Communications Corporation's home page on its Web server appear automatically. As you use the World Wide Web, you will probably find yourself returning to one page time after time. Sometimes you will go there three and four times a day to retrieve information. When you find yourself visiting a site this frequently, you want to make it Netscape's entry point into the world of the Web. It may be your personal home page or the introductory document for your company's Web server. There is more information on how to use the home page in chapter 8, "Finding Information on the Web."

To change Netscape's home page, simply follow these steps:

Tip

Due to the many new developments taking place with Netscape products every day, you may want to leave your Home Page option set to the Netscape Communications Corporation's home page. This way you can receive immediate notification of updates to Netscape as soon as you start the product.

1. If it is not already running, start Netscape by double-clicking its program icon.

2. Open the Options menu and select the General option.

3. Choose the Appearance tab (see fig. 3.11). You see an option labeled Start With:. This option allows you to either start Netscape with a blank page or to specify a home page.

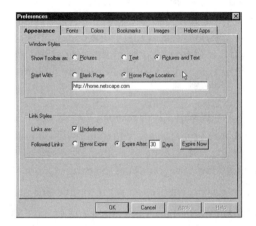

Fig. 3.11
The configuration screen for setting Netscape's home page and other general options.

4. Click the Home Page Location radio button.

5. Enter the URL of the site from which you want to start exploring the World Wide Web every day into the empty field below your Home Page Location radio button.

6. Choose OK to save your selection, and the next time you start Netscape you will see the site that you selected.

You do not need to worry about selecting a home page that does not include links to every site you visit often. Netscape includes a very advanced bookmark feature that allows you to keep a list of the sites that interest you. For more information on creating and using Netscape's bookmark feature, see chapter 9, "Netscape Bookmarks."

▶ See "Netscape Bookmarks," pg. 209

Saving and Printing Copies of a Web Page

Because the Web is used as a source of information on a myriad of topics, you often need to keep a copy of the material that you read. Sometimes you need to incorporate some of this information in another document, or you may simply need a hard copy to give to someone else. In either case, Netscape allows you to retain that Web site permanently with a click of your mouse.

Saving an HTML File for Future Reference

All Web pages are created from a text file that has special key commands stored in it that the Web browser reads. These codes allow us to see graphics, colorful backgrounds, bold text, and brightly colored links to other sites. You can save a copy of the original HTML file for future reference by following these steps:

1. Open the File menu and select Save As or press Ctrl+S.

2. The Save As dialog box appears, which allows you to direct Netscape to save a copy of the HTML code to a directory of your choosing. The default directory is c:\Program Files\Netscape\Navigator\Program.

3. Select the directory in which you want to save this page.

4. Place your cursor in the File Name: field and enter a name for this HTML document.

5. Choose Save. You have now saved a copy of this World Wide Web page that you can view at any time without actually connecting to the Internet.

Because you are saving pages, you must need to look at them at least every once in a while. The following steps assist you in reading a saved HTML document.

1. Open the File menu and choose the Open File option, or press Ctrl+O.

2. The Open dialog box appears. Change to the c:\Program Files\Netscape\Navigator\Programs directory, if you are not already there.

3. Click your mouse pointer on the name of the file that you want to open.

4. Choose Open.

Netscape opens the file, allowing you to continue working with that Web site. You do not have to retrace your steps, you can forge ahead finding the information you need to complete your tasks.

Printing Web Pages

Sometimes you simply need to capture the information that is on a Web page in the fastest way possible and you do not necessarily have to be able to look at it in electronic form. That is where Netscape's printing feature enters the picture.

1. Open the File menu and select the Print option, or press Ctrl+P.

2. Select the name of your printer from the Name drop-down list.

3. Set the number of Copies and the Print Range options to meet your needs.

4. When you're done setting up the printer, choose the OK button.

A window appears telling you that your document is being retrieved from the main Web site and that it is being formatted for the printer. This process should only take a few moments, and you can resume your search of the World Wide Web.

> **Tip**
>
> If you end up with a stack of printed pages and you're not sure where they are from, you will find the URL for that Web page located in the upper-right corner of the printout. This URL also allows you to go back to that site to get more or updated information.

Displaying Information on a Web Page

Netscape 2.0 allows you to look at a Web page in three different views. The first, and most common, is through the browser with all the HTML tags activated. This is the way you are going to automatically see all sites when you first jump to them.

The second method involves looking at the text file that makes up the body of the Web page. This is viewing the document source, and it is useful if you want to know how the Webmaster at that site achieved a specific look in her Web page. Of course, if you are just starting to program with HTML, you will want to look at a lot of Web sites in this view. It helps you learn the language, and the conventions that are used when writing HTML documents.

To view the source document of any Web page, open the View menu and select the By Document Source option. This opens a document viewer, generally the QuickView utility that comes with Windows 95 unless you have asked Netscape to use another. In this view you see the source code that is interpreted by the Web browser to create the graphical pages that you see on your screen.

II

Mastering Netscape

The third method shows you specific information about the Web page. Open the File menu and select the By Document Info option. This opens another Netscape window using a frame. In the top half of this window you see a copy of the main document. In the bottom half of this screen you see a summary listing about that Web page, as shown in figure 3.12.

Fig. 3.12
The Netscape browser window showing both the main Web page and the appropriate summary information on that file.

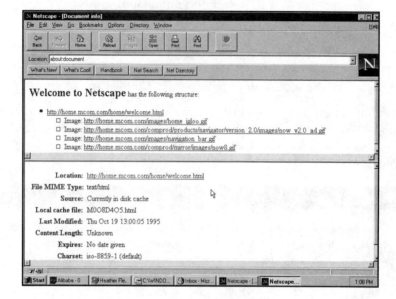

Getting Help for Netscape Products

Because Netscape is used by such a large base of Internet users, you can get product support quickly and easily from a variety of sources. Netscape Communications Corporation provides technical support to its licensed customers. UseNet newsgroups discuss how to use and configure Netscape to work in various situations. Listserv discussion groups also discuss the use of Netscape and how to make it perform specific required tasks. And once again there is the World Wide Web. The Web has many sites specifically designed to be viewed with Netscape. Many of these site owners will assist you in configuring Netscape to view their sites in the best possible fashion. You can generally contact the site owners by sending an e-mail message to *webmaster@the.site.name*.

Receiving Technical Support from Netscape

Netscape Communications Corporation provides its customers with many ways to get in touch with technical support, including e-mail, World Wide

Web pages, its online Help system, a printed handbook (for registered users), and technical voice support over a telephone.

Using E-mail

In this world of fast paced, practically instantaneous communication, electronic mail is becoming the best way to get information to and from your associates. Technical support services are also starting to jump on this bandwagon. Netscape has quite a few e-mail addresses from which you can get information. Some of them respond with a generic letter full of important information and answers to the most common questions that people ask. Others respond individually by qualified support or sales personnel.

Table 3.1 Netscape Corporation Electronic Mail Addresses		
For Help on...	**Department Name**	**E-mail Address**
The Netscape Test-Drive Servers	Technical Support	**test-drive@netscape.com**
Netscape Navigator 2.0 for licensed customers	Technical Support	**client@netscape.com**
Getting information about purchasing products	Sales—*automated*	**sales@netscape.com**
General product questions and answers	Sales—*automated*	**info@netscape.com**
Licensed Netscape Servers	Technical Support	**server@netscape.com**

When using a manually monitored system, include your name, return e-mail address, and product registration number in your message. Netscape provides support only to individuals who provide this information.

Referring to Netscape's Help System

Netscape's help system uses a series of linked HTML pages, some of which are located on your local computer, while others are located at Netscape's Web site. The Help menu in Netscape allows you to jump directly to important product support pages for your version of Netscape (see fig. 3.13). These pages include the Release Notes for your version, the related FAQs for Navigator, a Netscape Handbook, and a series of articles on how to get assistance and give feedback on Netscape's products. You can generally answer most, if not all, of your questions by reading these documents.

II

Mastering Netscape

Fig. 3.13
The available
Netscape Help
utilities located in
the Help menu.

Using Netscape's World Wide Web Pages

Netscape uses its Web site to provide much of its product support, not to
mention sales and marketing pushes. You can reach the Technical Support
pages by clicking the Assistance portion of the main Netscape imagemap located at the top of the Netscape home page. The address of Netscape Communications Corporation's Technical Support home page is **http://
home.mcom.com/assist/index.html**. Figure 3.14 shows you what to
expect.

Fig. 3.14
The main
Technical Support
Web page for
Netscape Navi-
gator.

When you get to this page you are greeted with product FAQs, search engines, a storefront, and a list of all the services Netscape provides for its products. You simply need to find the most appropriate services for the product
you have questions on, click its link, and continue down your path to a completely working product.

The Web site contains layers upon layers of information. If you see a topic
that might be helpful, jump to it and read it. If the site does not contain the
information you are looking for, choose Back and continue on to your next

option. You never know when a document is going to provide you with that one clue that solves your problem. Hey, even if it didn't solve your problem today, it may keep you from having another problem in the future.

Using Netscape Phone Support

For those of you who want to talk to someone voice to voice, you can get product support over the telephone. There are quite a few numbers you can call depending on the type of questions that you want to ask.

Table 3.2 Netscape Corporation's Support Phone Numbers		
For Questions About...	**Department**	**Phone Number**
Problems with the any Netscape servers	Technical Support	415-528-2727
Problems with a licensed version of Netscape	Technical Support	800-320-2099
Purchasing a product or checking on an order	Sales	415-528-2555
For assistance with Netscape Navigator Personal Edition	Technical Support	503.626.5475

Getting Help from UseNet Newsgroups

As mentioned earlier, UseNet newsgroups are one of the best ways for people with common interests to get together. There are many different newsgroups that discuss Netscape products. The following list names a few UseNet searching tools with some of the known sites that you can use to get into a UseNet discussion. I have also included specific instructions on how to use *Dejanews*, a UseNet newsgroup message searching utility that I have found helpful.

- *Launch Pad*—**http://sunsite.unc.edu/alt.fan.mozilla comp.infosystems.www.browsers**
- *TileNet*—**http://www.tile.net/tile/news/index.html comp.infosystems.www.misc comp.infosystems.www.users**
- *Dejanews*—**http://build1.dejanews.com/dnhome.html comp.infosystems.www.browsers.ms-windows**

The Dejanews system is very easy to use. The following steps enable you to search its entire message database for information specific to your problem with Netscape.

> **Note**
>
> Please remember that vocabulary and spelling are very important. You may refer to "e-mail" in a search, while someone else calls it "email," and another individual uses the phrase "Internet mail." Your search will not find the messages left by those other individuals. To do a thorough exploration, you need to search on as many different phrases and spellings as you can to get the broadest range of information out of your search.

1. In Netscape, enter the URL above as the address you want to visit.
2. Choose the Search option.
3. Click the AND radio button in the Define Operator list.
4. Enter your search criteria, such as **Netscape**, and choose the Search button, as shown in figure 3.15.

Fig. 3.15
The main Dejanews search utility screen configured to perform a search for all discussions of Netscape.

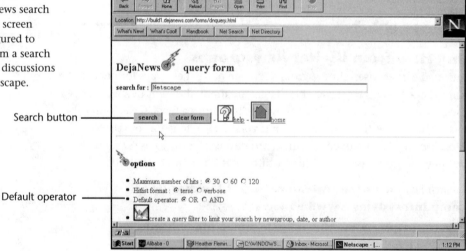

5. Choose Continue from the Security Warning dialog box.

Your screen now changes to a listing of all the messages and UseNet newsgroups that are currently discussing Netscape Navigator. This screen should be similar to the one shown in figure 3.16. You can read the UseNet discussions by double-clicking the highlighted message subject.

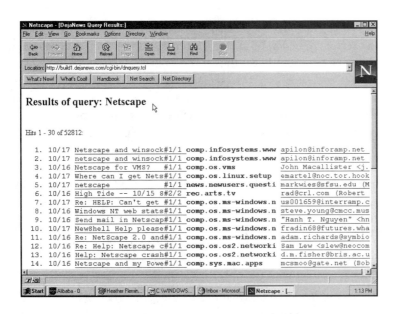

Fig. 3.16
The list of the
most recent
discussions about
Netscape that the
Dejanews service
could find.

Note

If you would like more details on using UseNet newsgroups with Netscape, please see chapter 15. To go directly to a UseNet newsgroup, type the address preceded by *news:* in the URL: field at the top of your Netscape screen.

For example, if you want to look at the **comp.infosystems.www.browsers.ms-windows** newsgroup, place your cursor in the URL: field on your main Netscape screen and type **news:comp.infosystems.www.browsers.ms-windows**. Press Enter to tell Netscape to search for that address.

▶ See "A UseNet Primer," pg.371

General Troubleshooting

There are more "little" problems experienced every day than all the technical support departments across the country could fix. So when you do have to call or write for technical support, have the following information handy to help the process along:

- ■ *Your name and registration number.* Most technical support services will not assist you unless you have a registered product.

- ■ *Version of the software you are using.* This narrows down the list of known problems so the support specialist can quickly switch gears to help you best with your product version.

II

Mastering Netscape

- *A short description of the problem.* For example, "I am able to connect to my service provider, John Doe's Internet Connections, but once I start Netscape I constantly get the error message `Netscape is unable to locate server: www.yahoo.com. This server does not have a DNS entry. Check the server name in the location (URL) and try again.` With this information the technician will know if your dial-up PPP connection is working properly, allowing them to narrow down the possible sources of your problem. They will also know the error messages that you are receiving in case this is a known problem they can fix in just a few minutes. When Technical Support personnel have to dig for information on a problem, it needlessly takes more of your time and causes you and them more frustration than the problem is worth.

- *The name and version of your operating system.* If you are running a product designed for Windows 3.1 under Windows 95, you may be having a known conflict with the operating system.

- *The type of Internet connection you are using:* SLIP/PPP or LAN.

- If you have a SLIP/PPP connection, know the brand and speed of your modem, and the name of the TCP/IP stack you are loading.

  If you have a LAN connection, know the name of the TCP/IP stack you are loading, the type of network card you are using, and the type of connection your network has to the Internet (e.g., T1 cable, 57600 baud line, etc.).

- Try other Internet applications, such as Ping or Telnet, and let the support technician know if they work properly.

- Know when the problem first started, and whether you recently added any new software to your computer around that time. Sometimes installing new software makes your old software not run properly. Many software packages come with their own versions of hardware drivers, and a new software package will often overwrite the version of the driver installed and used by a previously installed package.

Knowing this information in advance helps the technician to diagnose your problem, get you off the telephone, and back onto the Web faster. Without this type of information, you will be extending the time involved in solving your problem. Technical support personnel are highly trained individuals that really know their job. Remember that they are people, too, and can't read your mind, nor can they see your computer screen. They are dependent on your descriptions of a situation, or a screen to direct them to a solution. By providing them with as much information as you can, you are helping yourself and all the other people who are waiting on the phone lines.

CHAPTER 4

Loading and Configuring Netscape for the Macintosh

The Internet has traditionally been difficult to understand and use for two reasons: it's vast, and it's arcane.

The size of the Internet is easy to see. When Valvoline advertises its Web page address (**http://www.valvoline.com**/) during televised stock car races in the southeast United States, you realize that the Internet has spread into parts of our lives unimaginable 10 or more years ago. No one expects the Internet to become any less pervasive any time soon, if ever.

In the early days of the Internet, Internet access was difficult. Everyone involved in the Internet received access through their professional careers in academia and the military. Since the Internet was built primarily by linking computer systems that spoke various flavors of UNIX, UNIX knowledge became the required passport. When the Internet grew large enough that people could not hope to find what they needed just casting about by themselves, search tools were created with names like FTP, Telnet, Gopher, Archie, and Veronica. These tools were created for use by computer professionals, and were not designed for today's average user of the Internet.

Since 1990, the World Wide Web has been created as a user-friendly way to link many of these information resources and search engines together. The first Web browser, NCSA Mosaic, was a wonderful improvement in ease-of-use of the Internet. Since Mosaic's first version, many other Web browsers, including Netscape, have been developed. While there are many Web browsers, one study in the spring of 1995 estimated that three-quarters of all Web access was through a Netscape browser. This chapter discusses how to get Netscape 2.0 running on your Macintosh computer.

In this chapter, you learn the following:

- How to get Netscape onto your Macintosh
- What communications software you need in addition to Netscape, and where to get it
- How to configure Netscape

Getting Netscape

The two most likely ways for you to install Netscape on your Macintosh are either by downloading a newer version of Netscape with an already-installed older version of Netscape or other World Wide Web browser, or using floppy disks from a purchased copy of Netscape. If you are installing Netscape from a set of floppy disks, follow the instructions provided.

If you are using Netscape or another Web browser, the URL for downloading the most current version of Netscape is **http://home.netscape.com/comprod/mirror/index.html**.

If you have FTP (File Transfer Protocol) software, you can look for the FTP site **ftp.netcom.com**. If that site is busy, try **ftp2.netcom.com**, **ftp3.netcom.com**, **ftp4.netcom.com**, **ftp5.netcom.com**, **ftp6.netcom.com**, or **ftp7.netcom.com**. After you get through to the FTP site, look for the folder the files are stored in. As of this writing, the full path for the 2.0 beta release of Netscape is **ftp.netcom.com/2.0beta/netscape/mac/netscape2.0-b1.hqx**.

The Netscape Now! page is where you always find the most current version of the Netscape software (see fig. 4.1).

Fig. 4.1
Netscape Now!
page.

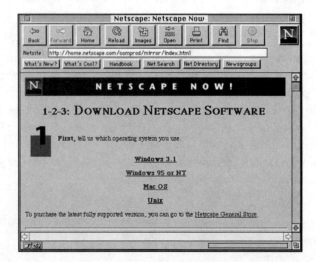

> **Note**
>
> If you already have Netscape and are installing a newer version, find Netscape on your Macintosh and note what folder the application is in. If you are downloading Netscape with an older edition of Netscape, choose the Preferences command from the Options menu, and then look at the Directories and Applications dialog box to see the default FTP download directory. If the default FTP directory is the same folder your current Netscape is located in, change the download folder to another folder. If you do not change the default download directory, you will overwrite your currently installed version of Netscape.

Follow Netscape's instructions on the following pages of its Web site. After you download the file, you need to uncompress the compressed file.

Installation Requirements

In order to install Netscape, you need a Macintosh that has a 68020 processor or better, can run System 7.0 or later, and has at least 3MB of free RAM and about 3MB of hard disk space.

> **Note**
>
> Netscape will not run on the Mac Plus, SE, Classic, Portable, or Powerbook 100.

Any helper applications you install will also want additional memory, from less than 400KB for StuffIt Expander to 2.5MB or more for Whurlwind. You also need at least a 14,400 baud modem.

The previous paragraph discussed the minimum requirements for Netscape on the Macintosh. A more realistic setup would have a Macintosh with the following:

- Either a 68040 or PowerPC processor
- At least 8MB of total RAM (not free RAM, although more RAM is always better)
- A color monitor (to take advantage of the image display capability of Netscape)
- The fastest modem you can find (28,800 external modems for the Macintosh are available for under $150 as of this writing)

Netscape, like almost every other application, performs better with more memory. For better performance and reliability, a good general rule for Macintosh software is to set the "minimum size" memory requirement to 25 percent higher than its default setting. Also, you can set Netscape's cache value higher, so that more images and Web pages are stored on your hard disk, which gives you faster response when jumping to a Web page you've visited in that session. With a large cache, your newsreader and electronic mail requirements, several helper applications (sound, video, uncompressing files, VRML, and so on), and your Netscape and helper applications folder (counting the additions created in the Preferences folder of the System Folder) could easily reach 6MB or more of memory and 20MB or more of hard disk space.

Installing Netscape

After you have the Netscape installer icon on your Macintosh desktop, double-click the icon to display the Netscape Installer window shown in figure 4.2.

Fig. 4.2
The Netscape Installer window.

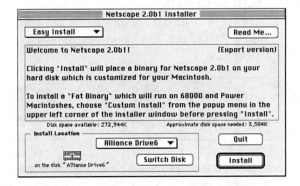

The Easy Install option, shown as the default selection of the pop-up menu in the upper-left of the window, installs a version of Netscape appropriate to your Macintosh (either a PowerPC-native version, or a version capable of running on 68000-series Macintoshes). If you choose Custom Install from the pop-up menu, you can install a fat binary version of Netscape that runs on both Power Macintoshes and 68000-series Macintoshes.

Note

Although a fat binary is larger than either a PowerPC-native application or a 68000-series version of the same application, sometimes a fat binary can be useful. At one time, I was commuting between a Power Macintosh at one location and a Macintosh SE in the second location. By carrying an external hard disk, I was able to travel with all my files and applications. Any processor-specific version of the several I used would have been inconvenient. However, available disk space on your system may recommend against wholesale installation of fat binaries.

If you have multiple disks attached to your Macintosh, use the Switch Disk button in the bottom center of the window to select the desired installation disk. Selecting the name of the disk next to its icon in the Installer window displays a pop-up list of the available disks and an option to select a folder of the current disk. If there is not enough disk space to install Netscape (about 3.5MB), the Installer will not allow you to install to that disk, and will display a message that you should select another disk. After you have decided where to install Netscape and checked to see if the chosen disk has enough memory (about 3.5MB), click the Install button in the lower-right corner of the window. An Installing window appears with a progress bar that fills in as the files are installed. A dialog box appears if installation is successful, and prompts you to quit the Netscape Installer or perform further installations (see fig. 4.3).

Fig. 4.3
The Netscape Installer window after a successful installation.

Macintosh Prerequisites: MacTCP and ConfigPPP

MacTCP is the Macintosh version of TCP/IP (Transmission Control Protocol/ Internet Protocol) used by research organizations, universities, and the Internet to allow different types of computers to connect with each other over a network.

SLIP (Serial Line Internet Protocol) and *PPP* (Point-to-Point Protocol) are protocols that use TCP/IP to make your personal computer a part of the Internet as long as the link to your ISP (Internet service provider) stays open.

> **Note**
>
> If you have Netscape or another World Wide Web browser running on your Macintosh already and are just upgrading your version of Netscape, you have MacTCP and some form of SLIP/PPP working already. Skip ahead to the "Setting Basic Preferences" section of this chapter for information on how to customize your version of Netscape to work best for you.

MacTCP is included with System 7.5, but was not installed if an Easy [System] Install was performed. If MacTCP is not in your Macintosh's System Folder, install the control panel with the following steps:

1. Insert Disk 1 of your set of System 7.5 floppy disks (or the CD, if your System disk shipped as a CD-ROM), and click the Continue button in the Welcome to System 7.5 window.

2. Click the Easy Install option in the upper-left of the Installer window, and select Custom Install from the pop-up list (see fig. 4.4).

Fig. 4.4
Custom Install.

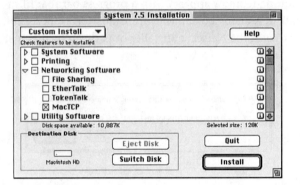

3. Click once on the triangle to the left of Networking Software to show the items in that folder. Click the checkbox to the left of MacTCP, and then click the Install button.

4. If you are using a CD-ROM, wait until you see a dialog box that says Installation was successful, and then click the Restart button to restart the Macintosh.

You also need either SLIP or PPP software to allow Netscape for Macintosh to talk to MacTCP. Apple does not supply SLIP or PPP software, but there are several shareware and freeware packages available.

> **Note**
>
> SLIP has almost entirely died out; almost everyone is using a PPP connection. SLIP software (such as InterSLIP) tends to be found in the same archive location as PPP software, so if you need SLIP, just follow my pointers to PPP software.

One place to find PPP packages such as MacPPP, ConfigPPP, and FreePPP is the Info-Mac HyperArchive. The URL of the TCP/IP-related software directory is **http://hyperarchive.lcs.mit.edu/HyperArchive/Abstracts/ comm/tcp/HyperArchive.html**.

After you download and uncompress the file, the PPP software will be a control panel with a README file. Install the PPP software by dragging the icons onto the closed System Folder, and then restart your Macintosh.

If you are installing MacTCP and ConfigPPP, you need several pieces of information from your Internet Service Provider or system administrator. If they support Macintoshes at all, they may have a set of instructions prepared for configuring MacTCP, ConfigPPP, and Netscape.

For MacTCP, you need to know the following information to enter into the window that appears when you select the More button from the MacTCP window (see fig. 4.5).

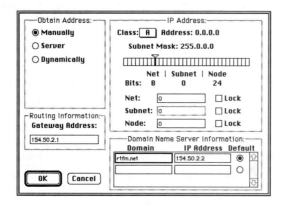

Fig. 4.5
The MacTCP 2.0.6 More window.

■ *How your system obtains the IP address*—Indicate this by choosing one of the radio buttons in the upper-left corner of the window.

■ *Gateway address*—This is typically four sets of one to three numbers with periods between the sets. A gateway address looks like this: 151.2.46.2.

■ *Class of the server*—The A that is visible is a drop-down menu from which you can select A, B, or C.

■ *Net, subnet, and node values*—These are three (normally) single-digit numbers.

■ *Domain name and IP address*—The domain is typically going to be the hostname of your Internet service provider, and normally is two or more words separated by periods. The IP Address field is the IP address corresponding to your ISP's domain name, and will look like the gateway address.

Mastering Netscape

For ConfigPPP, you need the following information to enter in the Config window:

- PPP server name
- Port speed of your Macintosh
- Flow control to use
- Type of telephone line (tone dial or pulse dial)
- Telephone number to dial
- Modem Init string
- Connect script for establishing connection

If you have difficulty configuring MacTCP and ConfigPPP, note these tips:

- If you are trying to enter values into the More window of MacTCP and the only fields you can enter values in are the Domain Name and IP addresses in the lower-right corner, you should set the Obtain Address buttons in the upper-left corner to Manually. Once you are done entering values in this window, remember to set the Obtain Address button to the correct choice.

- If you've entered all your information and you're having problems connecting, double-check everything. People often have trouble with typing errors. Get a friend or coworker to verify that all the information you have on-screen is correct.

- If you're still having trouble and there's another Macintosh that works with the network or service provider, find whoever is responsible for that Macintosh and double-check your settings with the settings on the working Macintosh. Remember that the connection script entered into ConfigPPP can include the username and password, so let the person responsible for that Macintosh preserve his privacy. You might ask him to make a copy of the Control Panels you need, delete his passwords from the copies, and give them to you on a floppy disk. Copying their setup to your Macintosh eliminates most of the setup this section describes how to do.

Configuring Netscape Preferences

Netscape can be customized in many ways. Most of the options ask you to choose which you prefer, more graphics or more speed. The Options menu contains controls for you to set many parameters of Netscape's appearance and behavior. There are four major windows and five toggled controls that can be selected from the Options menu.

The General Preferences Window

To view the General Preferences window, go to the Options menu and select the General command (see fig. 4.6).

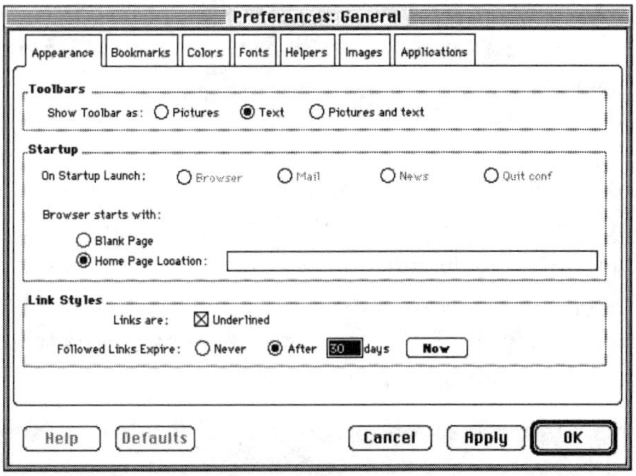

Fig. 4.6
The General Preferences window.

The General Preferences window has seven screens that let you control many aspects of how Netscape operates on your Macintosh. These seven screens are the following:

- Appearance
- Bookmarks
- Colors
- Fonts
- Helpers
- Images
- Applications

The Appearances Screen

The Appearances screen contains three panels: Toolbars, Startup, and Link Styles. The Toolbars panel controls whether the buttons on the main Netscape toolbar appear as text-only, picture-only, or pictorial buttons with text labels. If you want the window for your Web page viewing to be as large as possible, set this for text-only.

The Startup panel controls what Web page Netscape loads when it is first started, and what windows (for Web, mailbox, or UseNet news) are launched on startup. You can enter any URL (Universal Resource Locator) you like for the startup page.

TIP

One tip to speed Netscape's startup is to have your startup page be a page local to your computer, which doesn't have to be downloaded over your network connection. If you set the startup page to a local HTML file on your hard disk, Netscape typically takes less time to access a hard disk than to download a Web page over its Internet connection.

Link Styles controls whether or not you want links to appear on Web pages as underlined or not, and how long you want Netscape to keep a record of you following a given link. The default value of this Followed Links Expire option is 30 days, but you can set the time from 0 (a followed link never looks different from one you haven't looked at) to Never (a followed link will always look different than one you haven't looked at).

Expired Links as Trail Markers?

About now, somebody is thinking, "I can use these expired links as markers of where I've been!" True, but it's probably more efficient to mark your trail at just the interesting points, not every step along the path. On the other hand, expired links could be used in an experiment to research how people search for information.

The Bookmarks Screen

The Bookmarks screen lets you choose the folder your bookmarks are stored in on your Macintosh, and which bookmarks file you are using as well as the one you are adding to. For example, let's say you are researching multiprocessor operating systems, and you find the URL for AT&T Bell Lab's new operating system Plan 9. The designers of Plan 9 named their project after the Ed Wood, Jr. film *Plan 9 from Outer Space*, and they have included a Web link to a Web site devoted to this movie. With the Bookmarks screen, you can open your personal hobbies bookmarks file and add the bookmark for the movie to that file. You can then reset the bookmarks file to your operating system research list, and continue on with your work.

The Colors Screen

The Colors screen lets you set the colors for new links, links you haven't looked at yet, the text color, and the background color. For contrast and ease of reading, keep the text color dark and the background color light or vice versa, unless you like trying to read purple text on a black background. Instead of a color, you can set a background image file as the default background: a useful option if you are setting up Netscape for a presentation and want the company logo as a faint watermark-like image in the background of every page that does not have a defined background.

The Fonts Screen

The Fonts screen allows you to define the encoding format, the fixed font, and the proportional fonts used to draw the pages. You can also choose the display size of the fonts. If you find yourself leaning close to your monitor to read the words, and the text is in high contrast to the background, you could enlarge the text with these controls.

The Images Screen

The Images screen includes a choice that may improve Netscape's performance: Display Images either While, or After Downloading them. The default setting is to display an image as it downloads. If you are on a slow-to-medium speed connection, this lets you see the part of an image that has been downloaded, giving you the choice of whether to stop the download. If your computer is on a high-speed Internet connection, choosing the While Downloading option can be slower than After Downloading. Typically, a computer is idle between pieces of a downloading image. If the connection is faster than the computer can process the received information, you may have better performance if you choose After Downloading.

The Applications Screen

The Applications screen of the General Preferences window lets you select the supporting applications to use with a Telnet session (an older, terminal-based communication protocol explained in chapter 12), a TN3270 session (TN3270 is a fancy version of Telnet), and the application to choose to view the HTML source of a Web page. On a Macintosh, this is usually Simpletext. However, you can set the View Source application to any word processor or HTML editor you might have.

The Mail and News Preferences Window

The Mail and News Preferences window of the Options menu presents you with five ways to customize Netscape for sending and receiving electronic mail and reading UseNet newsgroups (see fig. 4.7). Chapters 12, "Accessing Other Internet Services with Netscape," and 15, "Reading UseNet Newsgroups with Netscape," cover this screen and its options in detail, so this section only covers the basics of what you need to do in order to get connected to your mail and news.

II

Mastering Netscape

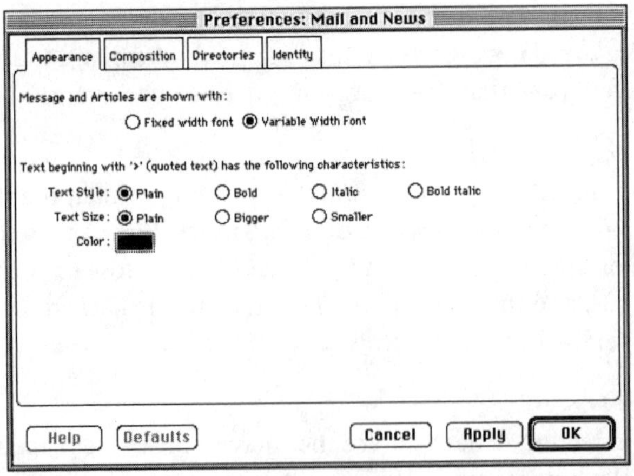

Fig. 4.7

The Mail and
News window.

> **Note**
>
> You will need to have the names of the computers, or servers, your Internet connection uses as the SMTP server, the POP server, and the NNTP server. You can get these names from your Internet service provider or system administrator.

To set Netscape's required preferences so that you can send and receive mail and read and post to UseNet newsgroups, follow these steps:

1. First, select the Directories tab. In the Mail panel of the Directories screen, enter the name of the SMTP (Simple Message Transaction Protocol) Server and the Mail POP (Point-of-Presence) Server in the first two fields at the top of the screen. The two servers may be the same, but they don't have to be.

2. In the News panel at the bottom of the Directories screen, enter the name of the news server.

3. Select the Identity tab. The Identity screen contains information Netscape uses to identify you to the outside world when you send a message.

4. Enter your name. This is the name you want the rest of the Internet to know you as, and does not have to be your real name.

5. Enter your e-mail address so messages you send can have a return address attached to them. Your e-mail address will look like words_or_numbers@more_words_or_numbers. Your POP user ID is the part of your e-mail address to the left of the @ symbol. Your reply-to address does not have to be the same as the address of the account you are sending from.

6. Click OK. To save your work, from the Options menu, choose Save Options.

The Network Preferences Window

The Network Preferences window contains settings that affect your connection to the network. The three screens of the Network window are the following (as shown in fig. 4.8):

- Cache
- Connections
- Proxies

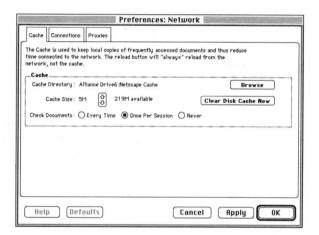

Fig. 4.8
The Network
Preferences
window.

The Cache screen lets you set the size of the cache Netscape uses on the local hard disk of your computer, and where you want the cache to be on your Macintosh. Netscape's cache does not have to be in the same folder or even the same disk drive where Netscape is located. If you decide to go back to a Web page that you've already downloaded, Netscape will look at the version you downloaded five minutes ago, instead of reconnecting to the network and downloading the page again (which probably hasn't changed in five minutes). Loading the page from your hard disk will always, except in very special circumstances, be faster than reloading the page from your network connection.

> **Note**
>
> If you think the page has changed in the last five minutes (for example, there are several people who have wired digital cameras to their Internet connection and update their Web page every minute with a snapshot of their office), selecting the Reload button will always load the page from your network connection, and not from the cache.

II

Mastering Netscape

Netscape's default setting for the cache is 5MB, and you can change this to a higher or lower value. Reducing the cache size to below 1MB is not recommended, as some individual Web pages and files can exceed 1MB in size. Reducing the cache too low causes Netscape to act as if it has no cache, which can severely limit performance.

The Connections screen lets you set the number of simultaneous connections Netscape can keep operating at any moment. When you connect to a Web page with many images, Netscape is actually trying to load four (the default setting) of the images at the same time. The only difficulty is that since your network connection doesn't grow in size as you raise the number of simultaneous connections, Netscape takes as long to download a Web page four connections at a time as it does to download the same page one connection at a time. You can probably avoid this screen and leave the default value of four in place, and never worry about changing the value.

Proxies are applications that are substitutes (that is, they act as a stand-in) for your same type of application. Proxies are rarely present for any other reason than to act as guards on the firewall on a network. You will need to ask your system administrator if there are any proxies present for use across a firewall, and what settings you need to make in Netscape in order to use them.

Individuals have different concerns over their privacy and personal security. While one resident of an apartment building may use only the latch lock on their door and leave the windows open all day, their neighbor may have two deadbolt locks on each door and bars on the windows. Netscape lets you choose how often you want to be shown an alert when the security level of the page you are looking at changes (see fig. 4.9).

Fig. 4.9
The Security window.

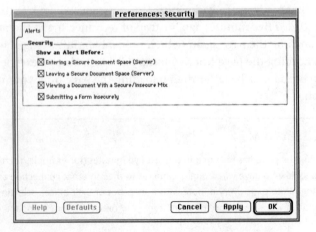

> **Note**
>
> Netscape's security is always working whenever you connect to a secure Web site. You cannot turn it off, either intentionally or accidentally.

The Security panel of the Options menu lets you choose how often you want to be alerted of changes in the security of your transaction. The four choices in the amount you want to be alerted are:

- *Entering a Secure Document Space (Server)*—When this option is on, Netscape displays a dialog box every time you enter a Netscape Commerce Server.

- *Leaving a Secure Document Space (Server)*—When this option is on, Netscape displays a dialog box every time you leave a Netscape Commerce Server.

- *Viewing a Document With a Secure/Insecure Mix*—When this option is on, Netscape displays a dialog box every time you enter a Netscape Commerce Server.

- *Submitting a Form Insecurely*—When this option is on, Netscape displays a dialog box every time you send a form response to an insecure server.

If you have all these options off, you can still detect if you are connected to a secure or insecure Web page by looking at the bottom left of the Netscape window and finding the key. If the key is broken, you are looking at an insecure site. If the key is a single piece, you are connected to a secure site. If the key image is enough for you, you can turn all of the options off. However, if the key image is small and unobtrusive enough that you might not remember to check the security status of your connection, you can turn on any or all of the various warning boxes.

The Preferences Menu Commands

Below the Preferences menu entries for the General, Mail and News, Network, and Security windows, the next portion of the Options menu is a set of five settings that can be toggled from this menu. If the command has a check next to it, the command is on. These commands are as follows:

- *Show Toolbar*—Shows the toolbar across the top of the Netscape window. If you don't need the buttons, turning off this option gives more area within the Netscape window to display images.

- *Show Location*—The field which displays the URL of the current Web page is optional. I keep this field for use in helping diagnose problematic URLs.

II

Mastering Netscape

- *Show Directory Buttons*—As with the toolbar, if you want a thinner top border to the Netscape window, turn this command off by leaving it unchecked.

- *Auto Load Images*—This command can be important for performance. If you're in a hurry, or if you don't care about pretty colored buttons, background textures and the full-page image of the Web page creator's favorite hermit crab, turn this option off to (often substantially) reduce the amount of time it takes to download a page.

- *Show FTP File Information*—When you look at an FTP site with Netscape, you see icons of folders and files with file information (size, date created or last changed, and so on). If you don't want to see this information, turn this option off.

The Document Encoding command lets you choose the document encoding standards. These options provide for more international use than earlier versions of Netscape.

The final command is important—Save Options preserves the changes you've made in this menu for the next time you start Netscape.

Technical Support: Where to Go

This chapter should be able to help you with most of your questions about where to find Netscape, how to install Netscape, and what you need in order to configure and run Netscape. In case you need some more assistance, here are some pointers.

If you have a problem with installing the MacTCP system extension, call Apple Computers at 1(800) SOS-APPL.

If you have a problem with ConfigPPP or another shareware or freeware PPP or SLIP system extension or control panel, look for the README file that comes with the software. If there is no README or Help file, throw it into the Trash, delete the file, and find another connection package.

The most likely problem you may have with getting Netscape is getting through to its site to download the software, especially if a recent version of the software was recently released. Look to the URL **http:// home.netscape.com/comprod/mirror/index.html** for a list of mirror sites—not operated by Netscape Communications—that have the most current publicly available version of Netscape.

If you can connect to the Internet using Netscape, look in your application's menus (Netscape 2.0 for the Macintosh moved the Help menu underneath the Apple Guide or Balloon help menu item in the System menu bar) for the entry Release Notes. This command takes you to the most recent official release notes for your version of Netscape.

For general assistance, Netscape has a large amount of information on its Web site. Netscape's technical support is on the Web at **http://home.netscape.com/assist/support/index.html**. In general, if you have a purchased version of Netscape, consult the materials you received with your purchase for consulting with technical support. If you are having problems connecting with Netscape and can't see the Web page in order to request technical assistance, technical support is available for Netscape Navigator Personal Edition at 1(503) 626-5475. Telephone support is available for the LAN Edition of Netscape Navigator at 1(800) 320-3099.

Note

As of this writing, Netscape Communication's support policy is free telephone support for 90 days to purchasers of the LAN Edition. If you did not purchase the LAN Edition within the last 90 days, telephone support is billed to your credit card (have it with you when you call) at $25 for the first 15 minutes and $2 per minute after the first 15.

You can also contact other people in your area (for example, within your office or university, or the local area Macintosh User Group) for advice and assistance. Your network system administrator or Internet Service Provider (ISP) technical support should also be able to help.

A final piece of advice: If you expend a great deal of effort solving a problem and succeed, write down how you did it. Preferably, write it down where you can find it again easily. Even if you choose not to be helpful to someone else if they run into the same problem, consider how much trouble you will have reinventing your solution.

II

Mastering Netscape

## CHAPTER 5

Loading and Configuring Netscape for UNIX

While Netscape on UNIX systems is much the same as it is on Windows PCs and the Macintosh, there are a number of significant differences, particularly with respect to installing and configuring the package. UNIX systems are multi-user, multi-tasking systems, and are considerably more complex than PCs. You may need help from your UNIX system administrator to get Netscape set up on the system.

In this chapter, you learn:

- The different available versions of Netscape
- How to download Netscape over the Internet using standard UNIX utilities and/or a Web browser
- How to install Netscape from the archive package you download over the Internet
- How to install Netscape you purchase from the CD-ROM distribution media
- How to configure Netscape to set it up so all users on your UNIX system can use it
- How to set up your own Netscape configuration so it looks and acts the way you want it to

You'll also want to look at chapter 16, "Configuring Helper Applications," where the setup of Netscape helper applications is covered for more UNIX-specific configuration instructions. Chapter 16 also describes some UNIX software on the CD-ROM that you can use as Netscape helper applications.

> **Note**
>
> All the information, including the figures, in this chapter are based on a beta release of Netscape version 2 for UNIX. The final release will be available by the time you read this, and you may or may not find differences between what you read here and what you see with the final version 2 release.

> **Note**
>
> Although Netscape is freely available for download over the Internet, you need to be aware that the downloadable version is substantially different than the version you might purchase in a computer store or directly from Netscape Communications Corporation. As we discuss in chapter 23, Netscape can communicate with some World Wide Web servers using data encryption to implement security in transactions, and hide confidential information such as credit card numbers, sensitive corporate information, or any other data you want to protect from Internet snoopers.
>
> The version of Netscape available on the Internet is considerably less secure than the one you can purchase. If you plan to use Netscape for the transmission of confidential information over the Internet, or you are otherwise concerned about the security of your Internet transactions with Netscape, you are well advised to purchase the secure version directly from Netscape Communications or in a computer store. The more secure version is not accessible on the Internet because it contains enhanced data encryption technology that the U.S. government considers to be a weapon of war. Consequently, this version cannot be exported. If you are in the U.S., you can, and probably should, purchase the secure, non-export version.

Downloading Netscape over the Internet

Although you can purchase Netscape in computer stores or directly from the manufacturer, you can also get a copy over the Internet using anonymous FTP or a World Wide Web browser, such as NCSA Mosaic or an earlier release of Netscape.

Getting Netscape with Anonymous FTP

If you don't already have some sort of World Wide Web browser working on your system but are on the Internet, you can use your system's *FTP* utility to download a copy. The TCP/IP file transfer protocol (FTP) is a standard part of virtually all UNIX systems; if your system is on the Internet, your system has the FTP utility. Although there are some graphical FTP tools available here and there for UNIX systems, they're not part of any vendor's standard UNIX installation, so I focus on the non-graphical user interface all provide. Later on, I cover how to use a Web browser to download Netscape.

The UNIX FTP utility is a non-graphical one, so you'll need to run it from the shell in a terminal window, such as a Sun *cmdtool*, AIX *aixterm*, HP-UX *hpterm*, standard X Windows *xterm*, or any ordinary terminal session. Figures 5.1 and 5.2 show the process of downloading Netscape using standard anonymous FTP.

In figure 5.1, you start up the FTP utility from the UNIX shell prompt, log in to Netscape's anonymous FTP server, named **ftp.netscape.com**, using the login name **anonymous**. For a password, type in your Internet e-mail address, such as *yourname@yourcompany*.**com**.

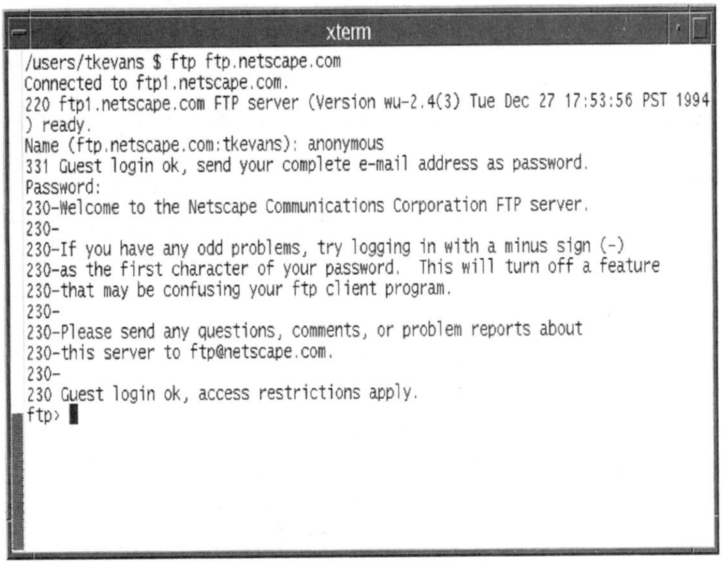

```
xterm
/users/tkevans $ ftp ftp.netscape.com
Connected to ftp1.netscape.com.
220 ftp1.netscape.com FTP server (Version wu-2.4(3) Tue Dec 27 17:53:56 PST 1994
) ready.
Name (ftp.netscape.com:tkevans): anonymous
331 Guest login ok, send your complete e-mail address as password.
Password:
230-Welcome to the Netscape Communications Corporation FTP server.
230-
230-If you have any odd problems, try logging in with a minus sign (-)
230-as the first character of your password.  This will turn off a feature
230-that may be confusing your ftp client program.
230-
230-Please send any questions, comments, or problem reports about
230-this server to ftp@netscape.com.
230-
230 Guest login ok, access restrictions apply.
ftp> 
```

Fig. 5.1
Accessing Netscape's anonymous FTP server.

Mastering Netscape

Figure 5.2 shows a directory listing from the server's /2.0beta/unix subdirectory with the several different versions of Netscape displayed. Several of the listing's lines are too wide for the screen shot so they are shown wrapped. (By the time this book is published, the directory name may have changed to simply /netscape/unix, as Netscape will have officially released version 2.) Figure 5.2 also shows the actual download taking place.

Fig. 5.2
Downloading a
copy of Netscape
for UNIX.

```
ftp>
ftp> pwd
257 "/2.0beta/unix" is current directory.
ftp>
ftp> dir
200 PORT command successful.
150 Opening ASCII mode data connection for /bin/ls.
total 47948
drwxr-xr-x    2 root     sys         1024 Nov  6 00:22 .
drwxr-xr-x    5 root     sys          512 Nov  5 05:07 ..
-rw-r--r--    1 999      999         1298 Nov  5 05:01 .message
-rw-r--r--    1 999      999         5473 Nov  5 05:01 LICENSE
-rw-r--r--    1 999      999         8726 Nov  5 05:01 README
-rw-r--r--    1 999      999      2141945 Nov  5 05:02 netscape-v20b2-export.alpha-de
c-osf2.0.tar.Z
-rw-r--r--    1 999      999      3500229 Nov  5 05:02 netscape-v20b2-export.hppa1.1-
hp-hpux.tar.Z
-rw-r--r--    1 999      999      2222789 Nov  5 05:02 netscape-v20b2-export.i386-unk
nown-bsd.tar.Z
-rw-r--r--    1 999      999      2200439 Nov  5 05:02 netscape-v20b2-export.i486-unk
nown-linux.tar.Z
-rw-r--r--    1 999      999      2415563 Nov  5 05:03 netscape-v20b2-export.mips-sgi
-irix5.2.tar.Z
-rw-r--r--    1 999      999      1819197 Nov  5 05:03 netscape-v20b2-export.rs6000-i
bm-aix3.2.tar.Z
-rw-r--r--    1 999      999      2699769 Nov  5 05:03 netscape-v20b2-export.sparc-su
n-solaris2.3.tar.Z
-rw-r--r--    1 999      999      1910943 Nov  5 05:03 netscape-v20b2-export.sparc-su
n-solaris2.4.tar.Z
-rw-r--r--    1 999      999      5618515 Nov  5 23:22 netscape-v20b2-export.sparc-su
n-sunos4.1.3_U1.tar.Z
226 Transfer complete.
1248 bytes received in 0.74 seconds (1.6 Kbytes/s)
ftp> bin
200 Type set to I.
ftp>
ftp> get netscape-v20b2-export.sparc-sun-solaris2.4.tar.Z
200 PORT command successful.
150 Opening BINARY mode data connection for netscape-v20b2-export.sparc-sun-solaris2.
4.tar.Z (1910943 bytes).
```

In figure 5.2, note the use of the FTP `pwd` (print working directory) command
to show we've switched to the /beta2.0/unix subdirectory, and the `bin`
(binary transfer mode) command. Finally, `get netscape-v20b2N-`
`export.sparc-sun-solaris2.4.tar.Z` downloads the Solaris 2.4 version of
Netscape, retaining its original file name. (The figure shows we've used the
standard X Windows cut-and-paste to highlight the file name, then paste it
onto the get command line—a nifty trick with long, complex file names like
this one.) You can, of course, change the file name by specifying a new file
name on the command line. At this point, you can download additional versions of Netscape if you have other UNIX systems from other vendors. To end
the FTP session, just type **bye**.

Downloading Netscape with NCSA Mosaic

If you already have a Web browser installed on your system, you can use it to
retrieve Netscape over the Internet. For example, in NCSA Mosaic, pull down
the File menu and select Open URL. When the dialog box opens up, type in
the URL **ftp://ftp.netscape.com/2.0beta/unix**. This will take you directly to the subdirectory on Netscape's anonymous FTP server containing
the various UNIX versions. Figure 5.3 shows this directory. Note the similar-
ity to figure 5.2, with the same file names shown. Note also the display of
graphical icons here; I discuss these icons and how they got into your
display in chapter 16, "Configuring Helper Applications."

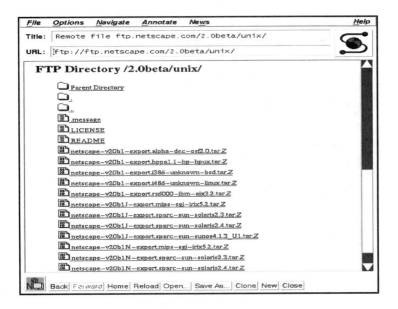

Fig. 5.3
Using NCSA
Mosaic to access
Netscape's FTP
server.

To download a copy, pull down Options and select Save to Local Disk, then
click the version you want. You'll see a running count of the bytes downloaded
displayed in the lower-left corner of the Mosaic window. After the download is
complete, a dialog box opens, prompting you to enter the file name to save the
download under; enter any name you want. Continue to click any other versions you want to download. Exit from Mosaic, or iconify it, when you're finished. (If you plan to continue to use Mosaic in this session, be sure to click
Options, then Save to Local Disk, to turn off the auto-download.)

Downloading Netscape with Netscape

If you're already using Netscape, you can use it to download a later version.
Click Open, then type in the URL **ftp://ftp.netscape.com/2.0beta/unix**.
This takes you directly to the subdirectory on Netscape's anonymous FTP
server containing the various UNIX versions. Figure 5.4 shows this directory.
(Of course, you can also reach this page from the Netscape home page at
http://home.netscape.com, which can be accessed by clicking the large
N icon in the upper-right corner of the Netscape window. From the Netscape
home page, click the Netscape Now icon, and then follow the prompts.)

II

Mastering Netscape

Fig. 5.4

Using Netscape to access Netscape's FTP server.

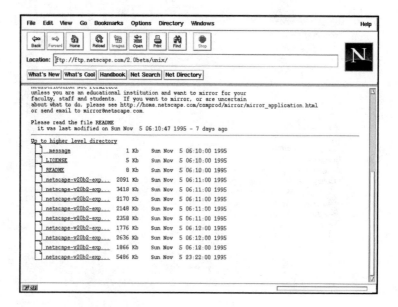

To download a copy of the latest Netscape, click the version you want. Netscape pops up a window, asking you to enter a name for the file you're downloading; the default is the same name under which it is stored on the FTP server. After you've entered a file name, or accepted the default name, the download starts.

Note

Version 2 now pops up a separate Download window in which the progress of an FTP file download is tracked (see fig. 5.5). (This new window also appears when data is being passed to a Netscape helper application as discussed in chapter 16, "Configuring Helper Applications.") You can use your mouse to drag the Download window out of your way and continue to use your main Netscape window while the download is taking place, scrolling the displayed page, or following other links on it. When the download completes, the separate Download window closes.

After your download is complete, you can exit Netscape or iconify (minimize) it.

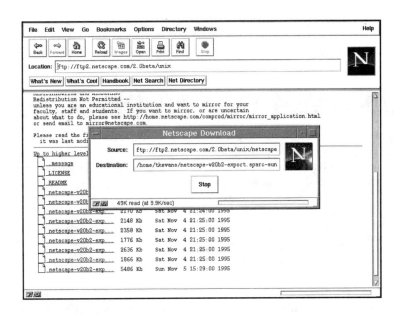

Fig. 5.5
Netscape version 2
Download window.

Installing Netscape on a UNIX System

Although you can install Netscape in your own user directory on a UNIX system, you or your system administrator will probably want to install it so it's accessible to everyone using the system. However you decide to do the installation, these are the steps to perform.

First, make a temporary directory into which to unpack the Netscape distribution. Be sure there's enough disk space available in the file system you pick; you'll need about 5MB of free work space. You'll be able to remove the work directory later. The example that follows creates the directory */var/tmp/ netscape*. (The hash mark (#) signifies the superuser, or root, shell prompt; yours may be a dollar sign, or a customized prompt of some sort.)

```
# mkdir /var/tmp/netscape
```

After you've created the directory, you can unpack the compressed Netscape distribution archive into it, using the commands that follow. Netscape is distributed in a simple compressed UNIX tar archive. The following commands assume you are working with superuser authority, have stored the downloaded Netscape tar archive in the directory /home/netscape, and have created the /var/tmp/netscape temporary directory.

```
# cd /home/netscape
# uncompress netscape-v20b1N-export.sparc-sun-solaris2.4.tar.Z
# cd /var/tmp/netscape
# tar xfv /home/netscape/netscape-v20b1N-export.sparc-sun-
solaris2.4.tar
```

Tip

Experienced UNIX users will recognize that the uncompress and tar commands can be combined into a single pipeline of commands. (Utilizing the vertical bar, or pipe, symbol (¦), UNIX pipelines allow the output of one command to serve as the input to the next command in the pipeline.) Here's the above sequence using this approach:

```
# cd /var/tmp/netscape

# zcat /home/netscape/netscape-v20b1N-export.sparc-sun-
solaris2.4.tar.Z ¦ tar xfv -
```

In either case, the unpacking of the archive will generate several files in the /var/tmp/netscape directory. Among them, you'll find a README file with detailed installation instructions. You can view this file online with the UNIX more or pg commands, or print it for reference. Also, you'll find a file named license.txt. Be sure to read this file so you understand Netscape's licensing terms. Use of Netscape is free to many users (primarily users in educational and nonprofit institutions), but others (primarily commercial users) are required to pay for it beyond the initial evaluation period.

Extracting Netscape from CD-ROM

Before moving into the actual install of Netscape from the temporary directory you've created, let's take a side trip and bring those of you who've purchased Netscape up to the same point we reached in the preceding section. After we've done so, we'll return to the final Netscape installation instructions, which apply both to the Internet-download and CD-ROM–purchase situations.

Rather than providing a separate CD-ROM for each supported UNIX system, Netscape distributes a CD-ROM containing versions for several different UNIX systems:

- Sun Microsystems (SunOS 4.1.x and Solaris 2.x for Sun SPARC hardware, though not for Solaris 2.x on x86)
- IBM RISC System/6000 (AIX 3.2.5, but not AIX 4.1.x)
- BSDI and Linux (two versions of UNIX for IBM-compatible PCs)
- Digital UNIX (formerly called OSF/1)
- Silicon Graphics (IRIX 5.x)
- Hewlett-Packard (HP-UX 9.x)

Here's a UNIX-style directory listing of the CD-ROM's top-level directory:

```
-r--r--r-- 1 root  6074 Apr 21 01:27 _readme.txt
dr-xr-xr-x 2 root  2048 Apr 21 01:12 aix.32
drwxr-xr-x 2 root  2048 Apr 24 12:40 bsdi
dr-xr-xr-x 3 root  2048 Apr 21 01:16 common
dr-xr-xr-x 2 root  2048 Apr 21 01:15 dec_osf1.20
dr-xr-xr-x 2 root  2048 Apr 21 01:15 hpux.903
dr-xr-xr-x 2 root  2048 Apr 21 01:15 irix.52
-r--r--r-- 1 root  9351 Apr 19 11:40 license.txt
drwxr-xr-x 2 root  2048 Apr 24 12:15 linux
dr-xr-xr-x 2 root  2048 Apr 21 01:15 solaris.23
dr-xr-xr-x 2 root  2048 Apr 21 01:15 sunos.413
```

Each of the supported systems has a different procedure for *mounting* the CD-ROM. You don't need a CD drive on every system, because you can install Netscape from one machine to another over your local area network using network file transfers, including using NFS-mounted file systems. After the CD-ROM is mounted, the procedure for installing Netscape is pretty much the same on all systems. Let's get the CD-ROM mounted first, then turn to the final installation instructions.

> **Note**
>
> UNIX device names for CD-ROMs (and other devices) vary, depending on the type of device, its type of hardware connection, the device configuration, and other matters. All the examples below use the default device name for the CD-ROM on the example system; your own device names may be different depending on your hardware setup. Check with your system administrator on the exact device name you should use on your system.

Mounting the CD-ROM on Sun Systems

On a Sun system running SunOS 4.1.x (also called Solaris 1.x), you'll need access to the root, or superuser, account to mount the CD-ROM. Insert the CD-ROM into its caddy and place it in the CD player, then type the following commands (as with the examples above, the # symbol represents the superuser prompt; you don't enter it):

```
# mkdir /cdrom
# mount -rt hsfs /dev/sr0 /cdrom
```

The system may tell you the /cdrom directory already exists when you type the first command; you can ignore this message. In the second command, the command-line arguments tell the mount command to mount the *high-speed* type file system device /dev/sr0 *read-only* on the /cdrom directory mount point. You can check to see that the mount succeeded by asking for a directory listing with the command ls /cdrom.

On a Sun system running Solaris 2.x (also called SunOS 5.x), you may or may not need superuser authority to mount the CD-ROM, depending on how the system was configured when it was installed. Ask your system administrator if the Solaris *Volume Management* feature is enabled. Volume Management is a new feature of Solaris 2.x that allows any user to mount and unmount CD-ROMs and floppy disks. If the package was installed, you can simply slip the CD-ROM into the drive and the system will automatically mount it for you. After a couple of minutes, you'll be able to change to the /cdrom/ cdrom0 directory and see the Netscape CD-ROM. (This mount point is the default one used by Volume Management; your system administrator may have changed this default, so check with her if the /cdrom/cdrom0 directory doesn't appear within a minute or so.)

Volume Management

Although instructions for mounting the Netscape CD-ROM in the absence of this package are provided below, Solaris Volume Management is a useful feature. You can check to see if Volume Management is running by searching the output of the UNIX ps command, like this:

```
# ps -ef ¦ grep vold
```

If you get nothing back, it's not running. Check to see if it has been installed with this command:

```
# pkginfo ¦ grep -I volume
```

If it isn't installed, you'll get back nothing but your shell prompt. You or your system administrator can install Volume Management from the Solaris distribution CD-ROM, using the pkgadd command.

If Volume Management is not running on your Solaris 2.x system, mounting the CD-ROM requires superuser access. Use the following commands:

```
# mkdir /cdrom
# mount -o ro -F hsfs /dev/dsk/c0t6d0s2 /cdrom
```

Mounting the CD-ROM on an IBM AIX System

IBM's UNIX, called AIX, also requires superuser authority to mount CD-ROMs. Here are the commands:

```
# mkdir /cdrom
# crfs -v cdrfs -p ro -d cd0 -m /cdrom
# mount /cdrom
```

You can also use the AIX System Management Interface Tool, using the smit command. Start up smit, select Physical and Logical Storage, Filesystems,

Add/Change/Show/Delete Filesystems, and, finally, CDROM File Systems. Fill in the blanks, then click DO to mount the CD-ROM.

Mounting the CD-ROM on a Silicon Graphics System

SGI's UNIX, called IRIX, automatically senses and mounts the CD-ROM when it is placed into the CD drive. Just pop the CD-ROM in and it will be mounted on the directory /CDROM.

Mounting the CD-ROM on an HP-UX System

HP-UX 9.x requires manual mounting of CD-ROM file systems.

```
# mkdir /cdrom
# mount -rt cdfs /dev/dsk/c201d2s0 /cdrom
```

As with the other examples in this section, this command uses the default device name for the CD-ROM device in HP-UX. Your hardware setup may differ, so see your system administrator if this command doesn't work.

Mounting the CD-ROM on a BSDI System

BSDI requires manual mounting of CD-ROMs by the superuser:

```
# mkdir /cdrom
# mount_cd9660 /dev/sd6a /cdrom
```

Mounting the CD-ROM on a Linux System

Linux requires manual mounting of CD-ROMs by the superuser.

```
# mkdir /cdrom
# mount -rt iso9660 /dev/scd0 /cdrom
```

Mounting the CD-ROM on a Digital UNIX System

Digital UNIX requires manual mounting of CD-ROM file systems.

```
# mkdir /cdrom
# mount -rt cdfs /dev/rz6c /cdrom
```

Unpacking the CD-ROM Distribution

Having mounted the CD-ROM on your UNIX system, you can unpack the distribution for your particular release of UNIX. We'll assume you've mounted the CD-ROM on the /cdrom mount point in the previous examples, and that you'll unpack the distribution into the temporary directory /var/tmp/netscape. As the earlier directory listing shows, there is a subdirectory on the CD-ROM for each of the supported UNIX versions, such as aix.32, bsdi, and so on. We'll use the convention ostype in our example commands; that is, where /cdrom/ostype is used, substitute the subdirectory name from the CD-ROM for your UNIX version for ostype. With the exception of Solaris 2.x, the command to unpack the distribution is exactly the same on all other UNIX systems:

```
# cd /var/tmp/netscape
# tar xfv /cdrom/ostype/netscape.tar
```

If your UNIX system is Solaris 2.x, substitute this command for the second one above:

```
# tar xfv /cdrom/cdrom0/ostype/netscape.tar
```

At this point, the Netscape distribution has been unpacked into the temporary directory and you can unmount the CD-ROM, then proceed to the final installation.

Final Netscape Installation

Whether you've downloaded Netscape over the Internet or purchased it on CD-ROM, you're now ready for the final installation of the package. With some small differences, which are explained in context (later in the chapter) as they arise, the procedure is the same on all the supported UNIX systems.

You now have several files in your working directory, including the following:

- readme.txt, or README
- license.txt, or LICENSE
- netscape
- Netscape.ad
- XKeysymDB
- hot-convert.sh.

We'll cover these files in the order listed. As noted, the README and LICENSE files provide installation instructions and licensing information, respectively.

The file named netscape is the Netscape executable program. Move the Netscape executable program into a directory accessible to all users on your system. A common place is the /usr/local/bin directory. Here's the command:

```
# mv netscape /usr/local/bin
```

Move the Netscape application defaults file Netscape.ad into a central location on the system:

```
# mv Netscape.ad /usr/lib/X11/app-defaults/Netscape
```

If you can't find the /usr/lib/X11 directory, you're probably on a Sun system, on which the app-defaults directory is /usr/openwin/lib/X11/app-defaults. Place the file in this directory instead. Since Netscape is an X Windows program on UNIX systems, you can control some of its behavior and onscreen appearance using X Windows Resources; the application defaults file contains those which pertain to Netscape. See "Netscape X Resources" later in this chapter for more information.

Move XKeysymDB, the key symbols file, into a central location on the system:

```
# mv XKeysymDB /usr/lib/X11 (or /usr/openwin/lib/X11)
```

This is a particularly important file for Sun users, since Netscape is a Motif application. The SunOS-supplied XKeysymDB file is set up for the (non-Motif) OpenWindows graphical user interface. The XKeysymDB file provided with the Netscape distribution contains the needed Motif keyboard bindings, linking various keystrokes to Netscape commands. If you don't install this file, Netscape will generate a large number of error messages on startup and some of the keystrokes may not work properly (or may not work at all). See your X Windows documentation for more information about the XKeysymDB file.

If you or other users on your system have been using NCSA Mosaic for Web browsing, you'll want to translate your Mosaic Hotlist into Netscape Bookmarks. The shell script hot-convert.sh can be use to do this. Install the supplied conversion file in a location accessible to all:

```
# mv hot-convert.sh /usr/local/bin
```

Later, users can run this script to do the conversion of Hotlist files into a Netscape Bookmarks files. The original Hotlist files are not changed.

That's it. You're done installing Netscape. You'll need to exit from your current X Windows session and start a new one before you start Netscape to put all the changes into effect.

Making Netscape Look Like You Want It To

There are a number of ways you can personalize the look of Netscape on your screen. These range from the size and position of the Netscape window to the font styles and sizes Netscape uses. In addition, you can control Netscape's background color and maximize the amount of information it can display.

Displaying More in Your Netscape Screen

Netscape uses a lot of on-screen real estate to display its various bells and whistles—in particular, the toolbar, directory buttons, and location. All these features of Netscape are convenient when you're just starting out. After a while, however, you might want to suppress the routine display of one or more of them, especially since they're all available from Netscape's pull-down menus. When you do, you gain a lot more space in the Netscape window for actual Web documents.

Removing the Toolbar, Directory Buttons, and Location

Figure 5.6 shows the Netscape Options menu. Notice the middle group of items set off by the horizontal lines—Show Toolbar, Show Location, and Show Directory Buttons. You can suppress the display of any of these by clicking the one(s) you want to suppress. Notice how the shading changes on the checkboxes beside the ones you select for suppression. To make your changes permanent, select Save Options.

Fig. 5.6
The Netscape
Options menu.

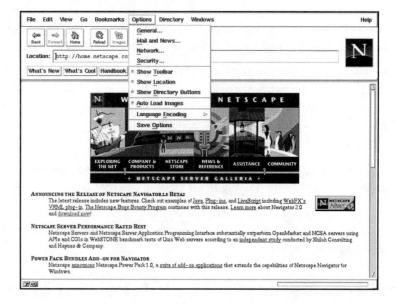

Changing Fonts, Window Size, and Colors

UNIX Netscape provides some Preferences for selecting the font, window sizes, and colors used to display text. In addition, there are a couple of other simple ways of setting fonts, windows and/or colors, along with some more complex ones:

■ Font Selection—Netscape's General Preferences, Fonts dialog box allows a choice of several font sizes.

■ Window Size—You can change the size of your running Netscape window by dragging a corner of the window, the same as you do with any other X Windows program. To start Netscape with a particular window size, use a command-line option. If your workstation has a large, high-resolution monitor, you might start Netscape in a large, 1024 × 768 pixels window, like this (be sure to include the equal (=) sign, as well as a blank space between it and the word geometry):

```
Netscape -geometry =1024x768 &
```

If you'd like to position your Netscape window precisely at startup, try this, which places it at the upper-left corner of your screen:

```
Netscape -geometry =1024x768+0-0 &
```

Command-Line Options

Like most UNIX programs, you can control the behavior of Netscape by giving it options on the command line when you start it. Experienced X Windows users, you may want to add a startup line for Netscape with your preferred command-line options to your X Windows startup file so it starts up every time you start X Windows. You'll find a list of the options Netscape knows about in the Frequently Asked Questions document, available on the Netscape Help pull-down.

- Colors—UNIX Netscape has only one easy way to let you change on-screen colors. You can select the background color with another command-line option at startup time. The figures in this chapter were made with Netscape using a white background to enhance their appearance. Here's how to start Netscape from your shell prompt with a white background:

```
Netscape -bg white &
```

Netscape X Resources

Besides command-line options, Netscape supports a large number of X Windows Resources, with which you can control many aspects of its operation and on-screen appearance. Installing Netscape X Resources allows you to make permanent changes such as background color, screen size, and many others, saving you from having to enter command-line options every time you start the program.

Netscape X Resources are listed in the Netscape.ad file distributed with the software and installed on your system. A common location for this file is the /usr/lib/X11/app-defaults directory; Sun, however, puts it in /usr/openwin/lib/X11/app-defaults. The file is named Netscape. You'll find a lot of documentation in this file in the form of comments. While these comments strongly suggest you not make extensive changes in this file, an example change might be to turn of Netscape's irritating (to many) use of the HTML <blink> attribute. As with other X Windows Resources, you can make changes in your Home directory, or make them system wide. To do the former, create the file Netscape (note the initial cap) in your Home directory, containing just this single line:

```
*blinkingEnabled: False
```

Save the file, then exit from your editor and run the following command at your shell prompt:

```
$ xrdb -merge Netscape
```

Some users prefer a single X resources file in their Home directory, usually named .Xdefaults (or .Xresources), containing all their customized X resources, rather than separate files for each application. If you're one of these folks, add the following line to your .Xdefaults file:

```
Netscape*blinkingEnabled: False
```

As you can see, you must include the application name (Netscape) in the .Xdefaults file; since this file refers generically to X Windows programs, you have to specify which one each entry in the file applies to. Once you've added the line, run the following command at your shell prompt:

```
$ xrdb -merge .Xdefaults
```

Earlier, I noted a Netscape command-line option that starts up Netscape with a white background. If you have tried this, you know that only part of the Netscape background actually comes up white (just the toolbar, Location, and the other housekeeping parts of the Netscape window). The rest of your window continues with the default Netscape gray background. If you'd like a completely white background, including not only the standard icons and the background of the actual text windows, use the *DefaultBackground Netscape X Resource. Do this in either the Netscape file in your Home Directory or .Xdefaults file, as follows:

```
*DefaultBackground:        #FFFFFF
```

You may recognize the right side of this entry as three hexadecimal (base 16) numbers, hex FF being equivalent to decimal 255. This entry uses a pure white background, and has been used for the figures in this chapter, to enhance their appearance. You can locate other available colors in the file /usr/lib/X11/rgb.txt on your system (/usr/openwin/lib/X11/rgb.txt on Sun systems). Each entry contains a color name and a set of three numbers referring to the respective amounts of red, green, and blue that make up the color. For example, the following are several entries from this file for shades of white:

248 248 255	ghost white
245 245 255	white smoke
255 250 240	floral white
250 235 215	antique white
255 222 173	navajo white
255 255 255	white

As you can see, white is shown with the three decimal color attributes 255, 255, and 255 in the rgb.txt file. You need to convert these numbers to hexadecimal to use them for this purpose. Decimal 255 is hex FF, so the entry FFFFFF represents white, while floral white would be FFFAF0 (255, 250, and 240 in decimal, per the rgb.txt file).

If you or your system administrator want to make Netscape X Resource changes effective system wide, make the changes in the /usr/lib/X11/app-defaults/Netscape file (/usr/openwin/lib/X11/app-defaults/Netscape on Sun systems). Users need to quit and restart Netscape to pick up the new settings.

II

Mastering Netscape

## CHAPTER 6

Loading and Configuring Netscape Personal Edition

Netscape Personal Edition version 1.2 was specifically designed for a SLIP/PPP Internet connection under the Windows operating system. You receive all the features of Netscape 1.2 and much, much more. This version of Netscape's Web browser includes:

- Full e-mail support through a cooperative link to Eudora Light
- Full support of UseNet news services
- Its own TCP/IP stack
- An audio player that works with most sound cards
- The Netscape Dialer

For those of us who like to have lots of help, Personal Edition places a copy of the Netscape Handbook on your hard drive during installation. It also has a Registration Wizard that automatically logs you in to the Internet service provider of your choice, and configures itself to work with that service. With all these features it is easy to see that Netscape Personal Edition is truly the home user's connection to the Information Superhighway.

This chapter assists you in installing and configuring Netscape Navigator Personal Edition. In this chapter, you learn:

- How to load Netscape Personal Edition
- How to configure for a service provider with the Registration Wizard
- How to set basic preferences after a custom installation
- How to get on the Web

Loading Netscape Personal Edition

Because Netscape Personal Edition includes an extra e-mail reader and dialer, you have the opportunity to decide who gets to make the installation decision—the computer or you. If you let the computer make the decisions, you are performing a *typical installation*. If you decide what you want to install and where you want it to go, you are performing a *custom installation*.

As with most programs, Personal Edition practically installs itself. There are very few questions to answer during an original installation. Even the custom installation requires only a few decisions on your part.

Note

If you are running the Microsoft Office taskbar, you need to shut it down while you are installing Netscape Personal Edition. The Office taskbar uses two files that are required by Personal Edition to complete its installation. If the Office taskbar is running when Personal Edition attempts to install, you will receive error messages when Personal Edition attempts to overwrite these files.

Installation Requirements

Netscape Personal Edition 1.2 has slightly different requirements than Netscape Navigator 1.2. The following lists the requirements for Personal Edition 1.2:

- IBM PC-compatible 386 or later
- 14,400 bps modem or higher
- 6MB free hard disk space (an additional 5MB is recommended for disk caching)
- 4MB RAM required, 8MB recommended
- DOS 5.0 or later
- Microsoft Windows 3.1, Windows for Work Groups 3.1, or Windows 95

Once you are sure that your computer system can run Netscape Personal Edition, you can start installing the program. Follow these steps:

1. Insert the CD into your CD-ROM drive.
2. Open the Start menu, and select Run from the available list of options.

3. Type **d:\netpers\setup.exe** to run Personal Edition's setup and installation program as shown in figure 6.1. If your CD-ROM uses a different
drive specification, replace the previous command with that drive
letter.

4. Click OK to continue with the installation.

5. The first screen that appears asks if you want to continue with the installation. Click Continue.

At this point, you must decide if you are going to do a typical or custom installation. The following list shows all the possible pieces that can be installed
by Personal Edition:

- The Netscape Navigator 1.2 Web browser
- The Eudora Light e-mail program
- Netscape's TCP/IP stack
- Netscape's Dialer program
- Netscape Personal Edition Handbook

The typical installation installs everything, and automatically creates an icon
for each piece. If you do not currently have a working Internet service from
your computer, the typical installation may be your best solution.

The custom installation allows you to decide which sections you want to install. You must install the Netscape Navigator portion of the software, but
you can skip the installation of either Eudora Light or the TCP/IP stack and
Dialer. If you select to install all the options shown in the Custom Install dialog box, you are performing the equivalent of a typical installation.

Note

If you choose to install the TCP/IP stack, Personal Edition automatically installs the
Dialer. They work as a package deal.

II

Mastering Netscape

Performing a Typical Installation

The most common way to install software is to allow the installation program to make all the decisions for you. Personal Edition's typical installation does exactly that. It prompts you for a few decisions and then off it races to complete the rest of the installation without you.

1. Select the Typical radio button and click Continue.

2. The installation program is now copying all the files from the CD to your hard drive. Once this process is complete you will receive notification that the installation is complete. As seen in figure 6.2, the installation program creates your program group. A notice appears that informs you of changes to your SYSTEM.INI, and that the original file was copied to the c:\netscape directory. Click OK.

> **Note**
>
> The program group created during a typical installation only shows the icons for the read.me file and the Registration Wizard. The Netscape and Eudora Light icons are created after the Registration Wizard has configured your system for you.

Fig. 6.2

The program group and its icons after completing a typical installation.

3. A dialog box now appears asking you to complete the final step in installing Personal Edition. Click the Restart Windows button to complete the installation and prepare to run the Registration Wizard. A discussion of the Registration Wizard occurs in the section, "Configuring for a Service Provider with the Registration Wizard," later in this chapter.

> **Caution**
>
> Be sure to exit all other programs that you have running before you restart Windows 95. Failure to do this could cause you to lose important information or corrupt the open files.

You cannot use Netscape Personal Edition until you run the Registration Wizard. At this point, you have neither a TCP/IP stack loaded nor the Dialer configured. Once you have completed the steps in the Registration Wizard you will be ready to start using the Internet through your new, or old, service provider.

Performing a Custom Installation

Performing a typical installation is always the easiest route to take, no matter what software package you are using. But sometimes you do not need the entire software package, you only need a few parts of it. In this situation it is generally best to perform a custom installation. Not only do you save hard drive space, but you often learn more about the product that you are using. To complete the custom installation of Personal Edition, simply follow these steps:

1. Select the Custom radio button and click Continue.

2. As you can see in figure 6.3, you can now select the directory in which you want Personal Edition stored, and the parts of the program that you want installed. Select the portions of the program that you need and click Install.

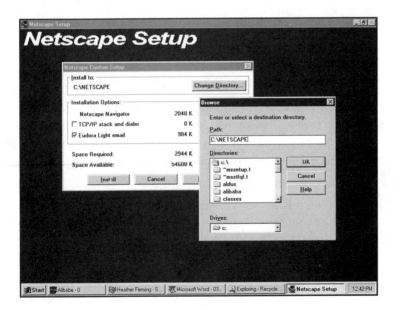

Fig. 6.3
The configuration screen for a custom installation.

> **Note**
>
> If you're using an e-mail reader you like, you probably won't need the Eudora Light e-mail option. Likewise, if you are currently using a 16-bit TCP/IP stack and dialer, or the Windows 95 SLIP/PPP dialer, you won't need to select the TCP/IP option. For the rest of this example I will be installing only Netscape Navigator and Eudora Light.

3. The installation program is now copying all the needed files from the CD onto your hard drive. The installation process creates your program group. As you can see in figure 6.4, it holds different icons than those installed with a typical installation. The Registration Wizard is not installed unless the TCP/IP stack and dialer are also installed. By not installing Netscape's stack, it is assumed that you already have a working TCP/IP connection and service provider.

Fig. 6.4
The completed program group and its icons after a custom installation is completed.

4. Click Restart Windows from the final installation screen.

Once you restart Windows, you can use Netscape Personal Edition. To learn many of its more advanced features such as e-mail and news, read the section, "Setting Basic Preferences After a Custom Install," later in this chapter.

> **Note**
>
> If you are using the Windows 95 TCP/IP stack and PPP dialer, you do not want to install Netscape's dialer. If you do install the Netscape dialer, you need to remove it before you can use the Windows 95 stack.

Troubleshooting

I want to use Netscape Personal Edition with my Windows 95 TCP/IP stack and its PPP dialer, but I can't get Netscape to talk to this stack. Is there anything I can do?

If Netscape is not working with the Windows 95 stack, you need to reinstall the TCP/IP protocol for your dial-up adapter in Windows 95. To do this, follow these steps:

1. Open the Start menu and select Settings, and then Control Panel.

2. From the Control Panel dialog box, double-click the Network icon.

3. Select the TCP/IP protocol, and then click the Remove button.

4. Click the Add button.

5. Select Protocol from the Select Network Component Type window, and then click Add.

6. Select Microsoft from the Manufacturers list, and TCP/IP from the Network Protocols list in the Select Network Protocols window.

7. Click OK.

You should once again see the TCP/IP protocol listed under your dial-up adapter. You need to restart Windows for this change to take affect.

Setting Basic Preferences After a Custom Install

Because the custom installation may not have installed the Registration Wizard or Eudora Light, depending on the selections you made, you must configure these programs for yourself. This is not a hard task; you just have to know something about your existing service provider. Some of the information you need includes your service provider's e-mail server address, news server address, and your full e-mail account name. Armed with this information, you should be able to configure Netscape and Eudora Light quickly and easily, and be surfing the World Wide Web in a flash.

Note

Netscape automatically updates your account information if you upgrade from a previous version of Netscape. You do not have to upgrade in the same directory. Your new version of Netscape grabs all the information that it needs from your previous version's configuration file.

Configuring Netscape for Sending E-mail

Personal Edition has the ability to send electronic mail, although it cannot receive it without the assistance of another e-mail program such as Eudora Light. To configure Personal Edition to send its own outgoing messages, you need to complete the following steps:

1. Open the Start menu, select Programs, Netscape Personal Edition, then Netscape.

2. When Netscape first starts, it automatically attempts to dial your service provider using your TCP/IP stack and PPP dialer. Click Cancel to stop this phone call, since you do not need to be connected to your service provider to change Netscape settings.

3. Open the Options menu and select Preferences. As you can see in figure 6.5, the Preferences dialog box has many tabs that allow you to control specific aspects of the program. Choose the Mail and News tab.

Fig. 6.5
Netscape's main configuration screen for e-mail and news services.

4. Place your cursor in the Mail (SMTP) Server field and enter the Internet address of your e-mail server. You might, for example, enter mail.george.net if your Internet provider were George Internet Services.

5. Place your cursor in the Your Name: field and type your real name. This is appended to the return address of messages so people know who they have received e-mail from.

6. In the Your Email: field, enter your entire electronic mail address. For example, I might enter heather@mail.george.net if my e-mail account name were heather and my service provider were George Internet Services.

Many other options can be set to control how Personal Edition handles the outgoing messages. For more details on how to configure these options look at chapter 13, "E-mail with Netscape."

▶ See "E-mail with Netscape," pg. 321

Configuring Eudora Light for E-mail

Eudora Light is an electronic mail program bundled with Netscape Personal Edition. This program is configured by the Registration Wizard. If you did not install the TCP/IP stack and Dialer, you must configure it manually. To do so, follow these steps:

1. Open the Start menu, choose Programs, Netscape Personal Edition, and then Eudora Light E-mail.

2. The first time you run Eudora Light, the Settings dialog box opens on your screen (see fig. 6.6).

> **Note**
>
> If you have used Eudora Light before, open the Special menu and select the Settings option to see the Settings dialog box. This dialog box opens to the Category screen that was last viewed. To continue configuring Eudora Light, select Getting Started from the Category scroll window on the left.

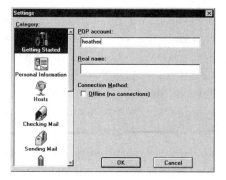

Fig. 6.6
The opening Settings dialog box for Eudora Light.

3. Enter your e-mail address in the POP account field.

4. Enter your full name in the Real name field.

5. In the Category list on the left side of this screen select Personal Information. The top two fields of this screen were completed when entering the information in the Getting Started category window. Select the Return address: field and enter your return e-mail address. For most people the return address will be the same as their mailing (POP account) address.

II

Mastering Netscape

6. Click OK to activate all the changes that you made to Eudora Light.

As you can see, there are many other settings included in the Eudora Light program. Look for a discussion of the remaining settings in chapter 14, "E-mail with Netscape Personal Edition and Eudora Light."

▶ See "Installing and Configuring Eudora Light," pg. 349

> **Note**
>
> In Netscape Personal Edition 1.2 for Windows 95, Eudora Light is not used. Netscape uses the Microsoft Exchange e-mail client that comes with the Windows 95 operating system.

Configuring Netscape for UseNet News

▶ See "Using Netscape to Read the News," pg. 379

Netscape Personal Edition comes with a UseNet newsreader. Chapter 15, "Reading UseNet Newsgroups with Netscape," discusses using UseNet news with Netscape in detail. To configure the main options allowing you to read UseNet news with Personal Edition, follow these steps:

1. Open Netscape using the Start menu.

2. Open the Options menu and choose Preferences. This will open the Preferences dialog box. Switch to the Mail and News tab if you are not already there.

3. In the lower half of this screen, there are options to set up a news service. Place your cursor in the News (NNTP) Server field and enter the name of your news server. Using my George's Internet Services example, you would enter news.george.net.

4. The News RC Directory should already contain c:\netscape\news, since that is the default directory used by the installation program for storing your news cache.

These are the main news settings that allow you to read news articles while surfing the World Wide Web. For more information see chapter 15, "Reading UseNet Newsgroups with Netscape."

Configuring for a Service Provider with the Registration Wizard

After you have completed a typical or a custom installation with the TCP/IP stack, you will need to run the Registration Wizard. This wizard automatically configures the Netscape Dialer for use with your new or existing service provider. It can also configure Eudora Light for sending and receiving e-mail from your new service provider.

1. To open the Netscape program group, open the Start menu, choose Programs, Netscape Personal Edition, then Registration Wizard.

2. The first screen you see, shown in figure 6.7, is a simple introductory screen to Personal Edition. To continue, click OK.

Fig. 6.7
The Personal Edition Registration Wizard's opening screen.

At this point, you must decide if you are going to use a pre-existing account or create a new Internet account with a new service provider. This should be a fairly easy decision to make. If you are currently using the Internet through a dial-up SLIP or PPP service and are happy with that organization, you will most likely want to stay with that provider. If you do not have an Internet account and want to create one, click the Create New Account button.

Using a Pre-existing Account

Let's assume that you already have an Internet account that is providing you with adequate service. You simply need to configure Netscape and the Dialer for that service. The following three items complete that process:

- Configure Netscape and Eudora Light with your account information.
- Configure your modem to work with Netscape's Dialer.
- Configure your dialer with the proper information about your dialing location.

Once these three areas are completely configured you can be off to explore the World Wide Web.

Configuring Netscape with Your Account

By selecting to use Netscape Navigator Personal Edition with your existing Internet account you have opened yourself up for a barrage of questions. These questions are about your service, yourself, and how your service works.

Before beginning this process make sure that you have the following information:

■ A list of the Internet addresses your server uses

■ The phone number you call to get Internet access

■ The IP addresses of the Domain Name Servers that your service provider uses

Once you have acquired all the information listed above, keep it handy while you perform the following steps to configure Netscape to work with your pre-existing account.

1. Click the Use Existing Account button in the Account Type dialog box. This is the second prompt you see after starting the Registration Wizard. This opens the screen shown in figure 6.8. This is the main screen for configuring an existing account. After you complete each main portion of the configuration you will be returned to this screen.

Fig. 6.8
The organizational screen for configuring Netscape to use an existing service provider.

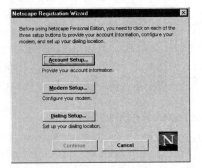

2. First you need to set up the existing account information. Click the Account Setup button to do this. This opens another dialog box letting you know what information you will need to continue the configuration. Click Next to continue.

3. Enter your name and organization (optional) in the appropriate fields; then click Next.

4. In the Login Name field, enter the name that you use to log on to your service provider. Your login name is usually some form of your real name or a nickname. You generally have the option of selecting this name when you set up your account. Because my login name at my service provider is heather, I would enter that here.

5. In the Password field, enter the password that you use to access your account. Some service providers allow you to select your own password or they assign you a password. Click Next to continue.

6. Enter the phone number that you call when connecting to your service provider. For example, if my service provider's phone number is 1-800-555-1212, I would type **800** in the first blank field and **555-1212** in the second field. Click Next to continue.

7. You must now enter your e-mail login name and password for use with Eudora Light into the appropriate fields. On many Internet systems, your main login name and your e-mail login name are the same. Click Next to continue configuring Netscape and Eudora Light.

8. At this point you are asked to fill in the IP address of your DNS (Domain Name Server). I would enter **191.138.163.1** for my primary DNS. If you do not know the address of your DNS you need to contact your service provider. Click Next.

> ### Note
>
> A *DNS* is the traffic cop of the Internet. It tells your computer how to get to where you want to go. You should always use the DNS closest to your current site, preferably only one to two jumps away. A *jump* refers to the way your request will travel from one computer to another searching for its final destination.

9. Place your cursor in the POP Server field and enter the name of your service provider's POP e-mail server. I might enter mail.george.net if I purchased my Internet access through George's Internet Services. If you do not know the complete names of your service's e-mail server give them a call.

10. In the SMTP Server field enter the name of the SMTP e-mail server used by your service provider. Some providers use the same address for both of these services.

11. The last field to fill in on this page is the NNTP Server field. This is the name of the news server used by your Internet service provider. News.george.net would be one possibility for me. When you are done, click Next.

12. This is the last screen you need to complete to have your account configured, and it only has one question. Check the Bring Up TTY Window When Connected checkbox if your service provider requires that you log in to their system manually. If you do not know the answer to this question, contact your service provider's help desk and ask them. Click Finish to continue the rest of the Registration Wizard.

The first step in configuring your existing Internet account to work with Netscape Navigator Personal Edition is now complete and there are only two more steps to go: Configuring your modem and your dialer.

Configuring the Modem

Personal Edition assumes that all its users have a modem of some type with which they can access the Internet. The Registration Wizard is capable of identifying this modem for you; although you do have the option of selecting it yourself. If you would like to configure the modem yourself, you can follow the steps in the section labeled "Creating a New Account—Configuring Your Modem," later in this chapter. To have Netscape select your modem for you, follow these steps:

1. Click the Modem Setup button located on the main Netscape Registration Wizard dialog box to configure your modem.

2. Because Netscape automatically attempts to find your modem, click the Next button.

3. You will see a screen checking each of your communications ports for your modem. After this process is complete and Netscape finds a modem that it recognizes, you are shown the name of the modem and its location (see fig. 6.9).

Fig. 6.9
Results of the
automatic modem
search.

> **Note**
>
> If the modem shown to you is not the type of modem that you have, you can change it by choosing the Change button, then selecting your real modem type from the following list. If you cannot find your modem in Netscape's list of supported modems, select (Hayes Compatible) from the modem Manufacturer list, and then the highest baud rate that your modem supports from the Model list. The Hayes-compatible modems generally work with all other brands.

4. Click Next to open the last dialog box associated with configuring your modem. Click Finish to complete the configuration of your modem and return to the main Registration Wizard window.

> **Troubleshooting**
>
> *When I ask Netscape to find my modem it tells me that there are none on my system. I know it is there. I can see it.*
>
> Some modems do not return information about themselves when queried by a program. Your modem is most likely doing this, or the messages that it is returning are not being recognized by Personal Edition. You will need to check your modem documentation to find your modem's brand and model name if you do not already know it.
>
> Personal Edition works best with 14,400 bps or faster modems and does not include many other speeds in its list of modems. You will need to manually select your modem from the supplied table, or use the Hayes Compatible option if your modem is not listed.

Configuring the Netscape Dialer

You have successfully configured your account and your modem. You are now ready to configure Netscape Dialer. To do so, follow these steps:

1. Click the Dialing Setup button. The Location Wizard dialog box appears asking for the area code that your modem phone line uses. It also reminds you to disable call waiting on your phone. The most common call waiting disable codes are included in the drop-down box to the right of the Call Waiting check box. Click Next to continue the configuration.

> **Note**
>
> You can generally turn off Call Waiting with *70, although this code depends on the phone company you use. If *70 does not properly disable your call waiting, you need to contact your phone company for the correct code.

2. The second Location Wizard dialog box asks for the code, if required, for getting an outside line. If you have to dial a special code to get an outside line, enter it in the First Dial field. You will also need to specify if you are using a Tone or a Pulse line from the phone company. If you are like most business and households you will have a tone line. Once you have made your selection, click Finish.

> **Note**
>
> In most office environments you must dial either an 8 or a 9 to get an outside line. If you are using Netscape Navigator Personal Edition in your home, you most likely will not have to dial this code.

3. You should be looking at the main configuration screen for the existing account setup. Click Continue to save your configuration to a file for use by the Netscape Dialer program.

4. In the Connection File Name field, enter the name under which you want to store your settings. Personal Edition uses the name MYACCOUN.SR by default.

5. In the second field in the Confirm dialog box, enter the label you would like to appear under your dialing icon. After entering this information, click Continue.

6. The Personal Edition Registration Wizard will finish creating the appropriate icons in your Netscape program group. To complete the installation and return to Windows 95, click OK.

Netscape Navigator Personal Edition is now installed for your existing Internet service provider. To run Personal Edition you simply need to double-click the Netscape icon in your Netscape Personal Edition program group. Or you can open the Start menu, select Programs, Netscape Personal Edition, Netscape.

> **Note**
>
> If you have decided at this point to use one of the service providers that Netscape Communications Corporation has arranged to be Personal Edition providers, simply run the Registration Wizard again. The second time you run the wizard you will want to make a new account.

Creating a New Account

Personal Edition allows you to easily subscribe to an Internet service provider. Netscape Personal Edition has established a working relationship with InternetMCI, NETCOM, and Portal. These Internet service providers are national or international providers of Internet services. They are very reputable and have a long-standing relationship with many of their customers. If you decide to use one of their services you will not be disappointed. Some of them have 800 numbers that you can call if they do not have a local number.

Entering Your User Information

Before Personal Edition lets you create an account on a new service provider, you need to enter your user information. The following steps take you through this process.

1. Click the Create New Account button located on the Account Type window to start your journey across the Internet with your new service provider. The screen that appears is the main organizational screen for creating a new Internet account (see fig. 6.10).

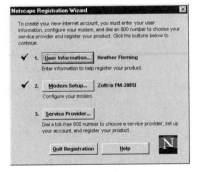

Fig. 6.10
Organizational screen for creating a new account with one of Personal Edition's providers.

2. Click the User Information button to set up a standard user profile for your new Internet service provider.

3. Fill in the appropriate registration information on your registration screen. It asks for your title, first name, last name, and the phone number that your modem uses. Click Next to continue.

4. The Registration Wizard also needs your organization's name (optional), your address, city, state, and ZIP code. Once you have completed this information, click Next.

5. This screen requires credit card information. This information is sent to Netscape only if you decide to use one of their Personal Edition providers. After Netscape has forwarded your credit card information to the service provider, they delete any reference to it from their records. Click Next.

Note

Netscape Navigator provides a very secure encoding system for sending credit card information across the Internet. With each new version of its product, this security system is getting harder to break. With the new technology that is available to create secure transfers of information, your credit card is just as safe being sent through Netscape Navigator as it is in your wallet.

---

6. The final query screen for setting up your user account asks if you would like to have your name removed from any lists that Netscape would share with other Internet-related companies. Simply check the box at the top of this dialog box to have your name removed from these shared lists, then click Finish to go to the next step of the complete configuration process.

7. On the final screen of the User Account setup, you will see a button asking you to fill out a user survey. If you would like to complete this survey click User Survey, answer the questions that follow. Click the Next button to go to the next screen of questions. Your answers to these questions assist Netscape in developing a marketing strategy and products that better meet the needs of their users. The Registration Wizard forwards the results of this survey to Netscape Communications Corporation when you register your software.

You are a third of the way there, you only have to configure your modem, and pick your service provider. As you continue running the Registration Wizard, start thinking about the amount of money and time that you might be spending on the Internet. Many Internet service providers allow you to only spend a set number of hours using their service without paying for extra time. Some providers allow you unlimited access for a flat fee. Others provide you with a choice of services. After you have arrived at an estimate for your expected Internet usage, you can easily pick the best provider for your situation.

Configuring Your Modem

To use Personal Edition you must have a modem or an existing LAN connection. The Registration Wizard assumes that you are using a modem and requests information on that modem. There are two ways that you can have Personal Edition configure your modem. The first is through the automatic detection system discussed previously. The second way involves just a bit of elbow grease on your part. Follow these steps to configure your modem yourself:

1. Click Modem Setup on the main Registration Wizard window.

2. Personal Edition allows you to select your own modem by checking the Don't Detect My Modem, Let Me Specify It checkbox. Click Next to continue.

3. As you can see in figure 6.11, you have the opportunity to specify the manufacturer and model of your modem. First scroll through the Manufacturer list on the left side of your window and select the manufacturer of your modem. After you have found the manufacturer, you will see a list of modem models on the right side of your screen. Select the appropriate model, then click Next.

Fig. 6.11
The Manufacturer and Model lists of modems for a manual modem selection.

II

Mastering Netscape

Note

If your modem manufacturer or model does not appear in the list, select the Hayes Compatible option from the Manufacturer list, and then select the speed of your modem from the model list.

4. You now need to specify the communications port used by your modem. Once you have specified the port that your modem uses, click Next.

Troubleshooting

How do I quickly locate the communications port for my modem?

Find the name of the COM port your modem uses by checking the Control Panel of Windows 95. To run the Control Panel, open the Start menu, and select Settings, Control Panel. Double-click the Modems icon in the Control Panel dialog box. If you had your modem attached to your computer when you installed Windows 95, it will appear in the modem list opened by this icon. Otherwise, Windows 95 will automatically find it for you. If you are using an external modem, make sure that it is on and plugged into the computer before starting this process.

Once you see a modem appear in your list, click the Properties button. This opens up a window showing you the name of the COM port used by your modem. To exit these screens click OK, then Close; then close the Control Panel by choosing File, Close, or pressing Alt+F4.

---

5. After you click Finish you are done configuring your modem to work with Personal Edition.

Selecting a Service Provider

You are now at the final stage in your voyage to Internet connectivity. After you have selected an Internet service provider you will be ready to place that first call and catch a wave of information. The following procedure assists you with this last process.

1. Click the Service Provider button on the main Registration Wizard screen to start configuring your dialer to connect to Netscape's Web server. From this server you are able to select a service provider and then complete the rest of your dialer's configuration.

2. The Dial Settings dialog asks for three pieces of information. The first asks for the code to disable call waiting if needed. If you have call waiting, check the Disable Call Waiting With checkbox and select the appropriate call waiting disable code from the drop-down list. Most phone companies use *70 to disable Call Waiting, but not all of them. If you have problems using the codes that are provided, contact your phone company for more information.

3. The second question you must answer is about a dialing code to get to an outside line. Most businesses have phone systems that require either

an 8 or a 9 be dialed before you can reach a number outside the office. Enter any required dialing codes in the First Dial field.

4. The third question deals with the type of phone service you have. If you have a Tone phone line select that radio button and click Continue, otherwise select the Pulse option and then Continue.

5. Your modem is now prepared to dial an 800 number that contacts Netscape and the World Wide Web site listing the available service providers. Click Continue to make the phone call.

6. You first see a screen showing that your modem is being initialized, then you will hear your modem dial and connect to Netscape.

Note

If your modem does not connect to Netscape the first time, do not worry. The Registration Wizard will attempt to make the call again. If the call fails a second time, a notification box appears and you will be returned to the main Registration Wizard screen. If this happens, you have to reset all dialing settings you filled in during the three previous steps.

---

7. Once the call is successfully completed, you see a screen similar to figure 6.12. This is the Netscape Registration server from which you can select a new service provider. To see more information about that provider click the button under the provider logo in the middle of your screen.

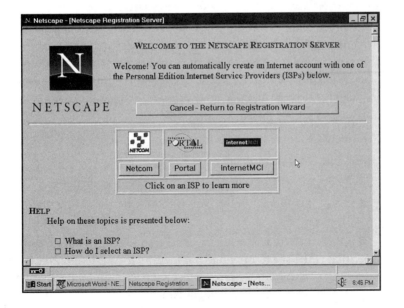

Fig. 6.12
The main Netscape Registration Server screen.

Note

Here is some information about each service provider that you can use when making your decision about the provider you want to work with:

	Setup Fee	Monthly Fee	Hourly Fee	Support
NETCOM	$25(waived)	$19.95 (includes 40 prime hours)	$2.00 (after first 40, free 7 days/week-ends)	24 hrs first 40
Portal	$19.95 (waived)	$9.95 (1st month free) $15 free hrs (1 time only)	$2.95 (US) $3.95 (Canada Puerto Rico)	9am-6pm Mon-Fri
InternetMCI	$18.95	$9.95 (5 free hrs/month) 800 Access: $6.50 /hr	Local Access: $2.50/hr	24 hrs 7 days/ week

There are also many cities that have local service providers. You can often find them listed in the Yellow Pages in the Computers section, or you can contact your local computer user group to find out which services are available.

8. Once you choose an Internet service provider, click its logo button on the main Netscape Service Provider Web page.

9. This opens a page full of information about that particular provider. Read through this information, it should answer any major questions that you have about the provider you have chosen, then click the Choose Provider button located at the bottom of this screen.

10. You will be asked to provide quite a bit of information, including the following:

   - Verify your credit card information
   - Verify your mailing ZIP code
   - Select an account name, password, and e-mail name
   - Select the phone number you will call when accessing their service
   - Often the service provider will ask you to select a "reserved word" that will assist in proving your identity if you should ever forget your password or want to cancel your account. Generally they will ask for your mother's maiden name.

> **Note**
>
> You are asked to select the nearest phone number to your location, although this may not be the most cost-effective number to dial. Check with your phone company for more information on minimizing your phone bill.

11. Once you have entered the information the service provider requested, click the Create Provider Account button. At this point you will be registering your copy of Netscape Navigator Personal Edition and subscribing to the Internet service provider you selected from the list.

12. You will then have to wait a few minutes for your account to be processed. Netscape will ask you to make changes to your account information if needed. After that has been completed, you must confirm your interest in creating an account with this service provider. To do this, click the Confirm Creation of Account button.

13. At this point you will have to wait a few more minutes for the final changes to your Internet service provider account to be finalized.

After the registration is complete, the Registration Wizard returns to add icons to your program group so that you can easily call your service provider. Click OK to close the Wizard and return to Windows. You are now ready to start surfing the World Wide Web.

> **Note**
>
> If for any reason you need to cancel your account with this service provider, you must call their customer service desk, give them your account name, password, address, phone number, and special reserved word when asked.

Getting on the Web

You are now ready to attack the World Wide Web. To load Netscape, open the Start menu, select Programs, Netscape Personal Edition, Netscape. This starts the Netscape Navigator program, and engages the dialer. The Netscape Dialer, as shown in figure 6.13, shows the current number that you are calling, your account name, and your hidden password. Once you have checked this information and you are ready to dial, click the Dial button.

Fig. 6.13

The Netscape
Dialer set to make
a call to the
NETCOM server.

▶ See "Moving
Around the
Web," pg. 145

▶ See "The Home
Page," pg. 168

◀ See "Connect-
ing to the
Internet,"
pg. 37

You should hear your modem dial, negotiate for a connection, and finally
connect to your service provider. At this point you will have to wait a few
moments for the dialer to log you in to your server and find Netscape's home
page. After this has occurred, you are on the road to finding more information than you ever thought you could use.

Troubleshooting

*I have installed the complete version of Netscape Personal Edition using the typical install
program, but I can't get on the World Wide Web. It keeps telling me that the DNS for
Netscape's home page is not valid.*

This error generally occurs when you do not have your TCP/IP stack loaded, your
TCP/IP stack properly configured, or you are not connected to your service provider.
Run the dialer by itself to connect to your Internet server. This should automatically
load your TCP/IP stack and connect you to your server. If you are not sure that you
are getting properly logged in to your server, start Netscape's Dialer, click the Properties button and then the General tab. Make sure to select the Bring Up TTY Window
option. Click OK and then click the Dial button.

If you are still getting that error, you will need to contact your Internet service provider to ensure that you are using the proper DNS address and domain name for
your server. If this information is incorrect you will not be able to contact other sites.

## CHAPTER 7

Moving Around the Web

Some people characterize the Web as confusing. They complain that it's not linear. It doesn't present you with a logical sequence of choices that you must make in order to move forward. You'll find through your own experience, however, that this is precisely why the Web is so intuitively easy. It's free-form, not linear. It more closely matches how people think: jumping from topic to topic as we see fit, as opposed to having order forced upon us.

Do you watch television? Read the news? Listen to your technically adept friends talk about the Web? If so, you've probably encountered a variety of metaphors that people use to explain how the Web works. Here are two:

- It's like our national highway system. It connects countless destinations together in a Web.
- It's similar to a spider's web. Nodes are joined together by tiny strands of silk.

The one concept that both of these metaphors have in common is that of joining, or linking, things together. This is in fact what the Web is all about, and represents one of the most important things you need to know about it. For example, you need to know that you can jump from one Web page to another by clicking on a link. You also need to know some other ways to get to a Web page without using links.

In this chapter, you learn about all these things and much more, including:

- Understanding how links work and how they look
- Learning about what a link can do
- Getting around with and without links
- Making Netscape load Web pages faster
- Configuring the way Netscape works with links

Understanding Links

By now, you've noticed the references in the margins of this book. They serve a similar purpose as links on a Web page—albeit a little low-tech. They refer you to other places in this book that might be useful or interesting to read. Without these references, you would have to resort to flipping through the pages looking for what you need.

Links on a Web page are even more vital. You have all the pages of this book right in front of you. At least you would know where to start looking. On the other hand, you have no idea where to find all the Web pages on the Internet. And there are too many to keep track of, anyway. Therefore, links are the only reasonable way to go from one Web page to another related Web page.

> **Note**
>
> *Hypertext* and *hypermedia* are two terms you'll frequently hear associated with the Web. A hypertext document is a document that contains links to other documents—allowing you to jump between them by clicking on the links. Hypermedia contains more than text, it contains multimedia such as pictures, videos, and sounds, too. In hypermedia documents, pictures are frequently used as links to other documents.

A link really has two different parts. First, there's the part that you see on the Web page—called an *anchor*. There's also the part that tells Netscape what to do if you click that link—called the *URL reference*. When you click a link's anchor, Netscape loads the Web page given by the link's corresponding URL reference. You'll learn about both parts of a link in the following sections. You'll also learn about the different resources to which a link can point.

Anchors

> **Tip**
>
> When you move the mouse cursor over a link's anchor, it changes from a pointer to a hand.

A link's anchor can be a word, a group of words, or a picture. Exactly how an anchor looks in Netscape depends largely on what type of anchor it is, and how the person who created the Web page used it. There are only a few types of anchors though: text and graphical. You'll learn about both types in this section.

Text Anchors

Most text anchors look somewhat the same. A text anchor is one or more
words that Netscape underlines to indicate that it represents a link. Netscape
also displays a text anchor using a different color than the rest of the text
around it.

> **Tip**
>
> Click and drag a link's text anchor onto your desktop. You can return quickly to that
> Web page by double-clicking the shortcut.

Figure 7.1 shows a Web page that contains three text anchors. In particular,
notice how the text anchors on this Web page are embedded in the text. That
is, they aren't set apart from the text, like the references in this book, but are
actually an integral part of it. Clicking on one of these links will load a Web
page that is related to the link. You'll find many text anchors used this way.

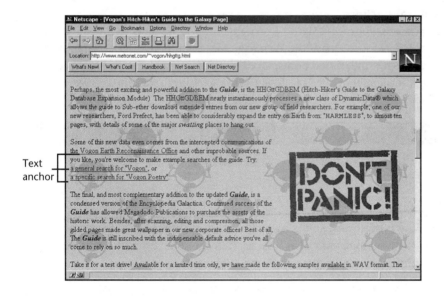

Text
anchor

Fig. 7.1
You'll find
Vogon's Hitch-
Hiker's Guide to
the Galaxy Page at
**http://www.
metronet.com/
~vogon/
hhgttg.html**.

Mastering Netscape

Figure 7.2 shows another Web page with a lot of text anchors. These anchors
aren't embedded in the text, however. They are presented as a list or index of
links from which you can choose. Web page authors frequently use this
method to present collections of related links.

Fig. 7.2
Yahoo (**http://
www.yahoo.com**)
is one of the most
popular indexes
on the Web. To
learn more about
Yahoo, see chapter
8, "Finding Infor-
mation on the
Web."

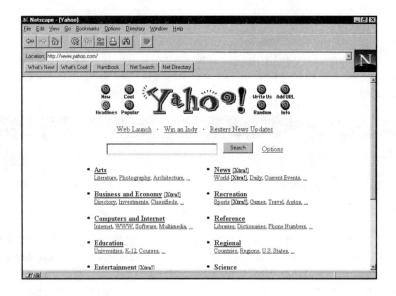

Graphical Anchors

A graphical anchor is similar to a text anchor. When you click a link's graphical anchor, Netscape loads the Web page that the link references. Graphical
anchors aren't underlined or displayed in a different color, however. And no
two graphical anchors need to look the same, either. It depends entirely on
the picture that the Web page's author chose to use.

> **Tip**
>
> Right-click a graphical anchor, and choose Save This Image As to save the image in a
> file on your computer.

Versatility is the strong suit of graphical anchors. Web page authors effectively use them for a variety of reasons. Here are some examples of the ways
you'll find graphical anchors used on a Web page:

■ *Bullets*. Graphical anchors are frequently used as list bullets. You can
click the picture to go to the Web page described by that list item. Frequently, the text in the list item is also a link. You can click either the
picture or the text.

■ *Icons*. Many Web sites use graphical anchors in a similar manner to the
way Windows 95 uses icons. They are common on home pages, and
represent a variety of Web pages available at that site. Figure 7.3 shows
a Web site that uses graphical anchors in this manner. Click the
ProShop icon to open the ProShop Web page, for example.

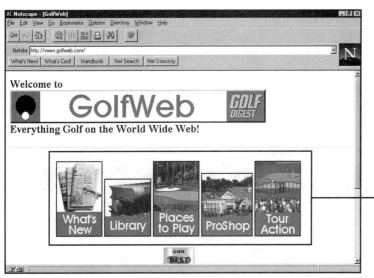

Fig. 7.3
You'll find
GolfWeb at
**http://www.
golfweb.com**.
GolfWeb's home
page uses graphical
anchors to repre-
sent a variety of its
pages you can
load.

Graphical anchors
used as icons

- *Advertisements.* Many Web sites have sponsors that pay to advertise on
  the site. This keeps the Web site free to you and me, while the site continues to make money. You'll usually find advertisements, such as the
  one shown in figure 7.4, at the top of a Web page. Click the advertisement, and Netscape will load the sponsor's Web page.

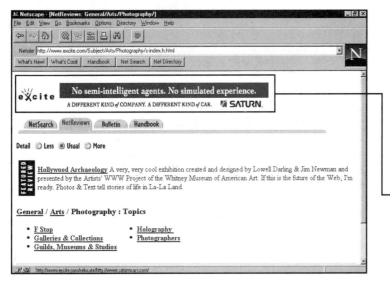

Fig. 7.4
Excite (**http://
www.excite.
com**) is an up-
and-coming Web
search tool that
uses sponsors to
keep the service
free to you and
me.

Graphical anchor used
as an advertisement

II

Mastering Netscape

URL References

The other part of a link is the URL reference. This is the address of the Web page that Netscape will load if you click the link. Every type of link, whether it uses a text or graphical anchor, uses either a relative or absolute reference. You'll learn about each type in this section, but when you're "surfing" the Web it really doesn't matter which type of URL reference a link is using—as long as Netscape loads the Web page you want.

Relative References

Tip

Choose View, by Document Source to tell for sure if a link is using relative references.

An URL reference to a file on the same computer is also known as a *relative reference*. It means that the URL is relative to the computer and directory from which Netscape originally loaded the Web page. If Netscape loads a page at **http://www.mysite.com/page**, for example, then a relative reference to **/picture** would actually refer to the URL **http://www.mysite.com/page/picture**. Relative references are commonly used to refer to Web pages on the same computer. Figure 7.5 shows a Web page that contains relative references to other Web pages on that site.

Fig. 7.5
Netscape's Web site is at **http://www.netscape.com**. The News and Reference section contains the latest information about the Web.

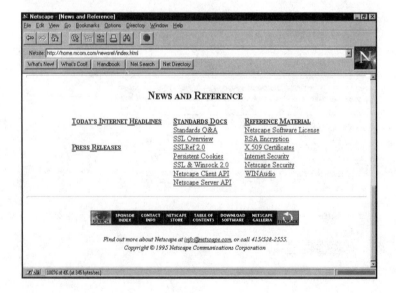

The primary reason Web authors use a relative reference is convenience. It's much simpler to just type the file name, instead of the entire URL. It also makes it easier to move Web pages around on a server. Since the URL references are relative to the Web page's computer and directory, the author doesn't have to change all the links in the Web page every time the files move to a different location.

Corporate Bulletin Boards

Many corporations such as Hewlett-Packard have created corporate bulletin boards that their associates view with Web browsers such as Netscape. These Web pages aren't on the Web, however. They're stored on the companies' internal network servers. They contain a variety of information that is useful to their associates such as the following:

- Meeting schedules and meeting room availability

- Announcements about corporate events

- Information about policies and benefits

- Recent press releases and financial statements

- Technological information

You can easily create a bulletin board for the corporation you work for, too. Part IV, "Building World Class Home Pages for Netscape," shows you how to build pages for the Web. The only difference between that and building a corporate bulletin board is in the type of information you choose to include on the page.

Absolute References

Tip

Hold your mouse over a link and look at Netscape's status line to see its URL reference.

An URL reference that specifies the exact computer, directory, and file for a Web page is an *absolute reference*. Whereas relative references are common for links to Web pages on the same computer, absolute references are necessary for links to Web pages on other computers.

II

Mastering Netscape

> **Note**
>
> You'll learn about HTML (Hypertext Markup Language) in chapter 24, "Using Netscape Gold and HTML." If you're curious about what a link with an absolute reference looks like in HTML, however, here's a sample:
>
> `<A HREF="http://www.yahoo.com/">Yahoo</A>`
>
> The first part of this link, the bit between the left (<) and right (>) brackets, is the URL reference. The word yahoo is the text anchor that Netscape underlines on the Web page. The last part ends the link.

Resources Links Can Point to

Links can point to more than just Web pages. They can point to a variety of files and other Internet resources, too. A link can point to a video, pictures, or even a plain text file, for example. It can also point to an FTP server, Gopher server, or a UseNet newsgroup. Table 7.1 describes the other types of things a link can point to and shows you what the URL looks like.

Table 7.1 Resources a Link Can Point to	
Type	**Sample URL**
Web Page	**http://www.mysite.com/page.html**
Files	**file://C:/picture.bmp**
Multimedia	**http://www.mysite.com/video.avi**
E-mail	**mailto:info@netscape.com**
FTP	**ftp://ftp.mysite.com**
Gopher	**gopher://gopher.mysite.com**
Newsgroup	**news:alt.fan.que**
Telnet	**telnet://mysite.com**

How to Move Around the Web

You didn't buy this book to learn how to load a Web page in Netscape, then sit back and look at it all day. You want to "surf" the Web—jumping from Web page to Web page looking for entertaining and useful information.

In fact, surfing is such an important part of the Web that both Netscape and the Web itself provide many different ways to navigate. You can use the links and imagemaps that you find on a Web page, for example. You can go directly to a Web page if you know its URL. You can also use some of the more advanced Netscape features such as bookmarks and frames. In this section, you'll learn how to use those features to move around the Web like a pro.

Clicking a Link

You learned about links earlier in this chapter. They are the primary method you use to go from the Web page you're viewing to another related Web page. All these links are provided by the Web page's author, and are usually accurately related to the context in which you found it.

Figure 7.6 shows a Web page with both text and graphical links. You can click Collabra Software, for example, to go to the Collabra Web site. The next time you see this link, its color will change, indicating that you've been there before. This helps you keep track of the links you haven't visited, so you don't waste any time. You can also click the graphical link at the right side of the Web page to get more information about testing out Netscape's server software.

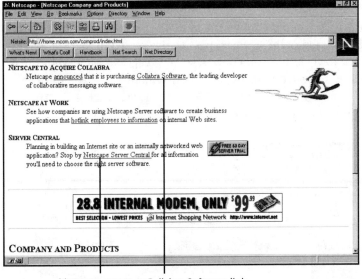

Netscape server   Collabra Software link
software link

Fig. 7.6
This Web page
(**http://
home.mcom.com/
comprod/
index.html**) has
a complete list of
Netscape products
and services at the
bottom.

> ### Client Pull on the Web
>
> You'll eventually run across a Web page that says something like "We've moved" or "This Web page has a new location." It'll display a link that loads the Web page at its new location if you click it. If you wait long enough, however, Netscape may automatically load the Web page at its new location.
>
> *Client pull* is the technology behind this behavior. Client pull allows the Web server to tell Netscape to reload the current Web page or load a different Web page after a set amount of time. One of the most common uses for client pull is the situation described previously. It's also used for simple sequences of Web pages, however, that work just like slide shows.

Clicking an Imagemap

▶ See "Using Imagemaps," pg. 699

Imagemaps are similar to graphical anchors, in that if you click an imagemap, Netscape will load another Web page. Imagemaps can load more than one Web page, however, depending on what part of the image you click. The image itself usually indicates the areas you can click on to load a particular Web page.

Figure 7.7, for example, shows the imagemap that Microsoft uses at its Web site. Each region of the imagemap is clearly defined so that you know where you need to click, and you know what Web page Netscape will load as a result. Click the area that reads "Microsoft Windows 95," and Netscape will load a Web page about Windows 95. Click the area that reads "Support" and Netscape will load the Microsoft Support Desktop.

Fig. 7.7
Microsoft's Web site is at **http://www.microsoft.com**.

Support clickable area

Windows 95 clickable area

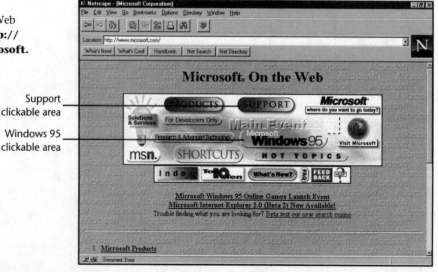

> **Tip**
>
> If you're having trouble deciphering a button bar, look for text links just below it.

A common use for imagemaps on the Web is *button bars*. Button bars are similar to the toolbars you've used in Windows 95 and other windowing environments. They don't appear to click in and out like buttons, however. They are, after all, just imagemaps. You'll find them at the top or, more frequently, the bottom of a Web page. Figure 7.8 shows a button bar from Netscape's Web site. Just like any other imagemap, each area you can click is clearly defined. You can click different areas to load different Web pages. You can click the Search button to search Netscape's Web site, or you can click the Netscape Store button to look at a catalog of Netscape products you can purchase.

Search clickable area ──

Netscape Store clickable area

Fig. 7.8
You'll find this button bar at the bottom of all Netscape Web pages.

Going Directly to a Resource

Which came first, the link or the Web page? If the only way to load a Web page was by clicking on a link, you'd never get anywhere. If a friend gives you an URL, for example, you need a way to tell Netscape to open that Web page without having to use a link. That's why Netscape lets you go directly to a Web page by specifying its URL in either the location bar or Open Location dialog box.

> **Tip**
>
> URLs are case sensitive. If you can't open a Web page, check for strangely capitalized letters such as **http://www.MywEbsiTe.com**.

Figure 7.9 shows the Netscape location bar with the drop-down list open. Type the URL of a Web page in Netscape's location bar, and Netscape will load the Web page. Netscape keeps the addresses of all the Web pages you've opened this way in the location bar's drop-down list. It keeps this list from session to session, too. That way you can always go back to that site by dropping down the list, and clicking on the Web page's URL.

Fig. 7.9
The drop-down
list keeps track of
only those Web
pages you've
opened using the
location bar.

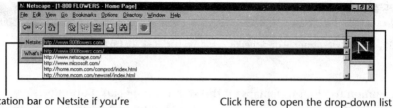

Location bar or Netsite if you're
viewing a Netscape Web page

Click here to open the drop-down list

Note

You don't have to type the **http://** part of an URL in the location bar, because
Netscape will add this for you. If you type just a company name, Netscape will add
www. to the beginning and **.com** to the end. If you type **netscape**, for example,
Netscape will load the Web page at **http://www.netscape.com**.

The Open button requires a few more mouse clicks, but it's just as easy to use.
Click the Open button on the Netscape toolbar. Type the URL of a Web page
in the Open Location dialog box, and click Open. Netscape loads the Web
page that you specified.

Moving Forward and Backward

After you've clicked on a few links and opened a few Web pages, you may
want to go back to a Web page you looked at earlier. Maybe you forgot something you just read, or something didn't seem that interesting then, but it
does now. Netscape provides two useful features to look at previously viewed
Web pages: the history list and the Back/Forward buttons on the toolbar:

Tip

In the History window, select a Web site from the list, and click Create Bookmark to
add it to your bookmarks.

■ The history list keeps track of all the Web pages that you've visited
   during the current session. You can get at the history list in one of two
   places: the Go menu, shown in figure 7.10, shows the last 15 Web pages
   that you've loaded in Netscape. Choose Go from the Netscape main
   menu, and then choose any of the Web pages on the menu. If you want
   to see a list of all the Web pages that you've visited during the current
   session, choose Window, History from the Netscape main menu. Figure
   7.11 shows the History window. You can scroll up and down the list,
   and double-click a Web page to open it in Netscape.

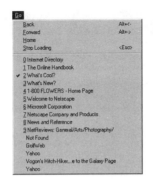

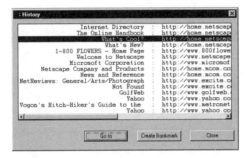

Mastering Netscape

- The Forward and Back buttons move you up and down the history list shown in figure 7.11. If you click the Back button, Netscape moves the highlight down the list and opens that Web page. If you click the Forward button, Netscape moves the highlight up the list, and opens that Web page. Once you've reached the bottom of the list, the Back button is disabled. Likewise, when you reach the top of the list, the Forward button is disabled.

Going to Your Home Page

If you start feeling a bit lost, it's sometimes easier to get your bearings by going back to your home page—starting over. Netscape lets you configure a home page that it uses for two purposes:

- Netscape loads your home page every time Netscape starts. It usually loads it from the cache so that you don't have to wait for Netscape to transfer it from the Internet.

- At any time, you can click the Home button on the Netscape toolbar to return to your home page.

Tip

Configure your home page to point to your favorite Web index such as **www.excite.com**, then it'll be only one click away.

Here's how to change your home page in Netscape:

1. Choose <u>O</u>ptions, <u>G</u>eneral from the Netscape main menu.

2. Click the Appearance tab, and Netscape displays the dialog box shown in figure 7.12.

Fig. 7.12
See the section "Changing the Way Netscape Works with Links," later in this chapter, to learn more about this dialog box.

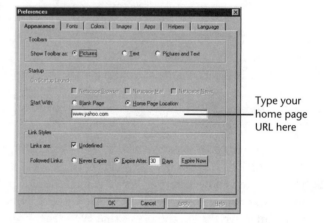

Type your home page URL here

3. Select <u>H</u>ome Page Location, and type the URL of your home page as shown in figure 7.12.

4. Click OK to save your changes.

Note

The term *home page* has two different meanings these days. First, a home page is usually a personal Web page where you would store links to your favorite Web pages, and maybe express yourself a bit. Second, many people refer to the opening page of a Web site as that site's home page. Hewlett-Packard's home page contains links for computers and peripherals, for example.

Saving Bookmarks to Web Pages

The easiest way to get back to a Web page that you visit frequently is to use Netscape bookmarks. *Bookmarks* let you save and organize links to your favorite Web pages. Unlike Netscape's history list, the bookmarks hang around from session to session. They are always easily accessible. Choose Bookmarks from the Netscape main menu. Figure 7.13 shows you what the Bookmarks menu looks like.

▶ See "Netscape Bookmarks," pg. 209

Fig. 7.13
Open a sub-menu or click a Web site to load it in Netscape.

Navigating a Web Site with Frames

Frames are a feature that is currently specific to Netscape. They allow the Netscape window to be split into multiple sections. Each frame on the window can point to a different URL. Figure 7.14 shows a Web page that uses a frame to present a button bar that's always available to you.

▶ See "Netscape-Specific and Future HTML Commands," pg. 721

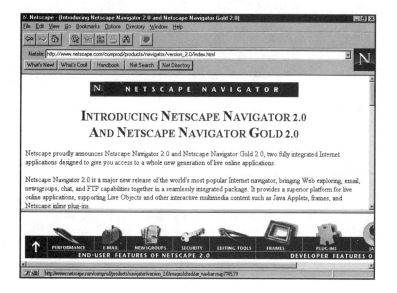

Fig. 7.14
At this site, the button bar will always be available in the bottom frame, regardless of which Web page the top frame is displaying.

II

Mastering Netscape

> **Note**
>
> You'll run across many Web sites that say "Netscape Enhanced, Best Viewed with Netscape," or something similar. They mean it. Many Web sites implement Netscape specific features that can't be viewed with other Web browsers. Frames are a typical example.

Many Windows 95 programs divide their windows into *panes*. They do it to make the organization of the windows' contents more obvious. A program that makes the resumes of a list of people available might have two panes: one to display a list of people and another to display the resume of the currently selected person. Netscape frames can serve a similar purpose, as well. Figure 7.15 shows a Web page that does the same thing as the resume program. It has three frames: one that shows a list of people, another for the resume of the currently selected individual, and a pane at the bottom to select a category.

Fig. 7.15
Frames make a Web site easier to use by organizing its contents in a logical fashion.

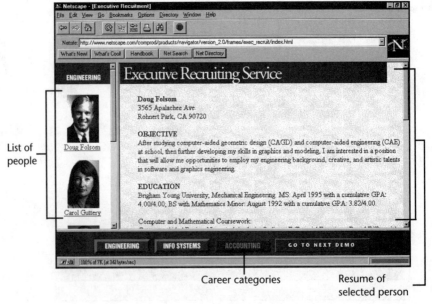

List of people

Career categories

Resume of selected person

Watching Netscape's Status

Netscape gives you a lot of feedback about what's happening after you click a link, or open an URL. Stars shoot past the Netscape logo while Netscape is transferring a Web page or file, for example. It also updates the status bar with information that'll help you keep track of what Netscape is doing. Here are some of the messages you'll see in the status bar:

Message	Description
`http://server/file`	The URL reference of the link to which you are currently pointing.
`X% of YK`	Netscape has completed X percent of a Y kilobyte transfer.

`Connect:`
`Contacting host:`
`server`
	Netscape is trying to contact the given server.

`Connect:`
`Host contacted.`
`Waiting for reply`
	Netscape has contacted the server and is waiting for a reply.

`Document: Done.`	The Web page is finished loading.

Getting Around Faster

If you're using a 14.4Kbps or slower modem, you'll eventually become frustrated with how long it takes to load some Web pages. Many Web pages have very large graphics that take a long time to download. Unfortunately, the use of large graphics is becoming more common as Web authors take it for granted that everyone on the Internet is using at least a 28.8Kbps modem.

Tip

Many Web sites provide links to text-only versions. Look for a text link that says "Text Only."

Fight back. Netscape provides a few features that make Web pages containing too many graphics more tolerable:

- You don't have to wait for the entire Web page to finish loading before you can click a link. Click the Stop button, and Netscape will stop transferring the Web page. If you change your mind and want to reload the page, click the Reload button. Also, most of the text links are available before Netscape has finished transferring the images for the Web page. You can click any of these links. Netscape will stop loading the current page, and start loading the Web page referenced by the link.

■ Most of your time is spent waiting for inline images to load. The irony is that the images on many Web pages aren't really worth the time if you have a slow connection. If you don't want Netscape to automatically load inline images, make sure that Options, Auto Load Images is not checked. If you want to view the images on a particular Web page, and you've disabled Auto Load Images, click the Load Images button on the Netscape toolbar. Figure 7.16 shows what a Web page looks like when it's loaded without inline images. Notice that Netscape displays *placeholders* where it normally displays the images. Netscape also displays alternative text to help you figure out to what the link points.

Fig. 7.16
You can click one of the placeholders to load the Web page it refers to, or you can click the Load Images button to see the inline images.

Placeholder

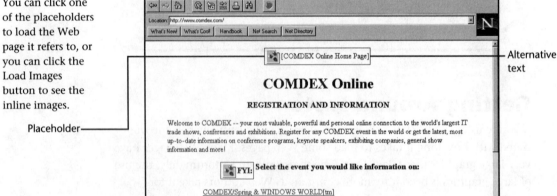

Alternative text

Changing the Way Netscape Works with Links

Netscape gives you a bit of control over how it displays links. It lets you choose whether or not they're underlined and what color it uses to display them.

Underlining Links

You learned earlier in this chapter that Netscape underlines a link's text anchor on a Web page. You can change that. Here's how to configure Netscape
so that it doesn't underline a link's text anchor:

1. Choose Options, General from the Netscape main menu.

2. Click the Appearance tab, and Netscape displays the dialog box shown
   in figure 7.17.

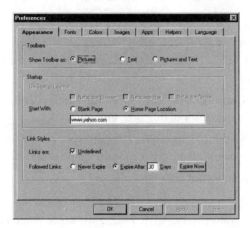

Fig. 7.17
Most of Netscape's
options can be
configured on one
of this dialog box's
tabs.

3. Deselect Underlined, and click OK.

Beginning with the next Web page that Netscape loads, text anchors won't be
underlined. You can still figure out where the links are, however, because
they are displayed in a different color than the text around them.

Using a Different Color for Links

If you don't like the colors that Netscape uses for links, you can change them.
If the default colors are hard to tell apart on your computer, for example,
you'll want to change the colors so you can easily see the links. Use the following steps to change the colors Netscape uses for a text link's anchor:

1. Choose Options, General from the Netscape main menu.

2. Click the Colors tab, and Netscape displays the dialog box shown in
   figure 7.18.

Fig. 7.18
Most of Netscape's
options can be
configured on one
of this dialog box's
tabs.

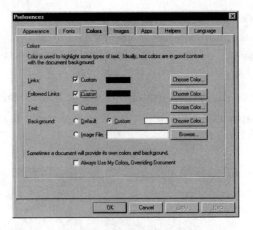

3. Select Links, and click the corresponding Choose Color button. Choose a color from the Color dialog box, and click OK.

4. Select Followed Links, and click the corresponding Choose Color button. Choose a color from the Color dialog box, and click OK.

5. Click OK to save your changes.

Beginning with the next Web page that Netscape loads, Netscape will display text anchors that you've never visited using the color you chose in Links, and text anchors that you've already visited using the color you choose in Followed Links.

Controlling Link Expiration

Netscape caches Web pages so they'll load faster the next time you visit that Web page. It takes much longer to load a Web page from the Internet than it takes to load it from the hard drive. So, Netscape stores every Web page it loads to your hard drive. The next time you point Netscape to that URL, it loads it from the hard drive instead of the Internet.

The problem is that if Netscape is loading Web pages from your hard drive instead of the Internet, you may be looking at a Web page that's out of date. Even if the Web page's author changes it, you'll still be looking at the older version.

Netscape let's you configure how long it will continue to get a Web page from the cache before it loads it from the Internet again. This is called the *expiration*. By default, Netscape expires a link after 30 days. If you find that the Web pages you use are updated more frequently, you can easily change it. Here's how:

1. Choose Options, General from the Netscape main menu.

2. Click the Appearance tab, and Netscape displays the dialog box shown earlier in figure 7.17.

3. Type the number of days you want Netscape to wait before expiring each link in Days. Alternatively, you can expire all of the links in the cache by clicking Expire Now.

4. Click OK to save your changes.

II

Mastering Netscape

## CHAPTER 8

Finding Information on the Web

You've probably heard some of the staggering numbers associated with the rise of the Internet and the World Wide Web: forty million global users increasing by millions each month, millions of Web pages containing countless documents—hundreds of new servers popping up almost daily. Just realizing that the enormous resources of sites like the Library of Congress are only one small part of all this vastness does a lot to explain the phrase information age.

How do you navigate such a universe? As a diligent infonaut perched at your computer, modem screaming, hard drive whining, you may begin to feel like a small spaceship drifting from one planet's gravitational pull to the next, with only the occasional burst from a new Web page's thrusters to point you in a new direction.

What we need is a map. All of this clicking around on links is great; but when you really need to find something (for instance, because your boss wants you to), surfing is about the last thing you want to do. But what if the Web had a table of contents—and some really strong search engines? Well, it does—sort of. And, Netscape makes the best of these engines easily accessible from the directory buttons on the browser window.

In this chapter you learn how to:

- Use Netscape's home page
- Specify your own home page
- Use the What's Cool and What's New buttons
- Perform category searches with Yahoo and other subject-search tools
- Find information using the most powerful Internet search engines

The Home Page

The home page, as you've likely discovered, is simply the first Web page that you see when you launch Netscape Navigator. By default this is Netscape Communications Corporation's Web site, but you have the option of changing your home page to just about any Web page on the Internet you want, as well as to a local (on your computer) HTML file.

> **Tip**
>
> When upgrading from Netscape version 1.x to 2.0, install Netscape in the same directory as the previous version (the Windows 95 default is c:\Program Files\Netscape\Navigator). This will retain your current home page settings, as well as your bookmarks file and any shortcuts you have in your Start menu or on your desktop. If you've not yet installed Netscape or you install to a different directory, Netscape automatically sets your home page to its Web site. For more information on downloading and installing Netscape, see chapter 3.

You'll also see the term *home page* used in a general sense to describe the main, or first, Web page of other people's and organizations' Web sites on the Internet. In my opinion, this is really the wrong way to use the term home page, but it's fairly well entrenched, so there's not much chance of changing it. If a page is the first page of a particular site, it's more correct to call it the *index page* or *default page* for that site. As far as Netscape (the application) is concerned, your home page is the first page that loads when you start your browser.

Selection of a home page is personal, and it depends on how you use the Web. Whether your interests are business or pleasure—or both—you'll have little problem finding a Web page out there that will suit your needs as you begin each browsing session. There are, however, some important things to know about the home page:

- You may return to your designated home page at any time by clicking the Home Page button.
- Netscape's own home page (**http://home.netscape.com**) is a great place to begin, especially if you're new to the Web.
- Netscape doesn't load the home page from cache on start-up (though it does cache after loading), so expect lag-time if you set your home page to a heavily-accessed server or URL that has specific time constraints.

- If you copy the source file for a Web page from another site and use it as your home page (loading it off your hard drive), you won't see any changes or updates from the original Web site.

- You may set your bookmarks file as the home page; however, your history file will not work as a home page.

- You may set your home page to bring up any number of files, including Windows 95 applications, helper programs, plug-ins and Java applets.

Let's look at this in a bit more detail.

The Home Page Button

Clicking the Home Page button once takes you to your home page at any time during a browsing session. Alternately, you may also select Go, Home from the drop-down menu bar.

You can think of the Home Page button as a mini-bookmark that contains only one hyperlink—a very important link with which you begin your Web session. Loading that page from the Home Page button is a bit different, though, than loading it at the start of a session, because of the way Netscape stores the home page in its cache.

Regardless of how you have your cache configured, the first time you load in your home page it does not use the files on your hard drive's cache. Netscape always travels to that first URL, updates the Web page, and then caches its contents in memory. This is especially important if you decide to change your home page to a site other than Netscape Corp's pages. Since Netscape must download all the files from your home page without the speed and support of the cache, connecting to a heavily used site or a Web page with a slow server can be frustrating.

Note

How Netscape uses its cache memory is a fully configurable option. See chapter 3 for more information on how to set up your cache.

Fortunately, the Home Page button—unless you've designated otherwise—acts as a regular URL, and uses the files from your cache.

The Home Page button is a little deceptive—it's a bit more powerful than it lets on. Though you can't move it, assign a macro to it, or change its appearance, you can use it to launch a number of Windows 95 files, as well as files that use a helper application, plug-ins, or Java applets. We'll see more about that in a moment. For now, let's take a close look at some of the benefits to using Netscape's own (default) home page.

Using Netscape's Home Page

As a veteran of the World Wide Web, Netscape has had the time and resources to put together an informative, flexible, and useful Web site (**http://home.netscape.com**), shown in figure 8.1.

Fig. 8.1
Netscape's opening page is now even easier to return to or reload thanks to client-side imagemaps.

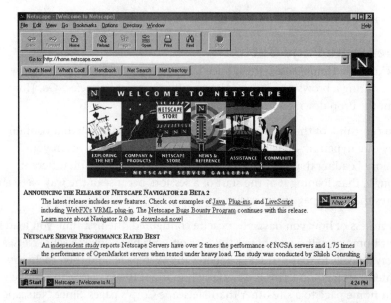

Netscape's home page offers a variety of resources and features a clickable imagemap with the following six options:

- *Exploring The Net* duplicates the same options that are reachable from the Netscape Directory buttons, namely, What's New, What's Cool, Handbook, Net Directory, and Net Search.

- *Company Products* divides itself into links about Netscape Products, Development Partners, About Netscape, Netscape Sales, Channel Partners, and Business Solutions.

- *Netscape Store* keeps you informed about Netscape software and publications with four links to Software, Publications, Support, and Bazaar, which allows you to buy t-shirts and boxer shorts sporting the Netscape Mozilla logo.

- *Assistance* points to sources that teach you more about the Internet.

- *Community* includes links to user groups and White Pages directories.

- *News & Reference* gives you access to a variety of news and information links, including Internet Headlines, Netscape Press Releases, Standards Docs, and Reference Material. A lot of technical information is available here.

Note

Reloading Netscape's home page is faster than ever, since the main imagemap that contains the most important links is now stored in your cache. For more details on client-side imagemaps, see chapter 28, "Using Imagemaps."

One of the most important links on this page is to the latest version of Netscape Navigator. You'll find it at the bottom of the Company & Products page under Netscape Products. You'll want to check this from time to time as Netscape updates the speed, reliability, and functions of its browser. Be aware, though, that the process of obtaining the latest version will take you through several pages of links to get to the download. You may be able to circumvent this to some extent by going directly to Netscape's FTP site. Do this by typing **ftp.netscape.com** in the address box, or use File, Open Location on the menu bar. Netscape's FTP server is often overloaded, but don't worry; if you get an error message you'll also get a list of dozens of mirror sites—FTP sites that contain the same files as Netscape's—that you can immediately access.

The Netscape Directory Buttons

Built in to Netscape's interface are links to certain pages on its Web site that can be of particular use to almost any Netscape user. Netscape, by default, displays these five buttons near the top of the browser. If you don't see these buttons, go to the Options menu and make sure that the Show Directory Buttons option is checked. Save your selection by clicking Options, Save Options.

Later in this chapter we look at the Net Directory and Net Search options for our discussion of search engines and techniques; right now let's look at the other three buttons.

What's Cool

The What's Cool button brings you to a collection of favorite Web pages, compiled and updated by Netscape. This is a good starting point for finding interesting Web sites. Figure 8.2 shows you what to expect.

Fig. 8.2
The Netscape Cool team is on the job, so there's some great surfing here!

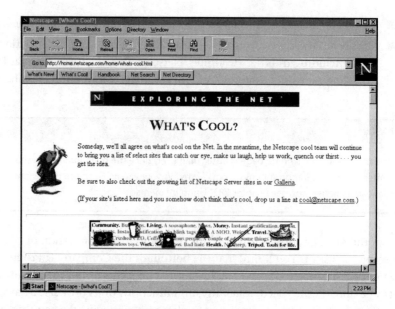

Also, check out the growing list of Netscape Server sites from the Galleria link; sites that use Netscape's Server software have native security features built-in for special use with Netscape Navigator.

▶ See "Netscape Forms and CGI-BIN Scripts," pg. 745

Be on the lookout for other cool-sites listings as you travel the Internet—many other Web sites compile, post, and update their favorite Web pages. You'll find a number of sites that also follow Netscape's practice of requesting you to submit your own cool links for inclusion in their pages. If you have some really cool Web sites you'd like to see in Netscape's What's Cool, submit them via Netscape's online form.

What's New!

The What's New! button takes you to an assortment of new Internet resources, archived monthly. This is an excellent place for introducing you to new Web sites; it will give you a good feel for just how fast the surface of the Web is spinning. Just as with the What's Cool pages, Netscape is interested in any new Web sites you want to tell them about. Of course this area is updated quite often, so your version of figure 8.3 will most certainly be a bit different.

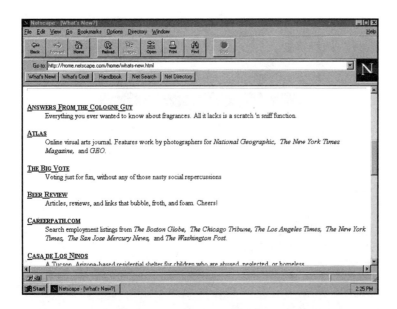

Fig. 8.3
Netscape's own list of some of the latest sites to appear on the Web.

Tip

Want some other examples of What's New sites? To keep up with the latest software on the Net, point your browser to Stroud's WSApps List, at **http:// cwsapps.texas.net//cwsa.html**, and Tucows, at **http://www.tucows.com/**. Both of these sites are meticulously maintained and updated daily, include reviews of the newest and best programs, and have direct links to FTP sites to download the freeware and shareware.

Using the Netscape Handbook

You may already have noticed that the Netscape browser really doesn't have much in the way of an online help file. That's because most of the documentation for the program is actually provided in Web format on Netscape Corp.'s Web site. The Netscape Handbook button takes you to all the information Netscape provides about the most current version of Navigator. In addition to the basics of using the Netscape browser, some elementary concepts of the Internet are explained (see fig. 8.4).

Perhaps among the most important links available from the Handbook button are links to the Release Notes for the current version of Navigator. It's on these pages that you can see what advances (and what problems, if any) have been introduced with the latest version of the program.

II

Mastering Netscape

Fig. 8.4

Here's Netscape's version of online help—the Netscape Handbook.

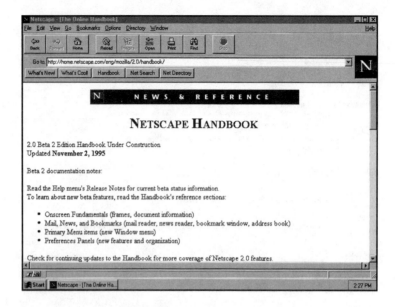

Using Another Home Page

As comprehensive as Netscape's home page is, you'll probably, at some point, find another you like better. You may discover that you change your home page as your needs change. For example, if you're heavily into e-mail, you may want your home page to be set to Netscape's e-mail window. If you become interested in a particular newsgroup, you may find yourself specifying the Newsgroups window as your starting point.

In fact, you can set your home page to load any valid, accessible URL on the Internet. And it's as easy as a few clicks. Just remember to watch out for slow servers or heavy Web sites—otherwise you'll become more intimate with the Stop button than you probably want to be.

To change your home page settings, select Options, General Preferences and then the Appearances tab (it's the default tab). The dialog box shown in figure 8.5 pops up.

Midway down you'll see the Start With text box. Enter the new URL there. You don't have to enter the protocol tag for most URLs, though some will require it. For example, if I'm setting my home page to Que's Web site, I type in

http://www.mcp.com/que or just **www.mcp.com/que**

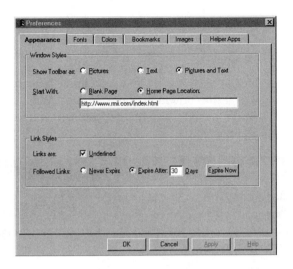

Fig. 8.5
Enter your new
home page in
the Start With
text box.

Notice that there is no Browse button that allows you access to your history
file, bookmarks file, or address box. You'll also find that Netscape doesn't allow you to paste a copied URL into this text box. This is an annoying setup
that Netscape should eventually fix in later releases. For now—unless you
have a photographic memory—you have to resort to pen and paper to write
down the URL, and then type it directly into the box.

Notice the two radio buttons above the box. The first one, labeled Blank Page,
should be checked if you don't want a start-up page to begin your Web sessions. Why do this? It keeps Netscape from loading *anything* when it starts
up. Perhaps you have different URLs you like to load first, depending on the
work at hand. Sometimes, for instance, I know I want to go straight to the
WebCrawler Web site to search for something. Other times I might want to
set off for Netscape's home pages or some other site I often call home.

The second radio button is the one you'll need to check if you're specifying a
home page other than Netscape's site.

Above the radio buttons are three checkboxes where you can specify whether
you want to start up with your home page, with Netscape's built-in e-mail, or
with the Newsgroups browser.

Using a Local File as Your Home Page

There are some distinct advantages to using a local HTML file on your hard
drive as your home page. A local file will load fast, and will always load (barring a badly fragmented hard drive or other local system problem). Again, a

▶ See "E-mail
with Netscape,"
pg. 321

▶ See "E-mail
with Netscape
Personal Edi-
tion and
Eudora Light,"
pg. 347

▶ See "Reading
UseNet
Newsgroups
with Netscape,"
pg. 371

II

Mastering Netscape

heavily accessed site sometimes means it takes quite a while for a remote home page to load. And, even if you specify a URL on the Web that's not heavily accessed, it's always possible that the site's server is down.

Perhaps the most important advantage to a local home page, however, is the control it gives you over the content of your start page. Write your own home page, and you can include exactly what you need and want—your own favorite links and graphics.

Finding the Internet—On Your Own Computer

When we talk about a local file, we're talking about a *client-side* file. If your computer is capable of only connecting to other computers, but cannot be accessed by any other machines, it is a *client*. If your computer can be accessed by other machines via the Internet or any network, it is referred to as a *server*.

Part of the evolution of the Web is its move toward an environment where its computers can be both clients and servers. As technologies like ISDN, wireless systems, coaxial cable, and optical fiber evolve—as bandwidth increases—a stronger server base emerges. Still, applications run much faster on your own system than if the bytes are moving through a data link. And, however quickly they grow, the faster access speeds will never be faster than your computer's processor.

The need for a large client-based cache that's only updated at user-specified intervals makes a lot of sense, then, while larger storage devices allow you, as a server, to make more interactive, snazzier content available to everyone else out there. This is especially feasible now, when storage devices (hard drives and CD-ROMs) sell for a tiny fraction of what they did a decade ago. For both clients and servers, the ready availability of electronic storage results in less reliance on the bandwidth of the connection.

What does this mean? It means that in the future in order to support new ways of finding and using the information and resources on the Internet, you'll store more and more HTML (Web) pages, graphics, videos, audio, applets, etc. on your own computer. As directories and indexes evolve, and as search engines and the like become more intelligent, interactive, and flexible, you'll need more and more of your own client computing power and storage to make your search for information as painless and fun as possible.

Of course, in order to specify a local file for your home page, you've got to have a file. One option is to create your own HTML page and use it as your home page.

Another option is to save the source code to any one of the millions and millions of URLs your browser can access. If you spend even a few minutes a day on the Web—and many of you spend far more time than that—you'll have already lost count of the number of Web pages you've visited. Just point your browser to the Web page you want to save, and:

1. With the page you want saved displayed in Netscape, open the File menu and choose Save As. The Save As directory box appears (see fig. 8.6).

Fig. 8.6
Save the downloaded file using the Save As option in the File menu.

Mastering Netscape

2. Select the directory or subdirectory where the file will reside using the Save in: drop-down menu.

3. Enter a name for the file.

4. Select the file type in the Save as type: drop-down menu. In this case, you want source (*.htm, *.html) option.

5. Click the Save button and the file will be downloaded to the location you specified.

To verify that the page was downloaded successfully, go ahead and load it into Netscape Navigator. From File, Open File, click the Browse button and find the folder you saved it in, highlight the file and double-click it or click Open. Look first in the address box after the file is loaded. Netscape, by default, displays your local file structure with UNIX specifiers:

file:///c|directory/subdirectory/filename.htm

where c represents the name of the drive the file is located on.

You'll notice, too, that your Web page has changed; the background and any inline graphics are now replaced by Netscape's little broken picture icons. We'll talk about this later in this chapter in the section "Starting Other Files with Your Home Page."

Specifying a Local File as Your Home Page

To change your home page to a local file, select Options, General Preferences, and the Appearances tab. Place your cursor inside the text box. Type the letter of the drive where the file is located, followed by a colon, backslash, the appropriate directories or subdirectories, and the file name. The file can be from any drive and any directory on your system.

For example, if I'm setting my home page to a file in the windows directory on my hard drive c, all I need to enter is:

c:\windows\myhome.htm

Ensure that the .htm extension is used (see fig. 8.7).

Fig. 8.7
Setting up a local file for your home page is no more difficult than setting up a URL.

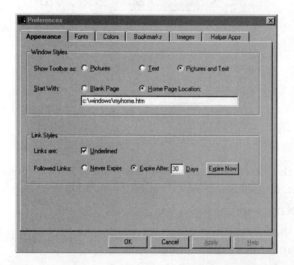

Not surprisingly, you may also enter the older UNIX version of the file name, which is a protocol handler file:/// followed by the letter of the hard drive, a vertical line or "pipe" (Shift+backslash key on a 101 or 102 standard keyboard), and forward slashes. The previous example would mutate into this:

file:///c|windows/myhome.htm

You can use either the DOS parameters or the UNIX specifiers; however, you may not mix the two styles.

Specifying the Bookmarks File as Your Home Page

You can also set your Bookmarks file as your home page. After you've been on the Web for a while and catalogued many of your favorite sites, this is a quick and easy option—it's also less clunky than fiddling with Netscape's View Bookmarks window. The file is located in your Navigator subdirectory and is simply named bookmarks.htm. Netscape's default installation for Windows 95 sets up the directory structure like this, where c is the letter of the hard drive:

▶ See "Netscape Bookmarks," pg. 209

c:\Programfiles\Netscape\bookmarks.htm

You may be tempted to try to use your History file as your home page. This would make some sense—the History file makes it easy for you to remember some of those dynamite Web sites you visited during your last session, but forgot to put in your Bookmarks file. Unfortunately, the file, netscap.hst, located in your navigator subdirectory, is just a text file that's used for reference to your cache, and is useless as a home page.

Starting Other Files with Your Home Page

As we saw earlier, if the Web page you saved from the Internet has any graphics or other media besides text, you get a surprise when you load that file—Netscape will not load in the other media with your home page. There's a simple reason for this.

The file you saved, of course, is an HTML file. Within the file are references to other files—graphics files—that were stored at the original server you downloaded from. The tags—the codes that HTML uses to display a document—within the HTML page gave the location of these files so that Netscape would know where to find them when displaying the page.

▶ See "HTML Primer," pg. 617

Unfortunately, when you saved the HTML file, Netscape *did not* save the graphics as specific files in the same directory, nor did Netscape do anything to change the code so the references would be renamed to work correctly on your hard drive. There are two ways to fix the problem:

- Return to the Web page at its original URL. While holding down the Shift key, click each graphic within that page one at a time, and save each picture to the same directory that holds the HTML file.

- Open up Netscape's Cache subdirectory in Windows Explorer and find the files. This will be hit-or-miss because the files are not saved with their original file names, but with a Netscape specific name that looks something like MO0#####. You can narrow your search by showing file extensions in Explorer—any graphics files will have an extension of

II

Mastering Netscape

either .JPEG or .GIF. Rename each file with the name referenced in the HTML document (you have to view the HTML code in Notepad or Wordpad to find the references to graphics files) and save each one in the same directory you used for your HTML file.

If this sounds a bit complicated, don't worry, it won't make much sense until you read Part IV of this book to learn how graphics are referenced in HTML files. But, since HTML is not much more difficult than using your favorite word processor, you shouldn't have much trouble.

Launching Netscape Helpers, Plug-ins, and Other Files

▶ See "Using VRML," pg. 491

▶ See "Sun's Java and the Netscape Browser," pg. 845

As you become experienced with the Web and begin to drool over some of its exciting new ways to deliver information, you may want to spruce up your home page with other applications. Though there's not much practicality in using a video or audio file to start your Web session (remember though, the file is also tied to your Home Page button, and you can click the button any time you choose), you may find a plug-in or Java applet works better than a regular HTML page, depending upon your particular needs.

For example, if you play the stock market and there's an available Java applet that updates a small spreadsheet to keep you informed of the daily averages, you may want to begin each session with this important information. Or, you may want to start your Web session off in three dimensions—using a VRML plug-in, you may intuitively find your favorite links quicker, easier, and a lot more fun. With the functionality and level of interactivity that Java and VRML promise to offer the Web, the possibilities are literally endless.

Run Your Other Windows 95 Apps from the Home Page Button

As it turns out, you can specify a number of other local files in Windows 95 to load from your Home Page button. More specifically, since Netscape communicates directly with the registry in Windows 95, it recognizes file extension associations located there—with the exception of executable files—and loads the associated application that supports your file. (Actually, Netscape *will* also recognize the exes directly, but you have to disable the Octet-stream MIME that still doesn't work exactly right. The result is not worth the effort.)

For example, if I want to launch a Microsoft Word document (and, by association, Microsoft Word) from my Home Page button, all I need enter into the text box located in the Options, General Preferences, Appearances tab is:

c:\directory\subdirectory\filename.doc

where c is the name of the drive the file is located in.

Netscape recognizes the file extension and has Windows launch Microsoft Word along with my document. Of course, it will not only load when I hit the Home button, but will also load at my home page every time I start Netscape.

Let's do a quick example with the WebFX VRML plug-in, which is freeware from Paper Software, Inc. You can find the latest version of the plug-in on the Netscape home page (**http://home.netscape.com**) or at **http://www.paperinc.com**, Paper's Web site. Download the WebFX plug-in into a temporary directory and launch its installation program. It will automatically configure and attach itself to Netscape. Make sure you have no other windows programs running while you're performing the setup.

Tip

It's always a good idea to close the MS Office shortcut bar, too, whenever you set up new applications.

Both Netscape and Paper, Inc. have links to a number of VRML sites and pages. Alternately, and the most fun, you can create your own VRML pages with the software on the CD-ROM included with this book. Once you've loaded in a VRML file, the look of the plug-in should be similar to figure 8.8.

Fig. 8.8
Mark Pesce's "Zero Circle"(**http://www.hyperreal.com/~mpesce/circle.wrl**) looks great in the WebFX plug-in.

Unlike an HTML file, a saved VRML file includes all its graphics and hyperlinks together in the same file. You'll find this to be true with Java applets, as well. Simply bring up the Appearances tab under Options, General Preferences again, and enter the name of the file as either a local file or the URL, depending on whether you've saved the file or you're accessing it from a remote system. Be sure to label the file extension as .WRL.

Net Directory: Searching the Internet by Subject

There's no question that using Netscape and the World Wide Web is the way of the immediate future on the Internet, and it's an amazing tool for gathering information. The Web metaphor, in fact, with its links spiraling out into the unknown, is an ingenious method of information retrieval—if only because it mimics the way most humans think—relationally.

But, sometimes things can feel a little disorganized. Especially when you're on a deadline or sick-to-death of *surfing* to find something. If you've ever used Gopher for information retrieval, then maybe you're feeling a bit nostalgic. Isn't there *some* way this silly Web can be organized?

Enter the Net Directory pages provided by Netscape. Click once on the Net Directory button on Netscape's interface and you're presented with a listing of available Internet directories scattered around the Web. This page is almost guaranteed to save you hours of surfing frustration more than once in your Web life.

What do we mean by directory? Directories generally provide an editorial service—they determine the best sites around the Web and include them in categorized listings to make finding information easier. Some directories actually combine two features—a directory of categorized sites and a search engine for searching both the category listing and the Internet.

There are a number of directories listed in Net Directory, the most well-known of which is Yahoo, known by many as the most outstanding attempt at organizing the Web yet.

The following are the options currently available in Net Directory:

- *Yahoo* is the grandfather of Internet guides. Easily the most comprehensive attempt at creating a table of contents for the Internet, Yahoo lets you get directly at listings of Web sites by category. Internet users send submissions to Yahoo, whose editors screen the sites for suitability.

There are a lot of sites that *aren't* covered in Yahoo...but many of the *quality* sites are.

■ *The McKinley Internet Directory* lists a database of World Wide Web, Gopher, FTP, Telnet, newsgroup and mailing-list links that are divided into categories. The database is searchable, and the sites are rated by an editorial team.

■ *Point* offers reviews of what they consider to be the top five percent of Internet sites. Sites are also allowed to submit their own selling copy, which is edited.

■ *World Wide Arts Resources* offers a digital outlet for more than 2,000 artists. This index page for the arts features links to galleries, museums, arts sites, an antiques database, and arts-related educational and government sites.

■ *World Wide Web Servers* offers a huge listing of Web servers. United States servers are listed by state.

■ *Virtual Tourist* is similar to the World Wide Web Servers information, but presented as a clickable graphical map.

◀ See "Clicking an Imagemap," pg. 154

The Yahoo Directory

The Yahoo Internet directory was created in April 1994 by David Filo and Jerry Yang, two Ph.D. candidates in Electrical Engineering at Stanford University, as a way to keep track of their personal interests on the Internet. The directory grew quickly in popularity after they made it available to the public and spent more and more time organizing sites into their hierarchy. In early 1995, Netscape Corp. invited Filo and Yang to move their files from Stanford's network to computers housed at Netscape.

Using Yahoo is a little like shopping for the best Internet sites. Instead of blindly following links to different Web sites, hoping that you'll eventually come across one that's interesting, you deal with Yahoo's pages for a while. As you move deeper through Yahoo's menu-style links, you get closer to Web sites that interest you.

Tip

Although Yahoo's primary role is as a directory for the Web, it also offers access to breaking Reuters NewMedia newswire stories. If you're a news hound, click the Headlines button at the top of Yahoo's index page.

II

Mastering Netscape

First you need to get to Yahoo. From the Net Directory page, click the link to Yahoo once. Starting at the top-most level, you choose the category of Web site you're interested in seeing, for instance, Computers and Internet (see fig. 8.9).

> **Tip**
>
> Yahoo's direct URL is **http://www.yahoo.com**. I'd even go so far as to recommend creating a Bookmark for Yahoo (or using it as your home page)...sometimes Netscape's Net Directory page is a bit slow to respond.

▶ See "Creating a Bookmark," pg. 211, and "Deleting a Bookmark," pg. 213

Fig. 8.9
Yahoo offers a directory listing of subjects from the Internet.

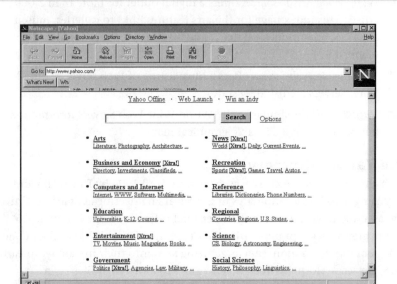

From there, it's as easy as clicking your way through the hierarchy as you get closer and closer to the type of site you're trying to find. In figure 8.10, for instance, I've moved down the line a little bit, having chosen to view Internet Providers, then Regions. Now I'm looking at a listing of different parts of the country. Pick one, and I'll get a list of links to the Web pages of Internet providers in that part of the country.

How Yahoo Works

What you first notice about the Yahoo directory is its 14 top categories. These categories, determined by the folks who designed Yahoo, are the basic structure of the Table of Contents approach. But how do you get your Web site included in this hierarchy?

This shows how far down into the hierarchy I am

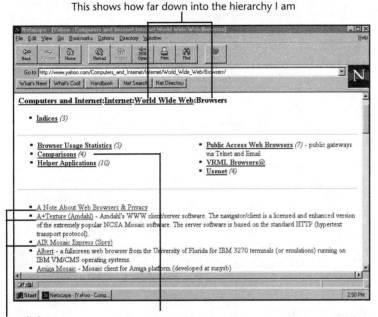

Fig. 8.10
Digging a little deeper into Yahoo gets you closer to the Web sites you're seeking.

These are links to specific Web sites

And this is another category level that I can dig into

Web site creators decide what category they feel is most appropriate for their Web site's inclusion in the directory. Once you get to the part of the directory you'd like your site to appear in, you click the Add URL button at the top of Yahoo's interface. You're then asked by Yahoo to fill out a Web form with information on their site, the URL, a contact's address, and other tidbits (see fig. 8.11). After reviewing the entry, Yahoo's staff decides if the site merits inclusion.

Why is this important? Two reasons. First, whether you're a Web user or a Web creator, it's significant to recognize that being included in the Yahoo directory is something of a make-or-break proposition. That's not to say that you can't have a successful site if you're not in the Yahoo directory (or, that it will be successful just because it *does* get included). But being in the Yahoo directory does, at least in a sense, suggest that you've arrived.

Second, it's important to note that being in the Yahoo directory is something you generally have to *actively* seek. These are, then, sites that *want* to be accessed. A lot of these sites are high-traffic areas with broad appeal...in fact, a good percentage of them are commercial sites. That is by no means always bad, but you should recognize that it is a limitation to what you'll find using the Yahoo directory.

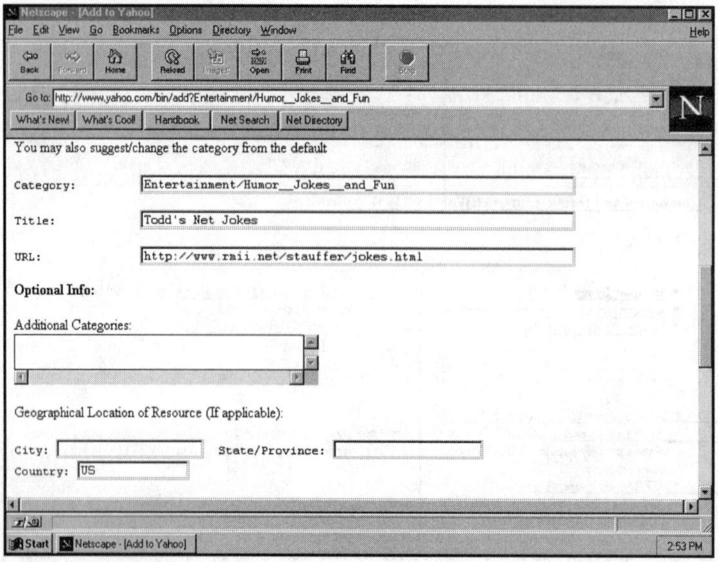

Fig. 8.11
Submitting your own Web site for inclusion in the Yahoo directory.

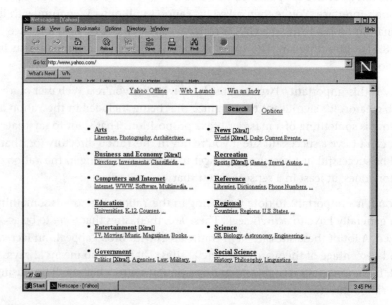

Searching with Yahoo

Clicking through the directory isn't the only way to get at Yahoo's listed sites. There's also a basic search engine that uses keywords to find interesting pages for you. Where do you do this searching? From Yahoo's main index page, enter a search phrase in the text box that sits above the category listings (see fig. 8.12).

Fig. 8.12
Yahoo lets you search its database for relevant sites.

By search phrase I simply mean a few keywords to help Yahoo limit the search. This takes some experimentation (as it does with all of the Internet search engines), and we'll discuss that later in this chapter in the section, "Searching on the Web." This simple search from the Yahoo index page assumes you want to find *all* the keywords you enter. By default it searches the names, URLs, and descriptions of all its Web pages.

What results from this search is a list of possible matches in Yahoo's database, with hypertext links to the described pages (see fig. 8.13). This gives you an opportunity to look at a number of different pages that may or may not include the information you're seeking.

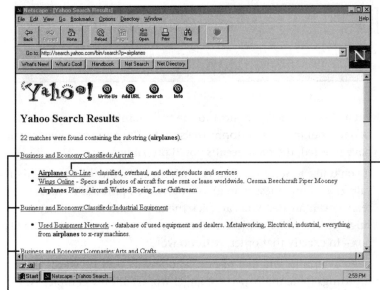

Fig. 8.13
The Yahoo search results page. Each of these results is actually a link to the site that's being described.

Click here to see a page that may be what you're trying to find

Results were found in these Yahoo categories

This is a pretty basic search, and, as I pointed out, it's based on a number of default assumptions about the type of search you want to use. If you're not having much luck, you may want to try taking a little more control over the search variables. For a more advanced search, follow these steps:

1. From the basic Yahoo index page, click the Options link, next to the Search button. The advanced Yahoo Search page appears (see fig. 8.14).

2. Type your search phrase or keywords into the text box.

Fig. 8.14
If you don't get good results from the simple Yahoo search, you can take more control of the variables.

Enter the search phrase here ——

Checkboxes determine what will be searched

Radio buttons help you widen or narrow the search

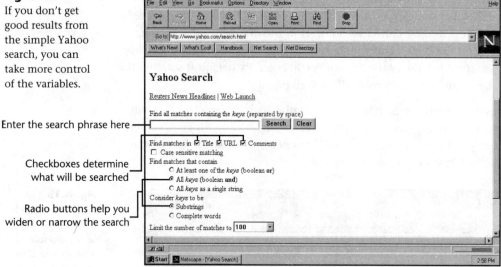

3. Put a check in the boxes next to the type of information you want Yahoo to examine as it performs the search. The more checkboxes you have selected, the more results you'll probably get.

4. If you'd like to see more results, click the radio button that allows results that contain less than all of your search phrases. To narrow the search even further, you can click the radio button for All keys as a single string, which looks for all of the words you entered in the text box—in exactly that order, with no words.

5. Then determine whether or not Yahoo treats your keywords as substrings (potentially parts of larger words) or only complete words.

Tip

You can eliminate a lot of erroneous results by telling Yahoo to assume your keywords should be complete words only. Why? Consider the keyword net. As a substring, it may appear as Net, Internet, and Netting. It may also, however, result in pages referencing the Netherlands and garnets.

---

6. Finally, choose the number of results you want shown. You can choose 100, 200, 300, or Unlimited. The more results you ask for, the longer it takes to get through them all.

7. Click the Search button to initiate the search.

What results is a page very similar to the search results page we saw with the simple Yahoo Search except, hopefully, it's more likely to have links to the sites you need to access. If not, you might want to keep trying if you feel like you can narrow or widen the search with the advanced options. If you feel like you've done all you can, it might just be that Yahoo doesn't have what you're interested in.

Don't worry, though. We've got plenty more directories and Internet search engines to consult.

The McKinley Internet Directory: Magellan

Offered by the McKinley Group, Magellan is another Internet directory and search service available from Netscape's Net Directory page (see fig. 8.15). Magellan offers a listing of over 1,000,000 sites—30,000 of which are reviewed, evaluated, and rated Web, Telnet, Gopher, and FTP sites. Like Yahoo, Magellan allows you to search its database directly for links that match certain keywords. You can also access the staff's recommended sites through a hierarchy of menus.

Fig. 8.15
From Magellan's index page you can search over 1,000,000 sites or browse around 30,000 reviewed sites.

Magellan isn't quite identical to Yahoo...it's both less and more of a directory than Yahoo is. While searching is more tightly integrated into the directory portion of Magellan, it does offer more description and recommendations than Yahoo does...at least for a limited number of sites.

Browsing the Magellan Directory

If you're looking for some of the best possible sites on the Internet, choose the Browse Categories link on Magellan's index page. This gives you a listing of categories to choose from, much like Yahoo's directory. Eventually you'll dig deep enough to find some sites that have been reviewed by the McKinley Group staff (see fig. 8.16). Here you'll see that many of the sites have been given a star rating to let you know how useful and impressive that particular site is.

Fig. 8.16
After choosing a category and a sub-category, here's a list of possible sites and their ratings.

Here you can narrow the listing with keywords

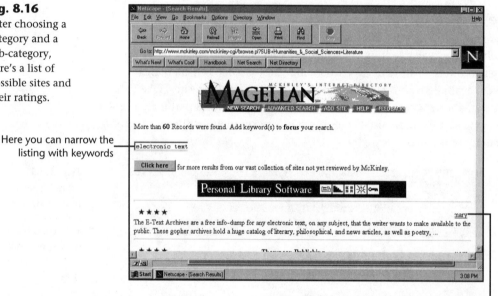

Click this link to visit the recommended sites

Notice also that you can limit the number of reviewed sites that appear in the listing by entering keywords at the top of the page and clicking the Focus Search button. This results in fewer listings in a particular category—most of which, hopefully, will include information that interests you.

Searching Magellan

As I mentioned before, you can also search Magellan for interesting Web sites. For a simple search, enter a search phrase in the text box on Magellan's index page and click the Search Magellan button. For a more advanced search, click the graphic marked Advanced Search. That presents you with the page in figure 8.17.

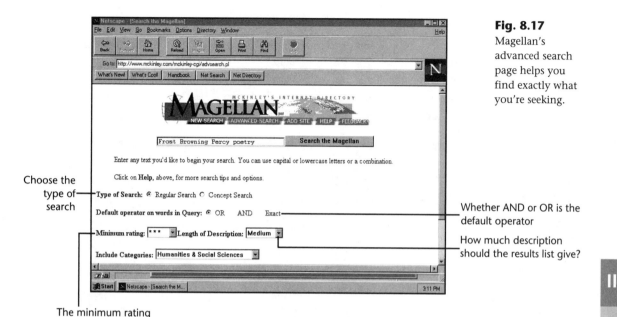

Fig. 8.17
Magellan's
advanced search
page helps you
find exactly what
you're seeking.

Choose the type of search

The minimum rating

Whether AND or OR is the default operator

How much description should the results list give?

Enter your search keywords in this box, then you've got some choices to make. Magellan allows you to do a straight keyword search or a concept search. For a concept search, Magellan generates a series of words that are related to the keywords you enter, and also searches for these. This generates resulting Web sites that don't necessarily include the specific keyword you entered, but may contain related information.

You are also asked to choose whether AND or OR should be assumed between your keywords (to, respectively, broaden or limit your search), the minimum rating for the pages to be returned and how much description you want to see in the resulting list. Once you've made these decisions, click the button marked Search the Magellan. Now you're off and running.

Tip

The advanced Magellan search engine can actually accept very involved (and somewhat complicated) keyword phrases. For more on Magellan's searching abilities, choose Help from Magellan's graphical interface, then click the Search the Magellan link.

Mastering Netscape

II

Point

Point is another widely recognized repository of Internet site reviews. Claiming to have links to the "top 5 percent" of Internet sites, Point is a great place to find some of what's cool on the Web (see fig. 8.18). To see a directory of the reviews that Point has to offer, click once on the Top 5% Reviews graphic in the top-left corner of Point's index page interface.

Fig. 8.18
Point offers
reviews of what it
considers to be the
best Internet sites
in various
categories.

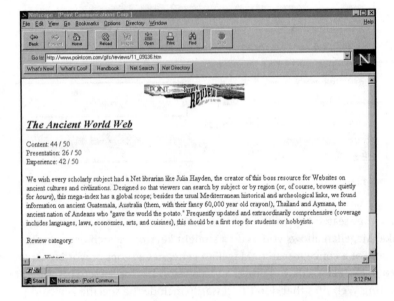

The reviews can sometimes be a little irreverent, fun and, as the Netscape Net Directory page puts it, pointed. Internet sites can also submit their own descriptions, which are duly edited. You search the reviews using keywords via the Point Search feature. If you want to submit your site for inclusion in Point's listing, you use the Submit feature.

> **Note**
>
> Interestingly, Point Communications, which puts out the Point directory and ratings, has recently been acquired by Lycos, one of the premier search engines on the Internet. According to the Point index page, this gives you access not only to the top 5 percent of sites, but, through Lycos, access to 90 percent of *all* the Internet sites around the world. We'll discuss Lycos in the "Net Search: Searching on the Internet" section of this chapter.

The Best of the Rest

There are a few other Internet directories available behind Netscape's Net Directory button. They're a little more specialized, but, if you're interested, you may find tons of links to the kinds of sites you want to visit.

World Wide Arts Resources

For anyone interested in the arts, the World Wide Arts Resources offers access to galleries, museums, an antiques database, related arts sites, as well as arts-related educational and governmental sites. The directory also presents the digital work of over 2,000 artists. There are a variety of resources within the directory, which have been actively compiled for well over a year now.

For example, if you are looking for the work of a particular artist, then use the Artist Index. Other resources include: Art Galleries & Exhibits; Museums, for international listings; USA Museums, which features a 20-page preview and has categorized both the museums and what is available at those museums; Important Arts Resources, which lists related arts sites; and Arts Publications, which features both electronic and conventional publications.

World Wide Web Servers

The World wide web Servers directory is a huge list of available Web servers from the CERN educational institution. The servers are presented alphabetically by continent, country, and state. Clicking the top-level country, for instance, lets you "drill-down" to the next geographic level, where you find listings of individual servers according to region.

North America is sub-divided into states, which are listed alphabetically. Also available is a listing of Federal government servers for North America. The directory is actually a listing of HTTP (HyperText Transmission Protocol) servers whose administrators have sent requests to **www-request@w3.org**, and other sites.

Virtual Tourist

The Virtual Tourist is similar in content to the World Wide Web Servers directory, but is presented in a visually appealing clickable map (see fig. 8.19).

When you click a specific area of the map, another screen appears to help you narrow down your search for geographically-sited Web servers.

Fig. 8.19
Virtual Tourist offers a clickable map listing of Web servers around the world.

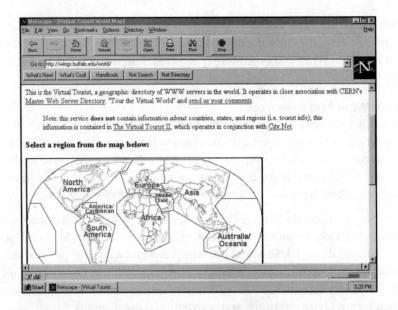

> **Note**
>
> Information about individual countries and states is not provided by Virtual Tourist. That sort of information is evidently available in The Virtual Tourist II, which is operated in cooperation with City.Net.

Net Search: Searching on the Internet

Now for that other button on Netscape's browser window, Net Search. Although some of these services overlap with the directories we found on Netscape's Net Directory page, you'll find that all of these are a little more oriented toward searching—and a little less interested in editorializing. For the most part, these search engines are here to help you find keywords in *titles* of Web pages. You won't see many reviews in these pages. You will, however, see hundreds of results to your queries—chosen from among millions and millions of possible Web pages.

The Net Search directory button takes you to the Internet Search page at Netscape Corp's Web site. Here you'll find a collection of easy-to-use search engines that allow you to find information and documents on the Internet.

There are a number of useful search engines listed, offering a variety of search techniques—for example, some search headers and document titles, some search their own extensive indexes of Internet documents and pages, and others rummage through the Internet itself.

The different search options available in Net Search are discussed in the next section. Here are some of the more popular engines:

- *InfoSeek Search* allows you to search the Web using plain English or keywords and phrases. Special query operators let you customize your search. Results include the first few lines from each Web site—often making it clear *how* your keyword is used, and thus, whether or not a site is actually interesting to you.

- *The Lycos Home Page* is an extremely comprehensive search engine that reportedly features a database of millions of link descriptors and documents. The engine searches links, headings, and titles for keywords you enter. It also offers different search options.

- *WebCrawler* lets you search by document title and content using words you enter into the search box. It's not as comprehensive as Lycos, but it's a quick and easy way to find a few hundred sites that match your keywords.

- *Deja News Research Service* allows you to search UseNet newsgroups in, what the company claims is, the world's largest UseNet news archive. A variety of search options are available.

- *Excite* allows you to search a database with over one million Web documents. You can also search through the past two week's worth of classified ads and UseNet news. Internet site content quality evaluations are also available through Excite.

- *W3 Search Engines* offers a variety of topics and subjects from the University of Geneva, although the list is not updated as often as the more mainstream search engine databases.

- *CUSI (Configurable Unified Search Interface)* features a single form to search different Web engines, provided by Nexor U.K.

How These Search Engines Work

Each one of these search services on the Net Search page is designed to give you access to a database of information related to Internet sites around the world. Some are Web-specific (like Lycos and WebCrawler) while others, like InfoSeek and Excite, allow you to search not only Web pages, but also UseNet newsgroups, online publications, and other archives of information.

What all of these do have in common is that they require you to come up with keywords to facilitate the search. There's definitely an art to this search—the more you try it, the more you'll see that it takes some patience and creativity. Let's discuss some of the basic concepts.

The key to a good search is good keywords. What you're trying to do is come up with unique words or phrases that appear only in the documents you want to access. For instance, one thing to definitely avoid are common terms, such as www, computer, Internet, PC, Mac, and so on. These terms come up time and again on pages that may or may not have material that interests you. Also consider that words like Mac not only appear in words like Macintosh, but also in Mace, Mach, Machine, Macaroni...you'll probably get a lot of bizarre results with such a common keyword. Articles and common English words like a, an, the, many, any, and others are generally unnecessary.

Most of these search engines also give you a choice of Boolean operators to use between keywords (AND, OR, NOT). Take care that you understand how these operators work. If you enter them yourself (in the search phrase text box), then an example might be:

Windows AND shareware NOT Mac

This results in pages that discuss shareware programs for Microsoft Windows, while it eliminates pages that include the word Mac, even if they *also* discuss Windows shareware. Remember that AND and NOT are used to limit searches; OR is used to widen them. Notice, for instance, that

Ford OR Mustang

generates many more results than either

Ford AND Mustang

or

Ford NOT Mustang

Presumably, the first only returns pages that have references to *both*, while the second returns pages that *do* reference Ford, but *do not* reference Mustang.

InfoSeek Search

InfoSeek is a very popular search engine that generates not only search results but also offers the first few lines from pages to help you determine if a Web site may have what you need *before* you leave InfoSeek to view it. While this can often save you time, the way InfoSeek reports its results (a maximum of 100 results, ten to a page) can take a little while to flip through. InfoSeek, therefore, is really designed for digging deep for a subject—perhaps when you've had less luck with other search engines.

What is InfoSeek Search?

You access InfoSeek by clicking the InfoSeek Search button on the Internet
Search page at Netscape. You can also start searching straight away by
entering search words in the text box under InfoSeek Search and pressing the
Search button on Netscape's Net Search page. This is a quick way to get results. The InfoSeek index page offers this same text box, but also includes a
quick directory of popular sites (see fig. 8.20).

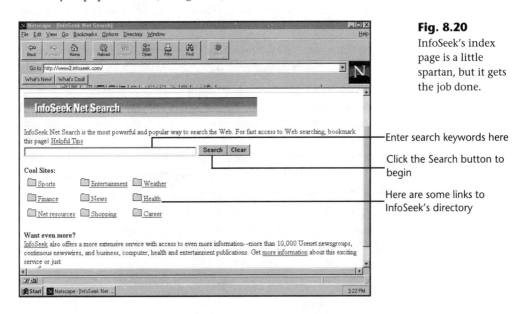

Fig. 8.20
InfoSeek's index
page is a little
spartan, but it gets
the job done.

Enter search keywords here

Click the Search button to
begin

Here are some links to
InfoSeek's directory

Mastering Netscape

InfoSeek is very easy to search. Simply enter keywords in the text box and
click the Search button. InfoSeek *assumes* an AND between each of your keywords, although it returns pages that don't include every keyword. Capitalization is important, though, so only capitalize words that you want recognized
as proper nouns.

InfoSeek offers this ability to search the Internet as a free service to the
Internet community; however, free searches are limited to 100 results per
search, and they don't cover the breadth of services that InfoSeek offers.
InfoSeek's commercial searching accounts may end up being something that
interests you, and more information is provided on their Web site.

Advanced InfoSeek Searches

At its most basic, InfoSeek is a quick and easy way to search the Internet. In fact, it's one of the few search engines that doesn't offer an advanced page with more control over the results. What you see is basically what you get with InfoSeek.

That is, at least, until you dig a little deeper. Then you realize that there is some customizing you can do to your searches. It all takes place in your search phrase (what you enter in the text box). The following little tidbits may help you get faster, and more reliable, results.

- Before authorizing any search for documents on the Internet, make sure there are no misspelled words and typographical errors in the text box.
- Don't use characters such as an asterisk (*) as wildcards.
- Unlike some other search engines such as Lycos, don't use Boolean operators such as AND and OR between search words, as InfoSeek looks at *all* words as search terms.
- When searching for documents, try both word variations (plural, adjective, and noun forms of the same word) and synonyms.
- If you want both the upper- and lowercase occurrences of a term, use only the lowercase word in the search text box.
- You need to separate capitalized names with a comma (for example, Bill Gates, Microsoft). You can also use a comma to separate phrases and capitalized names from each other.
- Quotation marks and hyphens can be used to identify a phrase.
- You can use a plus sign (+) to distinguish terms that should appear in every document. The + appears at the beginning of the term, with no space before the first letter of the first word (for example, +skiing Colorado, Utah).
- As an alternative to a plus sign, you can use a minus sign (-) to designate phrases or words not to be included in any document. This is useful if you have a word that is often used with another word in unison, but you want only documents containing the word and not both words to be retrieved (for example, desktop -computer).

Lycos

Lycos is a very comprehensive and accurate search engine that is also very popular. It consists of a huge catalog that, as of August 1995, claimed to include more than 90 percent of the Web. By late 1995, Lycos claims it will have cataloged more than 98 percent of the Web. As a result, you may find it often too busy to let you use it, especially during peak business hours. However, it is worth the wait; Lycos claims to already have included more than 7.98 million URLs and is adding to that number every day.

Lycos was developed at Carnegie-Mellon University, Pittsburgh. However, in June 1995, Lycos Inc. was formed to develop and market the Lycos technology. Lycos Inc. says that Lycos will remain free to Internet users, although, as a commercial venture, it will gain revenue from advertising and licensing the Lycos catalog and search technologies. Non-exclusive license holders of the Lycos technology already include Frontier Technologies and Library Corp., as well as Microsoft Corp. for use in the company's newly introduced Microsoft Network online service.

Searching with Lycos

The Lycos interface is similar to InfoSeek's in that you can just enter words and click the Search button. However, Lycos includes more options and contains a much larger database of indexed Web documents. You can begin by selecting the Lycos link on Netscape's Net Search page. That brings up the Lycos index page, where your search begins. A simple Lycos search works just like most of the other search engines. Enter your search keywords in the text box and click the Search button. Lycos finds any pages or documents matching any of the words you type into the search box.

For a more advanced search, choose the Search Options button next to the text box on Lycos' index page. Now you're presented with a new page, where you can spend a little more time tailoring your search (see fig. 8.21).

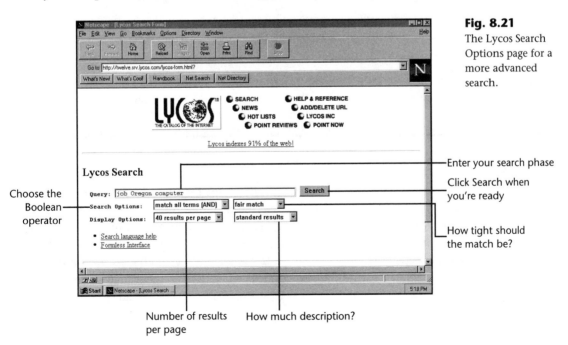

Fig. 8.21
The Lycos Search Options page for a more advanced search.

Choose the Boolean operator

Enter your search phase

Click Search when you're ready

How tight should the match be?

Number of results per page

How much description?

Here is where you can take a little more control of the search phrase. For instance, if you enter a number of keywords and you'd like to expand the search to show pages that match *any* of your keywords, pull down the first Search Options menu and choose Match Any Term (OR). You can also choose to match a certain number of keywords with this same menu.

Tip

If you're unsure how a keyword is spelled, type in a couple of different ways you think it might appear, then choose to match the number of terms that you know are spelled correctly. For instance, entering **Heron Hearon Huron senate candidate**, then selecting to match three terms would give me a good chance of finding information about this public figure whose name I'm not sure how to spell.

The second Search Options pull-down menu allows you to specify if you want close or not-so-close matches. If you are really just "fishing" for some leads as to where to concentrate your next search, make sure the "loose match" option is selected from the second Search Options menu. If you are pretty sure of the search criteria you typed in the Query box, then select "strong match." There are a number of choices in between, each becoming about 20 percent more lenient as they move down the list.

There are two Display Options pull-down menus—one dictates how many results are displayed on the page, and the second determines the level of detail for the specified search.

Although Lycos always allows you to access all the "hits" that resulted from your search, obviously all of them cannot be displayed at once. You can choose to display between 10 and 40 links on a page at any one time. This is done using the first of the two Display Options pull-down menu. To specify how many search results are displayed on the page at any one time, pull down the first menu and select the number you'd like to see.

The second pull-down menu lets you determine the level of information detail to be displayed about each search result. With this menu there are three levels of detail, each one on the list being a little more detailed than the one above it. The level of detail you specify will probably change with each search you do, depending on the documents you are seeking and the research you are trying to accomplish. If you don't specify any level, the default "standard results" takes the middle ground, reporting with a reasonable amount of detail.

How Lycos Works

So how does Lycos manage to cover so much ground on the Internet? There are actually three parts to Lycos, all of which are interconnected, and each requires the others to work properly. The first part of Lycos are groups of programs, called *spiders*, that go out and search the Web, FTP, and Gopher sites every day.

The results are added to the second part of Lycos—the "catalog" database—which contains such things as the URL address of each site found, along with information about the documents found at that site, the text, and the number of times that site is referenced by other Web addresses. As a result of the advanced search performed by the spiders, the most popular sites are indexed first. Whatever information and new sites are found by the spiders is added to the existing catalog.

The final element is the "search engine" itself. It's the real strength of the system for the end-user (us) because it can manage to access all of this information so smoothly and accurately. The engine sorts through the catalog and produces a list of hits according to your search criteria, listed in descending order of relevance. This means that, according to the search engine, the best and most accurate hits are at the top of the Lycos results list. So, the deeper you dig into Lycos' results, the less likely you are to find what you want...at least, according to Lycos.

WebCrawler

WebCrawler is one of the best search engines on the Web, not least because it is so easy to use and very fast. It is owned and maintained by America Online, which provides it as a public service to the Internet community. It's a great search engine to use when you're fairly sure that what you're looking for will appear in the title of a Web page...WebCrawler only searches titles of Web pages, not all text. For direct access, its URL is **http:// www.webcrawler.com/**. You can, of course, also access it from the Net Search page.

> ### Tip
>
> WebCrawler is also a great way to start out on a directed surfing expedition—that is, when you're not searching too closely. If you *want* to see 500 hits with the word Microsoft in the title, you'll find them the most quickly and easily with WebCrawler.

WebCrawler's interface is designed to be as uncomplicated as possible (see fig. 8.22).

Fig. 8.22
WebCrawler allows for easy searching and quick results.

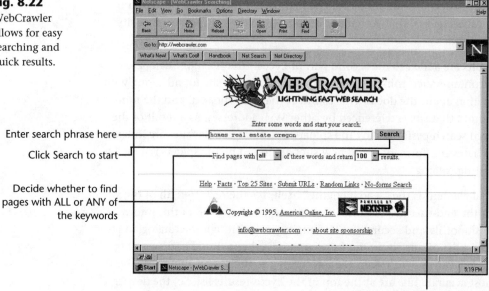

Enter search phrase here

Click Search to start

Decide whether to find pages with ALL or ANY of the keywords

How many results per page?

Instead of searching the entire World Wide Web for instances of your typed keywords, WebCrawler searches its own index of documents. This makes for quicker searches, although, with documents and pages being added to the Web at such an astounding rate, newer resources can be missed.

The result of your WebCrawler search is a list, with each item on the list underlined and colored indicating it is a hypertext link that you can click to retrieve that page from the Internet.

Down the left side of the search results is a list of numbers, with one number corresponding to each item on the list. The highest number is next to the first item on the search results list. This indicates that the first item is the most relevant according to your search keywords, which is why the numbers (from 100 to 001) are called *relevance numbers*. As you move down the list you notice that the number along the left side decreases for each item on the list—indicating that each of these pages offers fewer occurrences of your keywords than the previous item.

With a large search, not all the results are necessarily displayed on the first page. In fact, WebCrawler limits the results to 10, 25, or 100, depending on how many pages you specified in your search criteria. But if WebCrawler finds, for example, 500 pages that correspond to your search keywords and you chose to view 25 at a time, only 25 are going to be shown on the Netscape screen.

That doesn't mean you can't view the rest of the search results. To view the next 25 items in the resulting search list, click the Get the Next 25 Results button under the resulting list, and the next 25 items in the search are displayed. Keep doing that until you have viewed all the items in the list, if you need to see them. But don't forget, the further down the list you go, the less relevant the search results, according to your keywords.

Other Search Engines

There are a variety of other search engines available on the Internet, and some of the best have also been made available to users of Netscape's Internet Search page. These engines tend to be either more specialized—focusing on searching UseNet newsgroups instead of the entire Internet, for instance—or simply convenient ways to access the search engines we've already talked about.

Deja News Research Service

If you want to search UseNet newsgroups exclusively, then the Deja News Research Service is the place for you. Currently claiming over four gigabytes of searchable data, Deja News is updated every two days. You can even follow an entire newsgroup thread by just clicking the subject line when it appears at the top of your screen.

To get to the search engine page, choose Deja News from the Net Search page. Then, click the Search link on Deja News' index page. The Deja News query form page appears (see fig. 8.23).

For the simplest search, just type search words into the text box, click the Search button, and use the default options. However, for the best results, you should customize your search a little by following these steps:

1. Type your search words into the text box. You don't need to worry about capitalizing words because the search engine isn't case-sensitive. The engine automatically assumes there is an OR between multiple words.

2. Choose the maximum number of hits you want retrieved by checking either 30, 60, or 120 in the Maximum Number of Hits option. The default is 30. If more than the number specified is returned, a link appears at the bottom of the screen allowing you access to the next set of hits.

Fig. 8.23

Just enter words and click Search for simple searches. But you can perform more complex queries from this page as well.

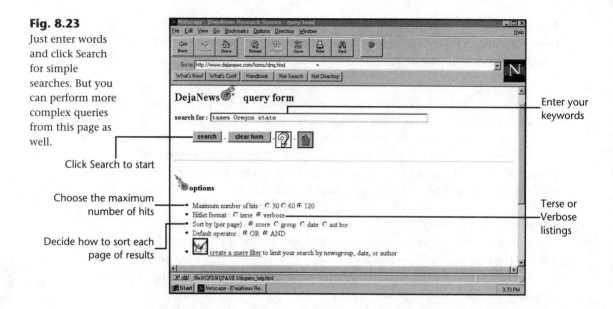

Click Search to start

Choose the maximum number of hits

Decide how to sort each page of results

Enter your keywords

Terse or Verbose listings

3. The amount of information retrieved about each site is determined by the Hitlist Format option. Click Terse for less information, or Verbose for more.

4. The Sort By option lets you emphasize score, group, date, or author.

> **Note**
>
> Score is just another way to say relevance number, as we discussed earlier. It's how Deja News determines how close each result is to your search phrase.

5. You can choose between default boolean operators using the Default Operator: OR or AND option.

6. Use the Create a Query Filter option if you want to use a filter to narrow down your search. A filter can be used to specify a date range, if you only want postings from a specific author, or if you know which newsgroups you want to retrieve (see fig. 8.19).

7. The age of the record can also be a factor in your search. If you want newer postings, check the Prefer New box, or if you want older ones, check the Prefer Old box. In addition, you can use the Age Matters option to tell Deja News how important it is that a message is relatively recent or a few months old.

There are some groups that are not included in the indexing, such as *alt., *soc., *talk., and *.binaries. Deja News says that this is either because they contain a large volume of postings that are mostly "flames," or else they don't lend themselves well to text searchings, such as binary groups.

In any event, Deja News is worth using if you want to search the enormous amount of UseNet newsgroups available. There are reportedly as many as 80MB of traffic posted on newsgroups each day! Newsgroups can be very useful for retrieving information if you know how to search and where to look.

Excite

Excite allows you to search through more than a million Web documents and the past two weeks-worth of UseNet newsgroups and classified ads. The user interface is as simple as other search engines available (see fig. 8.24).

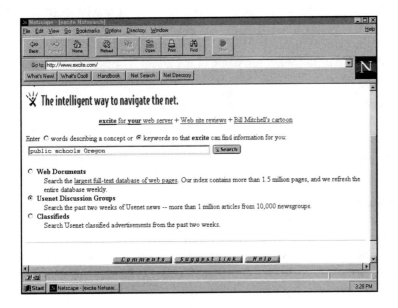

Fig. 8.24
The Excite database lets you search Web documents, UseNet news-groups, and classified ads.

Searching Excite is only slightly different from the other search engines. You start by selecting the *type* of search you want Excite to carry out—click the Enter...Keywords box if you want documents retrieved using regular keywords. You can also click the Enter...Words Describing a Concept box if you want the search engine to retrieve documents that seem to involve a subject that's related to the words you typed in the search box, and not just those documents that contain those words.

After you type in your keywords, you have another set of checkbox options. Check Web Documents if you want Excite to search its database of Web documents. Check UseNet Discussion Groups if you want to search through the last two weeks-worth of UseNet messages, or select Classifieds if you want Excite to search the last two weeks-worth of classified advertisements.

Excite uses both color-coded icons and percentage-style scores to indicate the relevance of retrieved results. When there's a red icon at the beginning of the result line, that is an indication that Excite thinks it's a good search match. On the other hand, a black icon means that it may not be such a good match. The colors are a quick way of identifying good matches at a glance.

The percentage is a better way of identifying the relevance of a search result, relative to the next search result. Obviously, the higher the percentage score, the better the match—at least in Excite's eyes.

The title of each result depends on whether it is a Web page or site, or a UseNet article. If it is a Web page, the page's title is displayed, or (if there is no title) it may just show the URL. If it is a Web site, then an Excite editor-selected site title is displayed. With UseNet listings, things are different. If a UseNet group is indicated, the name of the group is displayed. If a UseNet article is referenced, its Subject text is shown.

Excite also offers NetReviews (some of the best Web sites as chosen by the Excite staff) along with its database of Web pages and UseNet newsgroups. In fact, that's why you'll find Excite both on the Net Search and Net Directory pages. To access these reviews, click the NetReviews tab on the Excite index page.

W3 Search Engines

There are, in fact, many more searching services available on the Internet than we've even begun to touch on in this chapter. While InfoSeek, WebCrawler, and Lycos are some of the largest and most popular, that won't always mean they're the best for what you need to find. If you're not having much luck with the big name engines, head over to the W3 Search Engines page.

The W3 Search Engines page is basically an interface to many different types of search engines around the world (see fig. 8.25). You can search information servers (Web and Gopher, primarily), UseNet news, publication archives, and software documentation. You can even use these pages to search for people on the Internet in a variety of ways.

To use the individual search engine, just type in your search words in its text box and click the Search button next to that engine's description. You'll notice that you really don't have many options for these engines, but it is a convenient way to initiate simple searches for many different services.

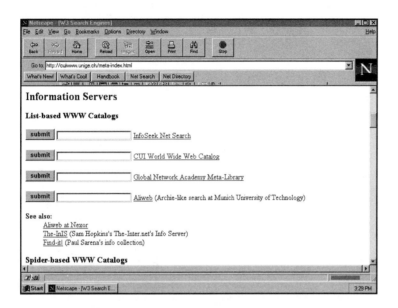

Fig. 8.25
Here are a few of
the search engines
you can use from
the W3 Search
Engines page.

CUSI (Configurable Unified Search Interface)

The Configurable Unified Search Engine (CUSI) allows you to quickly check related resources, without retyping search keywords.

This configurable search interface for a variety of searchable World Wide Web resources was developed by Martijn Koster in 1993 and is now provided as a public service by Nexor, which can be contacted at **webmaster@nexor.co.uk**.

CUSI offers a search text box for both manual Web indexes and robot-generated Web indexes, such as Lycos and WebCrawler.

## CHAPTER 9

Netscape Bookmarks

This chapter covers the use of Netscape's Bookmark feature. You can use Bookmarks to keep track of your most visited Internet sites. Placing them in your Bookmark list makes the site address instantly accessible from the Bookmarks pull-down menu in the menu bar.

In this chapter you learn about the following:

- Using Bookmarks and why they are useful
- How to create and delete Bookmarks
- Creating Bookmarks from your History list
- How hierarchical menus work
- Effective menu management
- How to turn your Bookmark list into a Web page

What Are Bookmarks?

The World Wide Web is a tapestry of millions of different documents and sites, all linked via references from other sites and documents. It is no surprise then that help was considered necessary for those exploring the links. One option available to all end-users of Netscape is the Bookmarks feature.

Bookmarks are an extremely useful feature of Netscape. They basically allow Netscape to remember whatever places on the Web you tell it to remember. Having taken note of the Internet address of a site, Netscape lists it in a pull-down menu that you access from the menu bar.

When you select an item on the list, Netscape enters the item's URL that it has saved in your Bookmark file and tries to connect to the site, document, graphic, or whatever it corresponds to.

Because of the complexity of Web URLs, it would be enormously tedious if you had to remember and manually enter every page's address each time you wanted to read it. And while you should always try and save a document or image on your local drive so as not to have to connect to it over the Internet, you will likely have a great many remote pages that you will want to access on a regular basis, because they will be continually updated with new information by the remote site's administrator.

Bookmarks take away that tedious task of having to write down or otherwise save each page's or document's URL address.

When you add an item to your Bookmark list, you are essentially keeping a record of that item's address on the Internet, along with a description of that item, and placing it in a pull-down menu that you can quickly access from the menu bar in Netscape.

◀ See "Understanding Links," pg. 146

When you want to go to that site or document or graphic, pull down the Bookmarks list, and select the item. Netscape automatically enters the item's URL and tries to access the address. Chances are you will be able to access the item without any problems, although the Internet being a global network, difficulties do sometimes occur.

> **Tip**
>
> The Bookmark list contains all the elements that go into making a normal Web page. However, when viewed as a hypertext document, the special HTML coding takes over and displays it with enlarged fonts and a visually pleasing composition that is easy on the eyes.

> **Tip**
>
> If a link doesn't work, one reason may be that the filename on the remote server has changed or it has been moved to another directory. Instead of using the entire URL, type in a truncated version listing just the main server address. That should get you into the remote server from which you can rummage around and look for the old file.

Saving Web Pages

Before you can begin to categorize and separate your Bookmarks into different sections, you need to create them by notifying Netscape that you want to save the URL of a specific Web page. Fortunately, Netscape makes adding a Bookmark to your Bookmark list a simple matter of pulling down a menu.

Creating a Bookmark

There are two ways to add a Bookmark to your Bookmark list. The first involves just pulling down a menu, while the second requires an extra step or two. Let's take the simple way first.

The easiest way to add a Bookmark to your existing Bookmark list is to just select <u>A</u>dd Bookmark (Ctrl+A) from the Bookmarks pull-down menu. The current page is added to the top of the list.

Note

Just as you can use your Bookmark file as your home page, you can also use it as any other Web page. This is because it is actually a normal hypertext document just like any other you come across when you go "Web crawling."

The second way of adding a Bookmark allows you to add a Bookmark without having to be at the actual site on the Internet in question.

To add a new Bookmark the long way, follow these steps:

1. Select <u>G</u>o to Bookmarks from the <u>B</u>ookmarks menu. The Netscape Bookmarks list window appears (see fig. 9.1).

Fig. 9.1
The Netscape Bookmarks list includes all your saved Bookmarks with their addresses.

2. Select a current item in the Bookmark list window. The new Bookmark appears directly below the current selection in the list. Alternatively, you can skip this step and go straight to step 3. Then, when the

bookmark has been added to the list, drag and drop the bookmark in the appropriate folder.

3. Select Insert Bookmark from the Item menu. The Bookmark Properties General sheet appears (see fig. 9.2).

Fig. 9.2
To add a new Bookmark's details, select Insert Bookmark from the Item menu in the Netscape Bookmarks list window.

4. Name the Bookmark in the Name: text box.

5. Enter the URL address of the new link in the Location (URL): text box.

6. You can include a lengthy description of the Bookmark in the Description: text box.

7. The Last Visited field shows when the site was last visited.

8. The Added On message shows the date that you added the Bookmark.

9. When all the particulars of the new Bookmark have been entered, click OK. The new Bookmark appears in the Bookmark list.

To go directly to your new Bookmark, either double-click the item in the list, or make the item the current selection and select Go To Bookmark from the Item menu. Alternatively, if you want to exit, click the close box in the upper-right corner of the Netscape Bookmarks window.

The newly added Bookmark now appears in the Bookmark list each time it is shown, or it can be accessed via the lower section of the Bookmarks menu. By default, the bookmark list file is called Bookmark.htm.

Note

After you begin categorizing a large Bookmark list, by adding headers and separators, for example, make sure you make a backup copy of the resulting file. If you get a hard disk crash and you have not saved the file, you will have to start constructing the Bookmark file again from scratch, which can be a very time-consuming process.

Deleting a Bookmark

Deleting a Bookmark from your Bookmark list is just as easy as adding it. Follow these steps to delete a Bookmark from your list:

1. Select Go to Bookmarks (Ctrl+B) from the Bookmarks menu. The Netscape Bookmarks list window appears.

2. Select the item to be deleted from the Bookmark list.

3. Select Delete from the Edit menu, or press the Del button. The item disappears from the Bookmark list.

4. Click the close (×) box in the upper-right to exit.

Creating Bookmarks from Your History List

Your History list keeps a record of the most recently visited Internet sites in case you want to return to a specific site while you are still in the Internet session. The History list disappears when you quit Netscape and end your current Internet session.

The History window consists of two columns, one displaying the title of the page visited, and the other showing the full URL. The most recently visited page is at the top of the list.

◀ See "Moving Around the Web," pg. 145

You may decide that you want to add an item from your History list to your Bookmark list, but for some reason or another, you neglected to do it when you visited the site and had the page displayed in the main Netscape screen. However, don't fret, you can still create a Bookmark from the current History list by following these steps:

1. Select History from the Window menu. The History window appears (see fig. 9.3).

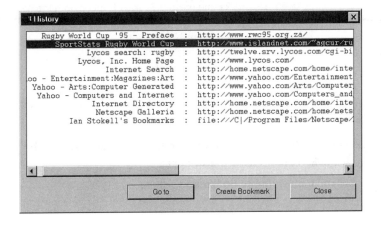

Fig. 9.3
You can create a Bookmark from the History list.

II

Mastering Netscape

2. Select the History item you want to make a Bookmark.

3. Click the Create Bookmark button under the list window. The selected item is added to your permanent Bookmark list.

4. Click the Close button to exit the History window.

Tip

You can access a numbered History list from the Go menu. Just click the numbered item you want to return to.

Changing Bookmark Properties

You may decide to change any number of Bookmark properties after you have placed the Bookmark in your Bookmark list. This next section tells you how to change such properties as the name, the URL link address, and the description. It also explains how to create a Bookmark shortcut using a function key.

Changing Bookmark Names

At some point, you may decide to change the name of a Bookmark. For example, the site name may change on the Web and you may want to have your Bookmark name correspond to the current name, or you may have organized your Bookmark list into categories and you want the name to reflect the category name.

Tip

When you initially save a bookmark using the Add Bookmark option from the Bookmarks menu, the bookmark is saved as per the original file or document name. You rename it via the Properties option of the Item menu in the Netscape Bookmarks list window.

Whatever the reason, changing the name of a Bookmark list item is a simple procedure; follow these steps:

1. Select Go to Bookmarks (Ctrl+B) from the Bookmarks menu. The Netscape Bookmarks list window appears.

2. Select the item from the Bookmarks list.

3. Select Properties from the Item menu. The Bookmark Properties list appears.

4. Change the name of the Bookmark in the Name field.

5. Click OK when you are done.

Adding a Description

As you add more and more Bookmarks to your list, and you find additional interesting sites that you want to return to, remembering what exactly it was that you liked at the site becomes more difficult. As a result, it is always a good idea to add a description to your Bookmark in order to remember exactly what the site includes. To add a description, follow these steps:

1. Select Go to Bookmarks (Ctrl+B) from the Bookmarks menu. The Netscape Bookmarks list window appears.

2. Select the item from the Bookmarks list.

3. Select Properties from the Item menu. The Bookmark Properties dialog box appears.

4. Add or change the description of the Bookmark in the Description field.

5. Click OK.

Changing a Bookmark Link

The Internet is a continually changing environment. Every day there are tens of thousands of documents added. In addition, documents are often moved from server to server, or directory to directory on the same server.

When this happens, the remote server administrator often places a note where the document used to be, telling anyone that comes to that address hoping to find the document that it has moved. In this case, there is usually a referring Web URL for you to change in your Bookmark list. Make a note of the new address and do the following to change the Bookmark URL:

1. Select Go to Bookmarks (Ctrl+B) from the Bookmarks menu. The Netscape Bookmarks list window appears.

2. Select the item from the Bookmark list.

3. Select Properties from the Item menu. The Bookmark Properties dialog box appears.

4. Change the URL address in the Location (URL) text box.

5. Click OK.

The new URL is now in effect.

> **Tip**
>
> Make sure you have included all the different sections of the URL correctly—the protocol used, the server name, the directory path, and finally, the filename. Without all these parts you may not be able to access the desired file.

> **Tip**
>
> Instead of trying to remember or physically copy a URL from the Go to: location text box in the main Netscape screen, use Netscape's cut and paste features to cut it from the Go to: box and paste it into the Bookmark properties dialog box.

◀ See "Understanding Links," pg. 146

Organizing Bookmarks

Bookmark lists are an extremely useful feature of Netscape. However, after you have added more than a dozen Bookmarks to your list, it needs to be organized in some way or else you will find that it is difficult to retrieve saved Bookmarks. The next few sections include advice on how to organize your Bookmark lists.

Hierarchical Bookmark Menus and Menu Management

A Bookmark list is extremely simple to use if all you do is keep adding Bookmarks to it and know exactly where each book item is in the drop-down list when you want to return to it on the Web. Unfortunately, things get a little more complicated than that.

As you travel the Web, you keep adding Bookmarks to your list, and before you know it, the list is long and cluttered. At this point, you need to think about organizing and categorizing the list into a hierarchical one, most likely with different subject categories divided into sections using headers and separators.

A well-planned Bookmark list, with common-sense headers and categories, and a visually uncomplicated set-up using separators, can take a lot of the frustration out of navigating the Web. A few seconds of forethought can save you many minutes in search time when you mislay that just-added Bookmark somewhere in your list of 300 items.

A Netscape hierarchical Bookmark list works much the same way as the Mac's folder-nested-within-another-folder, or the Windows 3.x/DOS subdirectory-within-a-directory format. With a hierarchical listing, you have top-level items, within which are at least one other sub-level category of Bookmarks.

That's how hierarchical Bookmark lists work. They have categories of items contained beneath headers or category titles. The items on the second-level appear indented in the Bookmark list to show they are on a sub-level (see fig. 9.4).

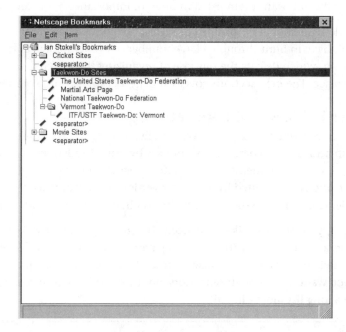

Fig. 9.4
A hierarchical Bookmark list contains indented items beneath higher-level folders.

A major benefit of a hierarchical system is that it allows you to display only the items that you want. You can just display the top-level headers by clicking each one header folder in turn. Top-level folder icons are shown as either closed or open. When the folder is closed, the items within it are hidden. When the folder is open, items are displayed in the Netscape Bookmarks window in a hierarchical listing.

If you only want the main folders displayed, just close all the folders in the window. Then, when you want to open up a specific header folder and access a particular Bookmark item, just double-click the top-level folder and the indented items appear in the list window.

If you have a lot of nested items within your Bookmark list and you want to locate one that is not immediately visible, use the Find Bookmark dialog box, which you access by selecting the Find option from the Netscape Bookmarks list in the Bookmark list window.

Organizing and Categorizing Your Bookmark List

When you get so many Bookmarks in your list that it overruns the list window, it is time to think about categorizing and organizing it. You can use headers and separators to visually distinguish between the different sections.

The categories you choose, of course, depend on the Bookmarks that you have listed, and the emphasis you want to place on the Bookmarks themselves; maybe you want them listed in order of importance, for example.

Bookmark items should be grouped in logical categories wherever possible, so you don't have to hunt through a large number of header folders in order to locate them, which defeats the purpose of organizing the Bookmark list in the first place. The next sections cover using header folders and separators.

Header Folders and Separators

Having decided what form your Bookmark list is going to take, one way to divide it up into easily recognizable sections is by using headers and separators. A header is essentially the title of a specific category group within your Bookmark list, and is represented in the newer versions of Netscape for Windows as a folder icon, while a separator is a physical line separating categories.

With both, you need to strike a balance between using too many headers and separators and not enough. Too many separators, for example, breaks up the flow of the Bookmark list and makes you scroll further down the list to get where you want. Not enough separators, on the other hand, can make deciphering a long list more difficult.

Note

You will typically be accessing your bookmark list from the Bookmarks menu, which displays only second-level folders. Scrolling down the list from the Bookmarks menu allows you to open up submenus.

Not enough header folders can also lead to you having to scroll down long lists of unrelated files in order to find the one you are looking for. Too many folders can also be a problem, as it often means you have to keep opening folders and sub-folders in order to display multiple lists and sub-lists, looking for the one item you need.

Bookmark list organization and planning are very important for efficient management once your list begins to get long.

Creating Header Folders

In the Netscape Bookmarks list window, folders represent category headers, into which you place individual Bookmark items. You should have a new header folder for each category in your Bookmark list.

Headers appear as folder icons, each with their own name, and are either open or closed. When open, an indented list of items within that folder are displayed in the Netscape Bookmarks window. When you double-click the opened folder, it closes and all items within it become hidden from view. To re-open that folder and display the enclosed list of Bookmarks, double-click the closed folder.

Creating a new folder header is a simple process; follow these steps:

1. Select Go to Bookmarks (Ctrl+B) from the Bookmarks menu. The Netscape Bookmarks list window appears.

2. Select the current item in the list, under which the new header folder is to appear.

3. Select Insert Header from the Item menu. The Bookmark Properties General sheet appears (see fig. 9.5).

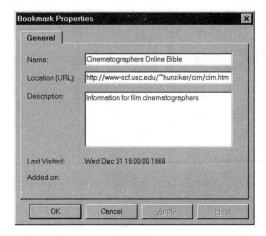

Fig. 9.5
The Bookmark Properties General sheet is where you fill in the details of the new folder header.

4. Name the new folder in the Name field.

5. Add a general description of the contents of the folder in the Description text box.

6. Click OK.

The new folder header appears in the Bookmark list, directly beneath the current item previously selected.

Tip

If you move or delete a header folder, all those items contained within that folder are also affected. Moving a folder is less cumbersome if you hide the contents first by double-clicking the open folder icon.

Just as you can have Bookmark items contained within header folders, so you can have folder icons within folders. To add a folder inside a folder, or indented beneath a folder in the Bookmark list window, just make the top-level folder the current item before selecting Insert header from the Item menu. The result will be a folder within a folder in the Bookmark list (see fig. 9.6).

Fig. 9.6

You can have folders nested within header folders in your Bookmark list.

The more Bookmarks you add to your list, the more useful nested folders become. Without the header folders, a long Bookmark list quickly becomes unmanageable.

In addition, because the bookmark list appears at the bottom of the Bookmarks menu, higher-level folders containing sub-lists of bookmarks are vital to maintaining order. Without folders, the Bookmarks menu can become unwieldy very quickly.

Drag and Drop Bookmarks

One of the primary benefits of upgrading to the Windows 95 operating system/graphical user environment is the ability to drag and drop files on the desktop. This is also true for using Netscape. It is a feature that is particularly useful for managing your Bookmark list.

To move Bookmark items within the list, just click on the item to be moved and, while still holding down the mouse button, drag the icon to the new location. When you get to the new location, release the mouse button and the icon moves.

If you are moving an item into a folder nested within another folder, make sure the sub-folder is displayed in the list. To do this, just double-click the top-level folder and the item/folders in the level immediately below the top-level folder are displayed.

If the current selection to be moved is a folder header, the header alone does not move. Everything belonging to that header—the sub-items attached and indented underneath it—also move up or down the list. In this way, you can save large amounts of time if you want to move entire categories of Bookmarks up the list. Think how long it would take to move everything individually after you have moved the header if drag and drop wasn't a feature of Netscape! Not to mention the time it takes indenting all the items that belong to the header!

Additionally, you can rearrange your Bookmark list items in the same way, simply by clicking the item and then dragging it to a new position in the same folder, or to another folder altogether.

Tip

Before moving items up the Bookmark list, it may be a good idea to collapse all the header items by clicking on the individual headers, so just the headers and not their sub-items are visible. Then you don't have so far to move the item.

Adding Items to a Specific Header

Having established your header category, you now need to indicate what items belong to it. You can specify which Bookmark items belong to a specific folder header by dragging and dropping them within that folder.

Dropping an item on a folder indents that item directly beneath the folder. This signifies that the item belongs to that folder. To hide the list of items in the folder, double-click the folder icon.

Adding and Deleting a Separator

Adding a separator is a similar process to adding a header, except you obviously don't get to name it! But be careful not to add too many. Separators can be very visually effective when used in the right amount, but too many can make a list look messy—especially if you want to use the list as a regular Web page as well as within the Bookmark menu.

To add a separator, follow these steps:

1. Select Go to Bookmarks (Ctrl+B) from the Bookmarks menu. The Netscape Bookmarks list window appears.

2. Select the current item in the list, under which the new separator is to appear.

3. Select Insert Separator from the Item menu. The Bookmark Properties General tab appears.

The separator appears directly beneath the item you selected as the current list item.

If you want the separator to appear directly beneath a header folder, and not as the first item in that folder's list, you need to close that folder icon, then make it the current item, before selecting Insert Separator from the Item menu. If the folder is open and selected as the current item when you click Insert Separator, the separator appears as the first item in that folder's list.

There will often come a time when you need to delete a separator from your Bookmark list. Deleting a separator is a simple two-step process; follow these steps:

1. Click on the separator that needs to be deleted from your Bookmark list, making it the current selection.

2. Select Delete from the Edit menu, or press the Delete key on the keyboard.

The separator is immediately deleted.

Using the Find Option in Netscape Bookmarks

When you first start saving Bookmarks, it's pretty easy to find items that you have added to the list. However, as time goes by and you begin to organize your Bookmark list into categories with headers, finding the Bookmark you want can get a little time-consuming. Sometimes you have to scroll through pages of items to get the one you want. Fortunately, Netscape includes a Find feature in the Netscape Bookmarks window that helps solve that very problem.

The Find feature allows you to search for titles in the Bookmark list. Found items match whatever you type into the Find dialog box, except that the word or letters are not case sensitive. To use the Find feature, follow these steps:

1. Select <u>G</u>o to Bookmarks (Ctrl+B) from the <u>B</u>ookmarks menu. The Netscape Bookmarks list window appears.

2. Select <u>F</u>ind from the <u>E</u>dit menu. The Find dialog box appears (see fig. 9.7).

Fig. 9.7
The Find feature allows you to easily find Bookmarks in your Bookmark list.

3. Enter the word, phrase, or letters that you want to find in the Find what box.

4. Click the Find Next button.

When you click the Find Next button, the search begins with whatever is the current selection and work its way down the list.

Obviously, if you want to search the entire list, it is best to make the top-most Bookmark item the current selection. That way the search begins from the top and works its way right through the list.

The item found becomes selected, at which point you can press the Find Next button again and wait for the next instance of the requested word, phrase, or letters to be located. The text you typed in the Find what box becomes selected if there is no match in your list.

The search also locates matches even if they are found within folder headers. If this happens, the header's folder list automatically unfolds, and the item that matches the search parameters becomes selected.

Using the What's New? Option

Instead of hunting through your entire list of bookmarks each time you sign onto the Web to see if there is anything new at the sites, you can have Netscape do it for you using the What's New? option. Here's how:

1. Select <u>G</u>o to Bookmarks from the <u>B</u>ookmarks menu.

2. In the resulting Bookmarks window, select the What's New? option from the <u>F</u>ile menu. The What's New? window appears (see fig. 9.8).

Mastering Netscape

II

Fig. 9.8
The What's New?
option allows you
to track new
additions to your
bookmarks
automatically.

3. If you want to check all the bookmarks on the list, click the All bookmarks radio button.

4. If you want to choose individual bookmarks from your list, check the Selected Bookmarks radio button.

5. Click the Start Checking button.

Netscape will check the selected sites and report any new changes.

Importing/Exporting Bookmark Files

There may come a time when you want to either let someone else use your Bookmark list—especially if you are involved in a workgroup project at work—or you want to use someone else's Bookmark list. This next section covers importing and exporting Bookmark lists.

Importing and Exporting Bookmarks

You can make your Bookmarks available for exporting to other users, just as they can make their Bookmarks available to you.

As you travel around the Web looking for information or research locations pertaining to your collective interest, you will no doubt run across a variety of sites you want to share with a group of friends or co-workers. If you create a Bookmark list for that day's search, for example, or update an existing Bookmark category list, you will then be in a position to export that list to other users.

Because documents on the Web are formatted using the platform-independent HTML language, the Bookmark list you save and want to export can be read on another platform without any converting. You just have to save it in the HTML format and pass it on, either via "sneaker-net" across the workspace, over a local area network within your building, or over the Internet as an e-mail message.

How To Import a Bookmark List

You can import another Bookmark list via the Netscape Bookmarks window. This is a particularly useful feature for office or education environments where a number of people are working on the same project and need to share research and information.

If your PC is connected to a local area network, you will probably be able to access other team members' hard drives, or at least a centralized server that can act as a holding pen for information collected by the different team members.

To import a list, follow these steps:

1. Select <u>G</u>o to Bookmarks from the <u>B</u>ookmarks menu. The Netscape Bookmarks window appears.

2. Select the current item from the Bookmark list window. The imported Bookmark list is added to the list directly under the current item selected.

3. Select Import from the File menu. The Import File As Bookmarks dialog box appears (see fig. 9.9).

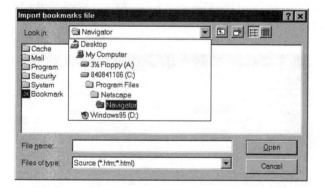

Fig. 9.9
You can import a Bookmark using the Import File As Bookmarks dialog box.

4. From the Import File As Bookmarks dialog box, select the file you are interested in from the list of available folders, drives, and file types. The selected file's name appears in the File name field at the bottom of the dialog box.

5. When you have the desired file listed under File name, click Open. The imported file appears in the Bookmark list immediately below the current item.

How To Export or Save a Bookmark List

After you have completed a new search or updated an old Bookmark list file, you can either send the file directly to other users using the company e-mail system, connect to their hard drives and place it in a place where they will find it, store it on the central information repository server, or leave it in a place on your own drive where those users will be able to retrieve it. Of course, the latter means you will have to keep your PC on all the time to allow them to access the new file.

> ### Tip
>
> Because your bookmark list is already in the form of an HTML file, called Bookmark.htm, you can save it as a straight text file and send it to someone else on the Internet via e-mail.

Turning your current Bookmark list into an export file for use by someone else is just as simple as importing a file.

To export your Bookmark list file, follow these steps:

1. Select <u>G</u>o to Bookmarks from the <u>B</u>ookmarks menu. The Netscape Bookmarks window appears.

2. Select Save <u>A</u>s from the <u>F</u>ile menu. The Export Bookmarks To dialog box appears (see fig. 9.10).

Fig. 9.10
Use the Bookmark List window to export your current booklist to another location.

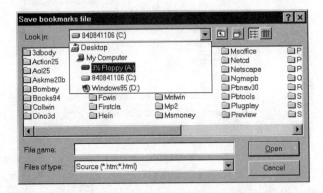

3. Type the name of the file as it will appear to others in the File Name field.

4. Select the type of file it will be saved as (for example, .htm for hypertext markup language) from the Save As Type drop-down menu.

5. Select the drive where the exported file is to reside from the Save In drop-down menu. If you are connected to a local area network, this can either be your own local drive, a drive on a distant user's PC, or a server on the network.

6. Select the folder where the exported file is to reside from the folder list.

7. Click the Save button. The file has now been exported to the specified location.

Bookmark Lists and Web Pages

Bookmark lists are actually Web pages in that they are already hypertext documents containing links to an item's URL address. Because they already contain the HTML special codes that allow a Web browser to arrange the text in the document as it was originally intended, you can use your Bookmark list as a Web page. The next few sections explain Web and home pages as they relate to Bookmark lists.

A home page is a sort of welcome mat to a server or a person's presence on the Web. It is the initial contact that an Internet user has to a remote server, and, as a result, contains a number of related documents that can be accessed from the home page. You can have a personal home page as well, and you can either store it on a remote server or on a local drive.

Your personal home page then should contain links to your favorite and most-used documents.

Storing your home page on a remote server has its drawbacks, though. If you configure Netscape to retrieve that document each time you log onto the Web, the server might be too busy to accommodate you, or the server might be down for maintenance.

However, if you want other people to be able to access your home page, for whatever reason, it should be placed on an easily accessible server that is available to other Internet users 24 hours a day.

But if you are going to be the only one using the home page, store it on your local drive in your PC. Then, when you start up Netscape, all the browser has to do is pull it up from your hard drive and won't need to go across the Internet to display it. It can save you time and trouble if you have your home page stored on your own hard drive.

A personal home page then, should feature a list of your most frequently accessed Internet sites for it to be of practical value. One way of doing this is to turn your Bookmark list into your home page.

To turn your Bookmark list into your home page, follow these steps:

1. Take note of the name of your Bookmark list file and the directory where it is stored.

2. Select General Preferences from the Options menu.

3. In the resulting Preferences dialog box, select the Appearance tab (see fig. 9.11).

Fig. 9.11
The Appearance
Preferences sheet
allows you to
specify your home
page.

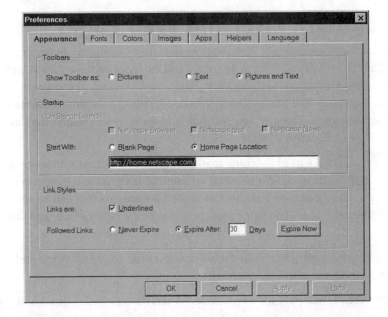

4. In the Start With: section, click the Home Page Location: radio button.

5. Enter the path to your Bookmarks list file stored on your local hard drive. For example, type **file:///C:\/PATH/BOOKMARK.HTM**, where PATH is the path from your C drive to the Bookmark directory, and BOOKMARK.HTM is the name of your Bookmark file.

6. Click OK.

▶ See "Choosing Your Web Publishing Tools," pg. 601

Your Bookmark file is now your home page and will appear on your screen each time you start Netscape, click the Home button on the toolbar, or choose Home from the Go menu.

CHAPTER 10
Using SmartMarks

Given the choice, which would you rather drive—a Geo Prism or a Lamborghini Countach? Both are automobiles and both can provide basic transportation. But in the Lamborghini, basic transportation translates to 420 horses under the hood, zero-to-60 in 4.7 seconds, and a top speed of 183 miles per hour, all provided by a 5.2 liter/315 cubic inch, double-overhead cam, fuel-injected V-12 engine. Placed side by side on an open road, it's a safe bet that most of the readers of this book would choose the Lamborghini, and not just because of the difference in top speeds. The Lamborghini surpasses the Geo in comfort, performance, handling, and even has a better stereo.

You could make the same type comparison between Netscape's old bookmark feature and Netscape's new bookmark utility, SmartMarks. In terms of features, functionality, and performance, SmartMarks is the Lamborghini and Netscape's old bookmark capability is the Geo Prism.

In chapter 9 you saw how you can use bookmarks in Netscape to keep track of important or useful Web sites you visit. While Netscape's bookmarks are a good and useful means of tracking your course as you navigate the Net, bookmarks are somewhat primitive in that they make up a purely mechanical means of recording Internet sites—you have to manually create and update each of your bookmarks. SmartMarks on the other hand, can be set to do a lot more than simply record the location of Web pages you browse. SmartMarks can be used as an intelligent monitoring tool that can alert you to changes in Web pages you decide to monitor.

In this chapter, you learn how to use SmartMarks to do the following:

■ Set up SmartMarks to intelligently monitor important Web sites and to alert you to changes in those Web sites

- Set up SmartMarks to read the new HTML extension "bulletins" on Web sites using bulletins
- Import your existing bookmarks into SmartMarks' smart folders
- Use SmartMarks to search the Internet and then save the search as a bookmark
- Back up and export bookmarks using the SmartMarks bookmark management features

What Are SmartMarks?

SmartMarks, by First Floor, Inc., is an advanced system of monitoring and organizing the bookmarks of Internet sites you visit. SmartMarks is an add-on application that lets you record the URL of Web sites you visit—the same as Netscape's standard bookmarks. But SmartMarks also allows you to organize your bookmarks and intelligently monitor the Web sites you visit and alerts you when those sites, or the links in those sites, change. More importantly, to save you from having to visit Web sites you regularly check for new messages or information, you can set SmartMarks to monitor those Web sites using the new HTML extension feature bulletins, and to record and save bulletin messages from those Web sites. Web administrators can insert bulletin messages in their Web pages to notify Web visitors of important news or information about the company or organization maintaining the Web site.

You can also use SmartMarks to conduct searches on the Internet using several of the popular search engines, such as Yahoo, Lycos, and WebCrawler. You can also save each search as a bookmark for quick reuse, or have SmartMarks monitor those search bookmarks for changes.

And best of all, SmartMarks will import your existing bookmarks into the SmartMarks system, saving you the time of having to manually re-enter your existing bookmarks, and allowing you to use SmartMarks' Web site monitoring features with your existing bookmarks.

Installing SmartMarks

Netscape distributes SmartMarks in the Netscape PowerPack and on its FTP site and its mirror FTP sites. This is probably where most of you got your copies of Netscape, even if you downloaded Netscape from its home page. If you look closely you'll see that the download link on Netscape's home page is actually a link to one of its FTP sites.

> **Note**
>
> To download one of the programs Netscape distributes over the Internet (e.g.,
> Netscape Navigator, SmartMarks, Chat) you usually click a download link on
> Netscape's home page, and then follow the prompts. If you are having trouble find-
> ing a download link, you can also click the icon link Netscape Now (it includes the
> Netscape N logo) and follow the prompts to download one of the Netscape software
> products.

To install SmartMarks, follow these steps:

1. Download SmartMarks. It is contained in the self-extracting file
   sm10r2.exe.

2. Create a temporary folder, copy sm10r2.exe into this folder, and run
   sm10r2.exe.

3. If you are installing SmartMarks from the Netscape PowerPack, insert
   the CD into your drive.

4. Run setup.exe and accept the defaults for the folder where SmartMarks
   will be installed. Follow the prompts to complete the installation. To
   save time later, set SmartMarks to start when you start Netscape. When
   the installation is complete, you will see a new menu item in your Programs menu, Netscape SmartMarks (see fig. 10.1).

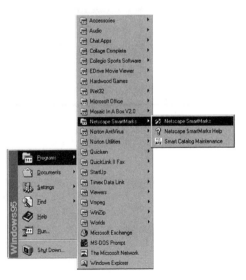

Fig. 10.1
SmartMarks menu
and icons after
installation.

II

Mastering Netscape

The Smart Window

SmartMarks' main screen, the Smart Window, is composed of six parts or sections (see fig. 10.2); four of which can be removed from view using the options on the View menu:

- *Main menu*—consists of the menu options for controlling operations within SmartMarks

- *Tree*—the display of folders shown on the left side of your screen; the tree can be removed from view, but if you do remove the tree, you have to use the Goto Parent command in the View menu to navigate your way through the folders

- *Viewer grid*—shows the contents of each folder in the tree

- *Web monitor*—displays bookmarks being monitored; can be removed from view, especially after your list of bookmarks grows substantially or you add more folders

- *Status bar*—displays the URL of the selected bookmark; can be removed from view especially if you turn on Smart captions

- *Toolbar*—composed of 10 icons displayed just under the menu; can be removed from view, but I don't suggest removing the toolbar because it is easier and quicker to use the toolbar rather than navigate through the menus

Fig. 10.2

SmartMarks main screen, also called the Smart Window, and the pre-installed bookmark folders.

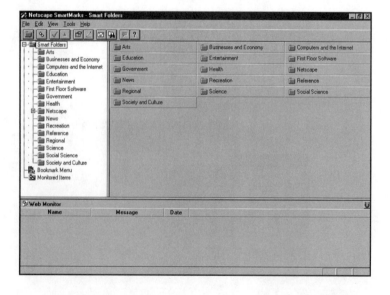

> **Tip**
>
> The View SmartMarks menu command opens the Smart Window, allowing you access to SmartMarks while running Netscape. You can also access the Smart Window by pressing Ctrl+V, or by choosing the SmartMarks icon on the Windows taskbar.

Using Smart Folders

When you start SmartMarks you will see that it already has a fairly extensive list of Web site bookmarks. Netscape includes bookmarks for about 300 of the most popular Web sites from Yahoo and pre-installs them into 16 bookmark subfolders under the main folder, Smart folders:

- Arts
- Business and Economy
- Computers and the Internet
- Education
- Entertainment
- First Floor Software
- Government
- Health
- Netscape
- News
- Recreation
- Reference
- Regional
- Science
- Social Science
- Society and Culture

These 16 folders make up what is called your catalog. A *catalog* is the definition used in SmartMarks to refer to a collection of bookmarks.

Creating a New Folder

One of the first orders of business is to create a folder or set of folders to contain the bookmarks of the Web sites you regularly visit. For example, if you are a football fan, you might want to create a folder called "Football," and inside the Football folder, create folders for "NCAA" and "NFL" so you can keep your college football bookmarks separate from your pro football bookmarks.

1. Start SmartMarks if it's not already running, or switch to SmartMarks from Netscape.

2. Select the folder Smart Folders so that the new folder you create is a subfolder of Smart Folders.

3. Click the New Folder icon (it's the first one on the left) or choose File, New Folder. This opens the Smart Folder Assistant dialog box (see fig. 10.3).

Fig. 10.3
Smart Folder Assistant dialog box for creating new bookmark folders.

4. Type **Football** in the Folder Name field. You can include a description if you want. Then choose Next.

5. Enter one or more keywords for this folder if you think you might want to conduct searches on this folder. Choose Finish to create the new folder Football.

6. To create folders "NFL" and "NCAA," select the Football folder and repeat steps 3 through 5.

If you've worked much with Netscape's bookmark header system, you can see how much easier it is to create a menuing system in SmartMarks to organize your bookmarks, and unlike Netscape's header system, the system in SmartMarks is automatically alphabetized. After you import your existing bookmarks into SmartMarks, if you already have bookmarks for football Web sites, you can move those bookmarks to your Football folders simply by dragging and dropping.

Importing Your Bookmarks to a Smart Folder

You can (and should) import your existing Netscape bookmarks into your SmartMarks catalog. This way you can use SmartMarks' monitoring features to monitor Web sites you are already visiting.

But, perhaps the best reason for importing your existing Netscape bookmarks into SmartMarks is that when SmartMarks is running with Netscape, your Netscape bookmarks are blocked from use by SmartMarks, and you only have access to the bookmarks contained in your SmartMarks catalog.

When you import your existing bookmarks they are placed into the folder *John Doe's* Bookmarks, where *John Doe* is your name.

Note

SmartMarks gets your name from the title of your bookmarks file, which is an HTML file. Your bookmark file got its title from the Mail and News information you entered in the Preferences dialog box. If your existing Netscape bookmark file has no title, when you import your Netscape bookmarks into SmartMarks, they are imported into a folder titled Unknown, rather than being imported into a folder called *John Doe's* Bookmarks.

The folder your existing bookmarks are placed in becomes the 17th subfolder under the main Smart Folders folder.

Here's how:

Caution

When you import your existing Netscape bookmarks into SmartMarks, make sure you have the topmost folder, Smart Folders, highlighted. When your existing bookmarks are imported they are placed in a subfolder of Smart Folders, and not a subfolder of one of the 16 pre-installed bookmark subfolders.

---

1. Launch SmartMarks.

2. Choose Tools, Import.

3. Select your Netscape bookmark file (see fig. 10.4). Its file name is bookmark.htm. Click OK to begin the import procedure. Depending on how many Netscape bookmarks you have in your bookmark file, this procedure takes anywhere from a few seconds to a few minutes. When completed, you see a new subfolder titled *John Doe's* Bookmarks (re-member, *John Doe* will actually be your name). Figure 10.5 shows SmartMarks after I imported my Netscape bookmarks.

Fig. 10.4

Selecting your
bookmark file to
import.

Fig. 10.5

Galen A. Grimes's
bookmarks
imported into
SmartMarks.

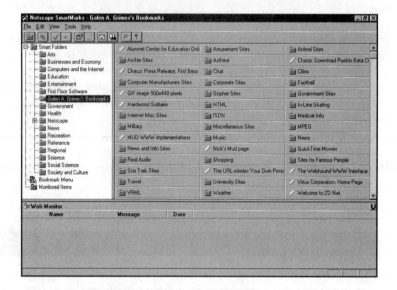

With your Netscape bookmarks imported into SmartMarks, choose Bookmarks and notice that the previous Bookmarks menu items in Netscape, Add Bookmark and View Bookmark, have been replaced with three SmartMarks enhanced bookmark menu items, Add SmartMark, File SmartMark, and View SmartMarks (see fig. 10.6).

Fig. 10.6

Netscape's
enhanced
bookmark menu
supplied by
SmartMarks.

In addition, you will notice an empty area directly below the menu item View SmartMarks. This area is part of your new enhanced bookmark menu and allows you to display parts of your SmartMarks catalog.

Enhanced Bookmarks Menu

When you are running both Netscape and SmartMarks, the normal Netscape bookmarks menu is replaced with an enhanced bookmarks menu (refer to fig. 10.6). This enhanced menu gives you the same bookmark functionality you had in Netscape (adding new bookmarks and viewing/modifying bookmarks), as well as access to SmartMarks and its advanced bookmark operations.

Caution

You have to have both programs—Netscape and SmartMarks—running to be able to take advantage of the enhanced bookmark menu. If SmartMarks is not running, the standard Netscape bookmark menu is used.

Adding a Simple Bookmark

You use the Add SmartMark menu command to add new bookmarks in SmartMarks. Here's how it works:

1. Jump to the following URL in Netscape:

http://www.nflhome.com/.

This is the home page of the National Football League.

2. Select Bookmarks, Add SmartMark (or press Ctrl+A) to save this Web site as a bookmark (or SmartMark).

3. Select Bookmarks again and you see that the Web site title is now included in your lower portion of the enhanced bookmark menu (see fig. 10.7).

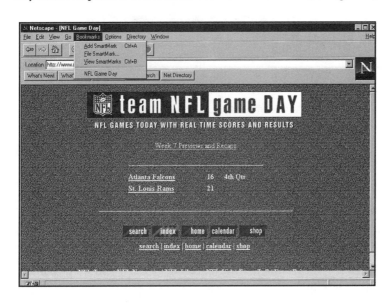

Fig. 10.7

Bookmark for the NFL home page added to SmartMarks and the enhanced menu.

As you continue to add bookmarks, they are added to the enhanced menu just like the bookmark for the NFL home page. SmartMarks treats the enhanced menu as a type of "holding area" for bookmarks you add, allowing you to come back later and file these newly added bookmarks to one of your catalog folders in SmartMarks.

You can also access Add SmartMark from the action menu in Netscape. Just right-click a Web page or a link and choose Add SmartMark to create a bookmark of the current Web page or the selected link.

Adding WWW Sites to Smart Folders

The File SmartMark menu command is another way you can add the current page as a bookmark to your catalog. The difference between the File SmartMark command and the Add SmartMark command is that the Add SmartMark command merely saves the bookmark title and URL to the Bookmark menu (which acts as a holding area for saving bookmarks "on the fly") but not directly to a Smart folder. The File SmartMark command, on the other hand, allows you to place the bookmark into one of your catalog folders and include descriptive information and monitoring specifications.

Caution

One part of the File SmartMark command that might seem confusing is that when you choose Bookmarks, File SmartMark, you bring up the Add SmartMark dialog box you see in figure 10.8.

Fig. 10.8
The Add SmartMark dialog box launched by the File SmartMark command.

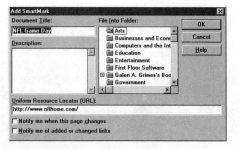

To add a bookmark using the Add SmartMark command:

1. In Netscape, jump to the Web page you want to add as a bookmark.

2. Open the Bookmarks menu and choose File SmartMark. This opens the Add SmartMark dialog box (refer to fig. 10.8).

3. Change the Document Title: (bookmark title) if you want to make it more descriptive.

4. Enter information in the Description: window if you want to describe some feature of this page.

5. Scroll down in the File in Folder list box and highlight the folder you want to place the bookmark into.

6. If you want to monitor this bookmark for changes to the Web page, select the Notify Me When This Page Changes box.

7. If you want to be notified if any of the links on this Web page change, select the Notify Me Of Added Or Changed Links box.

8. Choose OK to close the Add Smartmark dialog box and save this bookmark to the designated folder.

Tip

The File SmartMark command is not accessible from the Netscape action menu.

Monitor Your Favorite Web Sites

SmartMarks' greatest strength is its ability to automatically monitor your Web bookmarks for changes in content, links, or both. As you have seen, you can set SmartMarks to monitor Web pages and inform you when the pages change or when links in the pages change. You can also direct when SmartMarks checks Web pages for changes.

Before SmartMarks, if you wanted to monitor a Web page for changes, it meant you had to actually visit the Web page and visually inspect the page for changes. If you saw something you thought might be different from the last time you viewed the page, you had to remember what the page looked like the last time you saw it. You can see what a problem this is if the last time you saw a particular page was a week or so ago, and what a nightmare this becomes if you multiply the number of pages you're trying to remember by 20 or 30 and the time span is a month ago instead of a week ago.

You've seen previously in this chapter how you can set monitoring specifications when you add a bookmark to your catalog. You can also set monitoring specifications on any of the 300 or so bookmarks that come pre-installed with SmartMarks or the bookmarks you imported from your previous Netscape bookmark list.

Monitoring Existing Bookmarks

Here's how you set monitoring specifications on existing bookmarks:

1. Select the bookmark you want to monitor.

2. Open the File menu and choose Monitor Changes. This opens the Monitor Page dialog box you see in figure 10.9.

Fig. 10.9

Setting monitor specifications in the Monitor Page dialog box.

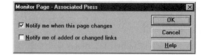

3. Select to monitor page changes, links, or both.

4. Choose OK to close the Monitor Page dialog box and place this bookmark into the Monitored Items folder (see fig. 10.10).

Fig. 10.10

Monitored Items folder and contents showing bookmarks being monitored.

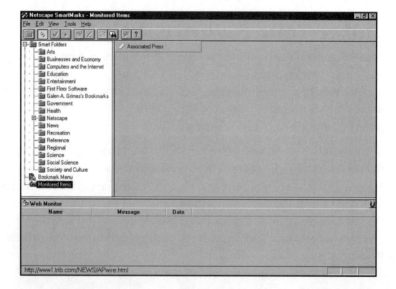

Note

You can also open the Monitor Page dialog box by clicking the bookmark you want to monitor and dragging it to the Monitored Items folder. Another way to open the Monitor Page dialog box to set monitor specifications is to right-click the bookmark you want to monitor and choose Monitor Changes from the action menu. If you want to change more than just the monitoring specifications, you can also use this menu to set Properties for the selected bookmark.

Setting the Monitoring Time Interval

After you select the bookmarks that you want to monitor, you need to set the time interval for how often SmartMarks updates the bookmarks you've selected.

Caution

Update usually means to "change" something, but in this case it means to "check" something—your monitored bookmarks.

To set the time interval, follow these steps:

1. Open the Tools menu and choose Preferences to open the Preferences dialog box.

2. Select the Internet tab (see fig. 10.11).

3. Select when you want updates performed.

Fig. 10.11
Internet tab of the Preferences dialog box where you set your Update time interval.

Mastering Netscape

Note

If you're wondering how often to set the update time interval, here are a few factors to consider. How many bookmarks are you monitoring? It usually takes about 5–10 seconds to update each bookmark. How often are the bookmarks you are monitoring likely to change? If the bookmarks are likely to change maybe once a month, it doesn't make much sense to set your update time interval to once every hour. A good compromise is to set the update time interval to run every time you start SmartMarks (select At Program Start-up). You can always manually update a particular bookmark by selecting the book-mark and then selecting the Update icon from the toolbar, pressing F4, or by right-clicking the bookmark and choosing Update.

---

4. Choose OK to close the Preferences dialog box.

Displaying Monitored Bookmarks and Messages

SmartMarks copies every bookmark you set it to monitor into its Monitored Items folder. Select the Monitored Items folder and SmartMarks displays all the folders it's monitoring (see fig. 10.12).

Fig. 10.12
Monitored bookmarks in SmartMarks' Monitored Items folder.

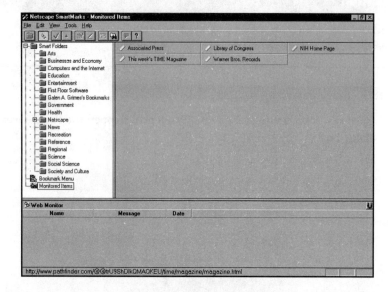

When SmartMarks updates your bookmarks, if it discovers changes to either the Web pages or to links, SmartMarks displays a message indicating the changes it has discovered in the Web Monitor section of the Smart Window (see fig. 10.13).

Fig. 10.13
Web Monitor section of Smart Window displaying bookmark updates.

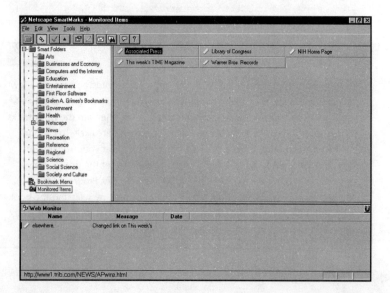

Once your update is complete, or if an update isn't scheduled for a while, you can hide the Web Monitor and use that portion of your screen for displaying bookmarks. Open the View menu and choose Web Monitor. If a checkmark is shown next to Web Monitor on the View menu, choosing Web Monitor removes the checkmark and temporarily hides the Web Monitor display (see fig. 10.14).

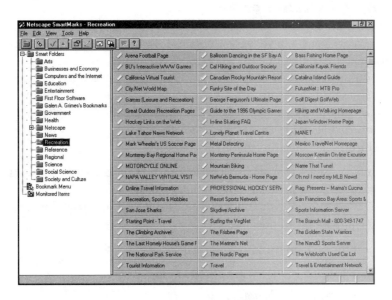

Fig. 10.14
Web Monitor hidden from view in Smart Window.

To redisplay the Web Monitor, open the View menu and choose Web Monitor again to replace the previously removed checkmark, and redisplay the Web Monitor.

SmartMarks and HTML Bulletins

SmartMarks is one of the first Internet products to support a new HTML extended feature called *bulletins*. Bulletins are text messages and descriptions that Web administrators can insert into Web pages and use to communicate with users but not force the users to visit the Web page to receive the communication. Now you're probably asking, why would anyone publish a Web page that they don't want users to visit and read? The purpose of bulletins is not to keep users away from Web pages, but actually to attract users to Web pages.

The use of bulletins by SmartMarks is an extension of the bookmark monitoring functions already detailed in this chapter. Without bulletins, SmartMarks can monitor Web pages to see if they have changed, but when a change occurs on a monitored Web pages, all SmartMarks tells you is that something on the page has changed. To see what that change is, you have to visit the Web page. With a bulletin on that monitored Web page, SmartMarks not only tells you that the page has changed, the Web administrator can communicate to you, through the bulletin, what the change is, and then you can decide if the change merits a visit to the Web page.

Locating Bulletins on Web Pages

Unfortunately, because bulletins are a relatively new HTML extension, their use on Web pages is not yet very widespread. To help you locate and become acquainted with bulletins, First Floor, Inc., the company that manufactures SmartMarks (Netscape licenses SmartMarks from First Floor), has created a list of Web sites using bulletins. The list is set up so that you can easily import it into your SmartMarks catalog and begin monitoring these Web sites using bulletins. First Floor has also promised to add Web sites to this list as they begin to incorporate bulletins into their Web pages.

The list of Web sites that are using bulletins is a Web page on First Floor's Web site. And because this list is a Web page, which means it is just a standard HTML document, you can import the list into your catalog the same way you imported your previous Netscape bookmark list.

To import the bulletin list into your catalog:

1. Start SmartMarks (if it's not already running).

2. Start Netscape (if it's not already running).

3. Jump to the Web page (it's shown in fig. 10.15) at **http://www.firstfloor.com/catalogs/bulletins.html**.

> **Tip**
>
> Because this page is subject to change as First Floor adds additional Web sites using bulletins, you might want to monitor this page using SmartMarks so you know when new links (pages) containing bulletins are added.

4. Open the Netscape File menu and choose Save As to save the currently displayed Web page as an HTML file. This opens the Save As dialog box. Save the file as bulletins.htm (see fig. 10.16).

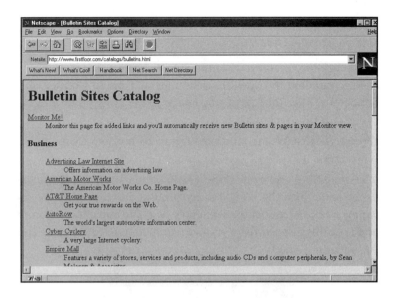

Fig. 10.15
First Floor, Inc.'s
list of Web sites
using bulletins.

Fig. 10.16
Saving Web page as
bulletins.htm.

5. Choose OK to save the file bulletins.htm and close the Save As dialog
   box.

6. Open the Bookmarks menu and choose View Bookmarks to open
   SmartMarks' Smart Window.

7. Select the First Floor Software folder in the tree.

8. Open the Tools menu and choose Import to open the Select a File to
   Import dialog box, and select the file bulletin.htm that you saved in
   step 5.

9. Choose OK to close the Select a File to Import dialog box and import
   the contents of bulletins.htm into your catalog. This operation should
   only take a few seconds.

Now that you've imported First Floor's list into your catalog, you need to monitor a bookmark before you can read its bulletin:

1. Right-click the Chamber of Commerce Web Site as the bookmark you want to monitor and open the action menu. Choose Monitor Changes to open the Monitor Page dialog box and select the monitoring specifications for this bookmark.

2. Choose OK to close the Monitor Page dialog box and to update this bookmark.

3. When the BUSY indicator stops flashing (indicating that the update is completed), open the Web Monitor window and right-click the monitor listing for the Chamber of Commerce Web Site and choose Comments and Bulletins to open the Comments and Bulletins dialog box and read the bulletin in the Web page you just updated (see fig. 10.17).

Fig. 10.17
Bulletin from the new Chamber of Commerce site.

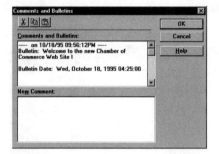

4. Choose OK to close the Comments and Bulletins dialog box after you have read the bulletin.

Now you have a monitored bookmark in your catalog to a Web page utilizing bulletins. The next time this Web page is changed, SmartMarks notifies you, and you can check the nature of that change by reading the bulletin instead of jumping to the Web site and reading the page.

As an individual user, this may not seem like such a time-saving device, but imagine a corporation using its Web site to communicate information to several hundred (or several thousand) customers and you can see what a time saver this could be to that customer base, especially if the information on the Web site changes daily.

Other Information Supplied by First Floor

In addition to keeping you updated on which Web sites are incorporating bulletins into their Web pages, First Floor, Inc. also keeps other useful bookmark catalog pages that you can import into your catalog. Two other catalog pages which you might want to take a look at are

■ *U.S. Government catalog from the Federal Internet source*—this is a listing of Web sites maintained by various government agencies and departments, which use their presence on the Web to convey information about the various services they provide

■ *Windows 95 catalog*—this is a listing of Web sites providing information about various aspects of Windows 95

Searching the Internet

SmartMarks would still be an good Internet utility if all it did was allow you to manage your bookmarks. But the developers of SmartMarks realized that an excellent Internet utility should also be configured to allow you to locate potentially new bookmarks, or to put it plainly, search the Internet. SmartMarks is configured to conduct and monitor searches using several of the most popular Internet search engines:

■ Yahoo

■ Lycos

■ WebCrawler

■ InfoSeek

If you are familiar with conducting searches using any or all of these Internet search engines, and are able to utilize their various search options, using these search engines through the SmartMarks Smart Finder interface should be no problem.

Yahoo

Yahoo, the Internet search engine started by two Stanford University graduate students, is perhaps the best known and most popular of the four search engines accessible through SmartMarks.

Through the Smart Finder interface you can conduct keyword searches on the Yahoo database similar to the keyword searches you can conduct directly with the Yahoo Web form.

Here's how:

1. In SmartMarks, open the Tools menu and choose Find to start the Smart Finder Internet search utility (see fig. 10.18).

II

Mastering Netscape

Fig. 10.18

SmartMarks' Smart Finder Internet search utility.

2. In the Search drop box, choose Internet - Yahoo.

3. In the first *where* drop box, decide whether you want to conduct your keyword search on the entire contents of the Web pages in Yahoo's database, or just on the titles, URLs, or the comments. The default choice is *Contents*, which conducts the search on the title, URL, and comments.

4. In the second *where* drop box, decide whether you want your keyword search to be an exact match (choose Matches) or just a substring match (choose Contains). The default choice is *contains*.

5. In the third *where* field, enter the keyword for the search.

6. If you want to enter a search using multiple keywords, choose the More button to open the second keyword field and the third *where* drop box which is used to determine if the search uses both keywords (keyword1 and keyword2), either keyword (keyword1 or keyword2), or treats both keywords as partial words, i.e., substrings (see fig. 10.19).

Fig. 10.19

Smart Finder set to conduct search with multiple keywords.

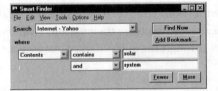

7. To start your search, click the Find Now button. Smart Finder passes your search through its interface to Yahoo, and then switches back to Netscape to display the results of your search (see fig. 10.20).

8. If you want to save the search parameters as a bookmark so that you periodically re-issue the search, select the Add Bookmark key to open the Add SmartMark dialog box. Select the folder you want to save the search bookmark in and give the search bookmark a file name. Choose OK to save the file and close the Add SmartMark dialog box.

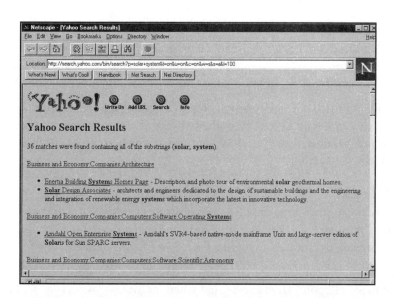

Fig. 10.20
Yahoo search
results.

> **Tip**
>
> Besides Yahoo, you can also save the search parameters for any of the search engines available through Smart Finder to a bookmark.

Lycos

Lycos, the search engine created by Carnegie-Mellon University in Pittsburgh, has one of the largest Internet search databases because it is a robot-search engine. A robot-search engine is a program that literally searches the Internet for file servers and then scans each server for information for its database. At the time of this writing, Lycos claimed that it had scanned 91 percent of the Internet and contained over 7.9 million URLs.

This differs from the database in Yahoo which consists only of entries submitted and then examined by the administrators.

The Smart Finder interface can conduct keyword searches on the Lycos database similar to the keyword searches you can conduct directly with the Lycos Web form.

Searches on the Lycos search engine and database operate almost identically to searches on Yahoo except that when multiple keywords are used in the search parameter, the search can only be conducted using either keyword (keyword1 or keyword2).

WebCrawler

The WebCrawler search engine and database also utilizes a robot-search engine, similar to Lycos, but is not believed to have as large a database. It began at the University of Washington, but is now operated by America Online.

Searches on the WebCrawler search engine and database operate almost identically to searches on Lycos except that when multiple keywords are used in the search parameter, the search is conducted using both keywords (keyword1 and keyword2).

InfoSeek

InfoSeek is another popular search engine on the Internet, and of the four accessible through Smart Finder, is the only one that charges for it services. You can however, use InfoSeek on a trial basis to see if you want to subscribe.

Searches on the InfoSeek search engine and database operate almost identically to searches on Yahoo except that when multiple keywords are used in the search parameter, the search is conducted using both keywords (keyword1 and keyword2), either keyword (keyword1 or keyword2), or one keyword or the other, but never both.

Back Up Your Catalog Using Bookmark Management

Periodically, you should make a backup of your SmartMarks catalog in the event a computer or disk error corrupts your catalog. SmartMarks includes its own maintenance utility for performing backups of your catalog (and restores, if necessary).

Caution

Before attempting to back up your SmartMarks catalog, make sure you have exited from SmartMarks. The catalog database must be closed in order to create your backup.

To back up your catalog:

1. Start the Smart Catalog Maintenance utility (see fig. 10.21).
2. Select Backup to begin the catalog backup operation. Depending on how many bookmarks are contained in your catalog, the backup operation takes anywhere from a few seconds to a few minutes.

Fig. 10.21
SmartMarks' Smart Catalog Maintenance utility main screen.

3. When you see the message indicating that the backup is completed successfully, choose Close to exit the Smart Catalog Maintenance utility.

Restore Your Catalog Using Bookmark Maintenance

The restore operation of the Smart Catalog Maintenance utility is only used to restore a damaged or corrupt catalog. In order to use the restore function, you must have previously created a successful backup of your catalog.

Caution

Just as when you created your catalog backup, SmartMarks must not be running when you are attempting to restore your previous backup.

To restore from your previous backup:

1. Click the Start button on the taskbar and choose Programs, Netscape SmartMarks to open the SmartMarks menu.
2. Click the Smart Catalog Maintenance icon to start SmartMarks maintenance utility.
3. Choose Restore to begin the catalog restoration operation. Depending on how many bookmarks are contained in your catalog, the restore operation takes anywhere from a few seconds to a few minutes.
4. When you see the message indicating that the restore is completed successfully, choose Close to exit the Smart Catalog Maintenance utility.

CHAPTER 11

Forms and Transaction Security

Browsing the Web is mostly a matter of downloading files from a Web server to view with your browser. But when you fill out an online form, you're sending data the other way—from your computer back to the server you're connected to.

Web forms are like paper forms; they are comprised of data entry fields, checkboxes, and multiple-choice lists. They open the electronic door to all kinds of exciting transactions on the Web. You can sign a guest book, sign up for a service, ask to be added to a mailing list, join an organization, request a catalog or brochure, and even make purchases by submitting forms over the World Wide Web.

We'll look at all of these possibilities in this chapter. You'll also learn the following:

- What different kinds of forms there are on the Web
- What the parts of a form are
- How to fill out and submit an online form
- What happens when you submit a form
- What security issues are associated with submitting Web forms
- How to make sure that your transactions (including credit card purchases) are secure and safe
- What the future holds for Web security

What Are Forms Good For?

Forms are the Web's standard method for letting you submit information to a World Wide Web server. They are used for four major functions:

- Searching for information in an online database
- Requesting a user-customized action, such as the creation of a custom map or table
- Registering for a service or group
- Online shopping

In each of these cases, forms give you the means to send specific information to the server you're connected to, so that you can receive a customized response back.

▶ See "Netscape Forms and CGI-BIN Scripts," pg. 745

> **Note**
>
> How does a Web site send a customized response back when you submit a form? Usually by running an associated program on the server called a *CGI-BIN script*. This specially-written program analyzes information provided by the form and performs the action(s) you request. Chapter 30, "Netscape Forms and CGI-BIN Scripts," covers how to write custom CGI-BIN programs to run on your own Web server.

In contrast, normal page links only allow you to click a link from a list to retrieve a "canned" response from the server. Forms let Web page creators send you information and services that are tailored to your specific needs, rather than broad, generic responses built for an audience constrained by "least common denominator" considerations.

Let's take a look at four real-world examples from the Web, one for each of these common uses of forms.

Searching

The most popular site on the World Wide Web is Yahoo at Stanford University. Yahoo is a combination Web index/search engine that lets you find just about any site on the Web in seconds. There are two different methods built into Yahoo for finding specific Web sites.

> **Tip**
>
> You can also find some interesting sites by clicking the New, Cool, Popular, and Random buttons in the Yahoo title bar, though these are more for Web surfers than for anyone trying to find specific information on the Web.

One search method is a standard hierarchical index (see fig. 11.1). While you can find a site by following the index through its ever-narrowing lists of topics and subtopics, this is definitely the brute-force approach, especially when you consider the tens of thousands of sites that are contained in Yahoo's index space!

The superior way to search Yahoo is to let it build a custom index to your personal specifications. You do this by filling out and submitting the simple one-line form near the top of the page (see fig. 11.1). You just click in the data entry field and type a list of keywords, then click the Search button. Yahoo then searches its database of Web site information and builds a custom index composed only of the entries that contain your keywords. This takes only a few seconds. Finally, Yahoo builds and transmits a custom Web page that contains an index that has been generated "on the fly" just for you.

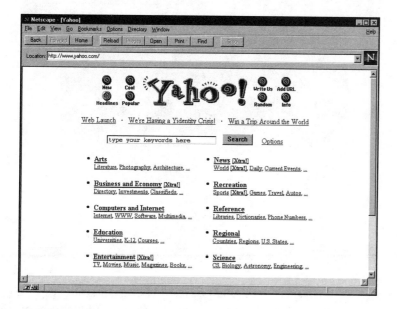

Fig. 11.1
Yahoo at Stanford University lets you search for Web sites in two very different ways. The best is to use its online form to search for keywords.

There are literally thousands of sites like Yahoo on the Web that let you use forms to search online databases and retrieve custom pages containing information on a myriad of topics. Just about every kind of information you can imagine (and some you *can't* imagine!) is available on the Web somewhere in a forms-searchable database. The following are a few good examples:

- Do a search in the AT&T 800 number directory (**http://www.procd.com/sr/freesrch.htm**)
- Search UseNet postings with DejaNews (**http://www.dejanews.com/**)

- Look up drugs on the Pharmaceutical Information Network (**http://pharminfo.com/**)

- Find interesting biographical notes in Britannica's Lives (**http://www.eb.com/calendar/calendar.html**)

- Do a keyword search for jobs (**http://www.occ.com/occ/SearchAllJobs.html**)

Requesting

Forms can also be used to ask a server to run a program to perform a specific task for you (see fig. 11.2). This is one of the most open-ended (and fun!) examples of interactivity on the Web.

Fig. 11.2
The Earth Viewer form lets you specify latitude and longitude for your point of view, as well as which satellite data to use. You can even generate a custom view from the sun or the moon!

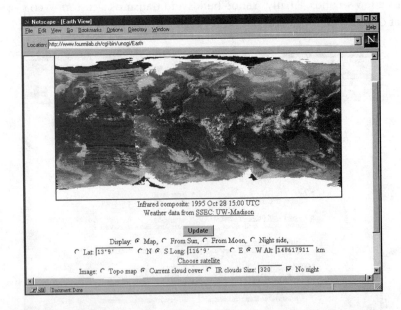

Because a Web server is a computer just like any other, it is fully capable of running any program that any other computer can run. So the types of actions you can request of a Web server are limited only by what the server is willing to let you do. The following is a quick list of a few of the actions you can request on the Web by submitting a form to the right site:

- Display an up-to-the-minute satellite view of the earth's cloud cover from a user-definable viewpoint using the Earth Viewer (**http://www.fourmilab.ch/earthview/vplanet.html**)

- Say something over the speech synthesizer in Rob Hansen's office at Inference Corporation (**http://www.inference.com/~hansen/ talk.html**)

- Operate a model train at the University of Ulm in Germany (**http:// rr-vs.informatik.uni-ulm.de/rrbin/ui/RRPage.html**)

- Generate custom tables of 1990 census data (**http:// www.census.gov/cdrom/lookup**)

While some of these activities are definitely more useful than others, they serve to illustrate what it is possible to do over the Web if the server you are connected to provides the right forms and support programs.

Registering

You can use online forms to sign up for just about anything somewhere on the Web (see fig. 11.3). You can enter contests and sweepstakes, join organizations, apply for credit cards, subscribe to e-mail lists on hundreds of different topics, and even sign a guest book at some of the sites you visit.

Most online registration forms ask you for the same information you'd supply on a paper registration form: name, address, phone, and—since this *is* the Internet, after all—e-mail address. Many places also require user registration before they allow you into the deeper, and hopefully most interesting, regions of their Web site. (Some may charge you for this privilege, some not.)

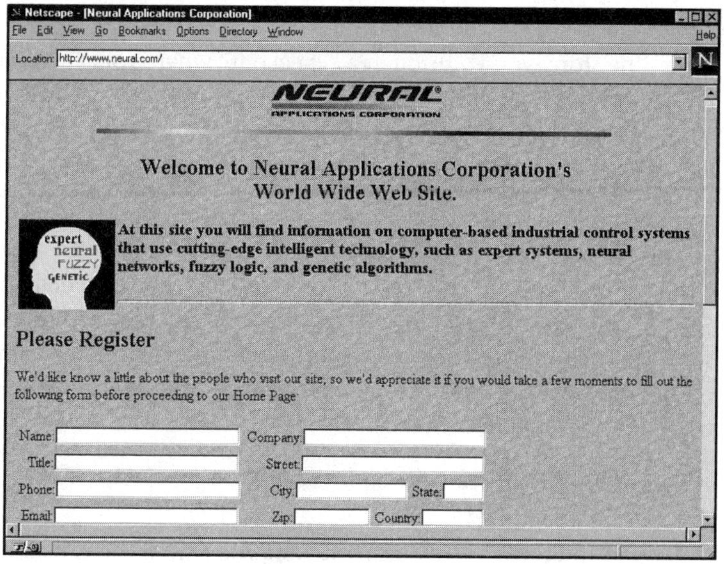

Fig. 11.3
Many sites, like this one, ask that you fill out a registration form before you are allowed to access the rest of their site.

Some of the places on the Web that ask you to fill out a registration form are the following:

- Neural Applications Corporation wants you to fill out a short registration form before you take a look at their home page (**http://www.neural.com**).

- Follow the links and enter your personal information and some keywords to win a new Toyota from Oxyfresh (**http://www.oxyfresh.com/Oxyfresh/Contest/**). (This particular contest ends April 1, 1996.)

- Apply for an AT&T "universal card" credit/phone card (**http://www.att.com/ucs/app/app_intr.html**)

- Subscribe to an e-mail list of properties for sale in San Francisco (**http://www.starboardnet.com/form.html**)

Shopping

You can shop 'til you drop without ever leaving home by cruising the electronic malls on the World Wide Web (see fig. 11.4).

Web shopping generally involves filling out an order form (or registering as a shopper) with your name, address, and credit card information. Many sites now even include an electronic "shopping cart." This allows you to browse a site, reading product descriptions and price information; when you find something you like, you just click the checkbox (an online form, of course) next to the item you want and it is added to your cart. When you get ready to leave the online store, you go through a "checkout" where your items are totaled and you are presented with a bill, which you can then pay with your credit card or "electronic cash." For more information on electronic cash, see the "Digital Money" section later in this chapter.

By "shopping" we really mean the process of requesting goods, "hard copy" information like catalogs or brochures, or services that require either the action of human beings or the transfer of physical objects through delivery services. Though this certainly can involve buying things, it also includes many other services. The following is a list of some more-or-less random examples: (Please note that we are not endorsing or recommending any of these products or services. Use at your own risk!)

- Enter Liechtenstein's $1,000,000 InterLotto lottery (**http://www.interlotto.li/**)

- Order free and low-cost government pamphlets from the Consumer Information Center (**http://www.gsa.gov/staff/pa/cic/cic.htm**)

- Click checkboxes to receive hundreds of free catalogs at the Mall of Catalogs (**http://www.csn.net/marketeers/mallofcatalogs/**)

- Request books or research services from a library. Though you'll have to check with your local or university library to see if they offer such services via the World Wide Web, Jim Robertson maintains a list of links to the kinds of forms commonly used by libraries at **http://hertz.njit.edu/~robertso/LibForms.html**

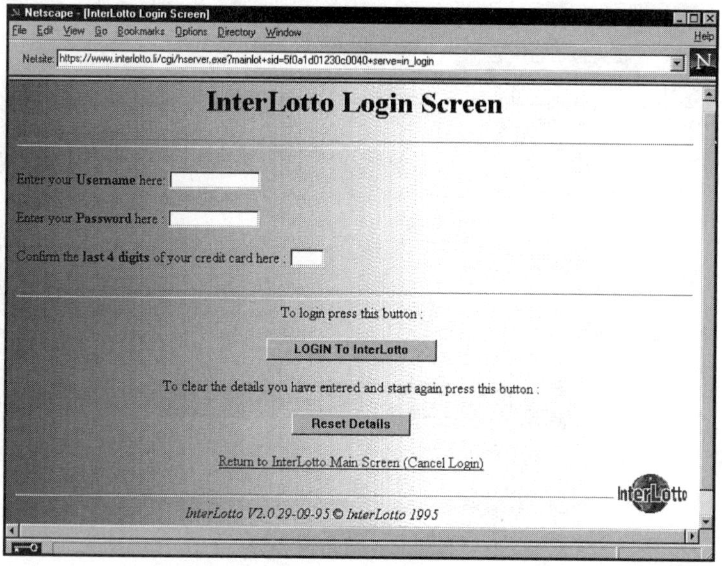

Fig. 11.4
You can enter Liechtenstein's national lottery directly through their secure server connection by filling out an online form.

A Generic Online Shopping Trip

Just so you'll know the steps that are involved, let's take a quick virtual shopping trip on the World Wide Web.

The first question is "Where to go?" A good place to begin is the All-Internet Shopping Directory at **http://www.webcom.com/~tbrown/**. It lists hundreds of online malls, catalogs, and stores.

From this list, a good choice might be "The Awesome Mall of the Internet." How could you pass by a place with a name like that?

The Awesome Mall lists the Cyber Warehouse online store; it's intriguing because they list a 28.8 modem for only $99.99, and you're tired of your slow 14.4 kilobit-per-second dial-up connection to the Web.

Scrolling down to the bottom of the page, you find a short form that lets you specify your preferred Delivery method, and Quantity to purchase (see fig. 11.5). Normal delivery is okay, and you only want one unit, so you can accept the default answers by clicking the button marked Add to Basket. This adds the item to your virtual shopping basket. Though you could add more items, you decide to be done for now. Selecting Shopping Basket from the bottom-of-page menu lets you examine your shopping basket's contents.

Fig. 11.5

You can use an online order form like this one to buy things on the Web.

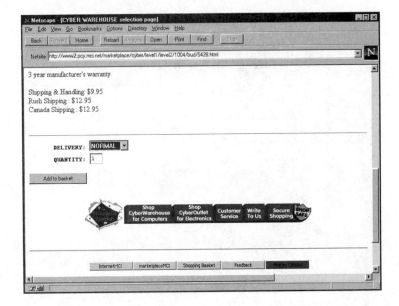

The shopping basket is private. Netscape pops up a Security Information dialog box to warn you that you're about to enter a secure space, and that all data transmissions from here on will be encrypted. Note that you haven't accessed any secure data yet, which means that the key icon in the lower-left corner of the screen will still look broken.

The shopping basket screen lists what you've purchased. At this point, the doorkey icon is unbroken, reminding you that this page is secure. (And you didn't have to do a thing to get a secure connection—Netscape did it all for you!) You could change your order now, but you decide you're happy so you just click the button marked Checkout.

That takes you to an online form where you fill out your shipping and credit card information (see fig. 11.6). The process is very similar whether you use a credit card or digital money, though many more sites take credit than "ecash." The key shows you still have a secure link.

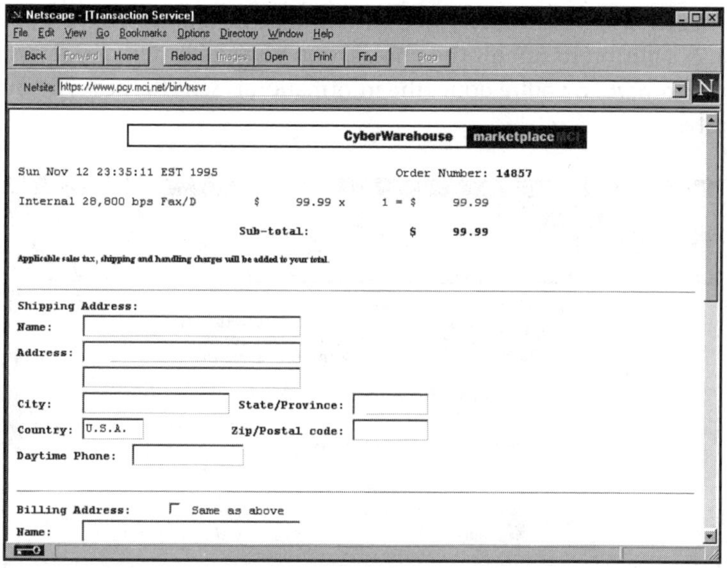

Fig. 11.6
When ready to make an online purchase, you are asked to fill out an order form through a secure connection (note unbroken key in lower left corner of screen).

Scrolling down to the bottom of this page, you find the credit card information part of the form. You know you can fill this out safely because your link is secure, and the data you send will be safely encoded by Netscape. When done, you press the Continue Checkout button, proceed though a couple of final messages, and you're done.

Form Formats

Web forms are created using the <FORM></FORM> HTML tag. Within this structure, many options are available to the Web forms designer to create a wide range of form elements. Online forms can include data entry fields, checkboxes, scrolling lists, and even push buttons.

You'll run into a wide variety of form formats on the Web. Among them are inline forms, full-page forms, multiple forms on a single page, and even hidden forms.

Inline Forms

If the Web page you're visiting needs only a single item of information from you, it's likely to present you with a much simplified form called an inline form.

The Lycos search engine is a good example of an inline form (see fig. 11.7). There is only one field to fill in and a single button to push when you're done. In fact, most forms that have only a single field don't even require that you push a button to submit the information you've filled in; if you just hit the Enter key when you're done, the information is sent to the server automatically.

Fig. 11.7
Lycos uses a single inline form field to ask for a list of keywords to search for.

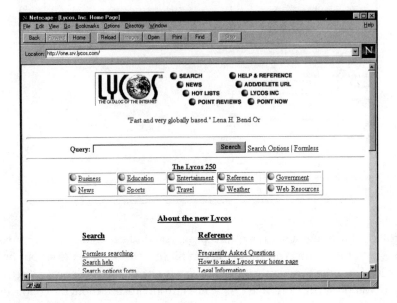

Full-Page Forms

You'll find many examples of full-page forms on the Web. These ask for a variety of information, and may make use of all the available form elements (push buttons, checkboxes, fields, scrolling menus, and so on). However, they probably also incorporate many other HTML design elements like style tags, formatted text, inline images, hypertext links, links to objects that launch helper applications, and even links to other sites. Sometimes it's hard to sort out which parts are the form and which parts are collateral material.

Yahoo's Search Options form is a good example of a full-page form with a variety of input field types (see fig. 11.8).

Multiple Forms

You can also put several separate forms on a single Web page. If there are multiple forms on one page, they are independent, each with its own SUBMIT button.

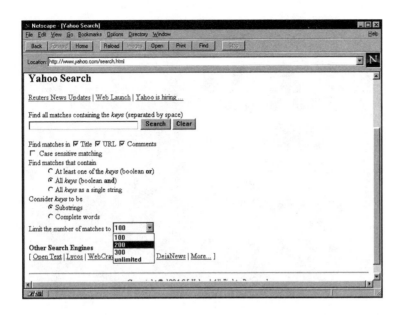

Fig. 11.8
Yahoo's Search
Options screen is a
good example of a
full-page form, and
it includes most of
the input field
types you'll see on
online forms.

Each individual form has its own associated program or script that is invoked when its SUBMIT button is pressed. Only the data from the associated form is passed to the server. Figure 11.9 shows an example of a Web page with multiple forms.

> **Caution**
>
> If you put more than one form on a Web page, make sure you don't nest one <FORM></FORM> construct within another. Forms cannot be nested within forms. According to proposed HTML 3.0 specifications, forms can only be nested within the following "parent" elements on an HTML page: BANNER, BODYTEXT, DD, DIV, FIGTEXT, FN, LI, NOTE, TD, and TH. Some older browsers have reportedly had problems displaying forms within tables; similar problems might arise from nested constructs.

Hidden Forms

You may have used forms without even knowing it. Sometimes forms are completely hidden. Forms can consist of nothing but hidden fields that send pre-defined data when an associated button, image, or link is clicked. Since there is nothing to see on a hidden form, we won't show an example here; however, we will discuss how they work a little later in this chapter.

II

Mastering Netscape

Fig. 11.9
Multiple forms
occupy William D.
Cross's All-in-One
Search Page at
**http://
www.albany.net/
~wcross/
all1srch.html**.

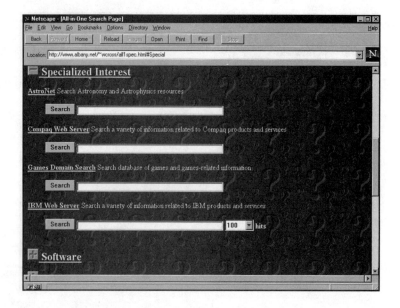

Filling Out a Form

Now that we've covered what forms are good for, and what different kinds of forms you're likely to run into on the Web, let's step through filling out a form page. We'll choose as our example a form that contains almost all of the different elements you're likely to encounter in real life.

▶ See "Netscape
Forms and
CGI-BIN
Scripts,"
pg. 745

Within a <FORM></FORM> form definition, most of the visible parts of a form are defined by three HTML tags: INPUT, SELECT, and TEXTAREA. These tags are discussed from a programmer's point of view in chapter 30, "Netscape Forms and CGI-BIN Scripts." For now, we'll concentrate on what they look like on the Web page, and how to fill them in.

Our sample form as displayed in figure 11.10 is defined in the short HTML script shown in listing 11.1:

Listing 11.1   HTML Source for a Sample Form

```
<HTML>
<HEAD>
<TITLE>Forms Test Page</TITLE>
</HEAD>
<BODY>
<H1>Forms Test Page</H1>
<FORM ACTION="http://www.test.com/cgi-bin/binfile" METHOD=POST>
Type text in this field:
<INPUT NAME="SomeText" TYPE="TEXT" SIZE="15" MAXLENGTH="30">
Enter Password:
<INPUT NAME="passw" TYPE="PASSWORD" SIZE="5" MAXLENGTH="10"><br>
```

```
Check all that apply:
<INPUT NAME="checkb1" TYPE="CHECKBOX" VALUE="check1" CHECKED>Checkbox
#1
<INPUT NAME="checkb2" TYPE="CHECKBOX" VALUE="check2">Checkbox #2
<INPUT NAME="checkb3" TYPE="CHECKBOX" VALUE="check3">Checkbox #3<br>
Select "Yes" or "No" (or "Maybe"):
<INPUT NAME="rad" TYPE="radio" VALUE="yes" CHECKED>Yes
<INPUT NAME="rad" TYPE="radio" VALUE="no">No
<INPUT NAME="rad" TYPE="radio" VALUE="maybe">Maybe<br>
[Here's a HIDDEN field...]
<INPUT NAME="hidd" TYPE="hidden" VALUE="secret!">
Here's an IMAGE:
<INPUT NAME="coord" TYPE="image" SRC="formtest.gif"><P>
<INPUT TYPE="submit" VALUE="Click Here to SUBMIT the form">
<INPUT TYPE="reset" VALUE="Click Here to RESET the Form"><P>
What's your name?
<SELECT NAME="Name" MULTIPLE>
<OPTION> Mary
<OPTION> Pete
<OPTION> Pamela SELECTED
<OPTION> John
<OPTION> Louise
</SELECT>
Enter comments:
<TEXTAREA NAME="address" ROWS=5 COLS=40>
I love what you've done with this page!
You are the Master of Web page design.
And I really, really mean this.
</TEXTAREA>
</FORM>
</BODY>
</HTML>
```

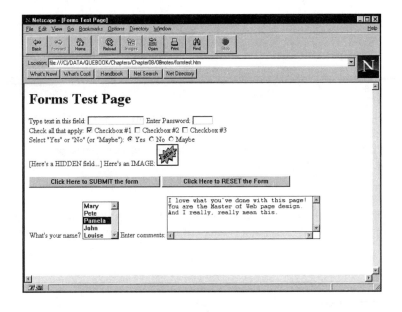

Fig. 11.10

Examples of the most visible parts of an HTML form as defined by <FORM> tags. Each part is explained below.

Mastering Netscape

The INPUT Tag

The <INPUT> HTML tag is what is used to define most of the input areas of a Web page form. It has eight commonly used TYPE options, each of which looks and acts differently on-screen.

The TEXT type is used for entering a single line of text. The SIZE attribute specifies the visible width of a text field, while the MAX attribute specifies the actual maximum number of characters that can be typed. (Though our example doesn't show it, you can also define a default value for input text that appears automatically in the text field by assigning VALUE="default text" in the INPUT tag line.) For example:

```
<INPUT NAME="SomeText" TYPE="TEXT" SIZE="15" MAXLENGTH="30">
```

To fill in a TEXT field, point and click in the field, then type. To move from one TEXT field to the next, use the Tab key.

Tip

When any form field is "active," your cursor and page up/down keys don't work to scroll the Netscape window anymore. Instead, they work to move around in the form field. To use them for scrolling the window again, just click anywhere in the window background.

A PASSWORD field is the same as a TEXT field, but for security purposes the screen doesn't display what you type. Instead, you see a string of asterisks (*). For example:

```
<INPUT NAME="passw" TYPE="PASSWORD" SIZE="5" MAXLENGTH="10">
```

You fill in a password field the same way you fill in a text field.

Note

Do you "fill out" or "fill in" a form? Webster, Strunk & White, and all of the other language authorities seem to have ordained no standard usage. I struggled with the "in/out" issue throughout the writing of this chapter, and finally settled on this convention: You "fill out" a form, but "fill in" a field.

The CHECKBOX type is for Boolean variables, variables which can take only one of two values. When a box is checked, the value of its VALUE attribute is assigned to the variable specified in its NAME attribute. If present, the CHECKED attribute indicates that the checkbox is checked by default. Example:

```
<INPUT NAME="checkb1" TYPE="CHECKBOX" VALUE="check1" CHECKED>

<INPUT NAME="checkb2" TYPE="CHECKBOX" VALUE="check2" >

<INPUT NAME="checkb3" TYPE="CHECKBOX" VALUE="check3" >
```

You check a checkbox by clicking it; you uncheck a checked checkbox by clicking it again.

The RADIO input type is for variables that can take any one of several different specified values. This is done by giving several (at least two) radio buttons the same NAME attribute with different VALUEs. Selecting one of the buttons causes any previously selected button in the group to be deselected, and assigns the VALUE to the NAMEd variable. The CHECKED attribute indicates which radio button is checked by default. For example:

```
<INPUT NAME="rad" TYPE="radio" VALUE="yes" CHECKED>

<INPUT NAME="rad" TYPE="radio" VALUE="no">

<INPUT NAME="rad" TYPE="radio" VALUE="maybe">
```

You select a radio button by clicking it. If the radio button you click has the same variable NAME as a radio button that has already been selected, the previous button will automatically be unselected when you select the new one.

Tip

Want to know which radio buttons share the same variable NAME, or what the default VALUE of a variable is? If the Web page creator hasn't been nice enough to tell you on-screen, the only way to know is to choose View, Document Source (Alt+V,S) from the Netscape menu and comb through the HTML code.

An input field of the HIDDEN type does not appear anywhere on a form, but the VALUE specified is transmitted along with the other values when the form is submitted. HIDDEN fields are not usually used on pre-defined Web page forms. They usually only appear on customized forms that are created "on the fly" by the a Web server you're connected to. They are used to keep track of information specific to your request. For example, if you request information from a server and it sends back a form asking for additional details, that form might include a hidden field type that defines a request number. When you submit the second form, the server is then able to tell which request

II

Mastering Netscape

number your second form referred to. Here's a simpler example from our test page, which simply returns the value secret in the variable named hidd:

```
<INPUT NAME="hidd" TYPE="hidden" VALUE="secret">
```

You don't (and can't) fill out a HIDDEN field. Its value is predefined. In fact, you probably won't even know it's there.

The IMAGE type is an advanced form of the SUBMIT type. (See below.) Instead of providing a push button, the IMAGE type lets you use a bitmapped image to submit a form. When clicked, the IMAGE field submits the entire form to the Web server, and can also be used to transmit the coordinates of exactly where the image was clicked. For example, if the IMAGE variable is named coord and the bitmap is 100×100 bits in size and you click the pixel at location 50,62, the server receives all of the form data, including the two clicked-coordinate values coord.x=50 and coord.y=62.

```
<INPUT NAME="coord" TYPE="image" SRC="formtest.gif">
```

If the INPUT type is IMAGE, you'll probably be asked to "Click somewhere on this image to submit this form," or something similar. If it is set up to transmit the coordinates of your mouseclick (that is, if it has a variable NAME), you'll probably be asked to click in different specific spots depending on what you want to do. In any event, you shouldn't click the IMAGE bitmap until you have filled in all the other fields on the form.

The SUBMIT input type creates a push button which, when selected, activates the ACTION specified in the FORM definition. In most cases, this means it sends the data from all of the form fields on to the server. The VALUE attribute of the SUBMIT type is actually the label that appears on the button. For example:

```
<INPUT TYPE="submit" VALUE="Click Here to SUBMIT the form">
```

When you are done filling out a form, click the SUBMIT button to finish.

> **Tip**
>
> SUBMIT buttons are often labeled something else, like "Done" or "Send." Don't let labels fool you. If it's a push button and it sounds like something you should only click when you're finished, it's probably a SUBMIT button.

RESET also manifests itself as a push button, but selecting it resets all of a form's fields to their initial values as specified by their VALUE attributes. Like the SUBMIT button, the VALUE attribute defines the button label text. For example:

```
<INPUT TYPE="reset" VALUE="Click Here to RESET the Form">
```

If you've totally mucked up filling out a form, click the RESET button to reset all the fields to their default values so you can start over.

There are other less-often-used or proposed-for-future-versions types for IN-PUT, but the types just covered cover 99 percent of what you'll run into on the Web. For information about other INPUT options, check out chapter 30, "Netscape Forms and CGI-BIN Scripts."

▶ See "Netscape Forms and CGI-BIN Scripts," pg. 745

There are two other common HTML tags besides INPUT that are used to create online forms: SELECT and TEXTAREA.

The SELECT Tag

RADIO and CHECKBOX fields can be used to create multiple choice forms. But the <SELECT></SELECT> element pair can be used to produce a neat multiple-choice field in the form of a pull-down list. If more than one choice is valid, the MULTIPLE attribute enables the selection of more than one option. Each choice is specified in a separate OPTION element. For example:

```
<SELECT NAME="Name" MULTIPLE>
     <OPTION> Mary
     <OPTION> Pete
     <OPTION> Pamela SELECTED
     <OPTION> John
     <OPTION> Louise
</SELECT>
```

To choose a SELECT option, click it. To select more than one option in a MULTIPLE-enabled list, click one option and drag to select more. To select non-contiguous options, hold the Ctrl key when you click additional items. Selected items are highlighted; if you can only highlight one option, then the MULTIPLE attribute isn't enabled.

The TEXTAREA Tag

The <TEXTAREA></TEXTAREA> HTML construct lets you type in multiple lines of text in a scrolling text box. As usual, the NAME attribute defines the variable. The ROWS and COLS attributes specify the width and height of the text area in characters. Default text (if any) is entered line by line between the <TEXTAREA> and </TEXTAREA> tags. For example:

```
<TEXTAREA NAME="address" ROWS=6 COLS=60>
     I love what you've done with this Web page!
     You are definitely the God of Web page design.
     And I really, really mean this.
</TEXTAREA>
```

To fill in a TEXTAREA field, just click it and type. You can use all of the standard editing keys (arrows, Delete, Page Up/Down, etc.) to move around and edit in the TEXTAREA box.

II

Mastering Netscape

Filling Out a Form by Uploading a File

Version 2.0 of Netscape adds the ability to upload the data for a form, rather than having to fill it all out online. This can save you lots of connect time when filling out long online forms. (Unfortunately, you can't upload data for just any old form—the Web form you're looking at has to be specially configured to accept a file as input.)

This is accomplished through the use of a new value for the <FORM> tag ENCTYPE, which defines the MIME type of a form submitted using the POST method. In the past, there has been only one valid value for ENCTYPE, application/x-www-form-urlencoded. The new value defined for input files is multipart/form-data.

A new INPUT TYPE has also been defined for FILE type input.

Here's an example of a short form that accepts file input (see fig. 11.11):

```
<FORM ENCTYPE="multipart/form-data" ACTION="http://www.site.com/
cgi-bin/getfile" METHOD=POST>
File to process? <INPUT NAME="file1" TYPE="file">
<INPUT TYPE="submit" VALUE="Send File">
</FORM>
```

Fig. 11.11
A short example of a Web form that accepts a file as input.

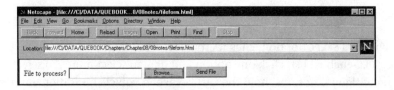

▶ See "E-mail with Netscape," pg. 321

▶ See "Configuring Helper Applications," pg. 395

The new INPUT TYPE="file" not only lets you upload a file in response to the form request, it even adds a BROWSE button that, when clicked, brings up a standard Windows file requester dialog box! It couldn't be much easier.

For Every Action...

Every FORM definition has an associated ACTION that determines how the server deals with the information it receives from the form. There are two possible form actions: GET and POST.

GET

The form GET action is no longer recommended, but you still see it used in forms on older sites. It's functionally identical to the POST action described later, but sends form data appended to the URL rather than as separate MIME urlencoded data. The following is an example:

```
<FORM ACTION="http://www.server.com/cgi-bin/doit" METHOD=GET>
```

When submitted, this sample form actually asks the server for a URL called **http://www.server.com/cgi-bin/doit&data&moredata&etc.**, where the items separated by ampersands at the end of the URL address are the various data fields you filled in on the form.

Tip

Don't worry if you see some strange-looking URLs containing lots of ASCII "garbage" in the location box on the Netscape Navigator screen. Some POST instructions (and all GET instructions) append form data to the URL. The server will know what it means, even if you don't.

Somebody somewhere decided this was sloppy, and came up with the POST action as an alternative. It keeps the URL request and the form data neatly separated.

POST and CGI-BIN Scripts

The form POST action sends form data back to the Web server you're connected to and (usually) launches a program called a CGI (Common Gateway Interface) script. The following is an example:

```
<FORM ACTION="http://www.server.com/cgi-bin/doit" METHOD=POST>
```

When submitted, this form launches a program called doit on the server, which processes your form data and performs the requested action(s).

CGI scripts may be written either in scripting languages like Perl, or in any other programming language, like C, Pascal, or BASIC (in which case they are more properly called CGI programs).

Tip

On many HTTP servers, CGI scripts are stored in a separate directory called cgi-bin, so if you see a pathname in Netscape's URL address line that includes /cgi-bin/ after submitting a form, it's almost a certainty that your submission has launched a CGI script or program.

Data sent to the CGI script by the POST action is MIME-encoded using the MIME data type application/x-www-form-urlencoded. URL encoding is not for security purposes; in fact, it's easily read by human eyes, if a bit strange looking. URL encoding is just a way for the server to identify POSTed data and receive it reliably.

URL encoding simply runs all the form data together as a single string. It then replaces spaces with "+" characters; replaces non-alphanumeric characters with their ASCII hexadecimal equivalent, preceded by a percent (%) sign; includes NAME= in front of every field; and puts an ampersand (&) between fields.

Here's an example. Let's say the form you are submitting (which uses the POST action, of course) asks you for values for variables named YOURNAME, YOURCITY, and CHOICE. You fill it out with the following data:

Mary Jones

Oklahoma City

Y

When you press the SUBMIT button, here's how the data is transmitted back to the server:

```
YOURNAME=Mary+Jones&YOURCITY=Oklahoma+City&CHOICE=Y
```

This line would be preceded by a MIME notice that the message is encoded in the MIME type/subtype application/x-www-form-urlencoded. Because the data is in a known format, the server can make some sense out of it.

Fortunately, all of this is totally invisible to you. You don't have to worry about how it works at all, because the process is fully automatic.

POST and MAILTO

The form POST action can also simply mail form data to a specified address through the MAILTO command. The following is an example:

```
<FORM ACTION="mailto:mbrown@neural.com" METHOD=POST>
```

Rather than launching a CGI-BIN script, the MAILTO command mails the same URL-encoded data string to the specified Internet mail address. Though not all browsers support the MAILTO command, Netscape does, and you'll find it used quite often on the Web.

The Form Submission Process Flowchart

So what *really* happens when you submit a form? The whole process is summarized in the flowchart shown in figure 11.12.

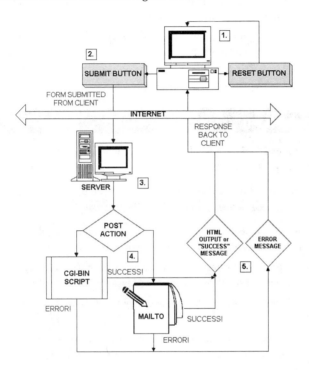

WHAT HAPPENS WHEN YOU SUBMIT A FORM?

Fig. 11.12
What happens when you submit a form.

Mastering Netscape

The following is the step-by-step process that occurs when you submit a form.

1. While filling out the form, you can move around and edit, and even press the RESET button to clear the form back to its default VALUE settings.

2. When you are satisfied with the data you've entered, pressing the SUBMIT button sends the form data to the server you got the form from via the Internet.

3. The server receives the data and performs the ACTION defined in the FORM statement.

4. If the METHOD is POST and the ACTION references a CGI-BIN script (or program), the CGI-BIN is run with the form data as input. If the ACTION is MAILTO, the form data is mailed to the address specified in the ACTION statement.

5. The server then sends a response back to you. If the action was successfully completed, you get a confirmation message or custom page, depending on the actions defined in the CGI-BIN script. If unsuccessful, you (hopefully) are sent an error message. If the action was MAILTO, the only feedback you get may be a Document Done message in Netscape's status bar at the bottom of the screen.

Troubleshooting

I pressed the SUBMIT button, but all I got back was some weird error message that I couldn't interpret. What gives?

There are a number of things that can happen when you press the SUBMIT button that result in you receiving an error message. The following are just a few:

- Between the time you received the form and the time you submitted it, the server you were connected to may have gone down.

- The server you're connected to may submit its CGI scripts to another server to be run, and that server may be down. (Hey—nobody said this would be easy!)

- The CGI program may be buggy, and might have choked on your particular data.

- The CGI program may be telling you that you filled out the form incompletely or incorrectly. Read the error message carefully to see if it's specific about the problem.

The fix is often no more complicated than pressing the Back button on the Netscape toolbar and filling out the form correctly. If you continue to get errors, your only solution may be to e-mail the Webmaster of the site where you're experiencing the problems. There's usually an address or link on most home pages for this purpose.

Forms and Security

The first time you click the SUBMIT button to order something using an online form, you may wonder if you should be afraid to use your credit card on the Web. But you might also wonder why no one seems to care about how much "insecurity" there is in more traditional uses of credit cards in stores, by mail order, and over the phone. It's really much more likely that someone will pull a receipt out of the trash at a store and steal your credit card number than it is that some hacker will latch onto it on the Web.

The real issue is this: How trustworthy is the party you're dealing with? Your major worry should probably be the chance of running into a dishonest employee or a bogus company—online or not—that wants to steal your number outright.

That being said, it should also be noted that there really are a few dishonest hackers out there who revel in gathering information through any means possible. Some of them even go on to use it for personal gain. When this happens, it doesn't matter that the percentages are low if it's *your* credit card number they're playing with! And, as commerce increases on the Web, it's likely to draw larger numbers of out-and-out professional thieves, too.

If nothing else, business and government are extremely concerned about security, and they won't trust their transactions to the Web until they're convinced that no one else can illegally tap in and see what's going on.

Clearly, the security of online transactions is not an issue that can simply be ignored.

Enter encryption. Public-key encryption, to be exact. Encryption uses a "key" number to change readable text into unreadable code that can be sent and decrypted back into a legible message at the receiving end. A public key system uses two keys: a public key number and a private key number. Messages encrypted with the public key can only be decrypted with the associated private key, and messages encrypted with the private key can only be decrypted with the public key. You keep the private key private and make the public key as public as you want, and you've guaranteed that all of your communications will be secure. Netscape incorporates public-key cryptography as part of its built-in Secure Sockets Layer (SSL) security.

(For more on public-key encryption, see the discussion on Netscape's Secure Sockets Layer technology later in this chapter.)

Of course it's more complicated than that, or this chapter would end right here.

Mastering Netscape

II

Tip

Point your Netscape newsreader to the **comp.security** newsgroups for the latest discussions of security on the Web.

The following are some of the other issues involved in making sure your online communications are really secure:

- Is your computer (the client in the transaction) set up in a secure manner?
- Is the server you're connected to secure?
- Is the connection between the two systems secure?
- Is there some way you can be sure your transaction is secure?

We'll address all four of these concerns (see fig. 11.13) in this chapter.

Fig. 11.13
The four areas of security concern.

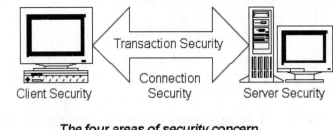

The four areas of security concern

Client Security

Frankly, client security is the only area in which you have much say. Your computer is yours, and you can choose how to set it up. The chain only being as strong as its weakest link, you want to make sure that your link in the security chain is not the one that's going to snap first.

There are three areas where you have can have some major effect on the security process: how you configure helper applications, how you set up proxy servers, and how carefully you keep your passwords.

Configuring Helper Applications

You can get into some real security problems if you configure helper applications without first thinking about security issues (see fig. 11.14). (See chapter 16, "Configuring Helper Applications," for detailed information on using the Netscape Helpers dialog box to set up helper applications.)

For example, if you configure Microsoft Excel as a helper app to view files with an extension ending in .XLS, what happens if a spreadsheet file you view while you're browsing the Web has an auto-execute macro that runs some hidden (and sinister) procedures? At that point, your system has been breached.

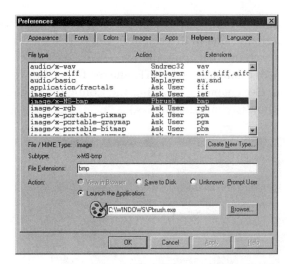

Fig. 11.14
You get to this dialog for configuring Helpers by selecting Options, General Preferences (Alt+O,G) from the Netscape menu.

You expose your PC to a great many security risks if you configure helper applications that aren't simply passive viewers or players, unless you are certain that downloaded files can never contain any malicious content.

Be careful about helper applications. Don't configure fancy helper applications that can be programmed to run sinister macros via the Web.

> **Note**
>
> Concern about sinister macros is no mere bugaboo. Recently, Microsoft addressed the issue of what it called a "prank macro" that was being distributed via a MS Word document on the Web. Though all this macro did was display a "playful" message, it could easily have done something much more harmful.
>
> Microsoft immediately issued a prank-macro-swatter program that would kill the macro and scan all Word documents for it, to eliminate it from your system completely.
>
> If nothing else, this real-world example illustrates how seriously Microsoft takes this issue.

Proxy Servers

Proxy servers—also called application gateways or forwarders—are programs that handle communications between a protected network and the Internet. Most proxy programs log accesses and authenticate users.

If you run Netscape from a machine on a network that is protected with a firewall (see "Firewalls" later in this chapter), you'll need to set up a different proxy server for each Internet application you want to use in conjunction with Netscape—for example, one for FTP, one for Telnet, one for UseNet news, and so on. (See chapter 3, "Loading and Configuring Netscape," for information on how to configure proxies.)

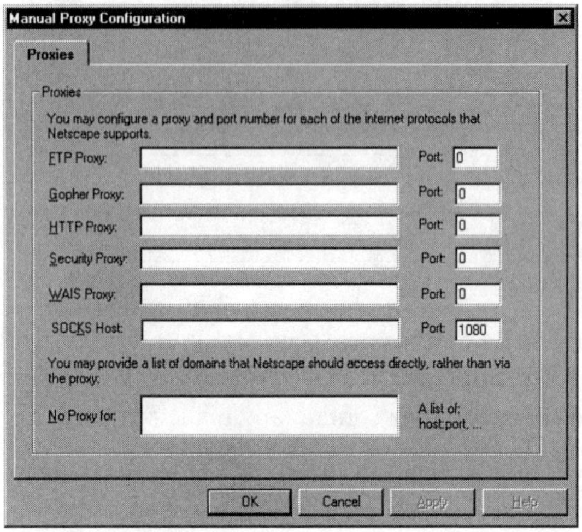

Fig. 11.15
You get to this dialog box for configuring Proxies by selecting Options, Network Preferences (Alt+O,N) from the Netscape menu.

Your major responsibility in this area is to make sure the proxies you use are secure and a good match to your network's firewall. In short, you should never use a proxy application that hasn't been approved by your system administrator.

If you connect to the Web via a commercial dial-up service like America Online or CompuServe, you don't need proxies and don't need to worry about them.

Passwords

If you ever want to rob a bank, just walk in at noon and check around the computer terminals of people who are out to lunch. The odds are very, very good that you'll find at least one person who has left their system password on a sticky note in public view.

Of course, you'll never have to worry about anyone stealing *your* password, because you follow the Five Basic Rules of Password Security, which are as follows:

1. Choose a password that isn't obvious.

2. Commit your password to memory.

3. Never write your password down anywhere that's accessible by anyone but you.

4. Change your password often.

5. Don't ever share your password with anyone.

If you're on a network, you already have a password for network access. Odds are, you'll register for additional access passwords on many Web sites, as well.

But there's also a password you can set for access to Netscape itself. To set your password, follow these steps:

1. Select Options, Security Preferences (Alt+O,S) from the Netscape menu.

2. Click on the Passwords tab to bring it to the front (see fig. 11.16).

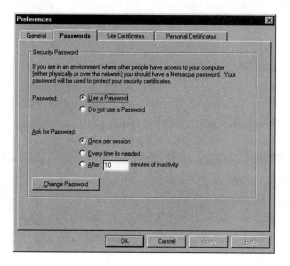

Fig. 11.16
Netscape's Passwords dialog box lets you set access password options.

3. Click the Use a Password radio button.

4. Under the Ask for Password option, click one of the following buttons, depending on your preference:

   ■ Once per session

   ■ Every time it's needed

   ■ After __ minutes of inactivity

5. If you selected the last option, enter an appropriate number in the minutes field.

6. Select the Change Password push button. You'll see the screen as shown in figure 11.17.

Fig. 11.17
Confirming that
you really want to
use a password.

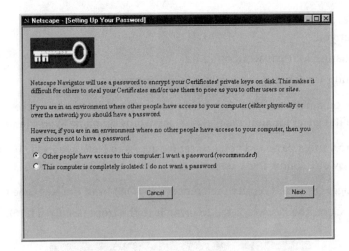

7. Click the radio button that indicates you want a password, then select the Next> button.

8. You are prompted to enter a password of more than eight characters, then retype it to confirm (see fig. 11.18). REMEMBER YOUR PASS-WORD!!! Netscape cannot tell you what it is if you forget.

Fig. 11.18
Entering a
password.

9. Choose the Next> button.

10. When the last window appears, select Finished. You'll be sent back to the Password window.

11. Choose OK to end.

Server Security and Firewalls

A poorly-managed Web server can be the source of many security compromises. For example, a poorly-written CGI script can accidentally allow malicious intrusions into a system. The Web server administrator is responsible for managing the server in such a way as to prevent such security compromises.

It's also important that the Web server software installed on the server machine be capable of handling secure transactions over the Internet. For example, the Netscape Commerce Server (Netscape's server software package) incorporates SSL (Secure Sockets Layer) security, with support for acquiring a server certificate and communicating securely with SSL-capable browsers like Netscape Navigator. (For more on the Netscape Commerce Server, see chapter 32, "Testing the Netscape Commerce Server.")

▶ See "Testing the Netscape Commerce Server," pg. 801

But perhaps the most important security concern regarding servers is the installation of a good firewall.

A better name for firewall might be traffic cop, because the main function of the group of programs that comprise a firewall system is to block some Internet traffic while allowing the rest to flow. There are a variety of ways that this can be implemented on a server system, but all firewalls perform similar functions.

Some allow only e-mail traffic, which limits security concerns to "mail bombs" and other e-mail–based attacks. Others allow a full range of Internet accesses. In any event, a firewall performs two major functions: user authentication and access logging. The first keeps out intruders; the second provides an accurate record of what happened in case one gets through.

Since all firewalls provide a single access point between the Internet and a network, they make it relatively easy to monitor communications should there be any suspected breaches of security.

Without some kind of firewall installed, a network system hooked up to the Internet is open to all kinds of security attacks.

Tip

For more info on firewalls, point Netscape to **ftp://ftp.greatcircle.com/pub/firewalls**, which contains the Firewalls mailing list archives.

Connection Security

Between point A (your computer) and point B (the Web server you're connected to on the Internet), there may be dozens of other computers handling the communications link. Obviously, the more computers in the chain, the more chances for some unknown someone to break into your transmission and steal your data.

II

Mastering Netscape

Unfortunately, you don't have much control over your Internet connection. That's even more reason to make sure you do as much as you can to make the things you do have some control over as solid and secure as possible.

Transaction Security

Transaction security is the area that most people think of when they think of security on the Web. Maybe it's because it's the area that encompasses the most high-tech and romantic aspect of computer security: cryptography.

There is, of course, much more to transaction security than just data encryption. Message verification and server identification are at least as important, if not even more so. After all, what difference does it make if a message is securely encoded if its source is someone impersonating you who is trying to use your credit card or steal your data, or if a message that you legitimately sent has been intercepted and altered in transit?

Note

What if your major concern is not making sure that data is transmitted securely, but making sure that it doesn't get transmitted at all? Many parents are concerned about (admittedly overblown) media reports about pornography and other objectionable materials that are available on the World Wide Web. They don't want their children to be able to access such data.

Parental lock-out systems can work in much the same way as the security measures employed in ensuring secure transactions. For example, a Web browser might have different accounts set up with different passwords and different encryption keys for parents' and kids' accounts. The parents' account might allow unlimited access, while the kids' account wouldn't properly decode transmissions from restricted sites. Such sites could be defined by looking for specific "ratings" tags sent by the Web server, or by setting up a list of forbidden sites.

There are many ways that parental lock-out could work. Netscape and two other leading Internet software companies (Microsoft and Progressive Networks) have formed the Information Highway Parental Empowerment Group to work on the problem.

The rest of this chapter is devoted to the topic of transaction security and how Netscape handles it.

Netscape Security

> **Note**
>
> Additional information on Netscape security is just a couple of mouse clicks away. From the Netscape menu, select Help, On Security (Alt+H,O) for access to the following helpful documents from Netscape Corporation's World Wide Web site:
>
> ■ Netscape Navigator Handbook: Security
>
> ■ Netscape Data Security
>
> ■ Using RSA Public Key Cryptography
>
> ■ The SSL Protocol

The Cracking of SSL

You may have read about it in the papers: Two University of California-Berkeley students and a researcher in France almost simultaneously posted messages to the Internet detailing their success in decoding a message that had been posted as a "Netscape security challenge." They discovered how Netscape 1.2 generates session encryption keys, enabling them to replicate the keys for that specific message with a moderate amount of computing power and, within a few days, they had deciphered it.

What was the problem? In a nutshell, Netscape was using a relatively small set of pseudo-random data (how many processes are running on the client computer, process ID numbers, the current time in microseconds, and so on) to generate a relatively large random number encoding key. This meant that the hackers didn't have to try every possible random 40-bit number to find the key.

The researcher in France used 120 workstations and two parallel supercomputers at three major research centers for eight days—approximately $10,000 worth of computing power. While this seems like a lot of effort to put into decoding just one simple little one-page message (and it is), it did serve to show that Netscape's security was crackable. If the same techniques had been applied to a security-critical message (for example, a hostile takeover bid for a major corporation), the consequences could be substantial.

The 40-bit key used in the "challenge" message is the international encryption mode used in export versions of Netscape Navigator. The 128-bit key encryption used in the U.S. version is export-restricted under government security regulations. It is much

(continues)

(continued)

more robust; it would have taken many years to break the challenge message if the same amount of computing power had been used had it been encoded with the U.S. version.

While no actual thefts of real-world information have ever been reported to Netscape Corporation, they worked quickly to provide updated software for free downloading from their home page on the Web. The new version 1.22 security patch increased the amount of random information used to generate keys from 30 bits to approximately 300 bits. With 10 times as much pseudo-random data to start with, keys in the latest versions of Netscape Navigator are now effectively immune from similar "brute-force" attacks.

The security features built into Netscape Navigator (and the Netscape Commerce Server) attempt to protect your Web transactions in the following three important ways:

- Server authentication (thwarting impostors)
- Privacy using encryption (thwarting eavesdroppers)
- Data integrity (thwarting vandals)

Netscape's Visual Security Cues

Version 2.0 of the Netscape Navigator includes some visual security indicators to let you know about security conditions. These indicators include identification of secure URLs, changing color bars, a broken/solid key icon, and the ability to view identification and security information associated with a Web page. You'll also see various warning dialog boxes from time to time, depending on how you have your security options set.

URL Identification

You can tell whether a Web page comes from a secure server by looking at the URL (location) field at the top of the Netscape window. If the URL begins with https:// instead of http://, your connection is secure (see fig. 11.19). Similarly, a news URL that begins with snews: instead of news: indicates that a document comes from a secure news server. In both cases the s stands for secure, of course, and in both cases it indicates that the HTTP requests are traveling through a Secure Sockets Layer.

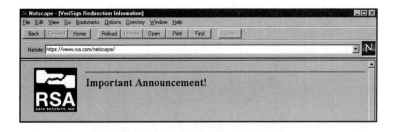

Fig. 11.19
If the server you're
connected to is
secure, Netscape's
URL bar shows the
address as begin-
ning with https://
instead of http://.

The Key and the Color Bar

To the left of the status message at the bottom of the Netscape screen, you'll
find a doorkey icon. The status of this key indicates whether or not you are
viewing a secure document. A broken key icon on a gray background indicates an insecure document; a solid key on a blue background indicates a
secure document (see fig. 11.20). The secure doorkey icon varies slightly
depending on the grade of encryption: The key has two teeth for high-grade
and one tooth for medium-grade. A mixed document with insecure information omitted is shown as secure; if the insecure information is included, the
status is displayed as insecure.

Fig. 11.20
The key in the
lower-left corner of
the Netscape
window is broken
(left) if your
connection is
insecure or mixed,
and solid (right) if
your connection is
secure.

Likewise, a blue color bar above the Netscape display window indicates a secure document, while a gray color bar indicates an insecure document.

Netscape Security Dialog Boxes

Several notification dialog boxes (or alerts) inform you of the security status
of documents.

When entering a secure document space, you are notified that the secure
document is encrypted when it is transferred to you, and any information
you send back is also encrypted (see fig. 11.21).

When leaving a secure document space, you are notified that the insecure
document can be observed by a third party when it is transferred to you, and
any information you send back can also be read by a third party.

When viewing a document with a mix of secure and insecure information,
you are notified that the secure document you just loaded contained some insecure information that will not be shown. If an insecure document contains

Mastering Netscape

secure information (either inline or as part of a form), this alert is not displayed. The document is simply considered to be insecure.

Fig. 11.21
One of Netscape's security alert dialog boxes; this one is to notify you of encrypted data transfers.

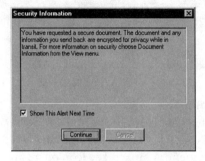

When you submit a form using any insecure submit process, you are notified that the submission process you are about to use is insecure (see fig. 11.22). This means that the information you are sending could be compromised by a third party.

Fig. 11.22
If a form you submit is insecure, you'll see this alert.

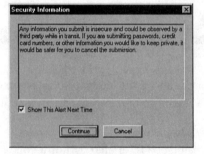

You are notified if the document was expected to be a secure document but is actually an insecure document (the document location has been redirected to an insecure document).

You can choose whether to receive these dialog boxes by setting the panel items in the Netscape Options menu (Alt+O).

Here's how to turn Netscape's security alert dialog boxes on or off:

1. Select Options, Security Preferences (Alt+O,S) from the Netscape menu.

2. Click the General tab to bring it to the front (see fig. 11.23).

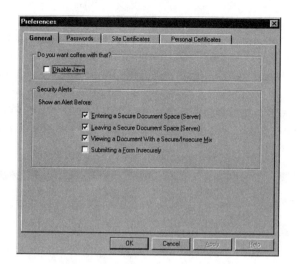

Fig. 11.23
You use Netscape's Security Preferences dialog box to set alert display options.

3. You'll see the following four different Security Alerts selections, labeled Show a Security Alert Before:

■ Entering a Secure Document Space (Server)

■ Leaving a Secure Document Space (Server)

■ Viewing a Document With a Secure/Insecure Mix

■ Submitting a Form Insecurely

Click the appropriate spaces to select or deselect the dialog boxes you want to see.

4. Choose OK to finish.

You can also simply uncheck a dialog box's Show this Alert Next Time checkbox if you decide you never want to see it again.

View Document Information

To view information about a displayed Web page, choose View, Document Info (Alt+V,N) from the Netscape menu. A new Netscape window (see fig. 11.24) displays the document title, the URL of the file, and document info, which includes file type, source, modification date, file length, expiration date, character set, and security level. This information is taken from the header of the document and from the server that supplied the page.

The Document Info window displayed in Netscape Navigator 2.0 uses another new feature, Frames, which enables independent sub-windows, or *frames*, within one page display window. In the Document Info window, the

II

Mastering Netscape

top frame shows the document title and its URL, and the bottom frame shows a list of information about the document. If you click the link to the document in the lower frame, the document itself is shown in the lower frame. If you then click the link in the upper frame, the lower frame displays the document information again. You can resize the relative sizes of the frames in the window: just put the mouse on the boundary until you see the mouse icon change into a split pair of arrows, then click and drag the boundary between frames.

Fig. 11.24
Netscape displays document information using its new Frames capability. This info is for a page at RSA, Inc.'s secure WWW server.

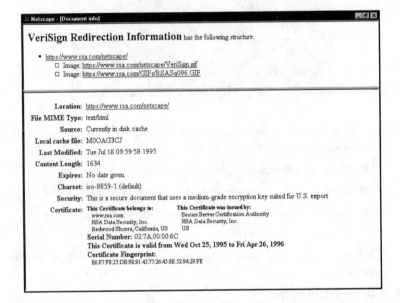

If a document is insecure, the security information panel notifies you that encryption is not used and there is no server certificate. If a document is secure, the security information panel notifies you of the encryption's grade, export

---

Note

Depending on where the Document Info window appears on your screen when it is invoked, you may need to move it (click and drag the title bar) to be able to use the scroll bar in the lower frame. You may need to scroll the lower frame down to where the security information line is, at the bottom of the list of document information, so you can see the lines of security information for the document.

control, key size, and algorithm type, and, in a scrolling field, the server certificate presents coded data identifying the following:

- Certificate version and serial number
- Issuer of the certificate
- Subject (organization) that is being certified

To ensure that you are communicating with the organization you want, examine the subject of the server certificate. The organization should identify itself with the name and location you expect.

Certificate information is protected by encryption to ensure authenticity and integrity. You can interpret the coded data as follows:

- *Country (C):* Two-character country code
- *State or Province (ST):* Unabbreviated state/province name
- *Organization (O):* Legal, registered organization name
- *Organizational Unit (OU):* Optional department name
- *Locality (L):* City the organization resides or is registered in
- *Common Name (CN):* The server's fully qualified host name (such as hostname.netscape.com)

To return to the main Netscape window, choose File, Close (Alt+F,C) to close the Document Info window, or use the window Close button.

SSL

The Secure Sockets Layer (SSL) protocol is Netscape's answer to transmission security over the World Wide Web. SSL is application protocol-independent and provides encryption, which creates a secured channel to prevent others from tapping into the network; authentication, which uses certificates and digital signatures to verify the identity of parties in information exchanges and transactions; and message integrity, which ensures that messages cannot be altered en route.

The Netscape Commerce Server and Netscape Navigator both incorporate SSL technology, and both (or compatible programs) are needed in order to establish a secure SSL connection.

SSL is layered beneath application protocols such as HTTP, Telnet, FTP, Gopher, and NNTP, and layered above the connection protocol TCP/IP (see fig. 11.25). This strategy allows SSL to operate independently of the Internet application protocols. With SSL implemented on both the client and server, your Internet communications are transmitted in encrypted form, ensuring privacy.

Fig. 11.25
How SSL fits into
transactions on
the Internet.

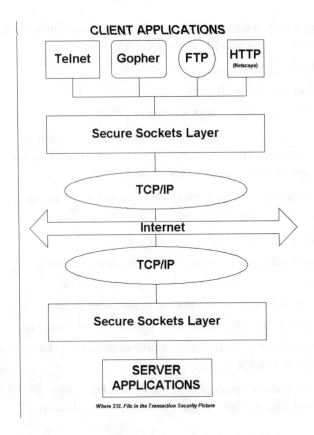

Where SSL Fits in the Transaction Security Picture

SSL uses authentication and public-key encryption technology developed by RSA Data Security, Inc.

Server authentication uses RSA public key cryptography (see the "RSA Public Key Cryptography" sidebar that follows) in conjunction with ISO X.509 digital certificates. Netscape Navigator and the Netscape Commerce Server deliver server authentication using signed digital certificates issued by trusted third parties known as certificate authorities. A digital certificate verifies the connection between a server's public key and the server's identification (just as a driver's license verifies the connection between your photograph and your personal identification). Cryptographic checks using digital signatures ensure that information within a certificate can be trusted.

RSA Public Key Cryptography

RSA (Rivest-Shamir-Adleman) public key cryptographic technology is at the heart of most Web security schemes, including Netscape's built-in Secure Sockets Layer protocol. The following is how it works, in a nutshell.

Encoding and decoding of messages is accomplished by using two large random numbers. One is called the public key, and is made public. The other is the private key, and is kept secret. Messages encoded with the public key can only be decoded using the private key, and vice versa. So messages sent to you can only be decoded by you, and messages you send can be verified as coming from you, since only your public key decodes them.

Because encryption is considered a national security issue by the federal government, U.S. products can't be exported to foreign countries with really high-level security built in. That's why the international version of Netscape uses only 40-bit keys, while the domestic version uses 128-bit keys.

The RSA encryption technology used in Netscape is owned by RSA, Inc., which also makes a stand-alone security product for Windows called RSA Secure. RSA Secure integrates into the Windows File Manager to provide RSA encryption for the Windows file system. The company offers a trial version for 30-day evaluation, and checking it out is a good way to learn more about RSA encryption. For more information on RSA, Inc., or to download the free evaluation version of RSA Secure, go to their secure (naturally) WWW server at **https://www.rsa.com.**

Public key cryptography has been around only a couple of years longer than the World Wide Web. Pretty Good Privacy (PGP) is a stand-alone public-key encryption program from MIT for multiple platforms that lets you play around with and learn about public key cryptography. You can also use it for serious purposes, like encrypting mail and files on your hard disk.

The latest version of PGP for Windows can be downloaded from **ftp://net-dist.mit.edu/pub/PGP**.

To learn more about PGP and public-key cryptography, point Netscape to **http://bs.mit.edu:8001/pgp-form.html**.

Note

The security of this system comes from the fact that the numbers used are very large. Though they can be discovered by factoring, the amount of computer time required to do so is highly impractical, often running into hundreds of years.

Server Certificates

To operate using security features, the Netscape Commerce Server requires a digitally signed certificate, which is a kind of trustworthy "electronic driver's license"—it's a unique identifier. Without a certificate, the server can only operate insecurely. If you are a server administrator and want to obtain a signed certificate, you need to submit a certificate request to a certificate authority, a third-party organization that issues certificates, and pay an associated service fee. (VeriSign, pg. 297, is one such company.)

When you request a server certificate from an online service, your server software generates a public key/private key pair and you choose a distinguished name. Online forms guide you through the process of submitting the form to the certificate authorization company.

The authenticity of each certificate request is verified (making sure requesters are who they claim to be). Upon approval, the certifier digitally signs the request and returns the unique digitally signed certificate through e-mail. You can then install the signed, valid certificate to enable security.

Setting Certificate Options in Netscape

You can examine and change Netscape's installed security certificates through the Options, Security Preferences (Alt+O,S) section on the menu bar.

Select the Site Certificates tab for a scrolling list of server certificates that Netscape is configured to handle (see fig. 11.26).

Fig. 11.26

You can set Site Certificate preferences through this Security Preferences dialog box.

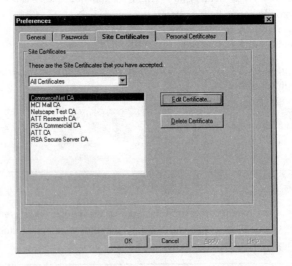

You can highlight an entry and select Delete Certificate to remove a certificate from the Netscape setup. You'll probably only want to do this if there is some major flap over bugs or breaches of a particular certification authority's certificates.

The Edit Certificate button brings up the certificate information dialog box shown in figure 11.27. Clicking checkboxes here lets you choose to allow or disallow connections to sites using the chosen certificate. You can also elect to see an alert dialog box when you encounter a site with the specified certification.

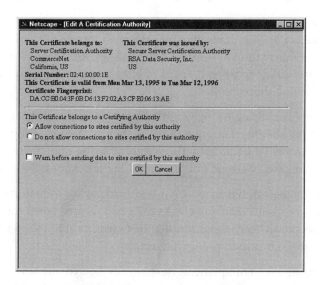

Fig. 11.27
Netscape displays detailed information about a site certificate.

II

Mastering Netscape

Note

Cookie files seem to be mentioned in passing in a lot of discussions having to do with security, without much associated definition or clarification.

Briefly, a *cookie file* is a small amount of data sent back from the server to be stored on your computer, which the server can then access later. This might be account information or any other information associated with your specific session that the server doesn't want to keep on hand, but needs to refer to again later.

Cookie files may be transmitted to your computer and back to the server in a secure or insecure manner (that is, with or without SSL security). So security with cookie files is, as with any data transfer, a separate issue to itself.

There are two things you can say about cookie files and security in general: There might be some extra measure of security in keeping your personal information on your machine rather than on the server itself, but there is also some additional security risk involved in transferring cookie file data back and forth between your machine and the server every time it's needed.

Business Transactions

First there was television which, from the very beginning, included commercials. Then there were those late-night infomercials for Ginsu knives and the Popeil Pocket Fisherman. Finally, with the advent of cable TV, there was the Home Shopping Network (and its many clones).

Though the Internet began life as an infrastructure for the exchange of scholarly information, it didn't take long for someone to figure out how to turn a quick buck online with mass postings and mailings. And it took even less time for those annoying all-text "spam" messages to give way to a plethora of Web-based online shopping malls.

Not that there's anything wrong with that (though some old-timers whine all night about the commercialization of the Web). Let's face it—people *like* to buy things. And buying things on the Web is no worse than buying them on the Home Shopping Network, or even at Wal-Mart. It's just different.

One of the toughest things to work out is how to pay for something you've ordered electronically. Cash and checks can't be squeezed down the wires, and most people are leery about posting their credit card numbers where they might be grabbed by unscrupulous hackers.

But enterprising Web entrepreneurs have already figured out how to take the electronic equivalents of credit cards and money electronically.

There are differences between using credit cards and using electronic cash, but the range of services available blurs the lines of distinction between the various methods of conducting financial transactions electronically on the Internet. Some schemes deal directly with banks, while some use second-tier arrangements, bonding-houses, and/or third-party secure-server services.

Digital Money

Digital money is a totally new concept. Even more radical in concept than the once-preposterous idea that paper bills could represent real gold, in its most basic form digital money involves transmitting an encoded electronic packet of information that is as secure and difficult to counterfeit as a dollar bill. (More so, really.)

Digital money is based on the same security encoding schemes as other secure transactions on the Web—encryption and authentication. But some of the proposed schemes go a step beyond.

For example, the two companies examined next have very different ideas of how digital money should work.

CyberCash

CyberCash has set up both debit and credit systems, but we're mostly interested here in the debit, or "cash" system.

In the CyberCash scheme, participating banks let a customer open accounts that amount to "electronic purses." Using the company's software, a customer moves money from the checking account into the electronic purse. As with an automatic teller machine, the customer then withdraws digital tokens from the purse and uses them to make purchases on the Net. Upon receipt, the seller queries the CyberCash computer to verify the token is valid and instructs CyberCash where to deposit the money.

To use the CyberCash system, you must install the client version of CyberCash software to work with your browser. It also requires that the Web server handling the transaction form must use the CyberCash system to decrypt order information.

CyberCash believes that most consumers want to have a record of their transactions to budget and account for their spending.

For more on CyberCash, visit their Web site at **http:// www.cybercash.com/**.

DigiCash

DigiCash operates a debit system that is similar to an electronic checking account. To set up a DigiCash account, you deposit money in a bank that supports the DigiCash system, and you are issued Ecash that can be used to purchase things through the Web.

But DigiCash has a philosophy that is much different than CyberCash's. DigiCash sees records as a threat to privacy, and has developed a method to create completely untraceable, anonymous digital cash. Without anonymity, they say, electronic transactions leave a detailed trail of activity that could enable governments, personal enemies, or commercial marketers to easily trace an individual's activities, preferences, and beliefs.

DigiCash, based in the Netherlands, has created electronic tokens that can be trusted as valid money regardless of who is spending them. An ingenious double-blind encryption method makes it impossible to trace transactions unless there is mathematical proof that fraud has occurred.

But the idea of total anonymity has scared off most bankers and has government officials worried as well. Total anonymity, they fear, could provide a haven for money launderers, arms dealers, and kidnappers.

For more info on DigiCash, check them out on the Web at **http:// digicash.support.nl/**.

Tip

For more information on digital money and the companies making it happen, check out the Yahoo index on the topic at **http://www.yahoo.com/ Business_and_Economy/Electronic_Commerce/Digital_Money/**.

Credit Card Transactions

If you're concerned about security risks when using your credit card over the Web, then you also should be concerned about giving out any personal information through a Web page. But then again, maybe you shouldn't buy raffle tickets from the neighborhood kids, either. Who knows what people will do with your personal information?

Using your credit card anywhere poses risks. Those risks are certainly more complex in the realm of Internet servers, browsers, and complex multifunctional systems. Secure communications does not eliminate all of an Internet user's concerns. The situation is analogous to telling someone your credit card number over the telephone. You may be secure in knowing that no one has overheard your conversation (privacy) and that the person on the line works for the company you wish to buy from (authentication), but you must also be willing to trust the person and the company.

That being said, let's look at a few of the schemes that are surfacing on the Web that claim to make using your credit card online as secure as (or even more secure than) using it at your local supermarket.

Netscape's Secure Courier

Netscape's Secure Courier protocol builds on their existing Secure Sockets Layer (SSL) protocol. Secure Courier observes the MasterCard and Visa security specification for bank card purchases on open networks.

While SSL encrypts data passing along the network between a client system and a server, Secure Courier keeps a transaction encrypted in a *secure digital envelope* when it arrives at a merchant's server or at other intermediate points on the Net. This means that the data remains *wrapped*, or protected, at any site at which it stops.

To find out more, connect to Netscape's Web page for the Secure Courier protocol at **http://home.netscape.com/newsref/std/credit.html**.

First Virtual

First Virtual Corporation is an online transaction handling company that operates a system that is designed for selling downloadable products, such as executable software files and information in text files. To get an account, you call them and give them your credit card information, and they issue you a First Virtual account number.

Whenever your First Virtual account number is used to purchase something online, you are notified by e-mail, and you must confirm the transaction before your credit card is charged. Once you verify, your card is charged for the purchase and the money is deposited in the vendor's First Virtual checking account.

The First Virtual method needs no software or hardware on either end of the transaction. It's designed to be simple, fast, and efficient.

For more detailed information, go to **http://www.fv.com/** on the Web.

VeriSign

VeriSign, a spin-off of RSA, Inc., is collaborating with Netscape to provide Digital IDs (digital certificates) for direct online transactions through the Netscape Commerce Server and Netscape Navigator version 2.0. The following four classes of ID are available:

- *Class 1*—Low level of assurance, to be used for secure e-mail and casual browsing. Non-commercial and evaluation versions are offered for free, with a VeriSign-supported commercial version for $6 per year.

- *Class 2*—Provides a higher degree of trust and security. Used for access to advanced Web sites. $12 per year.

- *Class 3*—A higher level of assurance for valued purchases and intercompany communications. $24 per year.

- *Class 4*—Said to provide "a maximum level of identity assurance" for high-end financial transactions and trades. Pricing is by quote.

The Digital ID system from VeriSign is being marketed as "The Driver's License for the Internet." RSA has the good fortune to own the patents on the encryption schemes used by SSL and SHTTP, so this gives the VeriSign system a boost.

For more info, see **http://www.verisign.com/**.

Open Market

Open Market acts as its own credit card company in a scheme that relies on their own Open-MarketPlace Server. It is unique in that it depends on the end-user having a browser that supports the S-HHTP protocol, not Netscape's SSL protocol. They'll be worth watching, if just to see whether a company other than Netscape can help set security standards on the Web.

You can check out their Web site at **http://www.openmarket.com/**.

Tip

For lots of links relating to credit cards, point Netscape to the Credit Card Network Home Page at **http://ccn-home.html**.

For an excellent detailed discussion of how credit card transactions work on the Web, check out this Netscape page: **http://www.netscape.com/newsref/std/ credit.html**.

The Future of WWW Security

Tip

For a lengthy discussion of current Web security issues, check out **http://www-genome.wi.mit.edu/WWW/faqs/www-security-faq.html**.

With a topic as hot as security, it's about as easy to get an agreement on the question of what's secure as it is to get two politicians to agree on a plan to balance the federal budget.

Though Netscape Corporation is in a powerful position, it's not powerful enough to simply dictate security standards for the World Wide Web. There are a lot of people out there—powerful, influential, and monied people in banking and credit and the government—who simply aren't convinced that Netscape's SSL protocol can protect their important transactions over the Internet.

That's why there are dozens of alternate proposals for security protocols for WWW transactions. Because of Netscape's position in the Web community, it's likely that SSL will be with us well into the future, but you're still likely to start running into some sites that want you to use another protocol. The following pages offer an overview of some of the most likely contenders for real-world implementation as WWW security protocols in the months and years to come.

S-HTTP

S-HTTP (Secure HTTP) has emerged as the major competitor to Netscape's SSL security protocol. In fact, it has gained such a following that most commerce on the Web will be supporting both protocols—including Netscape Navigator!

Developed by EIT, CommerceNet, OpenMarket, and others, S-HHTP extends the Web's standard HTTP data transfer protocol by adding encryption and decryption using paired public-key encryption, support for digital signatures, and message authentication.

Several cryptographic message format standards can be incorporated into S-HTTP clients and servers, including PKCS-7, PEM, and PGP. S-HTTP clients can also communicate with non-secure standard HTTP servers, though without security.

S-HTTP doesn't require (though it does support) client-side public key certificates or public keys, which means that you can initiate spontaneous transactions without having an established public key first.

S-HTTP also provides for simple challenge-response freshness authentication—that is, an "are you really you" and "yes, I'm really me" secure message exchange—to make sure no one is intercepting and changing transmitted messages. It can even consider HTTP's DATE header when determining freshness.

For more information on S-HTTP, visit the following sites: **http://www.eit.com/, http://www.openmarket.com/**, or **http://www.commerce.net/**.

Shen

CERN (the organization in Switzerland that created the World Wide Web) is developing a new high-level secure protocol called Shen. It approaches security by providing for weak authentication with low maintenance and no patent or export restrictions, or strong authentication using public key encryption. Since it's coming from CERN, which has the ear of the whole Web, Shen is bound to become a standard itself, or at least influence the development of other security standards.

For more info on Shen, point Netscape to **http://www.w3.org/hypertext/WWW/Shen/ref/shen.html**.

Fortezza

One of Netscape Corporation's latest security additions is integrated support for the Fortezza security card, which is based on U.S. government standard cryptography. Developed by the National Security Agency, Fortezza is a cryptographic system delivered in a PCMCIA card format, and is now mandatory for use in many government agencies. Fortezza cards are already being used by the Department of Defense and the U.S. intelligence community.

Support for Fortezza has been added to Netscape's Secure Sockets Layer (SSL) open protocol, and Netscape Corp. will be upgrading Netscape Navigator and other Netscape products to support the use of Fortezza cards.

Netscape is currently working with Litronic Industries to further develop the Fortezza cryptographic interface.

Because of its status as a top-secret government security protocol, information on Fortezza is difficult to come by. I know of no site on the Web that offers more than just a terse sentence or two on the subject.

Tip

Security is a hot topic on the Web. A good place to find out more about security online is the Virtual Library Subject Catalogue entry on the topic at **http://info.cern.ch/hypertext/DataSources/bySubject/Overview.html**.

Tip

For more details on Netscape's security technologies, see **http://home.netscape.com/newsref/ref/netscape-security.html**

An excellent source of links to security sites on the Web is at Xenon Laboratories WWW site: **http://www.xe.net/xenon/security.htm**.

## CHAPTER 12

Accessing Other Internet Services with Netscape

The World Wide Web was only created in 1991, and has since experienced explosive growth. However, the Internet was more than 20 years old when the Web was first developed as a graphical, point-and-click interface that would reduce the learning curve associated with navigating it. Finding anything on the Internet then was associated with understanding UNIX, and the tools developed for searching the Internet were only marginally more intuitive than being a systems administrator yourself.

This chapter will discuss some of Netscape's other capabilities besides looking at World Wide Web pages. One of the newest tools for navigating the Internet, Netscape incorporates many of the Internet access techniques that formerly required separate tools. In this chapter, you will learn:

- How to access an FTP site
- How to use Gopher to find information
- How FTP and Gopher are integrated into Netscape
- How to search FTP sites and Gopherspace with comic book characters
- The ancient art of Telnet

Accessing and Downloading from an FTP site

FTP (File Transfer Protocol) lets you examine the directories of remote systems on the Internet, and lets you transfer files between your computer and other computers. Almost as old as the Internet itself, FTP was designed to work with the systems of the time. You can think of FTP as being very much like using the cd and dir commands in DOS to move from one directory to another, and to see what's in that directory only when you get there. FTP lets you transfer both text files and binary files (programs).

Using Netscape for FTP

As a Netscape user, you have FTP incorporated into Netscape so that you really don't notice any difficulty. Netscape displays FTP information as a single column of links, each link being either a file or a directory link. An FTP directory viewed with Netscape looks very similar to the File Manager in Microsoft Windows. Each line of the FTP directory displays a small icon (either a file or a directory), the name of the file, the size of the file, and the date that file was added to the directory. FTP directories may include a README or an INDEX text file, which describes the contents of the directory, or the policies of FTP access for that site.

To reach an FTP server in Netscape, type the URL of the FTP server. If a link to an FTP server is on a Web page, select that link to jump to that FTP server. Netscape 2.0 reduces the effort needed to access an FTP site if the hostname starts with ftp. For example, typing the hostname **ftp.foobar.com** into the location field (without ftp:// before it) takes you to the URL **ftp:// ftp.foobar.com/**. For example, typing **ftp.kli.org** into Netscape's Location field takes you to the FTP archive of the Klingon Language Institute shown in figure 12.1, just as **ftp://ftp.kli.org/** does.

Fig. 12.1
The Klingon Language Institute's FTP server.

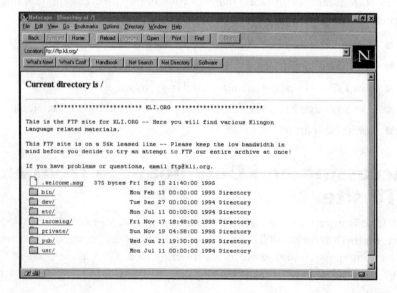

If, for whatever reason, a Web site you are trying to reach has named its Web server as ftp.whatever.com/, you can avoid the new default by specifying the protocol identifier. So typing the URL as **ftp.foobar.com/** or as **ftp://ftp.foobar.com/** starts an FTP session with the FTP server **ftp.foobar.com/**, but typing the URL as **http://ftp.foobar.com/** attempts to retrieve a Web page from the Web server. When you have found the file you want, downloading from an FTP archive with Netscape is as simple as selecting the appropriate link, and the file is transferred to your local system.

Tip

FTP directories and subdirectories almost always have a link at the top of the page named "Up to higher level directory." Clicking this link takes you one step higher in that FTP site's directory hierarchy—not back one Web page as the Back button in Netscape does.

Most FTP servers are set up to allow anonymous access—meaning that you do not need a login and password account set up specifically for that server. Typically, an anonymous FTP server accepts "anonymous" as the login, and your e-mail address as your password. Netscape is designed to try to log in anonymously when it encounters an FTP server.

Note

Because Netscape tries to log in anonymously, you need to have your electronic mail preferences set up in the Mail and News window of Netscape's Options window before you try. Most anonymous FTP servers request that you use your e-mail address as your password.

Using Netscape to FTP Non-Anonymously

In some instances, you have a username and password for a network, and need to log in to that network and download files. Netscape does support FTP access with a username and password. To start a non-anonymous FTP session with Netscape, add your username and the at (@) symbol before the FTP server's hostname. For example, if you had access to the servers at startup.com, and the FTP server's name started with ftp, you would type the following URL into the Location field at the top of the Netscape window:

ftp://username@ftp.startup.com/

II

Mastering Netscape

The next window Netscape displays is a prompt asking for your password. After you type in your password, you are logged into the FTP server, and may start downloading files.

There are some drawbacks to using Netscape for FTP. First, Netscape can require substantial amounts of RAM and system resources, especially if you have a large cache or several helper applications configured. If you have a lower-end system, you may encounter problems such as running short of available RAM. Second, Netscape does not allow you to send files via FTP, anonymously or not. The only way to send a file or document using Netscape is to send electronic mail, with the file attached to the mail. If you use FTP extensively, you may want to consider a separate FTP application. A stand-alone FTP application, such as WS_FTP, uses less memory than Netscape, lets you send FTP files as well as receive, and can be configured to retain the password for non-anonymous FTP sessions.

Archie: How to Search for Files to Remotely Transfer

The original problem with FTP was that, while FTP let you transfer a file from a remote computer system, you had to go to that remote directory with FTP first and find what you wanted. If the person administering the FTP server had not included an index text file describing the files in the directory, you had to guess if the file name you were reading was the one you wanted.

Archie was designed to create a centralized indexed list of files that are available on anonymous FTP sites. The Archie database, which as of this writing indexes over 1,000 anonymous servers and an aggregate of 2.4 million files, is mirrored at several locations around the world to reduce the load on individual systems. Over 50,000 queries are made to Archie databases every day. Many of the Archie servers now support inquiries using the Web forms capability discussed earlier in this chapter. Archie is accessible in three ways:

- Netscape
- Archie-specific client software
- Telnet

The Telnet protocol will be discussed later in this chapter. Archie clients are available for almost every platform, and may be found with the Web interfaces to the Archie database. To use Netscape to conduct Archie searches, use the URL **http://pubweb.nexor.co.uk/ archie.html** (see fig. 12.2).

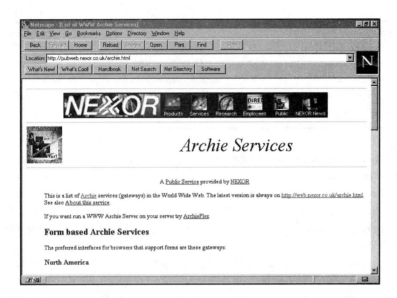

Fig. 12.2
The central index
of Archie servers
on the World
Wide Web.

This Web page presents you with links to many of the mirror sites of the
Archie database. One Archie server you can use is located at **http://
www.lerc.nasa.gov/archieplex/doc/form.html**, which gives you the
form shown in figure 12.3.

Fig. 12.3
The Archie form
for searching FTP
servers, as
provided by the
NASA Lewis
Research Center.

Mastering Netscape

Note

Whenever you are presented with a choice of multiple sites to connect to, it is polite to try the one closest to you first. International connections are often heavily loaded, and you may get a faster response from a host computer on the same continent that you are. However, if closer hosts don't respond, try the other hosts from the menu.

You may choose many ways to customize your Archie search. The default setting for matching your entry is a case-insensitive substring match, but you may choose other options from the drop-down list box. The results of your search may be given to you sorted by host or by date of the files, and you may choose a specific server from the next list box, or enter a domain in the field below that list box to restrict the search to only part of the world. To speed up your reply, you can reduce the number of answers. This is helpful if you have a good idea of what you're looking for. For example, if you know the exact name of the file you want, you probably don't need to receive the location of more than the first ten or so files matching that exact file name.

You can also set the "niceness" of your Archie search, from "Nicest" to "Not Nice at All." Niceness is a priority tag that determines how fast your Archie query is processed. If you are just about to leave for your lunch break, be considerate of other people and set your query as lower priority than normal ("Nice"), because you don't need your query answered immediately.

Gopher: Burrowing Through the Internet

Gopherspace is a common way to refer to the interlinked set of Gopher menus. Gopherspace, with its individually designed menus and no unifying taxonomy, but with frequent links from one Gopher menu to others, is generally considered to be the forerunner to the World Wide Web.

Gopherspace lacks some of the most visible features of the Web. Firstly, Gopher is text-based only, so there are no cool pictures, no odd little images usable as buttons or dividing rules on pages, and no large images used as menus. Second, Gopher servers don't know how to accept anything back from the Gopher client program you are running on your computer, so Gopherspace is one-way only. With no CGI-BIN support, nothing like a Webform for shopping or surveys exist in Gopherspace. With no e-mail capability, there are no hypertext links for sending e-mail with a single click. If you want to interact with someone or some site in Gopherspace, you will need to send e-mail or use the telephone.

However, Gopherspace has some strong points. The World Wide Web didn't exist five years ago, so anybody who wanted to set up a Web-like access before 1991 that didn't require the user to have a thorough understanding of UNIX had to use Gopher.

For you, the Netscape user, the biggest advantage Gopherspace has is that you don't have to do anything special. Netscape has full Gopher capability integrated into the point-and-click graphical interface of Netscape. A Gopher page appears to be a plain, but ordinary, Netscape page (see fig. 12.4).

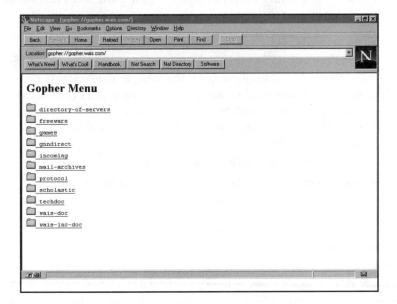

Fig. 12.4
A Gopher page viewed with Netscape.

Netscape displays a Gopher page as a single column of text links. Each entry in a Gopher menu consists of a small icon indicating the type of the file, and a description of the file. One major distinction between FTP directories and Gopher menus is that Gopher descriptions are typically in plain text, whereas FTP directories look like a directory listing from an operating system.

Some of the common Gopher link types you might see are:

- Menu—Another Gopher menu or directory
- Text—A text file
- Binary—An application (transferred via FTP if you select it)

- Telnet—Starts a Telnet session
- Search—Starts a simple Gopher search

A full list of Gopher document types is presented in table 12.1, in the section "How to Ask Veronica a Question: Search Strategies."

Veronica: a Gopher Search Tool

Gopherspace is too large to search randomly. In addition to the fact that Gopher has been around for several years longer than the World Wide Web, every Gopher menu was organized by the individual who created it, and there are no particular standards for organizing menus. "Tunneling through Gopherspace" may be almost as much fun as surfing the Web, but you are likely to take longer to find what you're looking for if you don't take advantage of some additional tools.

Note

The name Veronica is a crowning example of Silly Acronym Syndrome (SAS). Just as the UNIX variant GNU means GNU's Not UNIX, and the name of the e-mail reader pine is an acronym meaning Pine Is Not Elm, Veronica's creators were inspired to create a somehow-meaningful acronym around the name of one of Archie's cartoon girlfriends. Officially, Veronica means:

Very **E**asy **R**odent-**O**riented **N**et-wide **I**ndex to **C**omputerized **A**rchives.

You be the judge of whether you believe the words, or the acronym, came first.

Remember how Archie searches directories and file names available on anonymous FTP servers? Veronica is like Archie, but Veronica searches Gopher servers. While Archie is a good search tool to use if you know the exact file name you are looking for, Veronica can find items where Archie can't. Veronica's success derives from the fact that, while Gopher menus may be descriptive names, FTP shows just the file and directory names. For example, giving Veronica the words "martial arts pictures" may find you a GIF of Bruce Lee. On the other hand, Archie won't find the same picture of Bruce Lee unless you ask Archie to search for GAM_DTH2.GIF. If you don't know exactly what you're looking for, but have a good idea of what kind of thing you're looking for, Veronica is probably better than Archie.

Using Veronica is simple. After you get to a Veronica server from a Gopher server, you can enter keywords to search for. Veronica searches its index of Gopherspace looking for matches to your keywords. When Veronica's done, you receive a Gopher menu consisting of all the matches to your search.

> **Note**
>
> A Veronica menu of Gopher items is the same as an Archie page of FTP files and directories: you may not get the same result twice. If you run a Veronica search today and then again tomorrow, new files may have been made available by tomorrow, old files may have been removed, whole servers may be offline (or back online) tomorrow, and so on. The Veronica page you get today is an answer to your question today; the exact details of the answer may change tomorrow.

The following steps demonstrate a search from the home Gopher site at the University of Minnesota:

1. Once you have your Internet connection up and Netscape is running, enter the URL **gopher.micro.umn.edu** to jump to the University of Minnesota's Gopher server, as shown in figure 12.5.

> **Note**
>
> Remember that Netscape 2.0 allows you to skip entering the gopher:// portion of the URL if you are jumping to a Gopher server whose hostname starts with gopher.

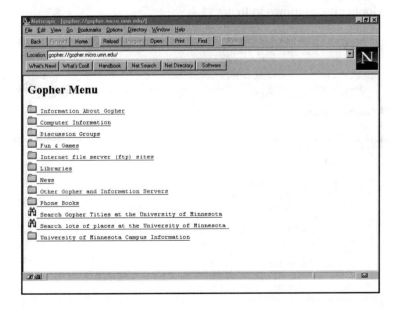

Fig. 12.5
The home of Gopher.

2. Select the Other Gopher and Information Servers item and the Gopher menu displayed in figure 12.6 appears.

Fig. 12.6

Other Gopher and Information Servers menu.

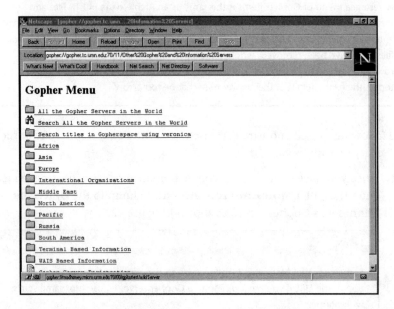

3. Select the Search Titles in Gopherspace Using Veronica item to see the Gopher menu shown in figure 12.7.

Fig. 12.7

Several Veronica servers.

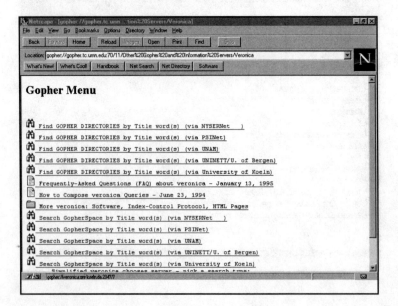

You should notice the two text file items in the middle of figure 12.7. The Frequently-Asked Questions (FAQ) about Veronica and How to Compose Veronica Queries text files can provide additional information on this search tool.

4. Select the Search Gopherspace by Title words (via PSInet) item to retrieve an Index Search dialog box as shown in figure 12.8.

5. Place the cursor in the text entry field and type anything you like. You may get a message that looks like Too many connections, please try again soon, or some variation. If you get this response, try another Veronica server, or just try again in a minute or two. Some servers may be busy at different times of the day or week.

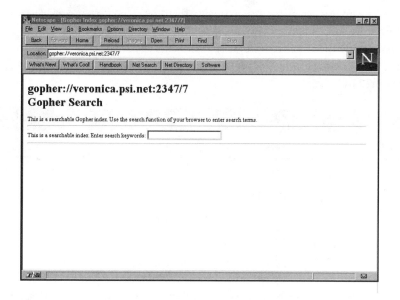

Fig. 12.8
A Veronica search input page.

Mastering Netscape

How to Ask Veronica a Question: Search Strategies

Veronica, like a hammer, extends your ability. A hammer lets you put nails into wood. However, a hammer also lets you hit your other hand (the one holding the nail) REALLY hard if you miss. Like any tool, Veronica can be used correctly or incorrectly. Because Veronica servers are always busy, search results can take time. If your search criteria are too narrow or just not quite right, you can eliminate the material you are looking for. If your search criteria are too wide, you can get a huge result (huge searches take even longer) that is not much better than tunneling through Gopherspace until you found the right file yourself. (What's the right file? The one you think fits the answer.) Here is some advice on how to ask Veronica the right question.

Remember that Gopher servers are set up individually—sometimes very individually. You can be creative in your search keywords as long as you are creative in the way others might have been creative before. You can use multiple words to quickly narrow your search. Veronica supports the Boolean operators NOT, AND, and OR. For example, the search TELEVISION AND DRAMA NOT DAYTIME gives you Gopher items for evening drama television shows, but TELEVISION AND DRAMA increases the size of the search result to include all Gopher items relating to daytime soap operas.

You can use an asterisk (*) as a wild card at the ends of words. A Veronica search for the keyword "director*" returns Gopher items for director, directory, directories, directorate, and so on.

A useful way to narrow your search is by file type. To narrow your search to return only results of a specific file type, add -t# to your Veronica search keywords, where the number sign (#) is a character representing a Gopher file type. The official Gopher document types and their signifying characters are presented in table 12.1.

Table 12.1   Official Gopher Document Types

Type Value	Description
0	Text file
1	Directory
2	CSO name server—read as text or HTML
3	An error of some sort
4	.HQX (also called binhex, a Macintosh compression format)
5	PC binary (an uncompressed application)
6	UUEncoded file (a UNIX compression format)
7	Full text index (a Gopher menu)
8	Telnet session—if you have a Telnet application configured, it will launch
9	binary file
s	Sound (an audio file)
I	Image (any format that's not GIF)
T	TN3270 session—if you have a TN3270 application (a fancy Telnet) configured, it will launch
g	GIF image

Type Value	Description
;	MPEG (a video file)
h	HTML (HyperText Markup Language)—a Web URL (Universal Resource Locator)
H	HTML URL Capitalized
i	Information (text) that is not selectable (like a comment line in a program)
w	A World Wide Web address
e	Event (not supported by Netscape)
m or M	Unspecified MIME (multi-part or mixed message)

For example, if you want to find Web pages on paleobotanical research in Turkey, you could use the Veronica search string `paleobotany AND Turkey -th`. If you know the Bruce Lee movie photo mentioned earlier was in GIF format, you could search for it using `bruce AND lee -tg`.

Jughead: Another Gopherspace Search Engine

Another Gopherspace search tool is Jughead, which was written by Rhett "Jonzy" Jones at the University of Utah. In keeping with the Archie comics motif for Internet search engine names, the acronym came first, and the name Jughead was justified as

Jonzy's **U**niversal **G**opher **H**ierarchy **E**xcavation **A**nd **D**isplay

Like Veronica, Jughead is a Gopherspace search engine. However, Veronica searches widely, over all of Gopherspace. Jughead is most commonly configured to search only the one Gopher server it is installed on, but Jughead can search that one Gopher server very thoroughly.

Jughead: If It's There, Use It

System administrators rarely bother to install Jughead on a Gopher server with a small file collection. If you find a Jughead search engine on a specific Gopher server, it's because someone thought it was better to install Jughead than to do without it.

For an example of how Jughead works, go to North Carolina State University's library Gopher server at **gopher://dewey.lib.ncsu.edu:300/7**. The Jughead search index of NCSU's library is shown in figure 12.9. Because the server's hostname does not start with gopher, you have to type the gopher:// portion of the URL.

Fig. 12.9
North Carolina
State University's
Jughead search
index.

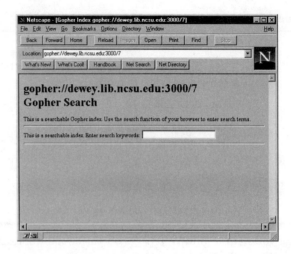

Entering search text into the field and pressing the Enter key gives you a Go-pher menu made up of all matching items in the site that the Jughead server indexes.

How to Ask Jughead a Question

Jughead accepts the same kind of Boolean search requests Veronica does, but Jughead has some special commands. The generic form for these commands is a question mark followed by the command (no spaces between the question mark and the command), followed by the string of characters to search for.

The special Jughead commands are as follows:

Command	Result
?all string	Returns all matches to the string
?help string	Returns the Jughead help document, as well as any matches for the string
?limit=x string	Returns up to x matches for the string
?range=x1-x2 string	Returns the matches between x1 and x2.

The ?range command is useful if the string matches a very large number of Gopher files.

> **Note**
>
> You can use only one special command per query. However, you can limit your Jughead queries to improve the response time. (It's also polite; other people may want to use that server, and asking Jughead for all matches to "IBM" may be a waste of processor time if the item you want turns out to be the third one returned.)

Jughead also restricts special characters for its own use. Almost all of the standard special characters are treated as a space. These special characters are:

!"#$%&'()+,-.?/\[@]{^}'~

This entire line is read as twenty-four spaces. Jughead treats a space as a Boolean AND, so it's probably best to use letters and numerals only in your search string.

Accessing a Telnet Site

Telnet is an ancient (as old as the Internet) way to access services on the Internet. When people speak of the Internet, they are generally referring to those computers that are on and connected to the Internet all the time.

> **Note**
>
> If you have a SLIP or PPP dial-up connection, your computer has an IP (Internet Protocol) address and is "part of the Internet." However, this only lasts as long as the connection. Generally, you need to have at least a leased-line connection before you can consider your local system as part of the Internet.

Telnet, like the World Wide Web, works because all the computers of the Internet are on and connected all the time, barring system crashes, backhoes accidentally cutting the T1 cable, and other things system administrators don't really like to think about.

You can think of Telnet as making your computer a dumb terminal for the system you are "telnetting" to. A dumb terminal was called such because it was only a keyboard and screen, directly wired into the host computer. Dumb terminals are called dumb because they have no processor inside. Terminals were manufactured in standard designs so they would be compatible with many different computers. A common type of terminal was the VT series manufactured by Digital Equipment Corporation. VT terminals came in several models (VT100, VT 102, VT220, and so on). Your personal computer is enormously more powerful than a VT100 terminal, so a Telnet terminal emulator acts like a terminal in order to let your computer communicate with computers that are set up to connect to VT100 terminals. In other words, every time you run Telnet, you are reducing your high-end state-of-the-art personal computer to the level of a keyboard and screen.

What you get for lobotomizing your great workstation is the ability to connect to many computer systems that, in some cases, don't have any other connectivity available. Also, because Telnet is the lowest common denominator of computer power, almost everyone can participate. Windows 95 and Windows NT include Telnet applications in the Windows folder.

You can configure Netscape to launch a Telnet application as a supporting application. Telnet applications are available from Netscape's Helper Applications Web page at URL **http://home.netscape.com/assist/ helper_apps/index.html**. To use these applications with Netscape, you need to download and uncompress the files, then configure the application as a helper application in the General window of the Options menu. You can find information on how to configure helper applications for Netscape in Part III, "Using Helper Applications," of this book.

Note

One specific Telnet application is Wintel, NCSA's Telnet application for Windows. Wintel is available through Netscape's Helper Applications Web page as listed earlier, or it may be downloaded directly from the FTP site **ftp://gatekeeper.dec.com/ pub/micro/msdos/win3/winsock/wintelb3.zip**.

Remember that, because the FTP site does not start with ftp, you have to type the URL type (ftp://) before the hostname.

If you have Windows 95 or Windows NT installed on your machine, you already have a Telnet application installed in C:\WINDOWS\ folder as TELNET.EXE.

Because Telnet and Gopher are both early Internet tools, many Telnet sites are most easily found through Gopher menus. For example, use Netscape to view the Gopher menu at URL **gopher://gopher.micro.umn.edu**, as you did earlier in this chapter. The Gopher menu shown in figure 12.5 is displayed. As you did earlier, choose the Other Gopher and Information Servers item and the Gopher menu displayed in figure 12.10 appears. Choose the Terminal Based Information from the bottom of the Gopher menu.

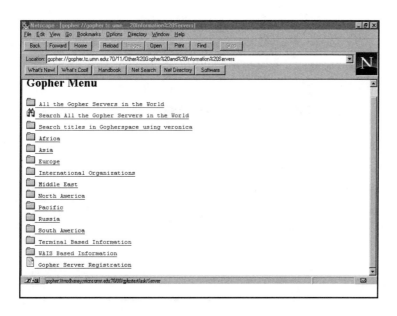

Fig. 12.10
The Terminal
Based Information
Gopher menu
item leads to a
menu of Telnet
applications.

When you choose the Terminal Based Information item, a Gopher menu appears as shown in figure 12.11.

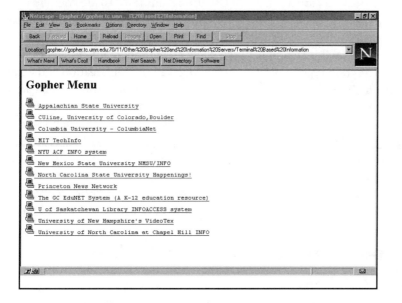

Fig. 12.11
Netscape displays
Telnet session
links in Gopher
menus as small
terminals.

Select the Telnet connection for Appalachian State University. If you have Netscape configured correctly, your Telnet supporting application launches, and the informational message Log in as 'info' appears before the Telnet

II

Mastering Netscape

window displays. When you see the "Enter username" prompt appear in the Telnet window, type **INFO** as your username. The main menu for Appalachian State University's information distribution server will appear, as shown in figure 12.12.

Fig. 12.12

A Telnet session with Appalachian State University.

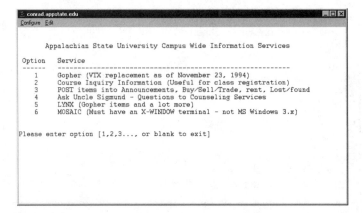

```
conrad.appstate.edu                                          _ □ ×
Configure  Edit

         Appalachian State University Campus Wide Information Services

 Option   Service
 ------   ------------------------------------------------------------
    1     Gopher (VTX replacement as of November 23, 1994)
    2     Course Inquiry Information (Useful for class registration)
    3     POST items into Announcements, Buy/Sell/Trade, rent, Lost/found
    4     Ask Uncle Sigmund - Questions to Counseling Services
    5     LYNX (Gopher items and a lot more)
    6     MOSAIC (Must have an X-WINDOW terminal - not MS Windows 3.x)


 Please enter option [1,2,3..., or blank to exit]
```

Appalachian State University provides a great deal of information to its students via its Telnet host computers. However, not all Telnet sessions are used for information gathering. Multi-User Dungeons (MUDs) are computer programs that people can explore by adopting a character and typing commands for the character to move, talk, and do other things. MUDs are commonly used for social interaction between people. There are many different types of MUDs, both in types of programming involved in their creation and extension, and in the types of interaction typically occurring. Some MUDs are socially oriented chat discussion, some are fantasy role-playing in nature, and others are oriented to foreign language practice. While Telnet applications may be used for MUDs, many of the various types of MUDs have specific client applications that were created to optimize some aspects of performance on a given type of MUD. For more information on multi-user games, see Yahoo's directory of multi-user games at **http://www.yahoo.com/ Recreation/Games/Internet_Games/MUDs_MUSHes__MOOs_etc_/**.

Troubleshooting Connection Problems

Sometimes you do not get where you want to go on the Internet. A site may be down, or a connection may have exactly too much interference in the lines to connect. A Web page you looked at yesterday may be deleted or moved today. This last section of the chapter offers some advice to improve your ability to get where you want to go.

Any address embedded in a link may be entered directly in the Locations field of your Netscape application. If the Web link is not the full link text, you can always see the link by moving your cursor over the link and not clicking the link. The full link description can be seen in the bottom edge of your Netscape window.

Normally, if the full URL (example: **http://www.yahoo.com/Recreation/**) has a slash at the end indicating the last part of the URL is a directory, Netscape adds the slash for you as it loads the default page there. If Netscape gives you an error Not Found, your first action should be to select the Reload command (either from the View menu, or the Reload button to the right of the Home button on the Netscape toolbar).

> **Note**
>
> An immediate Reload is not just an impatient, "Why won't this thing do what I want?" behavior, it's often the solution. Small errors happen all the time, and reloading may work more often than you think. Reloading is an especially good idea if images on a page are downloading badly and Netscape displays a "broken picture" image where the picture should have been.
>
> Reloading is exactly the right answer if you get a Too busy, try again later message when attempting to start an FTP or Gopher session. Gopher and FTP servers are often busy, and trying again is the same as redialing a telephone after you get a busy signal.

Your second attempt (if you were using a link from another page) is to look at the destination link displayed in the Location field between the two rows of buttons in the toolbar, and see what it looks like. Leaving the closing end off an anchor causes the rest of the page—from the beginning of the anchor, including the text label (if it was one), the image (if you used an image as the visible part of the link), and everything else to the end of the page—to become part of the destination address. If the location looks like a URL followed by words or file names, select the part of the address that doesn't look like a URL, and delete it. Try again.

Similarly, if you are typing in the address yourself, proofread the destination address. Fix any problems you see such as spaces accidentally inserted into the middle of the URL or capitalization errors, then select the Reload command. I recently encountered a non-functional link in a large Web site discussing HTML authoring. The Web page builder had typed /hyperext/ in the directory path where he meant to type /hypertext/. If a reload of the page doesn't work, or if you saw no problems with the URL, retype the URL, and

II

Mastering Netscape

try again anyway. If you got the URL from e-mail or an article you have electronically, try to copy the URL from where it is and paste it into the Location field in order to reduce interference from typing errors.

## CHAPTER 13

E-mail with Netscape

Netscape started life as a dedicated Web browser, and there's never been a doubt that it's a superior piece of software for that purpose. Netscape has also bent over backwards, for the most part successfully, to make other Internet services like FTP and Gopher accessible from Netscape.

But in one key area—e-mail—Netscape fell short. Early, 1.x versions of Netscape provided only the most rudimentary capability to access the Internet's most popular service. Users could only send mail with Netscape; they couldn't receive it. Needless to say, the designers of dedicated e-mail managers didn't find Netscape a threat to their business.

This is changing fast. In a bid to make its flagship program a full-service Internet client, Netscape has given version 2.0 a powerful mail manager that many users—particularly those at home—may find suits their needs.

In this chapter, you learn how to:

- Configure Netscape 2.0's e-mail servers and preferences
- Send and receive mail
- Organize your mail using folders
- Create an address book to speed your correspondence

Netscape's New E-mail Manager

In their first attempt to make their Web browser a full-service Internet client, Netscape's programmers have done a pretty fair job. The new e-mail manager provides most of the functionality that veteran Net users have come to expect from their software. It also offers a couple of very useful, Netscape-only twists.

The feature that, above all others, sets Netscape's mail package apart from its established competitors is the fact that it treats incoming messages basically as HTML documents. The mail reader is able to detect any URL mentioned in the text of a message and highlight it for one-click access by the user. Your mail becomes a separate, hotlinked gateway to the World Wide Web and the rest of the Internet.

Netscape doesn't stint on the standard stuff, either. You've always been able to use it to write and send messages, but now you'll find that you can easily reply to, forward, and carbon copy messages, just as users of third-party mail packages can. Message management is a snap because you have the ability to transfer your traffic to a set of custom, user-defined mail folders. Within those folders, you can tell Netscape to sort your mail by subject, sender, or date. You can also keep and maintain a list of your most frequently used addresses.

If you're a casual e-mail user, you'll likely find that Netscape's new built-in mail capabilities are all you need. And if it's important that you have the ability to tap into the Web directly from your message traffic, you'll find Netscape's mail manager indispensable.

But if you're accustomed to using other mail packages, programs like Eudora and cc:Mail, you'll soon see that Netscape's package isn't quite complete. Although some rough edges present in the Address Book and file attachment features of Netscape's early betas have been smoothed over, power users will miss high-end features like automatic message filtering.

All in all, if you're happy with your current mail program, you'll have to make the call as to whether you want to switch to Netscape just yet. You'd be well-advised, however, to watch carefully as it evolves in the future. It's quite clear that Netscape is serious about making its leading program the only Internet client most people will ever need.

But if you're a new mail user, or if you haven't found a package quite to your liking just yet, you'll probably want to give Netscape's e-mail facility a try. You may find that it meets your needs completely.

Setting Mail Preferences

Before attempting to use Netscape's mail facility, you must provide some basic information about yourself, your Internet provider, and your computer. Begin by choosing Options, and then select Mail and News Preferences. Netscape responds with a tabbed dialog box.

The best way to familiarize yourself with Netscape's mail settings is to step through each of the five tabs sequentially as you set up the program for the first time.

Appearance

The options on this tab, seen in figure 13.1, affect the way Netscape displays message text. Under Messages and Articles Are Shown With, your choice tells Netscape whether to use a fixed-width or variable-width font when it displays the text of your mail. The default is Fixed Width Font; in most cases you'll want to stick to that setting because Variable Width Font can ruin the formatting of many Internet messages. The settings under Text Beginning With > (Quoted Text) Has the Following Characteristics affects the display of message excerpts included in a mailing to establish its subject and context. They're largely self-explanatory; change them to suit your taste.

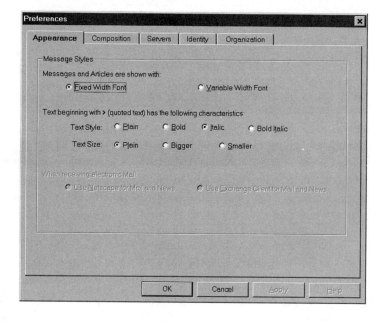

Fig. 13.1
The settings on the Appearance tab give the user control over the fonts Netscape uses to display the text of mail messages.

The remaining buttons on this tab, found under heading When Receiving Electronic Mail, tell Netscape whether to use its own built-in e-mail capabilities or those provided with every copy of Windows 95 by Microsoft Exchange. If you want to use Netscape's, click Use Netscape for Mail and News.

Composition

There are several key settings on this tab, seen in figure 13.2:

- The Send and Post setting determines how file attachments are coded. Allow 8-bit is the default and is recognized by most mail programs.

- The Deliver Mail setting tells Netscape whether you want to send each message when you're done writing it, or to hold it on disk. Choosing Automatically tells Netscape to send when you're done writing; Queue for Manual Delivery holds your message.

II

Mastering Netscape

Fig. 13.2

The Composition tab controls key settings for file encoding and message queuing.

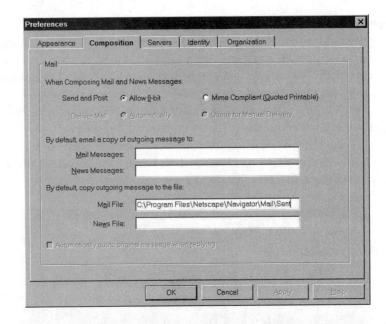

> **Tip**
>
> You'll probably want to queue your messages on disk if you do most of your work offline, as a dial-in Internet user. Send them by clicking File and choosing Deliver Mail Now.

- You can have Netscape send a copy of all your outgoing messages to a single address by entering that address in the Mail Messages field.

- The entry in the Mail File field tells Netscape where to store copies of your outgoing messages on disk. This is a key setting; in the following discussion of the Directories tab, we'll tell you how to avoid problems by reconciling it with that tab's Mail Directory field. If you don't care to keep copies of your outgoing traffic, you can avoid problems entirely by leaving this field blank.

- Checking Automatically Quote Original Message When Replying tells Netscape to insert the text of any message you answered with the Message menu's Reply option into the body of your answer.

Servers

This tab is probably the most important of the five on the Mail and News Preferences dialog box. On this tab, seen in figure 13.3, you tell Netscape how to get to your mail.

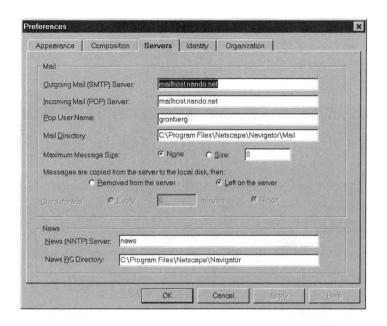

Fig. 13.3
Many of the controls that affect your use of Netscape's e-mail features are on the Mail and News dialog box. Here we're using it to enter information about our mail server.

Do the following:

1. Type the Internet addresses for your service provider's SMTP (send mail) and POP3 (receive mail) clients in the Mail (SMTP) Server and Mail POP Server fields, which are near the top of the tab. Get this information from your service provider if you don't already have it.

2. Type your e-mail name (in all likelihood, the one you use when you log into your Internet provider) in the Pop User Name box.

3. You should make sure Netscape's setup routine has provided access to the directory where your mail folders are stored by looking in the Mail Directory field. There should be some entry like C:\Program Files\ Netscape\Navigator\Mail, as seen in figure 13.3. The actual listing will vary depending on your Netscape setup.

4. If there's no path in the Mail Directory field, or you have reason to believe the path is incorrect, open Explorer, find the folder Netscape's installed in, and then find the Mail subfolder. Note the Windows 95 path, go back into Netscape, and type the path into the Mail Directory field.

Tip

You can use the Mail Directory field to tell Netscape to store your mail in any Windows 95 folder you want. Simply type its path in place of the one provided by Netscape.

II

Mastering Netscape

5. Click the Composition tab. Look in the Mail File field, near the bottom of the tab. The Windows 95 path listed there should match that in the Mail Directory field, with the addition of the characters, \Sent (see fig. 13.4). Netscape stores a copy of your outgoing messages in this file.

Fig. 13.4
Make sure the Composition tab's Mail File field refers to the same path as the Directories tab's Mail Directory field.

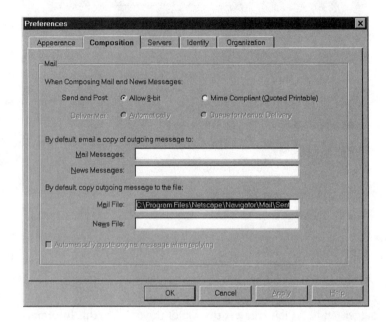

6. If it doesn't match, type the path in yourself. For example, if your Mail Directory is C:\Program Files\Netscape\Navigator\Mail, type **C:\ Program Files\Netscape\Navigator\Mail\Sent** in the Mail File field.

Troubleshooting

When I try to send mail, Netscape responds with an error message that says Can't open FCC file. *I've searched the Netscape directories and the rest of my hard drive and can't find an FCC file. Should I create one?*

No. This cryptic message is Netscape's way of telling you that the Composition tab's Mail File field isn't referring to the same Windows 95 path as your Mail Directory field. The Sent file has to be located in the same folder as the rest of your mail files.

This problem originally cropped up because the installation routines for the early betas of Netscape 2.0 wouldn't update the Mail File field when asked to install the program to any folder other than their default settings.

There are three ways to fix the resulting mess. Check the Mail Directory field, and then enter this path in the Mail File field, tagging the characters "\Sent" on the end. Alternatively, open Windows 95's Registry Editor and, using its search facility, find the phrase "Default FCC." It'll turn up among the HKEY_CURRENT_USER settings, as in figure 13.5. Click Edit, choose Modify, and enter the proper path in the field provided.

Your remaining option, if you don't consider it important to keep copies of your outgoing messages, is to leave the Composition tab's Mail File field blank. If you do, Netscape won't save any copies, but it won't pop up an error message either.

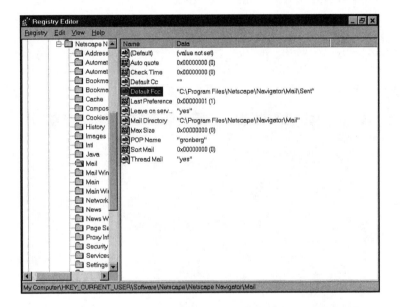

Fig. 13.5
You can use Windows 95's Registry Editor to reconcile the Mail Directory and Mail File fields. The path to the Sent file listed beside Default FCC should match the path beside Mail Directory.

II

Mastering Netscape

7. After you're comfortable with Netscape's mail features, you'll likely want to click the Removed from the Server button so old mail doesn't clutter your Internet provider's disk.

Identity

Netscape personalizes your outgoing messages by adding bits from the settings on this tab. You'll want to do the following:

1. Type your real name in the Your Name field.

2. Type your e-mail address in the Your Email field.

3. If you want replies to your outgoing messages sent to an address other than the one listed in Your Email, type it in the Reply-to Address field.

4. Fill in Your Organization if you want the name of your employer or the group you represent to appear on your mail.

5. If you want Netscape to append a signature file to your outgoing messages, use the Browse key next to Signature File on the Identity tab to search for and select a signature file from your hard drive. Your signature must be an ASCII text file. It should be hard-formatted and less than 80 characters wide. Internet etiquette would also suggest that you keep it short.

6. If you're concerned about retaining your privacy on the Internet, click either the Nothing: Anonymous User or A Unique ID Number button at the bottom of the tab. In most cases, however, you'll want your messages identified with Your Email Address.

Organization

The threading and sorting features of Netscape's mail manager are fully controllable from the mail window, but the program does allow you to designate their default settings. They're available on the Organization tab, seen in figure 13.6.

Fig. 13.6
The settings on the Organization tab tell Netscape how to sort and thread your message traffic.

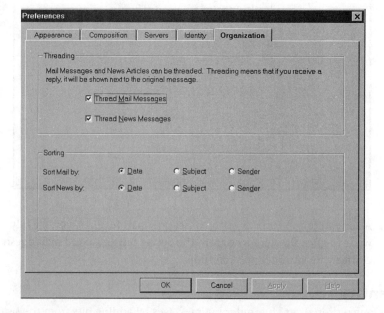

■ If you think you'll want your message traffic threaded (that is, with messages and replies on the same topic grouped together for easy reading), click the Organization tab and make sure the Thread Mail Messages box is checked.

■ You may also want to change the default sort order for your incoming message traffic. If so, click the Organization tab and choose one of the Sort Mail By selections. The available sort options are by Date, Subject, and Sender.

II

Mastering Netscape

> **Tip**
>
> For now at least, ignore the fields and buttons that control Netscape's newsreader functions. Read about them in chapter 15, "Reading UseNet Newsgroups with Netscape."

When you're satisfied with the changes you've made to the various tabs on the Mail and News Preferences dialog box, click OK to save your work. Clicking Cancel abandons it.

Using the Mail Package

At first glance, Netscape 2.0 appears no more a sophisticated mail package than its predecessors. The picture begins to change, though, when you click the Window menu and select Netscape Mail.

The program responds first by asking you to enter a password. In the Password Entry dialog box, enter verbatim the phrase your Internet provider told you to use when logging on to your mail server (see fig. 13.7).

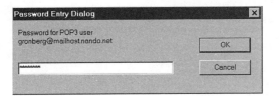

Fig. 13.7
Netscape demands that you enter the password for your Internet e-mail account every time you want to access its mail window.

There is, by the way, no way to save the password from session to session. You may consider this inconvenient, but Netscape apparently sees it as a security feature that can help keep the prying eyes of strangers away from your mail.

If you click OK, Netscape immediately tries to log on to your mail server. If it finds that you're not online, or that it can't log on to your server, eventually it will give up and flash an error message. If you've opened a mail window to work offline, you can avoid this problem by clicking Cancel in the Password Entry dialog box.

Understanding the Screen

Once in the program, you're confronted by a screen that reminds some users of the Microsoft Exchange e-mail client that comes with every copy of Windows 95. Don't be fooled: Netscape's mail facility is nowhere near as sophisticated as Exchange and nowhere near as resource-hungry. In actual use Netscape's mail facility compares favorably with such light-footed freeware and shareware packages as Eudora and Pegasus.

Let's get oriented.

- On the top left of Netscape's mail screen, you see a listing of your personal mail folders (see fig. 13.8). At minimum, this listing contains your inbox and your trash folder. After you've sent your first message with Netscape, you should see a Sent folder that holds copies of your outgoing traffic.

Fig. 13.8
Netscape's clean mail layout provides easy access to your message traffic and your personal mail folders.

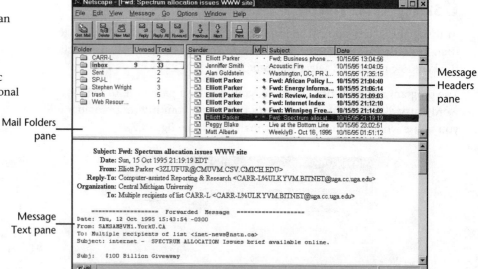

- On the top right, you see a scrollable listing of the message headers for every piece of mail in the folder you're looking at. The inbox opens by default when you first open Netscape's mail facility.

> **Note**
>
> Netscape highlights unread messages in bold. Folders that contain unread messages are also highlighted in bold. You open folders by double-clicking them.

- On the bottom of the screen, you see the text of the open message, along with headers indicating the message's subject, sender, sender's reply-to address, and the date it was sent.

One feature you'll learn to like may not be immediately obvious: If the message contains a URL, Netscape treats it as such, recognizing and highlighting it for immediate use. By clicking a URL, you can jump immediately to the Web page, FTP site, or other Internet service that it points to.

Tip

Netscape gives you one-click access to any URL embedded in an e-mail message displayed on-screen.

Note

You may notice at low screen resolutions that Netscape's mail display is a bit cramped. You can adjust the sizes of the various panes by clicking and dragging their frames. You'll find that the only real way to see what you're doing, video card permitting, is to use a higher screen resolution. Open Control Panel's Display properties, click the Settings tab, and set the Desktop Area slider to at least 800×600 pixels for a better look.

Composing and Sending Mail

Netscape 2.0's mail and news clients use the same front end for message composition. In the case of the mail client, you begin a message either by clicking the New Mail button on the toolbar or by clicking the Message menu and selecting New Mail Message. A message form like the one shown in figure 13.9 opens.

Netscape inserts the text of your signature file, if you use one, in the section of the screen reserved for message text. Fill out the rest of the message by following these steps:

1. Type the address of the person or organization you're writing to in the Send To field.

2. Type a short phrase in the Subject field describing the content of your message.

Tip

You don't have to open the Netscape Mail window to create a message. Click Netscape's File menu and choose New Mail Message to open a Composition window.

Fig. 13.9

Netscape uses a standard form for outgoing e-mail and UseNet articles. Here's an e-mail message ready to go.

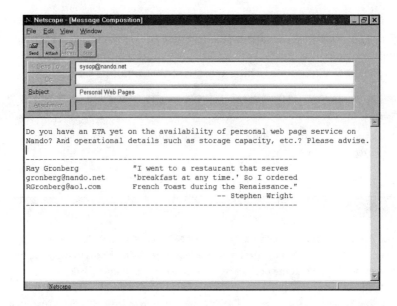

3. If you want to send copies of your message to third parties, click the View menu and select either Mail Cc or Mail Bcc. This adds a blank address field of the same name to your message header. Type the addresses of the additional recipients. Use Cc if you want to publicize the fact you've sent copies; use Bcc (blind copy) if you don't.

4. Click once in the main text box to set the cursor at the beginning of your message, and begin writing your text. Standard Windows 95 Cut, Copy, and Paste commands are available on the Edit menu.

> **Note**
>
> If the recipient of your message is using Netscape's e-mail manager also, you can pass along interesting and useful URLs in one of two ways. First, you can simply type the URL into a message. Or, if you're viewing a Web page or some other resource in the browser, you can click the File menu and select Mail Document. When you do, Netscape opens a new message window with the URL listed in the body of the mailing. In either case, when the person viewing your message opens it in Netscape's mail manager, the URL will appear as a hotlink. You need do nothing more than type; Netscape detects the presence of the URL automatically.

5. When finished, make sure you're online and then click the Send button on the Composition window's toolbar.

Netscape sends a new message as soon as you click Send, if its Composition preferences are set to deliver mail automatically. If they're set to queue messages, eventually you'll have to click the File menu and select Deliver Mail Now to send your outgoing traffic to your server.

Attaching Files and URLs to Mail

Most e-mail packages provide the capability to transmit binary files over the Internet by attaching ASCII-coded copies of them to your message traffic. Netscape is no exception. In fact, its attachment facility is one of the most versatile around.

You can attach files to a message any time before sending it. Open the Attachments dialog by clicking the Attachments button, which you'll see just below the Subject field. You may also click the Attach button on the message composition window's toolbar. Figure 13.10 shows the Attachments dialog box.

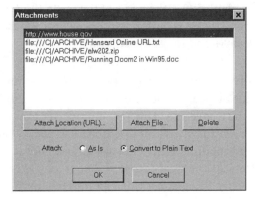

Fig. 13.10
You can attach a binary file to any outgoing message. Netscape will translate it using an ASCII coding scheme intelligible to most mail readers.

II

Mastering Netscape

Tip

If the Attachment button is grayed out, you can enable it by clicking any of the message's header boxes.

Once the Attachments dialog opens, you may add files to your message by clicking the Attach File button. Use the Enter File To Attach dialog box to select the file you want to transmit (see fig. 13.11).

Fig. 13.11
The Enter File To Attach dialog box looks and works like any other Windows 95 file-handling dialog box.

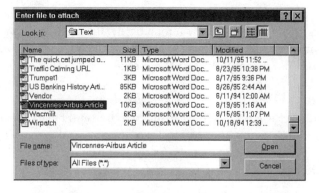

Once you've actually selected the file, you have a decision to make:

■ You'll want Netscape to code and transmit true binary files like a spreadsheet or a compressed archive using MIME rendering. Make sure it does so by highlighting the name of the file in the Attachments dialog and clicking the As Is button. Most e-mail software available automatically decodes and stores the attachment when it arrives on the receiving end.

■ You may ask Netscape to incorporate ASCII text files, such as those created with Notepad, into the body of the message itself. You do this by clicking the Convert to Plain Text button. Netscape does not, however, let you control where this insertion takes place. It always adds the new text to the bottom of the message. You will not see the text displayed in Netscape's message window, but as long as the file's visible in the Attachments dialog box it will appear in the finished message seen by your correspondent.

Tip

Bear in mind that you can always send an ASCII file As Is. If you do, Netscape will treat it as a binary file. This is perhaps the best way to handle heavily formatted plain-text files. Sending them in the body of a message could badly disrupt their formatting.

The Attachments dialog box also gives you the ability to e-mail a copy of an entire Web page—not just its Internet address. This new and exciting feature is unique to Netscape. If the recipients are using Netscape, they can view the Web page you're sending within a mail window.

Begin from the Attachments dialog box by clicking Attach Location (URL). Netscape opens the Please Specify a Location to Attach dialog box; type the full Internet address of the page you want to send (see fig. 13.12).

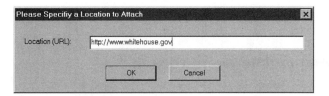

Fig. 13.12
Enter the URL of the Web page you want to send.

As with files, you have to decide whether to send the attachment as is or as plain text. If you know that the person to whom you're sending the URL is using Netscape 2.0 as a mail reader, click As Is. The result on the receiving end will be rather extraordinary (see fig. 13.13).

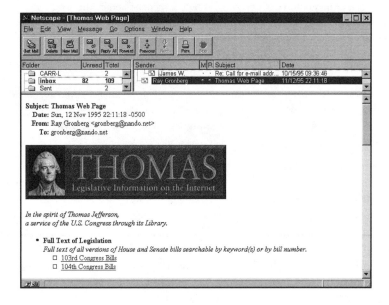

Fig. 13.13
Your friends don't have to seek out Web pages like this one from the Library of Congress. If they're using Netscape as a mail reader, you can send them a copy.

What you basically did is ask Netscape to mail the HTML source code of the URL to your correspondent. Because Netscape's mail facility treats every message as an HTML document, it is able to reconstruct a fully formatted and hotlinked Web page. Whatever you can do with that page from within a normal browser window, your friends can emulate within a Netscape mail window.

II

Mastering Netscape

If your friends don't have Netscape, all is not lost. By clicking Convert to Plain Text, you instruct Netscape's mailer to strip the HTML codes out of the page and send the remaining text. You may send it As Is anyway; they'll see pure HTML, but after saving a copy to disk they can always open and view the page in any Web browser. Bear in mind that they won't get any of the artwork that gives a Web page its distinctive look and feel.

Receiving and Replying to Mail

As explained earlier, Netscape tries to log on and retrieve messages from your mail server the first time you open the Netscape Mail window.

Troubleshooting

When Netscape tries to deliver my mail, it responds with a message that it's unable to locate the server. *What's wrong?*

One of four things, three of which you can do something about. The first thing you want to do is note the name of the server Netscape's trying to access. It'll be listed in the error message. It should be the name of your Internet provider's mail server. If it isn't, open the Preferences dialog box, click the Directories tab, and correct the entry in the Mail (SMTP) Server field.

If Netscape has the right address but can't get through, you may be working offline or you may have another program open that's got the mail server tied up. Get on-line by dialing in or logging on. Close any other program that uses SMTP or POP service before you try to use Netscape's mail manager.

The remaining possibility is that your Internet provider's mail server is down. If that's the case, you can do little but wait. If your provider has a help desk, you may want to call to let them know there's a problem.

You can also retrieve messages any time while the Netscape Mail window is open either by clicking the File menu and selecting Get New Mail, or by clicking Get Mail button on the toolbar. If you haven't already entered your mail server's password, Netscape requests it.

Netscape dumps all new mail into the inbox. Unlike some mail software, it can't automate the sorting of messages into user-specified folders. That's a job you have to handle yourself.

Like most e-mail packages, Netscape lets you respond directly to a message without having to address a new one from scratch. You do this by using the Reply, Reply All, and Forward buttons on the mail screen's toolbar.

By clicking either Reply or Reply All, you can tell Netscape to create a pre-addressed message. You can include the text of the message you received by clicking the mail window's File menu and selecting Include Original Text (see fig. 13.14). Trim the length of your quotation using the Edit menu's Cut, Copy, and Paste commands.

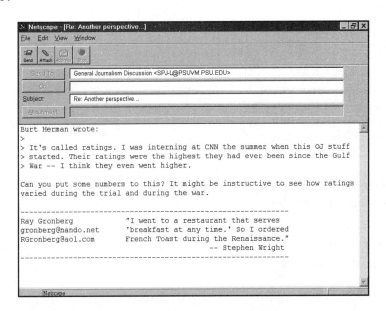

Fig. 13.14
By using the Reply and the Include Original Text commands, located on the mail window's File menu, you can draft understandable answers to your mail quickly and easily.

The Forward button works a bit differently. As with Reply and Reply All, clicking it creates a new message. This time, however, you supply the address of your intended recipient. But you'll notice that Netscape has filled in the Attachment field for you. By doing so, it tacks a copy of the text open in Netscape Mail window to the bottom of the message you're creating, including it for the benefit of your correspondent.

Organizing Your Mail

Fortunately, Netscape doesn't make mail sorting hard. You can add and name an unlimited number of folders and shift messages between them at your discretion (see fig. 13.15).

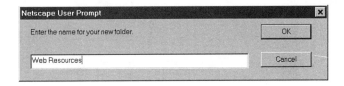

Fig. 13.15
User-created message folders simplify the task of organizing your mail.

Create a folder by clicking the Netscape Mail window's File menu and selecting New Folder. A Netscape mail folder is nothing more than a Windows 95 file, so you can give it a name up to 255 characters long. You may want to keep your names shorter than that, though. As it displays your folders, Netscape truncates the names of any that are too long to fit in the available window.

> **Note**
>
> Unlike many full-featured e-mail packages, Netscape does not offer any method of nesting folders within folders. High-volume mail users may find this a serious limitation that argues for keeping their current software. Low-volume users should be able to get along fine, but they may find it advisable to keep their filing system short and understandable.

Conversely, you kill an unused folder by clicking it once to highlight its name, and then selecting Delete Folder from the Edit menu.

The commands for shifting mail between folders—Move and Copy—are at the bottom of the Message menu (see fig. 13.16). Highlight either, and you'll find a list of your folders nested beneath them.

Fig. 13.16
The Move and Copy commands take only a single click. Highlight the directory you want to send the message to and release the mouse button.

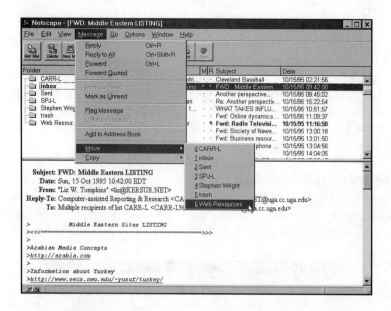

The Move and Copy commands work the same way:

1. Highlight the message you want to move or copy in the Message Headers pane by clicking it.

2. Click the Message menu and select Move or Copy.

3. A list of your folders will pop up next to the Message menu. Select the folder you want the message transferred to.

Choosing Move places the selected message into the destination folder and deletes it from the source. Copy puts a copy in the destination folder while leaving the contents of the source folder unchanged.

Within folders, Netscape gives users several options for sorting messages. All are accessible by clicking the View menu and highlighting Sort.

The three major options—Sort by Date, Sender, and Subject—are largely self-explanatory. Toggling the Ascending command tells Netscape to arrange messages in ascending or descending order.

Netscape's capability to organize messages into threads is both unusual and powerful. By toggling Thread Messages, you're ordering the mail client to override normal sort order in cases where a single message has inspired at least one reply. It groups the original and any replies, making the conversation easy to follow as it develops over time (see fig. 13.17).

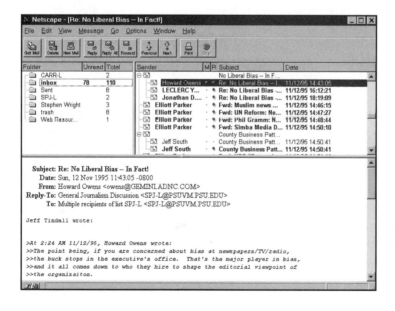

Fig. 13.17
The Windows Explorer-like tree structures indicate message threads.

You can send any highlighted message to the trash folder by clicking the Delete button on the toolbar, by clicking Edit and selecting Delete Message, or by transferring it there using the Message menu's Move command. Trash stays on your disk, however, until you click the File menu and select Empty Trash Folder. Unlike many mail packages, Netscape provides no way of automating deletions.

Using the Address Book

Any good e-mail software provides some quick and simple way of storing and retrieving the addresses of your most frequent correspondents. Most are very easy to use. See figure 13.18.

Fig. 13.18
Netscape's address book simplifies mailing chores by storing the names and addresses of the people you write the most.

Setting up an address book isn't difficult. In fact, Netscape gives you a couple of ways to do it. The easiest method is to open a message from someone you want to correspond with regularly, click the Message menu, and select Add to Address Book.

Netscape responds by opening a Windows 95 property sheet that has four fields (see fig. 13.19). If you're adding to your Address Book using the Message menu command, you'll find that two of them, Name and E-Mail Address, are already filled in.

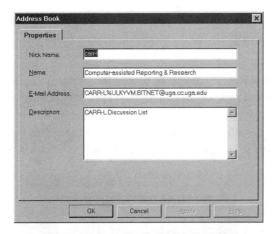

Fig. 13.19
Use the Address Book properties sheet to create and maintain your address list.

Troubleshooting

Netscape's Add to Address Book function filled out the properties sheet for the addition incorrectly. It didn't use the name and address of the person who wrote the original message. Why not?

There's an entry in the message's Reply To field. When it's creating an Address Book entry, Netscape always takes the name and address listed in Reply To. This avoids problems with mailings to a list or to a person who takes return mail at a different address. But it means more work for you; you have to take the time to enter the correct name and address yourself. Always check the entries in these fields the first time you create an Address Book entry.

The Description field gives you a place to write a short note about your correspondent.

The remaining field, Nick Name, gives you a place to enter a short, one-word phrase that can serve as a shortcut to your Address Book entry. Be sure to use lowercase characters only; Netscape won't accept a Nick Name that contains uppercase characters.

You can also create Address Book entries from scratch. Click the Window menu and select Address book. Once the address book opens, click the Item menu and select Add User. Netscape will open a blank Address Book properties sheet. You can also modify any existing entry in the Address Book by right-clicking the entry and selecting Properties.

Once you've created your Address Book, Netscape gives you three ways to use it. They work with any of the available address fields, Send To, Cc and Blind Cc:

■ The simplest way, once you've placed the cursor in the Message Composition window's Send To field, is to click the toolbar's Address button. Netscape opens a dialog box called Select Addresses (see fig. 13.20). Highlight the address you want to use, and then click the button that corresponds to the field you want it placed in. Click OK when you're done.

Fig. 13.20
Clicking either the toolbar's Address button or a message's Send To, Cc, or Blind Cc button opens the Select Addresses dialog box. Highlight your choice, click the button for the field you want it placed in, and click OK.

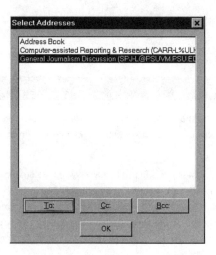

■ You may also open the Select Addresses dialog box by clicking any of the labels next to your message's various address fields. Unfortunately, once you've highlighted the address you want to use, you still have to place it in the proper field by clicking the corresponding button on the dialog box. You can't just click OK and expect the address to pop up where you want it.

■ If your memory is good, you can address a message quickly merely by typing an Address Book entry's Nick Name property in Send To, Cc or Blind Cc. Netscape will automatically fill the box with the name and e-mail address associated with the Nick Name as soon you move the cursor elsewhere.

You may notice that Netscape fills the message address boxes differently, depending on an Address Book entry's properties. If you've given the entry a Nick Name, it will use that until you close the Select Addresses dialog. Once you do, it will fill a field with both the name and the address of your intended correspondent. This is nothing to be alarmed about. As long as the e-mail address itself is bracketed by the < and > symbols, your mail server will be able to find it.

If you haven't given an address book entry a Nick Name, Netscape will only list the e-mail address in the proper field. The recipient's name won't appear. Again, no harm is done.

Because an address book is an HTML document—just like your Bookmarks file—Netscape gives you one other way of getting at it quickly. Just as with your Bookmarks file, you can load your address book directly into your browser.

Close your mail window, and then open the File menu and select Open File. You should find address.htm somewhere in your Netscape folder structure, most likely in the Program subfolder. If it doesn't open readily, use Windows 95's Find Files or Folders utility to search for it. When you find it, double-click to load it in Netscape (see fig. 13.21).

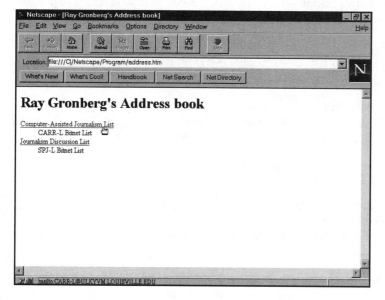

Fig. 13.21
Your address book is an HTML document you can see within Netscape. Load it, and you have the ability to address mail with a single click, just as you would from any Web page.

Once the file is there, you can create a new message, complete with pre-completed address information, merely by clicking one of the highlighted links. Because it's HTML, clicking a link opens a message composition window, just as it would if you had clicked an e-mail link embedded on a Web page.

And, again because it's HTML, you can also add your Address Book to your Bookmarks menu, putting it one click away any time you're using your browser.

Setting Up the Microsoft Exchange Client

There's more than one way to manage e-mail with Netscape 2.0. Starting with version 1.2, Netscape has shipped a connection to Microsoft Exchange with every copy of Netscape. Until recently, the Exchange client was the only thing that gave Netscape users full access to Internet e-mail services.

It was, and is, by no means a perfect solution. Exchange is a notorious resource hog that gulps RAM and virtual memory by the megabyte. It's also slow. For all that, it offers the Internet e-mail users little more than freeware programs like Eudora Light. You'll look high and low in Exchange, for example, and never find a high-end feature like automatic message filtering, which in a package like Eudora Pro, lets you tell the program to pre-sort incoming message traffic into mail folders.

Exchange shines as a corporate network messaging client. If you're not part of such a network, you're probably better off using Netscape 2.0's e-mail service, or acquiring a third-party mail package.

But if you are part of a corporate network, and if you're an Exchange user, you'll probably want Internet mail routed to your Inbox instead of relying on another program.

You don't necessarily need Netscape to use Exchange for handling your Internet mail. Microsoft provides its own POP3 client for Exchange as part of Microsoft Plus!. You can find instructions for setting it up in many publications, including Que's *Special Edition Using Windows 95*. The same references will tell you more about using Exchange on a day-to-day basis, which we also don't cover.

But we do tell you how to enable the connection to Netscape in the event you don't have Plus!. Just follow these steps:

1. From Windows 95's Start menu, open the Control Panel.
2. Double-click on the Mail and Fax icon.
3. On the Services tab, click the Add button.
4. Highlight Netscape Internet Transport and click OK (see fig. 13.22). A tabbed dialog box labeled Netscape Transport Configuration appears.

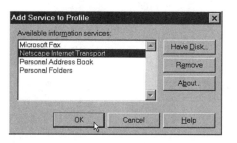

Fig. 13.22
Click OK to add the Netscape Internet Transport to your Microsoft Exchange user profile.

5. On the User tab, type your name in the Display Name box and your e-mail address in the Internet Address box.

6. On the Hosts tab, enter the addresses supplied by your Internet Provider in the SMTP Host and POP3 Host boxes (see fig. 13.23). These should match exactly those you entered in Netscape's Mail and News Preferences dialog box.

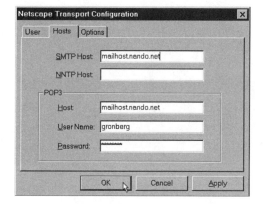

Fig. 13.23
Enter mail server and login information in the indicated boxes.

7. Also on the Hosts tab, enter your login name and password in the POP3 User Name and Passwords boxes.

8. On the Options tab, be sure to clear the Send RTF Text check box.

9. Click OK twice and close Control Panel.

10. Open Netscape's Mail and News Preferences dialog box by selecting it from the Options menu.

11. On the Appearance tab, click to put a check in the Use Exchange Client for Mail and News box.

II

Mastering Netscape

## CHAPTER 14

E-mail with Netscape Personal Edition and Eudora Light

As you learn in chapter 13, "E-Mail with Netscape," Netscape versions prior to 2.0 had only a limited send-only e-mail facility. To receive messages at all, or just to manage your daily flow of outgoing posts, you needed a dedicated Internet e-mail client.

Netscape tried to solve this problem in a couple of ways. Version 2.0 itself incorporates an e-mail package that provides many of the services available in competing software, along with a few wrinkles of Netscape's own. And since the release of version 1.2, Netscape has provided a tie-in with Windows 95's main communications package, Microsoft Exchange.

For many users, however, Exchange isn't the perfect solution because of its heavy demand for system resources such as hard disk space and RAM. And, for all the improvements found in Netscape's own e-mail package, it's hardly perfect either.

Netscape tried a different tack with Netscape Navigator Personal Edition 1.1 and 1.2, the first versions of its program sold in retail outlets. Both versions came bundled with a copy of one of the more useful e-mail packages around, Qualcomm's *Eudora Light*.

Even now that Netscape has beefed up its own e-mail capabilities, a freeware, dedicated mail package like Eudora still finds a niche with many users. Netscape's e-mail manager, for example, doesn't let you build a multi-level folder system to hold your old mail—something that's nearly a must if you have to deal with more than a couple of dozen messages a day. Nor does it let you attach more than one binary file to a single message—a real problem if you're a work-at-home type who needs to trade spreadsheets or word processing documents with clients or the home office. And its address book function is quite weak in comparison to that available in other packages.

Eudora Light shines in all these areas. And it's therefore still worth a trial run, even in the likely event that Netscape stops packaging it with later versions of the Personal Edition.

In this chapter, you learn how to

- Install and configure Eudora Light for use with your Internet connection
- Send e-mail messages
- Read incoming mail and manage your message traffic with Eudora's mailboxes
- Send and receive files attached to messages
- Sort and search your incoming and outgoing mail

What Is Eudora Light?

Eudora is a full-service Internet SMTP and POP3 client that has served users in various guises since 1991. Originally a Macintosh program, it was long ago re-written for use on PCs that run Windows 3.x or Windows 95. There's also a version available for the PowerPC.

All three versions are freeware, which means there's no charge for their use. You can download any of them from the Internet. If necessary, you can also buy a commercial edition, Eudora Pro, that provides features such as built-in spell-checking and the ability to password-protect your messages.

Eudora Light may be free, but it's no slouch in terms of performance and us-ability. It's useful on any system that runs the TCP/IP networking protocol, not just the Internet. You can set up your own mailboxes to store and man-age e-mail traffic, use it to send and receive binary files like programs and word processor documents, and configure it to automatically check your net-work for new messages.

What you can't do (so far) is use Windows 95 specialties like long file names and shortcuts. Eudora Light is a 16-bit Windows 3.x program. While it runs fine under Windows 95, it doesn't know about the new operating system's special features. And, as of this writing, Qualcomm has not announced plans for adapting Eudora Light to Windows 95.

Installing and Configuring Eudora Light

If you chose a Typical setup when you installed Netscape Navigator Personal Edition, Eudora Light is already on your hard drive and ready to run. You'll find it alongside Netscape in the C:\NETSCAPE folder.

You may have to complete the installation by creating a shortcut to Eudora by following these steps:

◀ See "Loading Netscape Personal Edition," pg. 122

1. Right-click the Start button and choose Open.

2. Double-click the Programs folder, and then double-click on the Netscape Personal Edition folder.

3. Open the File menu, click New, and then Shortcut. This opens Windows 95's Create Shortcut Wizard (see fig. 14.1).

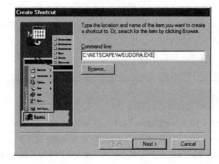

Fig. 14.1
Bind Eudora Light's command line to the shortcut using the Create Shortcut wizard.

4. Type **C:\NETSCAPE\WEUDORA.EXE** in the wizard's Command Line box. Click Next.

5. Name your shortcut. "Eudora" is a good choice, but you can choose another name if you want. Click Finish.

Windows 95 then creates the shortcut. From now on, you'll be able to open Eudora from the Start menu.

If you exerted more control over Netscape's setup by asking for a Custom installation, you'll have to put Eudora on your hard drive if you want to use it. You do this by clicking the Eudora Light Email checkbox in the Netscape Custom Setup panel (see fig. 14.2).

II

Mastering Netscape

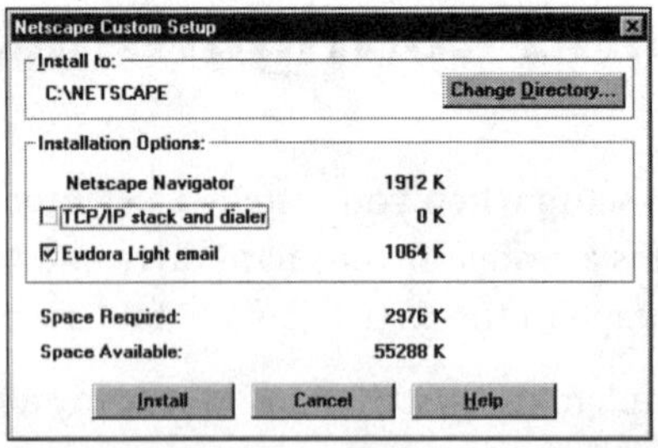

Fig. 14.2

The Netscape
Custom Setup
panel. To install
Eudora to your
hard drive, make
sure to check the
Eudora Light
Email checkbox.

Caution

A custom setup lets you install Netscape and Eudora to a directory other than
C:\NETSCAPE by clicking the Change Directory button. It will not, however, let you
install Netscape and Eudora in separate directories.

You can use Netscape Setup to add Eudora Light to your machine sometime
after you've installed Netscape itself. Run Setup, ask for a custom install, and
check the Eudora Light Email checkbox as above.

Note

If you're adding Eudora to a Netscape Personal Edition setup you've used for awhile,
be sure to back up your Bookmarks file by making a copy of it in another directory
(you can use Windows 95's file cut-and-paste feature in My Computer or under
Explorer). Netscape's Setup program is going to try to completely reinstall Navigator,
including its original Bookmarks file, whether you like it or not. Making a copy now
ensures that you don't lose track of your favorite Web sites if your bookmarks are
overwritten. Never assume that a software installation program knows to let the files
already on your disk alone.

Setting the Configuration Box

No Internet client program will work out of the box without some help from
the user. At minimum, you have to supply information about your Internet
service provider and the various servers available through your account.

As you might expect, therefore, the first time you open Eudora Light you
have things to do. You must provide the address of your Internet provider's
POP server, the system that handles and holds your incoming mail. You may
also have to provide the address of an SMTP server, which handles outgoing
traffic.

Open Eudora's Configuration dialog box by clicking the Special menu and selecting Configuration. Then follow these steps (see fig. 14.3):

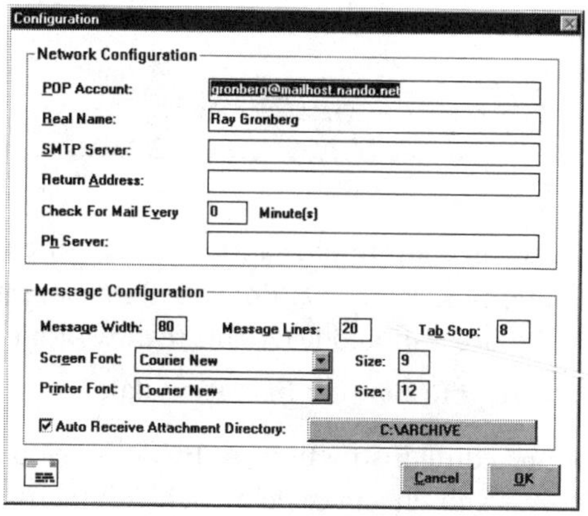

Fig. 14.3
Enter information about your Internet e-mail account using Eudora Light's Configuration dialog box.

Configuration

Network Configuration

POP Account: gronberg@mailhost.nando.net
Real Name: Ray Gronberg
SMTP Server:
Return Address:
Check For Mail Every 0 Minute(s)
Ph Server:

Message Configuration

Message Width: 80   Message Lines: 20   Tab Stop: 8
Screen Font: Courier New   Size: 9
Printer Font: Courier New   Size: 12
☑ Auto Receive Attachment Directory: C:\ARCHIVE

Cancel   OK

1. Type the name of your e-mail account in the POP Account box. In all likelihood, you'll use your regular e-mail address.

◄ See "Setting Basic Preferences After a Custom Install," pg. 127

Caution

In some cases—especially if your account is on a large system that uses aliasing to route mail to and through different servers—your POP Account's name may differ slightly from your regular address. Be sure you enter the correct name in the POP Account box by getting it from your Internet provider. This line has to be right or Eudora can't access your incoming mail.

2. Type your real name in the next box. Eudora adds it to your outgoing mail.

3. Enter the name of your SMTP Server in the next box, if your Internet provider tells you that it's different from your POP Account. If it isn't, leave this blank.

4. If you think you'll use Eudora to trade binary files with other e-mail users, go to the bottom of the menu and check the box to the left of Auto Receive Attachment Directory. Then click the large, unlabeled button to the right.

5. Use the dialog box that follows, Select Auto Receive Directory (see fig. 14.4), to choose a directory to hold incoming files. Click Use Directory when you've made your choice.

II

Mastering Netscape

Fig. 14.4
The Select Auto
Receive Directory
dialog box. This
user has picked
C:\TEMP to hold
incoming files.

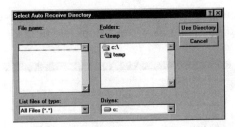

6. Networked users will want to plug a number into the Check For Mail Every XX Minutes box. With that done, Eudora can retrieve mail automatically. Dial-in users should leave this feature alone.

7. Click OK to accept your new configuration data.

If you followed the preceding instructions to the letter, you probably noticed that the Return Address and Ph Server fields were left blank. You enter something in Return Address only in the unlikely event that it's different from your regular e-mail address. Fill in the Ph Server field only if your Internet provider offers Ph address lookup services. If it does, enter the name of your server.

You'll also notice that you didn't touch most of the items in the Message Configuration section. These options alter the way Eudora displays new or incoming messages. You can't hurt anything by experimenting with them, but they default to some very useful settings.

Setting Switches Options

After Eudora Light's server configuration is set, you have some choices to make that affect the program's usability. You find them on the Switches menu (see fig. 14.5).

Fig. 14.5
The Switches
dialog box. The
configuration
shown is for a
typical dial-up
Internet user.

Open the Switches dialog box by opening the Special menu, and clicking Switches. What appears isn't for the faint of heart. This dialog contains 27 items, all user-changeable. Fortunately, most of Eudora's default settings will get you started. Depending on how you use your computer, however, you might want to reset some of them right away.

So you'll know what's available on the Switches dialog, here's a tour of the seven major switch groupings seen there. We go into detail only about the switches that affect Eudora's usability in a major way.

- The *Composition* group affects the display, composition, and storage of the messages you write. The major items you might want to change from the defaults are Use Signature (uncheck if you rarely or never use a signature file) and Keep Copies (check if you want Eudora to save copies of your outgoing message traffic).

- Moving clockwise, the *Checking* group controls the way Eudora downloads your mail. You'll probably want to put a check in the Save Password box so you don't have to reenter your server's password every time you receive mail.

- The *Switch Messages With* group sets up a hotkey to page between messages in your mailboxes. Check Plain Arrows if you want to use the cursor keys directly, Ctrl+Arrows if you want to use the Control key as a safety on the cursor keys. You make both options available by checking both boxes.

- The *Miscellany* options control a grab-bag of features, none of them really critical to the operation of the program. Leave the defaults alone for now.

- The *Sending* options, on the other hand, are very critical. Send on Check and Immediate Send are both on by default. You will want to uncheck Immediate Send if you're a dial-in user; doing so tells Eudora to send your messages to an on-disk queue rather than try to post them immediately. If Send on Check is enabled, Eudora posts any mail in your message queue when you check mail by clicking the File menu and selecting Check Mail. Otherwise, you have to post by clicking File and selecting Send Queued Messages, or leave Immediate Send checked.

- All the options in the *New Mail Notification* group are on by default. There's no real reason to change them.

- The commands in the *Send Attachments* group tell Eudora how to handle binary file attachments. Leave the Always as Attachment box unchecked if you want text files attached to your mail to show as text in the body of your message. If you check this box, they'll be sent separately as an encoded file. This control does not affect the handling of binary files. The radio button tells Eudora to use either MIME or BinHex coding as a default; you can override this choice later.

Troubleshooting

Eudora locks up mysteriously. After a short time, it produces a box that reads, `Error getting network address for 'your.server.name.' Cause: connection timed out (10060).` *What's wrong?*

You're probably a dial-up user trying to use automatic retrieval. Eudora can't log on to your mail server unless your computer is already connected to the Internet. Unlike Netscape and some other Winsock-aware software, Eudora can't make that basic connection by itself. Open the Configuration dialog box and set Check for Mail Every XX Minutes to zero to disable automatic retrieval.

If you are on a network and get this error, notify your system administrator immediately. There could be a serious problem with the mail server or your connection.

Upgrading Eudora Light

Netscape Navigator Personal Edition 1.1 comes equipped with Eudora Light version 1.4.5. The instructions in this chapter describe this edition of Eudora specifically.

But 1.4.5 is not the latest version of this program available—Internet users should have no trouble upgrading Eudora Light if they want.

Qualcomm maintains a Eudora Web page at **http://www.qualcomm .com/quest** (see fig. 14.6). It contains links to an FTP site, **ftp.qualcomm .com**, that always has the most recent version of Eudora Light available, which is 1.5.2 at the time of this writing. It also has information on Eudora Pro and a complete user's manual for Eudora Light in Microsoft Word format.

If you decide to upgrade, use Netscape or dedicated FTP software to download the package. It's a self-extracting ZIP file called eudor152.exe, and it is located in the directory /quest/windows/eudora/1.5. The same directory holds a user guide for Eudora Light 1.4 stored in a file called 14manual.exe.

After downloading your upgrade, copy it to the directory that contains your current version of Eudora Light. Highlight the new file in Explorer or My Computer, and run it by double-clicking it, pressing Enter, or right-clicking and choosing Open.

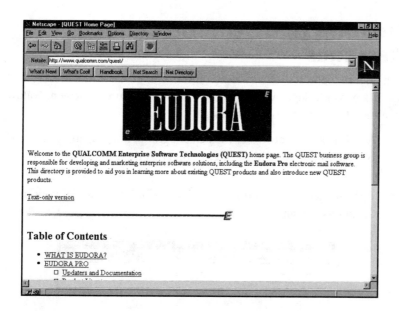

Fig. 14.6
Qualcomm's
Eudora home page
has links to the
latest and greatest
versions of its
popular e-mail
programs.

Eudora Light 1.5.2's installation is relatively user-friendly. It will not over-write your old copy of Eudora, so you can keep using it while you make the transition. Eventually, however, you will have to update your shortcuts to call "EUDORA.EXE" instead of "WEUDORA.EXE."

The new version sports a substantially cleaner interface. The major change: Qualcomm has consolidated the unwieldy Configuration and Switches dialog boxes into one wizard-like panel called Settings (see fig. 14.7). Access it by clicking the Special menu, and then Settings.

On the CD

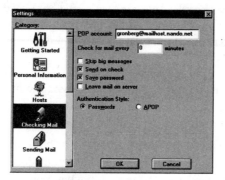

Fig. 14.7
The new version of
Eudora Light
eliminates the
Configuration and
Settings dialog
boxes in favor of
this cleaner
version called
Settings.

All the functionality of the former dialog boxes remains in this new one. This is not the place to go through it in any detail, but please believe me: if you can configure Eudora Light 1.4.5, you can handle 1.5.2 in your sleep.

Mastering Netscape

II

Creating and Sending E-mail Messages

With Eudora Light, it's easy to send Internet e-mail. Open the Messages menu and click New Message. A blank mail form pops up on your screen. Follow these steps to write and send a message:

1. Type the e-mail address of the person, group, or company you're trying to reach in the To field (see fig. 14.8). Press the Tab key to go to the next line.

2. In the Subject field, type a two- or three-word summary of your message. Press Tab again.

Fig. 14.8
This user has finished typing address information for a message and has begun to write its actual text. Note the gray line separating the message header from the text.

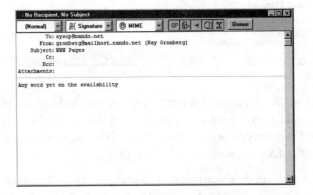

Tip

Keep your Subject summaries short but descriptive. A good subject description is like a newspaper headline: it'll make your messages stand out in a crowded In box on the receiving end of your correspondence.

3. You may want to send copies of your message to more than one person. If so, type the e-mail addresses of the additional recipients (separating them with commas) in the Cc field. Press Tab when you're done.

4. The Bcc field gives you a chance to send a "blind copy" of your message to other people. If you want, enter the e-mail addresses for the copies (separated by commas) and press Tab when you're done.

Tip

Bcc works almost exactly like Cc, except that the recipient listed in the To field gets no notice from your mail server that the added copies went out.

5. The cursor should now rest in Eudora's message window, just below the gray line crossing the screen. Now you're ready to type the text of your message. Go ahead and do it.

6. When you're done, click the button on the extreme right of Eudora's toolbar. Depending on your Switches settings, this button is captioned Send or Queue. Click it to send your new message directly to your mail server or to your outgoing message queue for later delivery.

7. If you're connected to the Internet, clicking the Send button will bring up a status indicator panel almost immediately. It has a button on it that you can click to cancel the outgoing message if you change your mind.

8. To send messages stored on disk once you're logged on, open the File menu and click Send Queued Messages. A status indicator pops up to let you watch the progress of your mailing.

Addressing Your Mail with Nicknames

The New Message procedure works fine if you're e-mailing a new or infrequent correspondent. But for people you keep in touch with every day, it's a little cumbersome.

You can use two Eudora Light features, Nicknames and Quick Recipients, to create and maintain a personal address book (see fig. 14.9). Open your Nicknames list by opening the Window menu and clicking Nicknames.

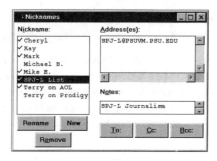

Fig. 14.9
Eudora's Nicknames and Quick Recipients features speed the process of addressing mail to your most frequent correspondents.

Creating a new nickname is simple. With the Nicknames window open, follow these steps:

1. Click the New button.

2. A dialog called New Nickname pops up (see fig. 14.10). Type the name of the person or group in the box under `What do you wish to call it?`

Fig. 14.10
Type the name of
your correspon-
dent in the box
provided on the
New Nickname
dialog box.

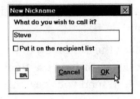

3. Check the Put It On the Recipient List box if you want to create a Eudora menu shortcut to the new nickname. Such shortcuts are called Quick Recipients. We'll discuss them in a moment.

4. Click OK. You'll see the new nickname highlighted on the Nicknames list.

5. Highlight any text appearing in the Address(es) box and change it so it reflects the correct e-mail address for this person.

Note

Eudora doesn't do a good job on its own of completing the Address(es) field for a new nickname. It will usually pick a random address from your Nicknames list to place in this box. Unwary users can mistakenly believe Eudora can divine the address from the name you assigned to the nickname. Whenever you create a new nickname, always double-check the address attached to it and edit as necessary.

Note

There is an even quicker way to create a nickname. Within any open message, click the Special menu and select Make Nickname. Eudora will ask you to supply a name as before. You should immediately open the Nicknames window and edit the Address(es) field. You'll find that Eudora copies both the Sender and Reply-To addresses to this field when you select Make Nickname; chances are you want to keep only one of them.

The Nicknames window controls input to a disk file that holds your address book. It stays open until you choose Close from the File menu or until you click Windows 95's close box. You can switch in and out of the Nicknames window at your convenience, using commands on the Window or Mailbox menus, while you work on your messages. If you change your Nicknames file in any way, however, Eudora won't let you close the window until you confirm or discard the modifications (see fig. 14.11).

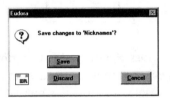

Fig. 14.11
Eudora gives you the choice of saving or throwing away changes to your Nicknames list.

Addressing Your Mail with Quick Recipients

Once your address book is fairly well settled, you won't want to open the Nicknames window every time you create a new piece of mail. Eudora lets you avoid that detour by letting you add your most useful addresses directly to its menus.

You got a hint of this capability when your created your first nickname. When Eudora asked you for the name, it also gave you a chance to put it on the Quick Recipients list. Try it now by creating a new nickname. Before you're done, check the Put It On the Recipient List box, just below the line where you enter the name (see fig. 14.12). Once you click OK, go to Eudora's menus and click Message, followed by New Message To.

Fig. 14.12
Adding a nickname to the Quick Recipients list at the same time you create it.

Use the Nicknames window to add existing nicknames to the Quick Recipients list. Double-click any name under the Nicknames list. When you see a checkmark pop up next to it, it's on Eudora's menu (see fig. 14.13).

Mastering Netscape

Fig. 14.13
Adding to the
Quick Recipients
list from the
Nicknames
window.

The Quick Recipients list gives you the ability to perform every basic Nickname function without ever opening the Nicknames window, which is a tremendous convenience. Eudora unfortunately hides it by scattering its various Quick Recipients commands among three different menu headings. Table 14.1 lists the commands now available to you.

Table 14.1 Eudora Menu Commands Using the Quick Recipients List		
Menu Command	**Menu**	**Action**
New Message To	Message	Creates a new message addressed to the Quick Recipient.
Reply To	Message	Creates a new mailing to the Quick Recipient that quotes an existing message.
Forward To	Message	Sends a copy of an existing message to the indicated Quick Recipient.
Redirect To	Message	Sends a copy of a message you've gotten to the indicated Quick Recipient, without changing the message's From field.
Insert Recipient	Edit	Adds a Quick Recipient to any of an outgoing message's address fields. Use the mouse to point to To, Cc, or Bcc first.
Add as Recipient	Special	Adds a highlighted e-mail address to the Quick Recipients list only. It will not add the address to the Nicknames list.
Remove Recipient	Special	Deletes a name from the Quick Recipients list only. It does not alter the Nicknames list.

> **Tip**
>
> You'll probably want to use the Quick Recipients feature for only your dozen or so most frequent correspondents. Beyond that the menus get a bit unwieldy.

Signing Your Mail

Eudora is capable of automatically adding what Internet users call a *signature file* to the end of your outgoing messages.

E-mail sigs—in their simplest form—offer readers more information about a message's sender, such as a corporate affiliation and a phone number. They've become part of Internet lore because there's a certain breed of Nethead who won't settle for simplicity. To these people, no sig is complete unless it includes a bit of elaborate ASCII artwork.

Eudora Light's Switches settings default to include a signature file at the end of your posts. You open this file by clicking the Window menu, and then clicking Signature. The file is blank when you start Eudora for the first time; it's up to you to create your own sig (see fig. 14.14). Type what you want. Store it by choosing Save from the File menu, or from the dialog that pops up when you click the Close box.

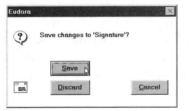

Fig. 14.14
By opening Eudora's Signature window, you can create and maintain a small text file that will close all your messages.

You can choose to leave a sig off any given message. Near the middle of the message toolbar, you see a box with the script letters "JH" inside. Click it, and a drop-down box opens to let you cancel the sig.

> **Note**
>
> Keep your sig simple. Name, address (via e-mail and/or snail mail), affiliation, and phone numbers suffice for most professionals. Artwork isn't essential, but it won't hurt anything as long it doesn't add to the length of your sig. Don't let it get more than about five lines deep; more than that and you're costing your readers connection time and, possibly, additional fees.

Reading and Managing E-mail Messages

Eudora's handling of incoming message traffic is probably one of the strongest parts of the entire package. Filing and keeping track of your old mail is a cinch, because the program lets you create a hierarchical set of mailboxes and you transfer messages between them at will. Each mailbox has what amounts to a table of contents that gives you a full rundown on the messages stored inside. And, if need be, you can save, print, and copy your messages just as you would with any other Windows 95 program.

When you're online, picking up your mail with Eudora Light takes two clicks of the mouse. Click the File menu, and choose Check Mail. Eudora will log on to your mail server and download every message that waits for you there.

> **Tip**
>
> If you've left the Switches dialog box's Send on Check option on, Eudora sends any outgoing message queued on your disk as soon as it's done picking up new mail.

Eudora deposits new messages in a database called the In box. You can tell Eudora, via the Switches dialog, to open the In box automatically when you have new mail. If you don't, click the Mailbox menu and choose In.

Understanding Eudora's Mailboxes

The In box is just one of three boxes Eudora uses by default. There's an Out box for mail you've sent or that is waiting in queue, and there's a Trash box for messages you've deleted. You can create additional mailboxes of your own.

No matter which mailbox you open—and they're all accessible from the Mailbox menu—Eudora will present some basic data about the messages it contains. The format is standard for every mailbox (see fig. 14.15).

Most of the fields in the Mailbox window are self-explanatory. Each line represents one message. There's a box that lists the address or Eudora nickname of the person who sent or received the message involved. There's another that indicates when it was sent and a small one that says how big it is. The largest field, the one on the right, reports on its subject.

Message size in kilobytes

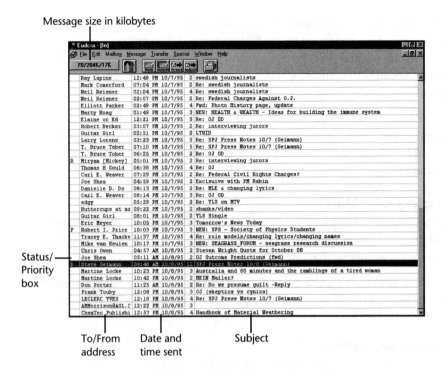

Fig. 14.15
Eudora Mailbox
windows offer
summary informa-
tion about the
messages they
hold.

Status/
Priority
box

To/From   Date and   Subject
address   time sent

The leftmost box is a bit more mysterious at first glance. In it you'll find, depending on the mailbox that's open, a series of one-letter codes that tell you
the message's status. These are the most important:

- A bullet next to a message in the In box window says you haven't read
  it yet.

- An R next to an In box listing means that you've posted a reply to the
  original sender.

- An S beside an Out box item means that the message has been sent.

- A Q seen beside an Out box listing means you haven't posted that message yet.

Aside from these, you may see a D or an F next to an In box item. They say,
respectively, that you've redirected a message sent to you by mistake or forwarded a copy to a third party.

Opening and Replying to Messages

You can open any message by double-clicking its mailbox listing. Alternatively, you can use the cursor keys to scroll through the listing and press Enter to open a message window.

With a message open or highlighted, create a return mailing by opening the Message menu and selecting Reply. Eudora opens a new message and pastes into it the text of the post you're answering. Use Windows cut, copy, and paste commands to reorganize and trim this quotation, and then type your reply.

On the Message menu you also see commands that let you forward copies of a given piece of e-mail to anyone you want, or redirect mail that came to your address by mistake. Clicking them pastes the text into a new message; you have only to fill in the address and click the Send or Queue button.

Storing Old Mail

There's nothing wrong with keeping old mail in the In and Out boxes and sending messages to the Trash box as they become obsolete. That works fine if you're a low-volume mail user.

But if you're not—say you get dozens of messages each week, some business-related, some personal, others from a mailing list or two—you'll want to customize your mailbox setup.

Creating New Mailboxes

Create new mailboxes by clicking the Mailbox menu and selecting New. Eudora responds by opening the New Mailbox dialog box (see fig. 14.16).

Fig. 14.16
This user is naming a new mailbox.

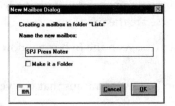

Enter a name in the line provided. Clicking OK creates the mailbox. You'll now find it toward the bottom of the Mailbox menu.

You can also nest menus under the Mailbox selector—which creates sub-categories for different posts—by checking the Make it a Folder box. Click OK, and you have another Mailbox menu item that can hold new mailboxes and folders of its own.

Note

Custom mailboxes do for your messages what Windows 95's Start menu likely has already done for your programs. But you have to think about how you want to organize your message traffic. You also have to set up a mailbox structure that makes your most important messages the easiest ones to reach. Don't go crazy nesting folders and mailboxes. After they pile up more than about three deep, it's easy to lose track of things.

Transferring Messages Between Boxes

The Transfer menu lets you shuffle messages between mailboxes. With one exception, it will mirror the look of your Mailbox menu. To move a message from one box to another, follow these steps:

1. Open or select the message you want to move.
2. Click the Transfer menu.
3. Scroll through your Mailbox hierarchy until you find the box you want to send it to. Click it.

The one thing you can't do with Transfer is move a message to the Out box. Eudora reserves the Out box for messages it has sent or is waiting to send.

Otherwise, the Transfer menu is quite flexible. You'll notice that it has a New command; it lets you create new folders and mailboxes on the fly as you're moving your mail around.

Need to reorganize the folders and mailboxes themselves? Click the Window menu and select Mailboxes. The window that opens lets you move them around (see fig. 14.17). It works like the Windows 95 Explorer: Click the folder icons on one side of the window until you find the mailbox you want to move, and then do the same on the other side until you've highlighted the destination. Click the Move button that points where you want to go.

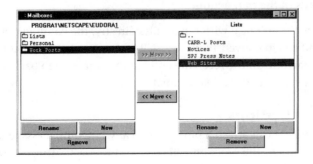

Fig. 14.17
The Mailboxes window lets you rearrange your mailbox and folders hierarchy. Here, we're about to move the Web Sites mailbox to the Work Posts folder.

Deleting Mail

Eudora Light gives the user several ways to get rid of old messages, but they all involve sending them to the Trash box first. Eudora continues to store messages there unless you tell it to clear the Trash box when you quit the program.

You can send a message to the Trash by

- Pressing the Delete key
- Pressing Ctrl+D
- Clicking the toolbar's menu icon
- Clicking the Transfer menu and selecting Trash

All of these commands work from within a message or from a mailbox window. All of them also work with groups of messages that you select from a mailbox window using the mouse with the Shift and Ctrl keys, just as you do when you're working with files in Explorer.

Clean out the Trash box by clicking Eudora's Special menu, and then selecting Empty Trash. Bear in mind that you're actually deleting files here; this operation is exactly the same as emptying Window 95's Recycle Bin, and it is just as permanent.

You can set Eudora to empty the Trash by itself. Open the Switches dialog from the Special menu, and click to place a check mark in the Empty Trash on Quit box.

Working with Attachments to Mail Messages

Work-at-home types will be glad to know that they can send and receive complex binary files like spreadsheets or word processor documents via the Internet's e-mail service. It is, however, a feat that demands a bit of wizardry on both ends of the transaction.

Internet e-mail can't deal with binary files directly; the computer on the sending end has to convert them to ASCII text before putting them on the wire. The machine on the receiving end has to change them back. Eudora has built-in software that does this automatically.

Encoding Options

With Eudora you can attach a binary file to any outgoing message. Depending on your orders, the program will convert it to ASCII using one of two popular encoding protocols, BinHex or MIME.

BinHex was originally developed within the Macintosh community and is still extensively used there. Until recently it was also widely used by the PC community. It's more than adequate for transferring text files, but it's not completely reliable for complex files like images and other multimedia.

Programmers developed the *MIME* protocol to answer this problem. Thanks to support from the creators of Web browsers like Mosaic and Netscape Navigator, MIME encoding is now virtually an industry standard. Almost all major messaging software packages—Microsoft Exchange and Lotus' cc:Mail included—support it.

Unfortunately, Eudora Light doesn't support another major protocol, UUEncoding, that's popular on UseNet's binaries newsgroups. Qualcomm supports this capability only in its commercial e-mail package, Eudora Pro.

Attaching Files

You'll need only a couple of mouse clicks to attach a file to an outgoing message. With a new message open, follow these steps:

1. Click the Messages menu and select Attach Document.

2. Eudora responds by presenting a standard Windows file selection dialog box. Work through your directory structure until you see the file you want, and then highlight it.

3. Click OK. The file's name and path should appear in your message's Attachment's field (see fig. 14.18).

Fig. 14.18
The author of this message has attached the file C:\ARCHIVE\ PGP262.ZIP and wants to send it out using the MIME protocol.

4. Choose an encoding protocol by clicking the drop-down box in the middle of Eudora's toolbar. Highlight your choice and release the mouse button.

Post your message in the ordinary manner. Eudora will encode and send the file after it's done sending the actual text.

Eudora Light requires almost no help from you to deal with incoming file attachments, as long as they're MIME- or BinHex-encoded. They're decoded automatically and stored in the directory you've specified in the Configuration dialog box.

Incoming file attachments that are UUEncoded need special handling. You'll have no trouble picking them out of your ordinary message traffic because they'll contain ASCII gibberish unreadable by humans. Save them to disk by clicking the File menu and choosing Save As, and then run them through a separate UUDecoding program like WinCode.

Mail Sorting and Message Handling

Keeping up with a heavy message load is a tough job. Mailboxes and folders help matters considerably, but they're not enough by themselves.

You would not, however, see them as a blessing if you had to pick through a half dozen mailboxes and a few hundred old mailings, just to find the since-forgotten post that told you how many people your boss was bringing to lunch.

Eudora fortunately has powerful sort and search features that make traffic control a manageable problem.

Sort Options

You can ask Eudora to sort a mailbox's message display in any of five ways by opening the Edit menu and selecting Sort. Most people find four of these methods useful:

- *Sort by Status* classifies messages by the entry in the mailbox's Status/ Priority box.
- *Sort by Sender* groups them by the address of the author or recipient.
- *Sort by Date* arranges them in chronological order, earliest to latest.
- *Sort by Subject* alphabetizes them according to the first letters in each message's subject field.

Note

The fifth sort option, Sort by Priority, isn't all that important unless you work in a large organization and use e-mail to communicate with your coworkers. Eudora gives you the option to assign a priority level to each outgoing message (accessible via a drop-down box on the extreme left of the toolbar). Most Internet users, however, don't bother with this feature.

Finding a Message

Eudora also gives you the ability to search for a message that contains a specific phrase or word. Just open the Edit menu, select the Find submenu, and then select Find (see fig. 14.19).

Fig. 14.19
Eudora's Find feature lets you search message headers or text for a specific word or phrase.

The dialog box that pops up has a place to enter the text you want to find. Checking the Match Case box tells Eudora to locate exact matches; leaving it blank tells it to report any instance of the word or phrase you're looking for.

The Summaries Only box gives you the option of telling Eudora to only search message headers. Leaving this box unchecked tells Eudora to ignore the headers in favor of searching the full text of each message.

You can repeat any search by opening the Edit menu and selecting Find Again from the Sort submenu.

II

Mastering Netscape

>

## CHAPTER 15

Reading UseNet Newsgroups with Netscape

CompuServe calls them forums. The Microsoft Network calls them BBSs (bulletin board systems). At your office, they're possibly known as cork boards. They are all places where people come together to exchange ideas and opinions, post public notices, or look for help. The Internet has such a place, too. On the Internet, it's called UseNet newsgroups, or just newsgroups for short.

You learn all about how newsgroups work and how to access newsgroups in this chapter. Here are some of the topics you'll find:

- How newsgroups work
- The different type of newsgroups on UseNet
- The organization of UseNet newsgroups
- Using Netscape's newsreader to access newsgroups
- Accessing newsgroups without using the newsreader

A UseNet Primer

Newsgroups are a bit more complicated than forums, BBSs, and cork boards. Not in a technical sense, but in a cultural sense. Newsgroups don't have official rules that are enforced by anyone in particular. They have unofficial rules that newsgroup peers enforce. Newsgroups concentrate cultures, from all over the world, in one place—a source of a lot of conflict as you can imagine.

So, take a few moments to study this section before you dive into newsgroups head first. Make sure that you understand how newsgroups and the UseNet culture works. Then, you'll learn how to use Netscape's newsreader to access one of the most dynamic parts of the Internet, newsgroups, later in this chapter.

Caution

If you're particularly sensitive or easily offended, newsgroups may not be right for you. Unlike the forums and BBSs on commercial online systems, no one is watching over the content on newsgroups. The material is often very offensive to some folks. You'll find plenty of nasty language and abusive remarks in some newsgroups, just like you'd expect to find in some pubs.

The Basics of Using Newsgroups

If you've ever used a forum or BBS on a commercial online service, you're already familiar with the concept of a newsgroup. Readers post messages, or articles, to newsgroups for other people to read. They can also reply to articles that they read on a newsgroup. It's one way for people like yourself to communicate with millions of people around the world.

Newsgroups are a bit looser, however. A newsgroup doesn't necessarily have a watch dog—other than the readers themselves. As a result, the organization is a bit looser, and the content of the messages is often way out of focus. The seemingly chaotic nature of newsgroups, however, produces some of the most interesting information you'll find anywhere.

Newsgroup Variety Is Good

The variety of content is exactly what makes newsgroups so appealing. There are newsgroups for expressing opinions—no matter how benign or how radical. There are other newsgroups for asking questions or getting help. And, best of all, there are newsgroups for those seeking companionship—whether they're looking for a soul-mate or longing to find someone with a similar interest in whittling. The following is a sample of the types of newsgroups you'll find:

- **alt.tv.simpsons** contains a lot of mindless chatter about the Simpson's.

- **comp.os.ms-windows.advocacy** is one of the hottest Window's newsgroups around. You'll find heated discussions about both Windows 3.1 and Windows 95.

- **rec.games.trading-cards.marketplace** is the place to be if you're into sports trading cards.

- **rec.humor.funny** is where to go to lighten up your day. You'll find a wide variety of humor, including contemporary jokes, old standards, and bogus news flashes.

Alternative and Regional Newsgroups

Not all the newsgroups available are true UseNet newsgroups. Some newsgroups are created to serve a particular region or are so obscure that they
wouldn't make it through the rigorous UseNet approval process. If something
looks like a newsgroup and acts like a newsgroup, however, it can find its way
onto your news server.

Here are some examples:

- Regional—Many localities, such as Dallas or San Francisco, have their
  own newsgroups where people exchange dining tips, consumer advice,
  and other regional bits of information.

- Alternative—The alt newsgroups are responsible for most of the variety
  on UseNet. Some of these groups have a reputation for being downright
  nasty (for example, pornography), but also have groups dedicated to
  your favorite TV shows, books, or politicians.

> **Note**
>
> If you have a child who will be using newsgroups, you might consider finding a
> service provider that makes the pornographic newsgroups, such as **alt.sex.pictures**
> and **alt.binaries.pictures.erotica**, unavailable.

Moderated Newsgroups

Moderated newsgroups are a bit more civil, and the articles are typically more
focused than unmoderated newsgroups. Moderators look at every article
posted to their newsgroup before making it available for everyone to read. If
they judge it to be inappropriate, they nuke it.

So what are the advantages of a moderated newsgroup? You don't have to
wade through ten pounds of garbage to find one ounce of treasure. Check
out some of the alternative newsgroups and you'll get the picture. Most the
alternative newsgroups are unmoderated. As such, they're a free-for-all—
profanity, abusiveness, and childish bickering. The value and quality of the
information that you'll find in moderated newsgroups is much higher than
their unmoderated cousins.

The disadvantages, on the other hand, are just as clear. Some people believe
that moderating a newsgroup is the equivalent of censorship. Instead of the
group as a whole determining the content of a newsgroups, the judgment of
a single individual determines the content of the newsgroups. Another significant disadvantage is timeliness. Articles posted to moderated newsgroups
can be delayed days or weeks.

Participating in a Newsgroup

Every Internet resource that you want to use requires a client program on your computer. Newsgroups are no exception. The program that you use to read newsgroups is called a newsreader.

A newsreader lets you browse the newsgroups that are available, reading and posting articles along the way. Most newsreaders also have more advanced features that make using newsgroups a bit more productive. Later in this chapter, you'll learn how to use Netscape's newsreader to access the news. You'll also find other ways to read the newsgroups without using a newsreader.

So How Do Newsgroups Work, Anyway?

NNTP (Network News Transport Protocol) is used to move the news from one server to another. It's very similar to e-mail in a lot of respects. Instead of all the messages sitting on your machine, however, they are stored on an NNTP news server that many other people can access. Therefore, the news only has to be sent to the server, instead of each user. Each user is then responsible for retrieving the articles she's interested in.

UseNet news makes its way to your news server using a process called flooding. That is, all the news servers are networked together. A particular news server may be fed by one news server, while it feeds three other news servers in turn. Periodically, it's flooded with news from the news server that's feeding it, and it floods all of its news to the news servers that it feeds.

Wading Through UseNet

Sometimes, you'll feel like you're knee deep in newsgroups. There are over 10,000 newsgroups available. Wading through them all to find what you want can be a daunting task. What's a new user to do?

It's all right there in front of you. There's a lot of logic to the way newsgroups are named. Once you learn it, you'll be able to pluck out a newsgroup just by how it's named. You'll also find tools to help you locate just the right newsgroup, as well as a few newsgroups that provide helpful advice and pointers to new users.

Newsgroup Organization

Newsgroups are organized into a hierarchy of categories and subcategories. Take a look at the **alt.tv.simpsons** newsgroup discussed earlier. The top-level category is **alt**. The subcategory is **tv**. The subcategory under that is **simpsons**. The name goes from general to specific, left to right. You'll also find other newsgroups under **alt.tv**, such as **alt.tv.friends** and **alt.tv.home-imprvment**.

Mastering Netscape

> **Tip**
>
> **alt.tv.*** is a notational convention that means all the newsgroups available under the
> **alt.tv** category.

There are many different top-level categories available. Table 15.1 shows
some that you probably have available on your news server.

Table 15.1   Internet Top-Level Newsgroup Categories

Category	Description
alt	Alternative newsgroups
bit	BitNet LISTSERV mailing lists
biz	Advertisements for businesses
clarinet	News clipping service by subscription only
comp	Computer-related topics: hardware and software
k12	Educational, kindergarten through grade 12
misc	Topics that don't fit the other categories
news	News and information about UseNet
rec	Recreational, sports, hobbies, music, games
sci	Applied sciences
soc	Social and cultural topics
talk	Discussion of more controversial topics

These categories help you nail down exactly which newsgroup you're looking
for. A bit of practice helps as well. If you're looking for information about
Windows 95, for example, start looking at the comp top-level category. You'll
find an **os** category, which probably represents operating systems. Under that
category, you'll find an ms-windows category.

> **Note**
>
> Exactly which newsgroups are available on your news server is largely under the
> control of the administrator. Some administrators filter out regional newsgroups that
> don't apply to your area. Some also filter out the **alt** newsgroups because of their
> potentially offensive content.

Searching for Newsgroups on the Web

Scouring the categories for a particular newsgroup may not be the most efficient way to find what you want. Here are a couple of tools that help you find newsgroups based upon keywords that you type:

- Point Netscape at **www.cen.uiuc.edu/cgi-bin/find-news**. This tool searches all the newsgroup names and newsgroup descriptions for a single keyword that you specify.

- Another very similar tool is at **www.nova.edu/Inter-Links/cgi-bin/news.pl**. This tool allows you to give more than one keyword, however.

Newsgroups for New Users

Whenever I go some place new, I first try to locate a source of information about it. Likewise, the first few places that you need to visit when you get to UseNet are all the newsgroups that are there to welcome you. It's not just a warm and fuzzy welcome, either. They provide useful information about what to do, what not to do, and how to get the most out of the newsgroups. Table 15.2 shows you the newsgroups that you need to check out.

Table 15.2 Newsgroups for the Newbie

Newsgroup	Description
alt.answers	A good source of FAQs and information about alt newsgroups
alt.internet.services	This is the place to ask about Internet programs and resources
news.announce.newsgroups	Announcements about new newsgroups are made here
news.announce.newusers	Articles and FAQs for the new newsgroups user
news.newusers.questions	This is the place to ask your questions about using newsgroups

Note

Don't post test articles to these newsgroups. Don't post articles asking for someone to send you an e-mail, either. This is a terrible waste of newsgroups that are intended to help new users learn the ropes. See the section "Practice Posting in the Right Place" later in this chapter to learn about a better place to post test articles.

news.announce.newusers

The **news.announce.newusers** newsgroup contains a lot of great articles for new newsgroup users. In particular, look for the articles with the following subject lines:

■ What is UseNet?

■ What is UseNet? A second opinion

■ Rules for posting to UseNet

■ Hints on writing style for UseNet

■ A Primer on How to Work with the UseNet Community

■ Emily Postnews Answers Your Questions on Netiquette

■ How to find the right place to post (FAQ)

■ Answers to Frequently Asked Questions about UseNet

Getting Real News on UseNet

UseNet is good for a lot more than just blathering and downloading questionable art. There's a lot of news and great information coming from a variety of sources. You'll find "real" news, current Internet events, organizational newsgroups, and regional newsgroups as well—all of which make newsgroups worth every bit of trouble.

ClariNet

You can be the first kid on the block with the current news. ClariNet is a news service that clips articles from sources such as the AP and Reuters news wires. They post these services to the **clari.*** newsgroups. These newsgroups aren't free, though. They sell these newsgroups on a subscription basis. You wouldn't want to pay for them, either, because they can be expensive. Many independent service providers do subscribe, however, as a part of their service.

ClariNet has more than 300 newsgroups from which to choose. My favorite ClariNet newsgroups are shown in table 15.3. You'll come up with your own favorites in short order. One ClariNet newsgroup that you definitely need to check out is **clari.net.newusers**. It's a good introduction to all the newsgroups that ClariNet offers.

II

Mastering Netscape

Table 15.3 Popular Clarinet Newsgroups	
Newsgroup	**Description**
clari.biz.briefs	Regular business updates
clari.local.*State*	Your own local news
clari.nb.online	News about the online community
clari.nb.windows	News about Windows products and issues
clari.news.briefs	Regular national and world news updates

For your convenience, table 15.4 describes each ClariNet news category. You'll find individual newsgroups under each category. Under the **clari.living** category, for example, you'll find arts, books, music, and movies.

Table 15.4 ClariNet News Categories at a Glance	
Category	**Description**
clari.news	General and national news
clari.biz	Business and financial news
clari.sports	Sports and athletic news
clari.living	Lifestyle and human interest stories
clari.world	News about other countries
clari.local	States and local areas
clari.feature	Special syndicated features
clari.tw	Technical and scientific news
clari.matrix_news	A networking newsletter
clari.nb	Newsbytes, computer industry news
clari.sfbay	San Francisco Bay Area news
clari.net	Information about ClariNet
clari.apbl	Special groups for the AP BulletinLine

Net-happenings

If it seems that the Internet is moving too fast to keep up with, you're right—without help, anyway. The **comp.internet.net-happenings** newsgroup helps you keep track of new events on the Internet, including the World Wide Web, mailing lists, UseNet, and so on.

The subject line of each article tells you a lot about the announcement. Take, for example, the following announcement:

```
WWW>Free Internet service for first 100 visitors
```

The first part tells you that the announcement is about a World Wide Web site. You'll find many other categories such as FAQ, EMAG, LISTS, and MISC. The second part is a brief description about the announcement. Most of the time, the description is enough to tell you whether you want to see more information by opening the article. The article itself is a few paragraphs about the announcement, with the address or subscription information near the top.

Regional Newsgroups

Is your geographical region represented on UseNet? A lot are. The Dallas/Fort Worth area has a couple of newsgroups, such as **dfw.eats**, **dfw.forsale**, and **dfw.personals**. Virtually every state has similar newsgroups. Other states might have special needs. For example, California users might be interested in the **ca.environment.earthquakes** newsgroup.

Using Netscape to Read the News

All that news is out there, just sloshing around on the news server, and you need a program to get at it. There are a lot of newsreaders out there, but you already have Netscape's newsreader. It's one of the cleanest and easiest to use newsreaders available.

Starting the Netscape newsreader is easy. Choose <u>W</u>indow, <u>N</u>etscape News from the Netscape main menu. Figure 15.1 shows the Netscape newsreader, and table 15.5 shows what each of the buttons on the toolbar do.

II

Mastering Netscape

Fig. 15.1

The Netscape newsreader window is divided into three panes: groups list, article list, and article body.

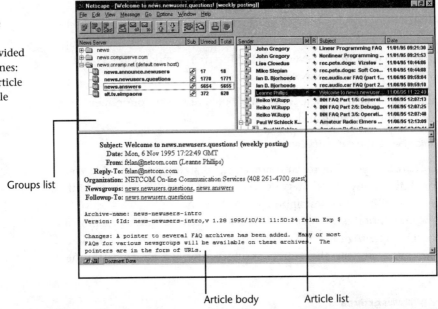

Groups list

Article body   Article list

Table 15.5 Buttons on the Netscape Newsreader Toolbar

Button	Name	Description
	Post new	Post new article to newsgroup
	Post reply	Post reply to newsgroup article
	Post and reply	Post and e-mail a reply
	New message	Create a new e-mail message
	Reply	Reply using an e-mail message
	Forward	Forward article to e-mail address
	Previous	Previous article in a newsgroup

Button	Name	Description
	Next	Next article in a newsgroup
	Mark thread read	Mark entire conversation as read
	Mark all read	Mark entire newsgroup as read
	Print	Print the current article
	Stop	Stop transferring from news server

Configuring Netscape to Read the News

To configure Netscape for your service provider, use the following steps:

1. Choose Options, Mail and News Preferences from the Netscape newsreader main menu, and click the Servers tab. Netscape displays the dialog box shown in figure 15.2.

◀ See "Loading and Configuring Netscape," pg. 59

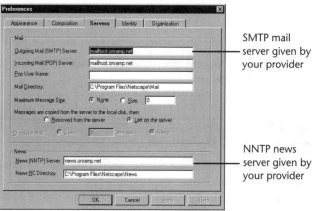

SMTP mail server given by your provider

NNTP news server given by your provider

Fig. 15.2
Your service provider should have given you the NNTP news server and SMTP mail server.

2. Fill in your NNTP (Network News Transfer Protocol) and SMTP (Simple Mail Transfer Protocol) servers as shown in figure 15.2, and click the Identity tab. Netscape displays the dialog box shown in figure 15.3.

II

Mastering Netscape

Fig. 15.3
You need to
provide a name
and e-mail address
so that other
people can
respond to your
postings.

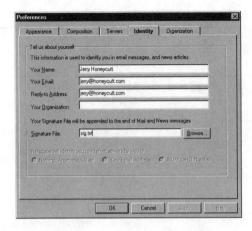

3. Fill in Your Name, Your Email, and Reply-to Address as shown in figure
   15.3. If you want to attach a signature file to the end of your postings,
   select a text file by clicking Browse. Click OK to save your changes.

Troubleshooting

Why do I get an error message that says Netscape couldn't find the news server?

First, make sure that you have a connection to your service provider. If you're definitely connected, make sure that you correctly configured your NNTP news server.
Don't remember the exact address your provider gave you? Try this: If your domain
name is provider.net, then add news to the front of it like this: **news.provider.net**.

Can I use Netscape to access UseNet through CompuServe?

Yes. The CompuServe news server is **news.compuserve.com** and the SMTP mail
server is **mail.compuserve.com**.

A Note about Signatures

You can easily personalize your postings with a signature. Save about three lines that
say something about yourself, such as your address and hobbies, into a text file.
Then, in step 3 of "Configuring Netscape to Read the News," select the text file you
created. Here's an example of a signature file:

```
Jerry Honeycutt ¦           jerry@honeycutt.com
                ¦                 (800) 555-1212
                ¦ Buy Using the Internet, Now!
```

Your signature can communicate anything that you want about yourself including your name, mailing address, phone number, address, or a particular phrase that reflects your outlook on life. It is considered good form, however, to limit your signatures to three lines.

Subscribing to Newsgroups

After you've configured the Netscape newsreader for your service provider, you need to download a complete list of the newsgroups available on your news server. Highlight your news server in the groups pane, and choose Show All Newsgroups from the main menu. Netscape displays a dialog box warning you that this process can take a few minutes on a slow connection. Click OK to continue.

Before you can read the articles in a newsgroup, you have to subscribe to it. When you subscribe to a newsgroup, you're telling Netscape that you want to read the articles in that newsgroup. Normally, Netscape only displays the newsgroups to which you've subscribed. Thus, subscribing to a handful of newsgroups keeps you from having to slog through a list of 10,000 newsgroups to find what you want.

Tip

Categories are indicated with a file folder icon, newsgroups are indicated with a newspaper icon.

Earlier you learned that newsgroups are named in a hierarchical fashion. Netscape takes advantage of this by organizing newsgroups the same way, using folders in the groups pane. Initially, all you see under a news server is the top-level categories. If you click one of the top-level categories, you see the sub-categories underneath it. Continue clicking categories until you see a newsgroup to which you can subscribe.

If you want to subscribe to **alt.tv.simpsons**, for example, follow these steps:

1. Click the **alt** top-level newsgroup.
2. Find **alt.tv** in the list under alt, and click it.
3. Find **alt.tv.simpsons** in the list under **alt.tv**, and check the box that is to the right of the name to indicate that you want to subscribe to that newsgroup.

II

Mastering Netscape

After you subscribe to all the newsgroups you want, you can tell Netscape to display only those newsgroups to which you've subscribed. Choose Options, Show Subscribed Groups from the main menu.

Note

You can sample the articles in a newsgroup before subscribing. If you click a newsgroup to which you haven't subscribed, Netscape displays that newsgroup's articles in the article pane. If you like what you see, subscribe to the group by checking the box next to the name of the newsgroup.

Browsing and Reading Articles

Tip

Articles that you haven't read have a green diamond in the R column.

Select a newsgroup in the groups Pane and Netscape displays all the current articles for that group in the articles pane. You can scroll up and down the list of articles looking for an interesting article. When you click an article in the article pane, Netscape displays the contents of that article in the body pane.

Notice that some of the articles are indented under other articles. These are replies to the articles under which they are indented. All the messages indented under an article, including the original message, are called a thread. Netscape indents articles this way so you can visually follow the thread. Figure 15.4 shows what a thread looks like in Netscape.

Troubleshooting

What happened to the articles that were here a few days ago?

It's not practical to keep every article posted to every newsgroup indefinitely. Your service provider deletes the older articles to make room for the newer articles. Another way of saying this is that a message scrolled off. The length of time that an article hangs around varies from provider to provider, but is usually between three days and a week.

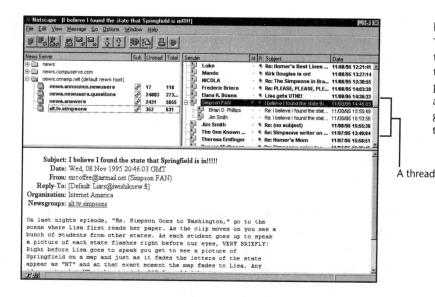

Fig. 15.4
The top portion of the message's body tells you who posted the message and what other groups they posted the message to.

A thread

Moving Around the Article Pane

When you click an article header in the article pane, the article's contents are automatically displayed in the body pane. After you read the article, you can click another article, or you can use the following options from Netscape's toolbar and menu to move around:

- Choose <u>G</u>o, Ne<u>x</u>t Unread from the main menu to read the next message you haven't read.

- Choose <u>G</u>o, Pre<u>v</u>ious Unread from the main menu to read the previous message you haven't read.

- Click the Next button to read the next article in the newsgroup—whether you've read it already or not.

- Click the Previous button to read the previous article in the newsgroup—whether you've read it already or not.

- Choose <u>G</u>o, <u>F</u>irst Unread to read the first message in the newsgroup that you haven't yet read.

Mastering Netscape

Troubleshooting

I opened an article, but its contents were all garbled.

You've probably opened an article that is ROT13-encoded. ROT13 is an encoding method that has little to do with security. It allows a person who is posting a potentially offensive message to place the responsibility for its contents on you—the reader. It essentially says that if you decode and read this message, you won't hold me responsible for its contents. To decode the article, right-click in the body pane, and choose Unscramble (ROT-13).

Downloading Files from Newsgroups

► See "Using Compressed/ Encoded Files," pg. 571

Posting and downloading files from a newsgroup is a bit more complicated than your experience with online services. Binary files can't be posted directly to UseNet. Many methods have evolved, however, to encode files into text so that they can be sent.

The downloading process works as follows:

1. A file is encoded, using UUEncode, to a newsgroup as one or more articles.

2. While you're browsing a newsgroup, you notice a few articles with subject lines that look like this (headings are provided for your convenience):

Lines	File name	Part	Description
5	HOMER.GIF	[00/02]	Portrait of Homer Simpson
800	HOMER.GIF	[01/02]	Portrait of Homer Simpson
540	HOMER.GIF	[02/02]	Portrait of Homer Simpson

These articles are three parts of the same file. The first article is probably a description of the file because it is part zero, and because there are only five lines in it. The next two articles are the actual file.

3. To download a file from a newsgroup, you retrieve all the articles belonging to that file. Then, you UUDecode the articles back into a binary file. See chapter 23, "Dealing with Compressed/Encoded Files," to learn how.

Replying to an Article

You'll eventually want to post a reply to an article you read in a newsgroup. You might want to be helpful and answer someone's question. You're just as likely to find an interesting discussion to which you want to contribute. Either way, the following are two different ways you can reply to an article you have read:

- Follow up—If you want your reply to be read by everyone who frequents the newsgroup, post a follow-up article. Your reply is added to the thread. To reply to an article, click the Post Reply button on the toolbar. Fill in the window shown in figure 15.5, and click the Send button.

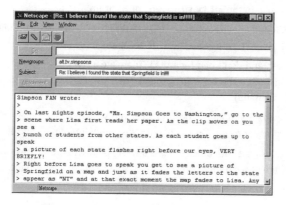

Fig. 15.5
The text that starts with the greater-than sign (>) is the original article. Delete everything that you don't need to remind the reader of what he posted.

- E-mail—If your reply would benefit only the person to whom you're replying, respond with an e-mail message instead. That person gets the message faster, and the other newsgroup readers aren't annoyed. To reply by e-mail, click the Reply button on the toolbar. Fill out the window shown in figure 15.6 and click the Send button.

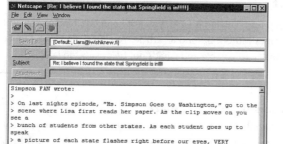

Fig. 15.6
Look carefully— the only difference between this window and the window in figure 15.5 is this window has the Send To field and the previous window as the Newsgroups field.

Stay out of Trouble; Follow the Rules

Etiquette, as Miss Manners will tell you, was created so that everyone would get along better. Etiquette's rules are not official rules, however; they're community standards for how everyone should behave. Likewise, netiquette is a community standard for how to behave on the Internet. It's important for two reasons. First, it helps keep the frustration level down. Second, it helps prevent the terrible waste of Internet resources by limiting the amount of noise.

- Post your articles in the right place. Don't post questions about Windows 95, for example, to the **alt.tv.simpsons** newsgroup.

- NEWSGROUP READERS REALLY HATE IT WHEN YOU SHOUT BY USING ALL CAPS. It doesn't make your message seem any more important.

- Don't test, and don't beg for e-mail. There are a few places where that is appropriate, but this behavior generally gets you flamed (a flame is a mean or abusive message).

- Don't spam. Spamming is posting an advertisement to several, if not hundreds, of newsgroups. Don't do it. It's a waste of Internet resources.

- Don't cross-post your article. This is a waste of Internet resources, and readers quickly tire of seeing the same article posted to many newsgroups.

Posting a New Article

It's no fun being a spectator. You'll eventually want to start a discussion of your own. To post a new article, click the Post New button on the toolbar. Fill in the window shown previously in figure 15.5 and click the Send button.

Note

Lurk before you leap. Lurking is when you just hang out, reading the articles and learning the ropes without posting an article. You'll avoid making a fool of yourself by learning what's acceptable and what's not before it's too late.

Practice Posting in the Right Place

You'll find a special newsgroup, called alt.test, that exists just for test posting. You can post a test article to that newsgroup all day long and no one will care.

In fact, you should go ahead and post a test article just to make sure that everything works. You'll get a good idea of how long it takes your article to show up, and you'll also learn the mechanics of posting and replying to articles.

> **Tip**
>
> Test your file uploads in the **alt.test** newsgroup, too, instead of testing them in productive newsgroups.

Posting a File

Netscape makes posting a file easy. Post a new article as described in the section, "Posting a New Article." Before you click the Send button, however, follow these instructions:

1. Click Attachment. Netscape displays the Attachments dialog box as shown in figure 15.7.

Fig. 15.7
You can attach more than one file to an article.

2. Click Attach File, choose the file you want to attach in the Enter File to Attach dialog box, and click Open.

3. Repeat step 2 for each file you want to attach to your article. Then, click OK to save your attachments.

After you've selected the files you want to attach to your posting, you can continue editing it normally. Click the Send button when you're finished.

Other Ways to Read the News

If browsing newsgroups with a newsreader seems like too much trouble, the tools described in this section might be just what you need. You'll learn to use DejaView, which lets you search UseNet for specific articles. You'll also learn how to use SIFT, a tool that filters all the newsgroup postings and saves them for you to read later.

Searching UseNet with DejaNews

DejaNews is a Web tool that searches all the newsgroup articles, past and present, for terms that you specify. Point your Web browser at

II

Mastering Netscape

dejanews3.dejanews.com/forms/dnq.html. Figure 15.8 shows you the DejaNews search Web page. To search UseNet, fill in the form as shown in figure 15.8, and click Search.

Fig. 15.8

Click the Create a Query Filter link to specify exactly which newsgroup, author, or date range to search.

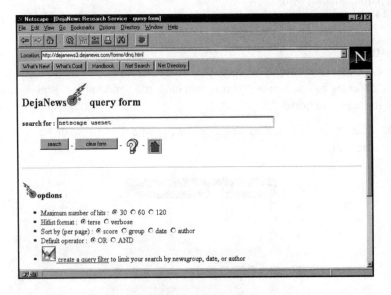

DejaNews displays another Web page that contains a list of the newsgroup articles it found. You can click any of these articles to read them, or click Get Next 30 Hits to display the next page full of articles. The following are a couple of other things you should know:

- The author's name is the last item on each line. You can click it to see what other newsgroups they typically post to.

- You can click the subject line of an article to display the complete thread that contains that article.

Filtering UseNet with SIFT

SIFT is a tool provided by Stanford that filters all the articles posted to UseNet. As an added bonus, it filters a lot of public mailing lists and new Web pages, too. You tell SIFT the keywords in which you're interested, and it keeps track of all the new documents on the Internet that match those keywords. Like DejaNews, this is a Web tool, so point your browser at **sift.stanford.edu**.

The first time you access SIFT, it asks you for an e-mail address and password. You don't have one, yet. That's OK. Type your e-mail address and make up a password. You'll need to use the same password the next time that you access SIFT. Click Enter to go to the search form.

The most effective way to use SIFT is as follows:

1. Figure 15.9 shows the SIFT search form. Select the Search radio button, and type the topics for which you're looking in Topic. If you want to make sure that some topics are not included, type them in Avoid.

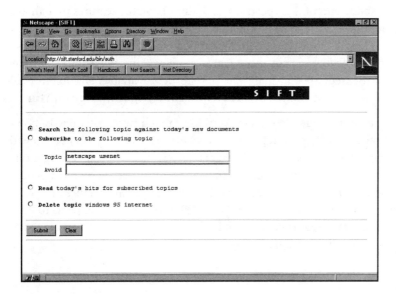

Fig. 15.9
You won't see the Read and Delete Topic choices until you've submitted at least one subscription.

2. Click Submit. SIFT displays a page, containing all of today's new articles that match your keywords, on each line. The most relevant line is at the top; the least relevant is at the bottom. Read some of the articles, Web pages, and mailing list messages by clicking them.

3. If you're happy with these test results, click Subscribe at the bottom of the Web page. Then, click Submit. The next time you log on to SIFT, you'll see additional lines at the bottom of the Web page, as shown in figure 15.9, that let you delete subscriptions or review the current day's hits.

4. If you're not happy with the results, click Search at the bottom of the Web page. Then, adjust the keywords in Topic and Avoid, and click Submit. SIFT displays a similar Web page using your new search keywords.

The Pros and Cons of Netscape's Newsreader

There's a wide variety of newsreaders available on the Internet. They range from the most basic (Qnews) to complex (Free Agent). Netscape's newsreader is at the basic end of this spectrum. It doesn't have the features that an avid UseNet junkie needs to be productive. Netscape doesn't let you choose a UUEncoded file, for example, then download and UUDecode it automatically. If you need more advanced features such as this, you should consider some of the freeware and shareware newsreaders available. Free Agent is available on the Web at **www.forteinc.com/forte/agent/dlmain.htm**.

Netscape's newsreader does have everything that a casual user needs, however. You can easily post, reply, and view articles—possibly easier than with the other newsreaders available. You can also view UUEncoded images on UseNet just by selecting the article in the list. This is about all most people use UseNet for anyway. Incidentally, the most important feature of Netscape's newsreader is how solid and well thought out it appears to be. Newsgroups are organized using an outline metaphor and the article list is easy to navigate, for example.

Part III

Using Helper Applications

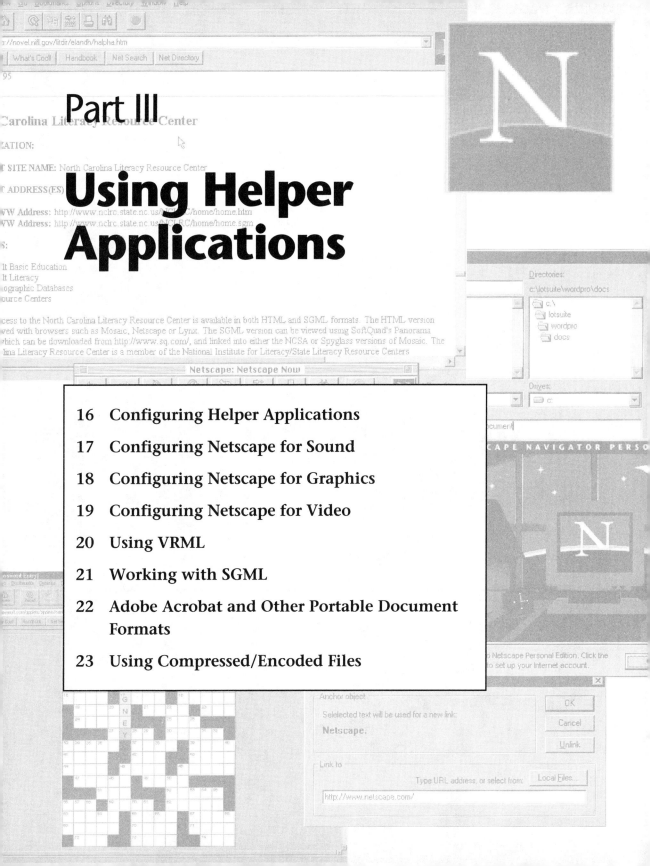

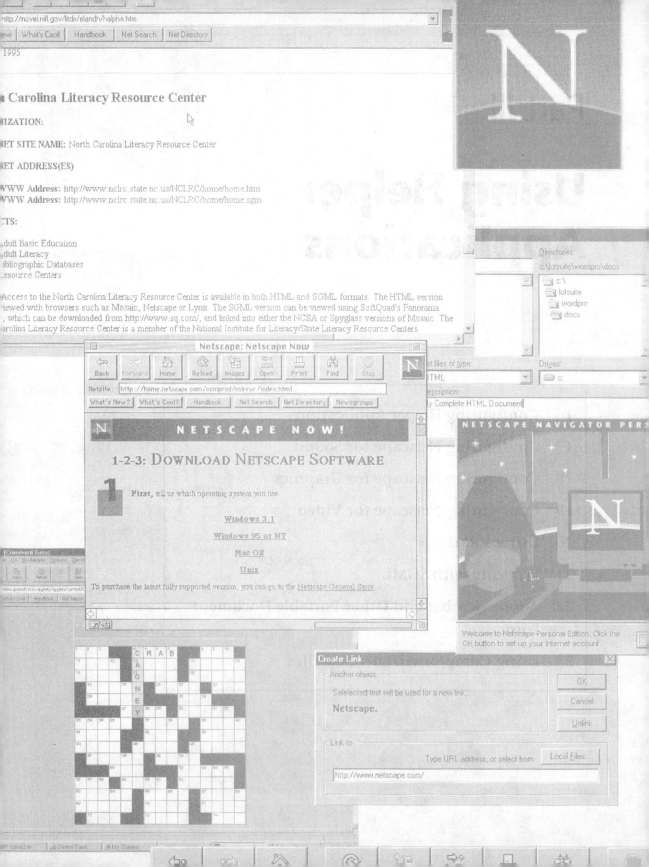

ew! | What's Cool! | Handbook | Net Search | Net Directory |

1995

Carolina Literacy Resource Center

IZATION:

ET SITE NAME: North Carolina Literacy Resource Center

ET ADDRESS(ES)

WWW Address: http://www.nclrc.state.nc.us/NCLRC/home/home.htm
WWW Address: http://www.nclrc.state.nc.us/NCLRC/home/home.sgm

CTS:

dult Basic Education
dult Literacy
ibliographic Databases
esource Centers

Access to the North Carolina Literacy Resource Center is available in both HTML and SGML formats. The HTML version
iewed with browsers such as Mosaic, Netscape or Lynx. The SGML version can be viewed using SoftQuad's Panorama
, which can be downloaded from http://www.sq.com/, and linked into either the NCSA or Spyglass versions of Mosaic. The
arolina Literacy Resource Center is a member of the National Institute for Literacy/State Literacy Resource Centers

Directories:
c:\lotsuite\wordpro\docs

c:\
lotsuite
wordpro
docs

st files of type: Drives:
HTML   c:

escription:
y Complete HTML Document

Netscape: Netscape Now

Back | Forward | Home | Reload | Images | Open | Print | Find | Stop

Netsite: http://home.netscape.com/comprod/mirror/index.html

What's New? | What's Cool? | Handbook | Net Search | Net Directory | Newsgroups

N   NETSCAPE NOW!

1-2-3: DOWNLOAD NETSCAPE SOFTWARE

First, tell us which operating system you use.

Windows 3.1

Windows 95 or NT

Mac OS

Unix

To purchase the latest fully supported version, you can go to the Netscape General Store.

NETSCAPE NAVIGATOR PERS

Welcome to Netscape Personal Edition. Click the
OK button to set up your Internet account.

[Crossword Entry]

CRAB
AGNEY

Create Link

Anchor object

Selelected text will be used for a new link:

Netscape.

OK
Cancel
Unlink

Link to

Type URL address, or select from: Local Files...

http://www.netscape.com/

## CHAPTER 16

Configuring Helper Applications

16

We can't always manage single-handedly everything that comes our way—sometimes we need a little help from our friends. Netscape is no different. It can't handle every single file type that it encounters on the World Wide Web. Sometimes it needs a little help from *helper applications*.

Fortunately, it's pretty easy to configure helper applications for Netscape. The hard part is figuring out which ones you need and where to get them. This chapter should help with the first, the enclosed CD-ROM should help you with the second.

In this chapter, you learn:

- Which file types require helper applications, and which don't
- What kind of helper applications are right for you
- Where to get helper applications
- How to configure helper applications to work with Netscape

The following chapters in this section will help you choose the best Netscape helper applications for:

- Sound
- Graphics
- Video
- VRML (Virtual Reality Markup Language)
- SGML (Standard Generalized Markup Language)
- Adobe Acrobat and other Portable Document Formats
- File decompression

What Are Helper Applications?

Though Netscape is a pretty versatile Web browser, you'll still run into files on the Web that it can't display: video files, audio files, odd graphics files, strange document formats, and even compressed files. To display or play these files, you need to set up helper applications.

A helper application is simply a program that can understand and interpret files that Netscape can't handle itself. Almost any program can be configured to act as a helper application for Netscape. The trick is figuring out which ones will be the most useful to you.

All Web browsers need helper applications. There are simply too many different file types on the Web for a browser to be able to handle them all internally.

Think about this: On a daily basis, you probably use a dozen or more different programs for word processing, spreadsheets, database management, electronic mail, graphics, and many other different applications. Each of these programs produces a different kind of data file, yet only a few of your applications are able to import even a limited number of different file types from other applications. And we're only talking about one person's files on a single computer! It's just not possible for Netscape to handle all the thousands of different file types it might encounter on the Web all by itself.

> **Note**
>
> Plug-ins are Netscape 2.0's new approach to handling animation, interactive multimedia, and much, much more. In a nutshell, *plug-ins* are add-on inline viewer modules for "live objects," which appear right on the Netscape screen alongside the text and inline graphics that Netscape can already display. With the proper plug-ins installed, Netscape can handle almost any file type inline, without spawning an external helper application. While this doesn't mean the end of helper applications, it is an exciting new capability of Netscape 2.0. For a detailed look at plug-ins, see chapter 36, "Netscape Plug-Ins."

Configuring a Helper Application

No matter what helper applications you choose to add, they all configure the same way. It takes only a few simple steps to set one up.

If you look at table 16.1, you'll notice that Netscape can't display .BMP and .PCX image files. These are pretty ubiquitous file types, and you'll run into them fairly often on the Web. A helper application is definitely in order.

Fortunately, Microsoft includes a program in Windows 95 that does a great job of displaying .PCX and .BMP files: Microsoft Paint—called Paintbrush in Windows 3.1 (see fig. 16.1).

Fig. 16.1
Microsoft's Paint comes with all versions of Windows. It makes a dandy Netscape helper application for viewing .BMP and .PCX image files.

To configure Paint as your .PCX/.BMP helper application for Netscape, follow these steps:

1. Open Netscape's Options menu, and select General.

2. Click the Helper Applications tab to bring it to the front (see fig. 16.2).

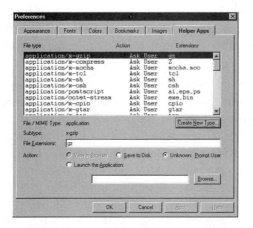

Fig. 16.2
The Helper Applications tab.

III

Using Helper Apps

3. Scroll down the list of MIME types until you see the image/X-MS-bmp entry. Click it to highlight it. The extension "bmp" appears in the File Extensions field (see fig. 16.3).

Fig. 16.3
Select the file type from the variety of types available.

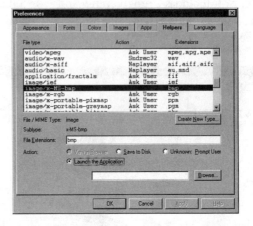

4. Click the Browse button. A dialog box appears. Find your Windows directory and double-click Pbrush (see fig. 16.4).

Fig. 16.4
Find the Pbrush.exe file and double-click it.

5. The full path name for the Paint program appears in the application box beside the Paint icon, and the Launch Application radio button is auto-selected. If you choose OK now, Paint will be configured as Netscape's helper application for .BMP files. But we want to use it to view .PCX files, too, so we'll go on.

6. Scrolling up and down through the list of MIME file types reveals that there is no entry for a file type with a .PCX extension, so we have to define our own. Click the Create New Type button to bring up the Configure New Mime Type dialog box. We can only enter one of the seven official MIME types in the Mime Type windows, so choose Image. We must make up our own MIME subtype because none is listed. We know that any "unofficial" MIME subtype must begin with "X-", and we need to follow that prefix with something unique, so let's just use the file name extension. Type **x-pcx** into the Mime SubType box and then click OK (see fig. 16.5).

Fig. 16.5
The Configure New Mime Type dialog box.

7. In the File Extensions box, type **pcx**. Because you already know the full path name for Paint, just type it into the File Path box, or you can enter it like you did before by Browsing. If the radio button labeled Launch the Application isn't auto-checked, check it manually (see fig. 16.6).

Fig. 16.6
Choose your file extension here.

8. Click OK to finish.

That's it! Paint is officially a Netscape helper application. The next time Netscape encounters a .PCX or .BMP image, it will automatically launch Paint to view it (see fig. 16.7).

Tip

You can also tell Netscape to automatically save a particular file type to disk whenever it is encountered, rather than configuring a helper app to display it. During the configuration process, just click the radio button labeled Save to Disk instead of the one marked Launch Application. You'll probably want to pick Save to Disk for files with an extension of .EXE (MIME: application/octet-stream) because these are usually executable programs.

III

Using Helper Apps

Fig. 16.7
Paint, now fully
configured as a
Netscape helper
application,
displays the flag.

What Kinds of Files Are on the Web?

Just about every type of file you can imagine exists somewhere on the World Wide Web (see table 16.1 for some examples). But this doesn't mean you'll run into them all.

Web pages themselves are almost always composed of just two elements: HTML-formatted text and inline graphics. All Web browsers can handle these, including Netscape; you don't need to worry about configuring helper applications just to be able to read Web pages. The problem comes when you try to access an external file by clicking a link to something other than a Web page.

Even then, the problem does not loom as large as you might fear, because the Web is mostly a compendium of hypermedia documents. That is, the hyperlinks on most Web pages jump to files with some sort of multimedia content: text, audio, graphics, or video. Even if these are in formats that Netscape doesn't speak natively, once you've configured helper applications for the half dozen or so most common multimedia file types, you may be able to go for months without encountering anything your Netscape configuration can't handle. (For some great online info about multimedia file types, follow the link in fig. 16.8.)

However, even if you do your best to avoid exotic file types, the day will come when you'll find a site that provides a link to some killer, must-have file that exists only in some weird format that you've never heard of before. Never fear. By configuring the proper Netscape helper application on the spot, you'll be able to play or display it properly. That's the beauty of helper applications. They make Netscape infinitely open-ended, extensible, and expandable.

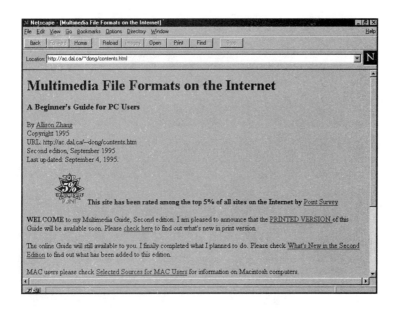

Fig. 16.8
An excellent reference to the kinds of files you'll run into on the World Wide Web is Allison Zhang's online book *Multimedia File Formats on the Internet* at **http://ac.dal.ca/~dong/contents.html**.

Netscape's Built-in Capabilities

Before we get into the topic of the helper apps you need, let's take a moment to find out which ones you *don't* need. Netscape already includes the built-in ability to display the three most-used graphics file formats on the Web, and bundles an external helper application that plays two of the most popular audio file types, as well.

Built-in GIF, JPEG, and XBM Image Display

You don't have to configure helper applications for GIF, JPEG, or XBM images. Netscape displays all three of these graphic file formats just fine all by itself.

There are good reasons for having graphics support built right into Netscape, though (see fig. 16.9). Web pages are more aesthetically pleasing if they combine text with inline graphics. But you'd be stuck with separate windows for text and graphics if Netscape had to launch a helper application every time it displayed an image. All Web browsers have to be able to display at least one graphic image format internally if text and graphics are to stay together on the page.

III

Using Helper Apps

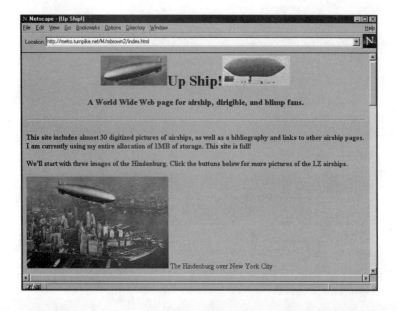

Tip

Have you ever wished that Netscape could display an inline graphic in its own window instead of inline? It can! Right-click the image and you'll see the menu of options shown in figure 16.10. Select View this Image and it will be displayed in its own window. You can also choose Save this Image As to save the image to disk, or choose Copy this Image Location to copy the URL of the image to the Windows Clipboard.

Most of the inline graphics on Web pages are GIF (Graphics Interchange Format) images, because that's what early Web browsers could display. Like all Web browsers, Netscape has built-in support for GIFs. But by today's image compression standards, GIF image files are just plain big. And when you're talking about a time-intensive medium like the Web, smaller is better.

JPEG images are much smaller than GIFs—in fact, a 16-million color JPEG graphic can be as little as 1/4 the size of the same GIF image in only 256 colors! That's why Netscape added built-in JPEG image display capability to its browser a couple of revisions back. Due in no small part to Netscape's support for the JPEG format, many Web sites now include inline JPEGs on their pages, which results in faster page downloads and much better-looking Web sites.

> **Tip**
>
> Look for sites with JPEG images in the new Progressive JPEG format supported by Netscape 2.0. They load up to three times faster than GIFs, and preview faster, too!

What about XBM images? Well, *XBM* is a monochrome image format used mostly on X Window systems running under UNIX. Frankly, these days you'll only run into XBMs on older UNIX sites where they haven't bothered to convert their images to GIFs or JPEGs yet. Because most Web servers are UNIX machines (with Windows NT and Windows 95 up-and-coming contenders), XBM isn't dead yet.

GIFs, JPEGs, and XBMs currently account for almost 100 percent of the inline graphic images on Web pages. With built-in support for all three, Netscape faithfully displays most of the images you encounter on the Web without requiring you to configure a single external helper application.

> **Caution**
>
> If you are designing your own Web pages, don't entirely abandon GIFs for JPEGs! There are still some people out there using older browsers that can't read JPEGs. And for small, simple images with few colors, GIFs can often be even smaller than JPEGs. Not only that, but GIFs support background transparency, which can improve the look of your pages—JPEG doesn't (at least not yet). For more information on how to implement graphics on your own Web pages, go to chapter 27, "Advanced Graphics."

▶ See "Advanced Graphics," pg. 673

Netscape's Included NAPlayer Helper Application

Multimedia just isn't multimedia without sound. Text, graphics, and animation only stimulate the eyes, but sound brings a whole different sense into play. By combining graphics with sound, you activate more of the brain and get your audience more involved. (Not convinced? Try watching TV with the sound muted!)

While Netscape doesn't have the ability to play sounds all by itself, it does come with a bundled stand-alone sound player called the *NCC Audio Player* (though most people know it better by its 8-character DOS file name: NAPlayer).

NAPlayer (see fig. 16.11) is a simple little program that plays two kinds of digitized audio files: Sun/NeXT sounds (.AU or .SND) and Mac/SGI sounds (.AIF or .AIFF). You can run NAPlayer by itself if you want to (it's located in the same directory as the Netscape program), but you probably won't. It's pretty unspectacular. If you do, you'll find that you can load sound files from disk and play them, fast forward, rewind, and pause. That's it. Let's face it, NAPlayer is not intended to do much—just play sounds for Netscape.

Fig. 16.11

NAPlayer, Netscape's bundled external helper application for playing .AU and .AIF audio files.

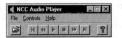

When you set up Netscape, NAPlayer is automatically configured as the helper application for .AU and .AIF sound files. You really don't even have to know that it exists. When Netscape encounters an .AU or .AIF sound file, it launches NAPlayer. NAPlayer appears briefly on the screen, plays the sound, and then disappears. That's how helper applications work. They just do their job and get out of your way. And most of the time, that's just exactly what you want.

Unfortunately, you'll run into more than just two sound file types on the Web. Lots more. Sounds that NAPlayer can't handle. The most obvious omission is Windows' own .WAV sound type. You probably have lots of .WAV files on your system right now (in your Windows directory, if nowhere else). There are also .MOD files, .MID files, and many others. (Chapter 17, "Configuring Netscape for Sound," covers how to configure helper apps for all of these audio file types.)

How Does Netscape Know When it Needs a Helper Application?

Before Netscape can tell if it can handle a file internally or whether it has to launch a helper application, it has to determine what kind of data it's dealing with.

If you've been using a PC for very long, you can probably identify many file types by their file name extensions. You know that a file named foo.exe is an executable program because the file name ends in ".EXE," and that one named boo.doc is a Microsoft Word document because it ends in ".DOC."

> **Note**
>
> By default, Windows 95's file-handling dialog boxes hide file name extensions. For example, a file named "picture.gif" is listed as "picture." File types are identified by icons. To tell Windows 95 to display file name extensions in all its file dialog boxes, follow these steps:
>
> 1. Run Windows Explorer.
> 2. Select the View, Options menu.
> 3. Choose the View tab.
> 4. Uncheck the Hide MS-DOS File Extensions box.

> **Caution**
>
> Not every file type can be correctly identified by its file name extension. Some different file formats share the same extension, and there are also many files on the Web that have arbitrary or misleading file names. Be sure to check for "context clues" that will help you identify a file's real file type. For example, if a file has the file name extension .exe but the text identifies it as an archive file, the odds are good that it's not an executable program, but a self-extracting archive.

Netscape can identify files on the Web by their file names, too. But that is only its *backup* method of determining what kind of files it's dealing with. Its primary method is by referencing a file's *MIME type*.

A Brief Course in MIME Types

MIME is an acronym for *Multipurpose Internet Mail Extensions*, but this is a little misleading. MIME type definitions are not just for Internet mail; they are used to identify any file that can be transmitted over the Internet.

A MIME type definition consists of two parts:

   type/subtype

Here's a real-world example:

   image/jpeg

It's pretty easy to see that this MIME type definition describes an *image* file in *JPEG* format.

Before a Web server sends a file to Netscape, it sends the MIME type definition for that file. Netscape reads this definition and looks it up to see if it can handle the file internally, or if there is a helper application defined for it. In the case of the example above, Netscape knows that the file it is about to receive is an image in JPEG format, which, of course, it can interpret internally; it won't try to launch a helper application.

If the server doesn't send a MIME type along before transmitting the file, Netscape uses the file name extension to identify the file type.

Troubleshooting

I thought I clicked a link to a graphic, but Netscape displayed a screen of unreadable text instead.

If Netscape has to identify a file by its file name extension rather than its MIME type, it can make the same kind of misidentification that a human would make with a misnamed or ambiguously named file. If Netscape tries to display a misidentified file type in its own display or in the wrong helper application, all you see is a garbled mess.

If this happens to you, hover over the file link with the hand pointer and read the file name in the status bar at the bottom of the Netscape window. If the file name extension looks wrong for the type of file you're trying to view, that's probably your problem.

In the rare case where you get a garbled inline image, you can view the file name by right-clicking the image. The file name will be displayed in brackets beside the View this Image choice on the pop-up menu.

You can also see file names by selecting View, By Document Source from the Netscape menu and looking for the file name in the HTML code.

If you can't figure out why a link isn't working right, you can always save the suspect file by holding down the Shift key and clicking the link. Then you can work with it later.

You can see a complete list of the MIME types that Netscape recognizes by choosing Options, General from the Netscape menu, then selecting the Helper Applications tab (see fig. 16.12), or you can look at table 16.1.

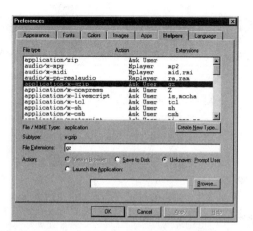

Fig. 16.12
Netscape can display this scrolling list of the MIME types it knows about. Just select Options, General from the menu and click the Helper Applications tab.

Table 16.1   MIME Types That Netscape Recognizes

Type/Subtype	Extensions	Description
application/x-gzip	.GZ	GNU Zip Compressed Data
application/x-compress	.Z	Compressed Data
application/x-mocha	.MOCHA, .MOC	Mocha Script
application/x-tcl	.TCL	TCL Program
application/x-sh	.SH	Bourne Shell Program
application/x-csh	.CSH	C Shell Program
application/postscript	.AI, .EPS, .PS	PostScript Program
application/octet-stream	.EXE, .BIN	Binary Executable
application/x-cpio	.CPIO	UNIX CPIO Archive
application/x-gtar	.GTAR	GNU Tape Archive
application/x-tar	.TAR	UNIX Tape Archive
application/x-shar	.SHAR	UNIX Shell Archive
application/x-zip-compressed	.ZIP	Zip Compressed Data
application/x-stuffit	.SIT	Macintosh Archive
application/mac-binhex40	.HQX	Macintosh BinHex Archive
video/x-msvideo	.AVI	Microsoft Video
video/quicktime	.QT, .MOV	QuickTime Video
video/mpeg	.MPEG,.MPG,.MPE	MPEG Video

(continues)

III

Using Helper Apps

Table 16.1 Continued		
Type/Subtype	**Extensions**	**Description**
audio/x-wav	.WAV	WAV Audio
*audio/x-aiff	.AIF, .AIFF, .AIFC	AIFF Audio
*audio/basic	.AU, .SND	ULAW Audio Data
application/fractals	.FIF	Fractal Image Format
image/ief	.IEF	
image/x-MS-bmp	.BMP	Windows Bitmap
image/x-rgb	.RGB	RGB Image
image/x-portable-pixmap	.PPM	PPM Image
image/x-portable-graymap	.PGM	PGM Image
image/x-portable-bitmap	.PBM	PBM Image
image/x-portable-anymap	.PNM	PBM Image
image/x-xwindowdump	.XWD	X Window Dump Image
image/x-xpixmap	.XPM	X Pixmap
*image/x-xbitmap	.XBM	X Bitmap
image/x-cmu-raster	.RAS	CMU Raster Image
image/tiff	.TIFF, .TIF	TIFF Image
*image/jpeg	.JPEG, .JPG, .JPE	JPEG Image
*image/gif	.GIF	CompuServe Image Format
application/x-texinfo	.TEXI, .TEXINFO	GNU TeXinfo Document
application/x-dvi	.DVI	TeX DVI Data
application/x-latex	.LATEX	LaTeX Document
application/x-tex	.TEX	TeX Document
application/rtf	.RTF	Rich Text Format
*text/html	.HTML, .HTM	Hypertext Markup Language
*text/plain	.TXT, .TEXT	Plain Text

Files that Netscape handles internally or via NAPlayer are marked with an asterisk ("").
You'll probably want to configure helper applications right away for the popular file types
that we've underlined.*

That certainly looks like a lot of different file types. Fortunately, you probably
won't run into most of them if all you're doing is cruising the Web. Many are
for specialized applications such as scientific document page layout, fractal
image generation, or UNIX shell scripts.

Types and Subtypes

There are only seven sanctioned MIME types: text, audio, image, video, multipart, message, and application. If somebody comes up with some hot new program or data file type, they have to fit it into one of these seven MIME types if a MIME-enabled application is going to recognize it.

However, there are both "official" and "unofficial" MIME subtypes. Official subtypes appear on the list without an "x-" prefix. That kind of gives away the fact that "x-" is the official way to label an unofficial MIME subtype. That a MIME subtype is "unofficial" in no way makes it a second-class citizen, however. It just means that the Internet Working Group, the organization that oversees the MIME standard, hasn't defined an official subtype for it...yet.

Missing MIME Types

There are several important file types that didn't make Netscape's internal list—for example, .MID (MIDI music) and .WAV (Windows wave sound files). Important file types that didn't make Netscape's internal list will be discussed by topic in subsequent chapters in this section.

You can create your own definitions for MIME subtypes that aren't on Netscape's list by clicking the Create New Type button in Netscape's Helper Applications dialog box, and entering a new type/x-subtype designation. Be sure to include the "x-" in the subtype name, and don't duplicate a name that's already on the list.

Of course, the rest of the world won't know about MIME types that you define, so Web browsers you connect to won't send file IDs that match your MIME types. Netscape will be stuck with identifying the file by its file name extension, which, in most cases, will work fine.

If Netscape encounters a file with an unknown MIME type and a file extension that is not on its internal list, it will try to display it as text. In most cases, this is definitely *not* what you want it to do. If you run into this problem, you can configure Netscape so that it automatically saves files of that type to disk by following these steps (see fig. 16.13):

1. Select Options, General from the Netscape menu.

2. Click on the Helper Applications tab to bring it to the front.

3. Choose the Create New Type button.

4. Enter a MIME type in the Mime Type field, and a MIME subtype in the Mime SubType field. (This should begin with an "x-".)

III

Using Helper Apps

Fig. 16.13
You must define both type and subtype for any new MIME type you define for Netscape.

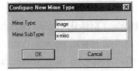

5. Enter the proper file extension(s) in the File Extensions field.

6. Click the Save to Disk radio button.

7. Click OK when you're done.

Caution

Once you've set up a new MIME type/subtype, you can't get rid of it—there's no Delete button in the Helper Applications configuration window. You can change the name of the application or the file name extension, and you can change the Action to Save to Disk or Ask User, but you can't get rid of it. The only way to do so is to manually edit the NETSCAPE.INI file under Windows 3.1 or the Registry under Windows 95.

Note

You can find out more about MIME types by obtaining the Internet Working Group's RFC document on the topic. It can be downloaded by pointing Netscape to:

ftp://ftp.isi.edu or **ftp://ds.internic.net**

Look for the directory rfc/ and the file name rfc1521.txt.

You can also enter into discussions about MIME on UseNet. Just point Netscape's newsreader to the group **comp.mail.mime**.

Troubleshooting

I configured a helper application for "type/subtype," but Netscape doesn't always seem to use it. And I sometimes get a Warning: unrecognized encoding *message. What's going on?*

◀ See "E-mail with Netscape," pg. 321

If this problem is only occasional, it's probably not Netscape or your helper application configuration that's at fault. The problem may be with the way the Web site you're connected to is sending MIME type information. Netscape may be receiving a self-contradictory or confusing MIME type identification, and it's trying to interpret the file without really knowing what it is. If you regularly run into this problem on a particular site, e-mail the Webmaster (usually *webmaster@site*) and inform him of the problem.

Separating the Wheat from the Chaff

So which file types do you actually need to worry about?

You can safely ignore the ones that Netscape handles internally. Though you *can* configure external helper applications to display the graphics files that Netscape normally handles, you generally don't want to do so; it disrupts the look and feel of Netscape's page display because helper applications don't appear inline. (However, this advice does not necessarily extend to the audio files that NAPlayer takes care of. Because audio isn't visual, and since NAPlayer is an external helper app anyway, you can't ruin the way a page looks by configuring a different audio player.)

Of the other file types in table 16.1, you'll probably want to configure helpers for many of the audio, graphics, and video file types listed. Subsequent chapters in this section help you decide which ones you're most likely to encounter. But to get you started, we've underlined the file types in table 16.1 that you'll probably want to get helper apps configured for right away.

The Three Philosophies of Helper Application Selection

There are three very different approaches to the process of selecting Netscape helper applications. One camp likes to configure a single monster, do-it-all helper app to juggle as many different file types as possible. Others like to use powerful stand-alone applications as helper apps so they can really manipulate the files they access. The last group prefers small, quick applications that display just one type of file. Let's look at this approach first.

The Zen Minimalist Approach

Netscape's own bundled NAPlayer is a good example of the type of helper application preferred by the minimalist. It's small, has very few features, and does just one thing—it plays sound files.

The advantage to this approach is that your helper apps load and play quickly. They don't eat up much memory, so they're perfect for systems with slower processors and less RAM.

The disadvantage is that you may have to install and configure lots of helper apps to handle all the different file types you might run into on the Web.

The minimalist approach is best if you're running Netscape on a computer with limited resources (like a notebook) or if your needs are utilitarian: catching up on news, doing mostly text-based research, and so on.

III

Using Helper Apps

The Control Freak's Preference

If you like to work "on the fly," you might prefer to use more powerful programs as helpers. For example, say you're involved in a project where you are downloading and converting hundreds of public domain graphics files to .BMP format. You could save yourself a lot of file manipulation time later if the helper application you have configured as your graphics viewer could convert and save them for you as you browse the Web.

▶ See "Configuring Netscape for Graphics," pg. 439

Paint Shop Pro is a good example of a powerhouse program that also makes a good Netscape helper application. It can read and convert three dozen different file types and manipulate graphics in scores of different ways, but it's easy to use and is compact enough to load relatively quickly. (Paint Shop Pro is discussed in depth in chapter 18, "Configuring Netscape for Graphics.")

Note

You won't want to spend a lot of time manipulating and converting files while you're online if you are using a dial-up connection that charges you for connect time. Instead, save the files you want to keep and work with them offline later.

Tip

You can save even more time if you don't view files while you're online. Just download them directly to disk. Instead of left-clicking a file's link to display it, right-click it and select Save this Link as. The file will be saved to disk without being displayed.

Tip

The true Netscape hacker knows that you never really even have to save a file you've viewed recently—it's already stored in Netscape's Cache directory (in pieces with cryptic file names!). If you're patient, you can find the file content you're interested in by scanning the cache using the Find, Files or Folders option on the Start menu in Windows 95, or by loading them one-by-one into Netscape using File, Open File. (Because older files in the cache are purged regularly, if you find something you want to keep you need to copy it elsewhere.) This process is not for the faint of heart, but if you know you looked at something just great on the Web yesterday and can't find it today, then happy hunting!

The Swiss Army Knife Solution

The advantage of having one helper application that handles everything is that configuration is quick and easy—you install one program, go through the configuration process once, and you're done.

The disadvantage is that do-it-all helper apps have a tendency to load slowly and hog system resources.

And, of course, there are no programs that will handle absolutely *everything* you might encounter on the Web. But you can come surprisingly close.

Take *VuePrint*, for example.

VuePrint is a program that is a veritable Swiss Army Knife for audio, graphics, and video. It comes in versions for Windows 3.1 and Windows 95, and can play or display all of these file types:

- Image files (.GIF, .BMP, .DIB, .RLE, .PCX, .TGA, .JPG, .TIF)
- Sound files (.MID, .WAV, .MCI)
- Movie files (.AVI, .MPG, .MMM, .MOV, .FLI, .FLC)
- Slide show files (.SLI)
- UUEncoded files (.UUE, .UU1, .01, .MSG)
- Zip files (.ZIP)

With a program like VuePrint installed on your system, you don't have to worry about running into files that Netscape can't handle. (VuePrint's capabilities are discussed at length in chapter 18, "Configuring Netscape for Graphics.")

Your Personal Setup

You'll most likely want to take an approach that's a compromise among these three extremes. Like most Netscape users, you'll end up configuring a handful of useful helper apps that expand Netscape's native capabilities without doing too much or too little.

Personally, I favor a "minimalist" approach. Because I connect to the World Wide Web via a 14.4KB dial-up connection, I keep helper applications configured only for the few file types that I run into all the time, like .AU and .WAV sounds, .BMP graphics, and .MOV and .MPG movies. For everything else, I just select Save to Disk when Netscape flashes its Save/Cancel/Configure dialog box for an unconfigured file type. Then I can view them offline, when I'm not paying for the connection.

III

Using Helper Apps

What Kinds of Programs Can You Use as Helper Applications?

Almost any program can be configured as a helper application for Netscape. But that doesn't mean you should go ahead and configure every program you own. Keep in mind effectiveness, efficiency, and utility.

Should You Use DOS, Windows 3.1, or Win95 Helpers?

If you're running under Windows 95, stick with Win95 helper applications as much as you can. If you're running Windows 3.1, use Windows 3.1 helper apps. I can't think of a single reason to ever use a DOS program as a Netscape helper, though you may discover a couple in the following chapters that are useful as offline file conversion utilities.

DOS applications don't integrate well with Windows. They don't make good use of system resources and don't multitask well with Windows applications like Netscape.

If you're running under Windows 95, you'll find that Windows 3.1 applications don't handle long file names, don't multitask efficiently, don't run as fast under Win95 as native 32-bit applications, and don't use the standard Win95 file dialog box.

Both you and Netscape will be happier in the long run if you use the most advanced, up-to-date programs your system can run as helper apps. But don't forget that you want your helper applications to be quick and resource-friendly, too.

Programs You Already Own

The first place you should look for helper apps is in the treasure trove of programs you already own. Both Windows 3.1 and Windows 95 come with a handful of small, efficient bundled applications that make excellent Netscape helper apps.

Fig. 16.14
You already own a copy of Sound Recorder, which can be configured as a Netscape helper application for playing .WAV audio files.

Win95 and Windows 3.1 both include a program that plays .WAV audio files: Sound Recorder. It lives in your Windows directory. The combination of

NAPlayer and Sound Recorder handle the three most popular digitized sound file types on the Web.

Earlier in this chapter, we discussed how to set up Paint, another program that is included with both versions of Windows, as a helper app for viewing .PCX and .BMP image files. With Netscape's native support for .GIFs, .JPEGs, and .XBMs, the addition of Paint instantly sets you up for viewing the Web's five most popular graphics image file types.

And you don't want to overlook Media Player, which is bundled with Windows 3.1 and Win95 as a player for MIDI music files (.MID) and Video-for-Windows videos (.AVI). (It plays .WAV audio files, too.)

By themselves, these three "free" Microsoft programs handle most of the multimedia files you'll encounter on the Web.

Windows 3.1's Notepad and Write can be handy helper apps for text file formats you want to display in a separate window. Windows 95 users can use QuickView or Wordpad, which also display Microsoft Word documents.

If you have Microsoft Office installed on your system, you can configure PPTView as a helper application for viewing online PowerPoint presentations (admittedly a rare thing). The Win95 version of Office includes Microsoft Imager, a graphics viewer and manipulation program that can handle *seven* different image file types.

All these programs are discussed in more detail in the appropriate chapters in this section. The point is, you may not have to look any further than your own system for the Netscape helper apps you need.

Freeware and Shareware Solutions

You should also be prepared to mine the Web itself for helper applications. There are literally thousands of freeware and shareware programs out there, free for the downloading. The chapters in this section discuss dozens of freeware and shareware programs that you can use as Netscape helper applications.

> **Note**
>
> So what's the difference between freeware and shareware? *Freeware* is just that: free. You can download it and use it forever without ever paying anyone a dime. *Shareware*, on the other hand, is software you can *try* for free, but if you *continue* to use it, you're expected to pay the author for the privilege. If you use it past the trial
>
> (continues)

(continued)

period stated in the program's license agreement, you are effectively stealing the program, just as if you had shoplifted it from a store shelf. Fortunately, most shareware license fees are so reasonable that they won't put much of a strain on your pocketbook.

So where do you go to get freely distributed helper applications?

On the CD

First of all, check out the CD included with this book. It includes most of the helper applications discussed in this section. The odds are good that you won't have to go any further to get all the helper applications you need.

▶ See "What's on the Netscape CD?" pg. 949

You might also want to check out the helpful advice that Netscape offers on its own Web site. While you're connected to the Web, choose Help, Release Notes from the Netscape menu and you'll find information on some of the most popular Netscape helper applications, as well as directions on how to download them.

Here are some other software archive sites to try on the World Wide Web:

- **http://vsl.cnet.com**—The Virtual Software Library
- **http://www.cris.com/~randybrg/win95.html**—Randy Burgess's Windows 95 Resource Center
- **http://www.pcworld.com/win95/shareware**—PC World Online
- **http://www.netex.net/w95/windows95**—Unofficial Windows 95 Software Archive
- **http://www.csusm.edu/cwis/winworld/winworld.html**—CSUSM Software Archive

For additional information on how to download files from the Web, see chapter 7, "Moving Around the Web." For more about finding files, see chapter 8, "Finding Information on the Web."

Many of the files you download from the Web will be compressed. To find out how to decompress the files you download, see chapter 23, "Using Compressed/Encoded Files."

▶ See "Using Compressed/ Encoded Files," pg. 571

Caution

Watch out for files you download that have an .EXE file name extension. Most are self-extracting archives, *not* usable executable files!

Commercial Programs

Of course, you could actually spend some money and *buy* programs to use as helper applications. If you're a real control freak, you might be considering using PhotoShop, PhotoStyler, PhotoFinish, or some other "name brand" commercial graphics, sound, or video program as a Netscape helper app.

But you should be aware that most of the programs you can buy for multimedia use are huge and eat up a lot of system resources. For most people, it would certainly be overkill to buy anything like the programs mentioned above just to use as Netscape helper applications.

But if you can find a small, elegant commercial program that you really like, there is certainly no reason why you can't buy it and configure it as a Netscape helper. If you're inclined to go this way, I advise you to read the reviews in popular computer magazines for guidance on which ones might be right for you. But try to steer clear of the huge "professional" packages. Odds are that they would just get in the way of browsing the Web.

Configure Now or Later, or Not at All

If you want, you can try to anticipate your needs and find and configure helper applications for all the file types you think you're likely to encounter in the future. Or you can just wait for Netscape to tell you that you need a helper app.

You may have noticed when we talked about MIME types, the scrolling list of file types that Netscape maintains under the Action heading also tells you what it will do when it encounters each of them (refer to fig. 16.6). If it handles the file internally, this entry says Browser. If it has been configured to launch a helper application, it lists the name of the application. (Note that the entries for .AU and .AIF are preconfigured for NAPlayer.) Most entries are simply labeled Ask User.

If you try to display a file that you haven't configured a helper application for (one that lists *Ask User* as its Action), Netscape displays the Unknown File Type alert shown in figure 16.15.

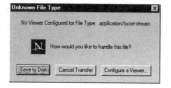

Fig. 16.15
The Unknown File Type alert lets you configure a helper application on the fly.

If you want, you can simply back out at this point by choosing Cancel Transfer, which returns you to the Netscape main window without viewing the file. You can also choose Save to Disk to load the problem file into your favorite application later. But if you select Configure a Viewer, Netscape jumps directly to the Helper Application configuration dialog box, just as though you'd selected it from the menu.

Fig. 16.16
You'll be able to browse for a helper application if you choose the Configure a Viewer button.

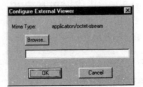

> **Tip**
>
> Advanced users may want to take a look at Netscape's helper application configuration settings in the Windows 95 Registry. You can do so by running RegEdit (in the Windows directory) and viewing HKEY_CURRENT_USER/Software/Netscape Navigator/Viewers.

Checking Your Work: The WWW Viewer Test Page

How can you make sure your helper applications are configured properly? Test 'em out!

The easiest way to test a Netscape helper application is to select File, Open File from the Netscape menu and try to open a file of the type you want to test from your system. If Netscape launches the right helper app and the file is displayed properly, you're in business.

If you don't have a file of the type you want to check, or if you simply prefer to test your helper app "under fire" on the Web, go to the Lawrence Livermore Labs Web Browser Test Page at **http://www-dsed.llnl.gov/documents/WWWtest.html**. This page presents a menu of buttons that send you dozens of different files to exercise just about any helper application you can think of (see fig. 16.17).

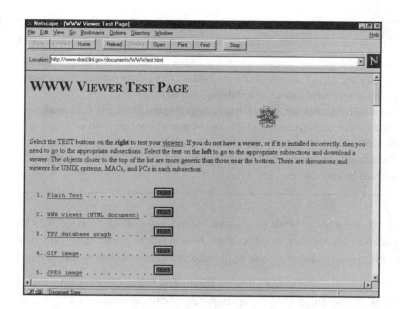

Fig. 16.17
You can test your helper application configuration by pointing Netscape to the Lawrence Livermore Labs Web Browser Test Page.

Netscape Helper Applications for UNIX

We'll cover how to set up helper applications for Windows 95 and Windows 3.1 in the following chapters. But if you're a UNIX user, read on for information on how to set up helper applications for the UNIX version of Netscape.

There's a rich set of UNIX programs that can be set up as Netscape Helper applications. Some of them are standard operating system utilities, while others are freely available on the Internet for retrieval and installation. This chapter can only cover a few of them: helper applications for viewing graphics files, displaying PostScript files, and playing audio and video files.

Setting Up a Helper Application for Viewing Graphics Files

We cover the steps of setting up helper applications in the next few paragraphs. As we set up a graphical image viewer, you'll learn important information about helper applications in general. While Netscape can handle several kinds of graphical image files, you'll encounter others; and you'll want a helper application to handle them. John Cristy's package ImageMagick contains just such an image viewer, called *display*.

III

Using Helper Apps

> **Note**
>
> The ImageMagick source code is included on the CD-ROM. This package contains not only *display*, but also several other valuable programs for manipulating images. For more information about ImageMagick, see **http://www.wizards.dupont.com/cristy/ImageMagick.html**. Like most available UNIX software, this package is distributed in source code form, and must be compiled before you can run it on your system. It will build on virtually all UNIX systems. The following paragraphs assume you've compiled and installed the ImageMagick package on your system.

Here are the steps to setting up ImageMagick's *display* as a Netscape helper application for viewing graphics files. As you follow them, you learn important information about helper applications in general that will be useful later.

In Netscape, pull down the Options menu and select General, and then click Helpers. Figure 16.18 shows the Helper Applications dialog box.

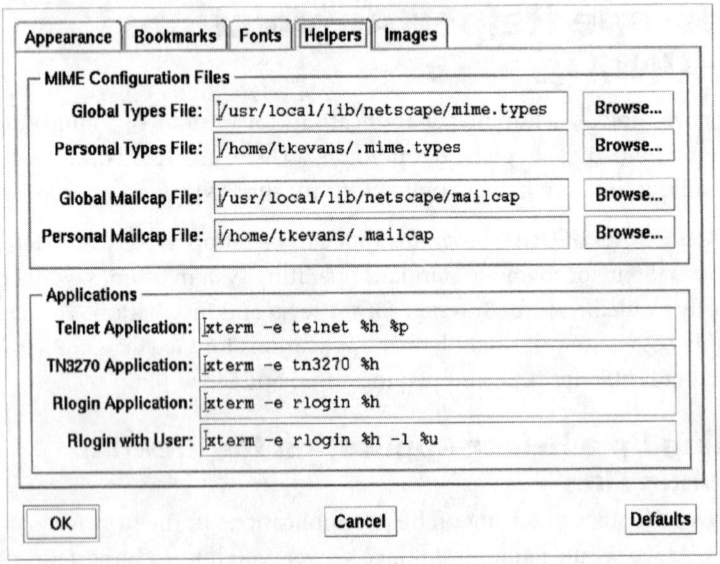

Fig. 16.18

The Netscape Helper Applications dialog box.

UNIX Netscape does not have the same graphical interface for setting up helper applications as do the Windows and Mac versions. In fact, this dialog box doesn't do very much of anything, but it does contain some very important information about MIME.

UNIX Netscape and MIME

Though we covered MIME basics earlier in this chapter, UNIX Netscape deals with MIME types a bit differently. While UNIX Netscape has built-in knowledge of MIME, and uses it to deal with the data it receives from a Web server, up to four MIME configuration files may be consulted by Netscape with each Web transaction. These four files, all of which need not exist on your system, are grouped into Global and Personal categories. Within these categories, Netscape uses the Types file and the Mailcap file.

In Netscape, MIME is used for linking file name extensions to types of files and, hence, from there to helper applications. Netscape already knows about the standard file name extensions and associates each with a MIME data type/subtype. For example, the file name extension XWD is associated with image files produced by the *xwd* (X Window Dump) program. (See your system manual for information about XWD.) Here's the entry from the Types file for XWD files:

```
image/xwd          xwd
```

As you can see, the MIME data type/subtype (on the left) is associated with the XWD file name extension, on the right. You can see the complete list of MIME data types/subtypes and associated file name extensions in the Global Types file.

Using MIME to Enable Netscape Helper Applications

You use MIME information—the association between the MIME data type/subtype and the file name extension—to set up your helper applications. For example, to enable Netscape to view graphics files with the *display* program as a Helper application:

- Check the Global Mailcap File to see if *display* (or some other program) has already been set up as a helper application for images. You can use the UNIX more or pg commands to view this file on your screen. Look for a line that begins with the MIME type/subtype "image/*;". If you find it, there should be something to the right of the semicolon; if it says display %s, you're already set up to view graphics with *display*. You may find another image viewer (a common one is xv) defined.

- If you didn't find *display* in the Global Mailcap File, or the file doesn't exist, set up *display* in your Personal Mailcap File. Usually called

.mailcap (note the leading period in the file name), create this file with any text editor, such as *vi, emacs,* or Sun's *textedit* editor. (As shown in the Netscape Helper Applications dialog box, this file is normally in your Home Directory.) Add the following line, making sure to include the semi-colon:

```
image/*; display %s
```

Note that the asterisk here is a *wild card*, meaning that you want to use *display* as your helper application for all images in Netscape.

The Global Mailcap File sets helper applications for all users on a UNIX system, which means that you or your system administrator can set up common helper applications (such as *display*) and make them available to everyone on the system. This minimizes the need for users to set up and maintain Personal Mailcap Files. If both files exist, your Personal Mailcap File overrides any conflicts with the Global File. For example, if you found an xv entry in the Global Mailcap file, putting the display entry in your .mailcap overrides the system default of using xv for you, but not for anyone else on the system.

Setting Up a Helper Application for PostScript Files

PostScript is a widely used graphic format. Defined as a device-independent standard for representing the printed page, you may think of PostScript in the context of printers. It's often useful, however, to view PostScript documents on-screen, so having a PostScript viewer as a Netscape helper application is important. Some UNIX systems include PostScript viewers as a standard part of the system. These include Sun's Solaris 2.x *imagetool*, SunOS 4.1.x *pageview*, and IBM's *showps*. You may also have the freeware package *ghostscript* installed on your system. To enable imagetool as a Netscape helper application for viewing PostScript files, add the following entry to either the Global or your Personal Mailcap File:

```
application/postscript;    imagetool %s
```

The Global or Personal Types file should contain a mapping of the MIME application/postscript data type/subtype to the file name extension .PS. You may also want to add the common PostScript file name extensions .EPS and .AI.

Configuring Netscape for Sound

As with images and PostScript, you use MIME information to configure a Netscape helper application to play sound files. Here are the steps; we'll use Sun's *audiotool* in this example. (You can substitute your system's audio player program—SGI's *sfplay*, for example—for audiotool.)

Check the Global and Personal Types files for an audio/basic entry. It should look something like this, with the MIME type/subtype and file name extension information:

```
audio/basic        au snd
```

As you'll recall, the Types file maps MIME data types/subtypes with file name extensions; in this case audio/basic is mapped to the file name extensions .AU or .SND. Add the entry to the Types file, if necessary.

Next, check the Global and Personal Mailcap files for an audio/basic MIME types/subtype entry, and add it, if necessary. It should look like this:

```
audio/basic;       /usr/openwin/bin/audiotool
```

Other Audio Types

So far, the discussion of audio has dealt only with the basic audio file format defined by Sun Microsystems and supported on other UNIX systems. You'll find, however, other kinds of audio files on the Web. One of the most common is the PC *WAV* format (audiotool doesn't support this audio format). To support this and other audio formats, you need to install another audio helper application. A no-cost audio player that works on most UNIX systems is *AudioFile*, which is on the CD-ROM in the back of this book. Alternatively, you can set up a custom Netscape helper application that uses an *audio file conversion utility* to convert the foreign audio format on-the-fly and pass it off to audiotool. SGI's *sfconvert* and Sun's *audioconvert* are two examples.

Netscape Helper Applications for Macintosh

The Helpers screen of the General Preferences window lets you choose which applications that are installed on your Macintosh are designated as helper applications for Netscape. Helper applications are used to process file types that Netscape is not designed to handle by itself. One example is Aladdin Software's Stuffit Expander. If Netscape is configured to pass received Stuffit files to Stuffit Expander, Stuffit Expander will launch, unstuff the .SIT file, expand the unpacked file further (if the unstuffed file is compressed in one of the several formats Stuffit Expander can process) until done, then close itself. Other helper applications are used to process sound or video that Netscape itself doesn't process natively.

Helper applications are discussed in detail in chapters 17–23 of this book. However, Netscape has a Web page that presents links to many of the most popular helper applications for Netscape for the Macintosh at **http://home.netscape.com/assist/helper_apps/machelpers.html**.

Configuring Netscape for Full Motion Video

As you might guess from the last few pages, configuring a Netscape helper application for viewing video files involves adding the correct MIME information to the Types and Mailcap files. Most UNIX systems, however, don't yet have video player software, so you'll need a helper application for this too. The most widely used MPEG (*Motion Picture Experts Group*, a widely used video data format) viewer for UNIX is called *mpeg_play*, and is available on this book's CD-ROM, where you'll find documentation on how to compile and install it, as well as the source code.

After you've installed mpeg_play in a directory that's accessible to you, you're ready to configure it as a Netscape helper application. First, check the Global Types file for a video entry, and add one if necessary. It should look like this:

```
video/mpeg          mpeg mpg mpe
```

Next, look for an MPEG viewer set up in the Global Mailcap file. It should look like this:

```
video/mpeg;         mpeg_play %s
```

If there's no entry, you or your system administrator can add one to the Global Mailcap file so everyone can access it, or you can add one to your Personal Mailcap file.

Other Kinds of Video

If you've ever used a Macintosh, you probably know about QuickTime videos. mpeg_play can't handle QuickTime or other video types. A good all-purpose video player for UNIX systems that handles QuickTime is Mark Podlipec's *xanim*, which is on the CD-ROM. You can set up xanim as your video helper application in the same way you do with mpeg_play. Because it can play several kinds of video, you may want to use xanim for all video, including MPEG video, and not use mpeg_play at all. To do this, add a wild card video entry to the Global Mailcap file.

```
video/*;            xanim %s
```

Check your Global Types file for the MIME type/subtype information for the other video types:

```
video/quicktime     qt mov
```

## CHAPTER 17

Configuring Netscape for Sound

Netscape is mute; by itself, it can't play sound or music files. But by setting it up with the right helper applications, you can turn Netscape into a veritable Caruso.

Of course, you not only need the right sound software—you also need the right hardware. Then you'll be ready to find some noisy places to visit on the Web. Fortunately, these are in ample supply.

In this chapter, you learn:

- How Netscape works with sound
- What kinds of audio file formats you're likely to run into on the World Wide Web
- Which Windows 3.1 and Windows 95 programs make good Netscape sound helper applications
- How to translate sounds for Netscape

Hardware Requirements for Netscape Sound

Back in the "old days" of personal computing—when "PC" was always followed by "XT," processor numbers were only four digits long, and software ran directly off of floppy disks—every PC shipped with a tinny little AM-radio quality speaker that beeped nastily at you any time you did something wrong. Some masochists (the kind who like to scrape their fingernails on blackboards) even wrote a few annoying DOS programs that played what they claimed to be digitized sounds on that little speaker. But no normal human being ever heard a single recognizable sound in the cacophonous din that emanated from a PC when those programs ran.

Now that we're in the high-tech age of multimedia computers—complete with 24-bit True Color animations, 16-bit stereo music soundtracks, and digitized CD-ROM voice-overs by the likes of Patrick Stewart—all PCs still ship with that same nasty, tinny little speaker.

Sure, Microsoft has a Windows driver that purportedly plays music and audio using only the internal PC speaker, but it freezes up your system when it runs, and everything still sounds like it's being fed through a weather-beaten drive-in movie speaker with a shorted connection.

To get real audio out of your PC, you need a sound card. If you bought your computer recently, or if you've spent a few bucks upgrading, the odds are good you already have a sound card. But if you don't, you can pick one up for anywhere between $30 and $800, depending on what you want it to do.

A good 16-bit stereo Sound Blaster Pro (or compatible) sound card does just about everything the average person needs done audio-wise, and does it for under $100. If you haven't invested in a sound card yet, drop this book right now, scan a few computer magazine reviews and ads, run to your local computer store, buy a sound card, and plug it in. You'll be glad you did, because PC speaker sound is almost worse than no sound at all.

How Computer Audio Works

Most of the sounds you hear coming from your PC are *digitized*. That is, the waves that make up the sound have been converted into a stream of digital bits and bytes by feeding them through some kind of analog-to-digital converter. You can do this yourself using the software that came with your sound board on any audio source, such as a microphone or tape player. Once digitized, the sound data is saved as a file on disk.

Digitized sound files vary in at least three important ways. First is the *sampling rate*, or the number of times each second the audio wave form is sampled as it is converted to digital data. PC sound file sampling rates generally range from 8,000 to 44,100 samples per second. (More samples = higher quality sound.)

Second is the way the data is organized in the file. For example, a digitized sound file may or may not include header information, which describes the file; may interleave the data from multiple sound tracks (i.e. 2 tracks for stereo); or may be comprised of a library of different instrument sound samples followed by a "play list" for using them to play a song.

Finally, the data in a sound file may be compressed in some way to save disk space and transfer time. For example, MPEG audio files are compressed at a 6:1 ratio.

There are a dozen or more relatively popular sound file types, each of which varies in the way it stores sound data. Most programs only play one or two kinds of sound files. Fortunately, if you have Netscape helper applications configured to play the three or four most popular types, you won't run into many audio problems cruising the Net. You don't have to worry about the rest unless you're a real sound freak or have some specialized application.

Note

You can find out more about audio file formats by checking out the Audio FAQ (Frequently Asked Questions) list on UseNet. You can retrieve the latest version by pointing Netscape to **ftp://ftp.cwi.nl/pub/audio**. Look for the files AudioFormats.part1 and AudioFormats.part2.

More information can also be obtained by reading the UseNet newsgroup **alt.binaries.sounds**.

How Netscape Works with Sounds

Web pages don't generally include audio files inline because Web browsers like Netscape can't play them without launching a helper application. Most Web pages that have an audio component make sounds optional; they ask you to click a link to load an external sound file.

Note

Plug-ins are a new feature in Netscape 2.0 that expand its multimedia capabilities in new directions. Plug-ins are basically add-on viewer modules for "live objects" that can be placed inline on Web pages. In the case of audio files, this means that they could be played automatically without having to launch a helper application when the page is loaded or when the user clicks a link. This doesn't necessarily mean that you don't need audio helper applications anymore, but it is an exciting new capability of Netscape 2.0. For a detailed look at plug-ins, see chapter 36, "Netscape Plug-Ins."

III

Using Helper Apps

▶ See "Netscape
Plug-Ins,"
pg. 933

Netscape comes bundled with its own stand-alone sound player helper application called *NAPlayer* (see fig. 17.1). When Netscape is installed, it automatically configures NAPlayer as your helper app for two digitized audio file formats: Sun/NeXT (.AU, .SND) and Mac/SGI (.AIF, .AIFF). NAPlayer is small, quick, and unspectacular.

Fig. 17.1
NAPlayer, the audio helper application that comes bundled with Netscape 2.0.

To cope with other sound file types, you need to configure additional audio helper applications. And because NAPlayer is so limited in what it can do, you may even want to configure a different player for .AU and .AIF sounds, as well.

Sound File Formats

Netscape recognizes audio files the same way it identifies all the files it accesses on the Web: by MIME type first, and then (if it doesn't receive a valid MIME type from the Web server it's connected to) by file name extension. (For more about MIME types, see chapter 16, "Configuring Helper Applications.")

◀ See "Configuring Helper Applications,"
pg. 395

The audio file MIME types and file name extensions that Netscape knows about are listed in table 17.1.

Table 17.1 The Two Audio File Types Recognized by Netscape		
Type/Subtype	**Extensions**	**Description**
audio/basic	.AU, .SND	ULAW Audio Data
audio/x-aiff	.AIF, .AIFF, .AIFC	AIFF Audio

This is certainly not a very extensive list. In fact, Netscape only acknowledges the two file types that NAPlayer can play. There are over a dozen other sound file types out there on the Web.

Table 17.2 lists some of the other audio formats you're likely to encounter while browsing the Web.

Table 17.2 Other Audio File Types You'll Find on the World Wide Web		
Type/Subtype	**Extensions**	**Description**
audio/x-fssd	.SND, .FSSD	Mac, PC
audio/x-iff	.IFF	Amiga
<u>audio/x-midi</u>	.MID, .MIDI, .RMI	MIDI music
audio/x-mod	.MOD, .NST	Amiga, Atari ST
audio/x-sf	.SF	IRCAM
audio/x-ul	.UL	US telephony
audio/x-voc	.VOC	Sound Blaster
<u>audio/x-wav</u>	.WAV	Windows RIFF

You'll probably want to configure helper applications for <u>underlined</u> file types right away.

The two you'll probably want to configure helper apps for right away are MIDI music files (.MID) and wave (.WAV) format digitized sound files.

Wave Files

The wave format is Window's own standard file format. All Window's warning beeps, whistles, and clangs live in your Windows directory as files with .WAV extensions. Because it is such a standard fixture on Windows computers, thousands upon thousands of wave files have made their way onto the World Wide Web.

Tip

In the Windows directory in both Windows 3.1 and Windows 95 is a little program called *Sound Recorder* that you can configure as a quick-and-dirty Netscape helper application for playing .WAV files. Use the MIME type audio/x-wav.

Most of the programs described in this chapter can play .WAV format files.

MIDI Music Files

MIDI music files (.MID, .MIDI) are completely different than other sound file formats. Originally developed to control electronic musical instruments, the MIDI file format has become extremely popular on PCs since the advent of MIDI-capable sound cards.

III

Using Helper Apps

MIDI files combine sound definitions called *instruments* with MIDI sequence control commands that tell a MIDI device (like your PC's sound board) which instruments to play when, for how long, and with what settings. In a way, a MIDI file is more like a printed sheet-music score than a digitized sound file. In fact, MIDI files don't contain digitized sounds at all, unless the file uses custom instrument definitions.

> **Tip**
>
> You guessed it! Microsoft has supplied you with a program that plays MIDI files, too. Also located in the Windows directory in both Windows 3.1 and Windows 95, *Media Player* can be configured as a Netscape helper application for playing .MID files. It also plays Video-for-Windows (.AVI) movies and, like Sound Recorder, wave (.WAV) audio files. Use the MIME types audio/x-mid and video/x-msvideo. Add audio/x-wav if you want it to play waves, too.

Sound Helper Applications for Netscape

> **Note**
>
> For information on where to find helper applications and how to configure them once you've found them, see chapter 16, "Configuring Helper Applications."

Now that we've finished the appetizers, we can get down to the meat-and-potatoes: Just what *are* the best audio helper applications for Netscape under Windows 3.1 and Windows 95?

There are dozens of programs that fill the bill, but we've culled only the very best for our discussion here. The following pages present a veritable smorgasbord of excellent freeware and shareware audio programs that will satisfy the most discerning Netscape user, whether you are a devout ascetic who only wants sustenance without fat, or a real gourmand looking for a plate-filling main course with all the trimmings.

Windows 95 Sound Programs

If you're a Windows 95 user, you want Windows 95 helper applications for Netscape. Not only do they understand long file names and have the unmistakable Win95 look-and-feel, they multitask better than Windows 3.1 programs and run faster because they're 32-bit applications.

Though Windows 95 is relatively new, there are already some good freeware and shareware audio applications out there. The following are some of the best.

MIDI Jukebox 2

Pocket-Sized Software's *MIDI Jukebox 2* is a simple little Win95 shareware program, and its main purpose is to act as a MIDI jukebox that plays background music as you work (see fig. 17.2). But it also makes a nifty helper application for Netscape. It can be configured as a helper app for playing both wave (.WAV) and MIDI (.MID, .RMI) sound files.

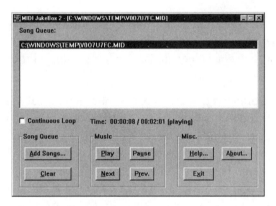

Fig. 17.2
MIDI Jukebox 2 can play wave and MIDI audio files for Netscape, and it's a great background music program, too.

The program is small (only 42KB) and offers a minimum of features: you can pause sounds or replay them. That's it. It's a perfect example of a helper application for the devout minimalist.

But if you like working to background music and have access to an extensive collection of music files, MIDI Jukebox 2's background music capability is a nice plus. It lets you load and play a list of MIDI and wave files from your hard drive or network, and you can jive all day while using very little in the way of system resources.

Because it was written for Windows 95, the program is fast and efficient and multitasks well. Best of all, the shareware fee is only $10.00.

If you're looking for a single, simple Win95 application to augment NAPlayer's .AU and .AIF sound-playing capabilities, you don't have to look any further than MIDI Jukebox 2.

TrueSpeech Internet Player

Any sound can be digitized, including speech. But sounds digitized in the proprietary TrueSpeech format by DSP Group, Inc., can be compressed and still retain excellent quality. DSP says that its technology can compress one minute of digitized speech to a file only 64KB in size. It licenses this technology to developers (for a fee) but provides a free real-time player called *TSPlay32* to users who want to play them (see fig. 17.3).

Fig. 17.3
The TrueSpeech
Internet Player
plays wave files,
and is optimized
for playing
digitized speech.

TSPlay32 is a Win95 program (there's also a Windows 3.1 version) that plays TrueSpeech files and regular wave files to boot. This program can easily be configured as a Netscape helper application for playing all the waves that come its way.

One of its best features is that it can play sound files in real time, as they are downloading; you don't have to wait for a file to download first. If you don't like what you hear, you'll know right away and can cancel the transfer in midstream. This can save you lots of expensive connect time if you're previewing many sound files, but keeping only a few. Of course, nothing is perfect—TrueSpeech sometimes gets ahead of a download and has to pause and wait for it to catch up, but you can always hit the play button to start the file playing over again from the beginning.

TrueSpeech is unique in that it is on the forefront of a new World Wide Web technology: programs that can access the Web independently of a browser. You can run TSPlay32 all by itself and choose to load and play a file from your disk or network, of course; but you can also tell it to load a URL and it will connect to the Web and play a file directly from the site where it is stored, all without the aid of Netscape or any other browser. This kind of independent program is going to open up the Web and make it seem like more of a wide-area network than a communications service. Look for more programs like TSPlay32 in the near future.

In the meantime, TSPlay32 also makes a good helper app for Netscape. Though at 266KB it's not exactly compact, it's not a monster, either. And you'll have fun playing sounds right off the Web when Netscape's not even running.

Sound Gadget Pro
If you're a control freak, just listening to sounds is never enough for you. You want to dissect them, tear them apart, and put them back together again in new and different ways.

If this is you, then *Sound Gadget Pro* (268KB) will be your favorite sound helper application for Netscape (see fig. 17.4). Not only can it load and play .AU and .SND files (thus replacing Netscape's wimpy NAPlayer), it also handles .WAV and .VOC (Sound Blaster) sound formats, as well as raw sound files.

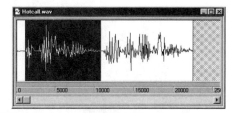

Fig. 17.4
Sound Gadget Pro lets you do much more than just listen to sound files. It lets you view and edit them, too.

Even though shareware author Nigel Magnay has chosen to inconvenience you a bit when this program is launched (you have to hit three randomly se-lected buttons before it will run), and even though files don't play automati-cally (you have to hit the Play button first), this program is such a nice sound editor you won't mind these minor inconveniences. Heck, you'll probably even figure out how much £10 is in American money and send Nigel his shareware fee.

Sound Gadget Pro lets you view a sound's waveform and manipulate it six ways from Sunday. You can reverse it, convert it to another format, change it from 8 to 16 bits or vice versa, and likewise from mono to stereo. You can fade, cross-fade, cut, paste, and even apply a dynamic envelope. You'll be turning staid voice-overs into Hollywood-style sound effect extravaganzas after only a few minutes of playing around with SGPro's highly intuitive Win95 interface.

If you're concerned about connect time, you might want to configure some-thing simpler as your Netscape audio helper app and just use SGPro on files you've saved offline. But either way, it's guaranteed to be good, sound fun.

Windows 3.1 Sound Programs

If you're running Netscape under Windows 3.1, you'll find that there are some excellent freely distributed sound programs on the Web (and on this book's CD, as well). Even if you're running Win95, some of these Windows 3.1 programs can nicely fill the gap until Win95 specific programs are avail-able that have similar features.

III

Using Helper Apps

Windows Play Any File

Windows Play Any File may have the largest name-to-program-size (47KB) ratio of any of the programs discussed in this chapter (see fig. 17.5). That's probably why most people (including the program's author, Bill Neisius) usually just call it WPLANY.

Fig. 17.5
WPLANY is a small sound player program whose sole purpose in life is to be launched by other applications.

WPLANY has no user interface of its own; it exists only to be called by other programs. If you do try to launch it by itself, all you get is the little info window shown above. But if you launch it from another program, it doesn't bring up a window at all; it just plays any of four different audio file types: .AU/.SND, .VOC, .WAV, and .IFF, in stereo or mono, in 8-bit or 16-bit format.

In other words, it's the perfect Netscape audio helper application. And it's not even shareware—it's free!

RealAudio Player

Like the TrueSpeech player we talked about for Win95, *RealAudio* plays sound files off the Web in real time, and can do so all by itself, without the assistance of a Web browser (see fig. 17.6). Unfortunately, it only plays its own proprietary (.RA, .RAM) files.

Fig. 17.6
The RealAudio Player only plays a proprietary audio format, but it does so in realtime.

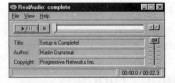

Still, it's a kick to hear audio in real time, without having to wait for the whole file to download before you know what it is. And it's fun to listen to files on the Web without having to boot up Netscape to do it.

Of course, you can configure RealAudio as a Netscape helper application if you want to, but you probably won't run into enough .RA files on the Web to make it worthwhile yet. You might want to wait to see if this new sound format achieves real popularity before you configure a helper app for it.

Tip

Netscape Corporation apparently has a high opinion of RealAudio—it is included in Netscape Power Pack ($54.95), Netscape's CD-ROM collection of five Netscape support utilities. The RealAudio player is in good company; the other applications on the Power Pack CD-ROM are Netscape Chat, SmartMarks, Adobe's Acrobat Reader, and Apple's QuickTime movie viewer. With Netscape support, RealAudio is bound to have a bright future on the Web.

Tip

A good place to find .RA files is the Internet Radio Network at **http://town.hall.org/radio/**. They have over 200 hours of files online, and regularly broadcast the proceedings of Congress over the Web in real time. (The files are available in .WAV format, too.)

But if you want to play with real-time audio on the Web, check this program out. For more info, take a look at Progressive Networks' home page at **http://www.realaudio.com**.

Waveform Hold and Modify

If the idea of editing as well as playing sounds appeals to you, you should like WHAM (see fig. 17.7). *Windows Hold and Modify*, its full, official name, plays .VOC, .IFF, .AU/.SND, .WAV, and raw sound files. But it also lets you edit those files in dozens of different ways.

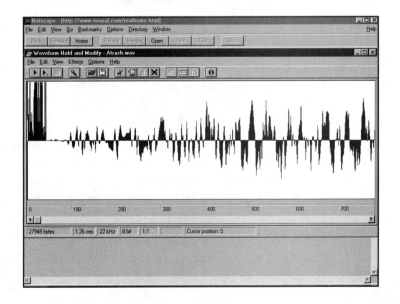

Fig. 17.7
Waveform Hold and Modify (WHAM) can play and edit five different kinds of digitized sounds.

III

Using Helper Apps

Like Sound Gadget Pro for Win95, WHAM lets you reverse, cut, paste, convert, and otherwise do just about anything you want to sound files. This 188KB program is a real audio powerhouse.

You can set WHAM up as a Netscape player in one of three ways.

If you configure it as you normally would configure any helper app, WHAM automatically loads a sound file when Netscape invokes it but does not play it. You have to do that manually.

If, however, you add a space and a "-p" to the end of WHAM's path name in the Launch Application field of the Helper Applications configuration window, WHAM plays the file as soon as it has loaded.

If you want WHAM to just play a file and then unload itself without ever opening a display window, make that a "-q" on the command line instead.

These command line options make WHAM one of the most versatile helper apps you can set up for Netscape audio. But no matter which way you configure it, WHAM is a great do-it-all sound application.

If you like WHAM and continue to use it, Australian author Andrew Bulhak requests a shareware fee of $25–$30.

XingSound

Xing Technology's demo of *XingSound* is only 30KB small, but when configured as a helper application, it lets Netscape play high-quality MPEG compressed audio files (see fig. 17.8).

Fig. 17.8

The freely distributed demo of the XingSound MPEG Audio player lets Netscape play some of the highest-quality sounds on the Web.

"MPEG? Isn't MPEG for video?" you ask. True. But MPEG videos also have audio content, and MPEG can be used to compress audio-only files as well as audio-and-video files. The advantage to doing so is that they retain high fidelity while being compressed from six to 15 times or more.

While there aren't a lot of MPEG audio files on the Web yet, this format is finding favor among professionals. That means that many of the *best* sound files on the Web are (or may soon be) MPEG compressed. That's a good enough reason for wanting to add an MPEG audio player helper app to Netscape.

The XingSound MPEG Audio Player only plays mono sound files. For full stereo, as well as MPEG digitizing and compression tools, you have to purchase full programs from Xing Technologies. But if all you need is a simple MPEG audio player helper application for Netscape, the demo program works just fine.

Midi Gate

Like MIDI Jukebox 2 for Win95, PRS Corporation's *Midi Gate* can be configured as a helper application to play MIDI music files for Netscape, or it can be used stand-alone (see fig. 17.9). When run by itself, it lets you compile a list of MIDI files that it can play in the background while you work.

On the CD

Fig. 17.9
Midi Gate can play MIDI files for Netscape or function as a MIDI jukebox for background music.

When invoked automatically by Netscape as a MIDI file helper application, Midi Gate thoughtfully runs minimized and hides in the corner of your screen. When it's done, it goes away. You couldn't ask for a more well-behaved Netscape helper app.

If you want to do a little more, all you have to do is click the minimized Midi Gate icon and it expands into the spartan window shown in figure 17.9. From here, you can scan the file for MIDI header information, pause or re-wind and replay the song, or save the file to disk.

Though it only handles .MID files, Midi Gate is a utilitarian little (34KB) freeware program that makes a handy Netscape helper app. And the back-ground tunes are nice, too.

Translating Sounds for Netscape

There are a couple of good reasons why you might find yourself interested in translating sound files from one format to another.

- If you find an absolutely must-have sound online in some strange for-mat and you don't have anything on hand that will play it.

- If you are creating your own Web pages and need to translate a lot of odd sound files that you have lying around to some more popular for-mat (like .AU or .WAV).

Either way, you have to find a program that can read the original and write the target sound file format. Many of the programs we mention in this chap-ter can do that to some degree. For example, if you want to convert a dozen .AU files to .WAV format, you can do it with WHAM on Windows 3.1 or Sound Gadget Pro on Windows 95.

But what if the formats you need to be able to read and/or write are real oddballs?

Well, the good news is, there's a solution.

The bad news is, you're going to have to run it from DOS.

That's because one of the most versatile tools for converting among various audio formats is a multi-platform application called *SOX* (Sound Exchange). It doesn't exist in Windows 3.1 or Win95 formats, but the DOS version is a very versatile tool.

SOX can read and write over a dozen different audio file formats. They are listed in table 17.3.

Table 17.3 Audio File Types That SOX Can Read and Write	
Extension	**Type**
.AIFF	Apple/SGI
.AU	SUN
.AUTO	Guess the Type
.CDR	CD Audio
.DAT	Text Data
.HCOM	Macintosh HCOM
.RAW, .UB, .SB, .UW, .SW, .UL	Raw
.SF	IRCAM
.SMP	SampleVision
.VOC	Sound Blaster
.WAV	Windows RIFF

In its simplest usage, SOX merely converts from one format to another. For example, to convert a file called bloop.au to one called bloop.wav, you would type:

sox bloop.au bloop.wav

DOS programs don't get much easier than that.

If you want to add special effects like tweaking the volume, changing the sampling rate, or converting from stereo to mono, SOX does all that too. But we're not going to get into all the subtle details of SOX here. If you want to perform such esoteric tasks, check out the SOX documentation.

## CHAPTER 18

Configuring Netscape for Graphics

If the World Wide Web were a box of Raisin Bran, text would be the bran flakes and graphics would be the raisins. While most of the Web's "nutritional content" may be in the text, the graphics are what make the Web tastier and just plain more fun than the rest of the Internet.

Netscape handles the most popular Web graphics file formats on its own, inline, but to view all the graphics on the Web, you need to set up a couple of helper applications. Fortunately, there are dozens of excellent Windows graphics programs out there that make great Netscape helpers.

In this chapter, we talk about:

- How Netscape works with graphics
- What kinds of graphics file formats you're likely to run into on the World Wide Web
- Which Windows 3.1 and Windows 95 programs make good Netscape graphics helper applications
- How to translate graphics for Netscape

Hardware Requirements for Netscape Graphics

Many older desktop PCs and notebook computers are limited in their graphics capabilities. If your machine can't display any more than 16 colors, this chapter probably isn't for you.

The minimum for cruising the Web these days is a 640×480 screen capable of displaying 256 colors. If your computer can do at least this well, you'll be able to view 85 percent of the graphics you find on the Web with no problem.

Of course, the *real* cutting-edge sites out there have pages that look good only on an 800×600 (or larger) screen, with 16-bit (65,536) or 24-bit (16,777,216) color palettes. Personally, I try to avoid such sites. They are a real killer on a 14.4KB dial-up connection.

> **Tip**
>
> Trying to view a big page on a small screen? No problem! Just use the scroll bar at the bottom of the Netscape window to move horizontally. Most people don't pay any attention to it on "normal" size screens, so they forget it's there when viewing pages that are a little wider than normal.

Still, some of those images are well worth waiting for. And once you've got them, you've got to have *some* way to display them.

I suggest you check the manual for your PC's display card and see what it's capable of. If your display card is more than a couple of years old, you may want to upgrade so you can handle those big, beautiful images. If your pocketbook says "no," don't despair. You can still look at them…if you're willing to compromise a bit.

> **Tip**
>
> Read your display card manual carefully! Even if your display isn't what you'd like it to be, it may be possible for you to plug in more video RAM and bring it up to speed. This is a much cheaper solution than buying a whole new graphics card!

How Computer Graphics Work

Computer graphics are *bitmapped images*; that is, they consist of a grid of dots called pixels that are mapped to a color palette. For example, the minimum Windows 95 display screen is 640 pixels wide by 480 pixels high (640×480), with a palette of 16 colors.

Many of the graphics images you'll encounter on the Web come in one of four "standard" sizes, which happen to match the screen sizes of common computer displays: 320×200, 640×480, 800×600, and 1024×768. However, you'll find bitmaps on the Web in sizes ranging from tiny "thumbnails" with dimensions of only a few pixels to images so huge your computer can't even load them, much less display them.

The number of colors in an image is dependent on how many bits are used to define the color for each pixel (see fig. 18.1). Table 18.1 shows how many bits are required for the five most common color palette depths.

Table 18.1 The Number of Bits Needed to Define Different Image Color Palettes	
No. of Bits	**Colors in Palette**
1	2
4	16
8	256
16	65,536
24	16,777,216

Fig. 18.1
The scenic Grand Tetons in eight bitplanes, four bitplanes, and one bitplane.

Tip

Don't forget that black, white, and gray are colors, too! A 2-color image (1 bit) is always monochrome (black-and-white). But 4- and 8-bit images are sometimes grayscale images, with each pixel's value indicating brightness, not color.

An image's color palette is generally defined in one of two ways.

For images with 16, 256, or 65,536 colors, the number that defines each pixel's color is usually a pointer into a table of predefined or user-definable colors. For example, a bit with the color "233" would point to the 233rd color defined in the color palette table. A color palette table defines colors using more bits than are used to indicate the color for each pixel. In this way, you can have images that, for example, use 256 colors out of a possible 24-bit color palette of 16 million.

But images with 24-bit color definitions usually indicate color values directly. This is done on a pixel-by-pixel basis using the same scheme that defines color palettes for entire low-color images—by splitting the number of bits for

III

Using Helper Apps

each color value into RGB (red, green, blue) values. (This is because a video monitor builds up an image from red, green, and blue dots.) For example, a 24-bit image splits the palette into 8 bits each for red, green, and blue values. That is, each color is made up of 256 different shades, each of the three colors, for a total of 16,777,216 possible colors in a single image.

How Netscape Works with Graphics

▶ See "Advanced Graphics," pg. 673

Most computer graphic images do not share the same set of colors. This can result in color "thrashing" if, for example, your computer tries to display two 256-color images with different color palettes on the same 256-color screen. You can also run into problems trying to display an image with more colors than your display can handle, like a 16-million color JPEG on a 256-color screen. Fortunately, Netscape is very clever about how it displays inline graphics. It handles these problems by using a process called dithering.

Dithering uses a pattern of available colors to create a visual illusion of displaying more. For example, if the Netscape screen palette had no orange available to it, it might try to "fake" orange by displaying a grid of yellow and red pixels. Your eye interprets the area as orange-ish, if you don't look at it too closely.

Note

Netscape actually does a very good job of dithering images. Dithering selection is automatic in Netscape 2.0, though you can change it manually.

To change Netscape's setting for dithering images, follow these steps:

1. Open the Netscape menu and choose Options, General.

2. Select the Images tab (see fig. 18.2).

3. The Automatic (Alt+U) radio button is checked by default. If you leave it checked, Netscape will continue to decide when it does and doesn't need to dither an image.

4. Choose Dither to Color Cube (Alt+D) to cause Netscape to always dither images to its internal "Color Cube" of reference colors.

5. Choose Use Closest Color in Color Cube (Alt+C) to turn off dithering alto gether; Netscape will always pick the closest solid color it has available.

6. Click OK to end.

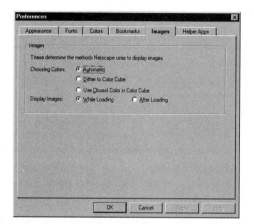

Fig. 18.2
Setting Netscape's
dithering options.

Note

Plug-ins are a new feature in Netscape 2.0. Plug-ins are basically add-on viewer modules for "live objects" that can be placed inline on Web pages. In the case of graphics files, this means that "foreign" image formats could be displayed inline just like GIFs, JPEGs, and XBMs, without having to launch a helper application. This doesn't mean that you'll never need another graphics helper application for Netscape, but it is an exciting new capability. For a discussion of plug-ins, see chapter 36, "Netscape Plug-Ins."

▶ See "Netscape Plug-Ins," pg. 933

Graphics File Formats

There are three different ways that images can be stored in files.

Most computer graphics file formats store image information as bitmaps. After all, that's how a computer displays them. All three of the image types that Netscape can display—GIFs, JPEGs, and XBMs—are bitmapped images.

Note

Okay, okay, we're lying. GIFs and JPEGs aren't really bitmapped image files; they're *compressed* bitmapped image files.

GIFs are 256-color (or fewer) images that are compressed using LZW compression, a technique similar to the file compression algorithms used in various archive file formats.

(continues)

(continued)

A JPEG image begins life as a 24-bit bitmapped image, then a very sophisticated image compression algorithm takes over. This analyzes the picture and compresses it to a very high ratio. JPEG compression is actually "lossy"—that is, it usually doesn't care if it throws away some picture detail in order to make the image a whole lot smaller.

XBMs are monochrome bitmapped images, but XBM files aren't binary bitmaps— they are C language source files, which represent images as numeric (hexadecimal) arrays; they can be read by C compilers, as well as Netscape and a few image display programs.

It just goes to show you that, when it comes to graphics image file formats, there are a *lot* of extremely different ways to store an image!

Fig. 18.3
JPEG compression at its worst. The rose on the left is a GIF image. On the right is a JPEG version of the same image compressed to the maximum possible degree (a compression setting of 1 out of 100, with optimized Huffman encoding).

Vector image files take a different approach—they actually describe how an image is drawn. When a computer displays a vector image file, it follows the instructions in the file to redraw the image. While it sounds tedious, vector images are much easier to rescale to different sizes, because the image doesn't have a hard-and-fast correlation between its definition in the file and the pixel-by-pixel image on the screen.

Metafiles use a combination of bitmapped and vector image definition. Windows Metafile (.WMF) format images are used quite often under Windows for clipart images that frequently need to be resized.

Note

You can find out more about graphics file formats by checking out the four-part Graphics FAQ (Frequently Asked Questions) list on UseNet. You can retrieve the latest version by pointing Netscape to **ftp://rtfm.mit.edu/pub/usenet/ news.answers/graphics/fileformats-faq** or **http://www.smartpages.com/**

faqs/graphics/fileformats-faq/part[1-4]/faq.html. This FAQ is also distributed monthly on the UseNet newsgroups comp.graphics, comp.answers, and news.answers as four separate files.

More information on graphics files can also be obtained by reading the UseNet newsgroup **comp.graphics.misc**.

Troubleshooting

I downloaded an image that looks just fine in [insert the name of your favorite generic graphics display program here], but the program I have configured as my Netscape helper application doesn't display it properly.

You're probably running into an older (or newer) version of that particular image file format. Though most image display and manipulation programs can handle older versions of various file formats just fine, some will "choke" on unknown variations. And standards groups are always updating file format definitions, sometimes coming up with variations that "break" older viewers. Because of the real-time nature of the Internet, these changes will often show up first on the Web. Make sure your Netscape graphics helper applications can always handle the latest versions of a graphics file format.

Netscape recognizes graphics files the same way it identifies all the files it accesses on the Web: by MIME type first, then (if it doesn't receive a valid MIME type from the Web server it's connected to) by file name extension.

◀ See "Configuring Helper Applications," pg. 395

Caution

There are several very different image file formats that share the file extensions .PIC ("picture") and .IMG ("image"). The only way to properly identify what kinds of images these really are is by MIME type or to use a program that actually reads and interprets the file's header information. Don't assume that either of these (or any other) file extensions can be used to accurately identify an image's real file type.

Netscape can display inline GIF, JPEG, and XBM images. These three formats account for almost 100 percent of the inline images on the Web. But external images are another matter. If you click a link and it leads to a file in a format that Netscape can't handle, you'll have to configure a helper application for it.

The graphics file MIME types and file name extensions that Netscape knows about are listed in table 18.2.

III

Using Helper Apps

Table 18.2   The Graphics File Types Recognized by Netscape

Type/Subtype	Extensions	Description
image/ief	.IEF	
image/x-MS-bmp	.BMP	Windows Bitmap
image/x-rgb	.RGB	RGB Image
image/x-portable-pixmap	.PPM	PPM Image
image/x-portable-graymap	.PGM	PGM Image
image/x-portable-bitmap	.PBM	PBM Image
image/x-portable-anymap	.PNM	PBM Image
image/x-xwindowdump	.XWD	X Window Dump Image
image/x-xpixmap	.XPM	X Pixmap
*image/x-xbitmap	.XBM	X Bitmap
image/x-cmu-raster	.RAS	CMU Raster Image
image/tiff	.TIFF, .TIF	TIFF Image
*image/jpeg	.JPEG, .JPG, .JPE	JPEG Image
*image/gif	.GIF	CompuServe Image Format

Images it can display internally are marked with an asterisk (*). The file type you'll probably want to configure a helper application for right away is underlined.

Of course, there are dozens more graphics image file formats in use on the World Wide Web. Table 18.3 lists some of these, though it is by no means an exhaustive list.

Table 18.3   Some of the Other Graphics File Types You'll Find on the World Wide Web

Extension	Description
.CGM	Computer Graphics Metafile
.DEM	Digital Elevation Model
.DXF	Autodesk Drawing Exchange Format
.IFF	Interchange File Format
.NAPLPS	North American Presentation Layer Protocol Syntax
.PCX	ZSoft Paint
.PIC	Pegasus Imaging Corporation Format
.PNG	Portable Network Graphics
.PSD	Adobe Photoshop
.RIFF	Microsoft Resource Interchange File Format

Extension	Description
.SGI	Silicon Graphics Image File Format
.SPIFF	Still Picture Interchange File Format
.TGA	Truevision (Targa) File Format
.WMF	Windows Meta File
.WPG	WordPerfect Graphics Metafile

The one you'll probably want to configure a helper application for right away is <u>underlined</u>.

> **Note**
>
> The hottest new graphics file type on the World Wide Web is the Portable Network Graphics (.PNG) format, which was created mostly as a response to the Unisys/CompuServe GIF graphics copyright controversy (which we won't go into here). According to the first drafts of the PNG specification, "The PNG format is intended to provide a portable, legally unencumbered, simple, lossless, streaming-capable, well-compressed, well-specified standard for bitmapped image files which gives new features to the end user at minimal cost to the developer." Look for PNG graphics to carve a major niche for themselves on the Web in the months to come.

Note that in each of these tables we've underlined a file type that you'll probably want to configure a Netscape helper application for right away. The two we've targeted are Windows Bitmaps (.BMP) and Zsoft Paint (.PCX) files. Though the GIFs and JPEGs that Netscape can handle internally are much more popular on the Web, you'll run into enough BMPs and PCXs to make configuring helper applications for these two file formats worthwhile.

Windows Bitmaps

Because BMPs are the native graphics file format of Microsoft Windows, you'll find quite a few of them on the Web. (And if not on the Web itself, on the rest of the Internet, at the very least.)

Most of the programs described in this chapter can display .BMP format image files.

> **Tip**
>
> In the Windows directory in both Windows 3.1 and Windows 95 is a little program called Paintbrush that displays both .PCX and .BMP images. For a step-by-step guide to setting up Paintbrush to work with Netscape, see chapter 16, "Configuring Helper Applications."

III

Using Helper Apps

Zsoft Paint Files

.PCX (Zsoft Paint) format files were really popular on the PC when all it could run was MS-DOS. The continuing popularity of .PCX files on the PC platform is a real testament to Newton's laws of inertia—.PCX files just don't seem to be fading away.

Fortunately, many of the programs discussed in this chapter can display .PCX files, too.

> **Note**
>
> Have Microsoft Office installed on your Windows 3.1 or Windows 95 system? Then you also have a little program available called *Microsoft Imager* (see fig. 18.1). (It may not have been installed automatically when you installed Office. If not, you can add it easily by running the Office Setup program again.) Imager can handle seven different graphics file formats: .BMP, .DIB, .GIF, .JPG, .PCD, .PCX, and .RLE. You can configure it as a Netscape helper for any of these file types (though you won't want to do so for .GIF or .JPG, since Netscape handles those inline). Microsoft Imager can also manipulate images in many different and interesting ways, since it's based on the popular graphics processing program HALO Desktop Imager.

Fig. 18.4
Microsoft Imager is included in the Microsoft Office package.

Graphics Helper Applications for Netscape

With GIF, JPEG, and XBM support built into Netscape, you already have direct access to the most popular graphics file types on the Web. But by adding helper applications for a few more, you'll never be caught by surprise by some weird file off a server in the backwaters of Timbuktu. The rest of this chapter discusses some programs that make excellent graphics helper applications for Netscape, whether it's running under Windows 3.1 or Win95.

> **Note**
>
> For up-to-date information about the latest versions of these and other graphics programs for Windows 3.1 and Windows 95, check out Brian Stark's excellent Graphic Utilities site on the World Wide Web at **http://www.public.iastate.edu/~stark/gutil_sv.html**.

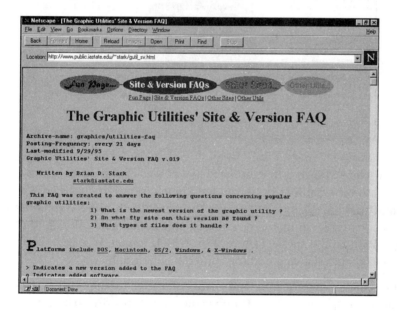

Fig. 18.5
Brian Stark's Graphic Utilities Site & Version FAQ.

Windows 95 Graphics Programs

Windows 95 helper applications are your best choice if you're running Netscape under Win95. They understand long file names, have the Win95 user interface, multitask better than Windows 3.1 programs, and run faster because they're 32-bit applications.

There are some good freeware and shareware graphics applications out there for Win95. In the following pages, we'll introduce you to some of the best.

LView Pro

Good news for graphics aficionados: *LView Pro* is now available in a Windows 95 edition (see fig. 18.6). A longtime favorite among Windows 3.1 users, LView Pro can view, manipulate, and convert among seven popular graphics image file formats: JPEG, BMP, TIFF, TGA, GIF, PCX, and PBM.

Fig. 18.6
LView Pro's most visible feature is its floating menu. It's a powerful graphics viewing and manipulation program that has a multitude of uses as a Web page creation tool. It also makes an excellent helper application for Netscape.

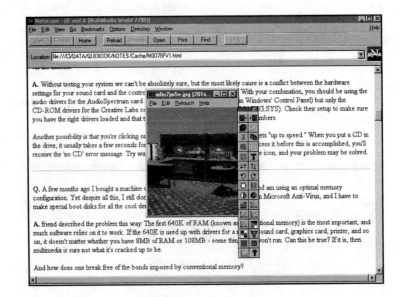

LView Pro (464KB) is a time-honored tool of Web page creators because of its ability to write transparent background color information in the GIF89a format. This is the means used to create Web graphics that let a Web browser's background color or image show through the background color of inline images. Without this special feature of the GIF89a format, Web pages worldwide would be stuck showing nothing but rectangular graphics.

Unfortunately, most graphics programs don't seem to support GIF background transparency. That's reason enough for Web artists to keep a copy of LView Pro on hand.

Add in its ability to view and convert other popular file formats and you have a very useful tool, indeed. Combine that with the dozens of ways LView Pro can twiddle images, and you've got a program you just can't live without.

Oh, yeah—you can use it as a Netscape helper application, too.

LView Pro is, quite simply, a must-have. MMedia Research requests a $30 shareware registration fee if you use LView Pro past the trial period.

PolyView

PolyBytes' PolyView displays and converts BMP, GIF, JPEG, Photo-CD, PNG, and TIFF images (see fig. 18.7). You can use it to adjust the brightness and contrast of images, and it displays a pretty nice slideshow. For a shareware fee of only $20, you couldn't ask for much more.

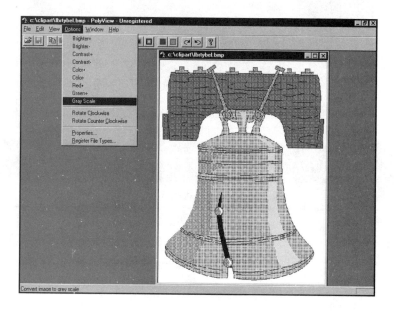

Fig. 18.7
PolyView is an elementary graphics viewer and converter for Win95.

Its Photo-CD and PNG support are worth noting. If these formats are important to you, setting up PolyView makes good sense. Though it's not small (662KB), if all you're looking for is a simple Netscape helper application for these file types, PolyView will do the job.

Vueprint Pro

If you're beginning to weary of all this talk about Netscape helper applications, and you're starting to wonder if you'll ever get helper applications configured for all of the file types we've talked about, have we got a deal for you!

Vueprint Pro is an all-in-one solution for displaying multimedia files (see fig. 18.8). It can be configured as a Netscape helper application for all of the sound, graphics, video, and compressed file formats listed in table 18.4.

Fig. 18.8
Vueprint Pro can display, play, convert, and manipulate dozens of different audio, video, and graphics file formats. It's a veritable Swiss Army Knife for multimedia.

Table 18.4 The 23 Multimedia and Compressed File Types That Vueprint Pro Can Display or Play	
Source	**File Name Extensions**
Images	.GIF, .BMP, .DIB, .RLE, .PCX, .TGA, .JPG, .TIF
Sounds	.MID, .WAV, .MCI
Movies	.AVI, .MPG, .MMM, .MOV, .FLI, .FLC
Slide Show	.SLI
Uuencoded files	.UUE, .UU1, .01, .MSG
Zip files	.ZIP

Not only can it display all of those file types, it can convert among them, print them, and twiddle them in lots of different ways. It can also install screen savers, display slide shows, and load multiple files at once. In short, Vueprint Pro will do just about everything you need to do with multimedia files.

With all that capability, you'd expect Vueprint Pro to be a huge program, and it is, though not as large as many programs that do much less: 672KB. Configured as a Netscape helper application, it takes a while to load. That's a good reason to consider configuring several smaller Netscape helper applications instead, saving Vueprint Pro for use as a stand-alone multimedia viewer/editor.

Either way, this is another must-have program for Win95. (A Windows 3.1 version is available, too.)

There's a $40 registration fee for this shareware program; you'll be reminded of that fact by a pop-up window every time the program is run or shut down, and by a banner across the middle of the screen in between. While these "re-minders" are about as subtle as having someone beat a tarantella on your head with a brickbat, the fee is certainly reasonable considering how much Vueprint Pro can do.

Drag and View

Drag and View is a very versatile little viewer program for Win95 (see fig. 18.9). Basically an expansion on Microsoft's own Quick View, Drag and View attaches itself to your right-mouse-button drop-down menu and lets you view a variety of common file types (many more than Quick View).

On the CD

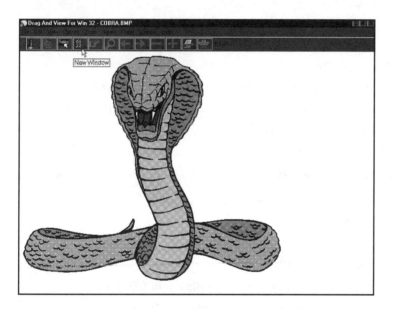

Fig. 18.9
Drag and View, a compact but capable file viewer for Windows 95.

III

Using Helper Apps

Tip

What? You haven't found *Quick View* yet? It should be right there on your right-mouse-button drop-down menu. At least that's where it is when you right-click a file that it can view (like WMFs, BMPs, Word DOCs, Excel XLS spreadsheets, text files, etc.). You can configure Quick View as a Netscape helper application for any file type it knows—it lives in the Windows\System\Viewers directory. If it's not there, you can add it by choosing Add/Remove Programs from the Control Panel.

The following file formats are viewable using Drag and View:

- ASCII
- Hexadecimal
- Microsoft Word and Word for Windows, including version 7
- Microsoft Works and Works for Windows, including version 3
- Windows Write
- Word Perfect and Word Perfect for Windows, including version 6
- Ami Pro
- Q&A Write
- dBASE
- FoxPro
- Clipper
- Excel, including version 6
- Lotus 123
- Symphony
- Quattro, Quattro Pro, and Quattro Pro for Windows
- .WMF, .BMP, .ICO, .PCX, .GIF, .TIF, .JPEG, and .TGA images
- .ZIP and .LZH archives
- .TTF TrueType Fonts

Support for even more file formats is added in the registered version ($35):

- CorelDraw version 3 (.CDR)
- AutoCad (.DXF)
- Micrografix Designer (.DRW)
- Microsoft PowerPoint (.PPT)
- Encapsulated PostScript/Adobe Illustrator (.EPS/.AI)
- Hewlett-Packard Graphics Language (.HPGL)
- Lotus (.PIC)
- Computer Graphics Metafile (.CGM/.CTM)
- WordPerfect Graphics (.WPG)
- Adobe Acrobat (.PDF)

Drag and View makes a great little (108KB) bare-bones Netscape helper application for all of the listed file types.

Windows 3.1 Graphics Programs

Windows 3.1 has been in existence long enough to serve as the operating platform for some of the best graphics programs around. Whether you're running Netscape under Windows 3.1 or are a Win95 user looking to augment your collection of 32-bit graphics programs, the following pages will direct you to some killer image display and processing applications.

Paint Shop Pro

You know how you feel when you get nostalgic about an old friend? Well, I feel that way when I talk about JASC's Paint Shop Pro (see fig. 18.10). I have used it every day for a couple of years now, both at work and at home, for creating graphics for software manuals and magazine articles. I used it to snapshot the screens in this chapter. Here's just how serious I am about Paint Shop Pro: I paid JASC the $69 registration fee. I just wouldn't have been able to live with my conscience otherwise.

On the CD

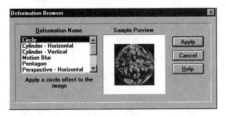

Fig. 18.10
Paint Shop Pro is the Cadillac of Windows image manipulation programs.

PSP directly supports 35 file formats, and can handle more through the use of external filters, including the ones shipped with Microsoft Office. PSP's native file types are listed in table 18.5.

Table 18.5	File Types Supported by Paint Shop Pro
Extension	**File Type**
.BMP	RGB encoded Microsoft Windows
.BMP	RGB encoded OS/2
.BMP	RLE encoded Microsoft Windows
.CDR	CorelDRAW
.CGM	Computer Graphics Metafile
.CLP	Bitmap Windows Clipboard
.CLP	Device Independent Bitmap Windows Clipboard
.CUT	Dr. Halo

(continues)

Table 18.5 Continued

Extension	File Type
.DIB	RGB encoded Microsoft Windows
.DIB	RGB encoded OS/2
.DIB	RLE encoded Microsoft Windows
.DRW	Micrografx Draw
.DXF	Autodesk
.GEM	Ventura/GEM
.GIF	Ver. 87a (interlaced) CompuServe
.GIF	Ver. 87a (non-interlaced) CompuServe
.GIF	Ver. 89a (interlaced) CompuServe
.GIF	Ver. 89a (non-interlaced) CompuServe
.HPGL	Hewlett-Packard Graphics Language
.IFF	Compressed Electronic Arts
.IFF	Uncompressed Electronic Arts
.IMG	New Style GEM Paint
.IMG	Old Style GEM Paint
.JIF	Huffman compressed Joint Photo. Expert Group
.JPG	Huffman compressed Joint Photo. Expert Group
.LBM	Compressed Deluxe Paint
.LBM	Uncompressed Deluxe Paint
.MAC	With header MacPaint
.MAC	Without header MacPaint
.MSP	New version Microsoft Paint
.MSP	Old version Microsoft Paint
.PBM	Portable Bitmap UNIX
.PCD	Kodak Photo CD
.PCX	Ver. 2 (with palette info.) ZSoft Paintbrush
.PCX	Ver. 3 (without palette info.) ZSoft Paintbrush
.PCX	Version 0 ZSoft Paintbrush
.PCX	Version 5 ZSoft Paintbrush
.PGM	Portable Graymap UNIX
.PIC	Lotus Development Corp.
.PIC	Pictor/PC Paint
.PNG	Portable Network Graphics

Extension	File Type
.PPM	Portable Pixelmap UNIX
.PSD	RGB or indexed Photoshop
.RAS	Type 1 (Modern Style) Sun Microsystems
.RAW	Un-encoded pixel data
.RLE	CompuServe
.RLE	Microsoft Windows
.TGA	Compressed Truevision
.TGA	No compression Truevision
.TIFF	Fax Group 3 compressed Aldus Corporation
.TIFF	Fax Group 4 compressed Aldus Corporation
.TIFF	Huffman compressed Aldus Corporation
.TIFF	LZW compressed Aldus Corporation
.TIFF	No compression Aldus Corporation
.TIFF	Pack bits compressed Aldus Corporation
.WMF	Microsoft Windows Metafile
.WPG	Version 5.0 WordPerfect
.WPG	Version 5.1 WordPerfect
.WPG	Version 6.0 WordPerfect

PSP can convert among all of these formats. It can also tweak graphics images in a plethora of useful ways, with features like edge detection, histogram functions, gamma correction, deformations, and even user-defined functions. You can use it as a versatile image capture program, and its file browser acts as a handy thumbnail graphic cataloger. PSP also includes built-in scanner support and a full set of paint tools.

All this does not come cheaply: Paint Shop Pro is an 843KB program, so only the most diehard control freaks will want to configure it as a Netscape helper application.

Still, PSP is such a handy all-around graphics tool that you'll want to keep it on hand for offline graphics work, if nothing else.

ACDSee

All ACDSee does is display images (see fig. 18.11). That's it. But sometimes, that's all you want. It's a medium-sized (449KB), quick little image viewer for Windows 3.1 that will display .BMP, .GIF, .JPEG, .PCX, Photo-CD, .PNG, .TGA, and .TIFF files. ACDSee has online help, and it works as both a nifty slideshow program and a Netscape helper application. The shareware fee requested by ACDSee is $15.

On the CD

III

Using Helper Apps

Fig. 18.11
ACDSee is a nice, tight little picture viewer that works great as a stand-alone graphics viewer or as a helper application for Netscape.

WinJPEG

Despite its deceptively small size (375KB), WinJPEG has a real graphics wallop (see fig. 18.12). It can display and convert among eight popular graphics file formats: .BMP, .GIF, .IFF, .JFIF, .PCX, .PPM, .TGA, and .TIF. It also packs a nice set of photo image processing features, such as edge detection, gamma correction, bit slicing, and color adjustment.

Fig. 18.12
WinJPEG is a tiny graphics power-house, displaying, manipulating, and converting eight popular graphics file formats.

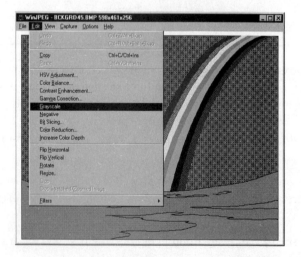

Of course, it makes a great Netscape helper application for graphics.

PVS asks a $25 registration fee for WinJPEG.

Translating Graphics for Netscape

Sometimes you just can't find a program that displays an image file you were told is a "must-have." When that happens, its time to fire up the ol' graphics converter.

Many of the programs discussed in this chapter will read, convert, and write files in several different formats. But if you're looking for something *really* exotic, it may be time to (shudder!) drop back into DOS.

First, though, we'll look at a couple of Windows 3.1 workhorses. If they can't handle your needs, we'll move on to two DOS programs that can convert image files among dozens of different graphics file formats.

JASC Media Center

Never one to leave a good thing half-done, JASC has expanded the program that was originally the image browser program for Paint Shop Pro and has turned it into a full-fledged multimedia cataloger, converter, and player system.

JASC Media Center, shown in figure 13.13, scans your directories and creates thumbnail catalogs of 37 different multimedia file formats (see table 18.6). Like Paint Shop Pro, it can support additional types through the use of external filters.

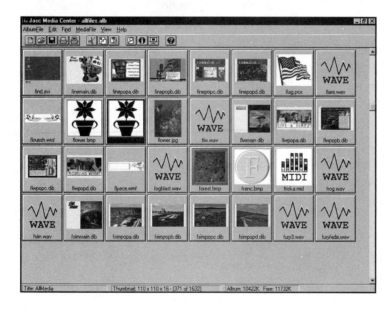

Fig. 18.13
JASC Media Center is a flexible multimedia organization system, file converter, and display program.

Table 18.6 Multimedia File Types That JASC Media Center Can Play or Display	
Extension	**Type**
.AVI	Video For Windows
.BMP/.DIB	OS/2
.BMP/.DIB	Windows
.CDR	CorelDRAW!
.CGM	Computer Graphics Metafile
.CLP	Windows Clipboard
.CUT	Dr. Halo
.DRW	Micrografx Draw
.DXF	Autodesk
.FLC/.FLI	Autodesk Animation
.GEM	Ventura/GEM
.GIF	CompuServe
.HPGL	Hewlett-Packard Graphics Language
.IFF	Electronic Arts
.IMG	GEM Paint
.JAS	JASC Proprietary Format
.JIF/.JPG	Joint Photo. Expert Group
.LBM	Deluxe Paint
.MAC	MacPaint
.MID	Musical Instrument Digital Interface
.MSP	Microsoft Paint
.PBM	UNIX
.PCD	Kodak Photo CD
.PCX	ZSoft Paintbrush
.PGM	UNIX
.PIC	Lotus Development Corp.
.PIC	Pictor/PC Paint
.PPM	UNIX
.PSD	Photoshop
.RAS	Sun Microsystems
.RLE	CompuServe or Windows
.TGA	Truevision

Extension	Type
.TIFF	Aldus
.WAV	Microsoft Windows
.WMF	Windows Metafile
.WPG	WordPerfect
.WPG	WordPerfect (Version 5.0 and 5.1)

Clicking on a thumbnail plays or displays the file; pressing Enter launches the editor you have specified for that file type.

Unfortunately, JASC Media Center (a relative lightweight for all it can do at 455KB) can only load files from its thumbnail albums, so it can't be configured as a Netscape helper application. But it can be used as an extremely flexible file type converter.

The shareware fee for JASC Media Center is $39, but if you register it in conjunction with Paint Shop Pro you can get both for $89.

Graphics Workshop

Though it doesn't work as a Netscape helper application, Graphics Workshop could be just the program you need if you're looking for a good all-around graphics tool for Windows (see fig. 18.14). You can use it to create thumbnail catalogs of your graphic files, then manipulate and convert them in dozens of ways. Graphics Workshop will read and write all of these graphics file types:

Fig. 18.14
Graphics Workshop is an image viewer, cataloger, manipulation and conversion program for Windows 3.1.

III

Using Helper Apps

- Graphics CompuServe   GIF
- Deluxe Paint   IFF/LBM
- Ventura   GEM/IMG
- Halo   CUT
- MacPaint   —
- Microsoft Paint   MSP
- PC Paint Pictor   PIC
- PC Paintbrush   PCX
- TIFF Images   TIFF
- Truevision Targa   TGA
- Windows 3   BMP/DIB
- Windows 3   RLE
- WordPerfect Graphics   WPG
- PFS: First Publisher   ART
- JPEG   JPG
- Kodak Photo-CD   PCD
- Sun Raster   RAS
- Slow Scan TV   HRZ
- AutoDesk Animations   FLI/FLC
- Windows Metafiles   WMF
- CorelDRAW Preview   CDR
- Corel PhotoPAINT   CPT
- QuickTime Movies   MOV
- Flexible Image Transport System   FITS
- UUencoded Graphics   UUE
- Windows Icons   ICO
- OS/2   BGA
- Portable Network Graphics   PNG
- MPEG Movies   MPG

Note that there are also three video file formats in that list: QuickTime (.MOV), Autodesk (.FLI), and MPEG (.MPG).

If you're terrified of DOS but have a driving need to convert graphics from lots of exotic file types, Graphics Workshop offers a nice, safe Windows 3.1 interface and lots of power under the hood. It's a good place to start.

Alchemy Mindworks requests a shareware fee of $40 if you use Graphics Workshop past the trial period.

Graphics Display System

Though it's a DOS program, the *Graphics Display System* has a mouse-and-menu system that makes for pretty comfortable use for a diehard Windows user, even if you haven't used DOS in years (see fig. 18.15).

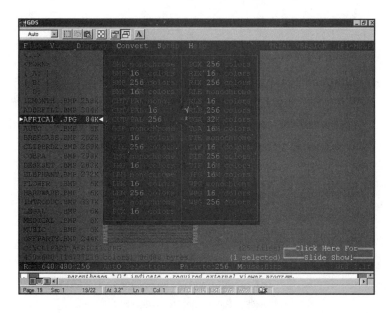

Fig. 18.15
Graphics Display System can convert among more different image file formats than you'll probably ever need.

Of course, you *can* run it from the DOS prompt with command-line options and never even bring up a user interface, if you prefer. In many ways, it's a very good compromise between DOS and Windows.

GDS is a very powerful graphics conversion program. It can read all and write most of the file formats listed in table 18.7.

Table 18.7   File Formats Handled by Graphics Display System for DOS

Extension	Type
.ANS	Color ANSI text—BBS
.TXT	Generic text—ANSI optional
.BBM	Deluxe Paint—IFF 'Brush'
.BMF	Corel Gallery Clipart

(continues)

III

Using Helper Apps

Table 18.7 Continued

Extension	Type
.BMP	Microsoft Windows Bitmap
.CUT	Media Cybernetics—HALO
.DIB	Device Independent Bitmap
.DL	'DL' Files (DL-VIEW.EXE)
.FLC	AutoDesk (FLXPLAY.EXE,FLIPLAY.EXE, QUICKFLI.EXE,
.FLI	
.FLX	PLAY.EXE, AAPLAY.EXE)
.GDS	Raxsoft/Photodex Scanning
.GIF	CompuServe GIF87/GIF89a
.GL	Grasp (GRASPRT.EXE)
.HAM	Electronic Arts—IFF/HAM
.ICO	Microsoft Windows Icon Files
.IFF	Electronic Arts—IFF/HAM
.IMG	GEM Raster
.JFI	JPEG—standard JFIF
.JPG	JPEG—standard JFIF
.LBM	Deluxe Paint—IFF/HAM
.MAC	Macintosh MacPaint Mono
.MP2	MPEG Audio (XING's MPEG.EXE)
.MPA	MPEG Audio (XING's MPEG.EXE)
.MPG	MPEG Video (XING's MPEG.EXE)
.PBM	PBMPlus Bitmap—mono
.PCC	ZSoft PC Paintbrush 'Brush'
.PCX	ZSoft PC Paintbrush
.PGM	PBMPlus Bitmap—gray
.PPM	PBMPlus Bitmap—true color
.RAX	Raxsoft/Photodex VideoGames
.RFX	Raxsoft/Photodex Fonts
.RLE	Windows RLE Bitmap
.SC*	ColorRIX
.TGA	TrueVision Targa—+RLE,Pals
.TIF	Tagged Image File Format
.WPG	WordPerfect Graphics—Bitmap

Items in parentheses "()" indicate a required external viewer program.

This little DOS program is a joy to use; it outstrips many Windows graphics programs. It has been a personal favorite of mine for years, and Photodex Corporation just keeps making it better and better.

Bonuses: GDS can also create catalogs of your images, and makes a nice little slideshow program, as well. The demo version is limited to handling 25 files at a time, cannot convert to JPEG format, and asks that you not use it for more than three weeks without paying the very reasonable shareware fee of $40.

DISPLAY

DISPLAY is tough to set up, but at least it has a DOS user interface that's a few steps above the command-line level. And if you're serious about manhandling graphics image files, DISPLAY handles more kinds than any other program. It can read, write, and preview all the following formats:

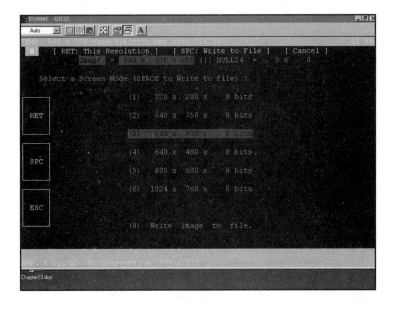

Fig. 18.16
DISPLAY is a DOS program that can handle just about any image file type you'll ever encounter.

Read:

GIF(.gif)	Utah RLE(.rle)
Japan MAG(.mag)	PBM(.pbm)
Japan PIC(.jpc)	PGM(.pgm)
Sun Raster(.ras)	PPM(.ppm)
JPEG/JFIF(.jpg)	PM(.pm)
XBM(.xbm)	PCX(.pcx)

Japan MKI(.mki)	PCPAINT/Pictor(.pic,.clp)
Tiff(.tif)	RAW GREY(.gry)
Targa(.tga)	Photo-CD(.pcd)
XPM(.xpm)	VORT output(.pix)
MacPaint(.mac)	WordPerfect Graphics(.wpg)
GEM/IMG(.img)	Windows ICON(.ico)
IFF/ILBM/PBM(.iff,.lbm)	ANSI screen file(.ans)
Windows BMP(.bmp)	Image INDEX(.idx)
QRT ray tracing(.qrt)	VIVID output(.img)
Mac PICT(.pct)	Thumbnail(.tnl)
VIS(.vis)	Dr. Halo(.cut)
PDS(.pds)	Japan PI(.pi)
VIKING(.vik)	PNG(.png)
VICAR(.vic)	DL(.dl)
FITS(.fit)	FLI(.fli)
Usenix FACE(.fac)	FLC(.flc)
IRIS/SGI(.sgi)	RAW(.raw/DMPEG)
YUV(.yuv)	MPEG(.mpg)
RAW RGB(.rgb)	AVI(.avi)
	GL(.gl)
	IFF/ANIM(.anm)
	RIFF/WAVE(.wav)

Write:

GIF	Sun Raster
JPEG	XBM
PBM	PGM
PPM	PM
Tiff	Targa
XPM	MacPaint
ASCII	Laser Jet
IFF/ILBM	Windows BMP
Mac PICT	VIS
FITS	FACE

PCX	GEM/IMG
IRIS/SGI	YUV
RAW RGB	Postscript
RAW GREY	WordPerfect Graphics
Windows ICON	Image INDEX(.idx)
ANSI screen file	Thumbnail
Dr. Halo	PNG

Preview:

GIF	JPEG
Windows BMP	PBM
PGM	PPM
Targa	PCX
MacPaint	Photo-CD
PNG	XBM
Sun Raster	Thumbnail
GEM/IMG	Windows ICON
WPG	FACE
IFF/ILBM	XPM
IRIS/SGI	

You'll note a couple of multimedia file types mixed in there with the graphics, such as .WAV audio files and Amiga ANIM animations. About the only omission worth noting is lack of support for Windows Metafiles (.WMF).

Though not for the rank amateur, DISPLAY can slice and dice graphics files like a pro.

III

Using Helper Apps

## CHAPTER 19

Configuring Netscape for Video

Arguably the hottest computer term these days is "multimedia," which means "more than one medium." With its combination of audio and animated graphics, computer video is what most people have in mind when they say that trendy word.

With the right helper applications, Netscape is perfectly capable of pulling down and playing video files directly from the World Wide Web. While it won't replace the television quite yet, video from the Web foreshadows even more exciting developments to come.

In this chapter, you learn:

- How Netscape works with video
- What kinds of video file formats you're likely to run into on the World Wide Web
- Which Windows 3.1 and Windows 95 programs make good Netscape video helper applications
- How to translate video for Netscape
- What the future holds for Netscape and multimedia

Hardware Requirements for Netscape Video

◀ See "Configuring Netscape for Sound," pg. 425, and "Configuring Netscape for Graphics," pg. 439

Video combines audio and graphics, so the hardware requirements for Netscape video are basically a combination of those spelled out in the previous two chapters (a 16-bit stereo sound card, plus a display card capable of displaying at least 640×480 pixel resolution in 256 colors).

However, because video files play sound and display graphics simultaneously, and because the images in video files *move*, you also need a fast processor and lots of RAM to keep things running at a smooth pace in real time. You'll want a big hard drive, too, if you're planning to keep many video files on hand—it's not unusual for a computer movie file to run 1MB or more, and I've seen plenty of them top 6MB and 7MB!

Tip

With videos more than with any other multimedia element, it's extremely easy to overrun your hard drive with downloaded files. At a megabyte or more apiece for the typical MPEG, .AVI, or .MOV file, it doesn't take long for your drive to fill up. If you regularly save video files to disk, make sure you also regularly purge unused files.

Tip

If you'd like to take a look at the self-proclaimed "biggest video on the Internet today," it's a 640×480 MPEG promo video for Television Associates that runs 15 minutes and 28 seconds. The file is 161.5MB, and it's located at **http://www.netvideo.com/netvideo/whatsnew.html**. Make sure your viewer (and system) can handle such a large file before you take the time to download it—most shareware video viewers have a built-in file size limit of 1MB. (You'll find that there are lots of good videos and excellent links on the netvideo site, too.)

Though the minimum requirements for PC video are often stated to be something along the lines of a 386SX20 with 4MB of RAM and a 40MB hard drive, if your system doesn't have at least a 486DX33 processor, 8MB of RAM, and a 540MB hard drive, playing video files may prove to be more of an exercise in frustration than an enjoyable experience.

Because video files are so huge, they take a long time to download. You want the quickest possible Internet connection if you want to get serious about video on the Web. This means you'll do best if you connect from work or school over a fast leased line, and if you're dialing up from home you'll want a 28.8 modem (even if you're a very patient person, you'll certainly want nothing less than 14.4).

MPEG, a popular video format covered later in this chapter, has special requirements. It incorporates file compression technology that works best with a dedicated MPEG decoder board. If you get serious about video on your PC, you may want to look into buying an MPEG board or a video card with MPEG built in.

How Computer Video Works

> **Note**
>
> Feel free to use the terms "video" and "movie" interchangeably when talking about moving images on the computer. (I certainly do in this chapter.) You can even throw in "animation" every once in a while and be totally correct, though most purists use that term only for motion graphics that are built up of hand-drawn or computer-generated images, rather than frames that are digitized from live-action footage.

Video playback under Windows and Win95 is usually handled though MCI (Media Control Interface) software drivers in your Windows\System directory, which can be called by any application. This means that you only need to install a driver for a particular video format once, and it can be called by any number of different viewer programs.

> **Note**
>
> You can find out more about PC video by checking out the video newsgroups on UseNet. Point your Netscape newsreader to **comp.multimedia**, **comp.graphics.animation**, **comp.os.ms-windows.video**, **rec.video.desktop**, and **comp.publish.cdrom.multimedia**.
>
> There are also many excellent multimedia resources on the Web. One good example is the University of Geneva's multimedia documentation directory at **http://tecfa.unige.ch:80/pub/documentation/multimedia/**. On this site you'll find a load of informative files, FAQs, demos, and so on. Check it out!

How Netscape Works with Video

Netscape needs helper applications to display video. You'll have to install two things for each video file format you want to handle:

- A video driver that will handle the format
- An application that can call the driver and display the video

You may need a different helper application for each of the different movie formats you'll find on the Web, or you may be able to find just one player you like that will handle them all. Viewers for a single video file format are often smaller, and sometimes have features and controls that are specific to that file type. Configuring an all-in-one viewer may mean having to load a bigger program at run time, but it also means you'll only have to learn the controls and quirks of a single viewer.

You may not even want to configure any real-time video helper applications for Netscape at all, especially if you're paying for connect time. Instead, you may want to set up all video files to be downloaded automatically to disk (see fig. 19.1). This lets you view them offline, where you can take your time playing them without incurring charges.

Fig. 19.1

You can use the Helpers dialog box to configure Netscape to save all videos to disk automatically, for leisurely offline viewing.

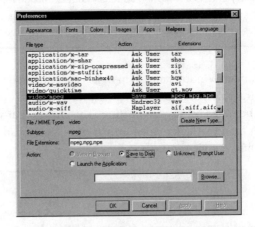

To set up your video files to be downloaded automatically to disk, follow these steps:

1. Select Options, General Preferences from the Netscape menu bar.
2. Click the Helpers tab to bring it to the front.
3. Scroll to the video/mpeg line and click it. It becomes highlighted, and mpeg,mpg,mpe appears in the File Extensions field.
4. Click the Save to Disk radio button. It becomes highlighted.
5. Repeat steps 3 and 4 for the video/quicktime and video/x-msvideo file types.

6. If you also want to save Autodesk animation files to disk automatically, click the Create New Type pushbutton. Enter **video** for the Mime Type and **x-fli** for the Mime Subtype, and select OK. Enter **fli** in the File Extensions field, and click the Save to Disk radio button.

7. Click OK to finish.

Tip

Netscape's disk cache (which is usually located in the Netscape/Navigator/Cache subdirectory) contains all the files you've viewed recently on the Web, with obscure file names but recognizable file name extensions. For example, if you recently viewed fishing.mov while browsing the Web, it might appear in the cache as something like MOOAAN4J.MOV. While it's almost impossible to figure out which *specific* file in the cache might be one you're interested in finding again, at least the file name extensions give you a clue. What's more, the file is still fully loadable into your regular video viewer. Happy prospecting!

Note

Plug-ins are a new feature in Netscape 2.0 that expand Netscape's multimedia capabilities. They are basically add-on viewer modules for live objects that can be placed inline on Web pages. In the case of video files, this means that they could be played automatically when the page is loaded or when the user clicks a link. Plug-ins won't make video helper applications become extinct overnight, but they are an exciting new addition to Netscape 2.0. For more information, see chapter 36, "Netscape Plug-Ins."

▶ "Netscape Plug-Ins," pg. 933

Video File Formats

Netscape recognizes video files the same way it identifies all the files it accesses on the Web: by MIME type first, then (if the Web server it's connected to doesn't send one) by file name extension. (See chapter 16, "Configuring Helper Applications," for more on MIME.)

◀ "Configuring Helper Applications," pg. 395

The video file MIME types and file name extensions that Netscape recognizes are listed in the following table: (If you plan to watch movies on the Web, you'll want to configure helper applications for all three of these file types.)

Type/Subtype	Extensions	Description
video/x-msvideo	.AVI	Microsoft Video
video/quicktime	.QT, .MOV	QuickTime Video
video/mpeg	.MPEG, .MPG, .MPE	MPEG Video

This next table lists the only other major video format that Netscape doesn't know about that you're likely to encounter while browsing the Web:

Type/Subtype	Extension	Description
video/x-fli	.FLI, .FLC	Autodesk Animation

You'll probably want to configure helper applications right away for all three of the formats that Netscape recognizes: Video for Windows, QuickTime, and MPEG. You may also want to configure a viewer for .FLI files, especially if you're into animation or CAD/engineering.

MPEG Files

MPEG (MIME: video/mpeg, Extensions: .MPEG, .MPG, .MPE) is an acronym for Moving Pictures Expert Group, the body in charge of the MPEG standard. Though it sounds like JPEG, the only thing they really have in common is that their standards groups are part of the same ISO (International Standards Organization) subcommittee, and the committees meet in the same place at the same time.

> **Tip**
>
> I've gleaned lots of useful information like this from Frank Gadegast's useful and entertaining MPEG FAQ (Frequently Asked Questions) list on UseNet. The latest version can be read online by pointing Netscape to **http://www.cs.tu-berlin.de/mpegfaq/**. (The .de means it's in Germany.)

MPEG exists because video files are big. The MPEG format compresses video files to a more reasonable size. Unfortunately, MPEG compression at its best requires a dedicated hardware decoder board. However, there are some MPEG software-only players that work pretty well on a fast processor.

There is no standard MCI driver for MPEG, though some players install their own and Microsoft has promised to provide one eventually. Many MPEG movie viewers choose to do their own internal decoding. Fortunately, you don't have to sort this out yourself; if a driver is needed for an MPEG viewer program, it's always included in the distribution file.

Video for Windows Files

Video for Windows (MIME: video/x-msvideo, EXTENSION: .AVI) is Microsoft's own native video format for Windows and Win95.

The most recent versions of the Video for Windows (including Win95) drivers incorporate several advanced codec (compression/decompression) algorithms for both audio and video. The latest are Intel's Indeo codec and Supermac's Cinepak codec, which allow for playback of color video images up to 320×240 at up to 30 fps (frames per second).

> ### Note
>
> A codec (compression/decompression) algorithm actually does most of the work in a video driver. Most video formats incorporate several different codecs, and different video files in the same format can use different codecs, depending on whether quality, speed, or some other factor is most important. Some codecs that you may see references to in various video file format specifications are the following:
>
> - Animation
> - Cinepak
> - Component Video
> - Graphics
> - Intel Indeo
> - Intel-RAW
> - None
> - Photo-JPEG
> - TrueMotion
> - Video
>
> In general, you don't have to worry about which codec a video file uses. Your driver will sort it all out and use the decompression scheme that matches the file's compression scheme without human intervention.

There are also hooks in Video for Windows that allow programmers to capture video sequences, add custom user interfaces, integrate text, music, and still graphics with videos, and so on. While this might not mean much to you directly, it does mean that it's relatively painless for programmers to create really nice video playback programs for the rest of us.

Video for Windows started out as Microsoft's answer to Apple's QuickTime, but it has become so popular on the Net that there are now Mac players for Video for Windows, too.

III

Using Helper Apps

The Video for Windows Driver

If you're running Win95, a 32-bit version of Video for Windows has already been automatically installed on your system. You only need to configure a viewer program to be able to play videos with Netscape.

If you're a Windows 3.1 user and you haven't played videos before, you may have to install the right driver first. To check, open the Drivers icon in the Control Panel and check the list. If the [MCI] Microsoft Video for Windows driver isn't there, refer to your Windows manual for details on how to install it from your Windows 3.1 installation disks.

If for some reason you don't have the Video for Windows driver available on your Windows 3.1 system, it can be downloaded from Microsoft's pages on the Web. Point Netscape to **http://www.microsoft.com/kb/softlib/mslfiles** and download the file wv1160.zip. This is version 1.1 of the Video for Windows driver—if there is a more recent version in the Microsoft library, grab that instead. Follow the instructions in the file for installation.

Once the Video for Windows driver is correctly installed, you can go ahead and find a suitable viewer to use as a Video for Windows helper application.

Media Player: The Windows Player for Video for Windows

Microsoft includes a program with Windows and Win95 called Media Player (see fig. 19.2), which plays .WAV digitized sounds, .MID MIDI music, and .AVI Video for Windows movies. You can configure Media Player as a Netscape helper application for all three of these multimedia file types, or for just one or two of them. It lives in your Windows directory, and is called mplayer.exe.

You can set Media Player's Options to make a video file repeat or rewind automatically at the end of the file, and you can optionally dither the image to a set of VGA standard colors. You can also scale the image size from 1/16 to full screen size, with specific selections for standard and double-size playback.

Fig. 19.2
Media Player, the multimedia player that comes with Windows, plays Video for Windows .AVI movies.

QuickTime Files

Apple's QuickTime video format (MIME: video/quicktime, Extensions: .QT, .MOV) was originally developed for the Macintosh, but quickly migrated to the PC platform. As the *original* microcomputer video format, QuickTime is very popular among creative types (who tend to prefer the Mac anyway) and it is the format of preference for many of the most experienced videographers on the Web. This means that many of the best Net movies out there are in QuickTime format.

Troubleshooting

I clicked on the link for a QuickTime movie, and it seemed to download and launch my viewer, but all I got was an error message. I've played QuickTime movies successfully before. What's going on?

Not all QuickTime movies are viewable under Windows. In order for a QuickTime file to be viewable on anything but a Macintosh, it has to be *flattened*; that is, it must be run through a converter program on the Mac that builds a cross-platform compatible file. (Unfortunately, there is currently no such converter for Windows or UNIX.) While most QuickTime videos you'll run into on the Web have been converted, you may run into one occasionally that has not been. If you find a QuickTime movie that won't play for you, this may be your problem.

Like Video for Windows, QuickTime also includes the Indeo and Cinepak codecs (among others), and can mix audio, still images, and text with video. The latest QT driver can even handle integrated MIDI music and—with a hardware card—MPEG compression.

However, the current Windows version of QuickTime (2.0.3, as this is written) lacks some of the more esoteric features of the Apple version, most notably support for capture, compression, PhotoCD display, SMPTE time codes (for tightly syncing audio and video tracks), and data references. These are promised soon for Windows.

The QuickTime for Windows Driver

The QuickTime for Windows video driver is not freely distributable. However, it has been licensed for distribution with many products, so you may already own a copy without knowing it. Check video collections on CD-ROM, CD-ROM magazines, or Windows graphics and animation programs. One of these may have even already secretly installed the QT driver on your machine. (Look for the file mciqtw.drv in your Windows/System directory.)

QuickTime can also be purchased online directly from Apple Computer at **http://quicktime.apple.com**. The current price is $10 for personal use. Upgrades are available on Apple's World Wide Web site at **ftp:// ftp.support.apple.com**.

Apple also occasionally makes QuickTime available free for the downloading. Check its site to see if now is one of those times. (It was at the time this book was written.)

The QuickTime Viewers

If you get Apple's QuickTime video driver from the archive file mentioned earlier, when you decompress the archive you also get two stand-alone viewer programs, one for still images and one for QuickTime videos.

The Picture Viewer displays Macintosh PICT (.PIC) and JPEG (.JPG) still images (see fig. 19.3). Though it can display more than one image at a time in scalable, zoomable windows, its lack of support for more than two file formats makes it pretty wimpy. You might consider using it as a helper application, though, if you regularly need to view Macintosh format images—if, for example, you're heavily into Mac desktop publishing and need to access Mac files from an online photo service.

Fig. 19.3
Apple's Picture Viewer for Windows comes archived with the QuickTime video driver, but can display only Mac PICT and JPEG format images.

The Movie Player plays QuickTime and MPEG movies (see fig. 19.4). The menus give you some control over image size and looping, and you can bring up a window that tells you some information about the movie you're playing. It can even handle multiple videos at once. Even though it's from the Enemy Camp (Apple), I've got to admit it's a pretty slick little video player.

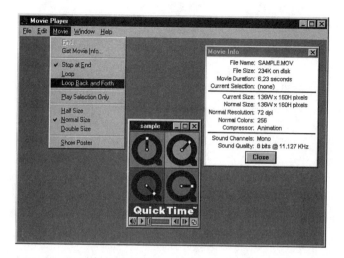

Fig. 19.4
Apple's Movie
Player for Win-
dows can play
both QuickTime
and MPEG movies.

Autodesk .FLI Animation Files

Autodesk is the publisher of AutoCAD, which is the most popular Computer
Aided Design program for the PC. Unlike traditional CAD programs,
AutoCAD is not limited to producing flat, monochrome, two-dimensional
images. It can also generate them in glorious 3D color, with realistic lighting
and shading. Not only that, but with the assistance of a couple of different
AutoCAD add-on programs, you can create 3D animations from AutoCAD
drawings.

Needless to say, engineers have had a lot of fun with the 3D animation capabilities of the AutoCAD system. This means that there are more than a few
animations available on the World Wide Web in the native AutoCAD .FLI file
format (MIME: video/x-fli, Extension: .FLI, .FLC).

If you're into CAD, engineering, or animation, you may find that you want
to set up a Netscape helper application to view .FLI animations. To do so, you
need the Autodesk Animator add-on driver and AAPlay player (see fig. 19.5)
in the file aawin.zip, which is available from many online FTP file download
sites, including **ftp://ftp.netnet.net/pub/mirrors/truespace/utils**
and **http://hyperreal.com:70/tools/pc/graphics/video**.

.FLI animations allow a surprising number of options, including associating
sound files, using scripts to tie together strings of animations, looping, color
cycling, and much more. You can even preload an animation into memory
for smoother playback, and hide the animation until it begins playing.
There's an option for setting the number of times the animation loops, and
you can specify a transition at the beginning and end of play. Soundtracks

III

Using Helper Apps

can be from CD or videodisc audio, .WAV files, or MIDI sequences. In short, you get a lot of options.

Fig. 19.5
AAPlay from Autodesk lets you play .FLI animations and edit animation scripts using a built-in editor.

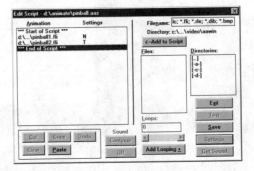

The only downside to all this is that the Autodesk software for creating .FLI animations is in the "professional" price category. But I suppose we should be thankful that we can, at least, play them back for free.

Video Helper Applications for Netscape

Assuming you've found and installed the video drivers you need, you now need to find just the right video viewer programs. Fortunately, they're not hard to come by in the multimedia-crazy computing community.

> **Note**
>
> You'll run into the same options over and over when previewing Windows video players. Here are the most popular:
>
> - *Looping*—This option determines whether a video stops at the end of play, or loops back and replays forever. Some viewers allow a specified number of loops, or add the option to simply rewind at the end of play.
>
> - *Color*—Many players let you choose to play videos back in monochrome, grayscale, colors dithered to a set palette, or full original color.
>
> - *Scaling*—Most videos are created to play back at a resolution of approximately 1/4 the size of a "standard" 640×400 computer screen size, or about 320×200 pixels. Most viewers let you choose other playback sizes, from 1/16 to full screen.
>
> - *Information*—You can usually pick a menu option to view information about the file you're playing, such as resolution, number of colors, and so on.

- *Playback Controls*—Most viewers have a Play button. Some have a Pause button, though this may be the same as the Play button. Others may include Fast Forward, Rewind, and Step by Frame Forward and/or Backward buttons. There may be a slider to select the current frame. If the player can play back sound, you may find a volume control as well.

- *File Options*—All of the viewers mentioned here let you load and save videos to disk. If you have a viewer you have configured as a helper application that automatically exits when the video is done playing, you may have to be fast with the mouse on the Pause button to stop the player so you have time to pick Save from the File menu.

- *Additional Options*—Look for the ability to save individual frames, print a frame to the printer, and so on. Some players offer a surprising number of additional options.

Note

For information on where to find helper applications and how to configure them once you've found them, see chapter 16, "Configuring Helper Applications."

Tip

Don't forget to look in chapter 18, "Configuring Netscape for Graphics," for graphics viewers and converters that can also display video formats. Specifically, see the listings for Vueprint Pro, Graphics Workshop, and JASC Media Center. And remember that they need to have video drivers installed before they can play movies!

Windows 95 Video Programs

When Microsoft designed Windows 95, they had multimedia very much in mind. Every aspect of Win95 is optimized for fast video, graphics, and audio throughput. They're no dummies at Microsoft—they know the future of computing is closely tied to multimedia, and they are eager for Windows to be the platform of choice for multimedia-hungry users well into the future. A couple of the very first applications to be released for Win95 are MPEG movie viewers.

III

Using Helper Apps

On the CD

MPEGPlay

Michael Simmons's Win95/NT shareware program MPEGPlay is a port of the Berkeley MPEG player for UNIX, a sort of standard in the computing community (see fig. 19.6). (It's also a descendent of the Windows 3.1 version.) The MPEGPlay distribution file includes two versions of the viewer, one of which includes support for the Microsoft WinG gaming library, which is also installed automatically when you install MPEGPlay.

Fig. 19.6
MPEGPlay is an MPEG video viewer based on the Berkeley standard source code.

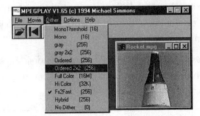

This player can play standard MPEG files that include P and B frame encoding, as well as large 354×288 movie files. It has several user-selectable display modes including monochrome, grayscale, color dither, and full color. (8MB of RAM is recommended for playing large image MPEG files.)

MPEGPlay offers several versatile color and scaling options, as listed in the table that follows:

Option	Description
Mono Threshold	Monochrome, white/black decision at 50 percent luminance
Mono	Dithered monochrome
gray	Luminance is mapped to 256 grays
gray 2x2	256 grays, scaled up by two, interpolates extra pixels
Ordered	Dithers to 128 fixed color palette
2x2	As above, but scaled up by two
Full Color	Luminance and chrominance are converted to 24-bit
Fs2fast	Fast error diffusion of 2 error values
Fs2	Error diffusion of 2 error values
Fs4	Error diffusion of 4 error values
Hybrid	Ordered dither for luminance, error diffusion for both chrominance channels
Image scaling	Actual size or stretched to fit scaled window
Bitmap color	Use palette colors or use palette indices defined in player

> **Note**
>
> What's all this about P and B frames? MPEG movies save file space by not including all the data from each separate frame in a movie file. There are actually three different video frame types in an MPEG file. I, or intra, frames are complete computer bitmap images (compressed, of course). P, or predicted, frames are predicted from the most recently reconstructed I or P frame; they don't contain complete image data, just difference information. B, or bidirectional, frames are predicted from the closest two I or P frames, one in the past and one in the future. The sequence of decoded frames usually runs: *IBBPBBPBBPBB... (repeat).* There are only 12 frames from I frame to I frame, because you need a fresh starting point 2.5 times per second. The interleave of P and B frames was arrived at mostly by experimentation.

MPEGPlay makes a great Netscape MPEG helper application. The unregistered version displays an About box at startup to remind you to pay the $25 shareware fee, and it will not handle MPEG movies larger than 1MB.

Ladybug

If you're looking for a small, neat, Win95-specific MPEG player, Ladybug should work well for you (see fig. 19.7). It has no menu bar; user options are all on a drop-down menu accessed by the right mouse button. It does little more than play MPEGs, but if that's all you need, this program will do it...and do it for free.

Fig. 19.7
Neat Software's Ladybug MPEG viewer has a spartan but Win95 optimized user interface.

III

Using Helper Apps

Windows 3.1 Video Programs

As of this writing, multimedia player development for Win95 lags somewhat behind Windows 3.1, which, of course, has a head start of several years. Though Win95 is sure to catch up eventually, it has a long way to go to match the variety of video players available for Windows 3.1.

VMPEG

VMPEG is the freely distributable demo version of a yet-to-be-released commercial MPEG viewer (see fig. 19.8). It can handle MPEG-1 audio in stereo as well as MPEG video/wave audio file pairs.

Fig. 19.8

VMPEG is a Windows 3.1 MPEG video viewer with an included MCI MPEG driver.

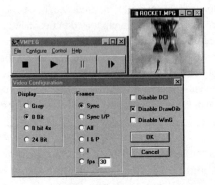

On a Pentium 90, VMPEG says it can display a 352×240 video sequence at up to 33 frames/second. It supports the following four display modes:

- 4×4 ordered dither normal size (8-bit)
- 4×4 ordered dither double size (8-bit)
- grayscale (8-bit)
- True Color (24-bit)

VMPEG also allows arbitrary scaling of the video output, and supports DCI enabled graphics cards for displaying full-screen, 24-bit, real-time movies.

Unlike MPEGPlay, which incorporates an integral MPEG decompressor, VMPEG installs an MCI (Media Control Interface) driver. This means that other programs—like Microsoft's Media Player, for example—can hook into VMPEG's driver and use it to display MPEG movies, too. In other words, if you want to you can install VMPEG, delete the player, keep the driver, and use Media Player to play MPEG movies. Very nice.

Xingit! Runtime Video Player

The Xingit! Runtime Video Player includes a Windows MPEG player, a DOS MPEG player, and an MCI driver for Windows (see fig. 19.9). If you choose to install the MCI driver, it can be used by other applications (like Media Player) to play MPEG video.

Fig. 19.9
The Xingit! MPEG player can even capture video and audio sequences, with the right hardware.

Xingit! provides support for WAV and MPEG audio playback, as well as video. Though Xingit! plays only MPEG movies, it offers you several user-selectable options—from border size to choosing which video card driver to use. If you own a Xingit! video board, the program even allows you to capture audio and video sequences. This program is a freely distributable demo, which is meant as an enticement to purchase Xing Technology Corporation's other multimedia products.

NET TOOB

If you want one program that will display all three of the major movie file formats—Video for Windows (.AVI), QuickTime (.MOV), and MPEG, you should take a look at NET TOOB (see fig. 19.10). Heck, it'll even display Autodesk Animations (.FLI) if you install a driver for them.

Fig. 19.10
NET TOOB displays .MPEG, .AVI, and .MOV videos (with the right drivers installed).

III

Using Helper Apps

The interface for this player is certainly nonstandard, though uncomplicated and pretty foolproof. The online documentation is cocky and quirky, too. But after you get things set up, NET TOOB does a good job of displaying videos.

Tip

Duplexx's FTP site at **ftp://cove.com/pub/duplexx/** has downloadable drivers for .AVI, .MOV, and .FLI files. Even if you decide to use another video viewer, you should check out this FTP site for one-stop shopping for drivers.

NET TOOB plays MPEG 2 audio files, allows you to play videos in 1/8, 1/4, or full-screen sized windows, and supports interleaved, synced audio. Duplexx also promises real-time playback of MPEG audio and video in a future release. NET TOOB can even act as a video screensaver, if you want.

If you decide to register NET TOOB, the fee is $15; if you decide not to, the software "cripples" itself after two weeks so that it can't play MPEG files at all, and it won't play other video files over 1MB in size.

Translating Video for Netscape

QuickTime is the video format of choice among Mac users; Windows users prefer Video for Windows. MPEG video is becoming more popular. It definitely represents the future of video on the Web.

If you're going to provide video content on your Web pages, the day will come when you'll want that video to be in MPEG format—and that day may come sooner than you think.

But be forewarned—the conversion process is not easy.

CONVMPEG3.ZIP

Mike Negus's CONVMPEG3.ZIP is an archive file that contains a toolkit full of DOS programs for converting .AVI files back and forth between .AVI and MPEG format. However, this is not a point-and-click operation. In fact, there are five separate tools in this archive, one for every step of the process. This procedure is not for those who are inexperienced with convoluted DOS file conversion processes. Still, if you must convert (bidirectionally) between .MPEG and .AVI formats, this is a set of tools that will get you there. You will also need a copy of Microsoft's VidEdit utility.

SmartVid

Converting between QuickTime and Video for Windows is much easier—you just need a copy of Intel's freely distributable SmartVid program, which comes in both DOS and Windows versions (see fig. 19.11). (I recommend the

Windows version for ease of use.) All you do is load a file of one format, select Convert from the menu, and type in a filename for the target file. That's
it. If all goes well, you get a .MOV file from an .AVI file, or vice versa.

Fig. 19.11
SmartVid doesn't offer many options. It's just a quick and simple program to convert .AVI files to .MOV format and vice versa.

If you need to convert a QuickTime movie to MPEG, you have to use both
sets of utilities: SmartVid to change the .MOV to .AVI format, and then the
CONVMPEG3 tools to turn the .AVI into an .MPEG.

The Future of Video on the Web

The major limitation to viewing killer video on the World Wide Web is bandwidth. Data compression, cable television network connections, ISDN lines,
and new technologies like Novell's NEST (Novell Embedded Systems Technology)—which promises to make computer networks available to a billion users
by the year 2000—could make bandwidth a dead issue. Until it does, viewing
video on the Internet is at best an exercise in patience.

> **Tip**
>
> For more on NEST—Novell's billion-user network that promises to interconnect
> everything from Coke machines to automobile factories to babies' crib monitors by
> the year 2000—check out Novell's NEST site at **http://nest.novell.com/**.

But there are always exciting new developments that foreshadow what video
on the Web might be like in the near future.

◀ See "The World Wide Web and Netscape 2.0," pg. 7

Multimedia Plug-Ins

Plug-ins are an innovative new way that Netscape 2.0 can expand its multimedia capabilities. Plug-ins are basically add-on viewers that allow Netscape
to display multimedia content inline in real-time. This means that sound,
video, and even interactive multimedia can be added to Web pages and
Netscape won't have to launch external viewers to display them; they can all
appear together on one page. Plug-ins for QuickTime video and Macromedia

▶ See "Netscape Plug-Ins," pg. 933

Director interactive multimedia presentations have already been announced by Netscape. Innovations like this will definitely change forever the look and feel of the Web.

Video Conferencing

Video conferencing involves two or more participants who transmit live video and audio to each other simultaneously. Most of the video conferences held today are between business people who use dedicated software and secure links.

However, that may end soon. Though there are still bandwidth problems with Internet video conferencing, some brave pioneers are testing the waters. One of the first "open-air" video conferencing experiments is Cornell University's CU-SeeMe Project (see fig. 19.12). With free software for PCs (and Macs), CU-SeeMe can link up two to eight participants at a time for black-and-white push-to-talk video conferencing through Internet "reflector sites" that take care of all the routing and trafficking problems. Hardware costs for hooking up can be as low as $100 for a cheap black-and-white CCD video camera with built-in interface, and view-only kibitzing is free.

Fig. 19.12
The CU-SeeMe site at Cornell tells you all about cheap (practically free) video conferencing. That could be *your* face in one of those little windows!

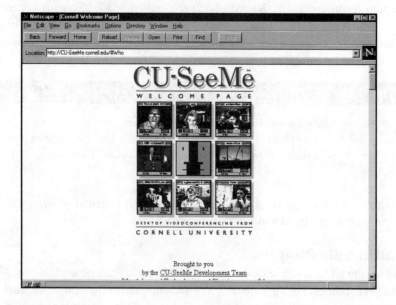

While it's far from a mature discipline, expect video conferencing to become a major player in the future of Internet communications.

For more information, point Netscape to Cornell's CU-SeeMe site at **http://CU-SeeMe.cornell.edu**. Or you can check out White Pine Software's site for information on the commercial version of CU-SeeMe at **http://www.wpine.com/cuseeme.html**.

MBONE: Live WWW Video Broadcasts

The MBONE (Multicast Backbone) is a network of computers on the Internet that form a backbone network for the transmission of live video and audio broadcasts. So far, it has been used for experimental broadcasts of events as disparate as scholarly meetings and a portion of a Rolling Stones concert. It is also capable of supporting live multipoint real-time audio and video conferencing.

The MBONE is a "virtual network" that is layered on top of the physical Internet. It packages real-time multimedia in such a way that normal networks (like Ethernet) pass it along without noticing that anything is other than normal. The MBONE network is composed of a string of network routers at different locations on the Internet, all running the MBONE software. These "islands" are linked by virtual point-to-point links called *tunnels*, through which pass the video and audio data packets of a live MBONE multicast.

Note

The MBONE is a more-or-less permanent arrangement, and requires a commitment at the network administration level. If you want your workstation-based LAN to become part of the MBONE, the IP multicast software is available by anonymous FTP. To find out how to download and set up the MBONE software, get the document mbone-connect from **ftp://genome-ftp.stanford.edu/pub/mbone/.** But first, read the MBONE FAQ (Frequently Asked Questions) list at **http://www.best.com/~prince/techinfo/** for more details about how MBONE works.

Though setting up an MBONE connection requires a real commitment of time and resources, and though there is not much live broadcast traffic on MBONE yet, it certainly shows that there is a lot of potential for video to grow and become a more important part of the World Wide Web. Look for MBONE (or a technology much like it) to make a real impact on the Web in a couple more years.

StreamWorks

StreamWorks, developed by Xing Technology, is a new commercial product for delivering live and on-demand video and audio (see fig. 19.13). The

III

Using Helper Apps

National Broadcasting Company (NBC) and Reuters news service are already using this technology for broadcast delivery of financial news programming to subscribers in the U.S. and Europe. New applications are being developed with StreamWorks for distance learning, corporate communications, news delivery, and computer-based training in corporate, educational, government, and health care markets. Xing says that it can even allow Internet providers to effectively get into the cable-TV-via-the-Web business.

Fig. 19.13

StreamWorks, Xing Technology's answer to delivering real-time multimedia via the Web and other networks.

StreamWorks can deliver live or on-demand multimedia content to multiple simultaneous users over local and wide-area networks like the Web. Xing's approach is built around international standards like UNIX and Windows NT servers, TCP/IP connections, MPEG video and audio compression, and HTTP/HTML client/server communication.

Expect many, many more players to get into the video-via-the-Web market in the coming months. There's a lot of money to be made in Web video, and there's no leader yet.

For more information on StreamWorks, point Netscape to **http://www.xingtech.com/streams/index.html**.

## CHAPTER 20

Using VRML

VRML, pronounced "vurmul," is the acronym for the Virtual Reality Modeling Language. VRML is defined as a subset of Silicon Graphics' Open Inventor three-dimensional modeling standard, but adds World Wide Web URL anchors for linking the flat Web pages and solid VRML worlds together. Silicon Graphics has released the VRML standard portion of Open Inventor into the public domain, and many people and companies are now involved in bringing three-dimensional depth and texture to the Web.

In this chapter, you learn about:

- The origins and history of VRML
- Some of the tools for VRML exploration and where to get them
- How these VRML tools work with Netscape
- Some of the non-VRML experiments in three-dimensional modeling for the Web

What Is VRML?

The *Virtual Reality Modeling Language* (*VRML*) is a language intended for the design and use of three-dimensional, multi-person, distributed interactive simulations. To put it in simpler language, VRML's designers intend it to become the building block of cyberspace.

The explosion of the World Wide Web was caused by its ease of use: anything reachable on the Web is reachable by one unique address, the URL (Universal Resource Locator). This flattening of the Internet has the effect of making the Web very much like a single, enormous hard disk. The Web's advantages can be seen in its rapid growth as people convert their Internet resources to HTML format, the enormous popularity of Netscape as a tool to access the Web, and the very existence of this book.

However, the World Wide Web is based on *HTML* (*HyperText Markup Language*), which was developed from the *SGML* (*Standard General Markup Language*) standard. SGML and HTML are fundamentally designed as two-dimensional text formatting toolsets. Mark D. Pesce, Peter Kennard, and Anthony S. Parisi presented a paper called *Cyberspace* at the First International Conference on the Web in May 1994 in which they argue that, because humans are superb visualizers and we live and work in three dimensions, extending the Web with a third dimension would allow for better organization of the masses of data already on the Web. They call this idea Virtual Reality Markup Language. The concept was welcomed, and the participants immediately began searching for a format to use as a data standard. A mailing list was started by Brian Behlendorf at *Wired* magazine, with Mark Pesce as the list moderator. About this time, the M in VRML was changed from Markup to Modeling to accentuate the difference between the text-based nature of the Web and VRML.

Note

The paper *Cyberspace* is available over the Web at **http://www.hyperreal.com/ ~mpesce/www.html**.

After intense discussion, Silicon Graphics' Open Inventor was settled on as the basis for creating the VRML standard. Open Inventor is an object-oriented (C++) developer's toolkit used for rapid development of three-dimensional graphic environments. Open Inventor has provided the basis for a number of standards, including the Keystone Interchange Format used in the entertainment industry and the ANSI/ISO's X3H3 3D Metafile specification.

The current VRML 1.0 specification was written by three people: Gavin Bell of Silicon Graphics (known as one of the two principal designers of Open Inventor), Anthony Parisi of Intervista Software, and Mark Pesce, moderator of the VRML mailing list.

VRML's design specifications were guided by three goals:

- Platform independence
- Extensibility
- The ability to work over low-bandwidth connections

All three of these are characteristics, already possessed by HTML and the Web, which the designers of VRML felt would be required if their standard was to have any popular acceptance.

VRML 1.0 is not the cyberspace of pop culture and science fiction: it defines the parameters for defining three-dimensional models (called *worlds*) and hyperlinking them by using the Web. The end of this chapter presents some thoughts for the future of the VRML initiative.

> **Note**
>
> The official VRML 1.0 specification can be found on the Web at **http://vrml.wired.com/vrml.tech/vrml10-3.html**.
>
> Instructions on how to join any of the several mailing lists on the Web that affect the decisions for the next version of the VRML standard are also on the Web at **http://vrml.wired.com/**.
>
> The VRML FAQ can be found at **http://www.oki.com/vrml/VRML_FAQ.html**.

VRML 1.0-Compliant Viewers

As this book went to press, there were only a few VRML browsers available. This is expected to change dramatically in the near future. For a current list of VRML browsers, point your Web browser to **http://www.sdsc.edu/SDSC/Partners/vrml/software/browsers.html**. This page is part of the VRML Repository (located at **http://www.sdsc.edu/vrml/**), one of the best locations on the Web for current information about the VRML initiative.

The rest of this section examines some of the tools presently available for use with Netscape 2.0 and Windows 95.

WorldView

WorldView for Windows is a VRML 1.0-compliant browser for three-dimensional image display (see fig. 20.1). The available version of WorldView is currently in beta release, but Intervista is expected to deliver a fully supported commercial release in the fall of 1995. At this time, WorldView includes support for 256 colors, a HotSpots menu option (similar to Netscape's Bookmarks, but for VRML locations only), multiple light sources, and texture mapping. The newest version of WorldView (as of this writing) supports collision detection (if your point-of-view runs into an object), as well as improved texture mapping and support for GZIP file compression.

Features that are expected to be part of the fall release include multiple camera angles as predefined options of the scene, the ability to display worlds with multiple levels of detail (in other words, fuzzier images of every object in the world for when that object is distant), context-sensitive help, and additional compressed file transfer capability for improved performance.

Fig. 20.1
The WorldView
for Windows
VRML browser.

WorldView runs under either Windows 95 or Windows NT 3.5 or 3.51. Microsoft's Reality Lab is also required, but it is included with your download of WorldView. To run WorldView for Windows, you should have at least an 80486DX/50 processor, 8MB memory, and at least a 256 color or better display driver and graphics card.

Note

Reality Lab is a three-dimensional renderer that converts the VRML code into a visual display on your monitor. Faster, but less flexible, than some of the other renderers such as OpenGL, Reality Lab ships with Windows 95.

Note

The WorldView installer file includes Reality Labs software as well as several sample VRML models, and is over 2.5MB. Downloading this file may take more than 30 minutes if you are on a dial-up connection of 14.4Kbps.

WorldView can run either in stand-alone mode or in conjunction with a World Wide Web browser. The WorldView initialization file (c:\windows\wrldview.ini) is preconfigured to run with Netscape. WorldView also works with Enhanced Mosaic 2.0 from Spyglass, but it requires modifications to the wrldview.ini file.

In addition to the official VRML 1.0 specification, WorldView supports the farDistance and nearDistance fields (in PerspectiveCamera mode) extension, which appears in many models available on the Internet. Intervista has announced it intends to recommend that these extensions be included in the VRML 1.1 specification.

WorldView's navigation model uses the following two types of movement:

- *Fly*—Moves you around the world
- *Inspect*—Allows you to move and tilt the 3D model, as if you were holding it in your hand

Note

Sometimes six dimensions of freedom can be confusing, especially with multiple movement modes available. If you ever have trouble moving about in a VRML world, every VRML browser I've seen so far has a Reset option that takes you back to the initial view of the current world.

For the Look and Tilt modes, the Alt or Control key acts as an accelerator. However, there is no "Fly Fast" accelerator key.

In addition to keyboard commands and the control arrows on the WorldView window, WorldView supports direct mouse control as a movement option. To steer your view with the mouse, find the crosshairs box in the lower-right of the WorldView window frame, and hold the left mouse button down anywhere within the box. Moving the pointer off the center of the screen causes the center to follow the pointer's movement until the pointer is again at the center of the display.

Moving the pointer above the crosshairs moves you forward; moving the pointer to below the crosshairs moves you backward. Moving the pointer left rotates your point of view left, and moving to the right rotates you to the right. Holding down the Shift key as you move the mouse left and right moves you in that direction without changing your orientation. For pitch and roll (tilting to the sides or forward and back), hold the Control key down as you move the mouse. You are not limited to the confines of the crosshairs box: You can speed up your movement tremendously by moving the pointer past the sides of the crosshairs box, out to the limits of your display.

You can download WorldView from Intervista Software's FTP server at **ftp://ftp.webmaster.com:80 /VRML/**.

For more information on the latest version of WorldView, visit their Web presence at **http://www.intervista.com/**.

WebSpace

Created by Silicon Graphics Inc. and Template Graphics Software, *WebSpace* has the advantage of being created by the same people who produce the Open Inventor modeling standard that VRML is a subset of. As WebSpace is a native Open Inventor application, it is robust in handling faulty VRML worlds. WebSpace also supports "moving" scenes through "engines." It is not surprising that WebSpace was the first production released VRML 1.0-compliant browser on the market. In addition to VRML 1.0 and Open Inventor 2.0, WebSpace also supports the Keystone Interchange Format (used in the entertainment industry), the ANSI/ISO's 3D Metafile specification, and uses the OpenGL 3D rendering engine.

WebSpace may be more powerful than an average user needs for a VRML browser. While WebSpace runs on a minimum configuration of an 80486/66 with 8MB of RAM and a 256 color graphics card, Template Graphics recommends that "you will soon want to have" a Pentium processor, 16MB or more of RAM, and a TrueColor graphics card that supports 24-bit color. WebSpace supports multi-processor machines and OpenGL accelerator graphics boards. On the other hand, if you already have the hardware, there is not another VRML browser as of this writing that takes advantage of a second processor.

WebSpace can be set up as a helper application for Netscape, and it can also be configured as the primary application, passing HTML information to Netscape and using Netscape's abilities to handle other file types such as sound or video.

Figure 20.2 shows WebSpace displaying one of the several sample files shipped with the application.

WebSpace uses Walk and Examiner as counterparts to WorldView's Fly and Inspect modes. In Walk mode, your WebSpace window has a T-shaped handle in the center of the lower edge, which you use to steer you in and around the world. For a VRML world that contains a single object, you can shift into Examiner mode by selecting the Examiner Viewer command from the View menu. The steering handle is replaced with a globe, which you can manipulate with the mouse. The object moves as you manipulate the globe.

You can download a version of WebSpace from **http://www.sd.tgs.com/ ~template/WebSpace/**.

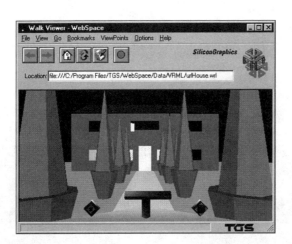

Fig. 20.2
WebSpace in Walk
mode.

Selecting the link `Getting WebSpace` takes you to the download page. If you
have a slow Internet connection, be careful about downloading this file: the
WebSpace installation file is enormous at over 4MB. Part of the reason for
this huge size is that WebSpace requires Microsoft OpenGL rendering software, which is included with the WebSpace application. As of this writing,
WebSpace is available in a commercial release for SGI, Sun Solaris, AIX, and
Windows NT (on Intel processors). The release version for Windows NT is
also the beta release for Windows 95. As with all beta software, you should
read the release notes for the most recent information on WebSpace.

> **Note**
>
> WebSpace is currently the only three-dimensional browser that supports both VRML
> 1.0 and Open Inventor 2.0 files, so you should configure Netscape for the (MIME
> type/subtype/extension) x-world/x-vrml/.wrl, application/x-inventor/.iv, and applica-
> tion/x-gzip/.gz data types. Adding the third passes GZIP'd VRML files to WebSpace
> for uncompressing, which dramatically improves your VRML travel speed.

WebFX

The Paper Software Company's *WebFX* is currently the only VRML viewer
available as a plug-in for Netscape. WebFX Plug-In for Netscape 2.0 allows
Netscape to display VRML worlds without launching a separate application.
The WebFX plug-in lets you view a VRML file inside an HTML document in
the same way you are used to viewing GIF or JPEG two-dimensional images.
Multiple VRML files may be displayed simultaneously within a single HTML
document. A set of VRML images contained within a Netscape table could be

used for many purposes, from a chart with depth displayed in its cells to a chess set. Figure 20.3 displays the human brain as a VRML object.

Fig. 20.3

WebFX uses Netscape's window to display VRML worlds, without launching a separate application window.

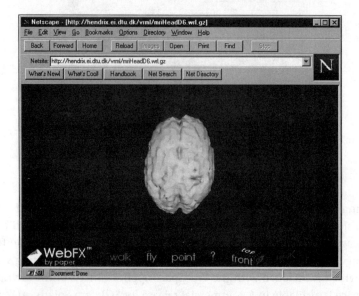

WebFX adds a toolbar across the bottom of the Netscape window. The three modes available in WebFX are Walk, Fly, and Point. Point lets you click anywhere in the visible window, and your viewpoint moves to that spot, and centers where you clicked as the center of your view. The question mark lets you display text information about your viewpoint in the current VRML world.

WebFX has some other convenient shortcuts in its controls, such as the perspective cube. In the right of WebFX's control bar, you can see a cube's corner, with the sides labeled top, right, and front. Clicking one of these sides gives you the view of the object from that perspective. The Reset button in the far right of the WebFX toolbar lets you reset the view of the current world to the viewpoint you started with when it first loaded.

Two interesting WebFX features work from the right mouse button. Clicking the right mouse button anywhere in the Netscape/WebFX window displays the WebFX pop-up menu. Another feature is that, by using the right mouse button instead of the left when the pointer is over a VRML object, you can fling the object to rotate constantly, just like reaching over to a globe and setting it spinning.

Paper Software also plans to provide a stand-alone VRML browser named *WebFX Explorer*. WebFX Explorer will incorporate many features of the Windows 95 interface such as object-oriented drag and drop, shortcuts, sorting, and customization capabilities within the Explorer's interface. As WebFX Explorer will provide full HTML support, it may be configured as a helper application to Netscape or be run independently of any Web browser.

Future plans are to provide plug-ins for other World Wide Web browsers, as well as adding Macintosh versions of both the various Web browser plug-ins and the stand-alone Explorer.

The stand-alone HTML/VRML WebFX Explorer's features will include texture mapping (.GIF, .BMP, .RAS, .RGB, and .JPEG formats), full GZIP support, limited support for Open Inventor format, and light, camera, and object manipulation. Some of the other features to be included are:

- IRC-based chatting with VRML avatars

> **Note**
>
> *Avatar* is originally a term from mythology, and meant the embodiment of a god come down to Earth. Neal Stephenson used the word in his 1993 novel *Snow Crash* to describe the visual representations of the characters as they interacted in a three-dimensional, worldwide, decentralized visual environment called the Metaverse. Stephenson's definition of avatar has already been adopted by many of those involved with VRML creation.

- Simple VRML authoring
- Extensions for collision detection, sound, and animated textures

WebFX requires Windows 95, NT, or 3.1, an 80486/33 computer with at least 8MB RAM, and a 256-color display or better. WebFX supports current three-dimensional acceleration hardware, such as Creative Labs' 3D Blaster board.

You can download WebFX (as of this writing in a "bleeding-edge beta release") from **http://www.paperinc.com/**.

Whurlwind for the Macintosh

While WebFX, WebSpace, and WorldView all promise to have Macintosh OS versions of their VRML browsers available, *Whurlwind* is (as of this writing) the only currently available VRML-capable browser that runs on a Macintosh. Primarily created for displaying 3DMF-format files created for use with Apple's QuickDraw three-dimensional imaging standard, Whurlwind also allows viewing of VRML 1.0-compliant worlds, as shown in figure 20.4.

III

Using Helper Apps

Fig. 20.4
Whurlwind for
Power Macintosh
displaying a
VRML-format
image.

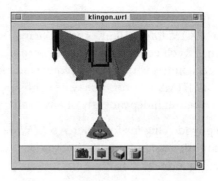

Whurlwind is a freeware application created by Bill Enright and John Louch
for viewing VRML and 3DMF format models. Whurlwind relies on
QuickDraw 3D, Apple's 3D graphics API, for rendering, picking, and navigation. Because QuickDraw 3D is optimized to run in 16-bit and 32-bit color,
QD3D runs faster with models created in these color depths than with models created in 8-bit color or 2-bit (black-and-white) depths.

At present, Whurlwind allows users to view VRML and 3DMF models from
different camera positions, and to jump to other Web sites. Future enhancements to Whurlwind are expected to offer scene navigation, allowing users to
wander around in virtual space.

QuickDraw 3D's minimum requirements (which become Whurlwind's minimum system requirements through inheritance) are a PowerPC-based
Macintosh with System 7.1.2 or up, and 16MB (or more) of memory.
Whurlwind itself is a PowerPC-native (only) application that uses 2.5MB of
memory.

You can download Whurlwind from Apple's QuickDraw 3D Applications site
at **http://www.info.apple.com/qd3d/Viewer.HTML**.

Configuring and Using VRML Browsers

Detailed explanations of how to set up all types of helper applications are
provided in chapter 16, "Configuring Helper Applications." For those of you
who feel comfortable with setting Netscape's parameters, table 20.1 summa-
rizes the MIME types, subtypes, and extension types required to configure the
various VRML viewers with Netscape 2.0.

Table 20.1   Settings for Configuring Netscape to Use VRML Browsers as Helper Applications

Application	MIME Type	Subtype	Extension
WorldView	x-world	x-vrml	.WRL
WebSpace	x-world	x-vrml	.WRL
	application	x-inventor	.IV
	application	x-gzip	.GZ
WebFX	x-world	x-vrml	.WRL
Whurlwind	x-world	x-vrml	.WRL
(Macintosh)	x-world	x-3dmf	.3DMF

For all of these helper applications, you should choose the option to launch the application.

Sample Worlds for Exploration

Example VRML 1.0-compliant worlds are installed in a \worlds\ folder. These world files may be loaded directly into WorldView, or loaded with Netscape's File, Open File command.

> **Note**
>
> VRML worlds are substantially larger than Web pages. Some of the worlds mentioned below are more than 500KB. As the transferred files are so much larger than the average Web page, you will become painfully aware of the speed of your Internet connection. The VRML specification calls for adequate performance over a 14.4 modem dial-up connection, which is a bare minimum. A more realistic assessment of the minimum connection speed for VRML browsing is as fast as you can possibly afford.

Out on the Web, one good model to look at is an M.C. Escher painting of a very odd house at **http://www.webmaster.com/vrml/models/escher.wrl**. This model provides good practice for navigating as you maneuver through turns and doorways.

The WWW Viewer Test Page at **http://www-dsed.llnl.gov/documents/WWWtest.html** provides sample URLs for a wide variety of content, which allows you to test your browser and how it hands data off to helper applications. It also has some other MIME pointers.

III

Using Helper Apps

In 1991, David Blair created a surrealistic film called *WAX: Or the Discovery of Television Among the Bees*. WaxWeb (at **http://bug.village.virginia.edu**) is Blair's entire feature-length film (2,000+ hypertext documents, roughly 1.5 gigabytes) accessible as a hypertext narrative. The VRML portion of the site consists of approximately 250 rooms worth of VRML, and will give you a feel for what other people might do later.

Serch is a searchable index of VRML sites, which may be viewed in HTML or VRML. The URL for Serch is **http://www.virtpark.com/theme / serch.html**.

> **Note**
>
> Appropriately, you can access Serch in VRML mode by using the above URL and replacing the .HTML extension with .WRL.

DOOM Conquers the World?

One enterprising project is a parser that converts a .WAD file (a map file from Id Software's incredibly popular first-person marine-kills-demons game) to an .IV (Open Inventor) file. So, to those of you who played DOOM and DOOM II on DOS, UNIX, and Macintoshes until carpal-tunnel syndrome set in, in a short time, you might be surfing a 3D shopping mall and thinking to yourselves, "This floor plan looks familiar… there's a pig-demon around the corner here! Don't go in!" To those of you who spent days designing fascinating layouts for others, don't wipe those .WAD files— they might be your VRML architecture portfolio.

Information on the wadtoiv project (and the source code) can be found at **http:// www-white.media.mit.edu/~kbrussel/wadtoiv.html**.

Non-VRML 1.0 Standards

Much in the same way that Netscape is extending the HTML standard by adding new enhancements, some of the VRML development initiatives are not waiting for VRML 2.0 to be defined before they release their own implementations of portions of the standard. Two of these are Chaco Software's IVRML (the I is for Interactive), used in its Pueblo software, and Worlds Inc. VRML+.

Chaco's Pueblo—VRMLizing MUDs

Chaco Communications, Inc. released a beta version of its Pueblo Internet game client in August of 1995. Pueblo helps role-playing game authors add multimedia features to current or new MUDs.

Note

MUDS (*Multi-User Dimensions*) have been popular on the Internet for years. A MUD is client/server-based software that has many clients operating on various computers, and a server that acts as the central point of communication between the many clients. Typically, a MUD server is connected to the Internet, and the clients Telnet to the server to participate in the play. The participants interact by typing messages to each other. Besides a decent typing speed, the ability to think quickly is important, as there will be people waiting for you to read their message to you and for you to compose and type your reply. MUD players interact in real time, unlike the participants in a UseNet newsgroup. A simple analogy of a MUD would be a text-based telephone party line. There are currently a few hundred MUDs of various types, most of which are active on a constant basis.

Chaco's built-in 3D graphics system *IVRML* (*Interactive Virtual Reality Modeling Language*) is based on VRML. As Mark Pesce stated in a Pueblo press release, "This is what I had in mind when I started VRML."

Pueblo is a MUD client that works with text-MUDs or hypermedia MUDs. On startup, you can see a hierarchy of existing MUDs. If you select a Pueblo-enabled world, the screen changes from a text-based terminal window to show a hypertext window, a command window, and a graphics window.

Pueblo includes the following capabilities:

- *IHTML*—Interactive Hypertext Markup Language
- *IVRML*—Interactive Virtual Reality Modeling Language
- Sound and music (waveform files and MIDI support)
- Flat images in a variety of formats, including .GIF and .JPEG
- Support for compressed transmissions
- A toolkit of C++ classes for world development

The freeware beta release of Pueblo runs on Windows 95 and Windows NT. A non-3D version is available for Windows 3.1. Pueblo is designed for Internet connection speeds of 14.4 kilobits/ second and greater. The Pueblo client is being distributed free from Chaco's Web server at **http:// www.chaco.com/pueblo/**.

III

Using Helper Apps

Worlds Chat—VRML+izing IRC

Worlds Chat is basically a three-dimensional version of the Internet's IRC (Internet Relay Chat) service. IRC was initially developed as an improvement to the UNIX talk program, allowing many people to communicate in real-time by typing. To communicate on IRC, you must have an IRC client, connect to an IRC server, and choose a channel. All users' input scroll up your screen, and you can join in as appropriate. Mostly, IRC is used as a recreational communications service.

The Worlds VRML+ incorporates three features absent in the VRML 1.0 standard:

- Avatar definitions (of yourself visible to others and vice versa)
- Motion (of others, visible to you)
- Text communication (between yourself and others)

Avatars are described using VRML. Each client sends a message to the Worlds Multiuser server that contains the description for that client's avatar. Due to packet size limitations, the avatar description message size is relatively small. One way to work around this packet size limitation is to send an avatar description message that consists of a WWWInline node pointing to a file containing a more fully detailed image of the avatar. This could eventually be extended so the avatar file included sound, animation, and so on.

Motion data contains information about the most recent positions of avatars in the three-dimensional space visible to the client, regardless of the physical location of the other clients. Motion has to be time-sensitive or it is meaningless information.

Simple text-based communication similar to the "chat" mode on many networks is the third major distinction between VRML+ and VRML 1.0. The ability to broadcast a message to multiple users, or just some of the multiple users within a range, may be added later.

More information on Worlds Inc. and its products can be found via the Web at **http://www.worlds.net/**.

The Future of VRML

VRML is in its infancy—everything in this chapter is likely to be no more than a paragraph in a similar book in a year.

VRML 1.0 is skeletal in design, and is missing many features that are looked on as mandatory for "true" VRML. The first major revision of the standard,

VRML 1.1, is expected to be an intermediate release incorporating several of the enhancements individually defined by various companies. Some of the features proposed for VRML 1.1 include ASCII text annotations for objects, integrated sound capability, and adding the i18n character set for international use. One suggested feature is the ability to cache inline objects. This would enable you to have a CD-ROM full of highly detailed VRML objects, and a VRML world could have an optional information field in the node, and the node would have a label that "item #1788 from the Gelbhart Models CD is here, turned this way." Admittedly, this solution requires that, to make best use of this site, everyone will want the model libraries. This information field would be defined by the VRML designer in a manner similar to the ASCII text description you can include in an image's anchor in HTML for a Web page.

VRML 2.0 is hoped to be a real and workable design for a language usable to model the interaction of multiple people located in an arbitrarily large geographic area.

Right now, while the current VRML browsers are all VRML 1.0-compliant, almost all of them have additional nonstandard enhancements, some of which might or might not become part of either the new VRML 1.1 or 2.0 standard. WorldView conservatively adds two perspective options that are not part of VRML 1.0—Paper Software's WebFX includes collision detection, and WebSpace is using features from Open Inventor. Pueblo and Worlds Chat are different enough that their creators chose to label their three-dimensional standards as IVRML and VRML+ respectively.

Many companies and organizations have announced their support for VRML-based three-dimensional graphics on the World Wide Web. A partial list of these companies includes: AccelGraphics, Inc., Brown University, CERN, Digital Equipment Corporation, Intergraph, NCD, NEC Technologies, net.Genesis Corporation, Netscape Communications, Oki Advanced Products, Radiance Software, San Diego Supercomputer Center, Spyglass, Tenet Networks, Viewpoint Datalabs International, Inc., the University of Darmstadt, Virtus Corporation, Wavefront Technologies, and 3Dlabs Inc.

Apple's QuickDraw 3D holds technical promise and some apparent advantages over the VRML 1.0 standard. One important advantage of QuickDraw 3D is the relative file size. A 3DMF file can be as much as an order of magnitude smaller than a VRML file of the same objects. The color depth issue mentioned earlier, that QuickDraw3D displays models created in 16-bit or 32-bit color depths in addition to models created in 8-bit color or black-and-white depths, means that QD3D models will be likelier to have more subtle color variations than VRML.

Using Helper Apps

However, the VRML standard has achieved a significant amount of momentum. VRML is based on a known standard with a significant existing user base. The VRML portion of the Open Inventor standard has been released into the public domain by Silicon Graphics, and is now an open standard that is being defined by the consensus of the participants.

If you're interested in learning more about VRML, the most important place to go is the VRML site at **http://vrml.wired.com**. You can subscribe to the mailing lists to see what has changed since yesterday. You can examine the archives of the mailing lists to backtrack conversational threads and see how the participants got to their current stage of a given discussion.

If you are interested in doing anything with VRML, get the fastest Internet connection you can find. While the designers of VRML have set their goals to be "acceptable performance on low-bandwidth connections," their specification of low-bandwidth is a 14.4 dial-up modem connection. This minimum requirement means that anything less than that is going to be almost totally unusable by any but the most patient.

VRML Author Software

This chapter has focused on VRML browser software. However, someone must build the VRML world before you can travel through it. VRML authoring software is being written almost as fast as browsers are. Silicon Graphics' WebSpace Author, Caligari's Fountain and World Builder products, and Paragraph's Homespace Builder are all currently shipping, with more VRML authoring tools expected soon. For more current information on the VRML authoring field, check the VRML Repository at **http://www.sdsc.edu/SDSC/Partners/vrml/software/modelers.html**.

Also, if you are interested in doing anything at all intensive with VRML and do not have a top-end graphics workstation, 3Dlabs is releasing graphics accelerator boards for PCs and Macintosh systems. Based around the GLINT three-dimensional graphics chip (which has been certified as supporting VRML 1.0), these cards are expected to improve the rendering capability of a given system by an order of magnitude. Apple has also released PCI-bus boards which are designed to accelerate QuickDraw3D operations as much as twelvefold.

## CHAPTER 21

Working with SGML

The announcement last fall that SoftQuad, Inc. would provide a free SGML viewer for WWW information brought the promise of a new dimension to information on the World Wide Web. The delivery of Panorama and Panorama Pro in the spring of '95 makes "SGML on the Web" a reality.

But what is SGML? What is its significance for the casual Web visitor? For the serious surfer? For the publishers of Web information? How does SGML relate to HTML? And, for that matter, what is HTML? What do SGML and HTML have to do with Internet and the World Wide Web? What does a Netscape user need to know in order to access SGML on the Web?

In this chapter, I give you a glimpse inside the "black box" to help you understand how HTML and SGML work on the Web, and then provide what you need to know in order to obtain an SGML viewer and use it with Netscape.

In this chapter, you learn:

■ The role of standards and markup languages in the way the Web works, including a brief explanation of the terms that you will hear—Markup, HTML, SGML, DTD

■ The relationship between SGML and HTML

■ The benefits that the SGML viewer adds to the delivery of Web information—for the information provider and for you the Web surfer

■ How to obtain the software you need to reap the benefits of SGML

■ How to configure Panorama for Netscape

■ How to use Panorama with Netscape to view SGML on the Web

> **Note**
>
> SoftQuad Panorama, developed for SoftQuad by Synex Information AB in Sweden, is available in two versions: a freeware version commonly called Panorama free and the commercial, supported version, Panorama Pro. When just the term Panorama is used, I am referring to generic capabilities available in both versions.

Panorama Today, Others Are Coming

Panorama (in both free and supported Pro versions) is the first SGML viewer available for directly displaying SGML on the Web. However, alternatives for delivering and viewing SGML on the Web are underway. *DynaWeb* by Electronic Book Technologies, Inc., delivers SGML source in *DynaText* electronic books via dynamic conversion to HTML, adding capabilities of its full text search engine. IBM is working on directly integrating SGML into its BookManager Web delivery products, but it delivers HTML via its Web server product(s) now.

Reports and rumors of other SGML viewing products under development are also in the air. The University of Waterloo's MetaClient prototype is due out in late November. According to information I have seen, it will use Java to bootstrap itself and will handle arbitrary language semantics including SGML. Reports are that Microsoft's next-generation Blackbird client for Microsoft Network is also SGML-based. According to an educated observer after viewing a recent prototype demonstration, Blackbird will deliver dynamic presentation of SGML into complex page layout with active widgets for aids and viewers. These two approaches, in particular, bear watching.

Hyper-G, with clients Harmony and Amadeus, offers an alternative approach to handling storage and delivery of Internet information, especially hyperlinks that it stores in a separate database. This "real hypermedia" technology guarantees automatic hyperlink consistency, which would solve the problem of broken links and provide other benefits. While I do not see SGML mentioned in the introductory literature nor in the report in *Byte Magazine*, November 1995, the approach seems to be handling all kinds of other formats—so SGML may not be far behind. Netscape's enhancements to HTML, being considered in the HTML 3.0 discussions, and its new Frames feature seek to address the pressure from Web publishers for more presentation control. But as far as I can tell, the developers are embedding the signals (markup) for this presentation into the document instances, an approach that negates the benefits of the SGML approach, discussed in the next section, "What is a Standardized Generalized Markup Language?"

What Is a Standard Generalized Markup Language?

Standard Generalized Markup Language (SGML) is an international standard designed to facilitate the exchange of information across systems, devices, languages, and applications. *HTML* is *HyperText Markup Language*, an implementation of the use of markup (information added to content) for distributing knowledge on the World Wide Web. The use of disciplined markup added to content is the heart of the method that enables authors all over the world to prepare information for Internet distribution, knowing that people using Web browser software on various platforms will be able to view it.

HTML & SGML—Two Paths to Convergence

SGML and HTML developed on parallel paths. Tim Berners-Lee and Dave Raggett, two physicists with offices down the hall from one another at CERN, each played a major role in the original development of one of the standards you know as HTML and SGML.

Discussion and debate about the importance of specific issues in the two approaches proceeded over the intervening years among purists in the overlapping communities that support the implementation of the standards. "Keep it simple," "Keep it disciplined," "Mark up for what it is, not how it will appear," "Style can be added at display time," "Hierarchy is important," "Conformance is important," "Flexibility is important," echoed through the discussions over the Net and when they met. To make a short story shorter, the need for both discipline (as the Web developed) and ease of use (as SGML usage increased), became obvious.

With the standardization of HTML 2 as conforming SGML in 1995, the two paths converged. The debate continues as pressure to add functionality increases with the spread of the Web and the discussion of enhancements for HTML 3.0, but the framework for resolving the pressure in conformance with the SGML standard is in place. The addition of SGML viewers to handle special requirements relieves the pressure to keep adding complexity to the basic HTML rules which have made the Web successful.

Definition of Terms

Standards are agreements about a common way of doing something, about doing the same things in the same way so that meaning is communicated.

Markup is information added to content—frequently, but not always, related to processing of the information. For example, printers use a blue pencil to note font and layout instructions on ad copy; word processing software uses embedded codes to retain specific, procedural markup for presentation format and style.

> **Note**
>
> Both *markup* and *content* are information, in fact content is *the* information or knowledge to be conveyed. However, I use the term content to distinguish the author's work from the additional information added to it.

Tag is a term used for SGML and HTML markup inserted into content.

Generic markup is the use of markup to identify the logical structure of information instead of how it is to be presented—`<Chapter><Title>` instead of `24 point Roman bold` to identify the lead-off line of a chapter. An extra benefit of implementing generic markup is that with it, one can use markup tags to identify content elements as well as structure, for example, product name, and hypertext link points.

> **Note**
>
> If you use the word processing style feature when you create documents, in a sense you are already beginning to identify the implied logical structure to which the style characteristics apply, such as headings and lists. You are already experiencing some benefits of "generic-like" markup, such as more consistent documents and less work to apply the presentation style features.

You might be interested in seeing an example of markup by looking at the HTML source in figure 21.1. The items of information between the angle brackets (< and >) are markup tags that identify the structural elements in the information.

An SGML *Document Type Definition (DTD)* is the specification of the rules for a set or class of documents with the same structure. The rule specification includes the following:

- Designating what elements can appear in a particular type of document and the generic identifiers or tags that are used to identify them.
- Defining the *content model*, the rules for where the elements can be used; for example, you might not want to allow a list to appear in a footnote.
- Specifying which attributes to make available to contain additional information describing a specific element (for example, security level).

- Defining external entities that can be used in conjunction with the content to provide information stored elsewhere (for example, graphic files, boilerplate text, or multimedia objects).

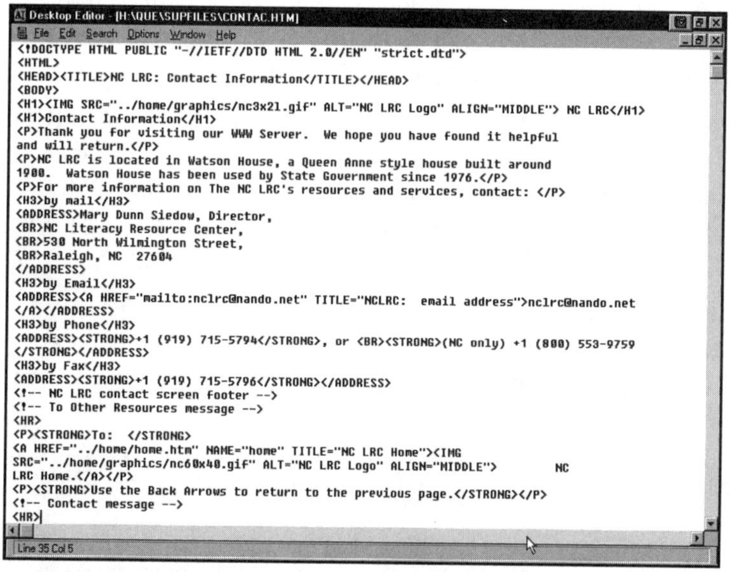


```
<!DOCTYPE HTML PUBLIC "-//IETF//DTD HTML 2.0//EN" "strict.dtd">
<HTML>
<HEAD><TITLE>NC LRC: Contact Information</TITLE></HEAD>
<BODY>
<H1><IMG SRC="../home/graphics/nc3x21.gif" ALT="NC LRC Logo" ALIGN="MIDDLE"> NC LRC</H1>
<H1>Contact Information</H1>
<P>Thank you for visiting our WWW Server.  We hope you have found it helpful
and will return.</P>
<P>NC LRC is located in Watson House, a Queen Anne style house built around
1900.  Watson House has been used by State Government since 1976.</P>
<P>For more information on The NC LRC's resources and services, contact: </P>
<H3>by mail</H3>
<ADDRESS>Mary Dunn Siedow, Director,
<BR>NC Literacy Resource Center,
<BR>530 North Wilmington Street,
<BR>Raleigh, NC  27604
</ADDRESS>
<H3>by Email</H3>
<ADDRESS><A HREF="mailto:nclrc@nando.net" TITLE="NCLRC:  email address">nclrc@nando.net
</A></ADDRESS>
<H3>by Phone</H3>
<ADDRESS><STRONG>+1 (919) 715-5794</STRONG>, or <BR><STRONG>(NC only) +1 (800) 553-9759
</STRONG></ADDRESS>
<H3>by Fax</H3>
<ADDRESS><STRONG>+1 (919) 715-5796</STRONG></ADDRESS>
<!-- NC LRC contact screen footer -->
<!-- To Other Resources message -->
<HR>
<P><STRONG>To:  </STRONG>
<A HREF="../home/home.htm" NAME="home" TITLE="NC LRC Home"><IMG
SRC="../home/graphics/nc60x40.gif" ALT="NC LRC Logo" ALIGN="MIDDLE">        NC
LRC Home.</A></P>
<P><STRONG>Use the Back Arrows to return to the previous page.</STRONG></P>
<!-- Contact message -->
<HR>
```

Fig. 21.1
Example of HTML markup for the NC LRC Contact Web page (Courtesy of NC LRC).

> **Note**
>
> HTML is a defined set of markup rules, a DTD, for a particular, widely applicable type of hyperlinked information that has several levels of headings, paragraphs, lists, and so on—most of the early information distributed via the World Wide Web. For more information about the specifics of the HTML rules for markup tags, see Part IV, "Building World Class Home Pages for Netscape."

SGML Is Not Complex—Information Is

Contrary to rumor, SGML is not necessarily more complex than HTML. The structure of the information itself and the owner's decision about what elements need to be identified determine the complexity of an SGML implementation, not the inherent characteristics of SGML. SGML can be used for very simple document structures, such as a memo with eight identified elements, or for exceedingly complex structures, such as the Department of Defense's CALS project, which uses a 100-page DTD with 300 pages of explanation.

A *markup language* is the syntax for defining rules and adding the markup to content.

An SGML *document instance* is a specific document or document component in which SGML markup has been added to content, according to the rules of the DTD for the type of information (for example, a particular Web page that includes markup conforming to the HTML DTD).

Conformance means meeting the requirements of the rules frequently confirmed via a program called a *parser,* which scans the instance and checks for conformance. Informally, one commonly hears "conforming SGML" or "conforming HTML" as shorthand for instances that conform to the rules of the applicable DTD.

Styles or *style sheets* is the term that refers collectively to characteristics used to determine presentation appearance—fonts, font size, font emphasis (bold, italic, and so on), formatting (spacing, alignment, indentation), color, and the like.

Note

By convention, I use the term *browser* for the software that you use to access the Web. Lynx, Netscape Navigator, NCSA Mosaic, Spyglass Enhanced Mosaic, and a jillion more coming on the scene are browsers. *Viewers* are additional *helper application programs* that work with the browser to access special features not (yet) handled by the browsers, such as special graphics, audio, animations, video, postscript, PDF, and now SGML. You obtain viewer programs in addition to your browser.

Benefits of Standard, Generalized Markup—The Way the Web Works

SGML and HTML were created to solve a problem: people using different computer systems and document processing tools had difficulty passing information to one another. Although the situation has improved somewhat with import filters, many of us remember the nightmares and extra work required to combine information created in different word processors or on a PC, a Mac, and a UNIX machine. Have you tried to take a document from Word and make it look right in WordPerfect or Ami Pro?

Identification of the logical structure and content elements in information makes it processable in a flexible way. The use of a disciplined standard allows automated processing and interoperability. Using generalized markup, rather than style characteristics, to convey the underlying structure enables the same information source to be presented in multiple ways.

For example, you can output the same SGML document instance and have it look one way online, another on CD-ROM, yet another on the printed page, and so on. Think of all the different ways you might want to deliver information. Using generic markup to identify the logical component rather than procedural presentation codes allows you the flexibility to take advantage of new technology developments quickly, without requiring costly effort to go back and reformat all of the instances of the information—especially when the generic tags are are vendor independent.

Another benefit of generic markup comes from separating the creation of the logical content from decisions about what it should look like when it is presented. This benefit can free you to concentrate on what you do best. Publishers of multi-author works such as magazines want the product to appear in a consistent style. Some people have an artistic gift for emphasizing important points, others suffer from "font-itis," some resent the time to learn how to use word processor style features when they are trying to convey a message.

Still another benefit of SGML is the capability to retain information about the implied logical structure of documents as they are converted for the Web. Markup becomes easier when the rules provide tags that fit the information. In fact, my company is even using SGML-tagged instances and entities to build simple directory databases.

A Personal Message for Those of You Who Like to Paint Pictures with Words

In today's desktop publishing environment, many people have become accustomed to controlling how the output of their work appears—"The Medium is the Message" and all that. They like it and become nervous when people talk about separating content creation from application of style. I am one of these people. Take heart. There is nothing that says one person cannot do both functions. They are just separated in time.

An experience I had when creating Web pages illustrates this point. Although committed to the principles of generic markup, as I proceeded to choose HTML tags for my information, I was tempted to violate the principles and select H4 or H5 tags for wordy second level headings so they would fit on one line—I wanted the page to look nice.

I suddenly realized that I actually had no control of how the output would appear to the reader, for two reasons. The predominant Web browser of that time (NCSA Mosaic) allowed the reader to specify the style for each element. If they desire, end

(continues)

III

Using Helper Apps

(continued)

users can make H4 bigger than H1. While most users accept the default styles (and the heading hierarchy), others (like me) prefer to change them in some way. Also, users can resize the window and the browser reflows the information. Oops. Tilt. I have no control.

This realization freed me to concentrate on the content, which turned out to be quite nice. I did not have to worry about whether to follow the principles and tag the real structure or to violate them for appearance sake. I also saved time reworking tags after seeing what the output looked like. My work went much faster and it actually looked pretty good.

I still sympathize with the providers who like to affect the appearance of their information; the medium does convey messages. But I also comprehend the value of reader control. One of the nice things about the Pro version of the new SGML viewer is that it allows providers to deliver one or more style sheets conveying how they intend the information to appear, yet the user can also create his own style files if he prefers his own way.

The essence of how the World Wide Web works successfully is the implementation of markup tags to identify the structure of information content in a disciplined standard way that allows others to write software (Web browsers) to present the information. Separating the process of identifying the information structure from the way it will be presented gives Web publishers the flexibility to take advantage of technological advances to display captured information content in increasingly new and fresh ways without having to revise it.

As the popularity of the Web has spread, an increasing tension—between the need to maintain the simplicity and discipline that make the Web successful and at the same time increase the flexibility to apply markup to additional types of information—manifests itself in the way the Web is changing as it grows. Some dominant themes are the following:

- HTML markup rules are evolving, accompanied by the difficulty of reaching agreement on what needs to be added—HTML 0, 1, 2, and now 3.
- Developers need the rules stabilized to avoid continually revising browsers that implement the markup with program instructions.
- Web publishers feel the constraints of following rules that do not fit new types of information structures.
- Information providers want to affect presentation style, for example, commercial advertisers want to show their wares. However, they do not

want to have to go back and redo embedded markup tagging when they want to change the look and feel of the presentation.

■ Various vendors are responding to this need with their own enhancements to HTML that only work on their browser. This causes headaches and dilemmas for the Web publishers and, in turn, for those who view the resulting information on the Web.

Into this tension comes a solution that adds the flexibility needed while still maintaining the standard discipline that makes things work.

The Relationship Between SGML and HTML

Although the development of HTML and SGML proceeded on separate intersecting paths, the paths have converged with the standardization of HTML 2.0 (and soon HTML 3.0) as conforming SGML.

HTML Is an Implementation of SGML

Hypertext markup language (HTML) is the implementation of a document type definition (DTD) for a specific document type with a widely applicable information structure. While SGML purists would assert that HTML, in particular early HTML, does not rigorously implement all the SGML principles—for example, hierarchical structure and elimination of presentation-specific markup from a document instance—documents that conform to the HTML 2.0 (and later) DTD rules now meet the SGML criteria.

SGML Is More Encompassing than HTML

The other day, a student reflecting on my explanation of SGML and HTML said, "Do you mean that when you use HTML you use rules created by someone else and with SGML, you can create your own rules?" In a nutshell, she understood the essence of the distinction between them. Using the fuller capability of SGML, authors can create their own rules to match the structure of their information.

While specific information on the elements included in the HTML DTD are discussed later in chapter 25, "HTML Primer," an example will help you see the difference between HTML and SGML markup.

You can see the difference for yourself in the figures 21.2 and 21.3 that show markup of the same information, the NC LRC page in the *Literacy Directory*. Figure 21.2 is the HTML version, figure 21.3 is the SGML markup. Note how much more descriptive the SGML tags are.

Fig. 21.2
HTML markup for
NC LRC page in
the *Literacy
Directory* (Courtesy
of NC LRC).

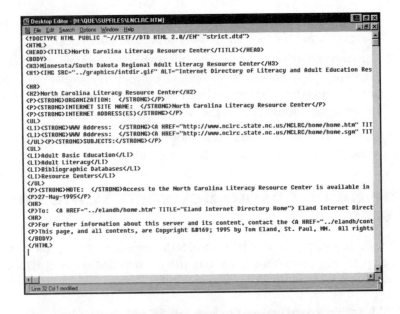

Fig. 21.3
SGML markup for
NC LRC page in
the *Literacy
Directory* (Courtesy
of NC LRC).

When I prepared a Web version of the *Internet Directory of Literacy and Adult Education Resources* (*Literacy Directory* for short), I converted the source information to SGML using specific tags for each item of information, for example, <SITE> for the Internet site name </SITE>, <ORG> for the organization that sponsors it </ORG>, <INETADDR><GOPHER>*gopher address*</GOPHER><WWW>*web address*</WWW>, and so on. In the HTML version, which I automatically generated, this information was simply tagged as <LI> list items.

> **Tip**
>
> If you are tempted to look at HTML source, a feature allowed by most popular browsers, you might find it helpful to know how to interpret the tag structure. The beginning of an information element is identified by a *start tag*, a tag name in angle brackets, for example, <SITE>. The end of the element is marked by an *end tag*, angle bracket followed by a slash, the tag name, and a closing angle bracket </SITE>.

You'll see the result of the differences later in the chapter after I introduce the SGML viewer.

The Benefits of SGML—Have Your Cake and Eat It, Too

The early Web browser programs such as NCSA Mosaic and Lynx include code to display each type of information based on the markup tag. When new tags are added to the rules, programmers have to change the code to handle them. Web publishers know well the frustration of preparing information and having it look different on browsers that are in different stages of implementing the changes; Web surfers note odd discrepancies in passing.

The new dimension that the announcement of an SGML viewer brings to the providers of Web information is the ability to add flexibility and style to Web information and at the same time maintain the simplicity and discipline that makes the Web successful. The SGML viewer provides a flexible way to meet special needs in a standard way. The new features of the SGML viewer provide significant benefits for providers of Web information. Providers in turn provide more, better, cleaner, quicker, and classier information for the readers who obtain the tool view it. Benefits of an SGML approach for special needs include the following:

- By adding the capability to handle special cases, the new SGML viewer reduces the pressure to keep changing the basic HTML definition. The HTML DTD can remain straightforward and simple, uncluttered by special needs and easy to use.

- For special types of information, providers can quickly create their own rules that match the structure and make markup more straightforward.

- The new viewer can display information with any defined DTD (set of tags). Reducing the need for browser program maintenance provides the flexibility to change as quickly as the needs are known.

III

Using Helper Apps

> **Tip**
>
> If you hear techies talk about an *arbitrary DTD*, they are referring to the capability to process information tagged with any set of conforming rules.

■ The new viewer allows publishers to deliver as many style sheets as they want with the information, so that users have a choice. The Pro version of the SGML viewer also lets users create their own. By using an SGML approach, providers gain style control without having to embed it in each document. They also can change the look and feel of a whole set of documents with a few clicks of the mouse instead of revising presentation tags, attributes, and frames in all the instances.

■ Maintenance of information is easier, quicker, and less prone to errors that confuse the reader. For example, the SGML entity feature allows single point maintenance of boilerplate information without requiring special programs.

■ The cost to the end user is right—there is a free version on the Net and an inexpensive Pro version for publishers and those who want additional features.

Examples of SGML on the Web

Now I'll let pictures tell the tale. Figures 21.4 and 21.5 contrast an HTML presentation with an SGML version of the same information and illustrate the result of what we've been discussing. I will use the "NC Literacy Resource Center" entry as it appears in the context of the *Literacy Directory* full alphabetical listing. Note the expandable table of contents, called a *navigator*, that runs down the left side of the page in the SGML version (see fig. 21.5). It is built with a couple clicks of the mouse. Note also the font and formatting differences. You cannot see the color, but the major headings are teal and navy blue. These, too, can be changed with a click of the mouse, which implements the change for all documents using the style sheet.

> **Tip**
>
> Note the plus and minus signs in the navigator. The user can click them to expand or contract the amount of detail he sees.

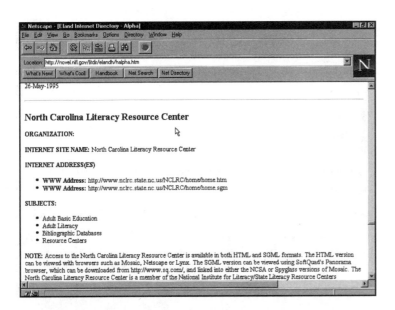

Fig. 21.4
View of the (HTML) NC LRC entry in the *Literacy Directory* via Netscape Navigator.

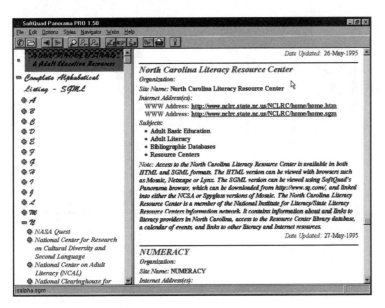

Fig. 21.5
View of the (SGML) NC LRC entry in the *Literacy Directory* via Panorama.

A second pair of examples, figures 21.6 and 21.7, show the HTML and SGML versions of the home page of SAGRELTO's InfoWorm Tutorials. Having the navigator on the screen lets you see what's coming and move quickly down the document.

Fig. 21.6
View of the (HTML) SAGRELTO InfoWorm Tutorials home page via Netscape Navigator.

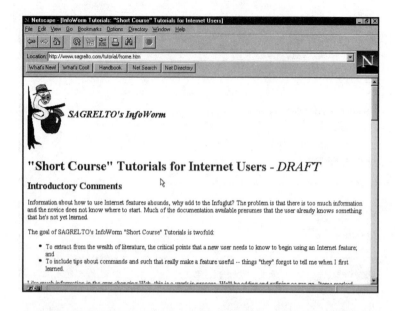

Fig. 21.7
View of the (SGML) SAGRELTO InfoWorm Tutorials home page via Panorama.

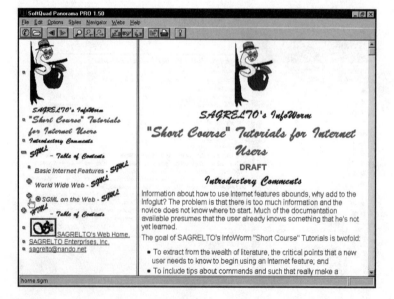

Obtaining and Setting Up an SGML Viewer

Hopefully, the previous discussion has piqued your interest and you are now ready to obtain an SGML viewer.

SQ Panorama is the first SGML helper application to enter the Web scene that can display SGML information from any set of rules (any DTD) without first converting it to HTML. Because Panorama is already available and because it illustrates well new features that can be provided by an SGML viewer, I will focus on it for the discussion in the rest of the chapter. In this section you learn how to obtain Panorama and configure it to work with the Netscape Navigator.

> **Note**
>
> In a sense, all Web browsers are SGML viewers because HTML is an implementation of SGML. However, I will reserve the term SGML viewer for software that can accept and display information for an arbitrary DTD, that is, any conforming set of rules.

> **Note**
>
> As of mid-October '95, Panorama is available only for MS Windows users (all flavors including Windows 95 and NT). The UNIX and Macintosh versions are in pre-beta testing and should be out late in the 4th quarter of '95 or early 1st quarter of '96.

> **Note**
>
> Other SGML viewing technology under development is likely to incorporate comparable features. My focus is to illustrate the advantages of SGML technology; my use of the currently available product for this discussion is not intended to slight other efforts.

Earlier I noted the distinction between a Web browser that you use to access WWW information and a helper application or viewer program that allows you to access special types of information. Panorama and Panorama Pro are viewers/helper applications. They work in conjunction with a compatible Web browser such as Netscape. The browser sends the request to download the information and delivers it to Panorama for display.

> **Note**
>
> The technical term for the technology that makes interaction between browsers and viewers work is *Common Client Interface (CCI).*

III

Using Helper Apps

Note

To use Panorama to view SGML documents on the Web, you also need a SLIP/PPP or a direct connection to the Internet.

Caution

Beginning with Netscape version 1.1 and Panorama 1.11 (July '95), Netscape Navigator joined the list of Web browsers that work with Panorama for viewing SGML Web documents. However, the code to implement the Common Client Interface technology in Netscape, via which the browser communicates with viewers such as Panorama, is so new (and new features are being added to Netscape so fast) that the interaction is still what I call "fragile." Beta versions sometimes interject some problems—for example, viewing local files did not work properly in the beta versions of 1.22, and a new problem that occurred in the first beta of version 2.0—as a message Unable to write file—prevented access to SGML Web files. In general, anomalies that occur relate to the interaction between Panorama and the browser rather than in Panorama itself.

The good news is that new features and fixes to problems come quickly, even in the beta mode; that is, Netscape 2.0 beta 2 seems to work best of all. The drawback is that you may encounter a few problems if development stages get out of sync. Be patient. I expect the stability to increase and settle down within one or two more versions.

Tip

SAGRELTO's Notes from a Panorama Beta Tester describes benefits of using the SGML with the new viewer, tips from our testing experience, and links to relevant resources. You can find this at **http://www.sagrelto.com/tutorial/sgetnote.htm**.

Finding and Obtaining an SGML Viewer

The first decision you must make is which version you want. The commercial version offers some features not available in the freeware version.

Both versions of Panorama allow you the same full capabilities to access and view SGML files on the Web. You may select between Styles and choose any Navigator (expanding Table of Contents) that the information provider makes available. For the curious, the capability to show tags and navigate the SGML tree are also available.

However, some features are available only in Panorama Pro that may make it desirable, even mandatory, and worth the $199 suggested retail price. Features available only in Panorama Pro include the following:

■ The ability to print, save, and open (local) files

> **Tip**
>
> As a prototyping tool for working with local SGML files, Panorama Pro is powerful—so powerful that I suspect the power surprised the vendors and became a major factor in their decision to reserve these capabilities for the Pro version. (They had to give us some reason to compensate them for the value they add with this invaluable SGML tool.)
>
> The capability to open files is desirable for those applications that want to make larger files available for download and local viewing. The ability to print is desirable for those who would like to create a special style and print camera-ready copy.

■ The ability to create your own Styles and Navigators (expandable Tables of Contents)

> **Tip**
>
> If you are preparing SGML information for the Web, you need the Pro version to prepare the style sheets and Navigators to deliver with your information.
>
> If you prefer your own styles to those provided by the publisher, this ability is a desirable feature.

■ The ability to create and manage Webs (a new facility for creating your own links among documents, bookmarks, and annotations)

■ The commercial version is supported software (the freeware version is not)

> **Tip**
>
> For Panorama, support is not a major issue; capabilities available only with the Pro version are. From experience, I know that SoftQuad does update its free software from time to time. Also, I experience fewer problems with SoftQuad products than with most software applications.
>
> However, support is an added benefit. I have found that the SQ support staff ranks among the very best, both in promptness and in competence.

III

Using Helper Apps

> **Tip**
>
> Some users may need the capabilities that the additional features provide; others may purchase it just because the features are fun to use. It's a very nice product to work with.

The fact that the less full-featured version is freeware makes the need to decide painless. You can try the free version first, then upgrade later.

Downloading the Free Version of Panorama

If you want the free version of Panorama, the file you are looking for is panofr10.exe, a self-extracting executable that contains a Windows installer program for the Panorama distribution.

> **Tip**
>
> If the free space on your hard drive is shrinking as fast as mine, you'll appreciate knowing that the size of the panofr10.exe (July '95) download file is a little over 1MB and the installed directory occupies a little more than 2.1MB. You'll also need room temporarily for the file extraction.

The following are three sites from which you can download a freeware version of Panorama:

- *The Wider World of SGML* is a special site set up when Panorama came out in May of 1995 to provide current information about Panorama free. It provides a way to obtain the software that you need to view SGML on the Web via the download features of a Web browser such as Netscape Navigator. The URL is **http://www.oclc.org:5046/oclc/ research/panorama/panorama.html**.

- NCSA is the central site for the distribution of free Panorama. The page for download via a Web browser is SoftQuad Panorama for Windows at URL **http://www.ncsa.uiuc.edu/SDG/Software/WinMosaic/ Viewers/panorama.htm**.

  If you prefer to use an FTP client, the URL is **ftp:// ftp.ncsa.uiuc.edu/Mosaic/Windows/viewers/panofr10.exe**.

  The file should also be available at NCSA mirror sites in the viewers subdirectory.

- A mirror site in Sweden is at the URL **ftp://www.nada.kth.se/ IPLab/megabiblion/panofr10.exe**.

General instructions can be found at the URL **http://
info.admin.kth.se/SGML/Bibliotek/PD-Program/Panorama/
Windows/**.

Panorama free is also licensed for distribution by vendors of browsers based
on Spyglass Enhanced NCSA Mosaic.

Obtaining Panorama Pro

If you want the additional features that are available in the commercial Panorama Pro version, you have three main choices, which are as follows:

- The starting point for vendor information and contact data is SoftQuad,
  Inc.'s Welcome Page (URL: **http://www.sq.com/**). You also may be
  interested in checking out the features of the Pro version described on
  the SQ Panorama Pro page at URL: **http://www.sq.com/panor-
  pr.html**.

- The Windows version of Panorama Pro is expected to be available on
  the shelves of major distributors and retail channels such as Best Buy,
  CompUSA, Computer City, Egghead Software, Media Play, Software Etc,
  and Staples in November 1995, followed by the Mac version in late
  January 1995, with an anticipated street price of $149 U.S.

- Panorama Pro can be ordered at a cost of $195 by U.S. Interleaf custom-
  ers for use in their document management and delivery systems by
  calling 800-955-5323 or sending e-mail to **i-direct@ileaf.com**. In
  Europe, Asia-Pacific, and Canada, customers should call their local
  Interleaf Offices for pricing and ordering information.

Also, you may contact SoftQuad directly at:

SoftQuad, Inc.
56 Alberfoyle Crescent, Suite 810
Toronto, Ontario
Canada
M8X 2W4
Telephone: (416) 239-4801
Fax: (416) 239-7105
e-mail: **mail@sq.com**
Web site: **http://www.sq.com**

Configuring Netscape for SGML

If you already have Netscape Navigator installed, the configuration step for
SQ Panorama free is easy because the Panorama setup includes configuration,
at least it did until Netscape 20b1. The installation of Panorama Pro is the
essentially the same, minus the download and decompression steps.

Note

Although my sources could not confirm it, I think the reason that Panorama does not automatically configure itself as a helper application (required for its operation) for Netscape 32e20b1j is that the Windows 95 versions are now using the Windows 95 Registry instead of .INI files. I'll tell you how to do it manually after the installation steps that follow and I expect that the vendor will make adjustments to continue doing it for you in a future version.

Tip

For those of you (like me) who need to maintain a stable system and are nervous about the impact of installing a new program, relax. Except for a panorama.ini file, which is placed in your Windows directory, Panorama files are all placed in the directory you designate.

To prepare a downloaded panofr10.exe for installation, perform the following steps:

1. Download the file from one of the sources listed in the "Downloading the Free Version of Panorama" section into a temporary folder.

2. Execute the self-extracting compressed file that you downloaded in Windows or DOS. For example, from the Windows 95 Explorer, double-click the panofr10.exe file name in the temporary folder.

3. Check the README.WRI file (by double-clicking it from the Windows 95 Explorer or opening it from WordPad).

Caution

To prevent a system hang in the early versions of Panorama/Netscape integration, an unresolved anomaly required you to take special precautions about the order in which you activated Netscape and Panorama. While the original problem is fixed now, my experience with implementing new browser versions is that old problems can reoccur and new problems occur, especially in beta versions. Be sure to check the information in the README.WRI file and follow the instructions.

From this point, installation of Panorama and Panorama Pro is essentially the same. You execute the SETUP.EXE program from the temporary folder or the installation disk folder, respectively.

To install the software, perform the following steps:

1. From STARTUP, select Settings, Control Panel. Click Add/Remove Software. Choose the Install/Uninstall tab and click the Install button. Click the Next button and when the window appears, enter the name of the temporary folder or disk followed by SETUP.EXE, or use the Browse button to locate the SETUP.EXE file in the appropriate folder. Then click Finish to start the SETUP process.

2. The SETUP program allows you to specify the directory where you want to put the program. You may accept the default or choose another path by typing over the default.

3. In most cases, if Netscape Navigator and/or other compatible Web browser(s) are already installed, the Panorama SETUP program looks for them and pops up a message box for each. The message asks whether you want SETUP to configure the browser for Panorama. In general, answer Yes for each of them.

> **Tip**
>
> For new versions, such as Netscape 2.0b1, SETUP may not find your browser, and you may need to follow the instructions to manually configure a helper application as directed below the list of steps.

> **Tip**
>
> If you are familiar with setting up helper applications or viewers described in chapter 16, "Configuring Helper Applications," you may be interested in what happens if you say Yes to the "Do you want to configure the browser?" question. If the answer is yes, the SETUP program adds a helper application for you for the MIME type text/x-sgml.

4. You are then asked which of the compatible browsers to set up for the initial execution of Panorama. If you are using Netscape Navigator, select Netscape.

5. When the SETUP program completes, you are ready to access SGML files on the Web. Connect to the Internet, bring up Netscape, and look for SGML on the Web resources.

III

Using Helper Apps

> **Tip**
>
> If you are installing Panorama Pro and are planning to access local files, you need one more step.
>
> In your browser, choose Options, General, and select the Helpers tab. Add a helper application for MIME type text/sgml using the following information:
>
> > MIME type: **text**
> > MIME Subtype: **sgml**
> > Suffixes (or extensions): **.sgml, .sgm**
> > Program: **xxx/panorama.exe** (where xxx is the path to the directory where you installed Panorama)

If you add Netscape after you have installed Panorama or the SETUP program did not recognize a browser that uses the Windows 95 Registry instead of an .INI file, the configuration step is still easy if you understand how to set up helper applications. See chapter 16, "Configuring Helper Applications."

In your Browser, choose Options, General and select the Helpers tab. Add a helper application for MIME types text/x-sgml and text/sgml using the following information which is the same for both except for the MIME subtype:

> MIME type: **text**
> MIME Subtype: **x-sgml** for one, **sgml** for the other
> Suffixes (or extensions): **.sgml**, **.sgm**
> Program: **xxx/panorama.exe** (where xxx is the path to the folder where you installed Panorama)

> **Tip**
>
> If you need to switch the browser with which Panorama interacts to (or from) Netscape, choose Options, Web Browser, and select the appropriate browser.

That's it. You're ready to go.

Opening an SGML Document

When you access a site with SGML information, Netscape brings up Panorama for you and starts loading the components as Panorama requests them. Just as many HTML documents contain graphics that are brought in separately from the text, SGML documents are made up from multiple components. Figure 21.8 illustrates one stage of what you see when you request an SGML resource from the Web.

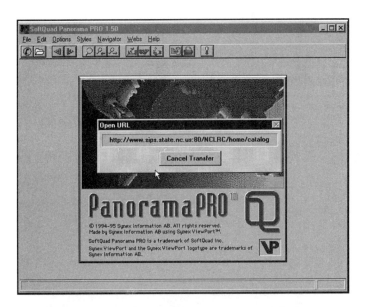

Fig. 21.8
Panorama coming
up for the first
time in a session.

Tip

You may notice a Cancel Transfer button in the message box that sits on top of
Panorama. It is like a Stop button on a browser—clicking it allows you to abort the
transfer. However, be aware of two things: First, you may have to do it multiple times
if there are more files to come (as you would in a browser if a file contained many
images); also, it is quite possible that you will receive a Parser Error message box at
the end (if any of the objects canceled are critical files, and it is likely that they will
be). In other words, you can do it if you want to, but aborting the download of an
SGML file is likely to have strange results.

Figure 21.9 looks like what you see when the download is finished.

Tip

In each of the Netscape versions since 1.22, something slightly different appears on
the screen as Netscape downloads the file and brings up the Panorama viewer. Don't
worry if the messages change a bit; the developers keep improving what you see. As
long as you see indications that several files are being accessed and Panorama comes
up, everything is as it should be. I'll explain more about the files below in the "Viewing and Saving SGML Files" section.

III

Using Helper Apps

Fig. 21.9
The end result of a
successfully loaded
document.

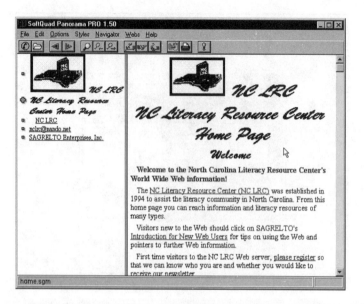

Tip

A technique that we adopted by necessity during the beta testing may be useful to
you when you start accessing SGML files with Panorama. You can arrange your
screen so that the browser and the viewer overlap but do not cover one another
completely. This allows you to click back and forth between them easily, especially if
you want to see what is happening in the other half of an interacting pair.

This kind of peripheral vision and the ability to cross over quickly that you gain are
very nice if things should go wrong. It is also kind of neat to watch the interaction
that takes place as multiple small files become an SGML document.

The components of the full SGML resource that may be downloaded from the
host site include the following:

- The basic SGML instance that you requested. It will have a suffix of
  .SGML or .SGM (if the basic information is maintained on a PC and
  uploaded to a UNIX server). This file contains a <DOCTYPE> line, which
  tells Panorama which DTD to get.

- A catalog file named "catalog" that tells Panorama where to look for the
  DTD and entity files, such as graphics and boilerplate.

- Another catalog-type file named "entityrc" that tells Panorama where to
  obtain the Style, Navigator, and Web files (I'll explain what these are
  used for in the "Viewing and Saving SGML files" section).

- The DTD file, usually with the suffix .DTD. This file provides the rules for this document to Panorama.

- One or more Style files with a suffix .SSH. Style files provide the information for formatting and dressing the display. Panorama will bring down the first one as it loads the document, and will go get others if you ask for them.

- One or more Navigator files with a suffix .NAV. Navigator files provide instructions for building the expandable Table of Contents that runs down the left side of the Panorama screen when the Navigator is activated.

- Zero to several entity files that contain information stored external to the basic SGML instance. Usually the suffix .ENT is used but it could be anything.

- Zero to several graphic files (for example, .GIF files) that contain any graphics that go on the page.

This sounds like a lot of downloading, and it is, but most of the files are very small. Also, Panorama keeps them around for a while and reuses them for other documents so it is not nearly as awesome as it sounds. However, the first document downloaded can take a while. Also be aware that because it is so easy to navigate through a large document quickly with Panorama, some of the publishers are providing large files. It takes longer to download them, but moving about in the information afterward is much faster than re-accessing the Web.

Note

Panorama is so new that there has not been time to complete research on how to maximize the performance. The Panorama developers and SAGRELTO are concerned about the download time and have made several significant improvements already. It can only get better.

If You Want to Have Fun One Day...

SAGRELTO is experimenting with the technique of storing small bits of information in entity files and then mixing and matching them to create multiple views of the same information.

(continues)

III

Using Helper Apps

(continued)

If you'd like to see the result of this technique, one day when you have a little time and you already have Panorama installed, request the *Literacy Directory* home page at **http://novel.nifl.gov/litdir/elands/home.sgm**. On that page, work your way down to the section that provides the links to the SGML versions of their information. Select one of the Browsing listings by Subject. If you want the full impact, choose the link for the Browsing listing of Web sites. This file is made up of about 100 small pieces. The message boxes in the browser and viewer open and close rapidly, almost like the clickety clack of a railroad train. It reminds me of how much faster gas seems to flow at a pump that displays the gallons and cents in three decimal places instead of two. The Gopher and LISTSERV sites are a bit smaller if you want a smaller dose.

This particular resource pushes the limits of the software so you may end up not being able to see the result, but that should be fixed soon, if it's not already.

Troubleshooting

After the components finish loading, I see a Panorama message screen indicating that Panorama was not able to find one of the pieces or has encountered an unexpected EOF (End of File). What's wrong?

This generally means either that one of the components was not available on the server or that something went wrong in the interaction between the browser's accessing the server to retrieve the data and passing it to Panorama.

You have done nothing wrong. And, there is not much you can do about the situation except try to reload. However, you may be able to view the data anyway. Try pressing the OK button and see if the information is readable. Generally, what is missing are the Styles or Navigator files, so it might not look as good as it should. If content is what interests you, you may have what you want.

If the problem persists, I know from experience that the Webmaster would appreciate hearing about it. It is usually very quickly fixed, but he may not know the problem exists.

Accessing SGML on the Web

SGML on the Web is a new technology. We are just beginning to see implementations that exploit its power to add power, style, and pizazz to Web information.

The general instructions for accessing SGML on the Web are as follows:

1. Connect to the Internet.

2. Bring up Netscape Navigator.

3. Request SGML information (via URL, bookmark, or a link from another Web resource such as NCSA/SoftQuad SGML on the Web). Netscape brings up a message box Viewing location and brings Panorama up automatically if the information you request is MIME type x-sgml.

> **Tip**
>
> I suggest that you add at least one item to your Bookmark list: a link to NCSA/SoftQuad SGML on the Web, the site that is currently the main reference for SGML documents on the Web:
>
> **http://www.ncsa.uiuc.edu/SDG/Software/Mosaic/WebSGML.sgml**
>
> If you find SGML interesting, you may want also to add a Header to store links to your favorite SGML sites as you discover them.

4. Explore the information via the features of Panorama.

Finding SGML Files on the Web

The dimensions that the SGML viewer adds to the power of Web information presentation are new. Many providers of Web information are just becoming aware of them. "SGML on the Web" information is sparse now but expect the sources of SGML information (and of products to view it) to grow rapidly as Web publishers learn to use the flexibility that the SGML viewer provides.

The following is a list of sites, primarily taken from the NCSA/SoftQuad SGML on the Web resource. I have investigated them and provided annotations to help you select from among them. I have tried to group them a bit by some common thread. The major groupings are: Locating SGML on the Web, Interesting Applications Referenced via NCSA/SoftQuad SGML on the Web, Information about SGML, and Promising Projects.

Locating SGML on the Web

The following two sites are, by design, central points for providing information about the SGML viewer and resources that have been designed to use it.

- *The Wider World of SGML on the Web* at URL **http://www.oclc.org:5046/oclc/research/panorama/panorama.html**

This site provides up-to-date information on how to obtain the free version of Panorama, the new SGML viewer that makes SGML available on the Web today. The site also provides SGML and HTML links to the NCSA/SoftQuad SGML on the Web site, as well as to other resources for those interested in SGML and HTML.

■ *NCSA/SoftQuad SGML on the Web* at URL **http://www.ncsa.uiuc.edu/SDG/Software/Mosaic/WebSGML.html**

This site is *the* primary resource for locating SGML information on the Web. Designed to be the focus of links to information about SGML, and especially to the newest sites that provide SGML on the Web today, this is a must visit for those interested in the new SGML viewer and the technology that it supports. The resources hot-linked here are also good resources to guide you to other information.

Tip

Designed as a focal point for collecting links to SGML information, the NCSA/SoftQuad SGML on the Web site will probably remain the best resource for some time. I know that in SAGRELTO's case this is true. As one of the first Web publishers to focus on preparing information for SGML on the Web, we plan to post our latest and greatest there. We'll also post a link to our home page where we'll link to the other SAGRELTO-prepared SGML resources as they roll off of the central list. On our home page, we'll also insert annotated links to others that we find particularly interesting.

Tip

If you are a provider of Web information as well as a surfer, note that implementing the new SGML technology gives you not only the opportunity to present your information with added power and style, but also adds the interest that draws visitors to an early adopter site.

Interesting Applications Referenced via NCSA/SoftQuad SGML on the Web

This large section is divided into subsections of similar themes and/or illustrations of Panorama features.

Two Sites that Demonstrate Interesting Features of Panorama

The following two sites that a new SGML explorer may want to visit illustrate SGML capabilities:

■ *Guide to Magellan Image Interpretation* at URL **http://
stardust.jpl.nasa.gov/mgddf/guidesgml.html**

The Jet Propulsion Laboratory's Guide to Magellan Image Interpretation. In this JPL Publication 93-24, there are 10 chapters and an appendix in SGML format, AAP Book DTD.

This resource provides a very nice example of SGML/Panorama Pro
features, including multiple style sheets and Navigators; thumbnail
images in a special Navigator that can be clicked to open larger images.

■ *SoftQuad Panorama Demos* at URL **http://www.oclc.org:5046/oclc/
research/panorama/demotbl.sgml**

An SGML file with links to explore for investigating Panorama features.

In the Newcomer Demos section, try clicking Greater Control to Display Styles and then follow the directions to use the Style menu to explore the use of multiple styles. Then browse other links to see other
features.

Literacy Resources

This section describes two applications that provide both SGML and HTML
versions of the content for the benefit of constituents in the Literacy Community. The SGML versions illustrate benefits gained from the presentation
control that Styles and Navigators offer to add pizazz to information. Check
out the following sites:

■ *Internet Literacy Directory—SGML* at URL **http://novel.nifl.gov/
litdir/elands/home.sgm**

The Internet Directory of Literacy and Adult Education Resources contains information and addresses for 164 sites of interest to the literacy
and adult education communities, compiled by the former Director of
the Minnesota/South Dakota Literacy and Adult Education Resource
Center. It now resides at the National Institute for Literacy where it
serves the national literacy community.

This SGML version shows examples of the use of styles and Navigators
to make directory type information more readable. It also provides
examples of the use of SGML entities to provide multiple browsing
listings.

■ *Internet Literacy Directory—HTML* at URL **http://novel.nifl.gov/
litdir/**

This Internet Directory of Literacy and Adult Education Resources contains information and addresses for 164 sites of interest to the literacy
and adult education communities.

■ *NC Literacy Resource Center Home Page—HTML* at URL **http://www.nclrc.state.nc.us/NCLRC/home/**

NC LRC's Web site provides information for literacy providers in North Carolina and for the literacy community across the world.

It features the beginning of an online catalog of literacy resources, newsletters, and other items of interest to the community it serves.

SAGRELTO Miscellaneous Web Sites

SAGRELTO's Web Home—SGML, at URL **http://www.sagrelto.com** contains resources distinguished by their colorful use of SGML viewer features for relatively traditional Web information—and relatively small files, including a collection of Internet tutorials and excellent examples and illustrations of SGML on the Web. Highly recommended.

Literary Works

The Literary category groups examples of SGML applied to sizable works in literature and related fields. Check out the following sites:

■ *Headwords from Bailey's 1736 Dictionary (Excerpts)* at URL **http://www.oclc.org:5046/oclc/research/panorama/contrib/liamquin/baileys/headwords.html#H**

This HTML page provides internal links to the alphabet and words. If you click the words, the SGML version comes up. An interesting use of black-and-white presentation with multiple fonts. This address lands you in the H section, which is relatively small for an SGML explorer.

■ *The Works of William Shakespeare* at URL **http://www.oclc.org:5046/oclc/research/panorama/contrib/Shakespeare/index.html**

Fans of Shakespeare with a little time can explore the use of SGML to view the master's works. The files are large but the server delivers them quickly.

The SGML is an example of how simple and straightforward use of style can facilitate viewing.

■ *Great Religious Texts* at URL **http://www.oclc.org:5046/oclc/research/panorama/contrib/religion/index.html**

If you are interested in the Bible, the Quran, or the Book of Morman, see the SGML version of these texts with markup credits to Jon Bosak of Novell, Inc. and the Free Text Project 1992-1994.

The SGML versions of books of the Bible and the Books of Morman are simply displayed and easily navigated by chapter and verse. The surahs of the Quran are colorfully or plainly displayed according to your choice from the Style menu.

■ *Public Domain Modern English Search* at URL **http:// www.hti.umich.edu/english/pd-modeng/**

This resource provides multiple ways to search a large collection of Modern English works. In the Bibliography and Browse section, you can browse a listing of the entire corpus with links to each work.

SGML and HTML versions of the full text of 314 works in the Modern English text collection, as well as a Table of Contents for each, are available via this link. Aesop, Louisa May Alcott, Dickens, Conan Doyle, Poe, DuBois, Edgar Rice Burroughs, and Tennyson are just a few of the authors' works presented here. Thomas Jefferson's Declaration of Independence and Maya Angelou's *On the Pulse of Morning* are two of the shorter works if you want a quick way to take a look at how the SGML turns out. The Style sheet and Navigator are preliminary, a simple way to access powerful information.

■ *Middle English Search* at URL **http://www.hti.umich.edu/english/ ME.html**

If you prefer the era of Chaucer and Everyman, this resource parallels the features of the Modern English Search.

There's a nice way to browse for the SGML versions of Middle English works, but the night I visited, the SGML versions were not available.

■ *Alice Freeman Palmer, The Evolution of a New Woman* at URL **http:// www.press.umich.edu/bookhome/bordin/**

The University of Michigan Press has provided a 756KB SGML version of this work by Ruth Bordin.

Text Encoding Initiative (TEI)

The Text Encoding Initiative has a group of sites listed on the SGML on the Web page. Because they seem to have similar characteristics, I have left them grouped together and have also included the related Center for Electronic Text for the Humanities. In general, I had more difficulties accessing the SGML on these sites, which are as follows:

■ *Text Encoding Initiative Home Page [new]* at URL **http://www.uic.edu/ orgs/tei/index.html**

Provides links to information about SGML and the Text Encoding Initiative.

- *The Electronic Versions of the TEI Guidelines* at URL **http://www.uic.edu/orgs/tei/info/elect.html**

  Following a link to this site brings you a link closer to SGML versions of information via a link to The TEI Guidelines: SGML Version, but you may find the file there too large for your time.

  Information about the TEI Guidelines in HTML form were linked here.

- *The TEI Guidelines: SGML Version* at URL **http://www.uic.edu/orgs/tei/p3/p3x/p3x.html**

  Following links to this resource brings you closer still to SGML versions of information, but here you find that the SGML versions are in a .TAR file over 5MB in size.

  Accessing referenced links on the page brought up files that looked like SGML files, but since they did not carry the .SGM or .SGML suffix, they were simply displayed as text. I tried adding a .p3x suffix to the MIME type text/x-sgml but it was a fiasco.

- *Oxford Text Archive Home Page: Revised Jan 1995* at URL **http://ota.ox.ac.uk/~archive/ota.html**

  This site looks very promising as an SGML resource, but the file is over 200KB and the server can be slow.

- *British National Corpus* at URL **http://info.ox.ac.uk:80/bnc/" ADD_DATE="815372928" LAST_VISIT="815387738"></A>**

  While this million word corpus, collecting samples of written and spoken current British English is an SGML work, I could not find examples of SGML Web offerings.

Technical Information

Several links to Intel's Component Technical Documentation leads off this section that groups resources of technical interest to one group or another. The following resources illustrate the use of SGML for technical material:

- *Component Technical Documents* at URL **http://techdoc.wais.net:2160/default.html**

  This HTML home page provides an introduction and links to other features including Contents and Search.

  You need to register to view the technical information, but it is easy to do so via a link from this page.

- *Contents* at URL **http://techdoc.wais.net:2160/contents.html**

  For those who like to browse to see what is available, this Table of Contents lists the available topics and provides links (with download size) to SGML, Acrobat, and PostScript versions of the information.

Note that the SGML files are significantly smaller than the other two formats.

- *Pentium™ Processor (610/75) Power Consumption, Rev 1.1* at URL **ftp:// www.wais.com/pub/techdoc/sgml/24241601/24241601.sgml**

  This link is to the smallest SGML file I found. The resource illustrates the use of SGML/Panorama features to provide a wealth of technical information, organized so that you can access what you need.

- *WG8 Home Page* at URL **http://www.ornl.gov/sgml/WG8/ wg8home.htm**

  International standards organizations responsible for SGML and related standards are represented by the Welcome to the ISO/IEC JTC1/SC18/ WG8 Web Service. This home page provides links to information about the work and meetings of the organization, an invaluable resource for those in the standards development world.

- *Journal of Electronic Publishing* at URL **http:// www.press.umich.edu/jep/jep-test.html**

  The University of Michigan Press project to make the Journal available in SGML as well as HTML is being tested. Works in Archive issue 1 are being made available in SGML or HTML.

- *Illinois Digital Library Initiative Project* at URL **http:// www.grainger.uiuc.edu/dli/**

  Building the Interspace: Digital Library Infrastructure for a University Engineering Community.

  If you choose the Testbed home page, you see some information alluding to a sample demonstration available to the public.

Information about SGML

This section focuses on resources that provide information about SGML. They are chosen from Bookmarks I have gathered over the last several years, and they are likely to provide good leads to further resources as well as what you find on these pages. Check out the following resources:

- *SGML Web Page* at URL **http://www.sil.org/sgml/sgml.html**

  This resource by Robin Cover, supported by SoftQuad, Inc. and the Summer Institute of Linguistics, looks like the beginning of a gold mine of information about all aspects of SGML. Of particular interest to explorers looking for examples of SGML on the Web, there is a link to Public SGML Software that discusses Panorama and promises to provide links to SGML resources in the future.

III

Using Helper Apps

Tip

Robin Cover's SGML bibliography has long been a major resource of information on SGML. As a well-known collector of information about SGML resources, his site should remain among the best places to look for SGML information and resources.

- *Public SGML Software* at URL **http://www.sil.org/sgml/ publicSW.html**

  In addition to providing lots of good information about public SGML software, you find a section on Panorama: SoftQuad's SGML Viewer for WWW on this page. This section is likely to be a continually enhanced source of links to SGML on the Web information.

- *Getting Started with SGML* at URL **http://www.sgmlopen.org/sgml/ docs/library/getstart.htm**

  This resource is a nice introduction to the concepts of SGML.

- *SGML Open—Information On SGML* at URL **http:// www.sgmlopen.org/sgml/docs/general/sgmldesc.htm**

  This site, a component of the SGML Open Web Service, is one worthy of recording in your exploration of SGML resources on the Web.

- *SGML Open Home Page* at URL **http://www.sgmlopen.org/**

  As the home page for the SGML vendor consortium, this resource is another centralized source of links to SGML information. Here you find links to the first SGML version of SGML Open information. If you browse the member vendor's information pages, you find additional SGML-related information.

- *Directory of ftp.ifi.uio.no/pub/SGML* at URL **ftp://ftp.ifi.uio.no/pub/ SGML/**

  The SGML Repository, located at the Department of Informatics, University of Oslo, Norway. Long the host of the active listserv and newsgroup **comp.text.sgml**, this site is one of the first that you learn about when becoming interested in SGML. No list of SGML resources is complete without it.

- *Graphics Communications Association* at URL **http://www.awa.com/ cgi-bin/cash?|http://www.awa.com/softlock/book2.html**

  The GCA is an organization involved in both the history of SGML and in conferences that are SGML-related.

- *Catalog of HyTime Architectural Forms and HyTime SGML Specification* at URL **http://www.sgmlopen.org/sgml/docs/goodies/hytime/ archform.htm**

  HyTime is an SGML-related standard.

- *DSSSL* at URL **http://www.jclark.com/dsssl/**

  The Document Style Specification Semantics Language standard is a standard related to SGML. Because of DSSSL's prominence and that of DSSSL LITE in current discussions, the site is worth noting and exploring.

Promising Projects

This section includes a sprinkling of project sources that caught my attention during my exploration to identify sources of SGML for Web viewing. Take some time to visit the following sites:

- *SGML: Academic Projects* at URL **http://www.sil.org/sgml/ acadapps.html**

  A link into Robin Cover's SGML Web Page site to the page where he describes academic projects involving SGML.

- *The Online Computer Library Center Home Page* at URL **http:// www.oclc.org:5046/oclc/research/**

  The Online Computer Library Center has been involved with SGML projects for a number of years.

- *SGML: Academic Projects—Duke University Finding Aids Project* at URL **http://www.sil.org/sgml/acadapps.html#dukeSpecial**

  A link to Robin Cover's SGML Web Page information that references the Duke University Finding Aids project.

- *SGML (Computer Interchange of Museum Information)* at URL **http:// www.nstn.ca/cimi/sgml.html**

  From the information available, it looks like this resource is an interesting SGML project, but at this early stage, some of the required components are not yet available.

- *HTI Resources in support of Panorama* at URL **http:// www.hti.umich.edu/sgml/panorama/**

  This site provides a list of links to information provided by the University of Michigan Humanities Text Initiative, which includes a significant SGML component.

III

Using Helper Apps

- *SGML and the Web* at URL **http://www.w3.org/hypertext/ WWW/MarkUp/SGML/**

As experienced Web surfers know well, you should also use your favorite Web search sites such as those linked via Netscape Search: InfoSeek, Lycos, WebCrawler, OpenText, and the others. I suggest starting with terms like SGML on the Web, Panorama, .SGM, and the like.

Viewing and Saving SGML Files

This section introduces you to the features of Panorama. I'll discuss and illustrate some of the features, but my main advice is for you to explore for yourself. Click around. Check the menus. There are lots of nice surprises. Try it, you'll like it.

Most people experienced with using Web browsers have little trouble using Panorama. The feel, if not the look, is intially very similar to other browsers. For example, the arrow buttons for moving back and forth between documents that you have viewed works the same in most browsers.

Tip

Note that the back arrow button may take you back within a document instead of directly to the previous document.

If you have been exploring many areas of a document, you may find it easier to choose the File menu and look below the commands, where in other applications you see a short list of previously opened files. In Panorama, this list is the abbreviated titles of documents you have opened and not closed. To return to a previous document, just click the title.

Now you are ready to explore the document and the features. Have fun! You shouldn't be able to do any damage moving around within a document.

Caution

One problem when following links to a number of SGML files is that information that previously looked fine starts to flow in odd ways. It appears to be related to a problem with the cache overflowing. The solution is to close pages that you are no longer using and, if necessary, close Panorama and come back in again.

> **Caution**
>
> A derivative problem that may occur when you close files using the same DTDs and style sheets is that you may see a Panorama message screen telling you that something is missing. Reloading the file may cure this problem. If not, close Panorama and come back in again.

Styles and Navigators

Two features that you may notice immediately, depending upon what features the Web publisher has chosen to use, are the Navigator and the Styles. The Styles are relatively obvious. Usually they are set up to provide a more sophisticated presentation than you see on a standard browser unless the author uses a lot of images. I'll mention a few things about them later, but first...what is a Navigator?

A Navigator is an expanding and contracting Table of Contents that runs down the left side of the screen. Click on any plus signs that you see to expand the Table of Contents, or the minus signs to contract it again. Click one of the items in the Navigator and watch the right side of the screen; it moves the text to the section you choose.

> **Tip**
>
> Be aware that while link items (usually colored text) may show up in the Navigator if the publisher chooses to put them there, clicking them will take you to the spot where they appear in the text, not to the other end of the link. To jump to the referenced document, you must click the link reference in the body of the document on the right side of the screen.

Panorama allows Web authors who prepare SGML for the Web to deliver multiple Styles and/or Navigators, if they so desire. For example, they might have a large type style for SVGA viewing, a small one for VGA, and yet another for printing. Likewise, different Navigators can provide different ways to move through the information.

III

Using Helper Apps

On the menu, choose Styles to see if more than one Style sheet is listed and try the others if they are available. Figure 21.10 is an example of a page that has multiple styles.

Fig. 21.10
An open Styles menu for a document with multiple styles.

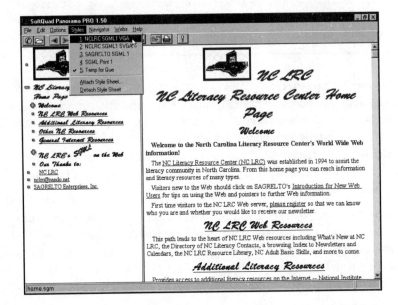

Panorama Pro allows you also to select Attach Style Sheet to create a new style file and set your own preferred look and feel. You then right-click an element to bring up an option box illustrated in figure 21.11, then use the Style Sheet Editor illustrated in figure 21.12 to set the style parameters for the element.

All Panorama users may select the Locate in Navigator or Locate in SGML tree options.

As illustrated here, Panorama Pro users may select Edit Style, which brings up the Style Sheet Editor as illustrated in figure 21.12, or they may select Navigator Entry with the result illustrated in figure 21.14.

You may set font characteristics for the Content and format characteristics for the Paragraph, Before and/or After element characteristics including text that should appear, and Misc characteristics such as background color or other special effects such as table formatting, and so on.

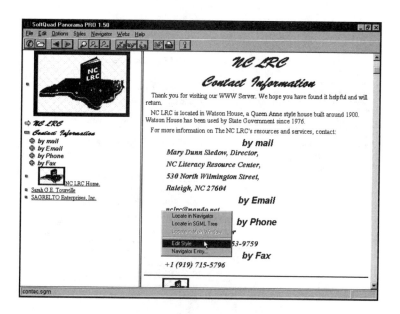

Fig. 21.11
Right-click an
element to bring
up an option box.

Fig. 21.12
The Style Sheet
Editor that comes
up when a
Panorama Pro user
chooses Edit Style.

Also, check to see if the author has provided more than one Table of Contents view by choosing Navigator from the menu bar. Figure 21.13 is an example of what you see.

Panorama Pro users may choose Navigator, Attach Navigator from the menu bar, and then right-click an element and select Navigator Entry from the option box illustrated in figure 21.11 to add or remove the element from the Navigator. When I was showing the "proof" copy of the Astrology Club page to my client, the city field was not yet in the Navigator. Figure 21.14 shows the Edit Navigator dialog box that came up when I right-clicked on the City element. In the dialog box, I clicked the Add button and the tree took on a new level that allowed the user to expand the Table of Contents by city as well as by state.

Using Helper Apps

Fig. 21.13
An open Navigator
menu for a
document with
multiple choices.

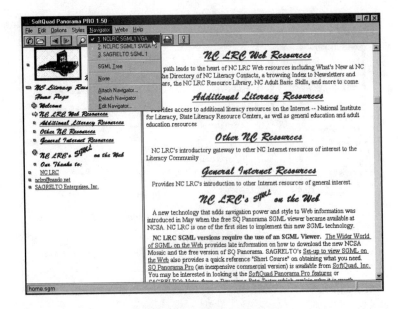

Fig. 21.14
An example
showing the Edit
Navigator feature.

Inside the Black Box—The SGML Tree and Show Tags

For those of you interested in seeing how things are put together, there are special features for you, too.

From the menu bar, choose Navigator, SGML Tree. The Navigator changes to show you a hierarchical diagram of the tags in the document. You can also navigate the document by clicking the element tags within the tree. Figure 21.15 is an illustration of an SGML Tree.

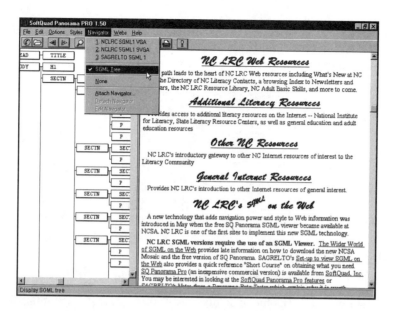

Fig. 21.15
Illustration of an SGML Tree.

A second feature is found by choosing <u>O</u>ptions, Show <u>T</u>ags from the menu bar. As figure 21.16 illustrates, the body of the document changes and the markup tags appear enclosed in little icons so that they stand out from the text. The NC LRC Contact page used in this example is the same as the one used to illustrate markup in figure 21.1.

Fig. 21.16
An illustration of the <u>O</u>ptions, Show <u>T</u>ags feature.

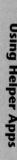

III

Using Helper Apps

Figure 21.17 illustrates the result of clicking a tag that has attributes (signaled by a little box in the tag with a hand cursor on it) with the left mouse button. Use this to check the address of a link that doesn't work.

Fig. 21.17

Illustration of looking at the attributes of an anchor <A> element.

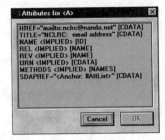

Links and Webs

In Panorama, ways to link to other information abound:

- Your basic HTML blue or colored text links via HTML anchor tags are supported. Try clicking the colored text in the body of the document until you find the color that the author used for links. Be aware however, that adding color is so easy with the style sheets that some of the color may be just for show or emphasis.

> **Caution**
>
> I haven't seen a standard HTML anchor that links to an e-mail (HREF="mailto:…") work as expected, yet. But then again, I haven't slowed down long enough to report the need to fix it either. I just didn't want you to be surprised.

- If the designer has implemented Hy-time linking (another SGML compatible standard that supports multimedia linking), you may see some small light blue circles or some very small globes. Little yellow light bulbs are likely to link to footnotes. The designer even has the option to create new icons of his choice. Try clicking every thing you see that looks unusual. There are lots of nice surprises and more to come as designers learn how to use the many features.

- Webs are ways for Panorama Pro users to create their own bookmarks, annotations, and links among/within documents. Quite frankly, we've been so busy implementing other features, we have not had a chance to do anything except look at the demos and try a time or two to see what they will do. We're excited about the possibility for both users and authors to add a Web of additional links and information. Let us know what you find if you get there before we do.

- Also click the icons and pictures in the text. To see one of my favorites, in Panorama's pandemo.sgm file, find your way via the Navigator to the "Notation Management" section and click the pictures—interesting things will happen for some of them. If a new window comes up, try clicking with the right and left mouse buttons. I leave the rest for you.

Searching

Explore the Edit, Search command for more neat goodies. When you do a search, watch inside your right scroll bar. It becomes a density barometer with little black lines wherever your term is found. The blacker it is, the more the hits. Just click the black spots to move to the hits. Also note that the hits for your search criteria are highlighted in the text.

Also note that you can now qualify your search by what SGML element the term occurs in, for example, your search criteria could be "home in <H1>". See the manual for more ways to qualify your search.

Printing, Saving, Opening (Local) Files and URLs

Unfortunately for Panorama free users, this section is short. These features are not yet available in the free version. (Quite frankly, I think that Panorama's power surprised the vendor and they had to hold back a reason for the professionals to compensate them for the power they unleashed.)

For Panorama Pro users, there is not much more to be said except these features work and function in the way a Windows or Windows 95 user would expect. From the File menu, you may select Open [local] File, Open URL, Reload, Save As ASCII file, Save As SGML file, Print, or other usual File options such as Close, Exit, or Printer Settings.

You can use the Styles, Attach Style Sheet and Style Sheet Editor illustrated earlier to set up element styles especially designed for printed output. Then you can select the Style Sheet that you created from the Styles menu, and choose File, Print from the menu to output really classy copy directly from the Web. You don't have to keep reworking the same content over and over and over again in word processing and/or publishing applications. Who needs to keep spending all your money on special products? Hmmm.

III

Using Helper Apps

## CHAPTER 22

Adobe Acrobat and Other Portable Document Formats

Every software program in the world has its own unique idea of what a data file should look like. And, consequently, the originating program is usually the only one that can read those files.

But what if you want to share files with somebody else? Maybe even with someone who owns a different kind of computer than you do? What if you want them to be able to read those files online in realtime on the World Wide Web?

You've just discovered some of the reasons for the existence of PDFs, or portable document formats.

Though the Adobe Acrobat PDF has gotten the most press, there are at least two other viable commercial portable document formats out there—Novell's Envoy and Common Ground from Common Ground Software. Not only that, there are also lots of ways to produce fairly transportable documents inexpensively. In this chapter, we examine several of these quick-and-dirty options, ranging from straight ASCII text to PostScript.

In the following pages, you learn:

- The reasons for using portable document formats
- What portable document formats exist, and how to create and view them
- How to set up Netscape to work with PDFs
- How to use ASCII text, PostScript files, and even Microsoft Word (or Windows 95 WordPad) files as cheap portable documents

Why PDFs?

To see how useful portable document formats can be, you need go no further than the World Wide Web. Web pages are created on a wide variety of platforms using a plethora of different page creation software. But the end result is a "portable document" written in HTML (HyperText Markup Language), which can be viewed on any platform with any Web browser.

> **Note**
>
> Adobe calls its Adobe Acrobat data files "Portable Document Format" files (with capitals), and the file extension for such files is .PDF. However, "portable document format" (no capitals) is in common use when referring to a portable file in any format, and PDF is the commonly used acronym for this generic term.
>
> While this can be confusing, and though we suppose that Adobe doesn't much care for it—just as Xerox Corporation doesn't want everyone referring to just any photocopy as a "xerox" (no capital)—the phrase does not appear to be trademarked by Adobe or anyone else. So we follow the common convention and use this term to refer to any and all portable document formats, not just Adobe's. When Adobe's file format is specifically referred to, we capitalize it.

Unfortunately, what a particular HTML page will end up looking like on the viewer's screen is a bit of a crap shoot. Even though HTML is a "standard," every WWW browser has its own idea of how HTML should be interpreted. Viewer windows can be sized anywhere from 640×480 to 1280×1024. Some browsers are all-text, while others can display only GIF images, and some now allow inline JPEGs and even video. Some browsers allow text to wrap around graphics, some don't. Each browser picks a different font and color set, both of which may be manually changeable by the user (see fig. 22.1).

Clearly, if you want your pages to look a certain way, you don't have much control over the end result with HTML.

What you want is something more like desktop publishing (DTP). In a desktop published document, you have very precise control (sometimes as close as .001 inch) over where elements appear on the page. Colors, images, and text wrap are all subject to your precise control. If you want this kind of control over what appears on your Web pages, then PDFs are for you.

A portable document is, in its simplest form, no more than a file that is the electronic equivalent of a printed page. A portable document keeps the on-screen display of graphics, fonts, and other page elements right where the creator put them. In short, they offer much greater visual "integrity" than HTML.

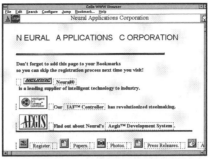
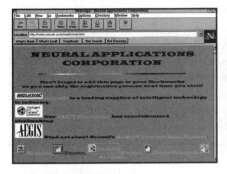

Fig. 22.1
The same HTML Web page interpreted in four very different ways. Clockwise from top left: UNIX Lynx text-only browser, Windows Cello browser, Netscape 2.0 browser (default settings), Netscape 2.0 browser (user-defined custom settings).

In addition, many PDF viewers offer special features like annotations (or "sticky notes"), HTML-like internal and external hyperlinks, and—possibly most important of all—cross-platform compatibility.

So who's that picky about their electronic documents? Try this short list for starters:

- Corporations who want to make sure their logos and "corporate identities" remain intact. Think of how much is spent each year impressing various brand names into your visual cortex, and you'll understand why companies like AT&T and McDonald's put a great deal of stock in PDFs.

- Software and hardware documentation creators, who want to make sure that information (especially tables and diagrams) remains as easy to interpret as when it left their computers.

- Government agencies like the IRS, who want to present accurate forms online.

- Marketing professionals who spend a lot of time and money creating brochures and want to make sure there are no discrepancies between their print and electronic versions.

- Instructors and trainers who don't want students messing around with prepared materials.

III

Using Helper Apps

Now that we have some good reasons for wanting to use PDFs, let's see how Netscape works with them.

How Netscape Works with PDFs

By now this should sound familiar: just as with video files, sound files, audio files, compressed files, et. al., to view portable document format files, Netscape calls upon helper applications.

▶ See "Netscape Plug-Ins," pg. 933

> **Note**
>
> *Plug-ins* are a new feature in Netscape 2.0 that may do away with some helper applications. Basically add-on viewer modules, plug-ins let Netscape display audio, video, and even PDFs inline, without having to launch helper applications. One of the first plug-ins for Netscape 2.0 is from Adobe, and it displays Acrobat PDF files in-line. The Adobe Acrobat plug-in is one of the five applications that Netscape Corporation is distributing on CD-ROM as the Netscape Power Pack ($54.95). For a detailed look at the topic of plug-ins, see chapter 36, "Netscape Plug-Ins."

A PDF is displayed using a viewer program (see fig. 22.2). Depending on the PDF type, the viewer may work only as a simple display program, or it may let you add hyperlinks and annotations.

Fig. 22.2
The Adobe Acrobat Reader program displays an accurate on-screen brochure which is unalterable by the end-user. However, the user does have control over zooming, movement, and printing.

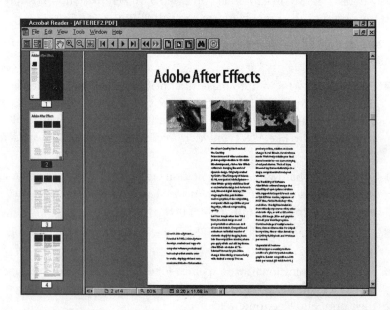

In any case, all PDF viewers are freely distributable. Naturally, the companies involved charge for their PDF file creation programs, but have to distribute the viewers for free. Otherwise, their portable documents wouldn't be very portable!

All PDF viewers let you navigate through portable documents using the keyboard keys, menu choices, or the mouse. Some let you click on small "thumbnail" images of a page or "bookmarks" to jump directly to the page you're interested in looking at. You can also load documents from disk, and print them to the printer.

All three of the PDF file viewers we talk about in this chapter—Acrobat, Envoy, and Common Ground—can be easily configured as Netscape helper applications.

PDF File Formats

Netscape recognizes PDF files the same way it identifies all the files it accesses on the Web: by MIME type first, then (if it doesn't receive a valid MIME type from the Web server it's connected to) by file name extension. (For more about MIME types, see chapter 16, "Configuring Helper Applications.")

◀ See "Configuring Helper Applications," pg. 395

Netscape doesn't natively know about any of the three portable document formats discussed in this chapter. None has an official (or even unofficial) MIME type defined for it, so we'll make up some logical ones (see table 22.1). In truth, Netscape will usually have to recognize PDFs by their file name extensions.

Note that we've left off the "x-" prefix for the Adobe Acrobat subtype, even though it's not an official MIME type. Though this is bad MIME type definition practice, there are enough sites on the Web that use the Adobe Acrobat MIME type without the "x-" in the subtype field that it has become common usage.

Table 22.1 The Three PDF File Types You Find on the World Wide Web		
Type/Subtype	**Extensions**	**Description**
application/pdf	.PDF	Adobe Acrobat
application/x-dp	.DP	Common Ground Digital Paper
application/x-evy	.EVY	Novell WordPerfect Envoy

The PDF you'll probably want to configure a helper application for is <u>underlined</u>.

III

Using Helper Apps

Adobe Acrobat

Adobe developed the Acrobat portable document format, so it's not surprising that its roots are in Adobe PostScript (see fig. 22.3). Around 1985, Adobe developed the PostScript page description language as a control language for some of the first laser printers. It became so popular among desktop publishers that a derivative, EPS or Encapsulated PostScript, became a common format for DTP clipart files. When the need arose for a truly portable document format for live display on computer media, Adobe turned again to PostScript to provide the base.

However, Acrobat is not PostScript. PostScript files are 100% text, but Acrobat files include blocks of non-human-readable LZW-compressed data. Though Acrobat is also a page description language, it is definitely a generation beyond PostScript.

Fig. 22.3
Adobe Acrobat
Reader v2.1
displays an
Acrobat brochure.
You can navigate
to different pages
by clicking on the
thumbnail images
at left.

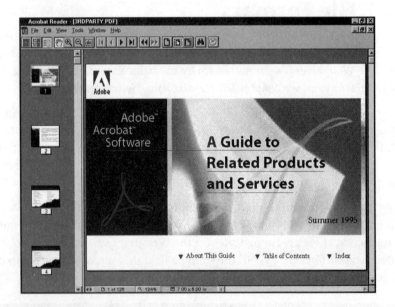

Creating Adobe Acrobat PDF Files

Acrobat .PDF format files are created using one of Adobe's commercial programs listed in table 22.2.

Table 22.2 The Adobe Acrobat Commercial Software Lineup	
Program	**Use**
Adobe Acrobat Capture	For scanning "legacy" documents and converting them to PDF format
Acrobat Exchange	Create .PDF documents, and add internal or external (URL) links, annotations, and security to PDF files (package includes PDF Writer, Search, and Reader programs)
Acrobat PDF Writer	A "virtual printer" driver that lets you print PDF files to disk from any application, like Aldus PageMaker or Microsoft Word
Acrobat Pro	Includes everything in Acrobat Exchange plus Acrobat Distiller, which converts PostScript files to PDF documents
Acrobat Catalog	Creates full-text indexes for PDF documents (included in Acrobat for Workgroups 10-user site license)
Acrobat Search	Lets you search through PDF files that have been indexed with Acrobat Catalog

For current pricing, or to view product brochures in Acrobat format, check out Adobe's World Wide Web site at **http://www.adobe.com.**

Displaying Adobe Acrobat PDF Files

You display Acrobat PDF files using the Adobe Acrobat Reader (version 2.1). Though all the document creation programs listed above are for sale, the reader is freely-distributable. It can be downloaded from Adobe's World Wide Web site at **http://www.adobe.com**/, and a copy is included on the CD-ROM supplied with this book. Versions are available for Macintosh, Windows, and UNIX platforms. There's even a v1.0 Acrobat Reader for MS-DOS.

On the CD

The Acrobat Reader can be configured as a Netscape helper application for the MIME type application/pdf with the file extension .PDF (see fig. 22.4). There are currently enough sites out there on the Web with .PDF files available that it makes sense to go ahead and configure the Acrobat Reader as a helper application.

III

Using Helper Apps

Fig. 22.4

The Adobe
Acrobat Reader
features user-
configurable
indexing, zoom,
and printing
options.

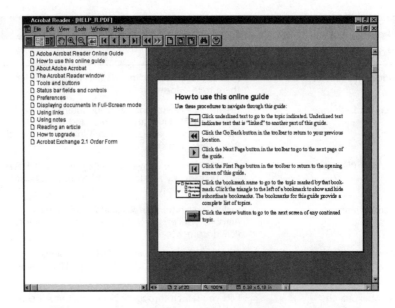

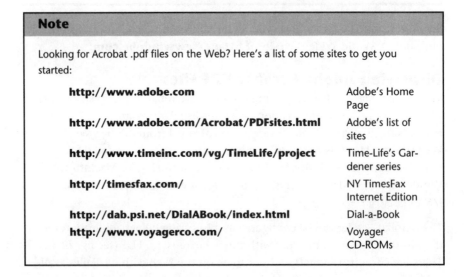

Note

Looking for Acrobat .pdf files on the Web? Here's a list of some sites to get you
started:

http://www.adobe.com	Adobe's Home Page
http://www.adobe.com/Acrobat/PDFsites.html	Adobe's list of sites
http://www.timeinc.com/vg/TimeLife/project	Time-Life's Gardener series
http://timesfax.com/	NY TimesFax Internet Edition
http://dab.psi.net/DialABook/index.html	Dial-a-Book
http://www.voyagerco.com/	Voyager CD-ROMs

The Acrobat Reader lets you pick a number of different zoom views of a .PDF
document. You can print the current page, a range of pages, or the whole
document to any Windows-configured printer—not just PostScript. The
Acrobat Reader also displays add-on notes, though you need the Acrobat
Exchange program to add them. You can copy text or graphics from PDF
documents to the Windows clipboard, then paste them into your favorite

Windows applications. You can even search for text, and display up to 10 documents at once.

Two "plug-in" modules are included with the Acrobat Reader. The Acrobat Movie plug-in plays QuickTime movies that are imbedded in PDF files (see fig. 22.5).

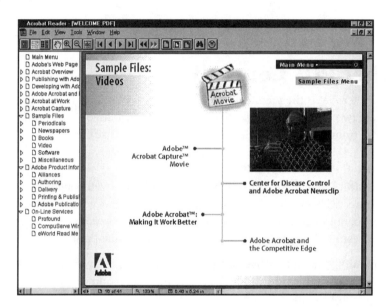

Fig. 22.5
In this Acrobat promotional file, a Quicktime movie (upper right) embedded in the .PDF file reports how the Center for Disease Control uses Acrobat to distribute time-critical disease reports to the world via the Internet.

The Weblink plug-in creates a link to your Web browser so that links can be included in Acrobat documents to URLs on the Web—when you click one, the Acrobat Reader launches Netscape and connects you to the linked site. Both plug-ins are totally automatic—you don't need to install them. The only thing you will need to do is let the Weblink plug-in know where to locate Netscape on your system. Here's how:

1. Choose Edit, Preferences, Weblink from the Acrobat Reader menu. You get the dialog shown in figure 22.6.

2. Click the Browse button and find your Netscape executable using the file dialog that appears. It's probably C:\program files\netscape\navigator\program\netscape.exe. Select the file name and click OK.

3. Click the Weblink Preferences OK button to finish.

III

Using Helper Apps

Fig. 22.6
The Acrobat Reader's Weblink Preferences dialog lets you set up the Reader to use Netscape for live URL links in Acrobat documents.

Other PDF Contenders

Though Acrobat is the premiere PDF in use on the World Wide Web today, there are two others also in use: Novell's WordPerfect Envoy, and Common Ground, from Common Ground Software. Each has its strong points.

Novell's WordPerfect Envoy

WordPerfect Envoy ended up a part of Novell when Novell bought WordPerfect Corporation. That may have hurt any chance it might have had to "be a contender" in the portable document format race, in that Envoy doesn't seem to have made it onto Novell's number-one-priority list.

Incorporating technology licensed from Tumbleweed Software Corporation, Envoy document files are said by Novell to be smaller and display faster than its competitor, Adobe Acrobat.

Without converting the same file to both formats and evaluating them side-by-side, this is difficult to determine. The Envoy .evy format files I've seen have all been smaller and seemed to have as much content as similar .pdf Acrobat files, but that doesn't necessarily mean that smaller size for Envoy files is a universal truth. However, the Envoy Viewer installation on my hard drive is certainly smaller than the Acrobat Reader installation: 1.2MB for the Envoy Viewer directory, vs. 2.6MB for the Acrobat Reader directory.

The Envoy Viewer is available for Macintosh and Windows (see fig. 22.7). It has all the basic features of the Acrobat Reader, and then some. It also allows you to highlight text, add annotations or "sticky notes," and attach files to Envoy documents using Windows OLE (Object Linking and Embedding). This means that an entire workgroup can use the free Viewer program to mark up and comment on an Envoy document; only the document originator has to have the purchased Envoy Publisher program to create the original document. To do the same with Acrobat, you would need to buy a copy of the Acrobat Exchange program for each workgroup member, at $195 apiece.

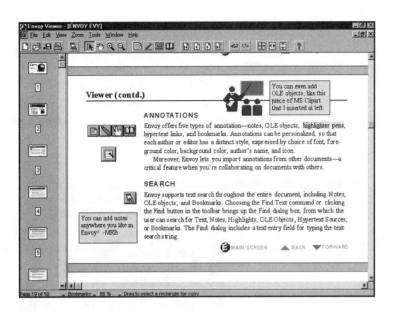

Fig. 22.7
Novell's free
WordPerfect
Envoy Viewer
program lets you
add notes and
links to any Envoy
document.

Envoy Publisher (which is included in Novell's Perfect Office program suite, or can be purchased separately) is simply a "virtual printer" driver for any Windows application; it's identical in function to Adobe's Acrobat PDF Writer. It can also be configured to save an Envoy file as a self-running document—that is, one with the viewer permanently built-in.

If you get the idea that I'm a bit more impressed with Envoy than Acrobat, you're right. If this book were about which portable document format product to invest in for your office, I'd heartily recommend Envoy over Acrobat. But it's not. It's about portable document formats for the World Wide Web. And the truth is, Adobe Acrobat is getting lots of exposure on the Web, while I have yet to see anything much at all in the way of Envoy files on any sites other than Novell's. So for the time being, at least, there is no real need to set up Envoy as a helper application for Netscape, unless you run into a site or sites that interest you which have files in Envoy format.

The latest version of the Envoy Viewer is available from **http:// www.novell.com/**.

Common Ground and "Digital Paper"

"Digital Paper" is such a cool phrase, I wish I'd thought of it myself. But I didn't. It's Common Ground Software's term for their portable document format files, which are displayed using the freely-distributable Common Ground Mini Viewer program.

Using Helper Apps

III

The Common Ground Mini Viewer, available for Mac and Windows, has the distinction of being the smallest of the three commercial viewers discussed in this chapter by far: only 243KB (see fig. 22.8). It is also the most limited, allowing only navigation, zoom, and printing options. To be able to highlight text, add bookmarks, add "sticky note" annotations, create links, etc., you'll have to purchase the Common Ground ProViewer. To actually create Digital Paper documents requires the commercial Common Ground document editing program.

Fig. 22.8
The Common Ground Mini Viewer displays "Digital Paper" documents.

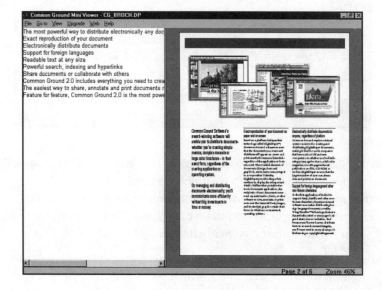

Common Ground Software has managed to ally itself with some heavy hitters in the PC marketplace—I would probably have never heard of Digital Paper if it hadn't been for the fact that Apple's Quicktime player documentation is distributed in Common Ground's format, and the Mini Viewer is included right alongside in the Quicktime ZIP file.

Still, there aren't enough Digital Paper files on the Web yet that you need to worry about configuring the Mini Viewer as a Netscape helper application, unless you happen to run into some Digital Paper format files during your journeys on the Web.

The latest version of the Common Ground Mini Viewer can be downloaded from Common Ground's Web site at **http:// www.commonground.com/**. A 30-day demo version of the Common Ground page creation program (approx. 7MB) is also available for downloading from this site.

The Bare Bones: Free, More-or-Less Portable File Formats

There is one disadvantage to using any of the commercial portable document formats discussed so far in this chapter—you can view them for free, but to create them you need to purchase a commercial document editor from Adobe, Novell, or Common Ground.

"Isn't there something that's almost as good, but free?" you ask. The answer is a qualified "yes."

To create and distribute truly free and portable documents, you have to sacrifice something: ease of use, document complexity, or degree of portability.

Table 22.3 lists the MIME types of several more-or-less portable document formats that Netscape is aware of.

Table 22.3 Portable File Types Recognized by Netscape		
Type/Subtype	**Extensions**	**Description**
text/plain	.TXT, .TEXT	ASCII text
application/rtf	.RTF	Rich Text Format
application/x-tex	.TEX	TeX typesetting files
application/postscript	.AI, .EPS, .PS	Adobe PostScript

ASCII Text

Probably the most portable of all file formats is straight ASCII text. Windows Notepad creates, reads, and saves ASCII text, as do a myriad of other programs on all platforms. ASCII text can be displayed directly in an MS-DOS or UNIX shell using the TYPE <filename> or MORE <filename> commands. It is by far the oldest of all "portable document" formats.

All an ASCII text file can contain is text, numbers, and punctuation marks—no graphics, no fancy formatting, no colorful fonts. But if the information you want to transmit is nothing but text, you can certainly send it as an ASCII .TXT file and be assured that just about anyone will be able to read it.

Netscape is set up to display MIME type text/plain ASCII text files with the extensions right in the Netscape window (see fig. 22.9). You don't need to do anything else to be able to display them.

To create, edit, or print .TXT files, all you need is Windows Notepad. You can also save files in ASCII text format from Microsoft Word or Win95's WordPad (as well as many other word processors) by selecting File, Save As from the menu, and then Save as type: Text Only [*.txt] from the Save As dialog box.

Fig. 22.9
Netscape displays
generic ASCII text
in its main display
window.

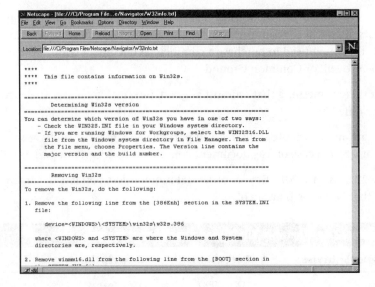

Rich Text Format

Rich Text Format (RTF) files are a giant step above ASCII text. Besides regular alphabetic, numeric, and punctuation characters, RTF files contain control sequences with formatting information for the file. This can include special characters not normally available in ASCII files, commands to insert footnotes or change paragraph formatting, etc. In fact, RTF files can include colors, fonts, graphics, and all the other elements that make documents interesting.

RTF files are not often seen on the Web, but there is no reason for them not to be. The fact that Netscape can recognize the RTF format right out of the box means that at least someone at Netscape Corporation thinks it's a viable format for use on the Web.

Microsoft Word can display RTF files, as can the WordPad program shipped with Win95. You can set up either program as a Netscape helper application for the MIME type application/rtf with the file extension .RTF.

Word and WordPad can also be used to create RTF files. To save a file in RTF format from either program, select File, Save As from the menu, and then Save as type: Rich Text Format [*.rtf] from the Save As dialog box, and click the Save button (see fig. 22.10).

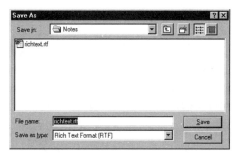

Fig. 22.10
Microsoft WordPad, shipped with Win95, can create, load, and save files in Rich Text Format. The Save As... dialog lets you choose the RTF file format (lower left of dialog box).

Microsoft Word Documents

At this point you might ask, "Why not just use Microsoft Word documents instead of RTF files?" Why not, indeed?

I've seen dozens of sites on the Web that haven't even bothered to translate their MS Word files into any other format. They just distribute them as Word .doc files. After all, it is the most popular word processor on the planet, so the odds are good that your intended recipient will own a copy of Word (or Win95's free WordPad program, which can also handle Word files) anyway.

Not only that, but Microsoft has, out of the goodness of their huge corporate heart, chosen to distribute a free stand-alone viewer for Word documents (see fig. 22.11). So now, everyone (at least, everyone with the Windows operating system) can easily view MS Word documents.

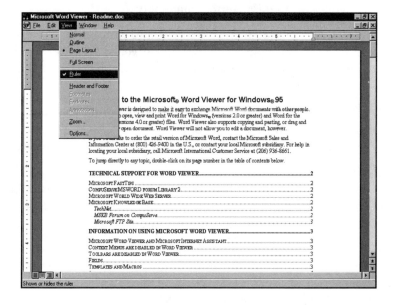

Fig. 22.11
Microsoft's freely-distributable WordView program displays a Word document.

III

Using Helper Apps

WordView is pretty bare-bones. It only loads Word .doc files and ASCII text .txt files (unfortunately, it won't handle RTF files). You can scroll around through a document, and pick your zoom level, as well as choosing normal, outline, or page layout views. You have control over page margins and printing options, and can copy text or graphics to paste into other applications. That's it. If you want more features, you'll have to buy a copy of Word.

The version of WordView shown in figure 22.11 is for Windows 95, but a Windows 3.1 version of WordView is also available. The latest versions of both can be downloaded from **http://www.microsoft.com/msoffice/ freestuf/msword/download/viewers/default.htm**.

> **Tip**
>
> Not all .DOC files are MD Word documents! Many are simply ASCII text documentation files for programs. This is usually not a problem, since Word, WordPad, and WordView also display ASCII text just fine.

TeX

TeX is a typesetting language originally developed by computer guru Donald Knuth to ease the process of typesetting complex mathematical formulas in his series of definitive computer programming books. It has since gained a tremendous following in the scientific community.

Netscape recognizes four MIME file types associated with TeX: application/x-tex, x-texinfo, x-dvi, and x-latex. However, unless you're a scientist yourself, the odds are good that you'll never, ever have to worry about encountering TeX documents on the Web.

TeX combines the complexity of typesetting with all the quirks and depth of a major programming language. It is not for the weak of heart. You should only delve into TeX if you have a great need for absolutely precise typesetting.

That being said, there are public domain implementations of TeX available on the Web for most platforms, along with TeX helpers like LaTeX and HyperTex, TeX fonts, and all the utilities and help files you need to get involved.

If TeX sounds like something you should be involved with, you can find out more through the UseNet newsgroup comp.text.tex; a FAQ is posted monthly. Another excellent resource is CTAN, the Comprehensive TeX

Archive Network at **http://jasper.ora.com/ctan.html**. Yahoo also maintains a good index of TeX resources at **http://www.yahoo.com/ Computers_and_Internet/Desktop_Publishing/TeX/**.

PostScript

As we mentioned in our discussion of Acrobat earlier in this chapter, Adobe developed PostScript as a laser printer control language sometime around 1985. It became immensely popular, and today you'll find thousands of .PS PostScript files on the Web.

> **Note**
>
> You can find out more about PostScript by checking out the PostScript FAQ (Frequently Asked Questions) list on UseNet. You can retrieve the latest version by pointing Netscape to **ftp://wilma.cs.brown.edu/pub/comp.lang.postscript/**.
>
> Adobe maintains an FTP site with lots of information on PostScript at **ftp:// ftp.adobe.com/pub/adobe**.
>
> More information can also be obtained by reading the UseNet newsgroups comp.lang.postscript and comp.sources.postscript.

Creating PostScript Files

PostScript is actually a programming language based on Forth, a control language often used to control industrial machinery. PostScript files are just ASCII text files; you can (and many do) write and modify PostScript program files by hand using a text editor like Notepad. Of course, you have to know and understand the entire PostScript programming language to be able to do so.

An easier way is to let your application programs—like Microsoft Word, FrameMaker, and Adobe Illustrator—create PostScript files for you. To do so, you need to set up a PostScript printer driver to print to a file on disk. Here's how to do this under Windows 95:

1. Open My Computer, then Printers. Double-click the Add Printers icon, and you'll get the Add Printers Wizard (see fig. 22.11).

2. Follow the Wizard's instructions to set up a PostScript Printer. The Apple LaserWriter is a good choice, because it's considered to be the baseline, generic PostScript device.

3. When you are asked to choose a port, select FILE:. This will create a PostScript file on disk whenever you use the Apple LaserWriter printer driver.

4. If you already have an Apple LaserWriter configured as a printer for Windows, you can temporarily change the driver's configuration by right-clicking on the Apple LaserWriter icon in the Printers window and selecting Properties from the pop-up menu. You'll get the dialog box shown in figure 22.12 (on the left). Click the Details tab to bring it to the front, then select FILE: as the port. Click OK to finish.

Fig. 22.12
Use the printer setup dialog box or wizard to configure Windows to create PostScript files from application programs.

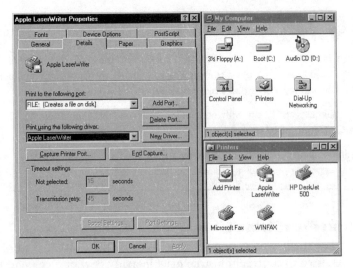

Once you have set up the Apple LaserWriter driver to print to FILE:, you can create a PostScript file using any of your Windows applications. Just print to the Apple LaserWriter and you'll be presented with a file dialog asking for a name for the PostScript file you're about to create. This file can then be used by anyone who has a PostScript printer or an on-screen PostScript viewer.

> **Note**
>
> If you have a PostScript file that you think would look good as a Web page, you can convert it using utilities created at Johns Hopkins University.
>
> The process is straightforward but involves a couple of steps. First, you convert the PostScript .ps file to straight ASCII text using a program called PS2ASCII. This output is then fed through a Perl script called PS2HTML. There are various caveats and exceptions to be aware of, so it's best to get the details from the Johns Hopkins server first.
>
> Information and executables can be had from **ftp://bradley.bradley.edu/pub/ guru/ps2html/ps2html-v2.html**.

Aladdin Ghostscript

Reading PostScript files online is a bit of a problem. Since PostScript is basically a printer control language, it's easy to create a hard-copy printout of a PostScript file—you just copy it to a PostScript printer. But reading a PostScript file online means you basically have to emulate a PostScript printer on your computer screen. Not that it can't be done. But it does take a suite of applications and support files to do it.

You need at least three different elements: a PostScript language interpreter, a set of PostScript Type 1 fonts (which every PostScript printer contains in its internal memory), and a viewer program to display the results.

Fortunately, the freely-distributable Aladdin Ghostscript interpreter has all of these elements, and more.

To set up Ghostscript, you need to download four files from **http://www.cs.wisc.edu/~ghost/index.html** (or just get them off of the book CD-ROM). When unarchived and installed, they provide all of the elements mentioned above. (I know we said three elements—the extra file is for the documentation.)

Ghostscript itself is a command-line-driven PostScript interpreter. Though you can feed it commands directly, that's not the easiest way to use it. The best way is to set up the GSView on-screen PostScript viewer program (see fig. 22.13) to use as a front end.

GSView is literally an on-screen PostScript printer emulator. With it, you can load and view PostScript printer files, zoom in and out, jump back and forth, search for text, and send the file to any printer. Yes, any printer, not just a PostScript printer (see fig. 22.14). It's the cheapest way I know of to get a fully functional PostScript printer on your desk. (GSView supports dozens of printers, so it's very unlikely that you'll not be able to find a driver that works well with your printer.)

GSView will also convert PostScript to EPS (Encapsulated PostScript) clip art format, and can extract text from a .PS file.

Note

One of the files in the Ghostscript distribution provides you with reasonable facsimiles of the 35 fonts generally provided with PostScript printers. You can also configure Ghostscript to work with additional downloaded Adobe Type 1 fonts. A good online pointer to free downloadable Type 1 fonts is the Internet Font Archives at **http://jasper.ora.com/comp.fonts/Internet-Font-Archive/index.html**.

Fig. 22.13
GSView (top left) is the on-screen PostScript viewer program that acts as a GUI for the Ghostscript PostScript language interpreter (bottom right).

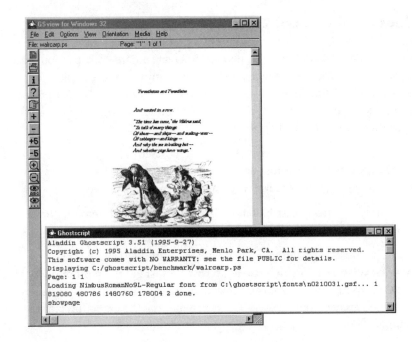

Fig. 22.14
The GSView printer selection dialog, which you see when you select File, Print from the menu.

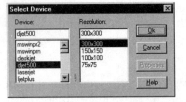

The on-screen display is faithful to the printed page, which is of very high quality. In fact, I'm willing to bet that you will be astounded at the print quality your faithful old dot-matrix or inkjet printer (color or black-and-white) can produce under Ghostscript control. And if you have an HP-compatible laser printer, the results will be virtually indistinguishable from an expensive PostScript printer.

GSView can, of course, be configured as a Netscape helper application for the MIME type application/postscript, with file extensions .PS, .EPS, and .AI. In fact, I heartily suggest that you do so.

CHAPTER 23

Using Compressed/ Encoded Files

File compression and encoding are not two of the most exciting topics you'll encounter on the Internet. Both are file conversion operations you'll likely perform sooner or later, but let's face it, they are about as exciting as watching grass grow.

You might be able to avoid binary file encoding if you have absolutely no interest in newsgroups, but you'll find it nearly impossible to escape using compressed files, especially considering the number of examples of .ZIP archive files that are used just in this book.

In this chapter, you learn:

- How Netscape works with compressed and encoded files
- What types of compressed files, beside .ZIP, you are likely to encounter on the Internet
- How to convert compressed and encoded files
- Where to find (or how to locate) the Netscape helper applications you need

What Is File Compression and How Is It Done?

Explaining file compression is relatively easy. Simply stated, it is a method of reducing the size of one or more files so the files can either be stored in a smaller space, or transmitted in a shorter time and later returned to their "normal" size. The .ZIP files (also called *archive* files) that are mentioned through this text are examples of one type of compressed archive file.

File compression works by examining a file for repeating characters (or bytes) or repeating sequences of characters, removing those repeating characters, and replacing them with a symbol representing how many characters were in the original sequence.

Here is a highly simplified example of how basic file compression works. For example, suppose a compression program examined a file and found the following sequence of characters:

XmmP XmmP XmmP AAAA AAAA XmmP XmmP XmmP AAAA AAAA AAAA

This sequence of characters could be replaced with the following representation:

3(Xmmp) 2(AAAA) 3(Xmmp) 3(AAAA)

Or, it could be replaced with this representation:

2(3(Xmmp) 2(AAAA)) 4(A)

In this example, the original character sequence is 55 characters (bytes) long (counting the trailing space). The first representation is only 32 characters long, and 58 percent as large as the original sequence. The second representation is only 24 characters long, and 43.6 percent as large as the original sequence.

Either of these "compressed" representations of the original character sequence can be used to re-create the original.

This is a highly simplified description of what is correctly referred to as a *substitutional compression scheme*. To paraphrase from several FAQs (specifically, Frequently Asked Questions 1/3, 2/3, 3/3) in the newsgroup **comp.compression**: The basic idea behind a substitutional compression scheme is to replace an occurrence of a byte sequence in a piece of data, with a reference to a previous occurrence of that sequence. There are two main classes of these schemes, named after Abraham Lempel and Jacob Ziv, who first proposed these schemes in '77 and '78.

The Lempel-Ziv 77 & 78 compression schemes have been the basis from which the following other compression schemes have been derived:

- LZ77 with hashing
- LZ77 using a tree data structure

- LZ77 with a history buffer
- LZRW1
- LZRW3-A
- LZFG

The original LZ77 scheme is the foundation on which many of the well known PC compression programs are built (for example, .ARJ, .LHZ, .ZIP).

Another popular compression algorithm that has spawned numerous derivations is called Huffman coding. Here's a reasonably accurate description of the Huffman coding scheme also paraphrased from several FAQs in the newsgroup comp.compression:

Huffman coding is a statistical data compression technique that reduces the average code length used to represent the symbols of an alphabet. Huffman coding is an example of a compression scheme that is optimal in the case where all symbol probabilities are integral powers of 1/2.

While all of the compression algorithms and their derivatives mentioned in this chapter perform the same basic function, they differ in how they sample the data they are compressing, and record exactly what data have been substituted and compressed.

What's important to remember is that you don't have to understand how compression schemes work their magic in order to use compression utilities. If, however, you have a greater interest in file compression and want more detailed information, check out the FAQs in the newsgroup comp.compression (for more information on reading FAQs in newsgroups, see chapter 15, "Reading UseNet Newsgroups with Netscape").

◀ See "Reading UseNet Newsgroups with Netscape," pg. 371

Compression Applications

Now that we've gotten past the theoretical, it's time to get down to the practical side of file compression, which is basically deciding what works best and getting that up and running.

Since Netscape is totally incapable of working with compressed archive files, you need another program to decompress archive files you download from FTP sites.

There are numerous programs you can set up in Windows, either 3.1 or 95, or DOS to work with Netscape to compress and decompress files. One of the best is WinZip, a Windows-based version of the popular PKZIP file compression utility.

WinZip

On the CD

WinZip, by Nico Mak Computing, is a shareware product patterned after the highly successful and ubiquitous DOS-based file compression utility PKZIP. Without a doubt you will find WinZip to be a highly useful and versatile Windows-based application for many of the following reasons:

- The vast majority of compressed files you are likely to download from FTP sites are in a .ZIP archive format.

- WinZip supports the native .ZIP format without the need for PKZIP or PKUNZIP, and also supports the .ARJ, .LZH, and .ARC file compression formats in the PC environment.

- WinZip is a Windows application and easily integrates into your Windows environment.

- WinZip 6.0 is a 32-bit application designed to work in the Windows 95 32-bit environment and supports numerous Windows 95 features, including long file names.

- WinZip also decompresses other popular Internet compression formats such as TAR, gzip, and UNIX compress.

In figure 23.1, you see the main operating screen for WinZip, version 6.0.

Fig. 23.1
WinZip 6.0 is the Windows 95 version of the popular file compression utility.

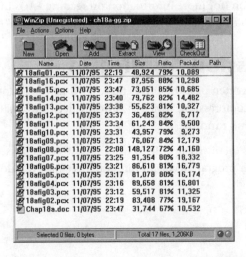

You can find WinZip on the WinZip page at **http://www.winzip.com/ winzip/index.html** (see fig. 23.2).

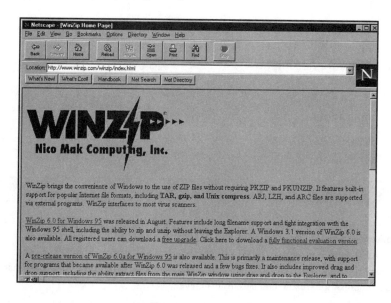

Fig. 23.2
The WinZip home page.

Installing WinZip

Because WinZip is a Windows-based program, you install and use it the same as most other Windows programs. To install the Windows 95 version of WinZip 6.0:

1. Copy the self-extracting archive file Winzip95.exe into a temporary folder and run the file to extract the installation files from the archive.

2. Run SETUP.EXE to install WinZip.

Using WinZip

Using WinZip to compress files into an archive is fairly simple:

1. Start WinZip and select File, New Archive, press Ctrl+N, or select the New icon.

2. Give the archive a name and select the folder (or directory) where you want the archive file stored.

3. Select the files you want to compress and place them in the archive. Select OK.

You can also configure it in Netscape to work as a helper application (for more information on helper applications, see chapter 16, "Configuring Helper Applications").

◄ See "Configuring Helper Applications," pg. 395

III

Using Helper Apps

You will want to use the following types:

- application/zip
- application/tar
- application/gzip
- application/x-compress

You will also want to create the following types:

- application/arc
- application/arj
- application/lzh

> **Note**
>
> Even though WinZip performs basic archiving operations without outside help, some advanced archiving features do require PKZIP and PKUNZIP from PKware, Inc., LHA.EXE from Haruyasu Yoshizaki, or the Shareware ARJ product from Robert Jung. Mainly these advanced archiving features center around creating archives rather than decompressing or extracting files from archives.

You can also create what are called *self-extracting archive files* using the WinZip Self-Extractor utility. A self-extracting archive file decompresses the files stored in its archive without the need for WinZip. This is becoming a popular method for distributing software. Netscape distributes its software products over the Internet in self-extracting archive files.

Self-extracting archive files have an .EXE extension instead of the .ZIP extension and are "run" the same as you would any other executable program to decompress the files stored in its archive. The WinZip Self-Extractor utility can also be downloaded from the WinZip home page.

PKZIP

PKZIP, created by Phil Katz, is one of the oldest file compression utilities in the PC/DOS world and by far the most widely used. Before it was PKZIP it was PKPAK and was designed to work with the .ARC archiving format, but a legal dispute with the creator of the original ARC compression program led to the creation of PKZIP and the now ubiquitous .ZIP format. Figure 23.3 shows PKZIP and some of its compression options.

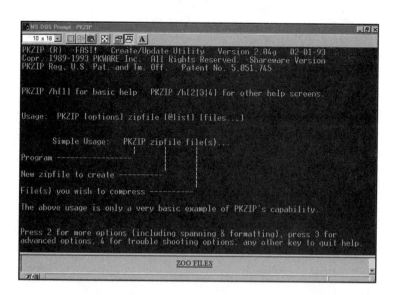

Fig. 23.3
PKZIP and the first of its three command-line help screens displaying its numerous file compression options.

PKZIP is a DOS-based program and is probably best run from a DOS prompt, but can also work in Windows in a DOS window. If you choose to configure Netscape to use PKZIP as a helper app, only configure it for type application/zip.

You can get a copy of PKZIP at **http://www.mid.net/MSDOS_A/ 00-files.html**. The programs that make up the PKZIP utilities come pre-packaged in the file PKZ204G.EXE, which is a self-extracting archive.

To install the PKZIP utilities, merely copy the decompressed files into a directory or folder that is included in your PATH statement.

ARC Files

PKPAK is the predecessor to PKZIP. This is the archiving/compression utility Phil Katz was sued over by the creator of the original ARC archiver. The terms of the settlement were sealed, but shortly after the settlement was reached Katz released PKZIP, which subsequently captured the lion's share of the PC/DOS file compression market. PKPAK can still be found on a few FTP sites and BBSs, and occasionally you still run across archive files with the .ARC extension. Figure 23.4 shows PKPAK and its file compression options.

PKPAK can also be downloaded from **http://www.mid.net/MSDOS_A/ 00-files.html** (see fig. 23.5) packaged as PK361.EXE, which is a self-extracting archive file.

III

Using Helper Apps

Fig. 23.4
PKPAK produces
the .ARC archive
file format.

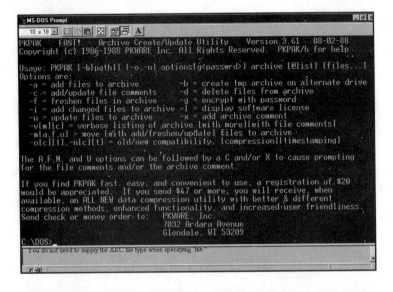

Fig. 23.5
Archiving Web
page covering file
compression
utilities from soup
to nuts.

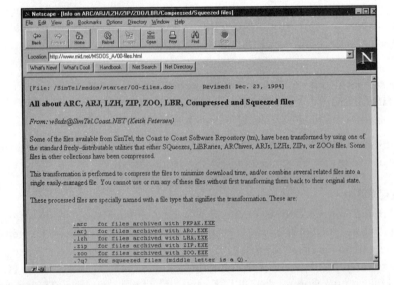

ARJ Files

ARJ, shown in figure 23.6, is yet another DOS-based archiving utility that is involved in archiving a fairly insignificant percentage of DOS-based archives (insignificant when compared to the percentage usage of PKZIP and PKPAK). Its main claim to fame is being fast and producing fairly small archives. You can download the complete ARJ utility as ARJ241.EXE from **http:// www.mid.net/MSDOS_A/00-files.html**. The file ARJ241.exe is a self-extracting ARJ archive file.

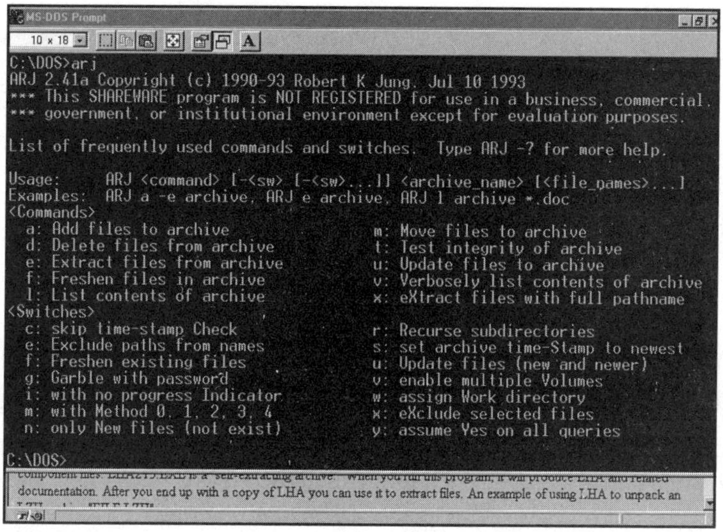

Fig. 23.6
The ARJ file
compression
utility.

LHA

Another competitor still in the PC/DOS file compression race is LHA, shown
in figure 23.7, by Haruyasu Yoshizaki. Despite the dominance by PKZIP, LHA
still maintains a small, loyal following, mainly because LHA is small, fast, and
free. It is distributed as freeware, not shareware. You can download a copy of
LHA version 2.13 from **http://www.mid.net/MSDOS_A/00-files.html**.
The file name to download is LHA213.EXE, which is a self-extracting archive
file.

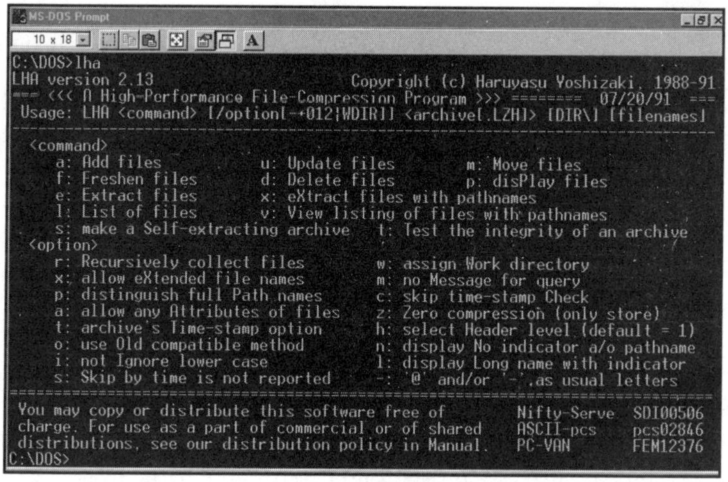

Fig. 23.7
The LHA file
compression
utility.

> **Tip**
>
> Besides downloading WinZip, go ahead and also download PKZIP, PKPAK, ARJ, and LHA. Install WinZip and use it as your primary archiving utility, but keep the other files handy because sooner or later, especially if you frequently download files from FTP sites and BBSs, you will run across a file requiring one of these DOS-based archivers.

The Hows and Whys of File Encoding and Decoding

While file compression can be viewed as a convenience (you really don't have to save time and space), file encoding and decoding are a necessity. File encoding grew out of the need to be able to post binary files on UseNet newsgroups.

The first UseNet was created in 1979 between Duke and the University of North Carolina using UUCP (UNIX-to-UNIX Communications Protocol, also called UNIX-to-UNIX CoPy). Then as now, UseNet was only set up to copy 7-bit ASCII files, since originally only text files (messages) were intended to be posted and sent between UseNet systems. Posting binary files presented a problem. Binary files, such as programs, graphic files, and even compressed archive files, require 8 bits. So in order to post binary files to newsgroups, either you change newsgroups to work with 8-bit files, or you need a means of converting 8-bit binary files to 7-bit ASCII files. The solution is what has been termed *UUEncoding*—encoding 8-bit binary files to a 7-bit ASCII text file format (and *UUDecoding* to convert the ASCII files back into their original binary format). Figure 23.8 shows what an encoded binary looks like.

> **Tip**
>
> As you might guess, whenever you encode a binary file to ASCII, the result is a larger file since it often takes several "text" characters to represent binary information. For this reason, it is a common practice to compress binary files before encoding them.

Another limitation of UseNet carried over from its earlier days is a 32KB limit on file and message size because some early computers could only handle files up to this size. This file and message size limitation is why you often see long messages and large files broken into two or more parts.

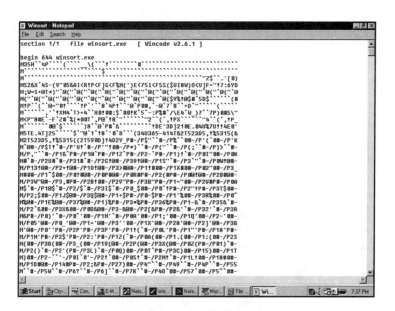

Fig. 23.8
A binary file encoded into 7-bit ASCII.

> **Note**
>
> Even though many newsgroup users still adhere to the 32KB limit on file and message size, many newer systems are not restricted by this limitation, so you still see files and messages exceeding 32KB.

Initially (back in the olden days of UNIX shell accounts), separate utility programs were used for encoding (UUEncode) binary to ASCII, and decoding (UUDecode) ASCII back to binary. This also meant that if you received the encoded file in several pieces, you had to edit the text file pieces back into one file before you could decode the ASCII file back into a binary format. You were lucky if the encoding program you were using had enough smarts to be able to put the pieces back together. Fortunately, now many newsreaders have built-in UUEncode/UUDecode functionality, allowing you to download/view or upload/attach binary files on the fly (and put the pieces back together). Netscape has thoughtfully included this functionality in its newsreader.

Encoding/Decoding with Netscape's Newsreader

In this chapter, we concentrate on encoding and decoding binary files using Netscape's newsreader and not on how to use Netscape's newsreader. (For more information on using Netscape's newsreader, see chapter 15, "Reading UseNet Newsgroups with Netscape.")

◀ See "Reading UseNet Newsgroups with Netscape," pg. 371

III

Using Helper Apps

Many of the binary files you see posted in newsgroups are pictures—pictures of animals, pictures of places and things, pictures of outer space, and lots and lots of pictures of people, mostly famous. A large percentage of the pictures you see posted are in either JPEG format (.JPG, .JPE, .JPEG) or in GIF format (.GIF).

Decoding a Binary File

Netscape's newsreader, like the Netscape Web browser, is configured to display JPEG and GIF files without using a helper application. This means that whenever you see a JPEG or GIF file posted, you can download the file by double-clicking it, and when the download completes, the Netscape newsreader immediately displays the file (see fig. 23.9).

Fig. 23.9

The Netscape newsreader displaying the USS Enterprise NCC-1701D.

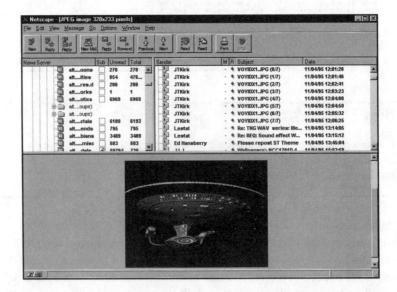

Encoding a Binary File

Just as the Netscape newsreader is configured to decode binary files on the fly, you can also use it to encode binary files you want to post to newsgroups. You create a message the same as you normally would and click Attach. When you attach the file, select the Convert to Plain Text radio button (see fig. 23.10).

Fig. 23.10
Encoding attached
binary (.JPG) file.

Getting Your Encoded Files Decoded

If you have problems with Netscape's newsreader encoding or decoding your
binary files, or if you have another newsreader you are absolutely in love
with and refuse to switch to Netscape's newsreader no matter what, there are
a number of encoding/decoding utilities available that let you encode and decode files manually.

There are a few you can find on FTP sites, and as we stated earlier, encoding
and decoding files is not flashy or sexy, and may just be slightly more exciting than watching paint dry.

WinCode

WinCode is one of two Windows-based encoding/decoding programs explained in this chapter, which you can use to manually encode or decode binary files (see fig. 23.11). WinCode is distributed as freeware, but the author
charges $5.00 if you want the Help file.

On the CD

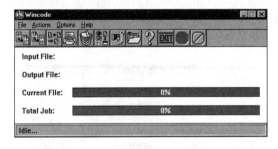

Fig. 23.11
WinCode, a simple
Windows-based
encoding/
decoding applica-
tion.

III

Using Helper Apps

Install WinCode from the CD that accompanies this book. You can accept
the defaults during the installation.

Start WinCode to open its main operating screen. From WinCode's main operating screen, you perform all basic encoding and decoding operations as

well as set options for both. WinCode creates a status report after each file coding operation you perform so you can see if there were any problems (see fig. 23.12).

Fig. 23.12
WinCode's file operation status report.

WinCode can also use PKZIP to archive large binary files prior to encoding. Select Zip/Unzip on the Options menu.

UUCode

UUCode is another fairly simple, UUEncoding/UUDecoding utility, much like WinCode. UUCode is distributed as shareware, which you can register for between $4 and $10, depending on whether you are registering a new copy or updating from an earlier version.

Install UUCode from the CD that accompanies this book. You can accept the defaults during the installation.

UUCode's screen is even simpler than WinCode's but is more than adequate for encoding and decoding binary files. UUCode can also be configured depending on how you need to encode files (see fig. 23.13).

Fig. 23.13
UUCode's encoding configuration screen.

Unlike WinCode, UUCode does ship with a Help file that explains the finer details of how the program functions (see fig. 23.14).

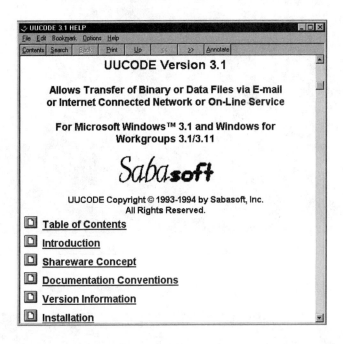

Fig. 23.14
UUCode's Help
screen.

Batch UUD for DOS

This program is about as plain and simple as you can get. As the name implies, this is a DOS-based program and only works one way—for decoding ASCII files back into their original binary format (see fig. 23.15). The one bright spot is that it does have enough smarts (sometimes) to figure out when a binary file has been split into two or more parts, and if you alphabetize the parts (for example, part-a.txt, part-b.txt, and so on) it makes a good effort to reassemble several ASCII files into one usable binary file.

To use Batch UUD for DOS, at a DOS prompt enter the command:

UUD file1 file2 etc.

Figure 23.16 shows Batch UUD for DOS in action, reassembling a binary .GIF file.

Fig. 23.15
Batch UUD for
DOS.

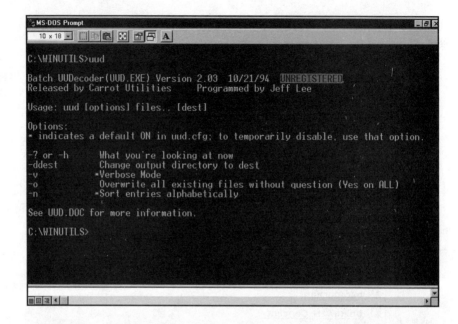

Fig. 23.16
Batch UUD for
DOS reassembling
EVEREST.GIF.

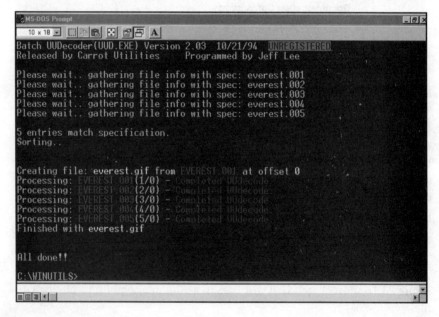

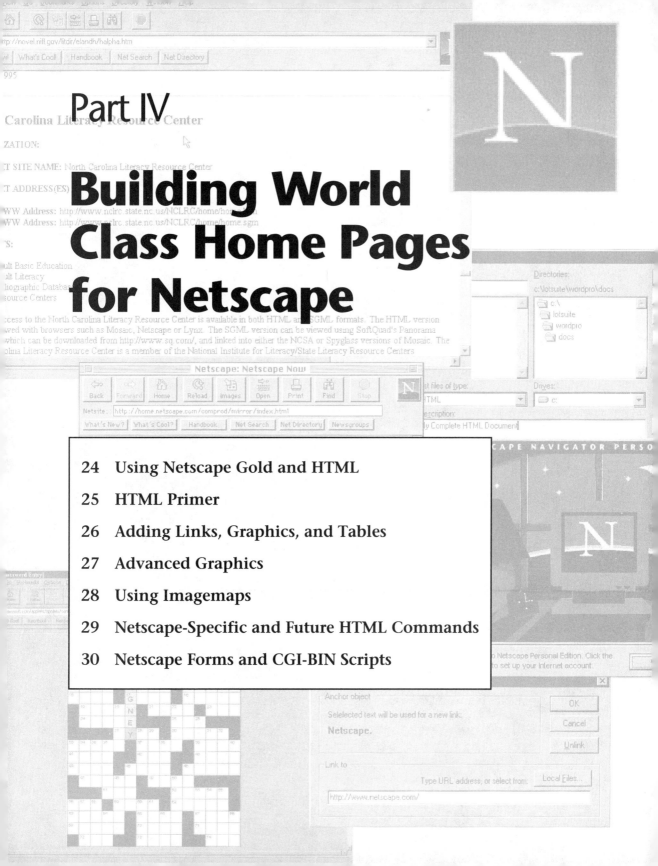

Part IV

Building World Class Home Pages for Netscape

ewl | What's Cool! | Handbook | Net Search | Net Directory |

-1995

Carolina Literacy Resource Center

NIZATION:

NET SITE NAME: North Carolina Literacy Resource Center

NET ADDRESS(ES)

WWW Address: http://www.nclrc.state.nc.us/NCLRC/home/home.htm
WWW Address: http://www.nclrc.state.nc.us/NCLRC/home/home.sgm

CTS:

dult Basic Education
dult Literacy
ibliographic Databases
Resource Centers

Access to the North Carolina Literacy Resource Center is available in both HTML and SGML formats. The HTML version iewed with browsers such as Mosaic, Netscape or Lynx. The SGML version can be viewed using SoftQuad's Panorama , which can be downloaded from http://www.sq.com/, and linked into either the NCSA or Spyglass versions of Mosaic. The arolina Literacy Resource Center is a member of the National Institute for Literacy/State Literacy Resource Centers

---

Directories:
c:\lotsuite\wordpro\docs

c:\
lotsuite
wordpro
docs

Netscape: Netscape Now

Back | Forward | Home | Reload | Images | Open | Print | Find | Stop

Netsite: http://home.netscape.com/comprod/mirror/index.html

What's New? | What's Cool? | Handbook | Net Search | Net Directory | Newsgroups

st files of type:
HTML

Drives:
c:

escription:
y Complete HTML Document

NETSCAPE NOW!

1-2-3: DOWNLOAD NETSCAPE SOFTWARE

1 First, tell us which operating system you use.

Windows 3.1

Windows 95 or NT

Mac OS

Unix

To purchase the latest fully supported version, you can go to the Netscape General Store.

NETSCAPE NAVIGATOR PERS

Welcome to Netscape Personal Edition. Click the OK button to set up your Internet account.

[Crossword Entry]

CRAB
A
G
N
E
Y

Create Link

Anchor object

Sellected text will be used for a new link:

Netscape.

OK
Cancel
Unlink

Link to

Type URL address, or select from: Local Files...

http://www.netscape.com/

## CHAPTER 24

Using Netscape Gold and HTML

Like the desktop publishing revolution of the last decade, computers are once again changing the way the written word is published and presented to readers. Last time, it meant everybody with a computer and a decent printer could develop a newsletter for their organization, advertising for their business, or their own greeting cards.

In the *electronic* publishing revolution, everyone now has the ability to create their own pages for the World Wide Web. And, just as with the early years of desktop publishing, Web publishing is growing easier to grasp by the day. As more of the big name companies start to include Web development tools in their products—and as a few smaller companies come to the forefront with revolutionary tools—Web page development will become something nearly anyone can do in the very near future.

For now, though, it still takes a little effort and education—hence the success of Web development firms and consultants. And, frankly, just because desktop publishing allowed more people than ever to dabble in the world of page layout, that didn't mean they all became commercial artists overnight. Most of the best stuff on the Web will continue to be developed by professional ad and design people. But the rest of us can put a page on the Web, too. In fact, that's what this and the next six chapters are all about.

In this chapter, you learn the following:

- The role of HTML and HTML standards in Web development
- What's currently possible with HTML on the Web
- How to set up your own personal Web site
- What a Web site should cost you
- Which tools you need to get started with HTML

What Is HTML and What Are the Standards?

The HyperText Markup Language, or HTML, is the standard by which documents on the Web are presented in browsers like Netscape. As the name implies, HTML is a method for taking standard text and marking it up in such a way that the browser knows what styles, sizes, and emphases to use when displaying the text.

In addition to text styles, HTML is also responsible for telling the browser when text on the page should be considered a link, where to insert graphical elements, and when to insert special elements like imagemaps, background graphics, mail-to commands, and other special features on the page. Figure 24.1 shows the behind-the-scenes HTML code for a sample Web page.

Fig. 24.1
The plain-text HTML codes behind a typical Web page. If you saw this in a browser, it would be pretty attractive.

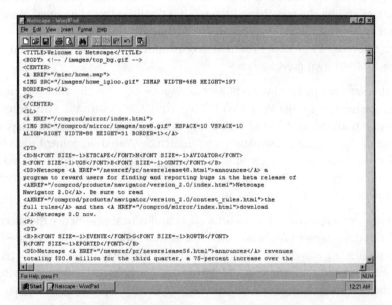

In figure 24.1, you might have noticed that HTML is all ASCII text. True to form for the Internet, we don't transmit a binary file from the Web server computer to the browser. HTML is all ASCII, which is then interpreted by the browser into formatted text and links.

Why Is HTML so Drab Looking?

If you're a veteran of DOS-based computing, you might notice that a raw HTML document looks a like a word processing document from a decade ago—like WordPerfect with reveal codes selected. And that's basically what

HTML is. Because it's an emerging technology, we're basically seeing a new file format (like WordPerfect's .WPD format or MS Word's .DOC format) as it develops.

And since it's ASCII (instead of binary, like .WPD or .DOC files), we can see all the special codes used to format the text. In fact, we can even enter them ourselves to create our own Web pages.

The HTML Standards

The key to the World Wide Web, in fact, is the HTML standard. By sticking to this predetermined markup language, all Web browsers are capable (in varying degrees) of translating HTML codes into attractive Web pages. And, although it seems like the whole world is using Netscape, that's hardly true. There are many different browsers available for Windows, Mac, X Windows, and even command-line UNIX. In order for all these different browsers to see something relatively similar, it's important to stick to the standards.

The Current HTML Standard

Of course, as with any good computer industry standard, HTML has gone through a few different incarnations. Each new version builds on the previous; although some HTML commands have fallen into disuse while others have gained popularity, most browsers will theoretically accept any standard HTML command, starting with the original HTML, referred to (by some folks) with hindsight as HTML 1.0.

> **Note**
>
> Actually, HTML has its roots in SGML, a more advanced hypertext markup language. See chapter 21, "Working with SGML," for more information.

The first real coherent standard was HTML 2.0, as defined by the Internet Engineering Task Force (IETF) in July 1994. This is really an ongoing process, and technically the standard hasn't been formally set in stone. The point is moot, however, since the HTML 3.0 standard is already being worked on (and implemented) by IETF, various application developers, and Netscape.

HTML 2.0 at its essence defines a fairly basic set of HTML commands that leave most of the formatting of a page to the individual browser. As the Web moves more toward a medium for graphic design (as opposed to just text-based document distribution), the standards are becoming increasingly more layout conscious.

The Emerging Standard: HTML 3.0

It's difficult to know *exactly* what additions the HTML 3.0 standard will make to HTML 2.0, but it's clear that the standard will be more design-focused. Very likely to be included are some of the elements that are already included in Netscape versions 2.0 and above, including table formats, flowing text around figures, and math functions within HTML code.

▶ See "Designing Web Sites for Netscape and Non-Netscape Users," pg. 736

HTML 3.0 is a clean superset of HTML 2.0, according to the IETF's documentation of the standard. That means that, as long as your documents adhere to the HTML 2.0 standard, browsers will continue to be able to read them, even as HTML 3.0 elements are introduced. This can be seen now, in fact, as Netscape has implemented many probable-HTML 3.0 elements, while still being able to cleanly display HTML 2.0 formatted documents.

Fortunately, the bottom-line mentality (and, ironically, what is probably slowing the standard-building process) is loyalty to the simplicity of HTML and HTML 2.0. While Web development is becoming an increasingly sophisticated and professional pursuit, it's difficult to maintain the universal goals of the original HTML—that just about anyone can learn it.

The Non-Standards: Netscape-Specific Commands

The fact that Netscape holds an estimated 70 percent of the browser market is a source of delight for some and heartache for others. With that sort of power in the market, Netscape Corp. has found it fairly easy to introduce its own extensions to HTML without suffering much backlash. Netscape's commanding lead in the browser market gives it a strong voice in formulating the standard while allowing it to react more quickly to customer desires (see fig. 24.2).

Fig. 24.2
Although some of these elements may eventually be part of the HTML 3.0 standard, they are currently Netscape-specific.

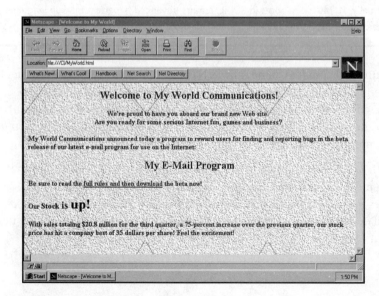

HTML features like blinking text and centered paragraphs are often confused for HTML 3.0 standard elements, but they're not. In fact, many of the HTML elements commonly found on the Web today—like different font sizes, flexible numbered lists, and background graphics—require Netscape or Netscape-compatible browsers to view. (You'll often come across Web sites that recommend using Netscape 1.1 or above for viewing.)

The question is, should you use Netscape commands in your HTML pages? You'll have to decide that for yourself. For the most graphical appeal, strongest layout, and flexibility, I'd have to say yes to Netscape commands. If your goal is to reach *all* Web users, you probably want to offer alternatives to Netscape commands on your Web pages.

▶ See "Designing Web Sites for Netscape and Non-Netscape Users" pg. 736

What's Possible with HTML?

HTML documents can be enticingly simple to create—only slightly more difficult than typing text into a word processor or text editor. And, as you get started with HTML development, that may be all that interests you. If your goal is to put something as straightforward as your resume, your academic papers, or just a clean little ad for your company on the Web, then nothing particularly advanced is necessary (see fig. 24.3).

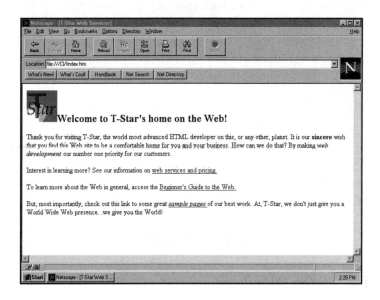

Fig. 24.3
An example of a simple HTML page. You can get your point across, even without heavy formatting or special elements.

At the same time, it's possible to make a career of HTML development (and many folks do). As you move up to more and more advanced concepts, though, you begin to see that HTML really does have some of the trappings of a programming language—as well as some concessions to the world of the commercial artist. It's never mandatory that you get this involved with HTML—just as no one is forcing you to use advanced mail-merge functions in your word processing program. But, in both cases, the functionality is there if you need it.

Text Formatting, Links, and Simple Graphics

▶ See "HTML Primer," pg. 617

▶ See "Adding Links, Graphics, and Tables," pg. 645

At its most basic, the goal of HTML is to present formatted text, hypertext links, and simple graphics that help make the text more readable or more communicative. The HTML 2.0 standard allows you to accomplish all of this; no further knowledge of HTML, Netscape commands or computer programming is necessary.

If your goal is to simply get on the Web, you really don't have that much to worry about. You should be up and ready after three chapters of reading and a few hours of work.

Serious Graphics and Clickable Maps

From the artist's point of view, one of the most popular advanced HTML elements is the imagemap. But don't let the name confuse you—these don't have a whole lot to do with maps of the world or road maps.

Imagemapping is a process by which specific parts of a particular graphic are designated as links to different Web pages or URL addresses. This allows the more advanced HTML creator to devise clever interface elements that make his Web pages more intuitive, more appealing, or, perhaps just more graphical (see fig. 24.4).

Fig. 24.4
Creating your own interface with imagemaps.

Each button sends you to a different Web page

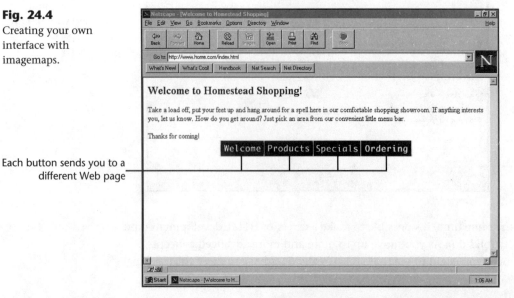

Perhaps you can see why this technique is so important and popular for Web development. Suddenly links can be hidden behind graphical interfaces that look a lot like multimedia kiosks or other graphics presentation mediums. Instead of drab underlined text and single-graphic links, the possibilities for a creative interface become boundless. Netscape's recent addition of support for client-side imagemaps makes this an increasingly enticing prospect, because now imagemaps are an even more efficient way to create stunning interfaces.

▶ See "Using Imagemaps," pg. 699

The High End of HTML

At its most extreme, HTML becomes a programming language—or, at least, it invites programming languages into the fray. With HTML we can also create forms for getting user responses, allow users to search our site using keywords and search fields, or even conduct transactions over the Web—accepting credit card numbers or similar payment information in exchange for products or services.

▶ See "Netscape Forms and CGI-BIN Scripts," pg. 745

Once the user fills in a form and sends it to your Web server to be processed, things are accomplished through what are know as CGI-BIN scripts. Created in Perl, C, and other popular scripting and programming languages, these mini-programs work behind the HTML scenes to generate on-the-fly responses to user queries (see fig. 24.5).

> **Note**
>
> The *CGI* in CGI-BIN scripts stands for *Common Gateway Interface*. In essence, CGI-BIN is simply the standard way to call other programs for behind-the-scenes processing of information received through HTML forms. The programs themselves are fairly easy to create if you have any experience with UNIX shell scripting, C, Perl, or similar languages.

Once again, Netscape is at the forefront with security and other options that make electronic commerce feasible and reasonably safe for the consumer and the Web developer. Beyond the text and graphics, the Web has emerged as a new medium for advertisement, customer service, and sales. But to get to that point takes some fairly acute HTML expertise.

> **Note**
>
> And then there's the next step: new Web-aware programming languages like JavaScript and Java. As these languages become more popular, CGI-BIN scripting may start to fade. See chapter 33, "Sun's Java and the Netscape Browser," chapter 34, "Java for C++ Programmers," and chapter 35, "JavaScript."

Fig. 24.5
Above: an HTML
form being filled
out. Below: the
results, after a
script processes
the form's
information.

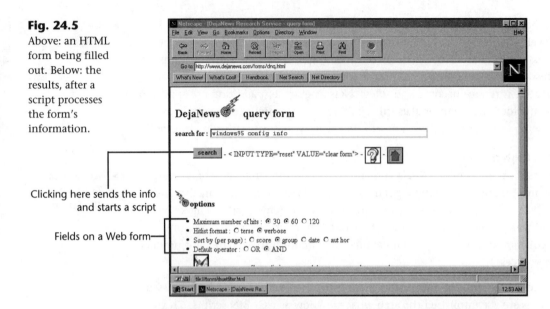

Clicking here sends the info
and starts a script

Fields on a Web form

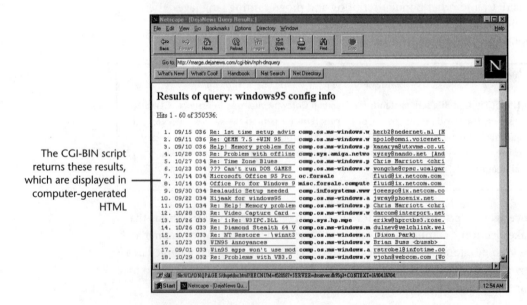

The CGI-BIN script
returns these results,
which are displayed in
computer-generated
HTML

Setting Up Your Web Site

For the most part, new HTML developers will be creating pages that will then
be made available on the Web by an Internet service provider (ISP) or an
Internet presence provider (IPP). You simply write the HTML documents, create all appropriate graphic elements, and upload the finished work to your

ISP. They then place the pages in the hierarchy of their Web presence, perhaps under a heading like Users' Pages or Business Pages.

> **Note**
>
> Organizations that call themselves Internet presence providers are generally Web publishers that don't offer Internet access. Internet service providers primarily offer Internet access (SLIP/PPP, etc.) but often offer Web sites to their users as well.

What becomes important here, then, are the services your ISP or IPP offer you, and how much it costs. As Web development becomes more specialized, you'll see rates for Web development that are similar to freelance design and writing costs. But what should you be paying if you do the Web development yourself?

How Much a Web Site Costs

The prices for Web site service vary dramatically from region to region and provider to provider. Those prices also tend to vary based on your needs—for instance, whether or not you'll be using the Web service for business or pleasure. For the most part, though, there are two basic factors that affect how much a Web site costs to the provider: disk space and page activity. These costs, in turn, should be passed on to you in a reasonably profitable way.

> **Tip**
>
> Look for special deals, especially in major metro areas. Many ISPs offer free or substantially discounted Web sites in exchange for your Internet service business. Others may offer cheap Web sites as a perk when you use their service for multiple Internet accounts or higher-priced corporate accounts.

Storage Charges

You'll need to consider the size of every HTML page you create, the graphics you add to it, and any other elements you add to your site, like imagemaps or scripts. A typical Web page, with small graphics and 30-40 lines of text, will take around 20,000 bytes of storage space. This should cost you only pennies per month to maintain.

> **Note**
>
> Your provider needs to be specifically set up to allow you to use imagemaps and scripts—and they may charge extra for these services.

Large corporate sites can be many megabytes in size, however, and depending on the ISP, charges per megabyte are generally somewhere in the $5-$10 per megabyte range. So, even if you have a very large Web site that is three megabytes in size (say, 50 highly graphical 80 KB pages), you might still be charged between only $15 and $30 a month to store that site.

Throughput Charges

Consider this, however. Many ISPs also charge you for the throughput that your site sees—that is, the amount of data that is transferred from the site across the Web to users. This number can also often be a dollar or a few dollars per megabyte. But, depending on the size of your site and the site's popularity, this arrangement can get expensive quickly. Consider a very popular corporate site that gets, for instance, 50 visitors a day—and an average visitor downloads two 25,000-byte pages:

50 visits * 50,000 bytes = 2,500,000 bytes per day

2.5 megabytes * $5 per megabyte = $10 per day

So, this site is costing you perhaps $15 a month for storage, but around $300 a month for throughput charges. Is this reasonable? It's on the high side of reasonable, to be sure. But $315 a month isn't too much to spend if this site generates sales or adds a worthwhile aspect to your customer relations. In fact, it's nothing compared to a typical business' advertising costs. If it's just for fun, though, you may be paying too much—or your site may be too large.

> **Tip**
>
> Some providers offer flat-fee service for personal and corporate Web sites. Generally this will be a happy medium price that has a limit to the amount of space you can use (often 500 KB or 1 MB) but no real limit to throughput. If you anticipate high activity on your site, one of these plans might be your best choice.

Other Charges

Be aware, too, that many ISP offer up other charges for your Web site. These can range significantly from an initial setup fee to a minimum monthly fee— or even a weekly or monthly maintenance fee that's a fixed, regular amount. Just make sure these fees seem reasonable. If not, shop around.

Also be aware that many ISPs and IPPs begin to act a lot like printing houses or ad agencies when it comes to creating the Web site for you. Rates of $50 to $125 an hour or more for creative services aren't uncommon. If you have graphics you need scanned, manipulated, or placed in your pages, be aware that those will cost you, too.

The key is to avoid being nickel-and-dimed on your Web site if your budget is tight. Learning a little HTML—at least enough to keep from being intimidated by it—can put you a little less at the mercy of the provider, and make you a smarter shopper. Once you realize that changing straight text into HTML documents really isn't that daunting of a prospect, you'll be much less likely to pay someone $50 or so per page to get it done.

Another big help is to pick the right provider in the first place. Like any growing industry, the Web services market is going to have its good companies, its not-so-good ones and some failures.

Picking the Right Provider for Your Web Site

Again, choosing the right provider for displaying your Web pages has a lot to do with how and why you plan to create a Web site. Certain providers offer services that benefit the individual users, while others are more capable of filling the more demanding needs of the corporate site.

Tips for All Types of Sites

Anyone creating a Web site should take care to explore a few things about a potential provider. First and foremost should be their pricing—in fact, pricing can tell you a lot about a provider. A good provider will have straightforward, cost-based pricing that charges you for services rendered, while not forcing you to pay for services you don't need. Disk-space and throughput charges are reasonable, but that doesn't mean all charges are.

The provider to be concerned about is one that has taken on more Web pages than its equipment—in this case its Web server—can handle. While shopping for a Web provider, spend some time on their Web site. Get a feel for whether or not the site reacts more slowly than other sites available locally or nationally. Do you notice a definite lag? Given that *any* Web server will experience occasional sluggishness, if you find that their server is regularly a bit slow, this is a good sign that their equipment isn't quite up to par.

> **Tip**
>
> Always be a little wary of ISPs that want or require long-term service contracts. If they offer discounts or increased services as an incentive for up-front payment, it may be worth the risk. But realize that it *is* a risk. There's no law that says an ISP has to stay in business.

Another sign is excessive charges for disk space, throughput, or high minimum charges for weekly or monthly Web service. A Web service company that focuses very closely on resource allocation may be doing so because their resources are limited. If things feel a bit tight at one provider, it may be in your best interest to shop around.

The Best Providers for Business Sites

Business users who intend to serve customers or generate sales from their Web site should consider that Web advertising is slightly different than most other types of advertising mediums. Why? Because customers have to seek *you* out. They have to know your URL and enter it in their browser (or click a link to your site) in order to see what you have to offer.

The savvy business Web site, then, is connected to a provider that actively seeks to help your Web site get hits—visits from Web users and potential customers. Sometimes a provider does this by setting up a virtual mall or an interesting home page for its users that point them in your direction (see fig. 24.6).

Fig. 24.6

Here's an attractive virtual mall site maintained by a Colorado-area Internet provider. This provides a service to both Web surfers in general and this provider's Web site customers.

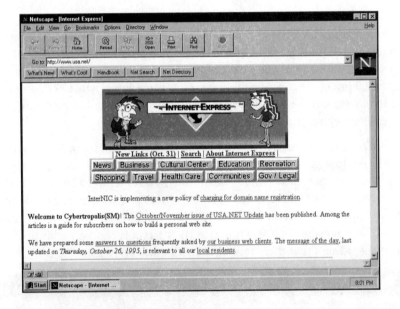

Other services they may offer you include lobbying to have your site included on popular Cool Sites or New Sites pages like those found at Netscape's Web site. Providers may also take it upon themselves to have your page registered with the Yahoo Web Directory, Infoseek, and other Web searching servers, so that your name comes up often when people all over the Web search for information and services you provide. At the very least, they should offer you some help in registering your site with these services on your own.

Getting Your HTML Files to the Server

The final question you may ask about a provider is, how easy is to maintain the Web site? Many providers will have you upload your pages to a central FTP server, and then they will take on the responsibility of adding or changing Web pages on your site. They may charge extra for this sort of maintenance, however, and it may take some time.

In other cases, you'll have a particular directory on the Web server to which you upload files, with the link to your page (from their virtual mall or users' home page) being a particular static file name like index.html (or index.htm for DOS-based servers). From there, you're free to create whatever links and additional pages you desire—even going so far as to create subdirectories on the site for organizing you materials. At least, you're free to do so as long as you don't go over any disk space or other limitations.

What's the best way to go? Whatever makes you most comfortable. If you'd rather have the provider take care of things, you'll probably have to pay for that service. But it may be worth it just to keep everything running smoothly.

Choosing Your Web Publishing Tools

The next step to successful HTML development is picking the right tools for the task. As HTML becomes a popular pursuit, there are more and more programs and utilities being developed to help you get a head start in HTML. Sifting through them can take some time, but you may find a gem that really is a considerable help.

You May Already Have Everything You Need!

If you're using the Netscape Gold edition, you already have an HTML editor built into Netscape. Just pull down the Window menu and choose the Editor command. This might be enough of an editor for all your HTML needs.

Even if you aren't using Netscape Gold, let me point out that you don't actually have to use *any* special program to create HTML pages. I've already mentioned that HTML is simply ASCII text, and it's true. So, a typical text editor (like Windows 95's WordPad, Mac's SimpleText, or UNIX's Emacs) is more than capable of creating any HTML page you can conceive.

Of course, the trick is that you need to know HTML pretty well to use just a text editor to create Web pages. That's why shareware and commercial HTML editors are popular alternatives to simple text editors. The better programs tend to make HTML creation much easier.

The Netscape Gold HTML Editor

Netscape Gold edition owners have a leg up on other Netscape users and Web developers—there's an HTML editor built into the program. It's a very robust, very useful WYSIWYG editor designed to integrate well with the Netscape browser.

Chapters 24–30 of this book are dedicated to teaching you HTML like a pro. But, honestly, the Netscape Gold editor takes a user-friendly approach to HTML development that allows you to get started without a lot of this knowledge. The Netscape editor sports a full-featured button bar for easily adding elements, full support for Netscape HTML commands, and an interface that makes creating HTML pages almost as easy as word processing (see fig. 24.7).

> **Tip**
>
> When you want to see the actual HTML source code for your pages, start by viewing the page in the Netscape browser window. Then select View, Document Source. The latest Netscape versions use color coding to show you the different HTML commands being used.

You'll eventually want to know more about HTML, and there are a lot of advanced features that the Netscape editor (and others) can implement. But, for now, you can get basic pages up quickly and easily, without a deep understanding of HTML.

Fig. 24.7
Included with the Netscape Gold edition is a very complete and useful HTML editor.

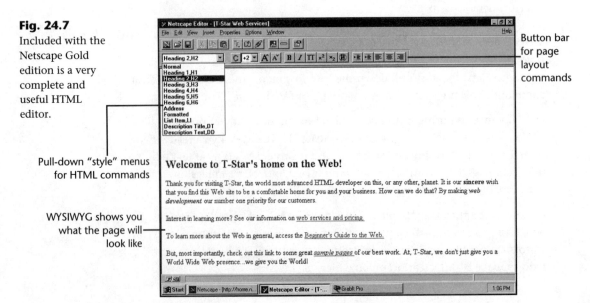

Button bar for page layout commands

Pull-down "style" menus for HTML commands

WYSIWYG shows you what the page will look like

One thing that's particularly impressive about the Netscape Gold HTML editor is its use of a "styles" metaphor for applying HTML commands. This gives you a quick and easy way to compare the different ways that HTML elements will affect your page. It also makes the task of turning basic ASCII text into HTML a straightforward process.

Basic HTML in the Gold Editor

You can start creating Web pages right away. With the Netscape Editor window open, click the window and begin typing. Don't worry about HTML elements right now—unlike other many other HTML editors, the Netscape editor doesn't require that you enter HTML commands while you're typing text. You can go back and add them later.

While you're typing, though, you may want to add emphasis to your text, like bold, italic, and teletype (monospaced), using the buttons on the editor's button bar (see fig. 24.8). You can also choose to align your text (by paragraph) by selecting one of the align buttons on the button bar as you begin each paragraph. You don't have to, though. You can still always go back and change things, just as if you were working in Microsoft Word or WordPerfect.

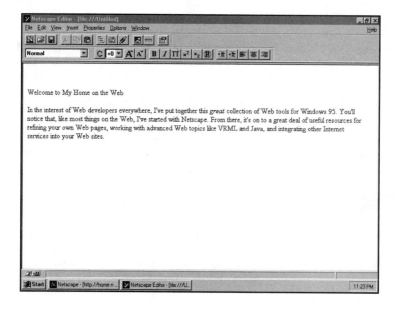

Fig. 24.8
Getting a quick start on your HTML page.

Once you've gotten the bulk of your text entered in the editor's window, you can go back and assign different HTML characteristics to the raw text. This is where the Styles pull-down menu comes in handy. Again, as in a word processor, these styles are designed to assign certain predetermined characteristics to the text. In this case, the styles assign HTML tags to the text that we select.

To change text to an HTML heading, for instance, select the text with your mouse as you would in any Windows program. (Double-click the text to select a word, or drag the mouse to select more than one word.) Now, from the pull-down menu, select one of the Heading styles. The text on your page should change to reflect its new HTML attributes (see fig. 24.9).

Fig. 24.9
Adding HTML commands in Netscape's editor is as easy as drag and click.

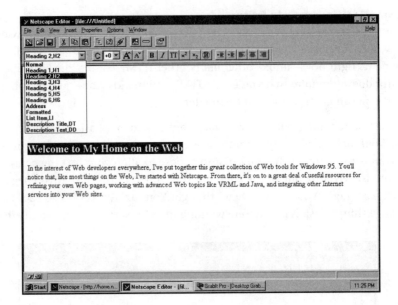

In fact, you can select text in the Editor window and assign to it nearly any of the HTML commands on the button bar, in the menus, or in the Style pull-down menu. You can even select multiple paragraphs, for instance, and use the align buttons to determine whether those paragraphs will be aligned against the left margin, centered, or aligned to the right margin.

> **Note**
>
> Notice that assigning any of the editor's commands to text—whether you use the style menu, the editor's menus, or the button bar—actually changes that text's *HTML* attributes. Different browsers are free to implement HTML in slightly different ways, so what you see in your Netscape browser may not reflect how it will look in other, non-Netscape browsers.

Simple HTML Lists

Netscape Gold's HTML editor makes creating simple bulleted lists a quick and easy process as well. To create a bulleted list from a series of items, simply enter the items and press Enter between each item and highlight the items in the editor window. Now, select List Item (LI) from the pull-down Style menu. The Netscape editor automatically adds bullets to each of the items, changing them to an HTML unnumbered list (UL).

To change the type of list generated by these steps, select the list and choose Container/List from the Properties menu. You can change the type of list (as well as the bullet or number types) in the resulting dialog box.

▶ See "Basic Formatting Tags," pg. 631

> **Tip**
>
> You can actually add more buttons to the button bar to help you with lists. Under the Options menu, select Browser. Click the Configure button for the Format button bar, and then place a checkmark next to the two list buttons. With your list items selected, you can now use these buttons to choose from different list styles.

Adding Graphics and Links

Once you have all your text arranged in a manner that pleases you, you can move on to adding hypertext links and graphics to your Web pages. Honestly, this is just about as easy as the more basic HTML commands in Netscape Gold's editor.

▶ See "Creating a Link," pg. 648

▶ See "Adding Graphics with HTML," pg. 657

To add a graphics image, place the cursor on the page where you want the image to appear. Now, from the Insert menu, select Graphic (there's also an Image button on the button bar). You'll be presented with a dialog box that will ask you what image file you want to load for this graphic and other attributes concerning how the graphic will appear on this page. Once you've made all the appropriate choices, the graphic should appear on the page.

To create a hypertext link on your page, select text in the editor and choose Insert, Link from the menu (or, choose the Link button on the button bar). Now you're presented with a dialog box that asks you for the URL for the Web page that you'd like this link associated with (or a path statement if the file is a local file). Enter this information in the dialog box and click OK (see fig. 24.10).

You can also select a graphic, a heading, or just about anything else in the editor window and use the same process to turn that element into a hypertext link.

Adding Advanced HTML Elements

With just these last two quick lessons we've got enough information to create a pleasant page for the Web. We've got text, graphics, and links—and that's most of what anybody really needs to get their Web site up and running. But the Netscape editor is capable of much more.

Fig. 24.10
Just highlight text and click the Link button to create a hypertext link for your Web page.

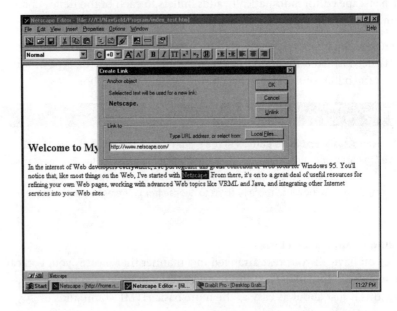

▶ See "Creating Tables with Netscape Elements," pg. 730

The Netscape editor allows for easy creation of advanced tables and forms, with pull-down menu items that cover Netscape-specific and HTML 3.0 commands. To create a table, for instance, just place your cursor on the page and choose Insert, Table. The resulting dialog box allows you to determine the number of cells, alignment, width, and other table attributes. From there it's simple to insert the cell data for your table.

The Netscape Gold editor also offers support for background graphics and colors, changing text color, and different style horizontal lines. It even includes built-in support for JavaScript and objects. Included with the Netscape Gold editing package is the Java Console, which lets you see the results of Java scripts you've built into your page.

If there's a drawback to the Netscape Gold editor, it's that the browser is, perhaps, too friendly. Most folks won't have a problem with this, but advanced HTML designers may find that the Gold editor hides too much of the raw HTML, not giving them enough control over their elements.

On top of that, the editor has a fairly strong Netscape bias, for obvious reasons, and it implements Netscape-specific elements somewhat recklessly. If you're interested in developing pages that conform to the "true" HTML 2.0 and HTML 3.0 standards, you need to be very careful with the Gold editor—and you need to be rather familiar with HTML itself.

> **Tip**
>
> Whenever you use Netscape-specific elements it's a good idea to warn your Web users with a statement like "This page is optimized for Netscape Navigator" or something similar on your site's index page.

HTML Editor Programs

Most HTML editors improve on standard text editors in two different ways. First, they offer menu items for changing the way text appears in your HTML document, allowing you to be free from memorizing all the different HTML commands.

Second, some of these editors present HTML documents in a WYSIWYG (What You See Is What You Get) mode. If you create HTML documents in a simple text editor, you'll need to load them into Netscape to test them. With a good HTML editor program, you'll see exactly what the page will look like as you create it.

> **Note**
>
> You might want to test your pages in browsers *other* than Netscape, too. Different browsers display pages in slightly different ways—you'll want to test your pages to make sure you look good in all of them.

The best of these programs do this in an intuitive way that really helps you create HTML documents quickly. Although you still need to understand how HTML works, some of the shortcuts offered by these programs will make your time spent creating HTML pages much more productive.

There are many, many HTML editors available for Windows, Windows 95, Macintosh, OS/2, and UNIX. My best suggestion would be to experiment with a few different offerings until you find one that you feel is the closest to what you need in an editor. A number of different editors for you to sample are available on the Netscape CD included with this book. The following examples aren't necessarily the programs that will be right for everyone, but they do represent some samples of what's available.

On the CD

HTML Notepad

Among the most basic, and yet elegant, improvements on the simple text editor is HTML Notepad for Windows. Although the presentation is sparse, HTML Notepad is capable of creating almost any HTML or Netscape element, including tables, forms, blink, and foreign characters (see fig. 24.11). In fact, Netscape elements are found in their own menu (Netscapisms), so you'll know instantly when you're creating a Netscape-specific page.

Fig. 24.11
HTML Notepad is a solid, small HTML editor that improves on simple text editors for HTML creation.

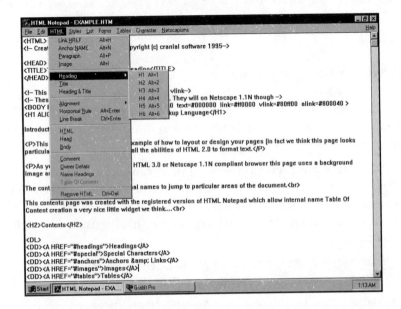

HTML Notepad provides no special WYSIWYG features, requiring you to load pages-in-progress into Netscape to test. It automatically loads Netscape for you after every save, if you choose to do so in the Preferences menu. On top of that, HTML Notepad offers a very complete Help file that not only points you to the right menu for commands, but gives you a nice overview of HTML in general.

HTML Notepad is a product of Cranial Software (Adam Fraser and Lee Griffiths) in Great Britain. It is distributed as shareware—after a reasonable trial period, the writers ask that you mail them the $30 registration fee. The latest version of HTML Notepad can be found at **http://www.u-net.com/ virtua/code/htmlnote/**. It requires at least Windows 3.1 and a 386-based computer.

CMed

This editor is unique as one of the first to take full advantage of Windows 95, although many will follow over the next year. Taking off at full 32-bit speed, CMed has an attractive and easy-to-use interface that is especially good at handling higher-end HTML creation, like HTML 3.0 and Netscape-specific commands (see fig. 24.12).

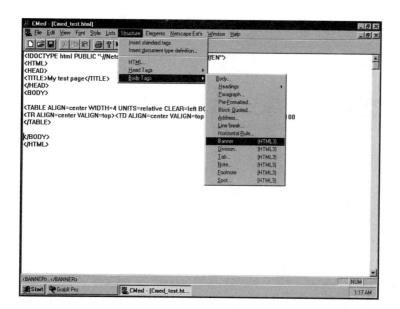

Fig. 24.12
The CMed HTML editor, specifically designed for Windows 95.

Another text-based (non-WYSIWYG) editor, CMed is aimed at the slightly more advanced HTML creator—there isn't quite as much friendly help and as many pointers here as there are with HTML Notepad. It is, ultimately, a little easier for the seasoned HTML user, and there seems to be more complete coverage of HTML 3.0 and other advanced elements.

Developed by Chad Matheson at the University of Western Australia as a school project, CMed has another distinct advantage—it's freeware. The latest version can be found at **http://www.uwa.edu.au/student/cmathes/**. It requires Windows NT 3.5 or Windows 95 to operate.

HoTMetaL Free and HoTMetaL Pro

HoTMetaL Free and HoTMetaL Pro take a fundamentally different approach to HTML creation. In a nutshell, you don't have to understand HTML. HoTMetaL is a completely WYSIWYG environment that is designed to shield you from the underlying HTML codes; a phenomenon that, earlier in this chapter, I suggested we would begin to see more frequently in Web design tools.

Instead of inserting HTML commands, HoTMetaL users simply enter text on-screen, select it, and choose the formatting or linking elements from the program's menus. Like WordPerfect of old, HoTMetaL then allows you to either hide or display the resulting HTML tags. Hidden, they provide you with a WYSIWYG representation of your page—even including graphical elements (see fig. 24.13).

Fig. 24.13
HoTMetaL Free
allows you to view
HTML in a
WYSIWYG
environment, with
or without HTML
codes.

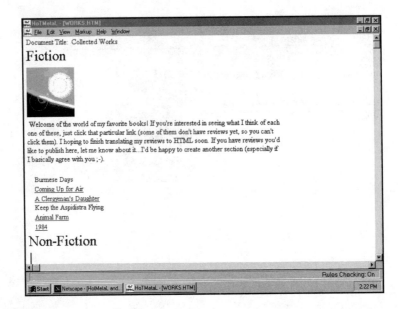

HoTMetaL Free is a scaled-down freeware version of the commerical application HoTMetaL Pro, which retails for an astounding $195. The Pro version does, however, offer just about everything you'd need to create HTML pages, including spell checking and thesaurus, search-and-replace, inline graphics display, tables support, templates, and forms support. Plus, an added bonus over many editors is the HTML parser, which actually checks to make sure your HTML documents are valid and correctly formatted.

Both are the work of SoftQuad, Inc. The HoTMetaL Free version can be accessed via SoftQuad's web site at **http://www.ptgs.com/links/sfq/ sfqhome.html**. HoTMetaL Pro is also available for the Macintosh, as should be HoTMetaL Free in early 1996.

HotDog Standard

Although not a WYSIWYG editor, HotDog Standard (along with HotDog Pro) remains an overwhelming favorite of folks all over the Web. With support for advanced HTML features, including *true* HTML 3.0 elements (along with Netscape-specific elements), HotDog is especially popular with folks on the cutting-edge of Web design.

One of the more impressive features of HotDog Standard is its built-in support for more easily creating tables and forms using dialog boxes that guide you through the process (see fig. 24.14). Just click the Table or Forms button on HotDog's button bar, and you're presented with a dialog box to help you create the element. This lets you avoid some of the tiresome, detailed HTML coding usually required.

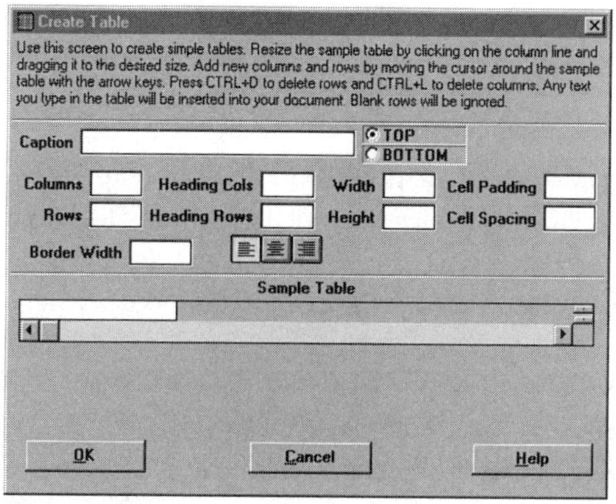

Fig. 24.14
HotDog Standard's
table editor lets
you avoid HTML.

IV

Building Home Pages

HotDog Standard is shareware, available for $29.95 from Sausage Software at **http://www.sausage.com/**. HotDog Pro is available for $99.95 and features spell checking, a built-in page viewer, HTML syntax checking, and the ability to convert ASCII files into HTML documents.

Note

You might want to check this out: Sausage Software uses the Netscape Commerce Server to allow you to securely purchase HotDog over the Web.

Note

Web Weaver for Macintosh is a popular editor for Mac users. It's considered semi-WYSIWYG, meaning it shows you a good deal of the formatting that will appear in your browser, but not necessarily all of it. Web Weaver uses floating palette windows to give you access to common HTML tags, while the rest are available as menu commands. You can also create your own custom palettes for getting at your favorite or most used elements.

Other Programs for HTML Creation

Aside from HTML editors, there are a couple of other programs you'll probably find useful for creating your Web site. Since graphics tend to be a focus on the Web, you'll want programs to deal with those. If you have access to professional graphics programs like CorelDRAW! or Adobe Photoshop, you'll definitely find good reasons to use them. There are shareware alternatives for graphics, though.

You may also want to create and make sound files available on your Web site. To do this, you may need still more shareware programs.

Graphics

LView Pro, a popular shareware image-manipulation application, is able to create transparent GIFs (graphics files with transparent backgrounds tend to look better on the Web; see fig. 24.15). It is available at **ftp:// oak.oakland.edu/SimTel/win3/graphics** and elsewhere.

Fig. 24.15

A transparent GIF on the World Wide Web. Notice how the graphic seems to be sitting almost directly on the background of the page.

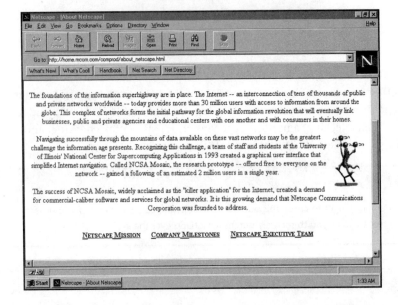

Another very popular, and very good, shareware graphics manipulation program is PaintShop Pro. PSPro rivals some of the commercial image programs for its depth of features and ability to work with various file formats. It can be downloaded at **http://www.winternet.com/~jasc/psp.html**.

You may also want to look into a Windows program designed to translate between common graphics file formats, like Graphics Workshop (gwswn11.zip), Image 'n' Bits (ima.zip), and Picture Man (pman155.zip), all of which are available from **ftp://gatekeeper.dec.com/pub/micro/msdos/win3/ desktop/** and other popular Windows FTP sites. Because most Web browsers support only GIF and JPG formats, you'll want to convert any graphics you have in other formats to one of these two.

Some of these applications are also capable of rudimentary image manipulation, and can be an inexpensive way to deal with images if you don't own a professional graphics package. Another popular program for image

manipulation is WinGIF (wingif14.zip), also available from **ftp://
gatekeeper.dec.com/pub/micro/msdos/win3/desktop/** and others.

Sounds

As your familiarity and interest in creating Web sites continues to grow, you
may also eventually want to experiment with programs that create sounds,
animations, and even digital movies. Tools like these can take some learning,
but, once you have your movies and sounds created, adding them to your
Web site is relatively easy.

For sound, look into Gold Wave (gldwav21.zip) at **ftp://
oak.oakland.edu/SimTel/win3/sound/**, a WAV to AU translation program that turns basic Windows sounds into AU format sounds—the standard
file type for sounds on the Web.

Emerging Tools: Page Layout and Word Processors

Not to be ignored are the growing numbers of tools and upgrades that add
HTML capabilities to programs that many of us already have. Of particular interest are add-ons for common word processing programs like Microsoft
Word and WordPerfect for Windows—both of which have programs available
that translate text from word processing documents into HTML documents.

Also in the works are improvements and upgrades to familiar desktop publishing programs, like Adobe PageMaker and QuarkXPress, that allow HTML
page creation. These are very interesting to commerical artists and other professionals who currently use these programs for publishing and advertising
layout. An easy transition to HTML will be welcome by all.

The question is, do these solutions do enough? For now, you still need to
know the basics of HTML and you need some sort of editor to do much creative layout in HTML. At the moment, you'll probably have more luck creating higher-end sites with a good HTML editor and some graphics programs
than you will trying to use print-oriented programs for HTML. It will take a
while for those programs to fully cover the ground between print and Web
publishing, while current HTML editors have been designed with the Web in
mind.

That said, we may not be too far from programs that will shield users from
HTML altogether. Soon, graphical interfaces and HTML conversion tools may
make learning HTML codes as useful as learning embedded codes in word
processing documents. Why type <bold>**boldface text**</bold>, when you
can just select the text and click a button on the program's interface?

HTML Tools for WordPerfect Users

Ease of HTML creation is the key to most of the add-ons and functionality built into the latest versions of popular word processing and desktop publishing programs. WordPerfect for Mac 3.5, for example, is rumored to include HTML tools as part of the program.

For WordPerfect for Windows users, Novell offers the WordPerfect Internet Publisher add-on as a free download from its Web site at **http://wp.novell.com/elecpub/intpub.htm**. This add-on turns WordPerfect into a WYSIWYG HTML editor, and even comes with a copy of Netscape for final testing.

HTML Tools for Microsoft Word Users

For Microsoft Word 95, Microsoft itself provides the Internet Assistant for MS Word 95 as a free download from its FTP site. This add-on allows you to create basic HTML pages in MS Word, then use the included translator to save your document in HTML format. The download is available at **http://www.microsoft.com/msoffice/freestuf/msword/download/ia/ia95/**.

Tip

Internet Assistant for MS Word 6.0 (for Windows 3.1) is also available from **http://www.microsoft.com/msoffice/freestuf/msword/download/ia/ia1z/default.htm**.

For all versions of Microsoft Word, including Windows 3.1, NT, Windows 95, and Macintosh (see fig. 24.16), Jill Swift has created ANT_HTML, a template and button bar add-on to MS Word that helps you create HTML documents. It allows you to create pages without worrying about HTML codes, translate HTML pages to WYSIWYG Word documents, and insert special characters into HTML documents. It's also a great tool for translating between HTML and .DOC, ASCII, .RTF, and other file formats.

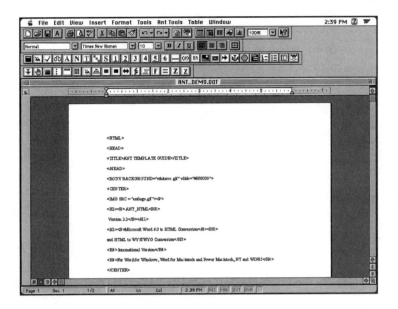

Fig. 24.16
Word for Mac
users get the same
HTML functional-
ity as Word for
Windows users
with ANT_HTML.

A demo of ANT_HTML (the template works for all Word 6.0 and above versions) is available at **http://www.w3.org/hypertext/WWW/Tools/**
Ant.html. The commercial version of the program is $39.

## CHAPTER 25

HTML Primer

As you've worked with the World Wide Web, you've most likely come across HTML, the underlying programming language that the WWW is based upon. While not as difficult to understand or use as other computer languages out there, HTML has its own quirks and idiosyncrasies that require you to spend some time learning about it. Unlike standard programming languages, HTML is a *formatting* language. You start with a page of pure text, and then add special HTML attributes that tell Netscape how to display that information on screen.

In the last chapter you learned how to prepare for building your own WWW site. That was only the first step. This chapter takes you right into HTML and serves as an introduction to build your own Web pages. In addition to learning all the basic markup tags, you'll become familiar with using horizontal lines, tables, and other popular HTML attributes.

Specifically, in this chapter you learn how to do the following:

- Use basic HTML tags
- Separate paragraphs of displayed text
- Include several types of lists in your HTML document
- Build a sample HTML document from scratch

Creating an HTML File

As mentioned in the last chapter, there are several tools available to make it easier to create HTML files. Some automated HTML editors take advantage of powerful drag and drop and WYSIWYG (What You See is What You Get) capabilities, which make writing HTML a much simpler process. Instead of memorizing dozens of different specific HTML tags and codes, editors allow you to concentrate on how your Web pages should look, not learning a new programming language.

Even if you are interested in learning the advanced specifics of HTML, you'll still want to use a specialized editor to take care of mundane HTML authoring.

HTML editors come in two basic formats. The first, such as Internet Assistant by Microsoft (**http://www.microsoft.com**), are complimentary add-on products that work with existing word processors. By integrating with Microsoft Word, Internet Assistant you can take advantage of all the tools of a word processor—such as a spell checker and revision marking. While most add-on products are free, you've got to own the corresponding word processor before they work.

The other types of HTML editors that exist are stand-alone products that are independent of existing word processors. Popular because they are geared specifically towards creating HTML files, you'll find all the needed tags and functionality built into programs such as HoTMetaL (**http://ww.sq.com**).

> ### Tip
>
> Regardless of which computer platform you use, HTML editors exist for virtually every type of computer out there. Everything from the PC to the Amiga has its own HTML editor. If you have trouble locating an HTML editor for your particular machine, check out Yahoo (**http://www.yahoo.com**) for a comprehensive list of HTML editors.

How to Save HTML Files

Unlike other programming languages, an HTML document is not compiled when you are finished writing it. All HTML files are saved strictly as pure text, or ASCII. When Netscape reads the ASCII text file, it interprets the HTML tags and codes you've included, and chooses to display information based on those characteristics.

Regardless of which text editor, HTML editor, or word processor you choose to work with, ensure that your HTML files are saved in strictly ASCII/text format. Typically, text editors and HTML editors take care of this for you automatically, but word processors such as Microsoft Word may not. Before you can make your HTML page available on the WWW, you might have to export from Word into text format.

> **Note**
>
> ASCII is a worldwide text standard that virtually all computer systems support. It enables any computer to read a text file and recognize all the letters, numbers, and characters stored inside.

Naming Conventions

By default, all HTML files should have an appropriate file extension so that both you and WWW browsers can recognize them. By following these standard naming conventions, you'll have an easier time recognizing other HTML files by their file names.

The most common way to identify your files is by using the .HTM or .HTML extension. Much as Microsoft Word recognizes files that have the .DOC extension, Netscape knows that files ending with .HTML or .HTM are specifically created for the World Wide Web.

- *.HTM*—the Windows 3.1 file extension
- *.HTML*—the file extension for HTML files created with Windows 95 and UNIX-based editors

Figure 25.1 shows how Microsoft Word automatically adds the .HTM extension to all files saved in HTML format.

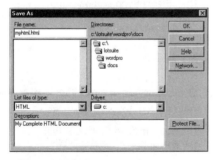

Fig. 25.1
The Save As dialog box in Lotus Word Pro 96 automatically takes care of adding the proper file extension.

> **Tip**
>
> Don't worry if you have other requirements that force you to use other naming conventions. WWW browsers use other methods to determine if a file is in HTML format when they don't recognize a file's extension. Using tags you'll learn later, Netscape recognizes HTML documents by the proper use of tags, not only the file naming conventions. Keeping a standard file extension is more useful for you, the HTML author, when keeping track of several files. Netscape can open a file regardless of its extension or file name as long as it is in ASCII format.

> **Note**
>
> Many UNIX WWW servers expect to find a file named INDEX.HTML in your main
> HTML directory. The server will display this file automatically when WWW visitors
> explore through the available directories. It's a good idea to name your initial WWW
> page INDEX.HTML (or INDEX.HTM) if your Web server supports this feature. Check
> with your Web administrator for more information. This feature of the Web is used
> when visitors forget to mention a specific document they want to reference within
> the URL. Visitors won't see the file name listed in the browser window, but Netscape
> knows to look for INDEX.HTML automatically.

In addition to ensuring that your HTML files uses common extensions, it is
more important that other files such as graphics, video clips, and sound clips
have the correct file extension. Without the correct file extension, Netscape
will not be able to properly display graphics, or load helper applications for
these external media types. Table 25.1 lists several other popular file extensions that you'll use when creating HTML documents.

Table 25.1 Proper File Extensions Netscape Recognizes

Extension	Description
GIF	The standard graphics format displayed with Netscape and most WWW browsers.
JPEG (JPG)	The other common graphics format used on the Web. This is a particularly good format to use with Netscape's new progressive rendering.
TIF	A less popular graphics format that requires an external helper application to view.
AU	Sound clips stored in a common audio file format that Netscape can recognize and play automatically.
WAV	The Microsoft Windows audio file format.
MPEG (MPG)	The popular video file format that was developed by the same people who created JPEG.
MOV (QT)	Apple's video file format that has quickly become one of the choice methods for providing video clips on the WWW.

Most HTML Tags Come in Pairs

Through a comprehensive set of formatting tags, Netscape knows which
text to display as a headline, where to separate two paragraphs, and how to
highlight vital information. Typically, these formatting tags come in pairs,

surrounding the text they intend to mark up. For example, marking a title on a page looks like this:

```
<TITLE> This is my Netscape title </TITLE>
```

When used in pairs, HTML tags are always related. The closing tag is just the initial tag with a "/" added within it.

While most tags come in pairs, you'll also encounter some HTML tags that appear alone, without a closing tag. These tags tend to separate paragraphs of text, or embed graphics on-screen, and don't change how text is formatted.

In this chapter, when a new tag is introduced, you'll always learn whether it has a corresponding closing tag, and if so, how to use the pair correctly.

Adding the <HTML> Tag

The first set of tags that you'll use in your HTML document is <HTML> and </HTML>. These tags should surround all pieces of HTML within a WWW document, indicating that HyperText Markup Language is being used. Add this set of tags so they appear like this:

- <HTML>
- </HTML>

WWW Browsers use the <HTML> tags to recognize that they are reading an HTML document. Without them, a WWW browser might not recognize the other markup tags that you've included in your document. As a rule, most browsers don't require the <HTML> tag, but using it is considered good practice. While Netscape is smart enough to recognize other HTML tags without <HTML>, future versions, and other WWW browsers might require it in order to recognize standard formatting tags.

Note

With the advent of VRML (Virtual Reality Modeling Language), Java (Sun Microsystems advancements for the Web), and future WWW enhancements on the way, using the <HTML> and </HTML> tags is really a must. Without them, Netscape may not understand which programming language is used in a WWW document, and how to display information correctly.

Understanding the HTML Section Tags

With your initial tag in place, you can start typing text and information into the HTML document. Using additional tags, you should organize WWW pages into two different sections: the header and body.

Using these section tags allows Netscape to take a quick snapshot of a document and recognize that it is separated into two components. This makes it easier to display information and keep the file organized.

Using the <HEAD> Tag

The <HEAD> tag marks an HTML document's heading. By default, the heading contains the document title, indexing information, and important settings for that specific page.

Also a container tag, <HEAD> and </HEAD> surround only a few lines of your file.

Netscape uses the information contained within the <HEAD> tags as a quick reference of the page while it is downloading the complete text and graphics. This allows Netscape to display the title before the rest of the document appears on screen.

Include the <HEAD> tags within the main <HTML> tags:

```
<HTML>
      <HEAD>

      </HEAD>

</HTML>
```

> **Note**
>
> If you plan on taking advantage of Netscape's built-in indexing capabilities, you should include the ISINDEX keyword within the document's header. When enabled, Netscape allows documents to be completely indexed and searchable automatically. This indexing characteristic is controlled by the WWW server running at your site. Check with your Web administrator for more information on whether your site is indexed.

Troubleshooting

I created a bunch of HTML documents, but I forgot to add the closing </HTML> *tag to the end of each file. Netscape doesn't seem to have a problem with this. Is this causing errors that I'm not aware of within Netscape or with non-Netscape using browsers?*

Currently, the </HMTL> tag is not required. When Netscape gets to the end of your HTML document, there is no more information to read, so it doesn't matter whether the </HTML> tag is there or not. Other popular WWW browsers don't have any trouble with this either. It is a good idea to add the closing tag in further updates in case WWW browsers become more picky in the future, but in general, including the </HTML> closing tag is considered good practice.

Using the <BODY> Tag

Used hand in hand with the <HEAD> tags, the <BODY> and </BODY> tags are used to signify the rest of an HTML document. These tags will surround most of your file. While the <BODY> tags don't affect how information is displayed within Netscape, they help keep the text file organized and indicate the main meat of a document.

By adding the <BODY> and </BODY> tags to your page, you have three sets of tags with no information to display:

```
<HTML>
     <HEAD>

     </HEAD>

     <BODY>

     </BODY>
</HTML>
```

Properly Titling Your Document

The first bit of text you'll type into your HTML document is the title. Like a book title, your document title is a concise statement that accurately reflects the contents of the document.

Your HTML title is the first piece of information people see when they visit a WWW page. In Netscape, the title appears in the title bar at the top of the screen, while the rest of the page is loading. Figure 25.2 shows where the HTML title appears within Netscape.

Fig. 25.2
The specified title
appears in the
Netscape title bar
running across the
top of the screen.

Title bar

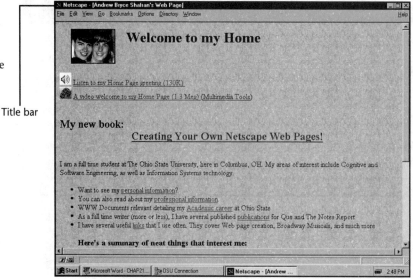

◄ See "Creating a
Bookmark," pg.
211, and "De-
leting a Book-
mark," pg. 213

In addition to appearing in the Netscape title bar, the HTML title is also the
information saved when a Netscape user adds a page to his list of bookmarks.

Using the `<TITLE>` Tag

Adding a title to an HTML document requires using the `<TITLE>` and
`</TITLE>` tags. Embedded within the document's header, titles can be any
length desired. To name a document "Andy's Home Page," add the following
line of HTML to your WWW document:

```
<TITLE> Andy's Home Page </TITLE>
```

Choosing a Good Title

Like any good book title, an HTML document's title should be focused, concise, and well thought-out to pique curiosity and attract attention. When
choosing a title, follow these tips:

- Describe the page accurately. The title should be a complete phrase that
  describes what appears in that file. If the HTML document is a particular scene within Hamlet, then a good title would be "Shakespeare's
  Hamlet: Act I, Scene ii."

- Keep the title short. Long titles may not fit in the Netscape title bar and
  are difficult to read and digest.

Adding Headers to Your HTML Document

Similar to using a document title, headers are also used to introduce a WWW page. Coming in six different sizes, headers are eye-catching bits of information that stand out when looking at a page with Netscape.

Add a size 1 header by surrounding text with the `<H1>` and `</H1>` tags. Figure 25.3 shows how the following tag appears within Netscape:

```
<H1> Dewey beats Truman!</H1>
```

Fig. 25.3
Headers are the real eye catchers of a WWW document.

Header sizes range from 1 (the largest) to 6, and can be added by using the corresponding number tag. For example, a size 3 header uses the `<H3>` and `</H3>` tags to mark specific text.

Figure 25.4 compares the six different sizes of headers and how they are displayed within Netscape.

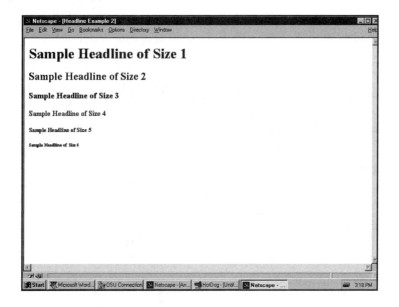

Fig. 25.4
Headlines come in all sizes.

Troubleshooting

Is there anyway I can add a more pronounced title to my HTML file to make sure people will always see the proper title?

As a standard procedure, many WWW developers include a size 1 header as the first piece of displayed text within an HTML document. Similar to the document's title, this header is much larger, more noticeable, and easier to read than the small title that is included in the Netscape title bar. Make sure you don't use the exact same text in the large header and title to avoid being redundant.

Organizing Paragraphs of Text

You're probably familiar with how a word processor works. After typing several sentences of information, you hit the Enter key and then start typing on the next line. This way you can organize your thoughts into separate paragraphs, making it easy for readers to browse through your document.

Formatting HTML doesn't work quite the same way. In an HTML file, you can use the spacebar and the Tab and Enter keys to make the source file easily readable, but without using the HTML in paragraph formatting tags, Netscape displays a jumbled mess.

Figure 25.5 shows how Netscape displays several paragraphs of text without using paragraph tags. Figure 25.6 is the same text, only formatted in a readable manner.

Fig. 25.5
Not even
Wordsworth could
read this mess.

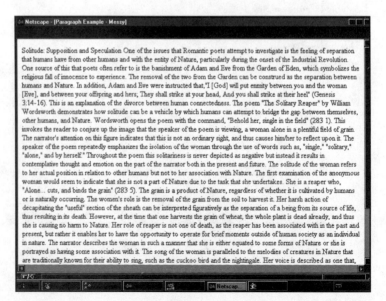

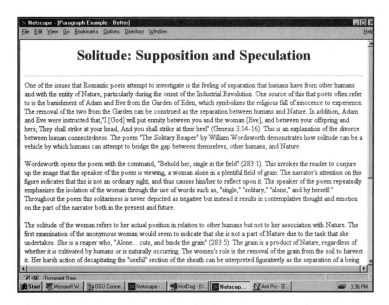

Fig. 25.6
A few short tags
makes quite a
readability
difference.

IV

Building Home Pages

With these paragraph organizing HTML tags, you can do the following:

- Organize and separate paragraphs of text on WWW pages
- Group pieces of related information together in an easy-to-read format
- Create itemized lists of information
- Focus attention on certain pieces of information on Web pages

Paragraph Breaks—<P>

The most common paragraph tag used on WWW pages is the <P> tag. This tag separates two paragraphs of information with a blank line. To use the paragraph tag, simply add <P> to your HTML file where you want to separate two lines of text. This tag isn't a container tag and can be added anywhere within your HTML document.

Figure 25.7 shows how the <P> tag formats the following information:

```
Typically, you'll want to separate paragraphs of information with
the HTML paragraph tag.
<P>
However, sometimes you want to use the <P> Paragraph <P> tag <P> to
<P> really <P> separate <P> pieces<P> of <P> text.
```

Fig. 25.7
The <P> tag is the most popular paragraph separation tag.

> **Note**
>
> Unlike most HTML tags, the <P> tag works both as a container tag (with the closing </P> tag) and as a separate stand-alone tag. Initially, WWW browsers (including Netscape) required that each separate paragraph of text was surrounded by the <P> and </P> tags. This was quite a hassle because the closing tag was often forgotten or not used. Nowadays, Netscape allows you to separate two paragraphs of text by only using the <P> tag.

Line Breaks—

Similar to the paragraph tag, the line break tag is also used to correctly place text on a page. The only difference is that the <BR> tag places text on the next line, without a blank line between two lines of text.

Think of the <BR> tag as hitting a carriage return on a typewriter. Whenever Netscape spots one, it automatically zings to the next line when displaying information. This tag is useful in telling Netscape where it can break up lines of text that are displayed on-screen. Figure 25.8 shows how the following snippet of HTML code appears in Netscape.

```
<H2>College Student Grocery List</H2>
      Milk <BR>
      Brownies <BR>
      Frozen Pizza <BR>
      Spaghetti <BR>
      Beer <BR>
```

Fig. 25.8
The <BR> tag is
popular for listing
several items on
subsequent lines.

IV

Building Home Pages

> **Tip**
>
> The header tags automatically include a carriage return and blank line after text
> surrounded with the <Hn> and </Hn> tags (where the n stands for the header level as
> described above) without worrying about using the line break or paragraph tags.

▶ See "
,"
pg. 727

> **Note**
>
> HTML also includes two derivations of the <BR> tag.
>
> The word break tag, <WBR> marks where Netscape should break up a specific word,
> should it need to wrap to a following line (particularly useful for long and extended
> medical terminology).
>
> The opposite of <BR>, <NOBR> and </NOBR> surrounds text that should never be
> wrapped on subsequent lines automatically by Netscape. The no break tag disables
> word wrapping.

The Horizontal Rule—<HR>

A different way to separate and organize paragraphs of information with
HTML is using the <HR>, or horizontal rule tag. The <HR> tag inserts a solid
line that goes completely across the Netscape screen to separate different
parts of an HTML document.

Not a container tag, adding a horizontal rule to a WWW page is as simple as
typing <HR> into the HTML file. Netscape supports a variety options that enable you to customize the appearance of horizontal lines on-screen, including
the length, thickness, and alignment.

▶ See "The <HR>
Element,"
pg. 723

Often, the <HR> tag is used to separate the main body of a document from the
title and footer. Figure 25.9 shows an example of how the solid horizontal
lines clearly define the different areas of the WWW document.

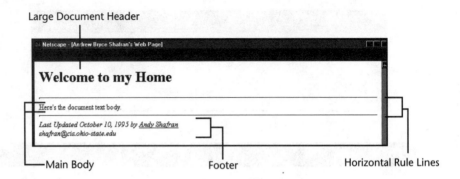

Large Document Header

Main Body

Footer

Horizontal Rule Lines

Predefined Text—<PRE>

Usually, Netscape ignores how text is placed within the actual HTML text file
without paragraph formatting tags. Tabs, extra spaces, and carriage returns
are all ignored by Netscape when deciding how to format a WWW page.

To circumvent this, use the <PRE> and </PRE> container tags to specifically arrange preformatted text to appear in a distinct manner within Netscape.

All tabs, carriage returns, and extra spaces are displayed exactly as they appear
within the <PRE> and </PRE> tags. By allowing users to predefine how text appears on-screen, Netscape lets WWW page creators create lists, tables, and
specially formatted bits of info without hassling with learning advanced
HTML tags.

Figure 25.10 shows how the following text appears, tabs and all, in Netscape:

```
<PRE>
<H2>How to pay for a wedding</H2>
<B>     Bride's Family    Groom's Family </B>
Reception  xxx
Alcohol                    xxx
Flowers    xxx             xxx
</PRE>
```

Other formatting tags such as headlines, italicizing, and bolding work fine
within the preformatted text tags.

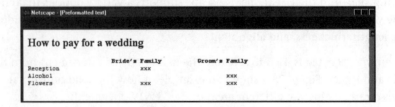

> **Note**
>
> When displaying preformatted text, Netscape uses a monospace font to ensure that each letter and character is the same width when displayed on the screen. This is so Netscape can guarantee that how you typed text within the <PRE> tags appears lined up correctly.

Basic Formatting Tags

Formatting paragraphs and chunks of text on-screen can be a harrowing task at best. In addition to organizing paragraphs of information, you've got to worry about how to make certain pieces of text stand out by using boldface, italics, text centering, and other formatting characteristics.

This section describes the popular HTML formatting tags and how they are used.

Strengthening Text—<B>

How often have you typed an entire paragraph, but wanted to make a single word or phrase stand out from the rest of the text? Maybe it's a special term, or the main focus of the paragraph. Either way, you want that word to jump out and catch a reader's eye on your WWW page.

Using the <B> and </B> container tags, surrounded text is displayed in boldface, making the letters appear thicker and darker on-screen compared to regular text.

> **Note**
>
> As mentioned in the last chapter, logical versus physical formatting is often a common debate among HTML programmers. Nowhere can this debate be better witnessed than in deciding how to make specific pieces of text stand out in bold or italics. The physical answer to this question is to use the <B> and <I> container tags to mark text as **bold** or *italics*.
>
> On the flip side, logical proponents suggest using the <STRONG> and <EM> (emphasis) tags to make text stand out. These two tags are used to describe how text should appear relative to normal text on-screen. Typically, the <STRONG> tag bolds surrounded text while the <EM> tag italicizes it, but this interpretation depends on each WWW browser's interpretation. For example, another browser might decide that <EM>phasized text should be bright red and in huge letters, while there's a much
>
> (continues)

(continued)

more standard approach to displaying <I>talic text—slightly slanted towards the right. With Logical Formatting tags, you're at the mercy of a WWW browser to interpret them however they like.

Nowadays, most HTML programmers tend to use the physical tags (<B> and <I>) because of the underlying uncertainty of how exactly WWW browsers will display text marked with logical tags.

Figure 25.11 shows how Netscape uses the <B> and <STRONG> tags to make important text stand out on a WWW page. Notice how Netscape tends to display the logical and physical tags in a virtually identical fashion.

Fig. 25.11
Boldfacing text adds significant character to specific words within paragraphs.

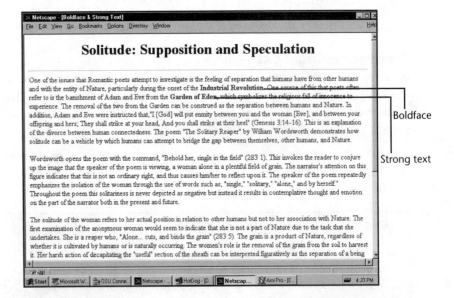

Italicizing Text—<I>

Another way to enhance the appearance of text within Netscape is by using the <I> and </I> italics tags. These tags indicate that text should appear italicized.

Italics can be used for highlighting a certain word or phrase, citing a published work, or for simply making a WWW page more readable. Look at figure 25.12 for an example of italicized (<I>) and emphasized text (<EM>) as listed:

```
After reading <I>The Body Farm</I> by Patricia Cornwell, I immedi-
ately had to go out and buy her other books. <EM>Postmortem</EM>
```

```
and <I>All that remains</I> are among my favorite hair-raising
whodunits!
```

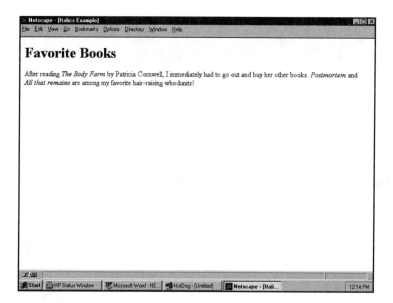

IV

Building Home Pages

Fig. 25.12
Italics comes in
handy when
referring to other
printed works, and
for highlighting
certain words in a
paragraph.

Note

You can use the italics tags alone, or in conjunction with other text formatting tags. For example, you could make some text appear boldface and italicized by surrounding it with `<B><I> YOUR TEXT </I></B>`. When embedding tags within one another, make sure you close the most recently opened tag first. Otherwise, you're more likely to forget to close a tag and have unwanted side effects.

Tip

Some older browsers don't support recursive formatting tags. If you mark text to appear in bold and italics, older versions of Mosaic and Netscape will only use the first formatting tag encountered.

Blinking Text—`<BLINK>`

Another lesser used text formatting feature is the `<BLINK>` HTML tag. Using this set of container tags, displayed text intermittently blinks on and off, quickly attracting the attention of someone visiting that WWW page.

Adding blinking text to a WWW page is as simple as surrounding text with the `<BLINK>` and `</BLINK>` keywords as shown in the following example:

```
<BLINK> <H1> On the Road Yet Again </H1> </BLINK>
```

> **Caution**
>
> At best, blinking text should be used extremely sparingly as a text formatting feature. Prudent use of the `<BLINK>` tag is required unless you want to create an unwelcome eyesore on the WWW. Visitors will never forget hundreds of blinking words that make a WWW page difficult to read and unmotivating to return to.

Centering Text—`<CENTER>`

A welcome addition to the HTML text formatting tags allows you to center headlines and text in Netscape. Using the `<CENTER>` and `</CENTER>` container tags, marked text always appears horizontally in the middle of Netscape's screen. Regardless of how skinny or wide your Netscape window is, text will be automatically centered for visitors.

This flexibility allows WWW page creators to practice more page layout and design techniques, as well as use more of the available Netscape window.

Figure 25.13 shows how a previous example changes when the main header is centered.

Fig. 25.13
You'll want to take advantage of centering text on-screen to make headlines and information stand out more distinctly.

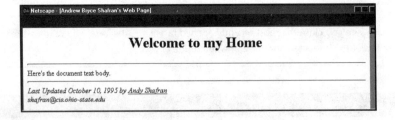

Additional Formatting Tags

In addition to bolding and italicizing text, HTML also supports several other popular text formatting tags. Table 25.2 outlines these additional HTML tags and how they make text appear in Netscape. These tags tend to be used less often and are not always supported by other non-Netscape browsers.

Table 25.2 Additional Logical Tags	
HTML Tag	**Tag Description**
`<BIG> </BIG>`	Makes selected text appear logically bigger than surrounding pieces of text.
`<SMALL> </SMALL>`	Makes marked text smaller in comparison to other text on-screen.
`<CITE> </CITE>`	A popular way of citing other reference materials.
`<TT> </TT>`	Fixed width font that resembles a typewriter.
`<BLOCKQUOTE> </BLOCKQUOTE>`	Used to make references of blocks of text from another reference.

Understanding HTML Lists

Everyday you make a list to organize various pieces of information in a specific order. Whether it's creating a grocery list to go shopping, or a to-do task list, keeping track of a lot of information is vital. Within HTML, lists are one of the most widespread and powerful tools used to display text with Netscape. The following is a list of several popular reasons to include a list in your HTML document:

- You can organize a lot of different types and pieces of information in one structured, easy-to-read format.

- You can describe a complicated step-by-step process in edible chunks of information.

- Create highlights of information in a table of contents fashion that points to other more general pieces of information.

Using the several different types of built-in lists, you can handle virtually any situation. You'll learn the differences among ordered, unordered, and definition lists, as well as learn the important syntax for displaying a list within Netscape.

Figure 25.14 shows an example of what a list looks like within Netscape.

Fig. 25.14
This simple
unordered list
could appear on
any WWW page.

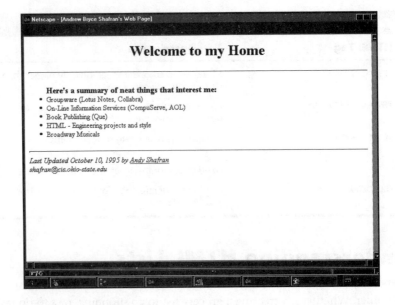

Creating Lists

In HTML, adding a list is not as easy as using a simple container tag. Several related HTML tags work together to allow you to select which type of list you want to display, how to delineate among different items within a list, and how to include a title for the list. For example, the HTML source code for the following list is shown:

```
<UL>
    <LH><B>Here's a summary of neat things that interest me:
        </B></LH>
    <LI> Groupware (Lotus Notes, Collabra)
    <LI> On-Line Information Services (CompuServe, AOL)
    <LI> Book Publishing (Que)
    <LI> HTML - Engineering projects and style
    <LI> Broadway Musicals
</UL>
```

The <UL> and </UL> tags select the list type (unordered). The <LH> and </LH> tags markup the list header, or title, and the <LI> or list item tag separates each list item from one another. Together, these three parts make up a complete list. By adding each tag in a step-by-step process, your list is finished.

Next, you'll learn how to include three different types of lists within HTML documents.

Adding an Unordered List

On the WWW, the unordered list is most commonly used. This list displays each list item with a bullet preceding each item of information.

To add an unordered list, follow these steps:

1. First add the `<UL>` and `</UL>` tags to your HTML document.

2. Within the unordered list tags, type in the text you want to appear as the list's header, and surround it with the `<LH>` and `</LH>` tags:

   \<UL\>

   \<LH\> Saturday Night Live Guest Hosts\</LH\>

   \</UL\>

3. Add the list item tag `<LI>` and type in that piece of information.

   \<LI\> Chevy Chase

4. Repeat the third step until you have every list item typed in and accounted for. Figure 25.15 shows the final unordered list created with the following text:

   ```
   <UL>
   <LH> Saturday Night Live Guest Hosts</LH>
   <LI> Chevy Chase
   <LI> Steve Martin
   <LI> Jim Belushi
   <LI> Dan Akroyd
   </UL>
   ```

Fig. 25.15
This simple unordered list was created in minutes.

Adding a Numbered List

Similar to an unordered list, the numbered list presents separate items displayed in an organized order. The main difference between the two list types is that the numbered list automatically numbers each list item according to its order of appearance within the list.

Creating a numbered list is virtually identical to creating an unordered one. Follow these steps to build a numbered list:

1. First add the `<OL>` and `</OL>` tags to your HTML document.

2. Within the numbered list tags, type in the text you want to appear as the list's header, and surround it with the `<LH>` and `</LH>` tags:

   \<OL\>

   \<LH\>Favorite baseball teams\</LH\>

   \</OL\>

3. Add the first list item tag <LI> and type in that piece of information. Remember that this first item will be numbered with a "1."

> **<LI>Cincinnati Reds**

4. Repeat the third step until you have every list item typed in and accounted for. Figure 25.16 shows the final numbered list created in this example:

```
<OL>
<LH>Favorite baseball teams</LH>
<LI>Cincinnati Reds
<LI>Seattle Mariners
<LI>Chicago Cubs
</OL>
```

Fig. 25.16
This simple numbered list is a good example of how numbered lists prioritize list items.

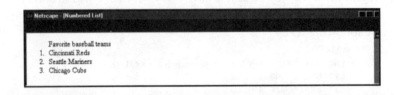

Tip

If you don't want to display the numbered list in straight numeric format, you can also number items with a letter (upper- and lowercase) or a Roman numeral. To change this Netscape only feature, add the TYPE= keyword to the <OL> tag. To use Roman numerals, your <OL> tag becomes:

```
<OL TYPE=I, II, III...>
```

To list elements with a letter instead of a number, try:

```
<OL TYPE=A, B, C...>
```

Adding a Definition List

Unlike the other common types of lists, definition lists have two parts to each item. Much as dictionary entries have two elements, the word and the definition, the definition list has two separate terms.

To add a definition list to your HTML document, follow these steps:

1. First add the <DL> and </DL> tags to your HTML document.

2. Within the numbered list tags, type in the text you want to appear as the list's header, and surround it with the `<LH>` and `</LH>` tags:

> **\<DL\>**
>
> **\<LH\>Important Web terms\</LH\>**
>
> **\</DL\>**

3. Unlike the other lists, which had a single component for each list item, the definition list has two. First type `<DT>` (short for definition term) and type in the term you want to define.

> **\<DT\> HTML**

4. Next type `<DD>` (definition definition) and type in the term's definition.

> **\<DD\> Hyper Text Markup Language**

5. Repeat the previous steps until you have every term and definition listed. Figure 25.17 shows the final definition list created in the following example:

```
<DL>
<LH>Important Web terms </LH>
        <DT> HTML
               <DD> Hyper Text Markup Language
        <DT> WWW
               <DD> World Wide Web
        <DT> VRML
               <DD> Virtual Reality Markup Language
</DL>
```

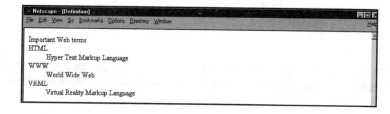

Fig. 25.17
This definition list is only a sample of the flexibility lists provide.

Notice how the definition term appears on one line, with the subsequent definition indented and on the following line.

Nesting Lists Within One Another

Like most other HTML elements, you can have lists within lists, allowing you to subcategorize a single list into many different pieces. Mixing and matching lists is permitted, although be careful when embedding a list within the definition list because of the separate types of list elements.

To embed a list within another list, first create the initial list:

```
<OL>
<LH>Favorite baseball teams</LH>
<LI>Cincinnati Reds
<LI>Seattle Mariners
<LI>Chicago Cubs
</OL>
```

Then, embed the `<UL>` `</UL>` (or whichever type of list you want to use) within the original list tags. For example, an expansion of the following initial list appears in figure 25.18.

```
<OL>
<LH><B>Favorite baseball teams</B></LH>
<LI>Cincinnati Reds
        <UL>
        <LH>Favorite Players </LH>
        <LI>Smiley
        <LI>Larkin
        <LI>Santiago
        </UL>
<LI>Seattle Mariners
        <UL>
        <LH>Favorite Players </LH>
        <LI>Johnson
        <LI>The Kid
        <LI>Buhner
        </UL>
<LI>Chicago Cubs
        <UL>
        <LH>Favorite Players </LH>
        <LI>Sosa
        <LI>Grace
        </UL>
</OL>
```

Tip

Notice how I used the `<B>` tags in the List Header above. This draws eyes to the description of the list before people start perusing it so they know what they are reading. Using formatting tags such as `<B>` or `<I>` are common within List Headers and List Items.

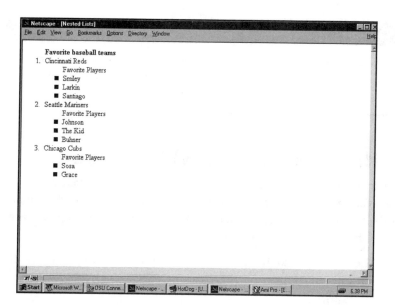

Fig. 25.18
Nested lists follow
the same rules as
single level lists.

Including Comments

In the world of programming, commenting sections of a program are virtually a required task. It is difficult to look back at work done several months
ago and exactly remember the reasons you decided to display information in
a certain format, or why you ignored specific conventions. Commenting
within HTML is just as important.

Comments are typed bits of information that can only be seen when a visitor
chooses to specifically view the page's source code. Standard comments
should include the last time a file was updated, who made the modifications,
and a description of recent changes. While HTML is usually straightforward,
some tags can be deceptive. Commenting on how the tag works, and why
you chose to use that tag is useful for future maintenance of that HTML
document.

To add a comment to your document, surround the commented code with
<!- and ->.

```
<!- My baseball Numbered list ->
<OL>
<LH>Favorite baseball teams</LH>
<LI>Cincinnati Reds
<LI>Seattle Mariners
<LI>Chicago Cubs
</OL>
```

> **Caution**
>
> Make sure you don't include private or confidential information within source code comments. Anyone who visits the page can see the original HTML text should they wish.

Building a Sample HTML Page

Now that you're finished with the HTML crash course, let's take a moment and review many of the different tags you've learned. Let's build a sample HTML document for a fictional local restaurant, trying to incorporate the many different HTML lessons learned.

1. The first step is adding the important tags that must be in all HTML documents.

   ```
   <HTML>

   <HEAD>

   </HEAD>

   <BODY>

   </BODY>

   </HTML>
   ```

2. Within the <HEAD> and </HEAD> tags, add a title to HTML document.

   ```
   <TITLE> OrangeBee's American Cuisine </TITLE>
   ```

3. Along the same lines as the title, add a large and bold header to the document.

   ```
   <BODY>

   <H1> OrangeBee's Fabulous American Cuisine on the Web </H1>

   </BODY>
   ```

4. Type in some basic information about the restaurant. Take care to separate the paragraphs of text using the proper tags. So far your sample HTML document looks like this:

   ```
   <HTML>
   <HEAD> <TITLE> OrangeBee's American Cuisine </TITLE> </HEAD>
   <BODY>
   <CENTER><H1> OrangeBee's Fabulous American Cuisine on the Web
   </H1></CENTER>
   <HR>
   Since 1991, OrangeBee's has been the fastest growing change
   of American cuisine and affordable eating. We offer a wide
   ```

```
variety of menu items, including several that contain under 5
grams of fat. <P>
<B>Stop by our nearest restaurants at: </B><BR>
Morse Road <BR>
Great Southern Shopping Center <BR>
Bexley <BR>
<HR>
<!- Created by OrangeBee's 1995 ->
</BODY>
</HTML>
```

5. Now the final step to this fictitious restaurant is to add a few menu items using a definition list. Try this list as an example:

```
<DL>
<LH><B>OrangeBee's famous menu</B></LH>
            <DT> Shrimp Cocktail
                <DD> <I>This succulent platter of shrimp
served with a tangy sauce. </I>
            <DT> Fat-free Caesar
                <DD> <I>Our homemade fat-free Caesar dressing
makes this salad ideal. </I>
            <DT>Steak and Eggs
                <DD> <I>Our cholesterol killer. This combo is
everything the '90s doctors say not to eat.</I>
</DL>
```

Figure 25.19 shows the final result of this sample WWW page. Read on to the next chapter to learn how to spice it up with graphics and links!

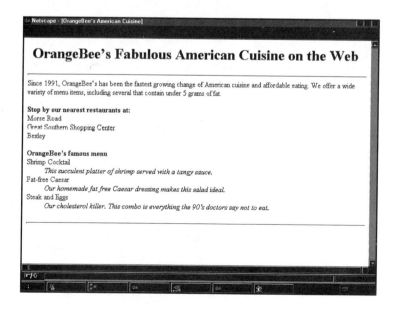

Fig. 25.19
OrangeBee's now has a simple and nice looking Web page.

Tip

When creating a lot of HTML files, most developers tend to create and use a standard template. This template has all the basic and necessary tags (such as <HTML> and <BODY>) already typed in, and follows a standard format (such as an unordered list). Once a template is created, all you have to do is fill in the blanks by typing the needed text, and the page is finished. Using a template saves you from always worrying about miscellaneous tags that are commonly forgotten.

## CHAPTER 26

Adding Links, Graphics, and Tables

Learning how to place and format text on WWW pages is the important first step to getting familiar with HTML. Numerous tags exist that allow you detailed control over how information is displayed when viewed with Netscape. But HTML offers a lot more than plain text formatting.

By this point, you're probably familiar with how to use hyperlinks to jump from site to site on the WWW. In this chapter you learn how to create and include those hyperlinks in HTML documents that you've created yourself. As you'll see, links come in all different shapes, sizes, and formats.

Along with links, graphics also spice up WWW pages and make them more interesting and informative to visit. HTML allows you to include a wide variety of graphics on WWW pages.

Like lists, tables are powerful layout tools which allow you to display and compare copious amounts of information within a columnized modular format. Tables include several new HTML tags that need to be used in the proper sequence to correctly organize information on the screen.

Specifically, in this chapter you learn how to:

- Understand HTML hypertext links
- Create standard links to other WWW pages
- Link Web pages to other Internet resources
- Add images with HTML
- Understand important image customization techniques
- Learn how to use graphics as links
- Create and incorporate a table into your HTML pages

Explaining HTML Links

The underlying premise behind the World Wide Web was to link information from all over the globe together in a single accessible format. People browsing the WWW in Rhode Island, for example, can have immediate access to information anywhere on the Internet. To accomplish this formidable task, every file and document on the Internet was given its own unique URL (Uniform Resource Locator), or address. Similar to a mailing address, the URL tells Internet browsers where to go when looking for specific information.

Once you know an URL, you can easily link into that spot on the Internet. By linking documents and files together from across the world, you create a virtual "web" of links back and forth, inspiring the name of the WWW.

Using Links

In Netscape, hypertext links typically appear as underlined blue text (see fig. 26.1). Using your mouse, you can click the underlined text and be brought immediately to the linked document. HTML authors can link to other local HTML files, specific anchored spots within the same HTML file, WWW sites elsewhere on the Web, and even additional Internet resources such as UseNet newsgroups, Gopher, and even e-mail can be linked to with HTML.

Fig. 26.1

In general, underlined text indicates a hypertext link.

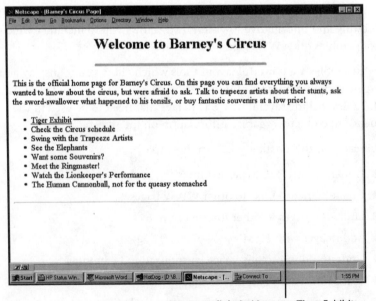

Hypertext links in Netscape Tiger Exhibit

Once visited, the linked text changes colors to indicate that you've already traversed that specific strand of the WWW. This serves as a useful reminder and map of where you've been and where you have yet to visit.

> **Note**
>
> Not all hypertext links appear in blue. Using advanced HTML characteristics described below, or setting Netscape preferences (see chapter 4 for more information) hyperlinks can appear in a variety of colors and formats. Typically though, hypertext links will be set out in a different color indicating that they are "hot" text.

There are no technical limitations to the number of different links available from a single HTML document. But WWW designers should be careful not to overwhelm their pages with hundreds of hypertext links to everywhere across the world—bigger is not always better.

Dissecting an URL

Not surprisingly, an URL is made of several distinct elements. Much as your mailing address requires a street address, city, state, and ZIP code to receive mail correctly, an URL has its own pieces as well. In general, all URLs look like this:

Internet Service://Host Name [:port] /path/and/filename

- *Internet Service*—The type of information Netscape is linking into. Most often you'll use http to link to other WWW documents, but e-mail, UseNet, and Gopher all have their own special name (described later). HTTP stands for HyperText Transfer Protocol and tells Netscape how to handle the linked information.

- *Host Name*—The electronic domain on the Internet that you are trying to connect with.

- *[:port]*—Indicates a special port on the Internet server to connect with. It is typically not required.

> **Note**
>
> Most URL's don't require a specified port address because by default, Netscape knows how to specifically communicate with the WWW servers on the Internet. Port addresses are more common when you need to include a link to a different Internet resource, such as Gopher or FTP because they tell Netscape which electronic data communications port is designated specifically for Gopher or FTP access.

- *path/and/filename*—The complete file name of the HTML document you want to access and the path required to reach it. If no file name is specified, Netscape automatically looks for a file called "index.html" in the directory specified.

Combining all the pieces together, here's the URL for Que, the publisher for this book:

http://www.mcp.com/que/

Creating a Link

Once you know the URL you want to link to, creating the link in HTML is a relatively easy process. As with everything else in HTML, adding links requires a special tag. HTML uses the <A> and </A> tags to create a link.

Follow these steps to add a hypertext link to an HTML document:

1. First identify the unique URL that you want to link to:

    http://www.mcp.com/que/

2. Add the HTML Anchor tag <A> </A> to the URL in the following fashion:

    <A HREF="http://www.mcp.com/que/"> </A>

    The HREF keyword indicates that you are creating a link to the HyperText Reference URL that you provide.

3. Indicate the text that you want to identify as "hot" in Netscape—appearing underlined and in blue, between the <A> and </A> tags.

    <A HREF="http://www.mcp.com/que/"> Link to Que Publishing </A>

Linking to Local Files

Linking WWW pages to other documents is as simple as knowing the complete URL to the linked document. However, if you want to link to other HTML documents that are located at the same site on the Internet, you can take advantage of several shortcuts.

This feature is called relative addressing because it allows you to give an URL that is relative to the original document. For example, to link to an HTML file named moreinfo.html that is located in the exact same subdirectory as the original document, you can use just the file name as the URL:

    <A HREF="moreinfo.html">Link to More Information</A>

Because keeping every HTML file in the same subdirectory can be confusing, with relative addressing, you can also indicate files within subdirectories as well. To link to evenmore.html in a subdirectory named INFORMATION, you can use the following link:

> <A HREF="INFORMATION/evenmore.html">Link to Even More Information</A>

Similarly, you can link to files that are one level higher than the current subdirectory in the hard drive structure:

> <A HREF="../themost.html"> The Most Information </A>

Using relative addressing makes it easier to organize a WWW file structure because you don't have to type the complete URL for every linked document.

Other Types of HTML Links

HTML also handles several other popular Internet resources that exchange and share information—UseNet newsgroups, e-mail, FTP, and Gopher are the ones you'll most likely want to use in your WWW pages. Each of these different types of information can be linked to directly with HTML by specifying their unique URL.

Note

Netscape also allows you to create hyperlinks to other different types of Internet resources including Telnet, WAIS (Wide Area Information Service), and other more obscure protocols. Each protocol requires its own unique keyword and has its own specific format. For more information on how Netscape integrates with other Internet services see chapter 5.

Using FTP Links

FTP traditionally allows any user to log on to an Internet domain, search through the file listings, and download the file to their personal computer. With HTML, you can directly link files to a WWW page and let visitors download a file simply by clicking the underlined link.

◀ See "Accessing and Downloading from an FTP Site," pg. 301

Follow the same steps outlined previously to add an FTP URL to an HTML document. An FTP URL looks similar to a standard URL except that it uses a different Internet service keyword. So **ftp://ftp4.netscape.com/pub/ smart/SM10R2.EXE** looks like

> <A HREF="ftp://ftp4.netscape.com/pub/smart/SM10R2.EXE"> Netscape's Smartmarks File</A>

when the proper tags are added. By clicking the highlighter text, Netscape automatically logs on to the Internet domain, finds the file to download, and starts retrieving it.

Caution

Adding an FTP URL as described previously assumes that the Internet site being connected to supports anonymous FTP logins. That allows everyone on the Internet free access to connect and download files.

Under some situations, anonymous FTP access is not allowed, and a user ID and password is necessary to connect. For those situations, the FTP URL looks like:

FTP://USERID:PASSWORD@ftp.netscape.com/file/smart.exe

Although you can include non-anonymous FTP links on a WWW page, make sure you understand the possible repercussions. Anyone who accesses that WWW page can view the HTML source code through Netscape and see the user ID and password.

Note

Another strategy often used when linking to files via the FTP protocol is to link to a directory instead of a specific file. By linking to a directory, Netscape brings up a list of files that you can download instead of linking to a single file. This is particularly useful because Internet files tend to change file names as newer versions are released. This saves you the hassle of constantly updating your HTML documents each time a file name changes.

To link to a FTP directory instead of a file, simply leave off the file name within the URL.

Using Gopher Links

◀ See "Accessing Other Internet Services with Netscape," pg. 301

As a precursor to the WWW, Gopher menus link to other worldwide menus in much the same way HTML links work. Over the years, enormous quantities of information have been placed on Gopher, and is not available in HTML format yet. Thousands of Gopher servers exist with vast information ranging from specific university information to the United States State Department Travel Advisories.

Fortunately, you can link to any Gopher server as long as you know the proper URL. Following the standard URL format, Gopher links tend to include a server port number, use extended file and directory names, and use Gopher as the Internet service keyword. The following is an example Gopher URL:

gopher://gopher.stolaf.edu:70/00/Internet%20Resources/US-State-Department-Travel-Advisories/Current-Advisories/australia

This URL tells Netscape to connect to the gopher.stolaf.edu server using port 70 and retrieve the current travel advisory for Australia. The following is how the link appears in full HTML, and figure 26.2 shows the results of clicking this link.

```
<A HREF="gopher://gopher.stolaf.edu:70/00/Internet%20Resources/US-
State-Department-Travel-Advisories/Current-Advisories/
australia">Gopher report on the US Travel Advisory on Australia</A>
```

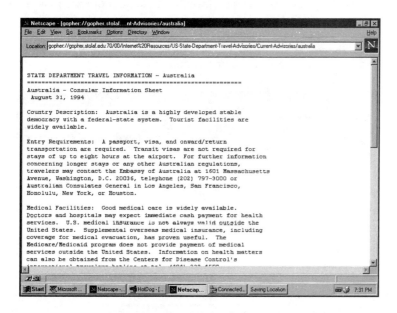

Fig 26.2
Unlike Netscape, Gopher offers a text-only outlook on linked information from around the world.

Tip

In the preceding Gopher URL, the "%20" is used to replace a space for the WWW link. Netscape can't properly recognize spaces in URLs and the %20 string is a standard replacement for them.

Using UseNet Links

UseNet URLs are much simpler than other types of URLs. They require the Internet resource keyword—news, a colon, and then the full name of the newsgroup:

news:alt.fan.dave_barry

UseNet URLs work differently because there is no central news Internet server. The URL tells Netscape to connect to the pre-customized news server and read that newsgroup.

The following is a complete HTML link to a newsgroup. Figure 26.3 shows the Netscape newsreader reading the newsgroup.

Fig. 26.3

Newsgroups are another integrated service available with Netscape and HTML.

Troubleshooting

I have a link on my WWW page to a specific UseNet newsgroup. I recently received e-mail from some people who don't have access to that newsgroup (alt.religion). They get an error message when trying to locate it. Is there a problem with my HTML encoding or any way I can help them out so they can read the newsgroup I am referring to?

Every site has its load of newsgroups that it carries. Because of the massive disk space that newsgroups use, few Internet servers can afford to provide access to every newsgroup. Lesser used and varied appropriateness newsgroups (especially the alt.hierarchy) are often not available on local news servers. Contact your System Administrator to ask your site to pick up a feed from a newsgroup that isn't currently available.

Using Mailto Links

Another important communication tool on the Internet is electronic mail. E-mail allows people to send personal messages to other individuals all across the world. With HTML, you can include an e-mail on a WWW page that lets visitors easily send mail to a specific address.

Using the mailto Internet services keyword, building an e-mail URL only requires knowing the e-mail address of the recipient. For example, to build a link to **shafran.5@osu.edu**, you would use the following URL:

> **mailto:shafran.5@osu.edu**

The full HTML for the e-mail link looks like:

```
<A HREF="mailto:shafran.5@osu.edu">Sample E-mail</A>
```

When clicked upon, Netscape brings up the Netscape mail window where users can type a message and send it on its way in a few moments (see fig. 26.4).

Troubleshooting

I'm looking for a specific URL of a neat World Wide Web page I found while browsing one day. Unfortunately I can't remember the complete URL or where I found the original link. Does Netscape know how to use a partial URL when looking around the Internet?

Netscape is limited only to the exact URLs that you supply. When looking for a specific URL to link to, try checking out Yahoo at **http://www.yahoo.com** and searching their index of WWW links. Good luck! For more information on using search engines, see chapter 8.

Fig. 26.4
Here's how
Netscape can be
used to send
e-mail.

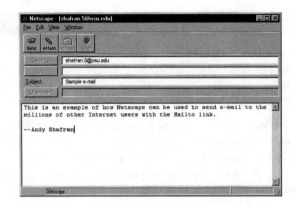

Understanding HTML Anchors and Targets

In addition to linking to other WWW files and Internet resources, HTML also has the ability to link and refer to internal points within the same document. Functioning like a table of contents, you can place multiple text anchors within an HTML document and create a centralized listing of them at the top of the file (or anywhere else). By clicking the hyperlinks, visitors aren't taken to a separate document, but to a different spot, called targets, within the *same* HTML file.

Primarily for large files, this internal referencing system requires two separate steps. First you've got to create the named targets within the HTML file, and then you must build the links to each of those specific targets.

Creating Named Targets

Adding named targets to WWW pages requires only a few steps. Follow these steps to add as many named targets as you want to your HTML document.

1. Choose a name for your target. This name should be succinct and to the point, but not too cryptic to be confusing.

   Mammals

2. Use the <A> and </A> tags to mark the text as a target, but instead of using the HREF keyword, use NAME instead.

   <A NAME="Mammals"></A>

3. Type in the corresponding text that you want associated with the named target. This is the text the target is attached to. Notice how other tags work within the anchor tags.

> **<A NAME="Mammals">**
>
> **<H3>Warm Blooded Creatures</H3**
>
> **</A>**

Once your named target is added, you're ready to move on to the next step and learn how to jump directly to it within the same file.

Tip

You don't have to associate any text with a specific named target. Instead, you can leave a blank between the anchor tags. Netscape places that line at the top of the screen when told to link to a named target. Not associating text with a target is useful when you want to associate one with a special list, table, or graphic.

Linking to Named Targets

Linking to a named target is identical to linking to other WWW documents with one minor difference. Instead of typing a complicated URL, you simply type in the target name with a "#" in front of it.

The following is an example of how to link to the previous example:

```
<A HREF="#Mammals">Mammals - Earth's Dominant Species</A>
```

As you can see in figure 26.5, links to named targets appear the same as standard links to other HTML files.

Caution

Don't forget the "#" in front of the target name. Without it, Netscape attempts to link to a separate file (located in the same current directory) with that target name.

Note

You can also link to specific named targets in other HTML files elsewhere on the WWW. To find out a target name, view the site's HTML source code and manually pick out the target.

Be careful though. Named targets tend to change considerably more often than HTML file names, and have a significantly better chance of becoming obsolete or invalid.

Fig. 26.5
Whether targets or
regular links, they
all appear the
same in Netscape.

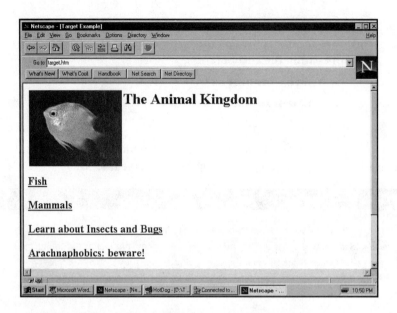

Important Link Tips and Traps

There are several important stylistic situations to be aware of when linking
HTML documents to one another. The following is a simple checklist to
evaluate your WWW links:

- *Test and re-test every HTML link.* Make sure that there are no typos or
  incorrect URLs included within your HTML documents.

- *Periodically check your HTML file for outdated links.* On the WWW, files
  occasionally move, are renamed, or even deleted. Regularly checking
  WWW links ensures that they are current and constantly maintained.
  For example, when linking to files, remember that file names change as
  new versions are released.

- *Organize lists of links.* If you need to include many links within a single
  document, use a list, table, or other organization technique to keep the
  list of links usable and readable.

- *In paragraphs, links should be invisible.* When linking a single word or
  phrase within a paragraph, the link should not affect the flow of the
  paragraph. Visitors should be able to read and understand the paragraph without accessing the link.

- *Associate relevant information to links.* Avoid linking the word "here" or
  other unimportant words. Pretend that you are only looking at the

"hot" text. You should be able to understand where that link will take you before clicking it. The word "here" doesn't describe where the link will take you.

Adding Graphics with HTML

Creating HTML files wouldn't be complete without learning how to add exciting and colorful images and graphics to them. In the multimedia atmosphere of the WWW, graphics are important tools because they can be used to jazz up a WWW page. You'll discover that most HTML documents incorporate graphics in their design because they immediately add variety to strictly textual information.

Other than aesthetic purposes, graphics can also have functionality within your WWW pages. Images can serve as hypertext links to other WWW pages, formatting tools to organize text around, or even replace extended pieces of information with an informative graphic.

This section introduces you to embedded graphics and images with HTML. While adding an image is easy, HTML offers a multitude of customization keywords and tags that allow you to "desktop publish" WWW documents.

The Different Types of Graphics

On the WWW, there are two popular graphics file formats that are widely supported and in use today. Of these two file formats, each has its own advantages and disadvantages for certain situations.

- *GIF (Graphical Image Format)*—The GIF format was developed by CompuServe (using technology from Unisys) and has been a worldwide graphical format standard for years. GIF files use standard compression techniques to properly handle a wide variety of colors and file size. Because of this, GIF files tend to have a significantly larger file size, but better detail and resolution than its counterpart, JPEG. If you had to choose an image format for Michaelangelo's Sistine Chapel, you'd choose GIF for the detail.

- *JPEG (Joint Photographic Expert Group)*—With the file size limitations of GIF in mind, the JPEG format was designed to be a high compression image format that stores similar GIF images in as much as 1/3 the space. Using recursive bit construction, JPEGs shrink an image several times to achieve quicker download times. Unfortunately, as a side effect, JPEG graphics tend to lose detail, especially for larger images. Because of the fuzziness that sometimes surrounds JPEG images, Monet's masterpieces would be perfect for this file format. Netscape's enhancements are refined towards loading JPEG images progressively. Netscape loads more detail into the image over several passes, allowing you to see the image form before your very eyes.

Initially, only GIF graphics were supported in the early WWW browsers. Nowadays however, virtually every browser (including Netscape) supports both GIF and JPEG and allows you to use them interchangeably. You should feel free to use whichever of the two image types you prefer.

Note

Be careful when including other popular image formats such as .TIF, .PCX, .PIC, or .BMP in your HTML pages. To view these images, individuals must have an external helper application built into Netscape.

This makes images of these file formats less ideal than backgrounds or embedded images, but acceptable as references to important information stored only in a specific graphical format.

Tip

Although not quite at par with GIF quality, JPEG graphics typically are much smaller in file size, and consequently download quicker.

Using the \<IMG> Tag

One of the most important HTML tags, the \<IMG> tag allows you to select which graphics to include on a page and how they are sized and formatted on the screen.

Without any special formatting keywords, adding a graphic is relatively easy. For example, the picture of the fish in figure 26.5 uses the following tag:

```
<IMG SRC="FISH.JPG">
```

When placed in an HTML document, this tag tells Netscape to display the graphic entitled **FISH.JPG** (which is located in the same current directory as the HTML file) on-screen.

You can also link WWW pages directly to graphics at another site. For example, if the file FISH.JPG were stored on the Que site (which it isn't), you could add the following tag to link your HTML document directly to the image:

```
<IMG SRC="http://www.que.com/fish.jpg">
```

Logically, when Netscape finds this tag, it first connects to **www.que.com,** retrieves the selected image, then displays it on your WWW page.

> **Caution**
>
> Linking images from other Web sites can cause performance problems for Web page visitors. That's because a visitor has to wait for the information to be retrieved from another site, *then* sent to their PC before they can see it. Sometimes this can be quite a slowdown. For better performance, ensure that displayed images are saved on the same Internet server as the HTML file.

Another popular way to include images within HTML documents is the use of thumbnailed images. Thumbnail images are miniature versions of a larger image that take up significantly less screen size and, thus, have a much smaller file size. Thumbnailed images are then linked to the full-size version of the image. This allows individuals the option of waiting to download the full-size image, or just being satisfied with the small, thumbnail version.

> **Note**
>
> Graphics can be stored and organized in separate subdirectories just like linked files. Using the method outlined previously in this chapter, you can direct Netscape to graphics stored in directories both higher and lower in the hard drive structure with no complications.

When placing graphics on WWW pages, the <IMG> tag offers a great deal of flexibility regarding how the image appears and is formatted on-screen. The following sections explain most popular <IMG> keywords that allow you to customize image placement in Netscape.

Alternative Text

Not all WWW browsers are created equal. While Netscape is by far the most robust and popular, others such as Lynx, are text only, and don't have the ability to display graphics and images.

Additionally, Netscape also allows users to customize whether or not to display graphics when visiting new WWW pages, because often times it takes too long to download and display all the embedded images.

To handle non-graphical browsers and Netscape's flexibility, it is standard practice to include alternative text in the <IMG> tag, which is displayed when the graphic isn't downloaded.

Use the *ALT=""* keyword to specify the alternative text to display instead of a graphic. Figure 26.6 shows how Netscape displays alternative text in the following example.

```
<IMG SRC="FISH.JPG" ALT="A cool picture of a colorful fish">
```

Fig. 26.6

Instead of the graphic, Netscape can display the alternative text.

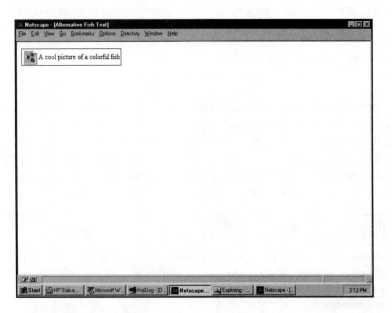

Alignment and Image Placement Options

When including graphics on a WWW page, you have several different choices where they are placed in the Netscape window. These alignment options are set with the *ALIGN=* keyword. With this keyword you specify not only where the image is aligned on-screen but also how text appears in relation to displayed images.

Table 26.1 lists the five unique ALIGN keywords and how they display graphics and text accordingly.

Table 26.1	HTML Alignment Options
Keyword	**Definition**
LEFT	Places the graphic on the left side of the screen. Text is displayed to the right.
RIGHT	The opposite of LEFT, the graphic is placed on the right margin with text on the left.
TOP	Lines up the graphic to the tallest item on the same line.
MIDDLE	Aligns the top of the text to the middle of a placed graphic.
BASELINE	Aligns the bottom of the graphic with the bottom of the line of text.

Although there are other ALIGN keywords, they are repetitive and not commonly accepted. For example, the BASELINE keyword is interchangeable and virtually identical with the BOTTOM and ABSBOTTOM keywords—just a different syntax for the same effect.

Figure 26.7 shows how the graphics are displayed on-screen using the following snippet of HTML:

```
<IMG SRC="fish.jpg" ALIGN=LEFT> Left Alignment<P>

<IMG SRC="fish.jpg" ALIGN=RIGHT> Right Alignment<P>

<IMG SRC="fish.jpg" ALIGN=TOP> Top Alignment<P>

<IMG SRC="fish.jpg" ALIGN=MIDDLE> Middle Alignment <P>

<IMG SRC="fish.jpg" ALIGN=BASELINE> Baseline Alignment <P>
```

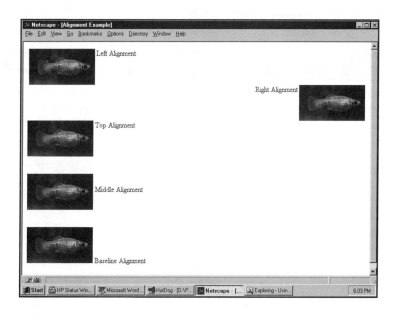

Fig. 26.7
With graphic alignment options, HTML designers have significantly more control over the appearance of their WWW pages.

> **Note**
>
> Another popular way to control graphics placement on-screen is to use Netscape tables. By using a table, you have more exact control on the position and area the graphic takes up on the screen.

Height and Width

Another advanced graphic option allows you to control exactly how wide and tall images appear within Netscape. By using the WIDTH and HEIGHT keywords, you can specify how many pixels of the screen an image should appear, regardless of what the original file's resolution was.

The HEIGHT and WIDTH keywords are typically used to create smaller, icon-sized versions of images that are easier to view on a WWW page. Using these two keywords is also an additional performance benefit within Netscape. Traditionally, Netscape must download all of the embedded images before it can format the text on-screen accordingly. When the WIDTH and HEIGHT keywords are used, Netscape knows exactly how much space to allocate for an image on-screen, and formats the page while the image(s) are downloading.

Use HEIGHT and WIDTH just like you would use the other IMG keywords described in this section. For example, to set an image to display *exactly* 300 pixels wide and 150 pixels tall, type in the following HTML:

```
<IMG SRC="FISH.JPG" HEIGHT=150 WIDTH=300>
```

Figure 26.8 shows an example of the same image with three different height and width dimensions.

> **Caution**
>
> Make sure you limit your HEIGHT and WIDTH pixel ranges to under 600 × 440. A standard VGA monitor displays 640 × 480 pixels across the screen, and anything larger virtually guarantees that visitors won't be able to easily see the entire graphic. 600 × 440 is the maximum recommended size to give clearance for standard Netscape options such as the title and scroll bars.

Vertical and Horizontal Distance

The next image placement keywords to become familiar with are HSPACE and VSPACE. These two keywords specify a specific horizontal and vertical distance away from an image that is blank space. This ensures that text remains a reasonable distance from the image by allowing the specified white space.

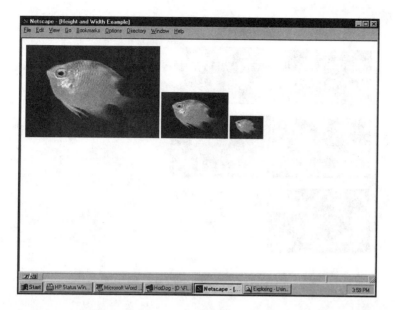

Fig. 26.8
All three sizes of
this image are
based on the same
original graphic.

Similar to the HEIGHT and WIDTH keywords, VSPACE and HSPACE require
numeric values in the form of pixels. As good practice, try to keep at least a
10 pixel border between an image and associated text. The following HTML
example shows how to use the HSPACE and VSPACE keywords to provide a
standard 10-pixel radius around an image:

```
<IMG SRC="FISH.JPG" VSPACE=10 HSPACE=10>
```

Borders

The last image customization tag is the BORDER width keyword. With this
setting, you can have Netscape automatically create a thick (or thin) black
border around any image included on your WWW pages.

Using the BORDER keyword, you can have a border thickness ranging from 0-
10 (the default is 0). The following example sets your image border thickness
to 5.

```
<IMG SRC="FISH.JPG" BORDER=5>
```

Figure 26.9 shows a sampling of five different border thicknesses ranging
from 1 to 9.

Fig. 26.9
Adding an outline
black border to
your images
frames them on
your WWW pages.

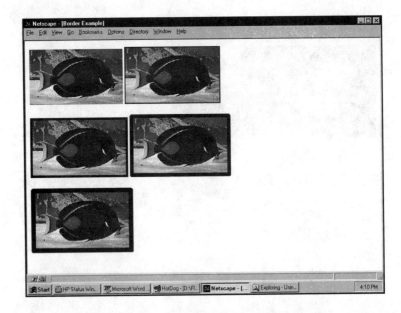

Wiring Graphics as HTML Links

Not only do graphics serve as pure visual eye candy, but they can also do double duty and work as hypertext links. By adding the proper HTML tags, embedded graphics and images can serve as links to other WWW documents and pages across the world.

Making an image serve as a link is a two step process. First you add the image along with the appropriate settings into the WWW document:

```
<IMG SRC="arrows.gif" ALIGN=LEFT>
```

Once you've added the image, now add a hypertext link in the same manner as you did earlier in this chapter, only instead of making a text phrase "hot" and surrounded by the link <A> and </A> tags, surround the IMG tag. You can also include text as well, so both the image and a text phrase link you to the same HTML document:

```
<A HREF="dir.html"><IMG SRC="arrows.gif" ALIGN=LEFT> <H2>Directions
to my House<H2></A>
```

Figure 26.10 shows how graphics can be used to link to different HTML documents. A blue outline border surrounds the graphics that are linked to other documents. By clicking upon the graphic, users are hyperlinked to the associated file.

IV

Building Home Pages

Fig. 26.10
HTML flexibility allows graphics to also serve as links to other WWW documents.

> **Note**
>
> Advanced Web developers tend to use graphics and images often to represent links to other WWW sites and pages. By using smaller icons to represent clickable buttons, WWW developers can create a graphical interface to their set of Web documents.

Creating Tables

Besides using standard lists and formatting tags, tables are another powerful tool for displaying information within HTML documents. Emulating the look and feel of a spreadsheet, tables allow you to specify rows and columns of information that are displayed within Netscape.

Tables are similar to lists (described in the previous chapter) because they allow a lot of information to be easily displayed in a small area. The main difference is that tables allow multiple columns of information—making it easier to compare and organize data.

Figure 26.11 shows an actual table from within Netscape.

Fig. 26.11
This easy to make
table lets you
compare facts in
a readable and
efficient manner.

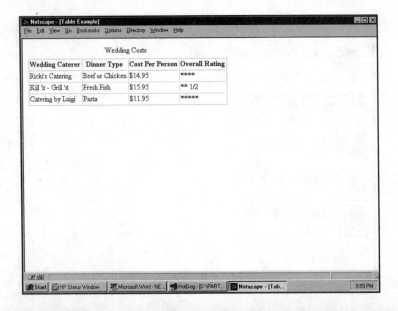

> **Caution**
>
> Although tables are popular with Netscape, their formal definition has not been
> accepted in HTML version 3, yet. The final HTML tags and codes that are accepted
> by all browsers could change slightly when HTML 3.0 is finally approved.

Adding a Table

Adding a table within HTML can be confusing because there are several different tags that need to be used in conjunction with one another. You've got
to specify each cell of every row and column individually, as well as the
table's header and other information.

Follow these steps to add a basic table to your HTML document:

1. First type the <TABLE> and </TABLE> container tags. This set of tags
   must surround the entire table. You can tell Netscape to draw the lines
   separating each cell of information from one another using the BOR-
   DER keyword:

   <TABLE BORDER=1>

   </TABLE>

2. Next type in the Table's Caption. This is a simple identifier that serves
   as a label for the table in general.

   <CAPTION> Wedding Costs </CAPTION>

> **Note**
>
> You can specify whether or not you want the table's caption to appear above or below the table by using the ALIGN keyword. By default, the caption appears above the table. To instruct the caption to appear below the table, you would use the `<CAPTION>` tag in the following way:
>
> `<CAPTION ALIGN=BOTTOM> Wedding Costs </CAPTION>`

3. Next type in the tags identifying each row of the table. The `<TR>` and `</TR>` tags surround every cell of information that appears within a single row. The number of `<TR>` row tags specifies the number of rows within your table.

4. Within the Table Row (`<TR>`) tags, you've got to specify the data in each cell with the `<TD>` tags. The number of `<TD>` and `</TD>` container tags indicates the number of columns within your table. Type the information for that cell within each set of `<TD>` container tags:

```
<TR>
    <TD>Ricki's Catering</TD>
    <TD>Beef or Chicken</TD>
    <TD>$14.95</TD>
    <TD>****</TD>
</TR>
```

5. When you are finished typing in each row and column, check out your table within Netscape. Make sure that each row has the same amount of columns and is lined up correctly.

> **Note**
>
> As a separate tag, you can also specify which cells of data should be boldface and serve as the Table Headers. Typically the first row and/or column of information is marked as a column or row header. Using the `<TH>` and `</TH>` tags instead of `<TD>`, Netscape automatically marks those cells in boldface so they standout. In this sample table, the first row of information uses the `<TH>` tags as below:
>
> ```
> <TR>
>     <TH>Wedding Caterer</TH>
>     <TH>Dinner Type</TH>
>     <TH>Cost Per Person</TH>
>     <TH>Overall Rating</TH>
> </TR>
> ```

The complete HTML code for the table shown in figure 26.11 is listed below:

```
<TABLE BORDER=1>
<CAPTION ALIGN=top>Wedding Costs</CAPTION>
    <TR>
            <TH>Wedding Caterer</TH>
            <TH>Dinner Type</TH>
            <TH>Cost Per Person</TH>
            <TH>Overall Rating</TH>
    </TR>
    <TR>
            <TD>Ricki's Catering</TD>
            <TD>Beef or Chicken</TD>
            <TD>$14.95</TD>
            <TD>****</TD>
    </TR>
    <TR>
            <TD>Kill 'it - Grill 'it</TD>
            <TD>Fresh Fish</TD>
            <TD>$15.95</TD>
            <TD>** 1/2</TD>
    </TR>
    <TR>
            <TD>Catering by Luigi</TD>
            <TD>Pasta</TD>
            <TD>$11.95</TD>
            <TD>*****</TD>
    </TR>
</TABLE>
```

Advanced Table Features

As a robust formatting language, HTML offers significant flexibility and customizability in creating tables that fit all sorts of different situations. A simple table forces you to ensure that every cell is typed in and offers a single straight forward format.

This section describes several ways to customize and modify how tables appear within Netscape using several different keywords. You'll learn how to create cells that span multiple rows and columns, customize the border thickness, and set text alignment within each cell.

Cells that Span Multiple Columns

Sometimes you'll want a particular set of information to be spread across more than one column. To accomplish this, you've got to add the COLSPAN keyword to the <TH> or <TD> tags for the cells you want to affect.

For example, in the sample table above, here's the following HTML to create a multiple column set of information (fig. 26.12):

```
<TR>
        <TH COLSPAN=2>General Info </TH>
        <TH COLSPAN=2>Hard Numbers </TH>
</TR>
<TR>
        <TH>Wedding Caterer</TH>
        <TH>Dinner Type</TH>
        <TH>Cost Per Person</TH>
        <TH>Overall Rating</TH>
</TR>
```

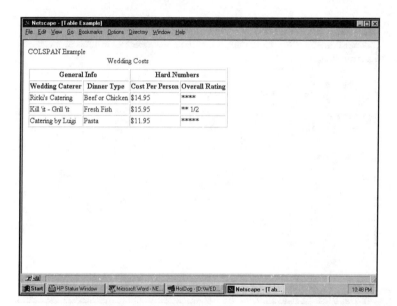

Fig. 26.12
Spanning multiple columns lets you organize information hierarchically.

> **Caution**
>
> When using the COLSPAN and ROWSPAN keywords (described below), make sure you correctly calculate the correct number of rows and columns that you combine. An incorrect number creates a disproportionate-looking table within Netscape.

Cells that Span Multiple Rows

Similar to the COLSPAN keyword described above, table cells can also be spread across multiple rows of information. Using the ROWSPAN keyword, you can specify how many rows a cell of information should span.

Figure 26.13 shows the multiple row spanning cells described below:

```
<TR>
        <TD ROWSPAN=2>Ricki's Catering</TD>
        <TD>Beef</TD>
        <TD>$14.95</TD>
        <TD>****</TD>
</TR>
<TR>
        <TD>Ricki's Catering</TD>
        <TD>Chicken</TD>
        <TD>$12.95</TD>
        <TD>**</TD>
</TR>
```

Fig. 26.13
Multiple row
spanning saves
you from typing
the same informa-
tion twice.

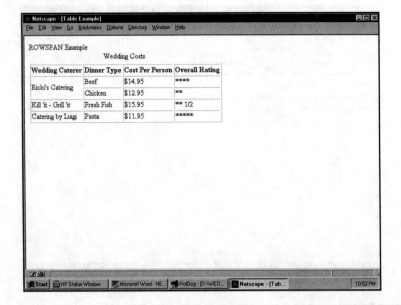

Cell Alignment

Like other text and image elements within HTML, you can also customize the text alignment within each cell of the table. By adding the appropriate keyword to the <TH> or <TD> tag you can specify both the horizontal and vertical alignment of data within the cell.

To set the horizontal alignment within a cell, use the ALIGN keyword. You can set alignment to be LEFT, RIGHT, and CENTER:

```
<TD ALIGN=CENTER>
```

To set the Vertical alignment, use the VALIGN keyword. VALIGN can be set as either TOP, MIDDLE, or BOTTOM:

```
<TD ALIGN=MIDDLE>
```

Vertical alignment is sometimes necessary when one column of information within a row has several lines of information.

> **Note**
>
> You can also embed graphics, other tables, and all types of lists within a specific table cell. By using the appropriate set of tags, images, lists, and tables are just as easy to include within a cell as straight data.

## CHAPTER 27

Advanced Graphics

World Wide Web pages benefit from the use of graphic elements, yet sophisticated graphics can significantly slow down the transfer of a site. Developing an attractive, and still responsive, site is the focus of this chapter. In addition to providing information on designing and choosing existing images, this chapter focuses on different image formats used on the Web and emphasizes the benefits and drawbacks of each. We explore the inherent graphic capabilities of Netscape, which allow the designer to make the best use of image download time through the use of thumbnail images. Finally, we look at Netscape's ability to modify a document's background and text colors.

In this chapter, you learn:

- Guidelines for developing graphics
- Which file formats are best for your Web site
- How to make interlaced and transparent GIFs
- How to convert images to progressive JPEGs
- Guidelines to optimize image download time
- How to develop and use thumbnail images
- How to modify backgrounds and text colors
- How to align images and wrap text

Developing Graphics for the Web

Developing graphics for use on the World Wide Web is significantly different than designing for the printed page. A closer analogy can be drawn between multimedia and the Web, as visitors to a Web page do not merely read information, but interact with the medium. In order to facilitate this interaction, care must be taken to develop an interface for a Web site that is useful and attractive. The ability to mix graphic elements with text and other media is much more limited in HTML than in other types of multimedia authoring. Often WWW pages are limited to the constraints of HTML, which was designed to display information in a vertical list. WWW page designers are also limited by differences in the user's connection to the Internet and his choice of browser. The popularity of Netscape is due in large part to its ability to allow designers more options for placing elements on the page as well as its excellent presentation of graphics.

Options for Developing Your Own Images

There are a number of excellent software products on the market for developing graphics. While shopping for these, pay particular attention to those designed specifically for working with graphics for the screen. As mentioned above, developing images for print and screen are two separate issues.

Graphics programs are usually designed to produce either vector or raster image files. *Vector* files contain mathematical equations describing the make-up of the image. This equation describes the relationship between objects in the image. For this reason, vector graphics are frequently used for Computer Aided Design (CAD) and images that contain distinct geometric shapes. Vector graphics were developed to print cleanly, much like the PostScript fonts. *Raster* files, also known as *bitmapped* graphics, store information about the individual placement and color of pixels in the image. Bitmapped graphics are primarily developed to be viewed on the computer screen. Printing bitmapped graphics is similar to printing bitmapped fonts in that they appear to be more jagged around the edges than their vector counterparts.

The image files currently supported by Netscape are all bitmapped graphics files. For this reason it is recommended that you purchase a graphics program that is capable of developing bitmapped images. The most popular graphics program for the World Wide Web is Adobe Photoshop. This piece of software has been the leading graphics design package for years due to its ability to produce original bitmapped images as well as touch-up existing images. Other leading bitmapped graphics programs include Deneba Canvas, Fractal Design Painter, and Fauve Matisse.

Options for Using Existing Images

Many times you will want to use graphics and images in your site that already have been developed. For example, you may want to include a professionally designed logo on your company home page, or maybe a photo of your cat on a personal profile Web page. Many times these images have to be converted to a digital format and possibly retouched in an image processing program before they can be used on the Web. There are a number of options available to help you with this process.

Desktop Scanners

A growing number of relatively inexpensive scanners on the market can capture photographs, line art, transparencies, slides, prints, and other two-dimensional images. Once captured, these images can be enhanced and resized in an image processing program such as Photoshop or Paintshop Pro, and saved in a format that can be used with graphical browsers.

Service Bureaus

A graphics service bureau or color separation house can scan images with a much higher degree of precision than is possible with desktop scanners. Some of these agencies may also convert your existing files to formats used on the World Wide Web. The use of a service bureau is generally the most expensive option for converting images to digital formats. Prices range considerably for individual services and between different locations in the country. You should explore the other possibilities first and if there is a particular need to have a high-resolution imaged scanned for your site, contact a number of service bureaus for price quotes.

Kodak PhotoCD

If the images you want to use are photographs, slides, or negatives, and you do not have access to a desktop scanner, consider having them placed on a PhotoCD. This method does require that you have an extended architecture CD-ROM drive and software capable of reading this type of compact disc; and most dual-speed, multi-session CD-ROM drives are compatible with this standard. Check the documentation of your graphics software to see if it can read the image format used for this process. PhotoCDs are capable of holding up to 100 photographs on each CD-ROM. The photos are scanned and saved on the CD in five different resolutions ranging from 128×192 pixels to 2048×3072 pixels. PhotoCDs can be ordered just about anywhere you can have prints made. The compact disc itself costs between $10.00 and $20.00, and each photo added to the CD costs between $1.00 and $2.00.

Digital Cameras

A number of cameras have appeared on the market in recent years that record images directly to disk in a digital format. These cameras are still relatively expensive, averaging around $700.00, and the images produced are generally of less quality than photographs converted by one of the previous scanning methods. The advantage to using digital cameras is the fact that they store the photographs directly in a digital format and the photos can be used immediately.

Stock Photo and Clip Art CDs

This option allows you to work with images that are already in a digital format. As a last resort, stock photo and clip art collections allow you to include some graphical elements into your Web pages where there would otherwise be none. There are a number of sites on the Web where you can download individual or libraries of clip art in file formats ready to use for your own site. For instance, Sandra's Clip Art Server at **http://www.cs.yale.edu/home/ sjl/clipart.html** archives a number of clip art collections. When using clip art from the World Wide Web or from CD-ROM, always read the copyright notice; although most can be used royalty-free, some require payment or simple acknowledgement.

Image File Formats

World Wide Web browsers support a limited number of file formats for inline images, and not all browsers are capable of displaying every type of image format within the same window as the HTML document. The two most popular formats supported by Netscape and most other graphical browsers are GIF and JPEG. Although the TIF and X-Bitmap formats can be used by some browsers, it is recommended that you use only GIFs or JPEGs.

Guidelines for Using GIF and JPEG Images

The *Graphics Interchange Format*, or *GIF*, was developed by CompuServe to provide an efficient way of storing and exchanging image files across platforms (see fig. 27.1). A file in this format can contain a maximum of 256 colors, or 8 bits per pixel. GIFs are the most popular images to use as inline images because they are supported by all graphical browsers. They are also the only format that supports transparent backgrounds and interlaced display.

The GIF format is best suited for the following types of images:

- Black-and-white line art and text
- Images with a limited number of distinct colors
- Graphics that have sharp or distinct edges—most menus, buttons, and graphs
- Graphics that are overlaid with text

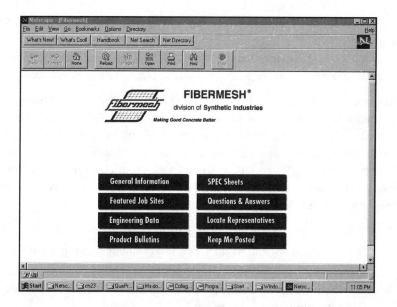

Fig. 27.1
GIF is the best
graphics format to
use for images
such as buttons
and menus.

The *JPEG* format was developed by the Joint Photographers Expert Group as a means of compressing images with a color palette of 24 bits per pixel, or 16.7 million possible colors.

For more information on GIF, JPEG, and other image formats, consult the World Wide Web FAQ at **http://sunsite.unc.edu/boutell/faq/ www_faq.html**.

The JPEG format is best suited for the following types of images:

- Scanned photographs and ray-traced renderings
- Images that contain a complex mixture of colors
- Any image that requires more than a 256-color palette

Using Interlaced GIFs

During download, a GIF file that is saved without the interlaced option appears on the viewer's Netscape window starting with the top of the image and filling down as it is received and decoded. The Netscape browser has been enhanced to take advantage of interlaced GIFs. An *interlaced GIF* stores the image in a sequence of nonadjacent sets, or what you might think of as layers. Netscape begins to process and display the image as it is received, which results in a gradual emergence of the image. Because the whole image appears in Netscape's window in sections rather than gradually filling in from the top down, viewers of the page can see much of the image before the download is complete. Interlaced GIFs should be used for all large graphics to allow the viewers of your page to see the entire image size immediately.

You can convert images to interlaced GIFs by using a number of commercial and shareware programs. The shareware program *Lview Pro*, developed by Leonardo Loureiro, includes the option to open a number of common file formats and save them as interlaced GIFs. The file formats that can be converted to and from GIFs and JPEGs using Lview Pro include JPEG, Windows bitmap, OS/2 bitmap, GIF, TARGA, PCX, PPM, and TIFF. To convert images to interlaced GIFs in Lview Pro, follow these steps:

On the CD

1. Open Lview Pro by double-clicking its icon.

2. Choose File, Open, and in the Open Image dialog box highlight the image file you want to convert. Click OK.

3. Once the image is open, choose File, Properties, GIF, and check the box titled Save Interlaced (refer to fig. 27.2).

4. Save the image as an interlaced GIF by selecting File, Save As. In the Save Image As dialog box, rename your image with the .GIF extension and select the GIF89a file type. Then click the Save button.

The image is now saved as an interlaced GIF.

Fig. 27.2
Check the interlaced GIF option when converting an image in Lview Pro.

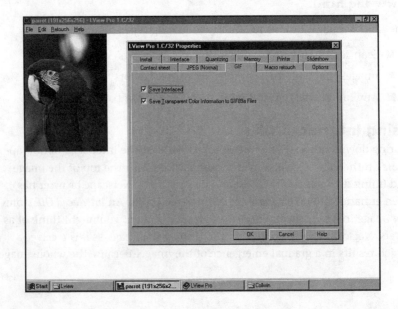

Using Transparent GIFs

An update to the original GIF format is *GIF89a*, which allows the image file to designate one of the colors in the image as *transparent*. Netscape supports the display of transparent GIFs, such as the one on the left in figure 27.3. Images that do not specify one of the colors as transparent are always displayed with a background on the browser's screen. This is fine if all your graphics are rectangular, but if you want to give your site a more polished look, you will want to include images that appear to be part of the background.

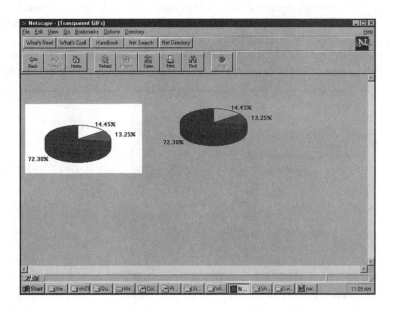

Fig. 27.3
Using transparent GIFs, such as the one on the right, gives your site a more polished look.

As with interlaced GIFs, there are a number of shareware utilities that convert images to transparent GIFs. To do so using Lview Pro, follow these steps:

1. Open Lview Pro by double-clicking its icon.

2. Choose File, Open; and in the Open Image dialog box, highlight the image file you want to convert, and then click OK.

3. Select Retouch, Color Depth. To save as a GIF, your image must be a palette image. Converting from True Color to Palette Image in Lview changes the color depth of your image to a maximum of 256 colors. In the Color Depth dialog box, select the Palette Image radio button (see fig. 27.4). Next you see options for palette creation and quantizing. Select 256 colors, uncheck the Dithering option, and click OK.

> **Note**
>
> A GIF image can contain up to 256 different colors specified in its color lookup table. In order to convert images with more than 256 colors in Lview Pro, you must first select the Palette image option to create a 256 color lookup table for the image. It is best to use the 256 colors (including Windows Palette) option when creating the palette unless you are sure that your image will look acceptable in 16 colors or simply black and white.
>
> Often in the process of creating a 256-color palette for an image, some colors in the original do not find a perfect match. The Enable Floyd-Steinberg Dithering option instructs Lview Pro to recolor an image using a technique that creates the look of more colors than the image actually has. Dithering should be avoided if possible because more complex images take longer to download.

Fig. 27.4
To make a transparent GIF, the image must first be converted to a palette image.

4. Now you're ready to identify the transparent color. Select Retouch, Background Color and you see the Select Color Palette dialog box. This window provides you with the color palette used by the image (see fig. 27.5).

5. If you can identify the color you want to make transparent, click once on that color in the Select Color Palette dialog box, and check the Mask selection box with either the white or black option. This masks your selection with either black or white, which enables you to see if the correct color for transparency was chosen. Don't be alarmed, the mask does not change the color of your image—it's just a helpful way of showing you the transparent selection.

6. If you have trouble seeing the exact color you want to make transparent, click the Dropper button in the Select Color Palette dialog box. The dropper, shown in figure 27.6, allows you to click directly on the image to indicate where you want the color to be transparent. Be careful: When the dropper is clicked on the screen, it disappears. However, the

color that you clicked will be highlighted in the Select Color Palette dialog box. You can test it by masking the selected color with black or white. If this is the correct color, choose OK; otherwise select the Dropper button again and click the desired color.

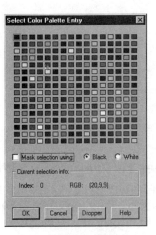

Fig. 27.5
The Palette dialog box shows which colors are used in the image.

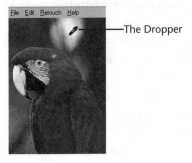

The Dropper

Fig. 27.6
The Dropper can be used to identify the color for transparency.

7. To save the image as a transparent GIF, select File, Save As; and in the Save Image As dialog box, select the GIF89a file type, as shown in figure 27.7.

More information about transparent and interlaced GIFs can be found on the World Wide Web at The Transparent/Interlaced GIF Resource Page **http:// dragon.jpl.nasa.gov/~adam/transparent.html**.

Tip

When creating images to be used as transparent GIFs, be sure that the desired transparent color is used only in those areas you want to hide.

Fig. 27.7
Transparent GIFs
must be saved as
GIF89a.

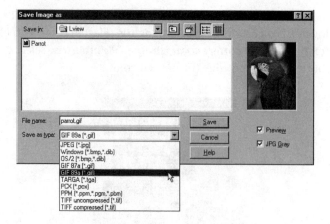

Converting Images to Progressive JPEGs

Netscape 2.0 includes support for a recent implementation of JPEG compression called the *Progressive JPEG*. Prior to version 2.0 of Netscape, use of inline JPEG images was limited to simple, or *baseline*, JPEGs. Baseline JPEGs store the image information as a top-to-bottom *scan* of the image. Baseline JPEGs appear in Netscape's window beginning at the top of the image and fill downward as image data is received. The progressive JPEG is similar to the interlaced GIF in that the image is stored as a *series* of scans. The first scan, or layer, of a progressive JPEG appears in the Netscape window as soon as the download begins.

The advantage of using progressive JPEG images in your Web site is that viewers of your page will begin to see the full size of images in rough detail as soon as the download begins. Existing baseline JPEGs must, however, be converted to the progressive format to take advantage of its features. To save images with progressive JPEG compression in Lview Pro, follow these simple steps:

1. Open Lview Pro by double-clicking its icon.

2. Choose File, Open; and in the Open Image dialog box, highlight the image file you want to convert, and then click OK.

3. When the image is open choose File, Properties, JPEG (Normal), and check the Progressive compression box as seen in figure 27.8.

4. To save the image as a progressive JPEG, select File, Save As; and in the Save Image As dialog box, select the JPEG file type.

For more information on JPEG consult the JPEG image compression FAQ at the URL **http://www.cis.ohio-state.edu/hypertext/faq/usenet/jpeg-faq/top.html**.

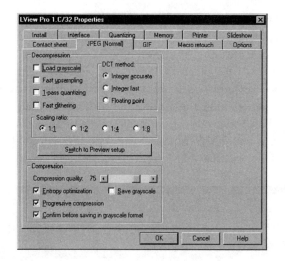

Fig. 27.8
Images can be
saved with
progressive JPEG
compression in
Lview Pro by
checking the
Progressive
compression
option.

Bandwidth Considerations for Image Use

When designing images for use on the Web, it's important to think about who the user is and what type of setup he has for viewing pages. Basic information relating to who is accessing your site can be found in the *http log* maintained by your server software. This log file records data about each visitor to your site. Log file statistics are generally no more than the date and time of access and the user's IP address. Unfortunately, http logs usually provide no information about the user's Internet connection, computer system, or monitor size and settings, all of which are important to consider when developing the graphics for your site.

A number of demographic reports and surveys have been published to present a better understanding of the general Web "surfer." These findings reveal the following:

- Over 90 percent are using graphical browsers
- Nearly 70 percent use the Netscape browser
- There is a fairly even distribution of Windows, Macintosh, and UNIX users
- Most users have a 14" monitor with a 256-color palette

Guidelines for Image Sizes

Because the majority of users are set up to view the Web on a 14" monitor capable of displaying a 256-color palette, you should consider that to be the standard for designing graphics for your site. The typical screen size of a 14" monitor is 640 pixels wide by 480 pixels high. When developing images to fit within this size, you should first consider that the user's browser will take up part of that viewing area. Depending on how it is configured, a browser may leave as little as 600 × 400 pixels as the viewing area. Also remember that Macintosh and UNIX browsers do not generally take up the entire width of the screen. As a general rule, the maximum width of any image on your site should be less than 500 pixels wide and 300 pixels high—a variety of image sizes are shown in figure 27.9. Images larger than this will not fit on most user's screens. They will also take longer to transfer.

Fig. 27.9
Images wider than 500 pixels may not appear in full on all viewer's screens.

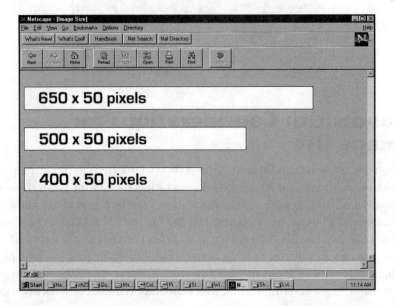

Using the Image Tag with Height and Width Attributes

One way to reduce the amount of time someone waits for your inline graphics to load is to tell the browser the size of the image in advance. Netscape uses this information when interpreting the final page layout; when it receives an HTML document, it spends a bit of time deciphering where to place the different elements on the screen. By knowing the exact dimensions of an incoming graphic element, Netscape can immediately lay out the text areas relative to where the graphic will eventually be.

◀ See "Using the <IMG> Tag," pg. 658

As you recall from chapter 26, the Image tag in an HTML document is comprised of two necessary elements: IMG and SRC. IMG signifies that it is an image, SRC denotes the *source*, or path to the image. Netscape can take advantage of the image tag appended with the height and width of the inline image to which it refers. This is done by adding HEIGHT and WIDTH attributes to the <IMG SRC> tag. The height and width of an image are measured in pixels. The use of this tag for an image with a height of 100 pixels and a width of 300 pixels would be written like this:

```
<IMG SRC="path_to_image" HEIGHT=100 WIDTH=300>
```

It doesn't matter whether the HEIGHT or WIDTH attribute comes first, but they must both be included along with the IMG and the SRC elements.

You can use any number of software programs to determine the dimensions of an inline image. Most professional paint and draw programs provide information about the dimensions of an open document. You may, however, have to change the preferences in a specific program to show the dimensional units in pixels rather than inches or centimeters because the Image tag elements must be written in pixels. Check the user manual for the specific paint program you are using to determine a document's height and width information.

Lview Pro can be used to determine the height and width of an image in pixel coordinates in the following way:

1. Open Lview Pro by double-clicking its icon.

2. Choose File, Open; and in the Open Image dialog box, highlight the image you want to measure.

3. When the image is open choose Edit, Resize (Ctrl+R). You see the Resize Image Window shown in figure 27.10. The size, in pixels, of the open image is reported at the top of this dialog box. The image width is the first number followed by the height.

Fig. 27.10
Lview Pro's Resize Image option shows the size of the open image and allows you to increase or decrease the size proportionately.

> **Tip**
>
> When you have determined the size of an image, write it down on a scrap of paper or add it to your HTML document immediately. Whatever you do, don't write down something like 137 x 281; if you're anything like me you'll forget which number is the height and which is the width. Getting these numbers reversed will change the shape of your image in Netscape's screen.

> **Note**
>
> Text is transferred much more quickly than images are. If width and height information is included for images, Netscape will begin to layout text as soon as it is received. Always include the width and height of an inline image in the HTML of the page so the reader can read the text on-screen while the image is loading. Paying attention to download time will increase satisfaction of those who visit your Web site.

Using and Developing Thumbnail Images

Thumbnail images on a Web page are small representations of larger graphics (see fig. 27.11). They are particularly useful on index pages as graphical links to the full-sized image. Because of the reduced size, thumbnails transfer to a user's browser more quickly than the full-sized graphics.

The easiest way to create a thumbnail is to reduce the size of the original image in a paint or image processing program. Photoshop and other image processing packages do an excellent job of proportionally reducing the size of an image. Many of the lower-end paint programs have options to scale images, however the result will most likely not produce a professional looking image. Lview Pro, however, does an excellent job of resizing images for use as thumbnails.

To produce a thumbnail image in Lview Pro, follow these steps:

1. Open Lview Pro by double-clicking its icon.

2. Choose File, Open; and in the Open Image dialog box, highlight the image from which you will create a thumbnail.

3. When the image is open choose Edit, Resize (Ctrl+R). You will see the Resize Image Window shown in figure 27.10. The size, in pixels, of the original image is reported at the top of this dialog box. The image width

is the first number followed by the height. To change the height or width of the image, simply type the height or width of the desired thumbnail image or use the slider bars below New Size/Current Size Ratio to adjust the percent of scaling. Be careful to check Preserve aspect ratio option if you want the image to be reduced in size proportionally.

4. Save the thumbnail image as either a GIF or JPEG by choosing File, Save as, and rename the image.

Tip

If the images you want to make thumbnails of are photographs, consider having them put on a Kodak PhotoCD. This process not only scans the images into digital files, but also provides you with duplicates of the images in a number of sizes.

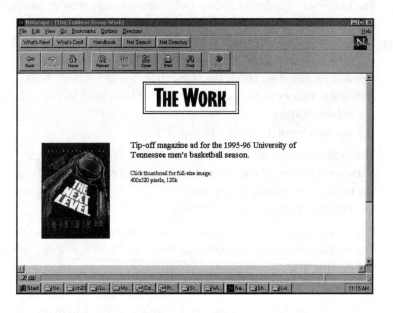

Fig. 27.11
Thumbnails are an efficient use of screen size and bandwidth.

As I mentioned earlier, Netscape and a few other browsers enable you to adjust the size of an image simply by changing the HEIGHT and WIDTH attributes in the image tag. Although this could be used to decrease the size of an image on the screen, the entire graphic still must be transferred to the user's browser. If your goal is to decrease the frustration time of potential viewers, this method will not help.

The image `HEIGHT` and `WIDTH` attributes can be used to alter the size of an image in the following ways:

- To reduce the size of an inline image, make its height and width proportionately smaller. For instance, an image 200 pixels high by 200 pixels wide can be displayed at half this size in the following way:

  ```
  <IMG SRC="path_to_image" HEIGHT=100 WIDTH=100>
  ```

  This image will appear on a viewer's Netscape screen at half its original size.

- To increase the sizeof an inline image, make its height and width proportionately larger. For instance, the same 200 by 200 image can be displayed at twice this size in the following way:

  ```
  <IMG SRC="path_to_image" HEIGHT=400 WIDTH=400>
  ```

  The image will appear on a viewer's Netscape screen at twice its original size.

- It is also possible to increase or decrease an image size relative to the viewer's Netscape window. In this case, the *percent* of increase or decrease is provided for either the `HEIGHT` or `WIDTH` or for both. For instance, an image can be displayed at half of Netscape's window size in the following ways:

  ```
  <IMG SRC="path_to_image" HEIGHT=50%>
  ```

  The image in this case will occupy 50 percent of the *height* of the Netscape window. The width will remain proportional to the height of the image, not to the window size.

  ```
  <IMG SRC="path_to_image" WIDTH=50%>
  ```

  This image will occupy 50 percent of the *width* of the Netscape window. The height will remain proportional to the width of the image, not to the window size.

  ```
  <IMG SRC="path_to_image" HEIGHT=50% WIDTH=50%>
  ```

  The image in this case will occupy 50 percent of the height and 50 percent of the width of the Netscape window.

Caution

Because individual users configure their browser windows to their own preferences, changing the aspect of an image with *both* a `WIDTH` *and* a `HEIGHT` percent will most likely distort your image.

Making Use of Cached Images

The Netscape cache function, which is explained in chapter 6, "Loading and Configuring Netscape Personal Edition," allows repeat images to appear more quickly than they did when they were first loaded. The browser's ability to store recent items can be used to decrease download time for graphics by using the same images on each page of your site for things such as title bars, menus, buttons, and bullets.

As you develop graphics for your Web site, consider taking advantage of the browser's cache. When Netscape downloads an image during a session, it keeps a copy of that image in your hard drive's cache. Subsequent requests for that image result in a faster display because the image is now stored in Netscape's cache and doesn't have to be retrieved from the server.

Images that appear on multiple pages on your site should be developed to take advantage of the viewer's cache. Designing shared navigation items such as menu buttons and image maps common to all pages not only increases the ease of use, but also decreases the amount of time a viewer will spend waiting for images to load, for instance, if you develop a series of images that are used as clickable buttons in your Web site.

> **Tip**
>
> To best keep track of images used on your Web site, it is best to keep them all in a common *images* directory. This practice can help eliminate multiple copies of the same image that can slow down your site by not taking advantage of images in the user's cache.

Design Tips for Graphical Web Pages

When developing graphical Web pages you can take advantage of Netscape's additions to HTML that affect the background and text of your page. Table 27.1 lists the additions to the BODY tag that include the use of background images and colors, as well as the designation of text and link colors. HTML extensions such as these make it easier to design pages that have visual impact. Chapter 31, "Creating a World Class Web Site for Netscape," further explores the use of background images and techniques that are used in world class Web sites.

◀ See "Creating a World Class Web Site for Netscape," pg. 777

Table 27.1 Additions to the BODY Tag	
Attribute	**Result**
BACKGROUND	Loads an image to use as a background
BGCOLOR	Specifies the browser's background color
TEXT	Specifies the text color
LINK	Specifies the link color
ALINK	Specifies the active link color
VLINK	Specifies the visited link color

Using Backgrounds and Text Colors

A welcome set of improvements to assist graphical development are extensions to the <BODY> tag. In Netscape it is possible for the designer of a Web page to distinguish the color and appearance of the end user's window, as well as specify the document's text and link colors. Most of the BODY attributes make use of the viewer's browser to change the page's appearance, thereby costing no more download time for viewing. The BACKGROUND attribute is an exception to the rule, it requires the use of an image to display as a background.

The BACKGROUND Attribute

Netscape and a growing number of graphical World Wide Web browsers support the BACKGROUND attribute of the BODY tag. As mentioned above, this extension does require the use of an image to be displayed as a background for the specific page. A GIF or JPEG image is appended to the tag in the following way:

```
<BODY BACKGROUND=<"url_of_image">
document
</BODY>
```

An image used as the background is tiled across and down the viewer's window. Because they are tiled in this fashion, background images must be created to appear in the browser's window without visible connection points—their edges must appear seamless. Textured graphics can be made seamless with the help of image processing software such as PhotoShop. There are also a growing number of WWW sites dedicated to background images, and many of the better ones include high quality seamless images you can download and use on your own site. Figure 27.12 shows one such site at the URL **http://funnelweb.utcc.utk.edu/~wallace/textures/textures.html**.

Caution

Background images require Netscape to fetch and download the specified graphic *before* the rest of the page is displayed. To minimize download time, always use the smallest image possible for backgrounds. A 100 by 100 pixel image should be the largest background image used.

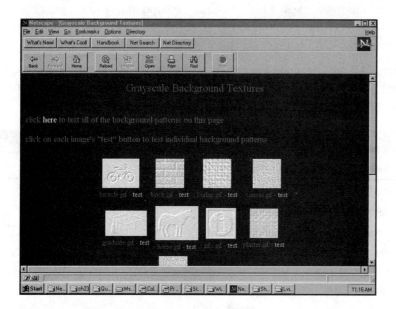

Fig. 27.12
There are a number of WWW sites dedicated to background images.

Note

Background images—like an inline image—are stored in Netscape's cache. You can increase access time to your site by using a common background image for all pages.

The BGCOLOR Attribute

The BGCOLOR attribute for the BODY tag is recognized by Netscape and a limited number of other graphical browsers. It differs from the BACKGROUND attribute in that the BGCOLOR changes the window color of a viewer's browser. This attribute does not require a viewer's browser to download and tile an image. For this reason, use of the BGCOLOR changes the window's background color immediately upon receiving the HTML tag and doesn't delay layout of the document. The primary drawback of using BGCOLOR is that there are a limited number of browsers that recognize it.

You use the BGCOLOR in the BODY tag like this:

```
<BODY BGCOLOR=#RRGGBB>
document
</BODY>
```

#RRGGBB refers to the hexadecimal color code made up of red, green, and blue. This code is interpreted as a color value in hexadecimal format. The red value of the desired color occupies the first two units, followed by two for green and two for blue. Each of these two color components must consist of one of 16 characters—numbers 0 through 9 followed by A through F—where 0 is the lowest value and F is the highest.

Table 27.2 outlines eight basic color combinations in hexadecimal code. Table 28.1 in chapter 28, "Using Imagemaps," contains the code for numerous other combinations.

Table 27.2   Hexadecimal RGB Color Codes

Color	Code
White	#FFFFFF
Red	#FF0000
Green	#00FF00
Blue	#0000FF
Cyan	#00FFFF
Magenta	#FF00FF
Yellow	#FFFF00
Black	#000000

Tip

When developing transparent GIFs for use as background images or colors, it is best to use the same background color as the image background when creating the image.

Text and Link Attributes

In addition to controlling the background color of a user's browser, it is possible to change the text and link colors. These extensions to the BODY tag use the same hexadecimal color code as BGCOLOR. The attribute for changing the color of a document's text is TEXT followed a specific color code. For example, to change a document's body text to green, the BODY tag would read:

```
<BODY TEXT=#00FF00>
document
</BODY>
```

Similarly, colors can be assigned to links as outlined in table 27.1. LINK specifies the color to be used for links that have not been followed. The ALINK attribute is the color a link momentarily flashes as it is clicked, or activated.
VLINK is a link that has previously been activated, or visited.

Note

If one or more of the body attributes for text and link colors are not specified, the
default color for those attributes is used: LINK=blue, ALINK=red, VLINK=purple.

An example of the BODY tag with all attributes designated—BGCOLOR set to
black, TEXT set to white, LINK set to yellow, ALINK set to magenta, and VLINK
set to green—is written like this:

```
<BODY BGCOLOR=#000000 TEXT=#FFFFFF LINK=#FFFF00 ALINK=#FF00FF
VLINK=00FF00>
document
</BODY>
```

Tip

You should always use the BGCOLOR attribute if you use BACKGROUND in the BODY tag.
If the image specified in BODY BACKGROUND fails to load or a user chooses to not load
images, all text and link colors will be displayed in their default colors. By including a
BGCOLOR that is similar in appearance to the BACKGROUND image, the text and link
colors will appear as you intended.

There are a number of excellent resources on the World Wide Web for previewing colors in hexadecimal code. Consult the following references on the
World Wide Web for more information on background colors and images:

■ Controlling Document Backgrounds: **http://home.netscape.com/
assist/net_sites/bg/index.html**

■ Yahoo's Index on Backgrounds: **http://www.yahoo.com/
Computers_and_Internet/Internet/World_Wide_Web/Pro-
gramming/Backgrounds/**

■ Background Color Index: **http://www.infi.net/wwwimages/
colorindex.html**

Image Alignment and Borders

By far the most influential feature of the Netscape browser is its unique extensions to HTML that allow text and inline images to be laid out on the screen in an aesthetic fashion (see fig.27.13). The additions to the IMG tag cause an image to float in relationship to other elements on the screen, hence they are referred to as *floating images*. The ALIGN attributes can be found in table 27.3, along with a brief description of the desired result. These recent additions are by far the most finicky elements in HTML. They are also the most important elements to master.

Fig. 27.13

An addition to the IMG tag allows images to be aligned on the right border.

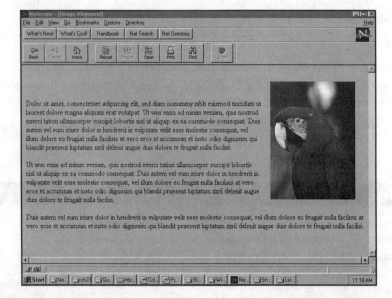

Table 27.3	Additions to the IMG Tag
Attribute	**Result**
ALIGN=LEFT	Aligns an image on the browser's left margin
ALIGN=RIGHT	Aligns an image on the browser's right margin
ALIGN=TOP	Aligns an image with the top of the tallest item on the same line, whether it is text or another image
ALIGN=MIDDLE	Aligns the middle of an image with the baseline of elements on the same line
ALIGN=BOTTOM	Aligns the image with the baseline of elements on the same line
BORDER=*pixel size*	Places a border around the image of the specified pixel size

The ALIGN attributes are used with the IMG tag. For example, to align an image on the browser's left margin, the tag would be used in the following way:

```
<IMG SRC="url_of_image" ALIGN=LEFT>
```

The image in this instance aligns itself on the left margin of Netscape's window. Elements specified after the IMG tag are positioned to the right of the floating image. The BR tag and its attributes are needed to end the effect of a floating image. These will be discussed in more detail in the following section, "Wrapping Text Around Images."

Note

Only one form of the ALIGN attribute can be used with each image. If two or more are included with the IMG tag, only the first one in the line will be used.

Wrapping Text Around Images

Netscape's additions to the IMG tag offer developers the ability to wrap text around floating images (see fig 27.14). This is an important component to developing both an attractive and useful site, as the World Wide Web was not initially developed with screen layout in mind. Prior to these attributes, using inline images with text resulted in a linear-looking page. Now it is possible to dictate the position of images in respect to text elements and graphics.

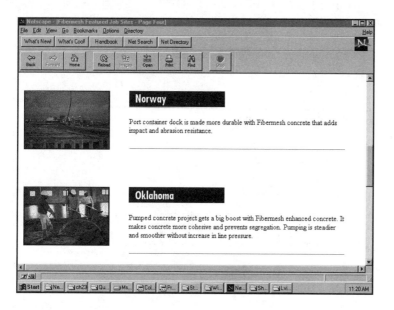

Fig. 27.14
Images and text can be positioned in sophisticated ways using the IMG ALIGN attributes.

To wrap text around an image on a Web page it is necessary to use one of the ALIGN attributes with the IMG tag. The desired text should then be included directly after the IMG tag. The result will vary with the attributes as follows:

- ALIGN=LEFT causes the image to align with the left margin of Netscape's window; text following this tag wraps to the right of the floating image.

- ALIGN=RIGHT causes the image to align with the right margin of Netscape's window; text following this tag wraps to the left of the floating image.

- ALIGN=MIDDLE causes the image to align with the left margin of Netscape's window; text following this attribute begins on the right side of the image at the middle point. Only the amount of text that fits between the right side of the image and the left margin of the window aligns with the middle of this floating image. All remaining text continues at the left margin below the image.

- ALIGN=TOP causes the image to align with the left margin of Netscape's window; text following this attribute begins on the right side of the image aligned with the top edge. Only the amount of text that fits between the right side of the image and the left margin of the window aligns with the top of this floating image. All remaining text continues at the left margin below the image.

- ALIGN=BOTTOM causes the image to align with the left margin of Netscape's window; the base line of text begins on the right, aligned with the bottom edge of the floating image (see fig 27.15).

Fig. 27.15
ALIGN=BOTTOM allows an image to serve as a part of the running text.

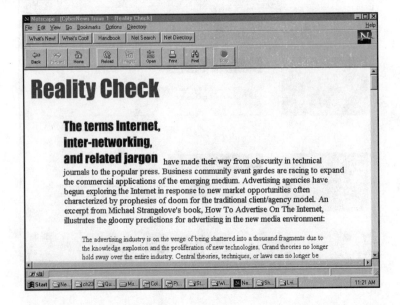

To get good results with floating images with text requires practice with extensions to the BR tag. The basic BR tag employed with text following an ALIGN attribute will merely break the line without stopping the effect of the floating image. In order to break the line and clear the margin to the right or left of the floating image, you must use one of the additions to the BR tag. These attributes are outlined in table 27.4. The BR tag with a CLEAR attribute is used at the point where you want to clear the right or left margin of a floating image. For example, if we aligned an image on the left with text wrapped to the right, it would be necessary to clear the left margin before another element could be placed there. The HTML would be:

```
<IMG SRC="url_to_image" ALIGN=LEFT>
text
<BR CLEAR=LEFT>
```

When in doubt as to which CLEAR attribute to use, begin with CLEAR=ALL. This clears both margins and allows you to safely add new elements to the page.

Table 27.4 Additions to the BR Tag

Attribute	Result
CLEAR=RIGHT	Breaks the line and clears the right margin
CLEAR=LEFT	Breaks the line and clears the left margin
CLEAR=ALL	Breaks the line and clears both margins

Caution

Aligning two images on the same margin without the appropriate BR attribute in between will cause one image to appear on top of the other.

## CHAPTER 28

Using Imagemaps

One feature you'll see in some of the more advanced home pages are *imagemaps*. These are simply pictures with certain designated areas that go to different URLs. Imagemaps are inherently easier to use than regular text links because there's no need to explain what the link does. A person doesn't have to read where a link might take him, he just sees it.

Though this may sound like imagemaps should be used everywhere, that's not true. There are some things to consider before using imagemaps. You also have to make sure it makes sense to put in imagemaps where you want them. All the information you'd want to know about imagemaps is covered in this chapter.

In this chapter, you learn:

- What imagemaps are and how they work
- How to choose appropriate imagemap graphics
- How to create an imagemap definition file
- How to reference your Imagemap in HTML
- Guidelines for using imagemaps
- Basic elements of laying out your imagemap

What Are Imagemaps?

Imagemaps allow for a friendly way for users to go to different Web pages by pointing and clicking in a picture. One of the big advantages of the Web over other Internet-related stores of information is that it's graphically advanced, which makes it more approachable to use. Instead of bland text menus, such as with Gopher clients, users can see what they want to get information on (see fig. 28.1).

Fig. 28.1
Instead of having people imagine what the Colossus might look like, you can use imagemaps to show them.

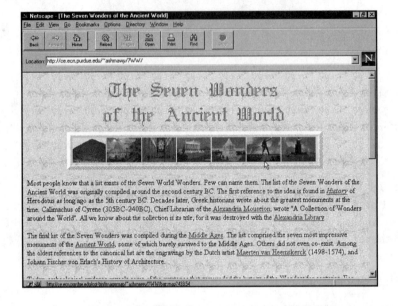

Imagemaps are simply pictures with areas that users can click on to go to different Web pages. Typically, the user sees an image which indicates where to click to go to different Web pages. There are a lot of different ways that the image can indicate clickable areas. Usually there is a border or something in the picture that indicates where users should click to go somewhere.

When the user clicks on the imagemap, Netscape sends the location of where the mouse click occurred in the image to the Web server. The server looks up which URL is referenced at that point and travels there. An imagemap that you may be familiar with is on the Netscape home page (see fig. 28.2).

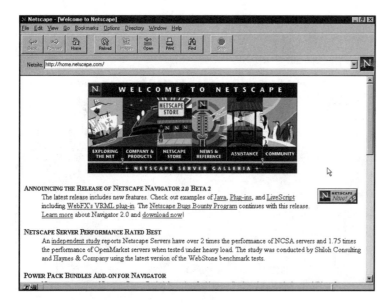

Fig. 28.2
The first imagemap almost everyone comes across is the one on the Netscape home page. Notice that when you move the mouse, different numbers appear at the bottom.

Strengths and Weaknesses of Imagemaps

There are some good and bad points to using imagemaps. Most are aesthetic points but a few are technical. Understanding the advantages and disadvantages of imagemaps is important if you want a popular Web site.

Advantages to Using Imagemaps

Imagemaps are most useful in the following situations:

- To represent spatial links, such as geographical coordinates, which would be difficult to layout using single image buttons or text links (see fig. 28.3).

- As a top-level menu bar which appears on each page in your Web site. The use of imagemap menus offers users the option of going anywhere in your site at any time.

- Creating the above mentioned common menu bar graphic for your site will save time in developing HTML documents, as this graphic will refer to the same imagemap reference file. Consistent menus also present a consistent look to a site which will ease user navigation. Instead of having to go into each page and put in links to other parts of your home page, you can just refer to the common menu bar graphic.

Fig. 28.3
Imagemaps make
it easy to represent
spatial links, such
as the area codes
for North America.

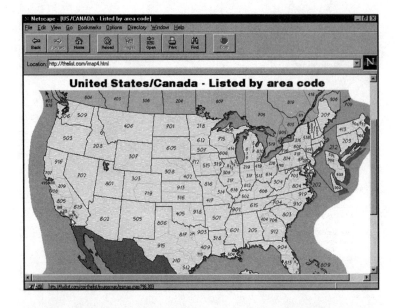

Fig. 28.4
No matter where
you go in the
Internet Movie
Database, you can
always go to the
most important
parts.

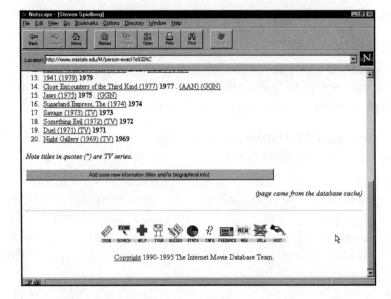

Disadvantages of Using Imagemaps

Obviously imagemaps aren't the end-all feature of Web pages, or else everyone would use them. There are certain situations where you *shouldn't* use
imagemaps. There are also some technical considerations before using them.

Imagemaps have a number of inherent drawbacks:

- Imagemaps cannot be used when running your site locally off a hard drive. This is only true if the server you're running locally doesn't have CGI scripts to support the imagemap. Also, some Web servers come pre-built with imagemap support. If you're not running of these "smart servers," you can't use imagemaps on your site.

- You can't test your imagemap until the HTML document is placed on a server. Because Netscape is merely an interface between the user and a Web server, CGI scripts are never used by it. Thus even things like imagemap interpretations are impossible without a Web server.

- Unless you provide an alternative text menu, there is no means of navigation for users who cannot load graphics or have turned graphics loading off (see fig. 28.5).

- Imagemaps tend to be larger than single-image buttons and, therefore, take longer to download.

- Use of a single imagemap menu for your site offers users the option of clicking on the reference to the page they are presently viewing. This can cause confusion in navigation.

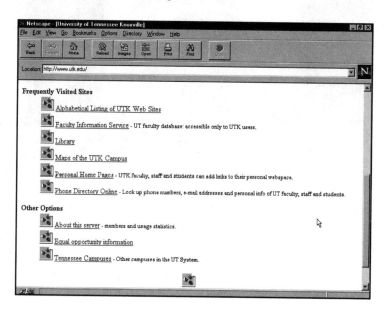

Fig. 28.5
This text menu provides a navigational alternative for the imagemaps that did not load.

Imagemaps and CGI

There is more involved in adding an imagemap to your Web site than simply creating an interesting graphic and referencing it in HTML. First of all, the use of an imagemap requires that your HTML document is located on a World Wide Web server. Its use also requires that the server is configured with an imagemap Common Gateway Interface (CGI) program, which will handle the mouse-click request from the user.

▶ See "Netscape Forms and CGI-BIN Scripts," pg. 745

When a user clicks one of the hot-spots of your imagemap graphic, the mouse's relative position on the image is sent to the Web server. Figure 28.6 shows an imagemap with buttons that represent the hotspots and take users to different URLs.

Fig. 28.6
An imagemap on this home page allows visitors easy access to chief information areas.

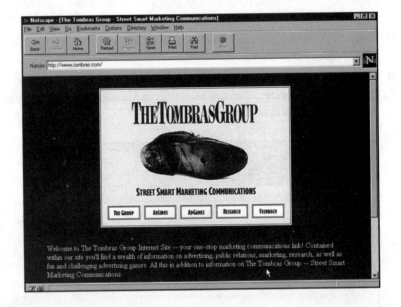

There are two primary types of imagemap definition file configurations, CERN and NCSA. They both hold the same information in an imagemap definition file, but it is presented differently. Both use the same region types (see "Elements of Imagemaps" later in this chapter) and the same coordinates. For this reason, you should check with the system administrator about the particular imagemap setup of the server you are using. For the following discussion we will assume that you have access to a Web server.

What the CERN Format Is

CERN is a group of European engineers who research a wide variety of topics. During the course of their research, they came up with the concept of the World Wide Web. They were the starting point for all sorts of WWW development and are rightfully labeled as "the birthplace of the Web." When the demand came for imagemap definition files, CERN came up with the following format:

    region_type coordinates URL

The coordinates must be in parentheses and the x and y coordinates must be separated by a comma. The CERN format also doesn't allow for comments about hot-spot regions. Here's an example of a CERN imagemap definition:

    rect (56,47) (357,265) http://www.rectangle.com/

How NCSA Is Different

The University of Illinois' National Center for Supercomputing Applications (NCSA) is also very important for its contributions to the Web. It's at NCSA that the first popular graphical Web browser, Mosaic, was born. They presented a slightly different format than CERN's for the imagemap definition file. Their format is:

    region_type URL coordinates

The coordinates don't have to be in parentheses, but they do have to be separated by commas. Here's an example of an NCSA imagemap definition:

    rect http://www.rectangle.com/ 56,47 357,265

Changing Things...Again

The standard-setting Netscape Navigator has taken a bite out of the complexity of imagemaps. Netscape Navigator 2.0 supports client-side imagemaps, which means that as a Web author, you don't need CGI scripts to figure out where you clicked. Netscape does the mouse interpretation and sends the correct coordinates to the Web server. However, you'll probably still need an imagemap definition file as it's the only thing that knows where the hotspots are.

Elements of Imagemaps

Several elements contribute to creating and using imagemaps effectively.

Imagemap, Image Map, Area Map, and Clickable Map

All of these terms are synonymous with what we refer to in this chapter as the imagemap concept: The use of an inline image in an HTML document that is configured to contain one or more predetermined hot-spots or regions, which represent active URL links. The imagemap is the complete embodiment of all the other elements of the imagemap itself.

Imagemap Graphic

An *imagemap graphic* is the actual inline graphic image that is displayed on your Web page. These images must be of the GIF graphics format and can be either interlaced or non-interlaced. It's also possible to have the imagemap graphic have a transparent background color (see "Choosing Imagemap Graphics," later in this chapter).

Imagemap Definition File

An *imagemap definition file* is a text file, usually denoted with the extension .*MAP*, that contains the coordinates for each hot-spot of a specific imagemap graphic. This file also contains the resulting URL associated with each region. Active regions may be made up of rectangles, circles, polygons, or points. Imagemaps may contain any combination of these figures. This file can also specify one default URL in the event that the user clicks inside an imagemap graphic that doesn't have a specified region. Be sure to find out from your system administrator whether the Web server accepts the CERN or NCSA format.

Imagemap Program

An *imagemap program* is a Common Gateway Interface (CGI) program running on a World Wide Web server. This program determines what URL to return to the browser depending upon where the user clicked on the imagemap graphic relative to the coordinates in the definition file. Some Webmasters don't let people run CGI scripts, so check with your system administrator before you begin.

The Imagemap Definition File Itself

The imagemap definition file is a text file which contains information about the active regions of a specific imagemap graphic. For this reason, a separate definition file will be necessary for each imagemap graphic you wish to use. The definition specifies the type of region located in the graphic as either a rectangle, circle, polygon, or point (see fig. 28.7).

These regions, obviously, reflect the geometric shape of the active region. Their coordinates are determined as pixel points relative to the upper left-hand corner of the imagemap graphic. The following list identifies basic imagemap shapes and their required coordinates.

- *rect*—Indicates that the region is a rectangle. The coordinates required for this type of shape are the upper left-hand and lower right-hand pixels in the rectangle. The active region is the area of the rectangle.

- *circle*—Indicates that the region is a circle. Coordinates required for using a circle are center-point and edge-point pixels. The active region is calculated as the area of the circle.

- *poly*—Indicates that the region is a polygon. Coordinates are required as a list of vertices for the polygon. A polygon region can contain up to 100 vertices. The active region is the area within the polygon.

- *point*—Indicates that the region is a point on the image. A point coordinate is one specific pixel measured from the upper left-hand corner of the imagemap graphic. A point is considered active if the click occurred closest to that point on the graphic, yet not within another active region.

- *default*—Indicates all of the area of an imagemap graphic not specified by any other active region.

The rect Region Type

This element indicates that the region is a rectangle. Coordinates required for using a rectangle are center-point and edge-point pixels. The active region is calculated as the area of the rectangle.

The circle Region Type

This type indicates that the clickable region is a circle. Coordinates required for using a circle are center-point and edge-point pixels for NCSA servers. The CERN servers require the center-point of the circle and its radius. The active region is calculated as the area of the circle.

The poly Region Type

When you want to specify any multisided region, you use the poly region type. Coordinates are required as a list of vertices for the polygon. A polygon region can contain up to 100 vertices. The active region is the area within the polygon.

The point Region Type

Small dots can be indicated with the point region type. A point coordinate is one specific pixel measured from the upper-left corner of the imagemap graphic. A point is considered active if the click occurred closest to that point on the graphic, yet not within another active region.

The default Region Type

What all other regions don't cover, the default region will. If a user clicks inside an imagemap and it's not within the bounds of any other region, the default URL will be retrieved.

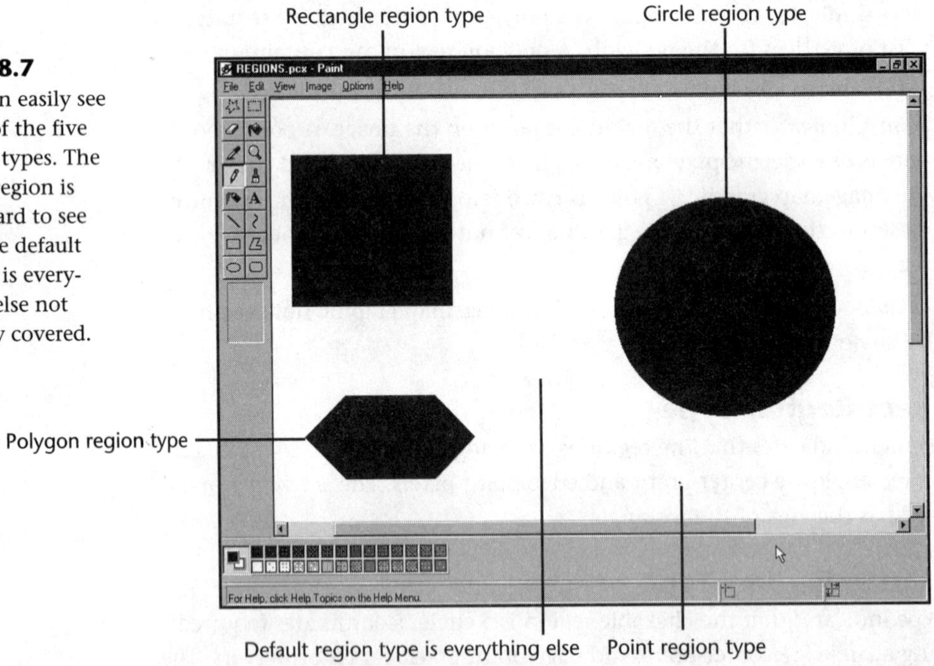

Fig. 28.7

You can easily see three of the five region types. The point region is very hard to see and the default region is everything else not already covered.

Rectangle region type   Circle region type

Polygon region type

Default region type is everything else   Point region type

Caution

An imagemap definition file should never contain both a point and a default region. The point region is activated by a click on the graphic closest to that point. The problem is that since the point region is so small, it's too easy for a user to *not* click it. As a result, the user could spend a lot of time trying to click on a point region and always getting the default URL.

Following each type of region in the imagemap definition file is the URL which will be returned to the user when a click within that area is recorded. The URL can be written as either a relative or an absolute path. Bear in mind that relative URL paths must be specific to the location of the definition file, not to the imagemap graphic. Active regions in the definition file are read from the first line down. If two regions overlap in their coordinates, only the one referenced first will be activated by the imagemap program.

On each line after the type of region and resulting URL there must be the integer pixel coordinates of the region. Figure 28.8 shows a sample imagemap definition file with the different region types and coordinates. The coordinates are all measured in pixels, starting from the upper left-hand corner of the imagemap graphic. The first number indicates the number of pixels the point is to the right of the left edge. The second number is the pixel measured down from the top edge.

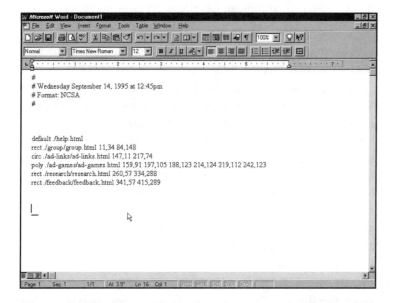

Fig. 28.8
An imagemap reference file contains information about the shape, resulting URL, and coordinates of active regions on the imagemap graphic.

Tip

An imagemap definition file should, whenever possible, be configured with a default HTML link. The default link will take the user to an area that isn't designated as being an active link. This URL should provide the user with feedback or helpful information about using that particular imagemap.

> **Note**
>
> The pound sign or hash character (#) can be used to comment a line in the imagemap definition file. Any line with the hash character at the beginning will not be executed by the imagemap program. It's useful for adding information such as the date of creation, the physical path to the imagemap graphic, or specific comments about the server configuration.

The Imagemap Process

An imagemap application can be one of the most confusing components in your site's development. For the most part, difficulties with the use of imagemaps result from a lack of understanding of the imagemap process. Therefore, let's look at what happens from the time you click your mouse on a spot in an imagemap graphic to when you are taken to the resulting URL (see fig. 28.9).

1. Let's assume you have clicked your mouse on one of the specified areas of an imagemap graphic.

2. Your browser will then send the location of the click back to the server. This information is sent using the HTTP GET method, the most common way of transferring information between Netscape and the server. You will notice that in Netscape's Location Window the URL is followed by a question mark and also the coordinates of where you clicked on the imagemap graphic. These numbers are referred to as *integer pixel coordinates*. They represent the distance in pixels from the upper left-hand corner of the imagemap graphic to the point where your mouse clicked. For instance, a pixel coordinate of 102,217 is 102 pixels to the right of the left edge and 217 pixels down from the top of the imagemap graphic.

3. The server receives the query from your browser and hands over the request to the imagemap program. This common gateway interface (CGI) program is given both the integer coordinates of where you clicked, as well as the location of the imagemap definition file. This file is essentially a lookup table for that particular imagemap graphic. It contains coordinates for the active regions in the graphic and their resulting action.

4. The imagemap program analyzes the click coordinate against the predetermined regions indicated in the imagemap definition file.

5. If the spot where you clicked matches with a region in the imagemap definition file, the imagemap program returns the resulting URL to the server. In the event that there is no match, an error message is sent to the server.

6. The server takes the information returned from the imagemap CGI and processes it. Typically, it sends the result back to your browser, which reacts by requesting the specified URL. If there was an error in the imagemap program or it failed to find a match for your request, the server sends an error message to your browser.

Different hot-spot regions go to different places

Fig. 28.9
The Macmillan Computer Publishing home page presents the user with several possible places to go. All the possible locations have clear and distinct borders around them.

Obviously imagemaps don't just magically appear on a home page, they have to be created. To create an imagemap, you're going to need an image and a tool to create the clickable regions. Since all of this information is going to be stored on a Web server, you'll need to know some information about it.

Things You'll Need on the Web Server

Since imagemaps depend heavily on pictures, you're going to need to know how much disk space you have on the server. For those who want to run a home page from their own Internet account, be sure to watch your disk quotas. Most service providers charge you money if you go over a certain limit.

It's also very important that you find out what type of Web server your home page is going to be running on.

You should contact your system administrator and find out if the Web server supports NCSA or CERN definition files. You should also find out if there are special restrictions for setting up your own home pages. Your service provider may have all their users' Web pages in one central location. This is information you'll need to know.

Mapping Tools

Obviously, one other thing you're going to need when creating imagemaps is a program that creates the imagemap definition file. These programs allow you to draw clickable regions on an image and then specify which URLs to go to. There are a number of mapping tools available for Windows 95 and Macintosh and a short description of each wouldn't do them justice. Mapedit is a good Windows 95 imagemap editor that you can get from **http:// www.boutell.com/mapedit/mapedit.zip**. A good Macintosh imagemap editor is WebMap, which can be found at **http://www.city.net/cnx/ software/webmap2.0b9.sea.hqx**.

Most map editing programs are the same. They all let you create and modify imagemap definition files, typically with the graphic loaded. They all provide for the three basic region types, rect, circle, and poly. The slightly more sophisticated ones also support the point and default region types directly. The only thing to really watch out for with imagemap editing programs is if it feels right for you. If the user interface is awkward, throw it out. There are many alternatives.

Creating an Imagemap

So far, we've been talking about everything related with the imagemap, it's time to talk about creating the imagemap itself. You should get a good idea of what type of imagemap you want to use. Do you want a menu bar that's everywhere? Do you want all your pages to have large imagemaps?

Choosing Imagemap Graphics

Now that you have a basic understanding of how the imagemap process
works, it's time to begin thinking about using an imagemap in your own
World Wide Web site. The best place to begin is by choosing an inline image
to be used as the imagemap graphic. Figure 28.10 is an example of choosing
the correct image for a particular imagemap.

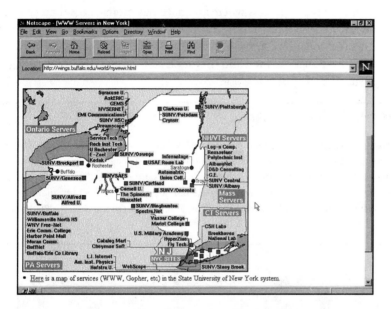

Fig. 28.10
Creating links
to geographic
information is a
common use for
imagemaps.

In chapter 27 you were introduced to guidelines for developing graphics for
use in World Wide Web sites. Many of these ideas are also useful when deciding upon the graphics to use for an imagemap. Let's review some of the more
important issues with respect to inline images:

- Inline images should be saved in the GIF file format whenever possible,
  as it is the only format supported by all graphical World Wide Web
  browsers.

- Save or convert images to be Interlaced GIFs. Saving or converting pictures as interlaced GIFs depends on which program you use, but most
  paint programs will do it. This format allows the graphic to be displayed
  in "layers" as it is transmitted from the server. That is to say the image
  is presented in ever-increasing detail as it's being received by Netscape.
  Users will begin to see the entire image area, without waiting for the
  entire image to download.

■ Develop graphics to be no more than 500 pixels wide and 200 pixels high. Most users will be viewing your site on a 14-inch monitor. Graphics that exceed the size of this recommendation cannot be easily viewed without scrolling for Macintosh users.

■ Graphics will download faster if they are created with a limited number of colors. Scanned images should be retouched to eliminate dithering. Dithering is the process where an image has more colors than can be displayed. When retouching a scanned image, simply change as many similar colors to a common color. For example, if you have a picture with three shades of red and they look very similar, then just change them all to be just one color.

Note

Transparent GIFs used as imagemaps present a problem with user navigation. Transparent GIFs are images where the background color is specified by Netscape. This makes the transparent image to appear to have no border and to "float" on the home page. Some of the active graphic will not be apparent to the user, so these imagemaps should contain some form of feedback or help as the default URL setting (see fig. 28.11).

Fig. 28.11
Yahoo's main masthead is a transparent GIF and the main user navigational interface.

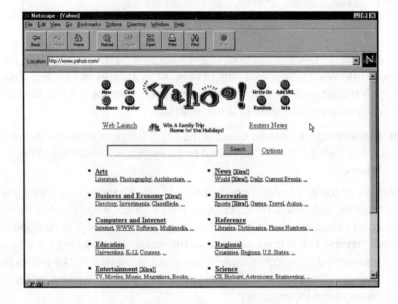

Creating the Imagemap Reference File

Developing the imagemap definition file will be the most difficult part of creating an imagemap for your Web site. Fortunately there are a number of shareware and freeware utilities to help you with this process.

An excellent utility for creating imagemap definition files for Windows 95 is the shareware program Mapedit developed by Thomas Boutell. Mapedit allows you to create definition files in the NCSA and CERN formats, as well as tools for defining active coordinate regions in the shape of polygons, rectangles, and circles. This program even gives you an opportunity to test your links prior to installing your document on a server.

To create an imagemap definition file using Mapedit 1.4 follow these steps:

1. To create a new imagemap definition file, first open Mapedit 1.4.

2. From the File Menu select Open/Create. Figure 28.12 shows the resulting dialog box that pops up.

3. Click on the Browse button to open an existing .MAP file. To create a new definition file, type in a name for this file in the Map Filename text box.

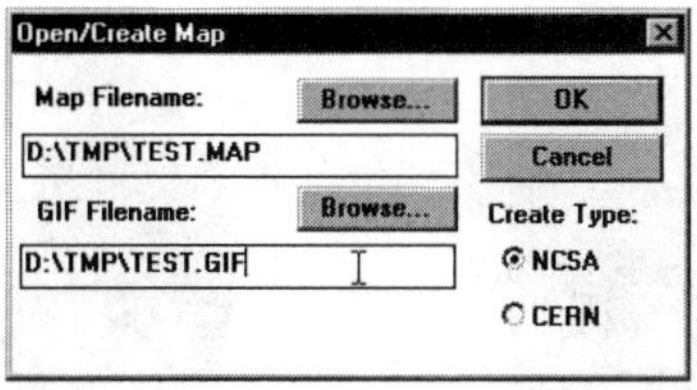

Fig. 28.12
Mapedit's Open dialog box.

Note

Most imagemap programs require the definition file to end with the extension .MAP. If this is the case with your server be sure to add this extension to all new definition files you create.

---

4. Under GIF Filename, click the Browse button and find the GIF image you wish to use for an imagemap graphic. Once you have chosen an image, the path to this graphic will appear in the GIF Filename window.

5. Click on either NCSA or CERN as the definition map format, then choose the OK button.

6. If you are creating a new imagemap definition file, Mapedit will display a Confirmation dialog box asking if you really would like to create this text file. Choose the OK button to continue.

7. Mapedit will open your imagemap GIF graphic in a window. To begin mapping active regions on this image choose one of the selections from the Tools Menu.

8. Selecting the Tools, Polygon Tool, Mapedit allows you to create the coordinates of a polygon on your image. To do so, click with the left mouse button onto the image where you would like to begin drawing out a polygon. You will notice that a line will stretch from the tip of your cursor to where you clicked on the image. Drag this line to the first vertex of your polygon and click the left mouse button again. The line will now be attached to that vertex. You will continue to click and stretch in this fashion around the area of your graphic to enclose the polygon—clicking the left mouse button on each vertex (see fig. 28.13). When you've reached the point where your polygon began, click the right mouse button.

Fig. 28.13
Click the vertices of a polygon to create the coordinates.

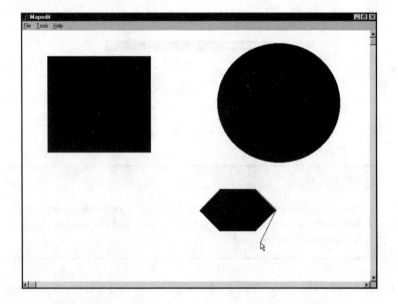

9. A window titled Object URL will appear asking for the URL to be associated with this region. In the text-area below URL for Clicks on This Object, type in a relative or absolute path to the desired URL.

Comments may also be added in the text box below Comments on This Object (see fig. 28.14). When you have typed in a URL and added a comment, click OK.

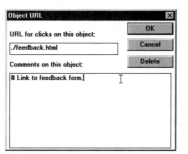

Fig. 28.14
Type in the resulting URL and comments for each region.

10. You may now continue creating additional regions on your imagemap graphic. The Circle Tool draws the radius of a circle out from where you click the left mouse button. Click the right mouse button to add a URL and comment to the circle region. Likewise, the Rectangle Tool traces a rectangle from the point where you click the left mouse button. To finish the rectangle, click the right mouse button. You may cancel any shape by pressing the Esc key or by clicking on the Cancel button in the Object URL window.

11. When you have finished mapping out the regions on an image, Mapedit allows testing of the active links. To test an imagemap, select Tools, Test+Edit. Clicking on an active region in this mode will highlight the region and open the Object URL window. If there are changes to be made in the URL or comments for this region, add this information to what appears in the Object URL window. Choose OK to continue testing your imagemap definition file. The Test+Edit functionality of Mapedit is built into the program itself and is not being run off the Web server. Also, there's no guarantee that any other imagemap creation programs will have this feature.

12. If you wish to include a default URL in your imagemap definition file choose File, Edit Default URL. This will allow you to specify a URL to be returned in the event that none of the regions match where the user clicked on the imagemap graphic. When you have specified a default URL, choose the OK button.

13. The last step is to save this document as a imagemap definition file. Choose File, Save. In Mapedit's Confirmation window choose OK.

> **Tip**
>
> A separate imagemap definition file is necessary for each imagemap graphic used in your Web site. A good rule of thumb is to keep the imagemap definition file and the related imagemap graphic in the same directory with a similar name. For example: main_menu.gif and main_menu.map

Referencing the Imagemap in HTML: the ISMAP Tag

As you recall from chapter 27, the Image tag <IMG SRC> can contain a number of attributes which determine the border, alignment, and alternative text name for the image. The Image tag is also the element in an HTML document that triggers the imagemap process.

The imagemap graphic must be made an active link in your Web page, much like the use of a single image button. As you will remember from chapter 22, inlined images can be used as clickable items as long as they are enclosed in the Anchor tag. That is, if you were to use a image named feedback_button.gif to link from your home page to a document in the same directory named feedback.html, the HTML would be:

```
<A HREF=feedback.html>
<IMG SRC=feedback_button.gif>
</A>
```

This tells the server that when the feedback_button.gif is clicked, a document named feedback.html is returned to the browser.

The ISMAP attribute appended to the <IMG SRC> tag builds upon the above process, and activates the imagemap. The link in the case of an imagemap is not to a specific document, such as feedback.html, but an imagemap definition file containing the coordinates for all the hot-spots of an imagemap graphic. The definition file, usually denoted with the extension .MAP, is analyzed by the imagemap CGI program on the requested server along with the coordinates of where the imagemap graphic was clicked.

> **Note**
>
> The physical location of your imagemap definition file will be subject to the configuration of your World Wide Web server. Most Netscape Commerce and Secure servers allow these files to be located anywhere within the http or Netsite directories. However, it is best to check with the system administrator on how your particular server is configured to handle imagemaps.

Regardless of your server's imagemap configuration, use of an imagemap in your HTML document must include the Image tag <IMG SRC> with the attribute: ISMAP. For instance, to reference an image on your home page named my_map.gif as an imagemap using the coordinates in the definition my_map.map, the HTML would be:

```
<A HREF=my_map.map>
<IMG SRC=my_map.gif ISMAP>
</A>
```

The link in this instance is not another HTML document, but the imagemap definition file which contains the coordinates for each region of the imagemap graphic, my_map.gif. The server receives the request for the definition file and the coordinates of the user's click in the form of a HTTP GET request. From there the imagemap CGI program is executed in order to interpret the request.

> **Note**
>
> It's acceptable to combine other Image attributes with ISMAP, however it is customary to place the ISMAP as the final attribute. For instance:
>
> ```
> <IMG align=left border=0 SRC=my_map.gif alt=My Map ISMAP>
> ```

Using Netscape to Test Your Imagemap

Once you've made your imagemap, the only thing left to do is to test it out. While most map editing programs let you test the imagemap regions you've outlined, nothing beats using Netscape. Testing it out as if you were an actual user, instead of the designer, is useful because there are things users catch that designers won't.

The best way to test your imagemap is to put it on your Web server. By testing the imagemap with Netscape, you'll see just how fast your imagemap comes through your modem and how distinct each clickable region is. It's also a good idea to have a friend at another service provider try out your imagemap, so you can check for valid URLs. No matter how detailed your imagemap might be, it's always a good idea to try it out a few times as if you were an ordinary user.

Providing an Alternative

While it's great to have imagemaps, you must also consider other people. There is a significant number of people browsing the Web who are using text-based browsers. You should provide for some means of letting them navigate around your home page. You can put in a separate section with a description of the links and the corresponding URLs. You can also have a link that takes the user to a text-only menu that has the same links as the imagemap. Whichever approach you take, be sure to put in an alternative for text-only users.

## CHAPTER 29

Netscape-Specific and Future HTML Commands

Having seen quite a bit of HTML, we're ready to look at the different levels of HTML (Netscape, HTML 2.0, and HTML 3.0) and consider whether or not you want to use these elements. In the previous few chapters you've been introduced to elements that fall under the purview of the HTML 2.0 standard. There's more to it than that, though.

Of particular concern in this chapter are two other types of HTML commands: Netscape-specific and HTML 3.0. Netscape-specific commands are HTML elements that have been introduced by the Netscape Corp. as proprietary elements that their browsers support for Web design. This doesn't *necessarily* mean that other browsers aren't able to deal with these elements. But it does mean there's a good chance that they can't.

HTML 3.0 is the emerging new standard for Web design. It hasn't yet been completely pounded out, but many of the elements that programmers are *assuming* will be included have already been recognized and included in browsers by Netscape and others.

In this chapter, you learn:

- The difference between Netscape and HTML 3.0 elements
- What the Netscape elements are and how to add them to your Web pages
- How to design your Web site so that Netscape and non-Netscape users can both access it
- How to design your pages for both Netscape and HTML 3.0
- The future of HTML

Netscape Versus HTML Commands

While not yet official, the HTML 3.0 standard for HTML elements is beginning to come into widespread use. Some of these elements are commands that Netscape (and others) have recognized for quite some time. In fact, Netscape is very active in the creation of the standard, and many elements that have been considered Netscape-specific for the last year or so will probably be included in the HTML 3.0 standard.

For now though, it's important for us to distinguish between Netscape and HTML 3.0 commands. As the HTML 3.0 standard comes into shape, we'll see where the standard deviates from Netscape-specific commands, and which will be included as they stand. And that will be important to you as a Web designer.

Why? While Netscape does control a considerable majority of the browser market, there are others out there. For that reason, it's important that you decide whether or not you're going to include any of these elements in your pages. Some browsers may not be able to view documents that include these tags, and others may, but with less than satisfactory results.

◀ See "What Is HTML and What Are the Standards?" pg. 590

As other browsers begin to lean toward the HTML 3.0 standard, they may have less reason to try to implement Netscape commands—especially where the two overlap. So for the best results, you'll want to stay as close to the HTML 3.0 standard as you can.

Adding Netscape-Only Commands to Your Pages

Netscape additions to HTML are of basically two kinds: extensions of the HTML 2.0 standard elements and new Netscape-only elements. Let's start with the extensions to HTML 2.0, then we'll look at the new types of elements you can include in Netscape-only pages.

Netscape's HTML 2.0 Extensions

Nearly all of Netscape's extensions work as attribute tags that are added to standard HTML elements—and, they are just about all designed to give the user more control over the look and feel of the page. This is, in fact, where Netscape tends to diverge from the spirit of HTML. These very specific tags allow you to decide with precision how the browser displays the HTML element. For the most part, the theory of HTML works against this—each individual browser *should* be left to doing the formatting on its own.

But, with 70 percent of the browser market, Netscape has made the ultimate overture to the more artistic of Web designers...more control over the page.

> ### Tip
>
> Remember, you should not use *any* of these Netscape-specific elements and tags if your goal is to create HTML 3.0 compatible pages. We'll talk about HTML 3.0 later in this chapter.

The <HR> Element

<HR> generally returns a horizontal rule in Netscape and other browsers. In Netscape, the default for this element is a shaded, engraved-looking line. But, thanks to new Netscape attributes, you can change this with the SIZE, WIDTH, ALIGN, and NOSHADE tags (see fig. 29.1).

◀ See "Basic Formatting Tags," pg. 631

Thickness changed to 5   Width is 75 percent

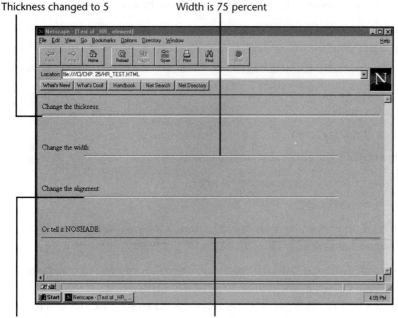

Fig. 29.1
The <HR> Netscape extensions in action.

This one is 75 percent and aligned to center   And this one has a NOSHADE tag

To change the size of an <HR> tag, the format is

```
<HR SIZE=number>
```

where *number* is the thickness of the horizontal rule.

Similarly, you can change the width of the <HR> tag from the default (whatever the width of the page is) to something more specific by formatting the tag as

```
<HR WIDTH=number>
```

where *number* is the exact length in pixels that you'd like the horizontal rule to be. You can also use a percentage (for example, 75 percent) to indicate that you want the line to be a percentage of the available window.

To align the horizontal rule on the page (this is only really useful if you've changed the WIDTH), the align tag is formatted as

```
<HR ALIGN=direction>
```

where *direction* is either left, right, or center. This, respectively, pushes the line up against the left margin of the available window, the right margin of the window, or it centers the line on the page.

Our final tag, NOSHADE, takes no variables, simply following the format <HR NOSHADE>.

HTML Lists

Another set of fully cosmetic tags can be added to the HTML elements: <UL> (bulleted list) and <OL> (ordered list) (see fig. 29.2).

To change the bullet style for <UL> lists, you can add the TYPE tag

```
<UL TYPE=style>
```

where *style* can be either disc, circle, or square.

Changing ordered list styles is very similar:

```
<OL TYPE=style>
```

In this case, *style* can be A for capital letters, a for lowercase letters, I for large roman numerals, or i for small roman numerals.

The <LI> element can also take the above tags, allowing you to change bullet types or order types in the middle of a list. For instance, <LI TYPE=a> changes this item's and all subsequent items' numbers (in an <OL> list) to lowercase letters.

The <LI> element can also accept the VALUE tag, allowing you to reset the number count in ordered lists, so that

```
<LI VALUE=5>
```

as the first element in an ordered list would cause the list to start counting from 5 (or V or E, depending on the type tag for that list).

Disc bullets

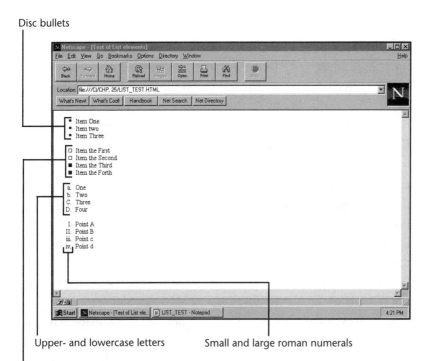

Fig. 29.2
The different ways
to show bullets
and numbers in
lists.

IV

Building Home Pages

Upper- and lowercase letters   Small and large roman numerals

Square bullets

Note

For the most part, an incorrect tag added to an HTML element returns that element to its default style in Netscape. For instance, adding the tag TYPE=circle to an ordered list causes the list to revert to standard numbers (for example, 6,7,8) even if the ordered list had been previously assigned a style tag for letters or roman numerals.

The `<IMG>` element

The image `<IMG>` element has a number of refinements that allow you to align the image with text, specify dimensions for images, decide how wide the border (or frame) for the image will be, and decide how much space should be left between images and text.

When you include the image in a line of text (that is, within the same paragraph), you can use the ALIGN tag, like

```
<IMG ALIGN=direction>
```

◀ See "Adding Links, Graphics, and Tables," pg. 645

to specify a number of different ways to align the image. The following are the different ways you can align the image:

- *left*—Image aligns with the left margin in the next available space down. Subsequent text is wrapped around the right margin of the image.

- *right*—Image aligns with the right margin of the page, and text wraps around its left side.

- *top*—The image aligns itself with the tallest item in the current line.

- *texttop*—Aligns the image with the tallest text in the line.

- *middle*—Aligns the middle of the image with the baseline of the current line.

- *absmiddle* (Absolute middle)—Aligns the image with the middle of the current line.

- *baseline* and *bottom*—Both of these align the bottom of the image with the baseline of the current line.

- *absbottom* (Absolute bottom)—Aligns the bottom of the image with the bottom of the current line.

You may ask, why the distinction between baseline and bottom? Or tallest item and tallest text? Because they can be slightly different, depending on the particular line of HTML coding in question, and that can be a little annoying to the HTML perfectionist.

Baseline is the bottom of a line of text that *does not* take into consideration the descenders in letters like y,j,q, and g. Notice that the bottom of the letters c and g are different, even on this page. The absolute bottom, then, is the bottom of the lowest letter in a line, generally one of these descending letters.

Similarly, the tallest *item* in an HTML line might easily be a graphic file, while the tallest text generally is a capital letter. Figure 29.3 shows why this might make a difference.

Aside from the ALIGN tag, the <IMG> element can also take five other tags: WIDTH, HEIGHT, BORDER, VSPACE, and HSPACE. Width and height generally appear together

```
<IMG WIDTH=number HEIGHT=number>
```

where each *number* is the dimension in pixels. This tag is essentially used to speed up the loading of a page—Netscape determines width and height when it loads the graphic, but it takes a second or so longer.

The change the size of a border, add the border tag

```
<IMG BORDER=number>
```

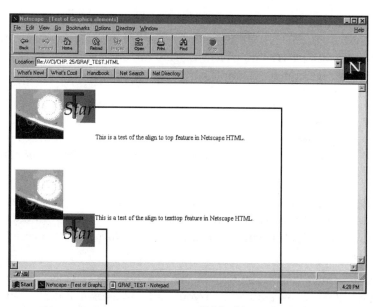

Fig. 29.3

Aligning an image
to texttop ignores
non-text elements
in an HTML line.

IV

Building Home Pages

This one is aligned to texttop   While this graphic is aligned to top

where *number* is the size of the border in pixels. Remember, the border is what
changes colors when an image is used as a hypertext link, so setting BORDER=0
may confuse your users into thinking that the image is *not* a link.

When you use the left and right ALIGN tags for images, you create what's
called a floating image that isn't attached to a particular line, but simply fills
the space left over by text. So, to keep these images from pressing up against
the text (and get a nice, clean word-wrap around the image) use the VSPACE
and HSPACE tags

    <IMG VSPACE=*number* HSPACE=*number*>

where the *number* for VSPACE is the number of pixels above and below the image that are to be kept clear of text, while the *number* for HSPACE is the number of pixels for the left and right margins of the image.

Adding some variety to the line break <BR> tag is the CLEAR attribute, which,
in the case of left- or right-aligned images, makes sure that the text coming
after the <BR> appears *below* the aligned image. For example

    <BR CLEAR=left>

will make sure text begins in the clear space below an image that is aligned
left.

New Elements

Netscape has also added some completely new Netscape-only elements that can be used just like HTML 2.0 elements, but can only be viewed by the Netscape Navigator browser (and any that are written to be Netscape-compatible).

`<NOBR>` and `<WBR>`

`<NOBR>` is a new element that allows you to create text that cannot be broken into a new line by the end of the Netscape window. It follows the format

```
<NOBR>text</NOBR>
```

where *text* is any text during which you do not want Netscape to create a line break. `<NOBR>` is especially effective when you have a series of words that you do not wish broken within a paragraph of text (like, for instance, a URL address).

The new element `<WBR>` is used in the rare instance that you have a `<NOBR>` section and you know *exactly* where you want it to break, if it needs to be broken by the Navigator window. You can also use it if you want to let Netscape know when a particularly long word can be broken, if it needs to be. Notice that `<WBR>` is only used if Netscape needs to create a line break in a particular line.

> **Tip**
>
> The `<PRE>`, `</PRE>` HTML element can also be used to create unbroken lines of text (like using `<NOBR>` and `<WBR>` in conjunction), with the additional benefit of allowing all white space and returns to remain intact.

Font and Basefont Size

Another new element created by Netscape gives you the ability to determine relative font sizes for normal text (see fig. 29.4). This is accomplished using the `<FONT SIZE>` tag, as in

```
<FONT SIZE=number>
```

where *number* is between 1 and 7 (3 is the default size). But, there is also another element, called `<BASEFONT SIZE>`. Why have the two different elements? Well, the `<FONT SIZE>` element can actually be made relative to the `<BASEFONT SIZE>` by using a plus or minus in front of the number, like this example

```
<BASEFONT SIZE=2>
<FONT SIZE=+2>
```

Now the font size for this particular text will actually be 4, which is the basefont's 2 plus the increase in the font size element. What good is this? By using relative <FONT SIZE> values throughout your HTML page, you can change the size of all fonts be simply changing the <BASEFONT SIZE> value.

I can change the font size up at every letter

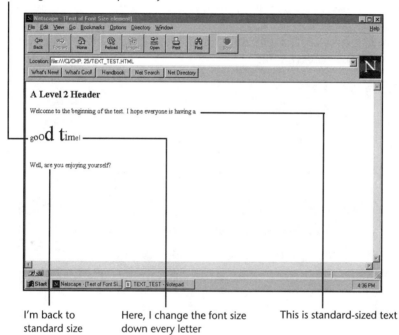

Fig. 29.4
You can change font size as much as you want, but for each change you need a <FONT SIZE> tag.

I'm back to standard size

Here, I change the font size down every letter

This is standard-sized text

You need to use a new <FONT SIZE> tag for every change in font size. In the example pictured in figure 29.4, there are eight different <FONT SIZE> tags in that one line of text!

> **Tip**
>
> Another way to make text stand out on the page is to use Netscape's <BLINK> *text* </BLINK> element, which causes a blinking gray box to appear and disappear over the enclosed text. Be aware, however, that there is fairly universal scorn for this silly little blink among the Web elite. Many folks find it annoying.

`<CENTER>`

Our final Netscape addition to HTML 2.0 is the `<CENTER>` element. Using this element, you can center any amount of text on the page, following the format

   `<CENTER>`*text*`</CENTER>`

where *text* can be a word, many lines, or even multiple paragraphs. In fact, the `CENTER` tag centers just about anything at all, including lists, images, and other elements (see fig. 29.5). Also, realize that Netscape inserts a line break at the end of the `</CENTER>` tag.

> **Note**
>
> Most `ALIGN` tags overrule the `<CENTER>` element, so if your images are set with `<IMG ALIGN>` they will continue to appear as they should, although the text that wraps around them will still be centered against the page.

Fig. 29.5
With the entire page set between `<CENTER>` and `</CENTER>`, you get some interesting results.

Creating Tables with Netscape Elements

Once again I should point out that Netscape tables are not the same as HTML 3.0 tables. To their credit, Netscape has been trying to implement tables that match the HTML standard for some time now, but the standard has been changed a few times.

What is a table? In HTML, creating a table allows you to present data in a way that is very similar to the way a spreadsheet looks. You have labels, rows, columns, and cells for your table that make information—especially reference data and financial and scientific findings—a little easier for your reader to consume.

With Netscape HTML, you start by creating a table, then adding a row and placing the header data (or titles of columns) in that row. Then you create more rows, and within each row you enter the data for the table. Each separate data entry creates a cell in the table (see fig. 29.6).

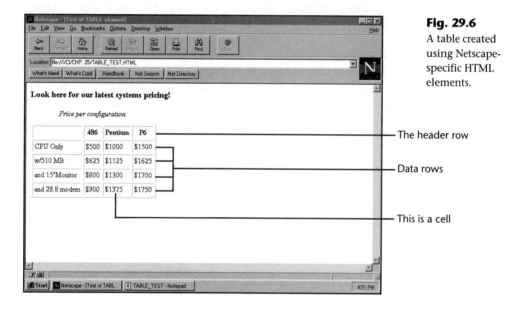

Fig. 29.6
A table created using Netscape-specific HTML elements.

The header row

Data rows

This is a cell

The <TABLE> element

To start your table you'll need to begin with the <TABLE> element, which wraps around all other table tags as such

```
<TABLE>
...all other table elements...
</TABLE>
```

In Netscape 1.1, the <TABLE> element has an implied line break before and after the table is shown. This has changed in Netscape 2.0, however, in anticipation of the HTML 3.0 standard for tables.

The <TABLE> element can also take a number of attributes, including the BORDER, CELLSPACING, CELLPADDING, and WIDTH attributes. All of these follow the format

```
<TABLE attribute_tag=number>
```

where *attribute_tag* is one of the four listed, and *number* represents how much of the attribute is applied. In the case of WIDTH, the number may also be a percentage, for example 75 percent.

What do these attributes do? The BORDER attribute is used to determine the size of the border around the table and between cells. CELLSPACING determines the amount of space that is placed between individual cells in the table. CELLPADDING determines the distance between a cell's data and the cell border. The WIDTH attribute determines the width of the table (default is whatever fits on the page). If you use a number for WIDTH, then it represents the number of pixels for the table; a percentage means the table should take up that portion of the available browser window.

Creating Rows of Data

The next step, after creating the table, is to fill it with rows. Beginning with a row for header information (if desired), rows are entered using the following element

```
<TR> data cells </TR>
```

where *data cells* are Netscape HTML data elements as described by the <TD> or <TH> tag (explained in a moment). The <TR> element can take either an ALIGN or VALIGN attribute, which becomes the default for all the cells in that row, so that

```
<TR ALIGN=Center> data cells </TR>
```

causes data to be aligned in the center of the data cells that you create for that row.

And how do you create data cells? With the <TH> (header cell) and <TD> (standard data cell) elements, such as

```
<TD> data </TD>
```

in which case, the data is any valid body HTML markup or text. How about an example? A simple table, including a header row and a few data rows, might look something like this:

```
<TABLE BORDER=2 CELLSPACING=4 CELLPADDING=3>
<TR> <TH>Job</TH><TH>Tues.</TH><TH>Wed.</TH><TH>Thurs.</TH> </TR>
<TR> <TD>Clean</TD><TD>Bob</TD><TD>Joe</TD><TD>Beth</TD> </TR>
<TR> <TD>Trash</TD><TD>Beth</TD><TD>Bob</TD><TD>Joe</TD> </TR>
<TR> <TD>Dishes</TD><TD>Joe</TD><TD>Beth</TD><TD>Bob</TD> </TR>
<CAPTION ALIGN=bottom><H3>Mid-week chore list</H3></CAPTION>
</TABLE>
```

Note

You might appreciate knowing that table data elements don't require the closing tag (for example, </TD> or </TH>)—especially if you type in your HTML manually. It's good form to include them, though.

I threw in the last major element for a Netscape table there at the end—the CAPTION element. This allows you to create a quick identifying line for your table, taking an ALIGN attribute (if desired) to align to the top or the bottom of the table (default is the top of the table). Netscape can accept any valid HTML between <CAPTION> and </CAPTION>, and the caption always appears centered with respect to the table (see fig. 29.7).

Tip

For a blank cell, enter **<td> </td>** instead of just a blank space (like <td></td>). This preserves the cell borders, making your table appear more complete.

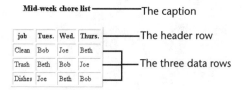

Mid-week chore list ————— The caption

————— The header row

————— The three data rows

Fig. 29.7
Assign your family chores over the Web? Well, maybe you can come up with a better reason for a Netscape table.

Background Graphics and Page Colors

Netscape HTML allows you to define certain graphics to tile behind your HTML codes, or colors to specify for the background and foreground. HTML 3.0 also allows you to add graphics to the background for Web pages, but doesn't follow Netscape's conventions for changing background colors. Again, it's up to you to decide if you should use these commands—just recognize that only Netscape-compatible browsers see these pages correctly.

Background

To add a background image to your HTML page, you simply add the BACK-GROUND attribute to the BODY element

```
<BODY BACKGROUND=path/graphic.ext>
...HTML document...
</BODY>
```

where *path* is the directory path to the graphic file on your server (either relative or absolute) and the name of the graphic file, with an appropriate extension, follows the path. (Of course, you don't necessarily need a path statement if your graphic resides in the same directory as your HTML page.) This causes the graphic to be tiled behind your text and other graphics so that the background graphic is displayed over and down the screen until the background is filled, depending on the size of the graphic (see fig. 29.8).

Note

There's a little file-size paradox here with background images—the smaller the image, the faster the page loads, but the larger the image, the faster it displays. So, if you use a single graphic background for your entire site, it's not *too* awful to have it a little on the large side; it will load once and display quickly from the cache. If you have many different backgrounds throughout your site, keep them smaller.

Fig. 29.8

A Web page with a background graphic. Notice that, since the graphic is smaller than the page, it is tiled to fill the screen.

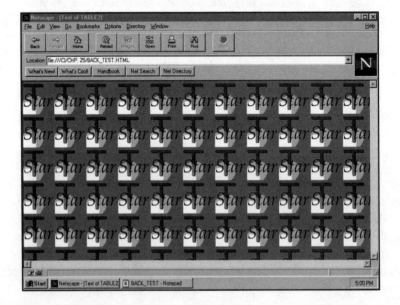

For Netscape only, you can define a background color for a page, and depending on the user's browser settings, it may or may not display. This is done with the BGCOLOR attribute to the BODY element

```
<BODY BGCOLOR=#rrggbb>
...HTML document...
</BODY>
```

where #rrggbb is the number sign and three hexadecimal numbers representing red, green and blue. An example might be

```
<BODY BGCOLOR=#000000>
```

which results in a black background. #FFFFFF would be a white background, #FF0000 for red, #00FF00 for green, #0000FF for blue, and so on.

Note

Here's a quick lesson in hex numbers. Hexadecimal means base-16, not base-10 (normal counting numbers), so each place past the one's column represents a multiple of 16, not ten. Since there are no single-digit numerals past 9 in our base-10 counting system, hexadecimal uses letters (A-F) to represent the remaining digits (10-15). An F in the 16's place, then, is 15*16=240. An F in the one's place represents 15, so the hexademical number FF equals the decimal number 255 (240+15).

◀ See "Advanced Graphics," pg. 673

Foreground

Once you've changed the background of your document, you might have a good reason to change your foreground colors, too—especially the color of your text and links. To do this, you use another attribute to the BODY element. For regular text, that attribute is TEXT, as in

```
<BODY TEXT=#rrggbb>
...HTML document...
</BODY>
```

where #rrggbb is another three hexadecimal numbers. You can also change the colors of links, realizing that there are actually three different link attributes: LINK, VLINK, and ALINK. LINK is the link before being selected, VLINK is a visited link, and ALINK is an active link. These are also attributes for the BODY element

```
<BODY LINK=#rrggbb VLINK=#rrggbb ALINK=#rrggbb>
```

where, once again, you enter the number sign and three hexadecimal numbers. Default for these values is blue for LINK, purple for VLINK, and red for ALINK.

Note

You may be wondering how you can see an active link (ALINK). This is the color the link changes to right after you've selected it, while the next page loads. It's also the color of a link to a sound, movie, or other file that you're in the process of downloading.

Realize that whether or not your users see these colors depends on how their browser is designed. If they don't Auto Load Images, for instance, then the background image won't be loaded, and (if you haven't also set a background color) Netscape will also ignore your link color attributes, working on the assumption that your changed colors may look bad on the default gray background.

Designing Web Sites for Netscape and Non-Netscape Users

Among Web designers who create pages with Netscape-specific commands, there are basically two different trains of thought. The first group, the others-be-darned group, designs pages with Netscape and HTML 3.0 commands, graphics, and area maps without concern for users who use other browsers; their emphasis is on the look of the page, not (necessarily) the content of the page. If you can read it, good. If not, get Netscape.

It's hard to condemn these folks—after all, Netscape commands give you the most artful control over your pages. In fact, many of them are even willing to offer a link to Netscape so you can download the browser for yourself. That's nice of them, but there is another way.

By using a *front door* to your Web site, you can give users a choice (see fig. 29.9). If you'd like, you can design sites that offer the same pages in two different formats: Netscape-specific and non-Netscape specific. Sometimes, for instance with tables, it takes a little creativity to create a non-Netscape page that still communicates everything you want it to. But, for the most part, Netscape additions are just cosmetic. It's easy enough to create pages that work for both Netscape users and non-Netscape users.

All you really need to do for your front door is offer two different links—one to an index page for your Netscape site, and another for your text-only or HTML 2.0-only site. Then, duplicate your pages for both types, taking any Netscape-specific elements or attributes out of one set of pages.

> **Tip**
>
> If you're developing a site for your business, it's almost imperative that you offer your users a choice of browsers. If not, you're cutting out 30 to 40 percent of your market!

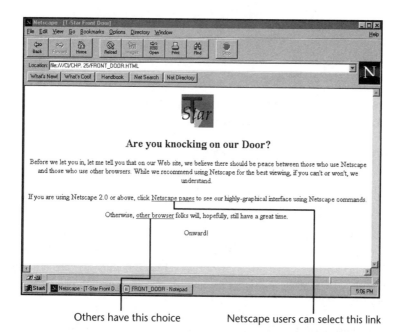

Fig. 29.9
A front door can let users decide whether or not they want to view pages that use Netscape-specific commands.

Others have this choice   Netscape users can select this link

Is there any way around this duplication? Actually, yes. Develop your pages without Netscape-specific commands. If that seems too limiting, consider developing your pages according to the HTML 3.0 standard instead of Netscape's HTML extensions. As time wears on, HTML 3.0 should be fairly quickly received by the folks who create Web browsers. You may have to give up a particular Netscapism or two, but that's a price to pay for reaching *everyone* who uses the Web.

For an exceptional Web-based reference for achieving Netscape-specific results using only HTML 3.0 standard elements and attributes, point your browser at Andrew B. King's pages at **http://ic.corpnet.com/~aking/ webinfo/html3andns/**.

Introduction to HTML 3.0

I think I've said often enough that HTML 3.0 is an *emerging* standard. But that does lead us to a couple of disclaimers that are important to make at this point; they are as follows:

> *HTML 3.0 may not yet be supported by all browsers.* At least for a while, you may have the same problems using HTML 3.0 elements that are new since HTML 2.0. It will take browsers a little while to catch up, although I imagine that the big names (Netscape, Mosaic, MS Internet Explorer) will support HTML 3.0 by the middle of 1996, assuming the standard stays relatively stable.

HTML 3.0 may change. As has happened a few times over the last couple of months, the HTML 3.0 standard may change a bit from what's presented here.

If you're interested in watching the progress of HTML 3.0 on the Web, you might want to check in at **http://www.w3.org/hypertext/WWW/ MarkUp/html3/CoverPage.html**.

HTML 3.0 vs. Netscape HTML

Before we look at the new elements that HTML presents us with, let's look at a few that have already been implemented in Netscape's version of HTML and figure out where the two disagree.

There's a rule of thumb here. Netscape, in general, errs on the side of *more control* over the layout of a page. Netscape also tends to create additional element tags for layout functions, whereas HTML 3.0 leans toward adding attribute tags to existing elements for layout—for instance, the Netscape <CENTER> tag.

Aligning Things in HTML 3.0. You may remember that the Netscape <CENTER> element tag is a catch-all—anything between the <CENTER> and </CENTER> tags gets centered, except for images that overrule that with their own ALIGN tags. HTML 3.0 doesn't offer the <CENTER> tag, however, since it's a purely aesthetic tag. HTML prefers to use the ALIGN attribute tag, added to different existing tags, such as

```
<P ALIGN=direction> Text </P>
```

where direction is left, right, center, or justify (solid left and right borders). This ALIGN attribute can also be added to the header tags (for example, <H1>, <H2>, and so on), <TABLE> tag, <TR> (table row) tag, and others.

But isn't this leaving something out? After all, the Netscape <CENTER> tag allows you to center any amount of anything that you want to center. That's more convenient, right?

Well, HTML 3.0 lets you center big chunks, too, with the <DIV> element tag. By adding the <ALIGN> attribute tag, you get something like

```
<DIV ALIGN=direction>
...a section of HTML...
</DIV>
```

where direction is, again, left, right, center, or justify. The <DIV> tag is creating a division within the body of the document. In essence, you're telling the browser that this is a particular portion of the body elements that needs to be treated in this special way. Advantage over Netscape HTML? It gives you more choices, while staying with the HTML 3.0 theory of no appearance-only element tags.

Creating HTML 3.0 Tables

If you've read through the process for creating Netscape tables, you may notice that HTML 3.0 tables aren't completely different. Most of the commands are the same; where the two diverge is basically in cosmetic differences. HTML 3.0 and Netscape tend to use different attribute tags for such things as centering text in cells.

Here's a quick sample of an HTML table:

```
<TABLE BORDER=1 ALIGN=CENTER>
<TR><TH>Pay<TH>Tuesday<TH>Wednesday<TH>Thursday</TR>
<TR><TD>Luis<TD>$25.00<TD>$40.00<TD>$30.00</TR>
<TR><TD>Marcia<TD>$15.00<TD>$30.00<TD>$50.00</TR>
<TR><TD>Rick<TD>$20.00<TD>$20.00<TD>$20.00</TR>
<TR><TD>Ellis<TD>$35.00<TD>12.00<TD>$40.00</TR>
<CAPTION ALIGN=BOTTOM>Pay per day for employees</CAPTION>
</TABLE>
```

As mentioned in the last section, the HTML 3.0 <TABLE> element takes the attribute ALIGN, which can be either left, right, or center. The <TABLE> element can also accept the BORDER, WIDTH, CELLPADDING, and CELLSPACING attributes as explained for Netscape tables.

The other differences are somewhat petty—if you get deep into creating tables, you'll want to explore them. In general, HTML 3.0 offers slightly fewer (and slightly different) attribute tags for the lowest level of table alignment and appearance.

Other Issues of Appearance

How about a couple more differences? HTML 3.0 does not recognize any of the text color and background color attributes that Netscape does (those hexadecimal numbers for colors). In fact, the <BODY> element can only be used to load a background graphic—you can't change *any* colors within it. So, our only choice here is

```
<BODY BACKGROUND=path/filename.ext>
...HTML document
</BODY>
```

where *path* is the directory path to the background file and *filename.ext* is the name of the background graphic and the appropriate extension.

HTML 3.0 also doesn't recognize the additional attribute tags for bullet lists, ordered lists, and the <HR> tag that Netscape offers. It does offer customizing attributes for these, but no browser currently supports them.

The <BLINK>, <NOBR>, and <FONT SIZE> elements are also lacking in HTML 3.0. In the last case, though, HTML does offer the <SMALL>, <SUB>, <SUP>, and <LARGE> tags for text, which (respectively) allow you to format text as smaller than the standard text, a subscript, a superscript, and larger than standard text on the page (see fig. 29.10).

Tip

It's a good idea to continue to use the header tags (<H1>, <H2>, and so on) when you're actually creating a header within your document. Use <SMALL> and <LARGE> only for body text.

Fig. 29.10
HTML 3.0 offers these alternatives to Netscape's <FONT SIZE> element.

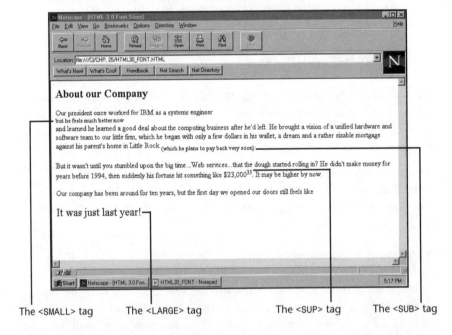

The <SMALL> tag   The <LARGE> tag   The <SUP> tag   The <SUB> tag

Finally, HTML 3.0 doesn't recognize most of the ALIGN characteristics for <IMG> elements that Netscape has added to HTML 2.0, like texttop, absmiddle, baseline, and absbottom.

The Coming Elements of HTML 3.0

In essence, HTML 3.0 is designed to add three major requests from the Web world: tables (discussed previously), text-wrap around figures, and the ability to show mathematical formulas in HTML documents. In addition to this, there are a number of appearance issues that HTML 3.0 addresses including the new <BANNER> element for more control of the top of a document, allowing you to fix corporate logos, back/forward controls, and other elements to keep them from scrolling as the rest of the page is scrolled.

The <FIG> element

This is basically a replacement for the <IMG> tag, although, of course, the <IMG> tag remains for the sake of backward compatibility. The new <FIG> element has three basic reasons for being.

- Text flows around a <FIG> defined image.

- A text-based description is part of the basic definition of the <FIG> tag, allowing nongraphical Web users to still get the gist of a graphic on the page (and access it if it happens to be a hypertext link).

- The <FIG> element allows you to create hotzones for client-side imagemaps.

Current imagemaps are server-based—you create the imagemap in a special program and, when accessed, it calls a map server program to determine where the user has clicked the graphic. That, in turn, determines which link it follows.

◀ See "Using Imagemaps," pg. 699

For client-side maps, then, no server interaction is required. The HTML describes what part of the graphics has been clicked, the browser interprets that click into the appropriate URL, and that URL is accessed.

> **Note**
>
> Netscape version 2.0 does not currently support the <FIG> tag, so if you access a page like this with Netscape, you only see the text options.

Math in HTML 3.0

This element can get really complicated, and if you're a math person, that might just be heaven. The <MATH> element for HTML 3.0 gives Web pages a standard way to represent complex mathematical formulas within lines of text. Up until now, the only choice for representing formulas in HTML has been to include them as graphics—perhaps creating them in a word processor or advanced math program first.

Although an amazing range of formulas and equations can be represented, I'll stick to a fairly simple example. Using the <MATH> tag, you can render the integral from a to b of f(x) over 1+x as

```
<MATH>&int;<SUB>a</SUB><SUP>b</SUP><BOX>f(x)<OVER>1+x</BOX>dx
</MATH>
```

or

```
<MATH>&int;_a_^b^{f(x)<OVER>1+x} dx </MATH>
```

Look complicated? It does to me. But, if this is the sort of thing you want to represent in HTML, you'll soon find that it's not terribly difficult. Notice that the first example uses the full HTML tags for the various different attributes you want assigned to the equation's variable (<SUB> for subscript, <SUP> for superscript). The second example uses HTML shortref characters for those same mark-up tags (_for <SUB>, ^ for <SUP>).

As the standard emerges, more information on markup and attributes for the <MATH> tag will be ready for you to use in your pages. To keep tabs on developments, check out **http://www.w3.org/hypertext/WWW/MarkUp/html3/maths.html**.

Non-Scrolling Elements

This tag is very interesting to serious Web designers. Using the <BANNER> tag in the <BODY> section of your page, you force the top of your page to be non-scrolling, allowing you to keep a corporate logo, back/forward controls, or a button-bar interface at the top of the screen at all times.

And, it's easy to implement! An example <BANNER> looks like

```
<BODY>
<BANNER>
<P ALIGN=Center>
<IMG SRC=logo.gif ALT=T-Star Consulting>
</BANNER>
...HTML document...
</BODY>
```

This results in a section at the top of our document that remains fixed, while the rest of the text scrolls as it normally would.

Finding HTML 3.0 Info on the Web

If you've got a handle on which Netscape tags you plan to use, whether or not you're going to use a front door, and if you keep in mind the ways that HTML 3.0 might change Web design in the near future, then you've gotten the most out of this chapter. From here, you'll probably want to head out on the Web for the latest in developments for both Netscape-specific and HTML 3.0 commands.

Check out the following good Web sites for this type of information:

http://home.netscape.com/assist/net_sites/index.html to keep abreast of changes and additions to new versions of Netscape and Netscape-specific HTML elements.

http://www.w3.org/hypertext/WWW/MarkUp/html3/ CoverPage.html to watch the HTML 3.0 specification change, shape up, and become a formal standard.

http://ic.corpnet.com/~aking/webinfo/html3andns/ for great advice from Andrew King on getting Netscape HTML and HTML 3.0 to work together on your pages.

Next up in this book you'll finish the discussion of the advanced Web site with a look at some of the programming that goes on under the hood, and a summary of the best elements and design techniques that make for the world-class site. Then it's on to some more emerging Web technology—a new programming language called Java.

## CHAPTER 30

Netscape Forms and CGI-BIN Scripts

The Web can seem a constantly changing, dynamic place. Netscape can give you a feeling of almost unlimited freedom and endless possibilities—a full tank of gas; wide, rough tires; and a wide, colorful horizon spreading off as far as you can see.

But sometimes, there's something more. Some sites on the Web seem thriving, somehow, even more exciting than the usual. It's hard to pin down, but some outposts in cyberspace seem almost alive.

What is it? What's the thing that separates these sites from thousands of others?

They're interactive! You can enter data and receive customized responses. You can make choices and alter the site as you like. You aren't just *reading* information, you're *controlling* it.

True interactivity—sites that let users do more than just browse—is the one thing that sets one bus stop on the Information Superhighway apart from another, that really defines the World Wide Web as a new medium. You use this interactively all the time, probably without thinking twice about it—but it sticks in your mind as something special, something worth remembering.

In this chapter, you learn:

- How CGI scripts and forms interrelate
- How to write CGI scripts in Bourne shell, Perl, or other languages
- What HTML tags are used to create forms
- The dangers you must be aware of when creating scripts and forms
- Where to go to get publicly available code for creating your own interactive Web site

Creating Web Interactivity

Two elements go into making interactivity on the Web possible: CGI scripts and forms. While these elements are probably two of the most misunderstood—and confusing—aspects of creating a Web site, they are also the two most powerful. With them you can do anything from asking the user to guess a number to taking an order for a pizza to offering free searches of your comprehensive Web database, as shown in figure 30.1.

Fig. 30.1
What makes Yahoo special? One thing is the ability to interactively search the entire site— something only CGI scripts and forms make possible.

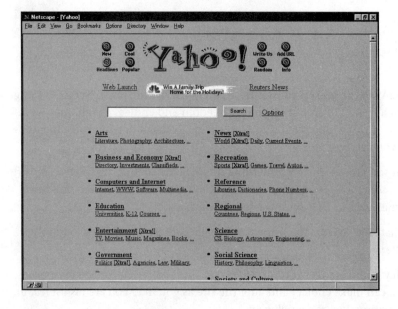

To get true interactivity on the Web, you need to understand and use both CGI scripts and forms, as they make up two halves of the same coin. Forms allow the user to enter data—information about himself, his request, his purchase order, or anything else—into Netscape and send it through the World Wide Web to your server. This is a "front end" that users see and interact with.

CGI scripts make up the "back end." They take the information sent to the server through the Web and process it—querying databases, placing orders, or simply logging accesses. It all happens behind the scenes, but it's where the real work takes place. The results are then passed back. Figure 30.2 is an illustration.

Though it can seem confusing, CGI scripts and forms are worth the trouble. They can transform your site from something static and predictable to something dynamic and exciting.

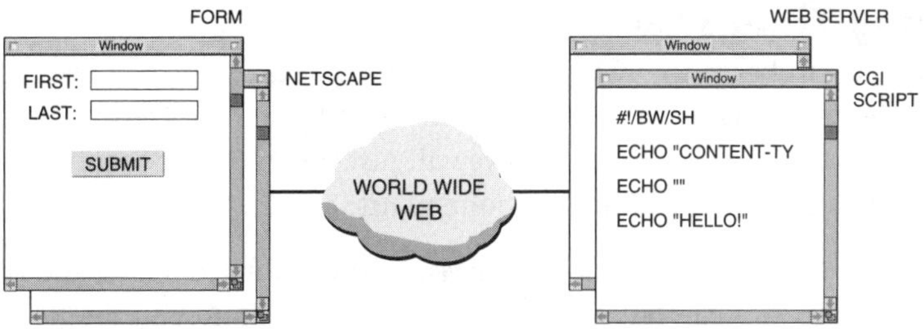

Fig. 30.2
Information is passed from a form to Netscape through the Web, to the server and ends up at a CGI script. The response is passed back through to the server, through the Web and back to Netscape.

CGI Scripting

The Common Gateway Interface is the full name of CGI, and it is a way for your Web server to extend its capabilities by running external programs—much the way Netscape uses helper applications to display a Word document, for example. CGI is a "gateway" to functionality not pre-programmed into your server, and allows you to use *all* of your computer's capabilities, instead of just those that are already part of the HTTP server software.

To a user, a link to a CGI program looks like a link to any other URL. It can be clicked like any other link and results in new information being displayed, just like any other link.

But a CGI program, under the hood, is much more than a normal Web page. When a normal URL is selected, a file is read, interpreted, and displayed by Netscape. When a URL to a CGI program is selected, it causes a program to be run on the server system, and that program can do just about anything you want it to: scan databases, sort names, send mail. CGI scripts allow for complex "back-end" processing.

CGI changes the definition of what Netscape can do. While normal pages are static and unchanging, CGI programs allow a page to be anything it wants to be.

Scripts Versus Programs

What's the difference between a CGI script and a CGI program? Semantics, mostly. The term script is left over from the early days of the Web, when it ran exclusively on UNIX machines. A UNIX script is a list of commands that are run in sequence, a lot like DOS batch files. The first CGI programs were written using these scripts, so the name CGI scripts caught on. Later, true programs (written in Perl or C, usually) were used to perform the same functions. There is no functional difference between scripts and programs—neither the user nor the server software can tell them apart—and both terms are used interchangeably in this chapter.

Setting Things Up

Before you can begin to use CGI scripts, you must take care of a few preliminaries. Because what follows really has nothing to do with Netscape—CGI
scripts live and run on the server—we will just touch on the requirements.
The following are some of these requirements:

- *You must have access to a Web server*, or the ability to install and configure one. This can be a complicated, tedious job and you should ask
  your company or school's system administrator or Webmaster if the
  facility is already set up.

- *You must know at least* some *UNIX*. Though Web servers exist for many
  different platforms and the concepts discussed in this chapter apply to
  all of them, the details contained here are UNIX-specific.

- *You must know a computer language*. CGI scripts are not written in HTML
  like normal Web pages. Instead of static instructions to be interpreted
  by the Netscape browser, they are actual computer programs. This gives
  them a flexibility that normal Web pages don't have, but also increases
  their complexity. Before you can write CGI scripts, you must know how
  to program.

While you can use almost any language to write your CGI scripts, the
most popular are Bourne shell (on UNIX), batch files (on Windows NT
and Windows 95), Perl, and C. Each has strengths and weaknesses, and
while a discussion of each is beyond the scope of this book, there are
many excellent references available.

For smaller CGI scripts, UNIX Bourne shell scripts or Windows NT or 95
batch files are a good choice. They are easy to write, easy to test, and
don't take much of a time investment. If a simple script needs to evolve
into something more complex—maybe it needs the ability to search a
text file—you can use the command-line tools, like grep, awk, sed, or
any number of others.

For medium-sized CGI scripts, Perl is a good choice. It's fast, flexible,
and easy to program. You can set variables, call subroutines, and do
everything a "real" language allows, without a lot of the hassle.

For large or time-critical CGI scripts, the most common choice is a true
C program. While C can be difficult to use and even harder to debug, it
is incredibly flexible and often the only way to get to external functionality—Microsoft's Telephony API (TAPI), for instance, can only be used
from C.

- *You must have permission to correctly install your script on the server.* For UNIX Web servers, by default, there is a subdirectory off of where the HTTP software itself is installed called *cgi-bin*. All CGI scripts go in this directory, though you will need specific UNIX permissions to access it. Again, talk to your system administrator or Webmaster for details.

CGI URLs

After the Web server is installed and you have correct access, the CGI script can be accessed like any other URL. A script called demo.sh, if placed right in the cgi-bin directory, would have a URL like:

http://www.server.com/cgi-bin/demo.sh

Subdirectories can be used as well, allowing for URLs like:

http://www.server.com/cgi-bin/marketing/demo/start.sh

These examples use the standard HTTP protocol to communicate with the CGI script. The Netscape Navigator, when connected to Netscape's Commerce Server, allows secure communication with CGI scripts by using the https URL type, like this:

https://www.server.com/cgi-bin/demo.sh

Sample CGI Scripts

Now that all the preliminaries are out of the way, the best way to see what CGI scripts can actually do is by writing a few and seeing how they perform. Following are four simple examples that demonstrate some of the power that CGI scripts give to Web pages.

Sending a Simple Message

While many CGI programs are extremely complex, they don't have to be. Probably the simplest example possible is the UNIX shell script in listing 30.1. This code produces figure 30.3.

Listing 30.1   A Very Simple CGI Script

```
#!/bin/sh
echo "Content-type: text/html"
echo ""
echo "<HTML><HEAD><TITLE>Listing 26.1</TITLE></HEAD>"
echo "<BODY>This is a <EM>simple</EM> CGI script.</BODY></HTML>"
```

Fig. 30.3

Listing 30.1 creates a page that looks like normal HTML.

A lot is happening in that five-line CGI program, and all of it is vital for the script to work as intended.

The first line of this program tells UNIX that this script is to run in the Bourne shell, one of the many available in UNIX. Bourne is the most common, however, and the only one that every UNIX ships with, so it is the most often used. If this program were a Windows NT or 95 batch file, this first line could be left off.

The second line tells Netscape what kind of information it is about to receive. The `Content-type:` is required for all CGI scripts and it must correspond to a valid, well-known MIME type.

MIME (or Multipurpose Internet Mail Extensions) is a method for delivering complex binary data over networks, and Web browsers like Netscape use it to invisibly encode and decode that data. The two most common MIME types used by CGI scripts are `text/html` for HTML output, and `text/plain` for flat ASCII text.

The third line is simply an empty space to tell the server that what follows is the data described by the `Content-type`. You *must* include this empty line, or there will be nothing to separate this header information from the main body of the message.

Caution

One common error when writing CGI scripts is to have an incorrect `Content-type` for the type of data that is being sent. If your script sends HTML, as listing 30.1 does, but the `Content-type:` is `text/plain`, none of the HTML tags will be interpreted by Netscape, leaving your page looking like HTML source code.

Note

While `Content-type:` is far and away the most common header sent from CGI scripts, Netscape (and most other browsers) understand another one as well.

If you have a `Location:` *URL* line, Netscape will automatically ignore any following content and jump to the new URL. This is how certain links can send you to a random URL—a CGI script picks from a database of URLs and returns a randomly generated `Location:` line.

The fourth and fifth lines are the actual HTML data that is to be sent to the Netscape Navigator. These lines are passed through the server and interpreted, just as the same instructions would be if they'd been read from an HTML file.

Troubleshooting

I keep getting errors when I try to run my CGI program. What do they mean? And what's the best way to debug my script?

The most common error is `500 Server Error` and it means that you either forgot to send the `Content-type:` line before your data or your CGI program failed somehow part way through. Both cases mean you have some debugging to do.

If you get `403 Forbidden`, you need to set certain permissions on your CGI script. When a Web server is installed, it is owned by a specific user on the system (usually root), and that user must be able to read and execute the CGI script itself and traverse the directories that contain it. Talk to your system administrator or Webmaster to correct this problem.

The best way to debug CGI programs is to execute them from the command line instead of through the Web server. Set any appropriate environment variables by hand—environment variables are discussed later in the chapter—and simply run your program. This allows you to see any errors your script generates instead of the generic `500 Server Error` message.

Sending a Dynamic Message

Of course, the simple CGI program above only outputs static data—no matter how many times you call it, the output doesn't change—and a user wouldn't be able to tell it from a normal Web page. The real power of CGI scripts can be seen when they go beyond this, when they start generating dynamic data—something that's impossible for a normal page to do.

This CGI script displays a new fortune each time you jump to it (see listing 30.2). The output is shown in figure 30.4.

Listing 30.2 A Dynamic CGI Script

```
#!/bin/sh
echo "Content-type: text/html"
echo ""
echo "<HTML><HEAD><TITLE>Fortune</TITLE></HEAD>"
echo "<BODY>Words of wisdom:<HR><PRE>"
FORTUNE=/usr/games/fortune
```

(continues)

Listing 30.2   Continued

```
if [ "$FORTUNE" = "" ]; then
        echo "A wise system administrator installs 'fortune' for his
➥users."
        echo "        -- Anon"
else
        echo $FORTUNE
fi
echo "</PRE></BODY></HTML>"
```

Fig. 30.4
Web users are given new words of advice from the UNIX fortune command each time they jump to this script.

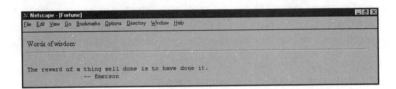

Instead of just printing out a pre-defined message, this script—through the UNIX fortune command—shows dynamic information each time it is run. If a user selects the link that runs this script twice in a row, it produces totally different results.

Just about any UNIX utility, or combination of utilities, can be used in place of the fortune command in the previous example. The real power of CGI scripts is to allow the entire capability of the computer to go into generating the Web page, and this example only hints at the possibilities.

If you're feeling adventurous—and know UNIX Bourne shell scripting—try modifying this script to do something other than print a fortune. Use finger to show who is currently logged on, or uptime to show how long the server has been running, or any command that you can think of. Be creative!

Using Server-Provided Information

While dynamic Web pages can be powerful, they can be even more so if they use some of the information that the server provides every CGI program. A CGI script that uses server information isn't doing anything special to get the server to provide that information, it's just taking advantage of what is always there.

When a CGI script is run by the server, several *environment variables* are set, each containing information about the server software, the browser the request came from, and the script itself. These variables can then be read by the CGI program and used in various ways.

For example, the program in listing 30.3 greets each user with the name (or Internet address) of his machine, and the name of the browser software he is using—Netscape, in our case. The results of this script are shown in figure 30.5.

Listing 30.3   A CGI Program That Uses Server Information

```sh
#!/bin/sh
echo "Content-type: text/html"
echo ""
echo "<HTML><HEAD><TITLE>Greetings\!</TITLE></HEAD>"
if [ "${REMOTE_HOST}" == "" ]; then
    REMOTE_HOST=${REMOTE_ADDR}
fi
if [ "${HTTP_USER_AGENT" == "" ]; then
    HTTP_USER_AGENT="a browser I don't know about"
fi
echo "<BODY>You are running ${HTTP_USER_AGENT}, on ${REMOTE_HOST}."
echo "</BODY></HTML>"
```

Fig. 30.5
This CGI program not only tells a user that you know where he lives, but what he's running, too.

This program uses three environment variables set by the server to find out the name of the machine running the browser: REMOTE_HOST, REMOTE_ADDR, and HTTP_USER_AGENT. REMOTE_HOST normally contains the Internet host name of the browser's machine—for example, my.server.com. But if, for some reason, this variable is empty, REMOTE_ADDR always contains the Internet address of the browser—123.45.67.123, for example. HTTP_USER_AGENT, if set, is an arbitrary string that describes the browser software the user is running—Netscape Navigator 2.0, for example.

That's all this program does—gets this information, does a little checking on it, and returns it to the user.

There are many variables like these. The most common are listed in table 30.1.

Table 30.1   CGI Environment Variables

Variable	Contents
REMOTE_HOST	The Internet name of the machine the browser is running on; may be empty if the information is not known

(continues)

Table 30.1 Continued	
Variable	**Contents**
REMOTE_ADDR	The Internet address of the machine the browser is running on
SCRIPT_NAME	The program currently running
SERVER_NAME	The Internet name or address of the server itself
HTTP_USER_AGENT	The browser software that the user is running

A complete list of CGI environment variables is available at **http://hoohoo.ncsa.uiuc.edu/docs/cgi/env.html**.

By using these environment variables creatively, you can do all sorts of neat things. Combining SERVER_NAME and SCRIPT_NAME can produce a URL to the currently running script, allowing it to reference itself.

Sending Continuous Data

Finally, there is another type of CGI script: the server push. When the user clicks a URL that points to a server push CGI script, the script does not simply send data to Netscape and shut down. It maintains the connection, and constantly pumps new data into the browser allowing such neat tricks as animating icons.

Writing server push CGI scripts is a complicated business, involving the creation of multi-part MIME documents, and it is well beyond the scope of this chapter. Fortunately, server push is losing favor as Java becomes the standard. While just as hard to program, Java animations are smoother and faster, as they don't depend on the speed of the network.

Creating HTML Forms

While CGI scripts are interesting in and of themselves and allow Web pages to come alive—through variation, personalization, and animation—their real power comes when they're combined with specific information received from the user himself. This is where forms come in.

Forms allow you to pose specific questions to a Netscape user and answer him based on the processing done in a CGI script. A form can be as business-like or as informal as you need it to be (see fig. 30.6). They can even add to the flavor of your site by being professional, friendly, or full of attitude. It's up to you.

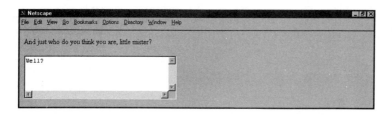

Fig. 30.6
A site poses a
specific question
to a Netscape user.

If CGI scripts are the "back end" of Web interactivity—taking care of all the
processing behind the scenes—forms are the "front end," the pretty, GUI
view that users see. CGI scripts and forms are two sides of the same coin and
to get the maximum use out of either, you must understand both.

A form in Netscape is almost exactly like a form in real life: it's made up of
spaces to enter text information in, lists of choices to check off, and options
to select from. But while a paper form must then be turned in or mailed off,
a Netscape form is instantly submitted—and instantly responded to.

There are four form tags that Netscape 2.0 understands, and they're used just
like any tags. The first, FORM, simply defines the beginning and end of a form,
and how and where the information collected in it will be sent. The other
three—TEXTAREA, SELECT, and INPUT—make up the part of the form the user
sees and interacts with, the actual text entry areas, menu selections, and push
buttons.

FORM

The <FORM> tag is used to mark the beginning of a form, while its compli-
ment, </FORM>, is used to mark the end. All the other form tags—TEXTAREA,
SELECT, and INPUT—are ignored outside of a <FORM>/</FORM> pairing, so you
must be sure to delineate both the beginning and the end of your forms.

> **Tip**
>
> It's good practice to add a </FORM> tag immediately after you create a <FORM>, then
> go back and fill in the contents. This helps eliminate accidentally leaving the end
> form tag off after you've finished.

The <FORM> tag has three attributes, and they define how a particular form behaves. While the contents of the form are set by the remaining tags, these
three attributes determine where the information entered by the user goes
and how it is sent there.

The first attribute is ACTION. A form's ACTION defines what URL the information entered into a form is sent to. It appears inside the FORM tag in the format:

```
<FORM ACTION="URL">
...
</FORM>
```

URL may be any URL, though for the data entered into the form to be processed correctly, URL should point to a CGI script that is designed to handle that particular form. If an ACTION is omitted, the URL of the page containing the form is used by default.

The FORM tag's second attribute is its METHOD. A form's METHOD defines how the information collected by that form is sent to the ACTION URL, and may be one of two choices, either GET or POST. The GET method is the simpler of the two, while POST allows far more data to be transmitted. Which METHOD you choose depends entirely on how the CGI program that processes the form data is written, but a well-written CGI program can handle both. METHOD has no effect on the form itself, only how the gathered information is sent.

> **Note**
>
> As the Web becomes bigger and the data sent across it more complex, the GET method is falling out of favor. Though it's easier to use, GET limits the amount of data that can be transmitted and does not hide that data from others using the machine the Web server is running on. For new or important Web sites, POST is the way to go.

> **Tip**
>
> It is almost always a good idea, when writing CGI scripts, to use a library that parses form data automatically, no matter which METHOD you use. These libraries are covered later in the "Encoding" section.

The METHOD attribute is used inside the FORM tag like this:

```
<FORM METHOD="POST">
...
</FORM>
```

> **Caution**
>
> Though it's possible to leave off a form's METHOD and have it work perfectly well, it's not generally a good idea. You should be as explicit as you can with your HTML, both to remind you what you intended to do in a specific case and to avoid relying on defaults that may change in the future or be different for non-Netscape browsers.

The third attribute—ENCTYPE—is rarely used. ENCTYPE defines the MIME content type that is used to encode the contents of the form when they are sent to the server. The default ENCTYPE is application/x-www-form-urlencoded, which is the standard URL encoding.

Of course, any or all of these attributes may be set for any particular form. For example, the following use of ACTION and METHOD is very common:

```
<FORM ACTION="http://my.server.com/cgi-bin/form.sh" METHOD="GET">
...
</FORM>
```

Once your form has defined how it will be used with the FORM tag, you must fill it with controls that the user can see and interact with.

TEXTAREA

The TEXTAREA tag allows users to enter free-form text information, in an open-ended edit field. This is useful for doing anything from sending comments to telling a story.

TEXTAREAs are defined with a beginning <TEXTAREA> and a closing </TEXTAREA>, with the default contents held between them:

```
<FORM ACTION="/cgi-bin/form.sh" METHOD="POST">
    Type your comment here:<BR>
    <TEXTAREA>
Everything was wonderful!
    </TEXTAREA>
</FORM>
```

This code sample produces figure 30.7.

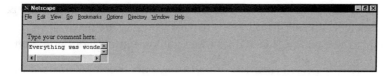

Fig. 30.7
A TEXTAREA can be created with defaults.

> **Caution**
>
> No HTML tags used inside a TEXTAREA pair are interpreted. If you use, say, the italics tag, <I>, you get three characters—less than, capital I, and greater than—instead of italics.

Like FORM, TEXTAREA also has attributes that may be set inside the initial tag.

The first attribute is NAME, and it defines the name of the TEXTAREA. What you set a TEXTAREA's name to is paired with the contents of the area when the user finishes his editing and submits the form. You must always give a NAME, as this is how the control is identified and its value retrieved.

The next two attributes are ROWS and COLS, each defining how big the TEXTAREA is to be, in character heights and widths. If left off, Netscape sets ROWS to one and COLS to 20, only allowing a very small typing area.

For example:

```
<TEXTAREA NAME="comment" ROWS=4 COLS=60>
I love your product!
I wish I had found it sooner.
</TEXTAREA>
```

This snippet of HTML results in the TEXTAREA shown in figure 30.8.

Fig. 30.8
This TEXTAREA is named "comment," and is 60 columns wide and four rows tall.

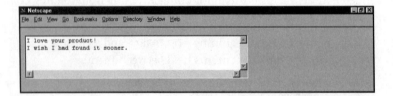

The final attribute is WRAP. WRAP affects how text appears within a TEXTAREA and may be set to OFF (which is the default) or to PHYSICAL or VIRTUAL.

If WRAP is omitted or set to OFF, the user must decide where each line entered into the TEXTAREA ends. If they continually type without hitting Return, the text will remain confined to the first line and the TEXTAREA will scroll to accommodate it. If WRAP is set to PHYSICAL or VIRTUAL, the text will wrap around to the next line, like it does when you type into a word processor.

The difference between PHYSICAL and VIRTUAL only becomes apparent when the data is sent to a CGI script. If WRAP is set to PHYSICAL, linebreaks are added to the end of each line, as if the user had pressed Return there. If set to VIR-TUAL, the text is delivered as if it had been entered all on one line.

SELECT

While TEXTAREAs allow users to enter free-form text information, it's often more desirable to allow them to make limited choices from a pre-defined list—just what the SELECT tag was designed to do.

The SELECT tag itself is simple, just a <SELECT>/</SELECT> pair with three attributes: NAME, SIZE, and MULTIPLE.

Troubleshooting

What happened? Everything after my prompt text is gone!

You forgot to include a closing </SELECT> tag. If left off, no other HTML tags are interpreted until the </FORM>.

NAME, like TEXTAREA, defines a name that is paired with whatever value the user selects.

SIZE defines the height of the list of selections to show the user. If it's left off, or if it's set to 1, the user is shown his choices as a pop-up menu, as in figure 30.9.

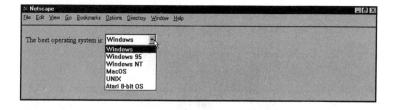

Fig. 30.9
Only the current selection is shown if SIZE is set to 1.

If SIZE is set to greater than one, the choices are shown as a list that the user may select from. If SIZE is greater than the number of actual choices available, empty spaces are displayed after the choices, as in figure 30.10.

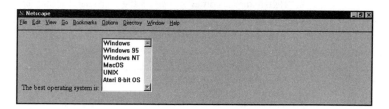

Fig. 30.10
With SIZE set to 7, the entire list—including empty spaces—is displayed.

The next attribute, MULTIPLE, takes no value and simply defines if this SELECT group allows multiple selections at one time. If omitted, the user is only able to make one choice from the list; if included, the user is able to make any number of choices, including zero. Also, as a side-effect of specifying MULTIPLE, the list is shown as a scrollable list, even if SIZE is set to 1.

After the SELECT entity is defined, OPTIONs must be defined within it. The OPTION tag defines each individual choice that the user will see and is only recognized inside a <SELECT>/</SELECT> pair. Like the LI tag, an OPTION's text does not need to be closed with </OPTION>, though it doesn't hurt:

```
<FORM METHOD="GET">
    Select your favorite food:
    <SELECT NAME="food">
    <OPTION>Cold pizza
    <OPTION>Cold Chinese
    <OPTION>Cold fried chicken
    </SELECT>
</FORM>
```

The OPTION tag has two attributes itself: VALUE and SELECTED.

The VALUE of an OPTION is what is associated with the NAME, if that option is chosen by the user. This is used by the CGI script to identify the option, but does not need to correspond to the text the user sees. Creative use of this can make selections easier to deal with from the CGI side of a form. If VALUE is omitted, it is defaulted to the text that follows the OPTION.

The second flag, SELECTED, simply defines which OPTIONs are selected by default when the choices are first displayed. If SELECTED is not sent on any OPTIONs, none of them are chosen; if more than one is marked as SELECTED, those are all marked. Usually, the single most common selection should be set as the default.

> **Caution**
>
> The SELECT tag's MULTIPLE flag only comes into play if the user selects something other than the default selections you have defined. If your SELECT is not MULTIPLE, it is still possible to have multiple selections returned—if more than one OPTION is marked as SELECTED by default.

If you want to allow customers to rate your service people, you might use something like the following. Note that the VALUEs of the OPTIONs relate to your scoring system, rather than the actual text of the OPTION.

```
<FORM ACTION="/cgi-bin/service_logger.sh" METHOD="GET">
    Please rate the service you received:
    <SELECT NAME="service">
    <OPTION VALUE="100">Excellent
    <OPTION VALUE="75" SELECTED>Good
    <OPTION VALUE="60">Fair
    <OPTION VALUE="50">Poor
    </SELECT>
</FORM>
```

This result of this is shown in figure 30.11.

Fig. 30.11
Web sites can offer
two-way commu-
nication, both
providing
information to
visitors and
generating it for
you.

INPUT

The final tag, INPUT, is far and away the most flexible and the most complex.
While TEXTAREA produces editable fields and SELECT produces lists of choices,
INPUT can be used to create six different input methods: TEXT, PASSWORD,
CHECKBOX, RADIO, HIDDEN, RESET, and SUBMIT.

Each kind of input is specified by an attribute of INPUT called TYPE. All the
other attributes to INPUT are based on what TYPE is set to.

TEXT

The TEXT attribute produces a single-line text entry field, like a single row
TEXTAREA.

If the TYPE of an INPUT is TEXT, a NAME must be specified, along with three
other optional attributes: SIZE, MAXLENGTH, and VALUE.

The SIZE of a TEXT INPUT is how many characters wide the text-entry field
will be; MAXLENGTH specifies the maximum number of characters a user may
enter into the field. If SIZE is bigger than MAXLENGTH, the text field will scroll
to allow the user to enter more data. If SIZE is excluded, the default is 20
characters; if MAXLENGTH is excluded, there is no limit on the amount of text
that may be entered.

The final attribute, VALUE, may be set to the default contents of the field, or
left off entirely if there are none. For example:

```
Please enter your name, first then last:
<INPUT TYPE="TEXT" NAME="first" SIZE="15" MAXLENGTH="13"
↪VALUE="John">
<INPUT TYPE="TEXT" NAME="last" SIZE="20" MAXLENGTH="18"
↪VALUE="Smith">
```

This result is shown in figure 30.12.

Fig. 30.12
Default values can
be used to show
the format of the
requested data if
no realistic
defaults are
possible.

PASSWORD

PASSWORD is a lot like TEXT—they share the same attributes—except that any
characters typed into a PASSWORD TYPE are hidden. This, of course, allows passwords and other secret data to be entered:

```
Password: <INPUT TYPE="PASSWORD" NAME="pass" SIZE="8"
MAXLENGTH="8">
```

If the user enters this code snippet, it appears like figure 30.13.

Fig. 30.13
No matter what
characters are
typed in, a
PASSWORD field
hides them from
prying eyes.

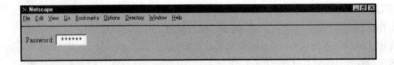

> **Caution**
>
> It is important to remember that even though a PASSWORD field prevents your secret
> data from being read off the screen, it is still passed over the network as plain,
> unencrypted text. It can even appear in the URL that way. Don't let PASSWORD lull you
> into a false sense of security.

CHECKBOX

A CHECKBOX is simply a toggle; it can be either on or off. CHECKBOX is great for
the simple, yes/no choices on your form.

CHECKBOX has three attributes: NAME, VALUE, and CHECKED.

NAME is the name that is delivered to the Web server, paired with the VALUE, if
the check box is selected when the form is submitted. If VALUE is left off, it is
automatically set to "on." If the final attribute, CHECKED, is included, the default state of the box is on instead of off.

```
Select the condiments you would like:
<INPUT TYPE="CHECKBOX" NAME="mayo" CHECKED> Mayonaise
<INPUT TYPE="CHECKBOX" NAME="mustard" CHECKED> Mustard
<INPUT TYPE="CHECKBOX" NAME="relish"> Sweet Relish
```

This HTML produces the check boxes shown in figure 30.14.

Fig. 30.14
CHECKBOXs allow for yes/no choices that are independent of each other.

IV

Building Home Pages

RADIO

RADIO is a lot like CHECKBOX, but only one toggle in a group may be selected at a time. All RADIOs in a single form that share a NAME are considered members of the same group, and if one is chosen by the user, any selected button is cleared. Otherwise, RADIO functions exactly like CHECKBOX, even down to the attributes it uses.

You may notice that this functionality sounds a lot like a non-MULTIPLE SELECT, and they accomplish almost exactly the same thing. Which one you choose depends largely on the look and feel you want your page to have.

The following code demonstrates the RADIO TYPE:

```
Select the type of bread:
<INPUT TYPE="RADIO" NAME="bread" VALUE="white" CHECKED> White
<INPUT TYPE="RADIO" NAME="bread" VALUE="wheat"> Wheat
<INPUT TYPE="RADIO" NAME="bread" VALUE="roll"> French Roll
<INPUT TYPE="RADIO" NAME="bread" VALUE="rye"> Rye
```

The result is shown in figure 30.15.

Fig. 30.15
RADIOs are designed for when you want the user to be able to make one selection from several choices.

> **Caution**
>
> As with SELECTs that are missing a SELECTED entry, if you don't specify a default value, it's possible that no member of a RADIO group will be CHECKED if you don't initially define a default. Always be sure to mark the most common choice as the default, with CHECKED.

HIDDEN

Different from all the other INPUT TYPEs, HIDDEN does not produce any graphics on the screen. It exists simply to allow the CGI script to receive a NAME and a VALUE that is guaranteed not to have been edited by the user.

There are several reasons to want to do this, but the most common is to maintain some sort of transaction number between server accesses. If, for instance, a CGI script generates a page that it wants to identify again, it inserts a HIDDEN element—containing some checksum, identification number, or password—that it can check for in the future.

RESET

The RESET TYPE creates a push button on the screen that clears the form and returns all the settings to their original default values. Its only attribute, VALUE, may be set to the text that you want the button to have. VALUE may also be left off, resulting in the text "Reset."

Consider this small bit of HTML:

```
<INPUT TYPE="RESET">
<BR>
<INPUT TYPE="RESET" VALUE="Clear Choices">
```

Its result is shown in figure 30.16.

Fig. 30.16
The top button is the default text for the RESET TYPE.

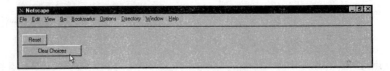

SUBMIT

The final TYPE, SUBMIT, works a lot like RESET but achieves an entirely different result—exactly the opposite, as a matter of fact. While RESET clears a form of user-entered values, SUBMIT gathers them up and sends them off to the Web server for processing, to the URL specified back in the ACTION. A SUBMIT button is the "Go" switch that every form must have to let the user say when he is done editing.

The only attribute to SUBMIT is VALUE, which sets the text of the push button. If excluded, the default is "Submit Query."

For example:

```
<INPUT TYPE="SUBMIT">
<BR>
<INPUT TYPE="SUBMIT" VALUE="      OK        ">
```

This code shows up as in figure 30.17.

Fig. 30.17
The top button uses the default text; the bottom, custom.

> **Caution**
>
> If the text of a button is very short, say "OK," the button usually ends up looking ugly. You can avoid this by padding the VALUE of the button with an equal number of spaces on both sides to widen it.

Bringing CGI and Forms Together

Now that you've got some basic background on both CGI scripts and forms, you're ready to bring them together to allow true user interaction with your Web site. The combination of CGI scripts and forms can bring a Web page to life, turning what was a static display of information into a customized and dynamic experience.

The program in listing 30.4 is a *guestbook*, an electronic version of the familiar visitor log used by hotels and museums. It first displays a list of signees, then uses a form to ask the current user to add his signature. It is written in Perl and uses a form-input library called cgi-bin.pl to *parse*—untangle—the data sent from Netscape. The result of the program is shown in figure 30.18.

Listing 30.4   A CGI Program To Process Form Input

```perl
#!/usr/local/bin/perl
print "Content-type: text/html\n\n";
# Load the library
do "cgi-bin.pl" || die "Fatal Error: Could not load cgi-bin.pl";
&ReadParse;
# Set the location of the guestbook
$guestbk = "guestbk.gbk";
# Get the sign-ins name
$name = $in{'name'};
# Only add to the log if they entered something
if (length($name) > 0) {
    open(FILE,">>$guestbk");
    print FILE "$name\n";
    close FILE;
}
# Show the current sign-ins
print "<HTML>\n<HEAD><TITLE>Guestbook</TITLE></HEAD>\n";
print "<BODY>\n<H1>Guestbook</H1>\n<H2>Current signees:</
➥H2>\n<HR>\n<UL>\n";
open(FILE,"<$guestbk") || print "You'll be the first\!\n";
while (<FILE>) {
    print "<LI>$_";
}
```

(continues)

Listing 30.4   Continued

```
close FILE;
print "</UL>\n";
# Request new sign-ins
print "<HR>\n<FORM METHOD=\"GET\" ACTION=\"$env{'SCRIPT_NAME'}\">";
print "Your name: <INPUT TYPE=\"text\" NAME=\"name\" SIZE=\"20\">";
print "<INPUT TYPE=\"submit\" VALUE=\"Sign in!\"></FORM>\n</
➥BODY>\n</HTML>\n";
```

Fig. 30.18
A guestbook is a
nice way to make
your site more
personal.

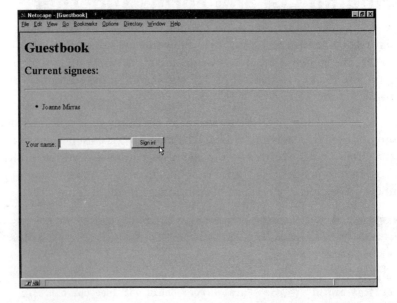

There are a few things to note about this CGI script. The first, and probably
most important, is that it is not only a CGI script—it does processing, like a
normal script, but it also generates its own form. The last three lines, in the
"Request new sign-ins" section, generates the HTML to request more information from the user.

This neat trick, where a CGI script also generates a form, is becoming standard practice on many Web sites. It allows a single program to both request
and process the data—it could even be expanded to generate its own error
message pages, too.

Secondly, you should note that the program uses the cgi-bin.pl library to extract the information the user has typed into the form. By using this utility,
the user-entered information is pulled out of the request, decrypted, and
stored in a Perl table called $in, easily and conveniently. You can get the
VALUEs of each form INPUT by asking $in for it, by referencing its NAME.

For instance, if a form INPUT has the NAME "address," the following line of Perl code would return the value the user entered:

```
$addr_variable = $in{'address'};
```

Of course, before you can use $*in*, you must have loaded cgi-bin.pl and called the library routine that sets up the table—lines four and five in listing 30.4.

Caution

When creating forms and CGI scripts, you should be aware that, normally, none of the data passed between the Navigator and the Web site is encrypted. This means that any private data (credit card numbers, love letters, and so on) can be "sniffed" by machines between the sender and receiver. Keep this in mind not only when designing your own forms and CGI scripts, but when using others.

Luckily, the Netscape Navigator, when used with its counterpart, the Commerce Server, has the ability to automatically encrypt data. If a connection is secure, Netscape makes the small key icon in the lower-right of the window whole instead of broken—making it impossible for intermediate machines to view the information you're sending. (Information on Netscape's secure Commerce Server is available at **http://www.netscape.com/comprod/netscape_commerce.html**.)

Stdin and stdout

So far, we've glossed over the details of how a CGI script accepts input from, and sends output to, the Web server. There are a few reasons for this, but the main one is that quite a lot can be done without ever having to understand how the mechanism works. Every one of the previous examples works without special knowledge of how the transfer is performed.

But in some rare instances, you need to know how this transfer takes place.

Every program running on UNIX has two channels, stdin ("standard in") and stdout ("standard out"). These two channels are how normal processes communicate with the world, and if the program is run from the UNIX command line, stdin reads from the keyboard and stdout writes to the screen.

But when a CGI script is executed from a Web server, it redirects these two channels away from the screen and the keyboard and takes control of them itself. This allows the server to send specific data into the script and receive answers back.

Every one of the previous examples, for instance, just echos or *prints* its output. Normally, this would just send the text to the screen, but because the script is run from the server, the output is captured and sent through the server to Netscape for viewing. Simple!

Reading input is a more complicated matter. While utility libraries like cgi-bin.pl automatically take care of the complexities of decoding input, you can do it yourself if you're feeling adventurous.

GET and POST

There are two ways to read the form data submitted to a CGI script, depending on the METHOD the FORM used. The type of METHOD the form used—either GET or POST—is stored in an environment variable called REQUEST_METHOD, and based on that, the data should be read in one of the following ways:

- If the data is sent from a GET METHOD FORM, the input stream is stored in an environment variable called QUERY_STRING. As noted above, this input stream usually is limited to about one kilobyte of data, which is why the GET METHOD is losing popularity to the more flexible POST.

- If the data is submitted from a POST FORM, the input string waits on stdin, with the number of bytes waiting stored in the environment variable CONTENT_LENGTH. POST can accept data of any length, up into the megabytes, though this is not very common yet.

Caution

While the GET METHOD is simpler for CGI scripts to handle, it limits the amount of data that can be sent, usually to slightly less than one kilobyte. If there is any chance that your form will generate more data than that, you should use the POST METHOD.

Parsing

After your CGI script has read the submitted data, it must parse it to pull out each NAME and VALUE that was sent from the form.

When a user clicks the SUBMIT button on a form, Netscape gathers all the user's choices and strings them together in NAME=VALUE pairs, each separated by an ampersand character.

```
<FORM ACTION="/cgi-bin/form.sh" METHOD="POST">
    <INPUT TYPE="TEXT" NAME="first">
    <INPUT TYPE="TEXT" NAME="last">
    <INPUT TYPE="SUBMIT">
</FORM>
```

This code snippet, if edited and submitted by Curly Howard, could produce the following data waiting on a CGI scripts stdin:

```
first=Curly&last=Howard
```

For your CGI script to actually use this information, it first must search for each ampersand to get each NAME/VALUE pair, then split the pair at the equal sign.

Encoding

There is more to getting the data a user enters into a form than simply reading and parsing it. The submission is encoded to protect it from 7-bit network layers that might silently strip significant bits from the data, damaging it in the process.

> **Caution**
>
> You should be careful not to confuse encoding with encryption. When data is submitted from a normal form, it is encoded simply to protect the integrity of the data while it travels over the network. This does *not* prevent it from being discovered, and decoded, by prying eyes.

The encoding format used when Netscape submits a form to a CGI script is determined by the ENCTYPE of the FORM, by default the MIME content type "application/www-x-form-urlencoded." This encoding format simply replaces spaces with the plus character and translates any other possibly troublesome character (control characters, the ampersand and equals sign, some punctuation, and so on) to a percent sign followed by its hexadecimal equivalent. So, using "application/www-x-form-urlencoded"-style encoding, the string

```
Here I am!
```

becomes

```
Here+I+am%21
```

After your script has read the submitted data, parsed it into NAME and VALUEs, it must finally decode it into the actual data that the user entered into the form. Then it is ready to use.

Protecting Yourself and Your Users

While programming CGI scripts and their forms is fun, the following are several things you should keep in mind—to protect yourself and your users.

- *Elegantly handle the submission of an empty form*—If a user just presses the SUBMIT button without entering any information into your form, what does your CGI script do? A well-written program handles this situation gracefully, without even trying to process the submission.

When you receive an empty request, you should either return an error telling the user what he did wrong or—even better—return the form that needs to be filled out. That way, as with the guestbook example, a single CGI script can both request and process the data, guaranteeing that both situations are handled. This is also handy for the first time the URL is jumped to, when the CGI script automatically presents the form to request data.

■ *Always be careful about trusting the data sent to you*—There are people out on the Web who would love nothing more than to cause you trouble. Purely out of a sense of vindictiveness, they will try to make your life as hard as it can be. Your CGI scripts need to take this into account.

For example, cleverly written queries can be used to gain privileges on your server that you never intended to grant. One common trick involves sending a shell command appended to some piece of requested data, so that when the CGI program uses that piece of data in an external command, the "piggy-back" command is executed as well.

Imagine a user entering **curly@stooges.com;rm -rf /** into a form. If you know UNIX, you'll recognize `rm -rf /` as the command that will delete everything on the computer. A badly written CGI script might simply add "finger" to the front of the request and execute it as a shell command, causing `finger curly@stooges.com` to be executed first, followed by `rm -rf /`.

Or, even worse, an unfriendly user could enter **curly@stooges.com;cat '+ +' > ~/.rhosts** and give the world login access to your Web server—the `cat '+ +' > ~/.rhosts` command removes password protection from a UNIX account.

■ *Be mindful that your users might not have a secure connection, and warn them if you are requesting sensitive data*—While both the Netscape Navigator and Commerce Server allow secure communication, most browsers don't; and there's no guarantee that the people who use your forms and run your CGI scripts will be using Netscape. At the very least, you should be wary of requesting sensitive data—bank account numbers, passwords—and, if you must, explicitly warn the user of the possibility (no matter how remote) of the data being sniffed.

Using Secure Forms

To ensure the security of any data submitted from a form, you must use Netscape's "secure HTTP" URL type, https.

If you know that a form will be sending data to a CGI script running on a Netscape Commerce Server, you simply need to change the "http" that starts the FORM's ACTION URL to "https" and the data will be encrypted and indecipherable to anybody "sniffing" the network. For example,

http://www.megaco.com/order.sh

becomes

https://www.megaco.com/order.sh

Any transactions made with the second URL are completely secure—the little key icon in the lower-left corner of the Navigator has become whole (see fig. 30.19). No other changes are needed, either to your form or CGI script.

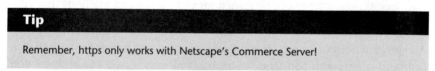

Tip

Remember, https only works with Netscape's Commerce Server!

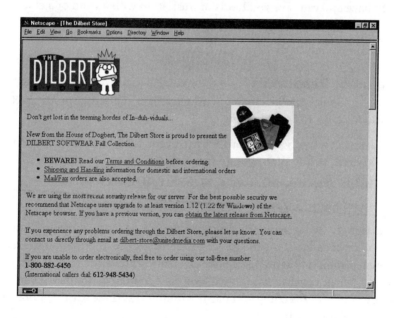

Fig. 30.19
When operating securely, Netscape makes the key icon whole.

Using the Public Domain

Form and CGI programming can be frustrating in the beginning. There are many rules to follow, most of which can be obscure or complex. Even getting a simple script up and running can be a chore.

One of the best ways to get over these first few hurdles and start CGI programming is to look at existing code. By reviewing (or simply using) already existing CGI scripts, you can not only save yourself a lot of time, but teach yourself new techniques.

Existing code almost always makes a good base to expand from. Instead of implementing a new script from scratch, an older program can often be expanded (or shrunk) to suit your needs. The earlier "guestbook" program, for example, could be modified to automatically add the name of the computer the user is connecting from, if that's what you wanted your guestbook to do.

Often rivaling the abilities of commercial offerings, many public domain CGI programs exist, free for the taking. Even if these scripts are too general for your specific needs, they can be mined for techniques and methods that you can then use in your own programs.

Also, experienced CGI programmers are almost always happy to share their code and talents with you. They've probably already solved any problem you might have and can save you hours of frustration with a word or a clue. Just ask.

And be sure to return the favor when you become an expert!

Available Resources

You can find many public domain CGI references and scripts on the Web itself. Good places to begin looking are:

> **http://www.yahoo.com/Computers_and_Internet/Internet/ World_Wide_Web/Programming/CGI**
>
> **http://ftp.ncsa.uiuc.edu/Web/httpd/Unix/cgi**
>
> **news:comp.infosystems.www.authoring.cgi**

Because every CGI program that receives data from a form must go through the bothersome decoding and parsing steps to get the information the user entered, common libraries have been created to handle the trouble for you. It is much, much easier to use this existing code than to go to the trouble of writing your own decoding and parsing routines, as these existing libraries come tested and are free.

> **ftp://ftp.ncsa.uiuc.edu/Web/httpd/Unix/ncsa_httpd/cgi/ cgi-lib.pl.Z** (for Perl)
>
> **ftp://ftp.ncsa.uiuc.edu/Web/httpd/Unix/ncsa_httpd/cgi/ ncsa_default.Z** (for C)

If you're adventurous (or you want to use an ENCTYPE other than "application/x-www-form-urlencoded," which all of these libraries are written for), you can try writing your own routines, but there really is no reason to—these work great!

Part V

Building World-Class Web Sites and Servers for Netscape

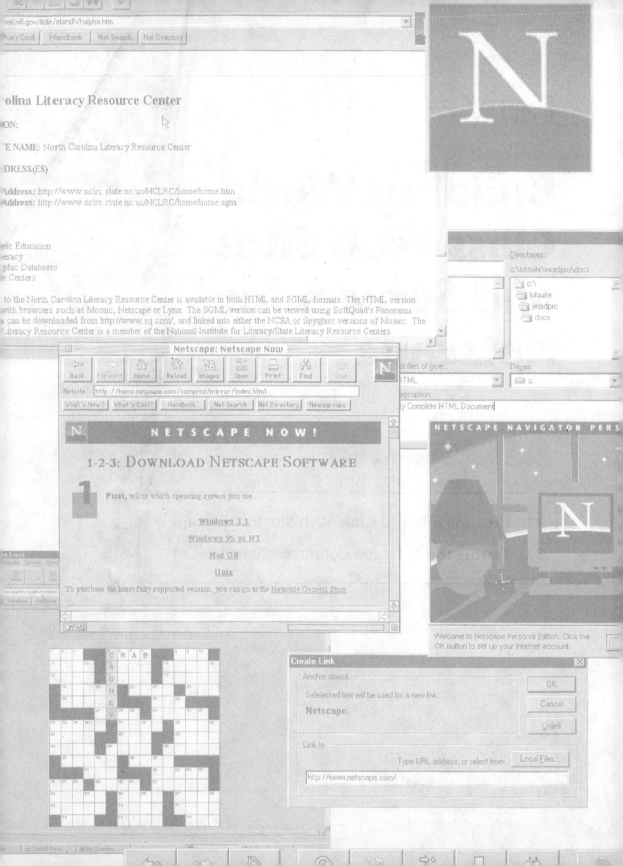

vel.nifl.gov/litdir/elandh/halpha.htm

hal's Cool | Handbook | Net Search | Net Directory

olina Literacy Resource Center

ON:

E NAME: North Carolina Literacy Resource Center

DRESS(ES)

Address: http://www.nclrc.state.nc.us/NCLRC/home/home.htm
Address: http://www.nclrc.state.nc.us/NCLRC/home/home.sgm

sic Education
eracy
phic Databases
e Centers

to the North Carolina Literacy Resource Center is available in both HTML and SGML formats. The HTML version
with browsers such as Mosaic, Netscape or Lynx. The SGML version can be viewed using SoftQuad's Panorama
a can be downloaded from http://www.sq.com/, and linked into either the NCSA or Spyglass versions of Mosaic. The
Literacy Resource Center is a member of the National Institute for Literacy/State Literacy Resource Centers

Directories:
c:\lotsuite\wordpro\docs

- c:\
- lotsuite
- wordpro
- docs

Netscape: Netscape Now

| ⇦ Back | ⇨ Forward | 🏠 Home | 🔄 Reload | 🖼 Images | Open | 🖨 Print | 🔍 Find | ⊘ Stop |

Netsite: http://home.netscape.com/comprod/mirror/index.html

What's New? | What's Cool? | Handbook | Net Search | Net Directory | Newsgroups

st files of type:
HTML

Drives:
c:

escription:
y Complete HTML Document

N   NETSCAPE NOW!

1-2-3: DOWNLOAD NETSCAPE SOFTWARE

First, tell us which operating system you use.

Windows 3.1

Windows 95 or NT

Mac OS

Unix

To purchase the latest fully supported version, you can go to the Netscape General Store.

NETSCAPE NAVIGATOR PERS

Welcome to Netscape Personal Edition. Click the
OK button to set up your Internet account.

		C	R	A	B		
		A					
		G					
		N					
		E					
		Y					

Create Link

Anchor object
Seleleted text will be used for a new link:
Netscape.

Link to
Type URL address, or select from: Local Files...
http://www.netscape.com/

OK
Cancel
Unlink

## CHAPTER 31

Creating a World-Class Web Site for Netscape

Remember the early days of desktop publishing, when it seemed that everyone with a personal computer and a page layout program was publishing his or her own newsletter? The common mistake made by many of these amateur publishers was an infinite mix of different typefaces and general lack of a basic sense of design. You may recall how difficult these homemade newsletters were to read, and for that reason few probably were read.

The World Wide Web draws many analogies to traditional print publishing; unfortunately, many of its early developers have made the same mistakes of the first desktop publishers. The world-class Web site is one that is not only rich in content and interactivity, but sophisticated in appearance. Developing the look of a World Wide Web site is a unique blend of interface design, graphic design, and manipulation of HTML elements.

In this chapter, you learn the following:

- Technical issues with running a Web site
- General Web page design issues
- How to create graphics with the illusion of depth
- Advanced page layout techniques using text and images
- Methods for incorporating interactivity into your site

Running Your Own Web Site

As much fun as running a Web site might be, there are a number of technical issues that need to be mentioned. You should consider all the points here before actually starting your own Web site. Most individuals really don't need to run their own Web site, while some companies should consider it. If you're sure you want to run your own Web site, try to make it look impressive (see fig. 31.1). The following are the most important components needed to run and maintain your own Web site:

- *A computer*—Most Web sites are run off of UNIX-based workstations because they are proven powerhouses. UNIX is more robust, reliable, and fault tolerant than Windows 95 or Macintosh. Any of the big name workstation makers, such as Sun, Hewlett-Packard, Silicon Graphics, and Digital, are good choices. Unfortunately, these machines cost a lot more money than PCs.

- *Web server software*—There are a lot of Web software programs out there, both free and for sale. The first, and best, choice is the Netscape Server because it supports all the features of Netscape Navigator. There are a number of alternative server software for all platforms, such as ZBServer for Windows 95, NCSA HTTPD for UNIX, and MacHTTP for Macintosh.

- *A connection to the Internet through an Internet service provider (ISP)*—If your company is already on the Internet, you can skip this requirement. Otherwise, don't worry; we'll discuss who to talk to and costs for this later in this chapter.

- *A system administrator*—Because you're going to have a computer running a Web server, you're going to need someone to manage it. If your company uses a lot of computers or is already on the Internet, you've got this covered already.

- *A person knowledgeable with HTML*—Since Web pages are written in HTML, finding someone who knows HTML is essential to your Web site. If you're lucky, you might be able to find a person who can both author your Web pages and act as a system administrator.

Fig. 31.1
Sophisticated Web sites incorporate interesting graphics, advanced HTML layout, and interactive elements.

Because there are so many factors involved in running a Web site, it's difficult to calculate the cost. The cost of the computer and Web server software vary from free to more than tens of thousands of dollars. A connection to the Net requires two costs, one to the telephone company and another to the ISP. The telephone company sells leased lines of various capacities for about $300 to $2,000 per month. A typical ISP charges around $500 to $1,000 a month to get Internet traffic routed to your site. Set-up costs for these are a little bit more expensive but are one time up-front charges. Finally, the position of Webmaster could be filled from people you already have, so an extra employee might not be needed.

Though these costs are pretty nebulous, the fact of the matter is that running a Web site is a full-time job. It requires a computer dedicated to being on the Net. In addition, the average yearly cost just for having such a computer on the Net starts at $10,000 a year and goes up from there. If you were to buy a new computer, the Web server software, and pay for a Webmaster, the cost could easily triple. That's not to say that average people can't run Web sites; it's entirely possible to run a part-time or slower-speed Web site for much less. Also, if you're already on the Net, you've already absorbed most of these costs, so starting a Web site could cost next to nothing.

Preparing the Web Site

In light of all the possible costs involved in running a Web site, the next thing you should think about is the purpose of it. Do you want a site that provides sales literature and generates revenue? Do you want a Web site that merely provides technical support for your existing customers? Do you want both of these? None of these? By answering these questions, you determine what type of site you want and what to put on it.

The first thing you should consider is what you want your Web site to do for you. If you want to just provide sales literature and generate revenue, you probably won't be sending a lot of graphics to people. As a result you can get by with a much slower Internet connection, which would reduce your set-up costs. For such sites, a 28,800 baud connection to the Internet should suffice. On the other hand, if you want to provide technical support for your existing users, you can't get away with a slow connection. It's not that you'll necessarily have graphics-heavy Web pages, but that you'll be sending more data across your Internet connection. It's far easier for people to go to your Web site and get the latest patch to your software than to contact your company for it. This type of Web page may require a very fast connection to the Net and increase set-up costs. Such a connection would be a 56KB line or above, which requires special hardware on your site's end.

The second thing you should consider before creating the Web pages for your site is your target audience. Are you looking to have your Web site accessed by everybody on the Internet? If so, you're going to have to think about providing more disk space to store the extra home pages (see later in this chapter). You might also want to look at getting a higher capacity connection to your ISP, if this is the case. Will your audience want to, and be able to, buy your products from your Web page? This will seriously affect which Web server software programs are available to you. Possible legal problems might also arise if a customer's credit card number is somehow compromised. Finally, you should ask if your target audience is even going to see, or care about, your home page. If you're running a sidewalk cafe, putting up an entire Web site probably wouldn't do much for your business.

Basic Design Issues Do's and Don'ts

The usability of a Web site was not much of a concern to developers in the early days of the Web. In the beginning, most of us were tickled that we could put a couple of links and a simple graphic on our home page. Over the past year, World Wide Web sites have become much more sophisticated. One of the most important changes taking place is that designers are beginning to address the overall look of their sites. The Netscape browser has been instrumental in this evolution, as it has given developers a broader range of tag extensions with which to work. If you're fully convinced you want to start a Web site, there are a few basic design issues to be mindful of.

◀ See "HTML Primer," pg. 617

The interface design of your page relates to how easily a user can interact and access information in your site. The design of Web sites has become a legitimate concern as the number of sites competing for our attention has increased. Sites that are well designed are more frequently visited than those that are laid out in a sloppy or haphazard fashion. Good examples of well-designed Web sites are Yahoo (**http://www.yahoo.com/**) and the Internet Movie Database (**http://www.msstate.edu/Movies**).

Organizing Your Web Page

Before you sit down and start creating your Web site, you should think about how it's going to be organized. Whether it's for a company or an individual, the most important thing is to decide what information you want to present. Are you going to put answers to common technical support questions? Are you going to put a directory of employees and their phone numbers? Next, figure out logical groupings for these bits of information. For companies that sell lots of products, organizing your Web site by product lines is a good start for how to group your Web pages. Build your Web site around these groupings, so that people can easily find what they want.

A good way that people like to organize their sites is by writing little descriptions for each category (see fig. 31.2). This makes it easier for people new to your site to find out what you have and how to get there. This also makes it very easy for you to add new information later on, such as for a new product. The only problem with this approach is that sometimes others might not understand your particular groupings.

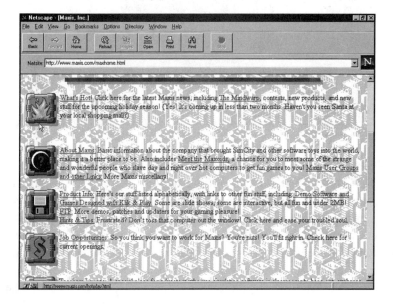

Fig. 31.2
A popular method for organizing Web pages is to put short descriptions about what each link does. Here, people using either a text browser or a graphical browser can access the links they want.

Making Sure Your Message Gets Across

A mistake that some people make when designing their Web sites is that they get too flashy. They figure that because they *can* put in lots of graphics and flashing text, they *should*. This is wrong. Typically, this makes the Web page very busy, and it's difficult for people to get the information they want. It's a confusing background image, a bad color scheme, or whatever. As you might be able to tell from figure 31.3, the background color of this Web page is too close to the link color. Just remember what information you're trying to get across and save the emphasis for later. The blinking text, cool animation, or large images impress people the first time, but become tiresome the fortieth time.

Fig. 31.3

The links aren't very clear against the background color. Good color selection helps to make a home page more enjoyable.

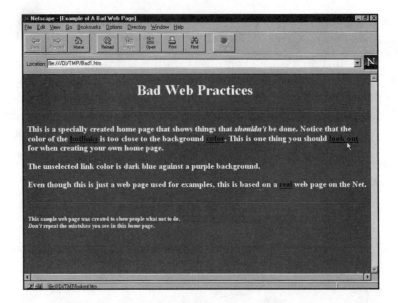

Letting Everybody See What You've Got

Many new Web page authors are putting graphics-heavy Web pages on the Net. Don't. While Netscape is the best browser around, not everybody uses it. Add to this the fact that not everybody has an extremely fast connection to the Net. For these two reasons, you should be very careful about using any sort of graphics on your Web site. Don't make your imagemaps and inline pictures so large that it takes a long time for people to see them (see fig. 31.4). The bigger the image, the longer it takes for people to see it. Just because a 200K GIF looks good in the HTML editor doesn't mean everyone has the patience to see it. Know your audience and design your site around them.

Helping the User Out

Even the best-designed and thought-out Web sites might be confusing to some. As a result, when designing pages for your site, make sure to put in navigational aids for the user. Give the user a way back to the main home page and other important links (see fig. 31.5). If possible, cross-index your Web pages to each other, so related pages are just a click away. Nothing is more frustrating to a user than to go down a path of links, not find what he wants, and find no way to help him get there. Try to anticipate other related categories that a person might be interested in on each page and put links to them. If a person has selected a Web page that lists jobs in Los Angeles, put in links to job listings for other Southern California cities. A few buttons here and there or a menu bar that's always around go a long way in helping users. The more you help them out, the more likely they'll come back.

Fig. 31.4
Sun mainly sells computers to companies, not individuals, so it can get away with this large imagemap. Can you?

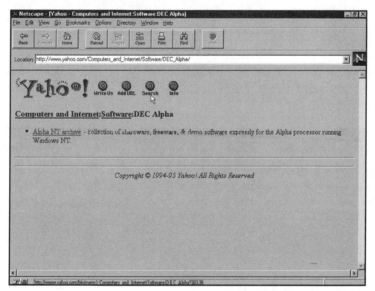

Fig. 31.5
When putting in menu bars for your Web site, be sure to put them everywhere. No matter where you are at Yahoo, you can always find the menu bar.

Make Everything Look the Same

Web pages usually aren't created in one sitting or by one person and, as a result, each page often has a different look and feel. By having an inconsistent look and feel to your Web site, users get the feeling that you threw the pages together (see fig. 31.6). It won't seem professional and it won't be a site they'll eagerly return to.

Fig. 31.6

Here we see another example of a page with a bad color scheme. This time we see black links on a white background.

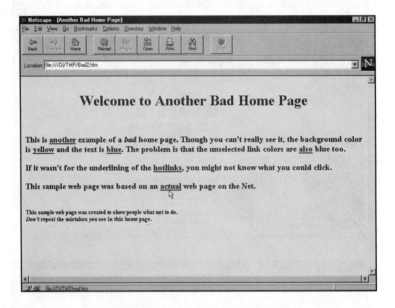

Each page of your site should make consistent use of text size, headers, navigational aids, and menus. Before adding new pages, look at the existing pages already on your site.

> **Tip**
>
> A good way to check whether your Web site is consistent is to try it out yourself. Put the page on the Web site and go to your own home page. Go through all the various links and see if the pages all feel the same. Do they all look pretty much the same? Are the fonts and colors the same? These are things you might not see when creating each Web page.

Working with Frames

As you read in chapter 29, "Netscape-Specific and Future HTML Commands," frames are a new creation with Netscape Navigator 2.0. Because frames can affect other frames or other windows or can just stay put, they're an excellent tool for your home page. They can provide for a static menu bar on all your home pages, which helps your site look consistent and helps the user read it (see fig. 31.7). Because frames can affect other frames, you can use them as a way of offering better search capabilities. Instead of having the user go back and forth between the search page and the results page, you can have the search frame update the results frame. This feature is also especially useful for offering all your product literature online. You can offer all your products in one frame, and when a user selects a particular product, the corresponding literature pops up in the modified frame.

Tip

As with everything else, make sure that the frames are consistent. Make sure that each page allocates the same amount of space for the frame. Change the frame size only or remove it all together only when absolutely needed.

Fig. 31.7
Frames offer your Web site consistency and offer the user a static menu bar.

Checking for Consistency

A very easy way to see if your Web site is consistent is to try it out for yourself. Pretend to be an average user who has stumbled across your home page. Poke around your own site and check for some of the following:

- Do the pages pretty much look the same?
- Are the fonts and colors the same?
- Are the background images similar to each other?
- If you have menu bars, do they look the same or similar?
- Is the tone of your Web pages consistent?

> **Note**
>
> Along with your e-mail address, you should also include a phone number and postal address in key areas of your site. This allows customers to contact you for more information. If you're not running a Web site for a company, you might not want to put this information on your home pages.

Adding Color to Your Site

After you've created your Web pages and are ready to add some pizzazz to them, here is some advice. A few touches of color here and there make a site more enjoyable. But just like planning out your Web pages, you should plan out your color scheme. You don't want text colors to look too much like the background color. You don't want a link color to look too much like the color used in a background image. Use color with caution, and you can liven up your Web pages a great deal.

Color Considerations

Before using color in your Web pages, there are a few things to think about. You might want to consider using distinctive colors for emphasis, rather than just using regular HTML tags. Also, if you're planning on running a commercial Web site, try to avoid using black as a background color. Some people might want to print out a particular page on your site, and a black background throws off some browsers.

Appropriate Use of the BODY Tag for Backgrounds

Attributes for the `<BODY>` tag were introduced in chapter 27, "Advanced Graphics." There are attributes for background colors and background images. The background color tag, `<BODY bgcolor=#RRGGBB>`, instructs the browser to display a particular color as the background for the HTML document. These colors are represented in respect to their red, green, and blue makeup. The body background image tag, `<BODY background=URL_of_image>`, causes an image to be tiled across the background of the user's browser (see fig. 31.8).

The following are a few design guidelines for using background colors and images:

■ Text is more legible against a light background. Most images, however, are enhanced against a dark background.

- A white background on most computer monitors is too harsh on the eyes for pleasant reading. It is better to use a light gray or a pastel color on pages that have extended passages of text.

- Busy background images should not be used, as they will greatly reduce the readability of text and irritate your audience (see fig. 31.9).

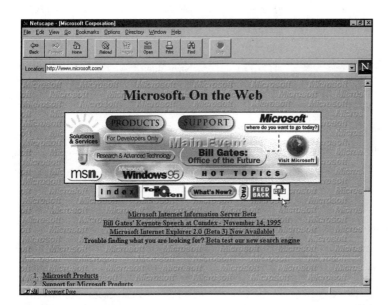

Fig. 31.8
Well-designed backgrounds enhance images without sacrificing readability.

Text and Link Colors

In addition to background color and image, the BODY tag can specify a text color and various link colors. These attributes were introduced in chapter 27, "Advanced Graphics," and are worth discussing here as they relate to the interface design of your site (see table 31.1). You may recall that they are specified with a letter or number indicating their red, green, and blue makeup.

Table 31.1 Background, Text, and Link Colors

Color	RGB Code	Color	RGB Code
Aquamarine	#70DB93	Medium Blue	#3232CD
Baker's Chocolate	#5C3317	Medium Forest Green	#6B8E23
Blue Violet	#9F5F9F	Medium Goldenrod	#EAEAAE
Brass	#B5A642	Medium Orchid	#9370DB
Bright Gold	#D9D919	Medium Sea Green	#426F42
Brown	#A62A2A	Medium Slate Blue	#7F00FF

(continues)

Table 31.1   Continued

Color	RGB Code	Color	RGB Code
Bronze	#8C7853	Medium Spring Green	#7FFF00
Bronze II	#A67D3D	Medium Turquoise	#70DBDB
Cadet Blue	#5F9F9F	Medium Violet Red	#DB7093
Cool Copper	#D98719	Medium Wood	#A68064
Copper	#B87333	Midnight Blue	#2F2F4F
Coral	#FF7F00	Navy Blue	#23238E
Corn Flower Blue	#42426F	Neon Pink	#FF6EC7
Dark Brown	#5C4033	New Midnight Blue	#00009C
Dark Green	#2F4F2F	New Tan	#EBC79E
Dark Green Copper	#4A766E	Old Gold	#CFB53B
Dark Olive Green	#4F4F2F	Orange	#FF7F00
Dark Orchid	#9932CD	Orange Red	#FF2400
Dark Purple	#871F78	Orchid	#DB70DB
Dark Slate Blue	#6B238E	Pale Green	#8FBC8F
Dark Slate Grey	#2F4F4F	Pink	#BC8F8F
Dark Tan	#97694F	Plum	#EAADEA
Dark Turquoise	#7093DB	Quartz	#D9D9F3
Dark Wood	#855E42	Rich Blue	#5959AB
Dim Grey	#545454	Salmon	#6F4242
Dusty Rose	#856363	Scarlet	#8C1717
Feldspar	#D19275	Sea Green	#238E68
Firebrick	#8E2323	Semi-Sweet Chocolate	#6B4226
Forest Green	#238E23	Sienna	#8E6B23
Gold	#CD7F32	Silver	#E6E8FA
Goldenrod	#DBDB70	Sky Blue	#3299CC
Grey	#C0C0C0	Slate Blue	#007FFF
Green Copper	#527F76	Spicy Pink	#FF1CAE
Green Yellow	#93DB70	Spring Green	#00FF7F
Hunter Green	#215E21	Steel Blue	#236B8E
Indian Red	#4E2F2F	Summer Sky	#38B0DE
Khaki	#9F9F5F	Tan	#DB9370
Light Blue	#C0D9D9	Thistle	#D8BFD8
Light Grey	#A8A8A8	Turquoise	#ADEAEA

Color	RGB Code	Color	RGB Code
Light Steel Blue	#8F8FBD	Very Dark Brown	#5C4033
Light Wood	#E9C2A6	Very Light Grey	#CDCDCD
Lime Green	#32CD32	Violet	#4F2F4F
Mandarin Orange	#E47833	Violet Red	#CC3299
Maroon	#8E236B	Wheat	#D8D8BF
Medium Aquamarine	#32CD99	Yellow Green	#99CC32

Advanced Graphic Design

Incorporating sophisticated graphics into your World Wide Web pages can make the difference between a run-of-the-mill site and one that stands out from the online crowd. The following are a few design elements that add a look of sophistication to your site:

- *Drop Shadows*—Soft-edged drop shadows on text and graphics make them appear to float above the browser's background and add depth to the page (see fig. 31.9). The use of a dark drop shadow with a slight offset can make text more legible against a dark background. Several leading graphics packages, such as Fractal Design Painter, provide options to add drop shadows to images. Furthermore, Photoshop plug-ins, such as The Black Box filters, offer a wide range of user options for adding drop shadows to selected objects.

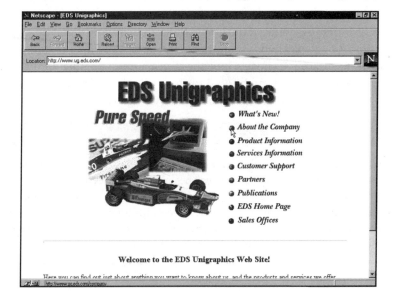

Fig. 31.9
Drop shadows incorporate a sense of depth to a Web page.

■ *Emboss*—As with the use of drop shadows, images that have embossed edges stand out on the viewer's screen. Embossed images make good buttons and menus, as they mimic buttons found on VCRs and cassette players (see fig. 31.10). They also break up the visual monotony of browsing two-dimensional Web pages. Developing embossed images is best done in sophisticated graphics packages such as Photoshop (employing the use of plug-ins such as The Black Box filters) or Adobe Gallery Effects.

Fig. 31.10
Embossed buttons and menus mimic buttons found on VCRs and cassette players.

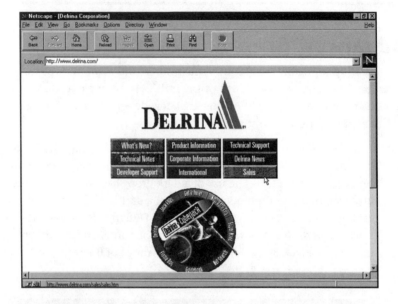

■ *Ray Tracing*—Ray-traced images provide a much more dramatic three-dimensional experience than those with embossed edges or drop shadows. Ray-traced 3D images give the appearance of floating on the viewer's screen and can be used to show off a new product or package or can simply add impact to your page (see fig. 31.11).

Note

When developing graphics with drop shadows or embossed edges, decide on the angle of a common light source before you begin. Most graphics programs that create embossed images and drop-shadowed text allow you to preview the light source configuration. Use this feature to decide on a good light source position, and keep it consistent with other similar images. Individual light sources for each object confuse viewers and suggest a lack of organization in the site's development.

Fig. 31.11
Three-dimensional images break up the visual monotony of browsing two-dimensional pages.

The `IMG LOWSRC` tag

The `LOWSRC` attribute to the `IMG` tag was designed to allow a low-resolution graphic to initially load on the viewer's Netscape screen, replaced by a higher-resolution image during the final layout of the page. This attribute allows developers the ability to present the general look of a page quickly to the viewer, replaced with more detailed images as the download continues.

The `LOWSRC` attribute is appended to the `IMG` tag in the following way:

```
<IMG SRC="url_of_high-resolution_image" LOWSRC="url_of_low-
➥resolution_image">
```

The `LOWSRC` image can further take advantage of download time by specifying the height and width of the final image. As discussed in chapter 27, "Advanced Graphics," on using thumbnail images, an image can be resized on the browser's screen by specifying the `HEIGHT` and `WIDTH` attributes for the image. This can be used with the `LOWSRC` by loading a thumbnail image as the low-resolution image with the specified `HEIGHT` and `WIDTH` attributes of the high-resolution image. For instance, with a high-resolution image of 200 pixels wide by 100 pixels high and a thumbnail image with the dimensions of 20 pixels wide by 10 pixels high, you could use the `LOWSRC` in the following way:

```
<IMG SRC="url_of_high-resolution_image"
➥LOWSRC="url_of_thumbnail_image">
```

In this instance, the LOWSRC image stretches to fit the final image area of 200 pixels wide by 100 pixels high on the browser window. The final image replaces the stretched thumbnail image on the final pass.

Developers have taken advantage of the LOWSRC attribute to incorporate the appearance of simple animation. Because the original LOWSRC image is replaced by the final image, it is possible to leave out part of the final image in the LOWSRC image, thereby giving the viewer the illusion that the image is being "filled in." This LOWSRC trick can be used, for instance, to "morph" an old logo into a new one, or initially load a black and white image replaced by a full-color graphic.

Caution

The image used as the LOWSRC must be the same size as the final image. The final image won't be loaded directly over the LOWSRC image if the sizes aren't the same. Similarly, make sure that the HEIGHT and WIDTH of the final image are the same as the LOWSRC's image.

Advanced Layout Design

While there are a lot of features in HTML, the language doesn't provide nearly as much control for the HTML author as a desktop publishing (DTP) program. Something as simple as indenting a paragraph is impossible with standard HTML, because spaces before and after words are ignored. Similarly, there's no provision within the HTML standard to give the HTML author any margins to work with, unlike most DTP packages. Because of such limitations of HTML tags, here are some tricks. Most of these tricks aren't widely known, because they either require a bit of work or aren't intuitive. All of these provide for much better control over the flow of the text, which makes your page stand out more. A few of these have problems under certain conditions, but by and large, you can use them to make a dazzling page.

Aligning Text and Image with BLOCKQUOTE

The BLOCKQUOTE tag is used widely in the development of sophisticated Web pages. To see why, look at the text in a printed book such as this one and then look at the text on a WWW page. What are the differences? The first thing you might notice is that the book has a right and left margin, whereas, most likely, the text on Netscape's window runs from edge to edge with no discernible margin. The BLOCKQUOTE tag allows you to pull the text in from the edges of the browser's window and create a margin on both the left and right sides. This makes your long passages of text more readable, as it is easier for the eye to catch the left edge of text as a viewer scans down the page.

The BLOCKQUOTE tag is also a unique way to create the look of multiple columns when combined with floating images. As discussed in chapter 27, "Advanced Graphics," floating images are those graphics specified with an ALIGN attribute in the IMG tag. Text following a floating image naturally wraps around the image based on the ALIGN attribute. For instance:

```
<IMG SRC="url_of_image" ALIGN=LEFT>
text passage
```

This image is aligned on the left, and the related text passage wraps around the right edge of the image.

Using BLOCKQUOTE before the text in the previous example creates a margin between the image and text, as well as the appearance of a two-column layout for the page. Figure 31.12 shows the result of aligning an image on the left with a BLOCKQUOTE between it and the following text. The text continues to flow down the page in this fashion until the appropriate BR attribute is specified to clear the browser's margin:

```
<IMG SRC="url_of_image" ALIGN=LEFT>
<BLOCKQUOTE>
text passage
</BLOCKQUOTE>
<BR CLEAR=LEFT>
```

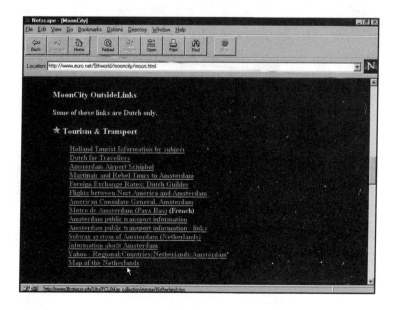

Fig. 31.12

The BLOCKQUOTE tag, when used with a floating image, can create a column of text.

Layout Using Hidden Images

One of the simplest tricks employed by experienced World Wide Web developers is the use of hidden images in the layout of a page. As discussed in chapter 27, "Advanced Graphics," the GIF89a image format can allow for one of the colors in the image to appear transparent. GIF transparency is generally used to hide the background of the image on the browser's screen. However, it is possible to create a single-color GIF that is completely transparent to the browser. These images can take on the same attributes as visible images and can be used to manipulate text layout.

Figure 31.13 demonstrates the use of a hidden image combined with a border background and BLOCKQUOTEd text. The hidden image is a single-color, transparent GIF that is the same width as the left border used in the background image. By aligning the hidden image with ALIGN=LEFT, it becomes a floating image allowing the BLOCKQUOTE to push the following text away from the background's left border. The HTML for this example is as follows:

```
<BODY BACKGROUND="url_of_background_image">
<IMG SRC="url_of_hidden_image" ALIGN=LEFT>
<BLOCKQUOTE>
text passage
</BLOCKQUOTE>
<BR CLEAR=LEFT>
</BODY>
```

Fig. 31.13

A hidden image allows text on this page to be pushed away from the background's borders.

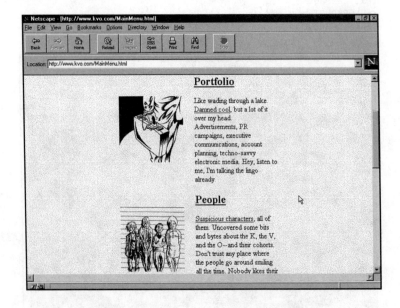

Caution

As nice as figure 31.14 looks, the thing to remember is that it *only* works with the BLOCKQUOTE tag. Most other HTML tags only indent the first line and have the rest end up in the left margin. Also, horizontal rule tags completely ignore this trick.

Hidden images can be used in a variety of ways with text and other images on a page. For instance, a transparent GIF with the width of 25 pixels and the height of 10 pixels can be used to indent paragraphs if placed before the line of text to be indented. Figure 31.14 shows how such indentation can be done, while figure 31.15 shows what the transparent GIF really looks like.

The HTML would be written as follows:

```
<IMG SRC="url_of_hidden_image>first paragraph of text
<P>
<IMG SRC="url_of_hidden_image>second paragraph of text
<P>
```

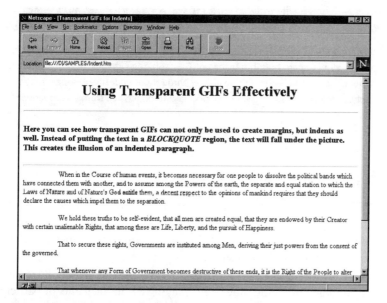

Fig. 31.14
The use of a hidden image used to indent a paragraph as it appears on the user's browser screen.

Caution

When Netscape is low on memory, using transparent GIFs to indent might not work. The hidden images suddenly turn white in these situations. The only easy way to avoid this problem is to not overload your pages with a lot of graphics.

Fig. 31.15
Revealing the
actual size and
placement of the
image.

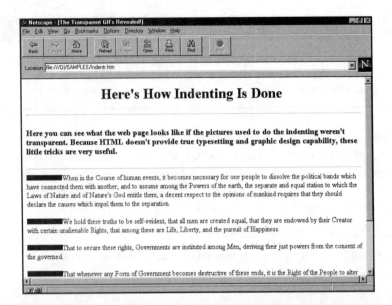

> **Tip**
>
> Hidden images, like any inline image, can take advantage of Netscape's disk cache. When developing pages using transparent GIFs as hidden images, develop a limited number of sizes and use these same images throughout your site. Once an image is downloaded to a user's browser, it will not have to be fetched from the server when called for again.

Adding Interactivity

One way to get people's attention to your Web site is to provide for user interaction. This basically means that users have a certain amount of control over the Web site. It's not as frightening as it might sound, since this is always under your control. Your site can give the user as much, or as little, interaction with whatever you want them to have on your system. Be it clicking a link to start an automatic slide show, playing an online game, or participating in an online forum, you control it all.

Creating Dynamic Documents

Netscape has added the ability to create what is known as "dynamic documents" in a Web site. To understand this mechanism, it might be helpful to review the relationship between a browser and server. The World Wide Web has been based upon a static document principle, in which the browser requests a document from a server when there has been some form of user input—such as clicking a text or graphic link. When the request has been received and processed by the server, the connection to that browser is broken until another request is made. *Dynamic documents*, on the other hand, allow the browser and server to maintain a dynamic relationship through one of the following techniques:

- *Client Pull*—The HTML document received by the Netscape browser contains a directive tag that instructs the browser to either reload the current document or fetch another document after a specified period of time.

- *Server Push*—The connection between browser and server remains open as directed by the server. This is usually done through a CGI program that sends new information to update the browser's screen.

Server push generally requires writing a Common Gateway Interface (CGI) program, which is beyond the scope of this discussion. Client pull, on the other hand, is an element in the HTML document and can be incorporated quite easily into any Web page. A popular use for client pull is the development of a series of HTML documents similar to a slide presentation program (see fig. 31.16). Incorporating this type of self-running presentation into your Web site provides visitors a guided tour of the most important areas of your site.

Writing client pull elements into an HTML document begins with the META HTTP-EQUIV tag, followed by the subsequent action to be taken by the browser, the length of time before the action is taken, and the result of the action. The META tag is always placed within the HEAD section of the document where the length of time before the action is specified in seconds. For instance, if we were to use client pull to move from an HTML document named slide1.html to a document named slide2.html after a period of 30 seconds, the HTML would read as follows:

```
<HTML>
<HEAD>
<META HTTP-EQUIV="Refresh" CONTENT="30; URL=path_to_slide2.html">
```

Once received, the META HTTP_EQUIV tag in slide1.html instructs the browser to fetch the document named slide2.html after a period of 30 seconds. Using client pull with the META HTTP_EQUIV within each document of a slide show allows you to guide a visitor through the most important elements of your Web site (see fig. 31.16).

Fig. 31.16
Dynamic docu-
ments can be used
to create online
presentations such
as this campus
slide show at
**http://
www.utk.edu**.

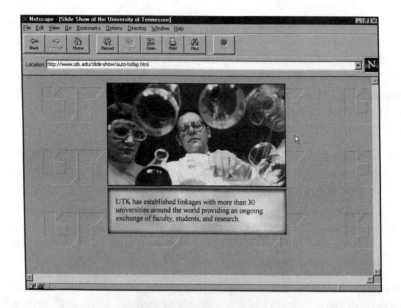

Caution

Try to avoid putting dynamic documents in your main home page. Every time a Web
page is loaded, or reloaded, the dynamic document is also loaded. This means that
whenever someone goes to your main home page, even if he's been there a long
time, he'll see the dynamic document. Forcing users to see documents they've already seen could make them mad.

Caution

The browser receiving a client pull begins to count the seconds before reload as soon
as the HTML document is received. Be sure to specify enough time for the complete
download of all elements on a page before sending a user to another page. Test your
client pull documents on a variety of Internet connections to ensure that visitors with
even the slowest connection have sufficient time to download and comprehend each
page before being sent on.

Advanced Interactive Elements

The best World Wide Web sites are those that allow visitors to interact with
elements contained within the site. The simplest form of interaction is the
use of text and graphics links to other documents within your site or elsewhere on the Web. More advanced forms of interaction usually require specific CGI programs to handle the user requests. Developing CGI programs is

much more sophisticated than HTML and is covered in chapter 30, "Netscape Forms and CGI-BIN Scripts." There are a number of good online references to programming CGI scripts and a number of sites that have simple programs available for downloading. Many of these programs can be used "as is" or are easily converted to use on your site. Unique CGI programs for your site can be written for a number of interesting purposes.

User Feedback and Discussion Forums

One of the primary concerns for most companies developing a presence on the WWW is how to encourage repeat visitors to their sites. Incorporating user discussion areas into Web sites is an interesting way of dealing with this problem (see fig. 31.17). A site can develop a community of its own by providing an online forum for visitors to ask questions about the company's products, provide answers to frequently asked questions, and allow users a means of communicating with each other. The following are several different types of discussion programs that are used on the Web:

- *Chat Areas*—Similar to the chat areas of commercial online services such as America Online and CompuServe. World Wide Web chat areas allow users to interact with the site and post messages in real time. This type of discussion program is useful for live, online interviews, as well as question and answer areas that require immediate feedback.

- *Threaded Discussion Forums*—Threaded discussion programs on the WWW are similar to UseNet newsgroups. With this type of discussion area incorporated into their sites, companies can begin threads of discussion based upon the needs and interests of visitors.

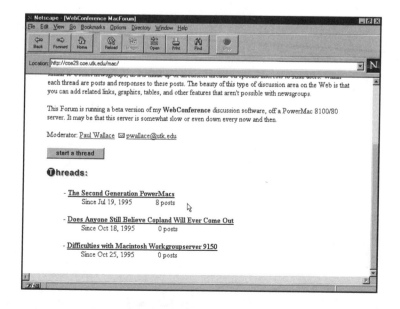

Fig. 31.17
Discussion forums incorporated into a Web site help develop a community of repeat visitors.

Online Games

Incorporating games into your site is another example of how to increase visitors through interaction. Games and sweepstakes can be changed periodically to encourage users to visit your site on a regular basis (see fig. 31.18). Examples of games on the World Wide Web can be found at Yahoo's index on Interactive Web Games at the URL **http://www.yahoo.com/ Recreation/Games/Internet_Games/Interactive_Web_Games/**.

Fig. 31.18
Mystery games, such as this one at **http://www. tombras.com** encourage visitors to search through an entire site in order to find clues.

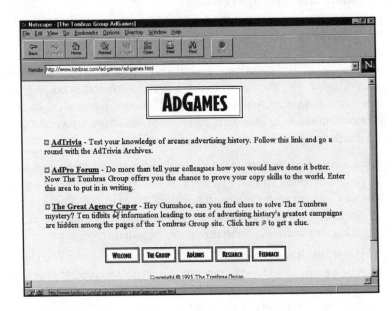

## CHAPTER 32

Testing the Netscape Commerce Server

One of the features that caused Netscape Navigator to make such a big splash when it was first introduced was its capacity to conduct secure transactions over the Internet. For businesses and others who wanted to transact private business using the Internet, this was a major step forward; the introduction of Netscape's secure transaction capabilities led many organizations to finally venture out onto the Net.

The Navigator software is only one half of the security solution created by Netscape. The other half resides with the software that runs the Web site, called the server.

Netscape actually produces several variations of its server products. In this chapter, we'll cover the basics of "test-driving" the Netscape Commerce server, which is used to handle secure transactions.

In this chapter, we discuss:

- Netscape's offer to let you try their server for 60 days without charge
- The technical requirements for setting up a Netscape Commerce server
- How Netscape's Secure Sockets Layer security works
- Getting a copy of the software
- Installing the software
- Basic configuration of your server software
- Setting up security on your server
- How activating security affects the way users see a Web site

Caution

Obviously, there's more involved in setting up and configuring a Web server than we could possibly hope to cover in one chapter. Our goal here is to provide the basic information that someone (either with a fairly good idea of how Web servers work, or a fairly good book on the subject of setting up Web servers available as a reference) would need to get and try the Commerce server software. This chapter assumes that you have familiarity with either Windows NT or some variant of UNIX at a server management level.

Nevertheless, even if you don't have advanced experience with running NT or UNIX servers, you may find the information on how the Web server interacts with Netscape Navigator to be interesting or at least helpful in understanding how your transactions are protected when you sign on to a secure server.

Have They Got a Deal for You!

Whereas Netscape's Navigator Web browser is a relative bargain for the level of increased functionality it brought to the Web at under $40 for a licensed copy, Netscape's server software is generally seen as a fairly high ticket item—a single copy of the Commerce server generally costs an organization over $2,000 (and that's before you pay for the machine and the connection to the Internet!).

Because most organizations aren't willing to lay that much money down on a product sight unseen, Netscape has created a way for companies to test out their server software before they purchase it, following the same "shareware" concept they employed to make their Navigator software the de facto standard of Web browsers.

Netscape calls their "try-before-you-buy" offer the Test Drive program. The deal is pretty straightforward; after filling out and submitting an application form to Netscape (which can be done over the Web), you receive an account name and password that can be used to download a copy of the server software.

The copy of the software that you receive is fully functional. Unlike many shareware producers, Netscape does not disable any of the features in their Test Drive version.

Sometime shortly before the two months are over, you are contacted by a member of Netscape's sales staff, who reminds you that if you don't purchase their server software, you need to stop using it when the 60 days are up.

Netscape banks on the fact that by the time the 60 days are over, you won't be able to think about parting with their server software, and you'll be much more willing to part with the cash instead.

The only key feature that you don't get through the test drive offer is support from Netscape's technicians. In order to get support for Netscape's server products, you must buy a support contract, and you must have a licensed copy of a Netscape server to purchase the support contract.

Netscape does offer some help facilities for its test drive customers. Netscape has established in-house newsgroups (called Netscape User Groups, or NUGgies) that promote the exchange of information among users of Netsape's products. Many of the questions you may have about the configuration of your system can be answered by participants in these newsgroups.

You can also always order a copy of the documentation for the particular type of server you're using. There are two manuals for the Netscape Communications and Commerce servers; there's a Server Administration Guide and a Programmer's Guide for each. Unless a change has been made recently, the only difference between the Communications Server guides and the Commerce Server guides is the cover. Although the documentation is a little thin, you may want to order copies of both the Administration Guide and the Programmer's Guide as a reference.

Test Drives on Most Netscape Servers Available

Netscape's offer is not limited to just their Commerce server software. If you want a more robust regular Web server but don't need the security capabilities of the Commerce server, you might consider trying the Communications server. If you need to set up a secure firewall for a collection of systems, you may want to use the Test Drive offer to try the Netscape Proxy server.

The difference between the Commerce server and the Communications server is that the Commerce server includes programs necessary to do secure transactions and the Communications server software does not. In terms of administration and configuration, the two types of servers are practically identical. A copy of the Commerce server can be used to transmit insecure documents the same way a Communications server would. You are also allowed to run more than one copy of the server software on a machine at a time (provided that your machine is powerful enough to handle it.) Therefore, if you needed to transmit both secure and insecure documents from your server, you could run two copies of the Commerce server—one with security turned on and the other with it turned off—rather than buying two different versions of the server software.

Requirements for Running a Netscape Commerce Server

In order to be able to run a Netscape Commerce server, you're going to need access to some heavy-duty resources (that is, beyond the scope of your average home user). Before you go to the trouble of downloading the software, let's take a minute to review the minimum requirements for setting up a Commerce server. These requirements can be broken into three main categories: operating system, hardware, and Internet connection.

Operating System Requirements

At the time of this writing, Netscape only produces versions of its server product that run under Windows NT (3.5 or later) and commercial variants of UNIX produced by Digital (OSF/1 2.0), Hewlett-Packard (HP-UX 9.03, 9.04), IBM (AIX 3.2.5, 4.1), Silicon Graphics (IRIX 5.2, 5.3), Sun (Sun OS 4.1.3, Solaris 2.3, 2.4), and Berkeley Systems Design (BSDI 1.1, 2.0). Therefore, a user running Windows 3.1, 3.11, 95, or a Macintosh running some version of the MacOS, won't be able to run this software.

> **Note**
>
> Not only must you have access to a system running one of these operating systems, you must be able to access this system as a privileged user. (On UNIX-style systems, you will probably need root access.) If you are only a user on a system with multiple users, you may want to ask your system administrator to install a version of the Commerce server for you. System administrators can configure the Netscape server software to give individual users the ability to set up personal Web sites, which can use many of the Netscape server features. For security reasons, however, it is quite likely that your system administrator will prohibit you from using the server's most interactive features, especially those that require running programs.

Windows NT may be more familiar to a novice Webmaster, especially if you have limited knowledge of the UNIX operating system at the administrator level. Choosing NT as your operating system might be the right choice if your organization lacks the in-house knowledge necessary to maintain a UNIX-based system.

Nevertheless, you should be aware that running a Netscape server on a Windows NT system also somewhat limits its functionality. Many programmers find that it is much more difficult to get NT to perform the types of variable exchanges most frequently employed in CGI scripts.

For these reasons, if in-house programming and UNIX system administration help is available (or if you *are* the in-house programming and system administration expertise), you may want to lean towards a UNIX-based system, if possible.

Note

Although Linux is dearly loved by many, there is, at the time of this writing, no port of the Netscape server software for Linux. If you plan to run a Netscape server on a PC, you'll have to use either Windows NT or BSDI.

Hardware Requirements

There are a number of considerations that should go into the selection of the hardware platform for your Netscape Commerce server Web site. The type of system to use, memory, and the kind of connection you have all play important roles—depending upon your objectives for your server.

Intel 386, 486, or Pentium-based PC

You have two big options with respect to running a Netscape server on a PC—Windows NT or UNIX? Windows NT may provide a familiar operating environment that makes the leap onto the Web easier, but our experience shows that PCs running BSDI perform quite valiantly as servers. A particularly bulked-up machine (such as a high-speed Pentium with lots of available memory) functions nearly as well as much more expensive equipment options.

Digital Alpha

A Digital Alpha system can run either Windows NT or OSF/1, Digital's variant of UNIX. According to Netscape's specifications, a DEC Alpha running Windows NT 3.5 only requires 16MB of memory to run the server. We still recommend having more, but if you're in a pinch and are limited on resources for your test, this is an option.

Silicon Graphics

Silicon Graphics (SGI) actually offers several configurations of their machines, called the WebFORCE product line, which come bundled with a bunch of tools for creating HTML documents and graphics for Web sites. A copy of any version of the Netscape server software can be added to the package at a discount from Netscape's own price. Our experience setting up servers on SGI equipment has been extremely positive. SGI's X Window desktop is a very intuitive, very user-friendly interface that, in our experience, has proven to be a great help for beginner-to-intermediate level system administrators who want to focus more on the operation of the Web site than on the maintenance of their machine.

Furthermore, SGI has taken substantial steps to provide support for their customers by publicly announcing the solutions to complex technical problems, such as getting a server to answer to several distinct IP addresses so that multiple Web sites can be run on one machine. However, unless you happen to have a spare SGI system just lying around, this can prove to be a fairly expensive solution. (A low-end system can still cost more than $10K.) While I wouldn't suggest buying one for your test drive, you might very well consider purchasing one as your permanent server if your test drive is successful.

Sun Systems
Like Silicon Graphics, Sun has bundled systems aimed at organizations getting onto the Internet. Once they are set up, Sun's SPARCstations and Netra servers perform well as servers. Users who are unfamiliar with UNIX (and even some experienced users) may find Sun's X Window interface clunky and cumbersome. Sun's systems remain aimed at more advanced system administrators, but because they comprise a larger percentage of Sun's market, you will also find a larger number of ready-to-use tools that have already been debugged and compiled for Sun systems.

Hewlett-Packard PA and IBM RS/6000
Whereas Silicon Graphics and Sun have engaged in public alliances with Netscape to support their server products, IBM and Hewlett-Packard have not, which probably explains why many corporate users don't necessarily think of these platforms when planning their corporate online presence. Nevertheless, Netscape's server products work on these platforms. If available, they are a fine platform for your test drive.

Necessary Memory
Memory plays an important factor in figuring out how many people will be able to connect to your site at any one time. Each connection consumes a certain percentage of your system's memory resources. When these resources are fully allocated, your server refuses to take any additional connections. Therefore, it's important to be sure that you have sufficient memory to accommodate a reasonable number of users simultaneously.

According to Netscape, the minimum memory necessary to run their server under Windows NT is 16MB. However, 16MB is a little light just for running Windows NT, let alone a heavy-duty server. 32MB should be your minimum for running your system; 64MB is common for sites that receive moderate traffic. If you are planning for your site to have a very high volume of traffic, you probably need to plan for even more memory to handle the burden.

Similarly, Netscape lists the minimum memory configuration for UNIX-based servers at 32MB. During configuration, you need to set the maximum number of processes that can be run by Netscape to serve users. This number is limited by the amount of available memory on your system. While 32MB of memory may be sufficient for the purposes of testing your new server, you probably want more memory on your completed system.

Necessary Internet Connectivity

Theoretically, any type of connection to the Internet that provides the server with its own unique IP address can be used to provide access to a Web server. There are, however, some practical considerations that make certain types of connections more practical than others.

To be successful, your site needs to have its own unique name and IP address. Your server should therefore be attached to a system where it is given a unique and unchanging IP address.

Likewise, there needs to be a sufficient amount of available bandwidth for users to reach your site. The term *bandwidth* refers to the amount of information that can be transferred to and from any particular site on the Internet at any point in time. Moreover, the connection needs to be stable and dependable, or users become frustrated while trying to access your site and may never come back.

It is therefore no surprise that the most successful Web sites are on networks with high-speed connections to the Internet, such as a T1 line, or a fractional T1 line. For smaller organizations and businesses with only moderate traffic on their Web site, a 256K connection (one-fourth of a T1 line) may be sufficient. Web sites with higher volumes of traffic may require even more bandwidth. Just remember that it makes no sense to invest in high-end server software and a powerful machine to run it if no one can connect to your site.

Caution

Some Internet Service Providers (ISPs) offer plans that provide a minimum amount of bandwidth regularly, with the option to automatically bump up to a higher volume of bandwidth if demand requires it.

Because these pricing models tend to be based on the maximum bandwidth demanded at any one point during a month, this is a particularly dangerous strategy for a Web site.

(continues)

(continued)

Web sites can become popular almost instantaneously; mention of your site on the right index or UseNet newsgroup can generate a tremendous amount of interest literally overnight. Therefore, demand for access to your site could skyrocket, far outstripping the amount of bandwidth that you had budgeted to support.

Be sure to choose a plan that lets you define the maximum amount of bandwidth being provided so you don't end up with a surprisingly high bill at the end of the month. Choose an ISP that provides you with regular reports of your bandwidth usage. If you find that you are regularly using the maximum amount of bandwidth available, you may want to consider increasing your connection. Just don't put that decision into the hands of the users who decide to visit your site.

Getting the Software

Once you've set up the machine on which you'll be running your server, you can start the process of getting a copy of the software. The process has the following three steps:

1. Apply to participate in the Test Drive program.
2. Receive a username and password from Netscape.
3. Log in to Netscape's Test Drive system and download the appropriate version of the software for your system.

The next few pages guide you through the process of applying for the Test Drive program and downloading the software. Most of the directions that you need are available on the Test Drive pages of Netscape's Web site.

Submitting an Application

The first step is submitting an application to participate in the Test Drive program. To do this, you should open up Netscape Navigator and connect to their site at **http://test-drive.netscape.com/**.

There are three main portions to the application. The first phase asks for contact information for the person downloading and using the software. Netscape uses this information to contact you to see if you want to purchase the software when your 60 days are nearly over.

Note

Sometimes people are tempted to enter incomplete or inaccurate information in these forms, primarily because they don't want to be bothered in the future by solicitations. This is probably one of those situations where that's not such a good idea. Think of it this way, if the nice salesman were letting you take a $50,000 car out for a spin, you would think it completely reasonable that they'd want to know how to reach you.

The most important part of this segment of the application is your e-mail address. Double- and triple- check to ensure that it's properly entered. Netscape uses this e-mail address to send you the access password you need to download the software.

The second section of the application asks for contact information of a Value-Added Reseller of Netscape products. If you've already been dealing with a specific reseller of Netscape products, you should enter this person's information. Then he will be the person bothering you in 60 days instead of someone from Netscape in Mountain View.

Note

There are two ways to buy Netscape's products: directly from Netscape or through an intermediary company called a *Value-Added Reseller*, or *VAR*. Some organizations, such as government agencies, may be required to purchase all of their software through one or another VAR. In this case, you should identify who that VAR is, as that salesperson probably knows more about special arrangements for pricing of software than a more general salesperson for Netscape.

VARs can also be a secondary source for support of the products that they sell; although Netscape doesn't provide technical assistance for Test Drive users, a VAR may very well have a technician who can help you work out problems to get your site set up and running.

The third phase of the application is a participant survey. These questions are aimed at providing Netscape with a better consumer profile so they can better target the development of new products. Answer all of the questions, and then click the Submit button to send the information to Netscape.

Getting a Password and Downloading the Software

Shortly after you submit your application (within a few hours to a few days), you should receive an e-mail message to the account listed in your application giving you a username and password to use to download the Netscape server software.

Troubleshooting

It's been over a week and I still don't have a password!

If you've submitted an application and haven't heard anything back within a week, that probably means that the application didn't make it through.

That doesn't mean that they don't love you and won't let you try their software, it just means that somewhere along the line the form didn't process properly.

Go back and re-submit your application. This time, be sure to very carefully check your e-mail address before you submit the application. If after a few days you still haven't received a password, try calling the Test Drive program directly. They can probably take an application from you directly over the phone.

To download the software, follow these steps on the computer that will server as the Web site:

1. Log in to the Test Drive server at the address listed in your response e-mail; the address is probably **http://test-drive.netscape.com/download/**.

2. Once you connect, you should see a dialog box that looks like the one in figure 32.1.

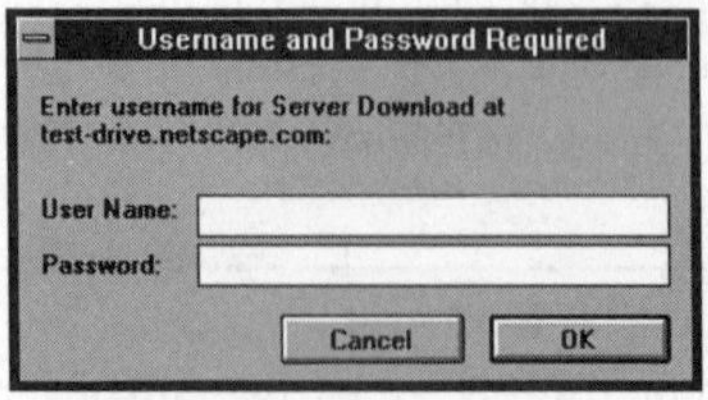

Fig. 32.1
The Test Drive download login dialog box.

Enter your username as indicated in your e-mail from Netscape (probably your e-mail address) and your password where prompted. Be careful when typing the password to specify capitals and lowercase letters exactly as you received them from Netscape.

3. Read the Test Drive License Agreement. If you agree, click the button that says you agree to move on. If you don't agree, the process of downloading the software will end, and you'll be returned to Netscape's home page.

4. After you agree to the License Agreement, a form like the one shown in figure 32.2 appears.

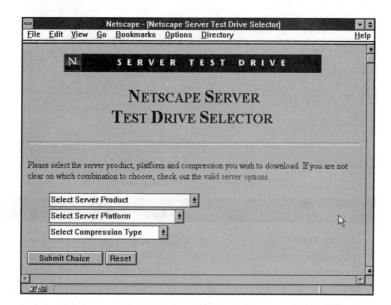

Fig. 32.2
The Test Drive Download Request form.

5. Select the operating system that you'll be using.

6. Select the type of server (Communications, Commerce, Proxy) that you want to download.

7. Select the compression type that you want. For NT servers, you can choose either .EXE or .ZIP compression types; for UNIX, you can choose between .Z and .gz compression. Choose a compression type that you know is usable on the computer that will be running the server.

8. Click the Submit button. This opens a dialog box that allows you to specify where the file should be stored. In the dialog box is the name of the specific file that Netscape will be sending (usually PICK.CGI); you need to replace this generic name with the full path of the working directory where you will be unpacking the file and the full name of the file provided by Netscape in the Downloader form, as shown in figure 32.3.

Fig. 32.3
The Downloader
form.

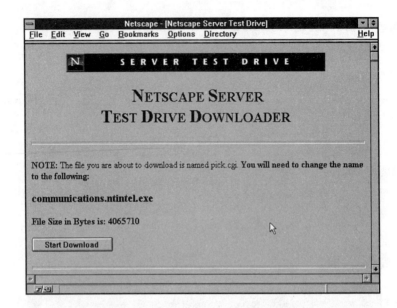

Netscape - [Netscape Server Test Drive]

File Edit View Go Bookmarks Options Directory   Help

SERVER TEST DRIVE

NETSCAPE SERVER
TEST DRIVE DOWNLOADER

NOTE: The file you are about to download is named pick.cgi. You will need to change the name to the following:

communications.ntintel.exe

File Size in Bytes is: 4065710

Start Download

> **Caution**
>
> The name of the file as it's stored on Netscape's server, where it must be distinguished from all of the other versions of the software, is different from the name of the archive as it should be stored on your computer to let the installation scripts work. Therefore, you must change the name of the file when it is downloaded to the name specified by Netscape. This will likely be COMMERCE.EXE, COMMERCE.ZIP, commerce.tar.gz, or commerce.tar.Z, depending on which compression type you've chosen.

> **Note**
>
> Netscape starts the clock on your 60-day test drive from the first time you try to download the files. So before you start the download, make sure that you have sufficient hard drive space on your machine to hold the file. The download is about 2.5MB; when uncompressed, the files may take up to 30MB.

9. Click the Accept button. This should start the download process. Keep an eye on it, and shut down the connection when the file is done transferring.

Installing the Netscape Commerce Server Software

Once you've downloaded the software, you'll need to unpack and install it. On both UNIX and NT systems, this is simply a matter of running a simple script, which copies files to the appropriate directories and automatically starts a special installation server so you can perform whatever configuration needs to be done.

The next section has separate sets of instructions for starting the Installation server on NT and UNIX systems. Once Netscape appears and the installation server is started, skip forward to the section "Configuring Your Netscape Test Drive Web Server."

Starting the Installation Server on an NT System

To start the installation process on an NT server, follow these steps:

1. Decompress the files into a working directory. When you started the download, you specified which type of compression you wanted to use. If you chose .EXE, you can simply type the name of the file at a DOS prompt or double-click the file name in File Manager and the archive will be decompressed.

   If you chose .ZIP as your compression style, use your favorite .ZIP utility (such as WinZip) to uncompress the files into a working directory.

   > **Note**
   >
   > Name your working directory something other than \NETSCAPE. The \NETSCAPE directory is where the install program will want to put the completed files; it will have a hard time if the installation files are in the same directory.

2. Run the program SETUP.EXE from your working directory. When prompted, click the Continue button to install the server files.

3. At this point, you need to specify a path to store the server files. By default, the SETUP program wants to put the files under a subdirectory called \NETSCAPE. Unless there's a big reason not to use this default, you should use it. It doesn't matter if your current version of Netscape is already stored there; the Netscape server needs the Navigator client to finish configuration. The path that you specify at this point is what is called the *server root*. Remember this path because you need it while configuring your server.

4. You will then be asked whether there is an existing Domain Name System (DNS) entry for your server through a dialog box like the one shown in figure 32.4. The DNS is a cross-referencing database of computers by name and IP address. If the administrator of your domain has already given you the name of your server, click the DNS Configured button. If you do not have a specific domain name for your system, click the No DNS Entry button.

Fig. 32.4
The DNS Configuration dialog box.

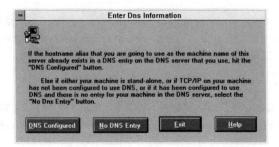

5. If you clicked the DNS Configured button, you will be prompted through a dialog box to enter the DNS name of your server.

   If you clicked the No DNS Entry button, you will be prompted through a dialog box like the one shown in figure 32.5 to enter your system's IP address.

Fig. 32.5
Enter your system's IP address in this dialog box if your server doesn't have a DNS entry.

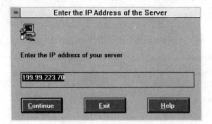

6. Once you've entered the requested information, you should see a dialog box like the one shown in figure 32.6 telling you that the files have been successfully installed.

7. Click the OK button. This should start a copy of Netscape and bring up a screen that looks like the one shown in figure 32.7. You should now skip forward to the section on configuring your server.

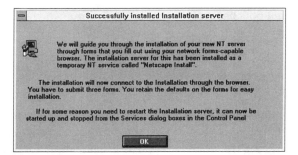

Fig. 32.6
The installation
server files have
been successfully
installed.

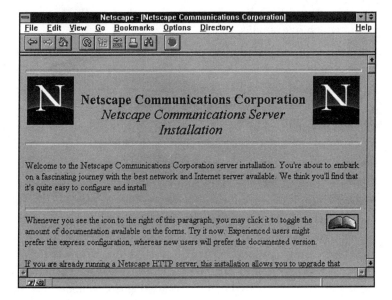

Fig. 32.7
The Netscape
Server Installation
home page.

Starting the Installation Server on Your UNIX System

Starting the installation of the Netscape Server on your UNIX system is a matter of running a simple script. On a UNIX system, you need to create a user that will own the processes created by the server system. Create your new user before you start the installation.

To run the QuickStart installation script, follow these steps:

1. Decompress and untar the file you downloaded from Netscape.

If you have gzip on your system, type the following command:

> **gzip -d** *filename*

where *filename* is replaced by the name of the file that you downloaded from Netscape.

2. You should now have a .TAR archive file in your working directory. To unpack the .TAR file, type

   tar -xvf *whatever.tar*

   where *whatever.tar* is the name of the tar file that resulted when you decompressed the file in step one.

3. When you untar the file, you should end up with a directory called either httpd, if you're test driving the Communications Server, or https, if you're testing the secure server. The installation script is stored in a subdirectory called install under this directory. Change into this directory by typing either **cd httpd/install** or **cd https/install** depending on which one applies.

4. Once you're in the install directory, type **./ns-setup** to start the installation script.

5. When prompted, enter the full name of the server, complete with the domain name.

6. You will then be prompted to indicate what browser you will be using to configure the server. If you are at the terminal that controls the server, you can just press Enter, and a copy of Netscape will connect to the Installation Server and appear on your screen.

   If you are installing the server software remotely or on a system that does not have its own monitor, type **NONE** at the network navigator prompt. You will need to access the Installation Server through a copy of Netscape on your remote system. To access the server, enter the URL **http://*servername:portnumber*** where *servername* is the name of the server that you entered in step five, and where *portnumber* is the port number that the installation script points you to before prompting you for the name of your browser.

7. At this point, the installation server should be running, and you should see a screen that looks like the one in figure 32.7. You can now proceed to the next section on configuring your server.

Configuring Your Netscape Test Drive Web Server

There is little difference between the configuration of a UNIX-based server and an NT-based server. Both use Netscape as the user interface, and the forms for the two systems are practically identical.

There are three sections to the configuration of a Netscape server. These are Server configuration, Document configuration, and Administrative configuration.

If you follow these steps, you can easily complete all three sections and get your server configured right away.

1. From the introductory page, select the option Install a New Netscape Server from Scratch and click the Start the installation! button.

2. This brings up the Installation Overview page, as illustrated in figure 32.8. Although you can do the three parts of the configuration in any order, it's probably best to do them left to right, as shown on the page. Click the Server Config button.

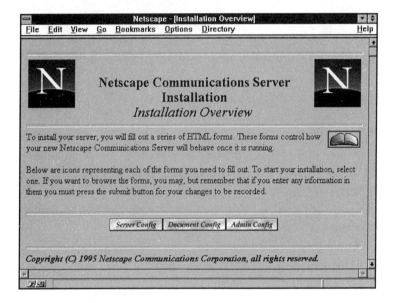

Fig. 32.8
The Installation Overview form.

3. The Server Configuration form shown in figure 32.9 lets you enter information about the server itself.

    - *Server Name:* Check the server name and make sure it's the same as the one you entered when you started the setup program.

    - *IP Address:* Enter the IP address of your system. This information is used primarily for systems that are running multiple Web sites off the same computer through a process where one computer answers to multiple IP addresses. Even if that's more complicated than you want to get right now, enter your IP address so that if you want to run multiple servers down the line, that option will be available without having to shut down and reinstall your original server.

Fig. 32.9
The Server
Configuration
form.

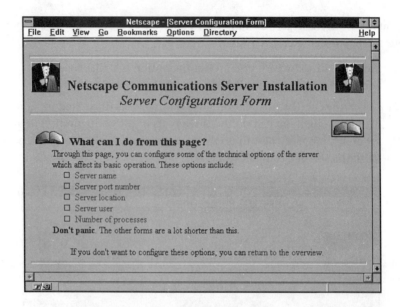

- *Server Port:* The regular port for a Web site is port 80. Unless you really have a need to change this, leave it on 80.

- *Server Location:* This is the server root directory. The default server root on a UNIX system is /usr/ns-home; the default root on an NT system is \NETSCAPE\HTTPD.

- *Server User:* On UNIX systems, you need to specify the name of the user that you created that will own the server's processes. For a variety of reasons, you should not leave the default username "nobody" as the user. Create a real user and enter that name in this slot.

- *Number of Processes/Threads:* Unless you know that your use is going to be either very light or very heavy, you should leave these numbers as they are.

- *Recording Errors:* By default, the Netscape server logs its errors to its own error file. If it is more convenient for you to have them directed to the system error log, you can indicate that here.

- *Hostname Resolution:* If you leave this option turned on, the Server will attempt to resolve the hostnames of users entering your system. This can be very helpful for monitoring your system's usage.

- *Access Logging:* By default, the server keeps a log of all users who access the site. If you're extremely short on disk space or if you expect that the volume to your site is going to be so large that trying to keep a record would not be of any value, you can shut the logging off at this point.

4. When you're done entering the Server Configuration information, click the Make These Changes button. This takes you to the Document Configuration form.

5. The Document Configuration form shown in figure 32.10 lets you tell the server where your HTML files will be stored and how to present files to users.

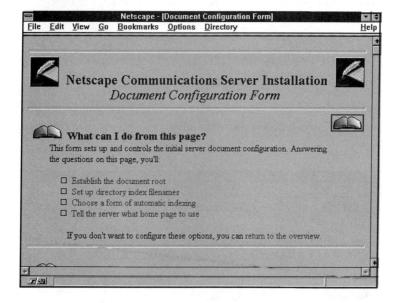

Fig. 32.10
The Document Configuration form.

- *Document Root:* Enter the name of the directory where you have stored the HTML files for your server.

- *Index Files:* When a user asks for a specific directory, the server usually sends an index of the directory. On Web sites, there is usually an HTML document that spells out the contents of a specific directory called the index file. These files are usually named index.html, but if you want to call them something else you can. Just enter the name of your first page documents in this line.

- *Automatic Indexing:* When a user asks for the index of a directory that does not have an index.html file, they get a listing of the files that the server has available in that directory. If you leave Fancy Indexing checked, the Netscape server will send little icons to indicate the file type as well as the name of the file. Checking Simple Directory Indexing provides the user with only a directory of files.

- *Home Page:* This option lets you specify a particular document that will be the first thing users see when they come to your site. Normally this is the index.html file stored in the server root, but Netscape allows you to specify any document you'd like.

6. When you have completed entering your document configuration information, click the Make These Changes button to continue to Administrative Configuration.

7. Netscape servers have lots of features beyond those that you configure during installation. All the administrative features are handled by another smaller server, called the Administrative Server. The administrative Configuration form shown in figure 32.11 lets you configure this server so you can access the more advanced options of your Netscape server.

Fig. 32.11
The Administrative Configuration form.

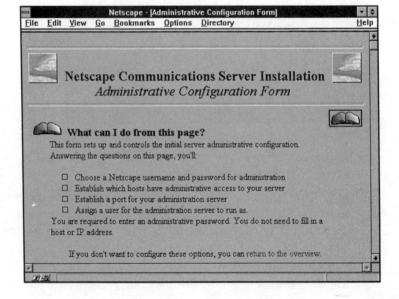

- *Administrative Username and Password:* Pick a username and a password that you'll use when accessing the Administrative server. Remember these, or you'll pretty much have to reinstall the server software to reconfigure the Administrative server.

- *Administrative Access Control:* By default, the only place you can access the Administrative server is from the server console. If you want to be able to access the server remotely, enter the specific domain names or IP numbers in this slot.

- *Administrative Server Configuration:* You will be prompted to enter a port and the user ID of a real system user that will own the processes generated by the Administrative server. Just as the traditional Web server port is 80, the traditional Web server administration port is 8080. The administrative user should probably be a user on your system that can run system-wide processes. You may want to make it the root user on a UNIX system or the administrative user on an NT system.

8. When you're done configuring the Administrative server, click the Make These Changes button.

9. You should now see a form that indicates all the information you've entered for your server (see fig. 32.12). Check through it to make sure there are no mistakes, and then click the link that says "Go for it!!!"

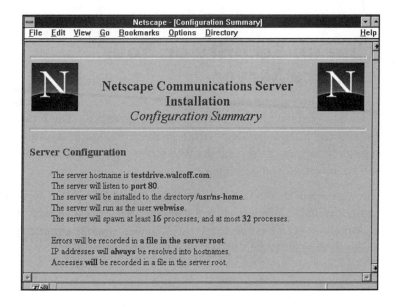

Fig. 32.12
The Server Configuration summary.

10. The Installation server will copy the server files to their appropriate locations and start your Web server. When the process is complete, you will see a page that starts with the image shown in figure 32.13.

Fig. 32.13
The server has been successfully installed.

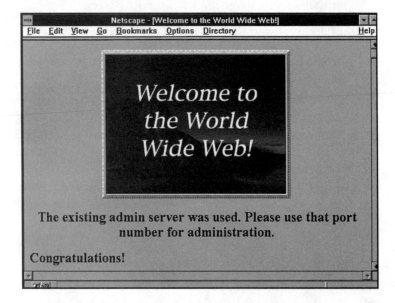

Your server is now up and running. You have successfully started your test drive.

Setting up Security on Your Commerce Server

In order to make transactions with their Commerce server "secure," Netscape has employed a strategy called the Secure Sockets Layer (SSL). The Secure Sockets Layer uses a three-part approach to make sure that messages are transmitted securely between a user and the Web server. These three steps are *authentication*, *encryption*, and *data integrity*.

The first two steps of this strategy, authentication and encryption, depend on a fairly fundamental concept in current computer security called *public key encryption*. Before we examine how Netscape implements public key encryption in its own software, let's take a look at how it works generally.

What Is Public Key Encryption?

The types of code making and breaking that most people are familiar with are called *secret key encryption*. In secret key encryption, both the sender and receiver know what the "key" is in order to decrypt the message. The problem with secret key encryption is that both the sender and the receiver need to be in agreement as to what the key is. Usually, somehow you need to get the key from one person to another; thus, the plots of hundreds of spy movies involving codebooks and microfiche hidden in teeth are created. Obviously, the problem with secret key codes is that once the secret key is no longer a secret, all messages sent using that key are compromised.

In 1976, Whitfield Diffie and Martin Hellman created a new system of cryptography that they called *public key cryptography*. In public key encryption, three separate mathematical factors are used. Two of these factors, called a *public key pair* are made available publicly. The third factor is actually the result of a particular mathematical relationship involving the other two factors. This third factor, called the *private key* is protected and not made available to anyone except for the user who receives information. The text of the message itself becomes a fourth factor in a very complex mathematical equation.

When the text of a message is processed in relation to the public key factors, it results in a value that can only be retrieved by someone who knows the private key factor or by someone who has sufficient computer resources to try all possible factor combinations until the private key factor is determined and the original message is decoded. The theory is that, given sufficiently complex factors, the amount of resources necessary to factor out the private key and the message text from the result of the mathematical relationship is far greater than the value of the information contained in the message.

Sending and Receiving Messages
Using Public Key Encryption

Suppose that a sender wants to issue a private message to a receiver. In cryptography, the original message is called the *plaintext*. The sender retrieves the receiver's public key pair (two of the three factors) and encrypts the message using these two factors. The resulting encrypted message, or *ciphertext*, can only be decoded if the third factor, the private key, is also known. Since the private key factor is only known by the receiver, he should be the only person capable of decoding the message. When the message is sent through the system, it can be intercepted, but unless the third factor is known, it cannot be read.

> **Caution**
>
> Obviously, this system depends on the fact that the private key is kept private and is not made generally available. When your private key is known, all three factors are available to the person who wants to read messages intended for you. Later in this chapter, we'll discuss some common-sense approaches to keeping your secure information secure.

Avoiding Message Tampering through Authentication

The second problem of sending messages through an open system (after the possibility of private information being intercepted) is the problem of ensuring that a received message is actually from the person who supposedly sent it.

On the Internet, the process of verifying that the sender of a message is actually who they claim to be is called *authentication*.

Public key encryption can also be used as a system for authentication. Using the private key, a sender does a computation involving the private key and the message itself. The result of this computation is attached to the message and both are sent. When the message is received, the receiver performs another computation using the message, the signature, and the sender's public key. While this computation does not yield the private key factor, it does show whether or not the factors could exist within the mathematical relationship that should exist among the known factors. If the mathematical relationship does not hold, either the signature or the message may have been altered.

> **Note**
>
> For more information on data encryption, check out RSA's Web site at **http:// www.rsa.com**. Lists of answers to Frequently Asked Questions about cryptography, public key encryption, and digital signatures can be found at **http:// www.rsa.com/rsalabs/faq/**.

How Is Public Key Encryption Used by Netscape?

In 1977 Ron Rivest, Adi Shamir, and Leonard Adelman invented a type of public key encryption that they named RSA (using the first initial of each of their last names). This process was patented and is licensed by a variety of companies for use in products that maintain secure transmission of materials.

Netscape has licensed the RSA public key system for use in its server and client products. Netscape has incorporated the RSA encryption mathematical formulas or algorithms into their message transmission security system, which they called the Secure Sockets Layer. As we mentioned earlier in this chapter, the Secure Sockets Layer actually involves three separate strategies: authentication, encryption, and data integrity verification.

Authentication

The first step of the Secure Sockets Layer approach is a variation of the public key authentication discussed earlier. When a user tries to connect to a Web site, the user's copy of the Netscape Navigator Web browser client sends a request for information to the Commerce server. When a Netscape Commerce server receives this request for information, it sends the Netscape Navigator client software a package of information, including the server's public key pair and a copy of a *signed digital certificate*. A signed digital certificate is an electronic document from a trusted third party (called a *Certification Authority*) stating that the public key pair sent is authentic and actually belongs to the server that the user is trying to reach.

As the name suggests, the signed digital certificate contains its own public key information. When the Netscape Navigator client receives this information, it authenticates the signed digital certificate by checking it against the public key pair at the Certification Authority. It then checks the content of the server's public key pair. Once the public key pair has been mathematically verified by the Netscape Navigator client, the server has been *authenticated*.

At this point, the Netscape Navigator client then generates a *session key*, or a temporary public key. Using the server's public key, the client encrypts this session key and sends it to the server.

Encryption

Once the client has received and authenticated the server's public key and sent a copy of its session key to the server, both sides have copies of the other's public key. Information can now be transferred between the server and the client using standard public key encryption techniques. Encrypted information, while available to many other systems on the Net, are of little value without the factors necessary to decipher them.

Data Integrity

Like most Internet transmission protocols, Netscape's Secure Sockets Layer system uses an integrity checker to ensure that data hasn't been tampered with or warped in transmission between the server and client. SSL's Message Authentication Codes (MACs) work much like the system that FTP uses to ensure that a packet has been properly received.

Why Go to All This Trouble?

Let's suppose someone figures out how to fool the DNS system into sending requests for a server at www.goodguy.com to a server at www.thief.com. Since, like most Internet client applications, the Netscape Navigator software depends on the DNS system for navigation, as far as it's concerned, www.thief.com looks exactly like www.goodguy.com.

Let's also say that our thief is particularly diligent and has made copies of all of the available files on the www.goodguy.com site. This means that the site looks exactly like www.goodguy.com.

Here's the thief's problem: If the thief uses the public key pairs from www.goodguy.com (which he could get), he can't decrypt any of the information he received without the www.goodguy.com private key.

If the thief tries to resolve this problem by creating his own set of public keys, they won't match the signature on the signed digital certificate, and the client will know that it's not talking to the right server.

The Great Netscape Security Debacle of 1995

In September of 1995, Netscape faced a public relations nightmare when two Berkeley students (Ian Goldberg and David Wagner) announced to computer hacker groups and the press that they had figured out a way to crack the public key encryption system used by Netscape. (Check out **http://www.tezcat.com/web/security/items/ssi-news.txt** to read the announcement.)

Unlike the server's public/private key set, which is generated only about once a year, the Netscape Navigator client generates a new session key each time it encounters a new secure server. Versions of the Netscape Navigator client up to version 1.1 used a limited set of variables to generate the client's session key.

Armed with some limited knowledge about the origin of these variables and their eventual use, these students were able to use sheer computing power to eventually crack a session key. Once the session key was known, it was possible to decrypt messages from the server to the client, revealing a potential flaw in the security system.

Netscape responded by raising the number of variables used to create the session key from 30 to 300, thus raising the number of potential combinations considerably and making this particular type of attack much less feasible. Versions of the Netscape Navigator client 1.2 and above incorporate this feature. An upgrade patch was also sent to users of the Netscape Commerce server software that prevents users of versions prior to 1.2 from logging in to a Netscape Commerce server.

Establishing SSL Security on Your Commerce Server

The process of setting up security on your Netscape Commerce server is less an exercise in computing skills than it is a challenge to get through red tape. The following are four steps to establishing security on your server:

1. Generate your private and public keys.
2. Request a signed digital certificate from a Certification Authority.
3. Install your signed digital certificate.
4. Activate security through your administrative server.

Before you get started, do the following to get your server ready to handle secure data:

- Get rid of any programs that aren't absolutely necessary to run the Commerce server. Users should only be accessing this computer through the Commerce server.

- If this is a system that lets users log in through accounts, get rid of all of them except for the account that runs the server. If certain accounts need to be left in place for server maintenance, make sure they have passwords and have all external accesses locked out.

- Eliminate physical access to the system as much as possible.

- Place the server in a locked, climate-controlled computer server room, if possible, and limit access as much as possible.

- Set up an adequate backup system that copies all relevant files to tape on a regular basis. (These tapes also need to be protected, as they contain copies of your private key file.)

> **Note**
>
> Why go through all the bother of taking these precautions? If the information that is stored on this system is sensitive enough to require protection through encryption, you'll want to make sure that unauthorized parties are blocked at all potential entrances. After all, once the data gets to your server, it's no longer encoded and can be viewed clearly by someone who can get access to your system.

Generating Private and Public Key Pairs

The first step to setting up SSL is generating public and private keys for your server. Early versions of the Netscape Commerce server allowed the administrator to generate key pairs using a form that could be viewed through a Netscape Navigator client attached to the administrative server. This system used a set of conditions on the system to generate a set of random numbers that provided the basis for the keys. This system was later discovered to be insufficiently secure.

The new method of generating key pairs requires input from the server administrator to serve as the random seed for generating the key pair. Once you run the program, you are prompted to enter input at the keyboard. The key generating program records the random lengths of time between input keystrokes and uses them as the random seed for generating the key pair.

To start the key generation program on a UNIX system follow these steps:

1. Log in as root by entering the command **su root**. When prompted, enter the root password.

> **Note**
>
> If you are Telnetting to the server, you should not be able to log in as directly as root. Log in through another account with permission to access the server and use the superuser (su) command to log in as root. If you are able to Telnet in to the server as root, go back and disable root login through Telnet before continuing. If you are unsure how to do this, check your server administration manual.

2. Change to your server's root directory. This is not the directory where your HTML documents are stored but rather where the server programs are kept. If you did a standard installation of your Commerce server,

these files are found in the directory /usr/ns-home. To change to this directory, type **cd /usr/ns-home**.

3. The key generation program is stored in the directory bin/https/admin/bin. Change to this directory by typing **cd bin/https/admin/bin**.

4. Run the key generation program by typing **./key**.

5. At this point, you can begin generating the key pair files.

To start the key generation program on an NT system, follow these steps:

1. Through a DOS window, change directories to where the key generation program is stored.

2. Run the key generation program by typing **key**.

3. Begin generating the key pair files.

Generating the Key Pair Files

Once the key script has been started, you are prompted to provide a path for the new key pair file. Usually, this file is stored in the secure server's configuration directory. If you did a standard installation of your Commerce server, this directory would be /usr/ns-home/https-443.###.###.###.###/config (where ###.###.###.### is replaced by the IP address of the server) on a UNIX system or \netscape\https\config on an NT system. The default name for the key pair file is SERVERKEY.DER.

> **Note**
>
> You may change the default locations of these files if you want. In fact, changing these locations may be desirable, if you feel fairly confident in your skills with UNIX, as placing the files in an unorthodox location makes it harder for system intruders to find the files, should they manage to somehow gain access to your system. If you decide to place this file in a location other than the default, be sure that the directory where you put it is accessible *only* by root (and don't forget where you put it).

Once you've entered the path for your key files, you are presented with a progress meter above your command line. When prompted, begin to type on your keyboard. You can type anything; the text isn't really important, though I'd avoid "The Quick Brown Fox." Any text you're not familiar with (even this paragraph) will do. The program reads the time between your keystrokes and uses them as the random seed for generating your key files.

> **Note**
>
> Do not use the automatic repeat feature by holding down a single key to fill up the progress meter. The time between keystrokes of a held-down key is not random, and makes your resulting keys much more vulnerable to attack.

Once you have filled up the progress meter, the program uses your random input to generate a key pair file.

After the key pair file is generated, you are prompted to enter a keyfile password. This password should be at least eight characters long and should include at least one non-alphabetic character. The password should also not be found in any regular dictionary of terms. Birthdates, family member names, and the like are all bad choices because someone might be able to use this information to crack your keyfile password. Once you select a password, you should memorize it and not write it down. You also need to remember it; should you forget your keyfile password, you'll need to generate a new key pair and request a new signed digital certificate (for which the Certification Authority will probably charge a fee to your organization).

> **Note**
>
> When you request a signed digital certificate from a Certification Authority, they ask for the name of one key Web administrator who has responsibility for the security of the system. This should be the person who creates and knows the keyfile password.
>
> In many organizations, it's considered regular business practice to make sure a copy of your passwords are available should something happen to you and someone needs to access your files. This should be an exception.
>
> The worst that can happen if something happens to you or the keyfile is somehow "lost" is that a new key pair needs to be generated and someone needs to have a new signed digital certificate produced by the Certification Authority, proving the validity of the new key pair. Though frustrating, the total potential loss is some downtime on your server and the cost of a new signed digital certificate (about $100).
>
> By contrast, if the integrity of the keyfile password is violated, the information on your server can be vulnerable for an indefinite period before you discover that someone else is copying and decrypting your data. These potential costs by far outweigh the cost of generating a new keyfile password.

Caution

Whenever the secure server is restarted, the administrator is prompted to enter the keyfile password so the keyfile can be decrypted into the public and private keys for use by the server. Since the keyfile password is required to be entered, secure servers must be restarted manually, unlike Communications servers which can be started by a script when the server starts up.

Once you have generated the keyfile, you can request a signed digital certificate from a Certification Authority.

Requesting a Signed Digital Certificate

There's some paperwork you need to do before you can perform the computer side of this task. The red tape involved with getting a signed digital certificate is largely related to proving that you are who you say you are.

Certification Authorities are companies whose job it is to verify that a given public key actually belongs to the company that purportedly owns it. Through their digital signature on your digital server certificate, users are able to authenticate that the server they've reached is the one they think they're addressing.

What Is Verisign?

Verisign is the Certification Authority most generally affiliated with Netscape Commerce servers. The directions in this chapter assume that you are getting your signed digital certificate from Verisign. If you get your certificate from another Certification Authority, the process may vary slightly, but the requirements are generally the same.

Note

You can find out more about Verisign's signed digital certificate services at their Web site (**http://www.verisign.com/**).

Documenting Your Server

Before Verisign will process your request for a signed digital certificate, they require that you send them the following information:

- The name, address, and contact information of the person who will be serving as Webmaster of the secure server, as well as the name of the specific server that will be running the Commerce server software. Verisign usually requires that this information appears on corporate letterhead above the signature of someone with authority to delegate this authority on behalf of the company. This information proves that the person interacting with Verisign is authorized by the stated company to do so.

Note

A template for generating this letter is available on Verisign's Web site at **http://www.verisign.com/netscape/index.html**.

- The company's business license or articles of incorporation. This information proves that the company has the right to engage in commercial transactions.
- A purchase order or check for the cost of issuing the signed digital certificate.

In order to expedite the processing of requests for signed digital certificates, Verisign asks that applicants fax a copy of this information to them before submitting the request for the certificate. Verisign begins processing the request but does not issue the certificate until the hard copy of all materials reaches them by mail.

Note

Certification Authorities tend to be very strict about their rules. It can take up to two months for a Certification Authority to issue a signed digital certificate, depending on the ease with which they can validate the information submitted with the certificate request.

This stringency is actually good for everyone, as it helps to prevent fraudulent behavior that could damage online commerce for everyone. If the CA requests additional verification or supporting information, do your best to provide the information as soon as possible.

If it is impossible to provide a specific piece of information requested by the CA, contact them and explain why. There is usually an alternate form of proof that the CA finds acceptable.

Requesting a Signed Digital Certificate from a Certification Authority

Once the proper documentation has been submitted to your selected Certification Authority, you can issue your online request for a signed digital certificate. This is done through a form accessible through the Administrative server.

Starting the Administrative Server

To start the Administrative server on a UNIX machine, follow these steps:

1. Log in as root by typing the following at a command prompt: **su**. When prompted, type in the server's root password.

2. Change the server's root directory. For a standard installation of the Netscape Commerce server where the root is stored in the directory /usr/ns-home, type the following command: **cd /usr/ns-home**.

3. Run the Administrative server program by typing the following: **./start-admin**.

   The server returns a message that tells you the port through which the Administrative server can be reached.

To start the Administrative server on a Windows NT machine, follow these steps:

1. Change to the directory where the Netscape server programs are kept.

2. Run the Administrative server program by double-clicking it.

Accessing the Administrative Server

Once you have started the Administrative server, you can access the security configuration forms using the Netscape Navigator client. To do this, follow these steps:

1. Start a copy of Netscape.

2. Open a connection to the Administrative server. You can open a dialog box to enter the Administrative server's address by clicking the Open tool, or you can enter the address into the Location field below the Netscape toolbar.

   The administrative server's address is the name of the server followed by a colon and the number of the port through which the Administrative server can be accessed.

Note

The Administrative server tells you what port it can be reached at when you start it; the default setting is port 8080. The name should look like this:

http://www.servername.com:8080

Once you enter the Administrative server's address, you are presented with a dialog box asking you for the name of the Administrative user and password, as illustrated in figure 32.14.

Fig. 32.14
The Administrative server login dialog box.

Note

The username and password requested at this point are the administrative username and password you entered when you first installed the server software. If you have forgotten this name and password, you may need to remove the software and reinstall it.

When the appropriate username and password are entered, you see an HTML document that looks like the one shown in figure 32.15.

3. Scroll down to the section titled Configure Server Security, as illustrated in figure 32.16.

Click the Request or Renew a Certificate link. This brings up the form shown in figure 32.17.

4. Fill out the form to request your certificate.

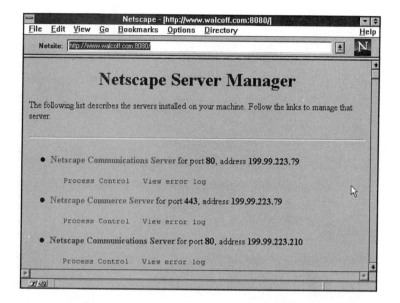

Fig. 32.15
The Administrative
server index page.

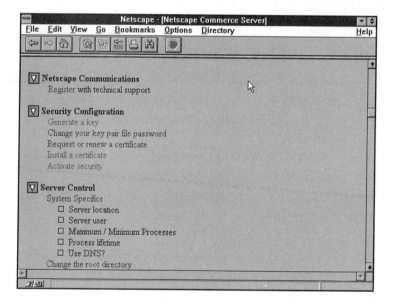

Fig. 32.16
Options for
establishing
security on your
server.

Fig. 32.17
Use this form to
request a signed
digital certificate.

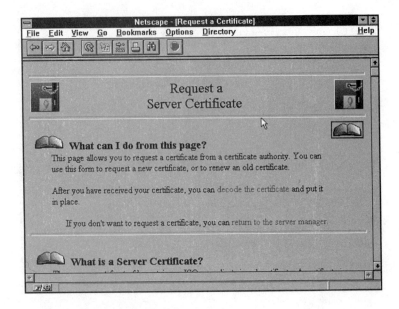

You need to enter the following information:

- The e-mail address of your Certification Authority
- The path to your keyfile
- Your keyfile password (used to decrypt the keyfile so a copy of the public key can be sent to the Certification Authority)
- The "distinguished name" of the server that will be running the secure server
- A phone number so the Certification Authority can contact you if any problems arise

5. Once you have entered the appropriate information, click the Make These Changes button.

The Administrative server then runs a script that decrypts your keyfile and attaches a copy of your public key to a message that is sent to the Certification Authority using the e-mail address you supplied.

Shortly after you submit your request, you should receive a confirmation by e-mail that your request has been received. Before you can do anything else, you need to wait for the Certification Authority to validate your information. Within a few days or a few weeks, you will receive a second e-mail message containing the signed digital certificate. Then you can proceed to install it and activate security on your server.

Installing a Signed Server Certificate

Once the Certification Authority has verified the authenticity of your request for a signed digital certificate, they send you an e-mail containing your server certificate.

The critical piece of this e-mail is marked with lines that say

```
--- BEGIN CERTIFICATE ---
```

and

```
--- END CERTIFICATE ---
```

This is your signed digital certificate that is used by clients to authenticate your server. You can either edit the e-mail and save this text in a file, or you can cut and paste this text directly into the appropriate form.

To install the certificate, follow these steps:

1. Start the Administrative server. (This is covered in detail in the previous section.)
2. Log in to the Administrative server through your Netscape Navigator software.
3. From the Server Manager index page, click the link called Install a Server Certificate. This opens up the hypertext document shown in figure 32.18.

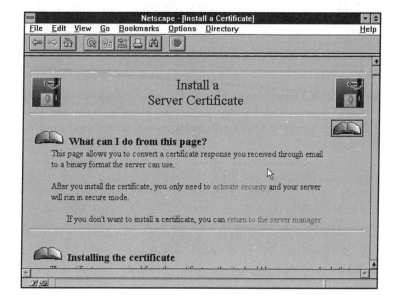

Fig. 32.18
The Server Certificate installation form.

4. Insert the text of the certificate from the e-mail message. If you have already saved the contents of the certificate into a file, specify the full path of the file where the file can be found. If you have decided to cut and paste the certificate contents, open up your e-mail program in a window and copy the lines saying Begin, End, and everything in between, and paste them into the section of the form designated for this purpose, as shown in figure 32.19.

Fig. 32.19

The contents of a server certificate pasted into the installation form.

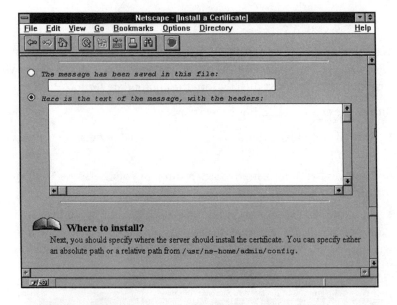

Note

As discussed earlier in this chapter, server certificates are related to specific keyfiles. If you requested server certificates for several servers at the same time, be absolutely sure that the server certificate you install matches the keyfile and the server.

5. Specify where the certificate file will be kept. As a default, the file is called SERVERCERT.DER and is stored below the directory where the main server files are stored in a subdirectory called /admin/config.

> **Note**
>
> If you are running a UNIX system and decide not to store the file in the default location, make sure that the SERVERCERT.DER file is not kept in the root directory or in another generally accessible directory. Although many clients access and read this file, you don't want anyone to be able to tamper with it. If this file is tampered with, users of your site will be unable to authenticate your server and will therefore be unable to log in.

6. Click the Make These Changes button. A script runs, and your server certificate is installed in the appropriate directory.

Now that the certificate is installed, you need to tell your server to turn its security features on.

Activating Security and Enabling (/Disabling) Ciphers

Once you install the server certificate, the server's response should provide you with an opportunity to proceed and activate security on the server.

If you elected not to follow this option at the time you installed the server certificate, or if for some reason you decided to leave security deactivated, you can get to the Security Activation form by following these steps:

1. Activate the Administrative server, as discussed previously in the section on generating a key pair.
2. Log into the Administrative server using your Netscape Navigator client.
3. From the Server Manager index page, select Activate Security or Enable a Cipher. This reveals the HTML document shown in figure 32.20.

Once you have entered the Activate Security or Enable a Cipher form, you have to supply the basic information that the server needs to pull all of the previous efforts together. Follow the next series of steps to fully activate security on your server:

1. Select the option that says you want to run in secure mode.

> **Note**
>
> Once you have activated your server's secure mode, users with Web clients that do not support SSL are no longer able to communicate with the server. At this time, only users running Netscape Navigator can access your secured server. These users will also experience some changes to their interface that alert them to the fact that they are communicating with a secure server. These interface changes are discussed in the next section of this chapter.

Fig. 32.20
This form allows
you to turn on
your server's
security features.

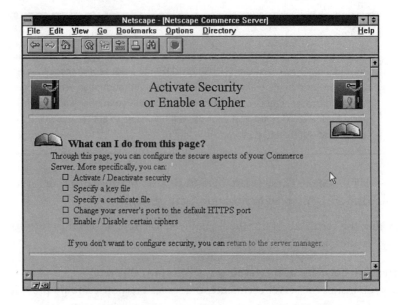

2. Select a port number for your server. The default selection is 443; this
   port is the standard for secure Web servers. Unless you have a really
   good reason to change it, you should probably leave it alone.

3. Enter the path of the keyfile that you generated before you requested
   your server certificate. This points users to your public keyfile to enable
   the encryption section of SSL.

4. Specify the path to the server certificate that was installed in step 3.
   This allows users to authenticate your public key by verifying your
   keyfile with the Certification Authority.

5. Select which ciphers you want to activate. Unless you have a specific
   reason to shut one off, you might as well choose to leave them all
   turned on.

6. When you have supplied all of this information, click the Make These
   Changes button.

Once the Administrative server runs the appropriate script, the security features of your server are activated.

How Users See a Secure Server

Once security is activated on your server, users who can access the site will
notice several key changes in the way their Netscape Navigator responds to
your site.

The most important change is that any users who had previously connected to your server using software other than Netscape Navigator (or some other SSL-compliant Web browser) will no longer be able to access your site.

> **Note**
>
> The patch to the Commerce server that solved the security problem related to key generation also added an option for redirecting users who do not have either SSL software or a version of Netscape Navigator beyond 1.1 to another HTML document. If you are running an insecure Communications server on the same machine as your secure Commerce server, these users can be redirected to an insecure version of your site (which does not accept credit card numbers or exchange other sensitive information).

Second, the prefix to the URL of your site will change from http:// to https://. Thus the insecure server http://www.walcoff.com/ would become https://www.walcoff.com/. This new URL tells the host (www.walcoff.com) two key things: first it connects to the machine at the secure port (number 443); second, the preliminary request to the server activates the sequence of exchanging keys that is necessary for secure communications.

Third, users will notice some changes to the look of their Netscape Navigator window that indicate the activation of secure communications. These include the addition of a blue bar below the toolbar, and the "joining" of the broken key into a dark blue key in the lower-left corner. Both of these modifications are illustrated in figures 32.21 and 32.22.

Additionally, if the user has not deactivated them, dialog boxes will appear as the user moves in and out of secured documents, alerting them to the transition from insecure to secure communications.

If all of these features are working, then you have correctly installed your Commerce server. The question of whether you like the software well enough to buy a copy is up to you, but if you do decide to buy it, your installation and signed digital certificate are still valid. No further configuration is necessary; all that is required is the payment of the appropriate fees to Netscape.

Fig. 32.21
Connections to
insecure servers are
marked with a
broken key in the
lower left hand
corner.

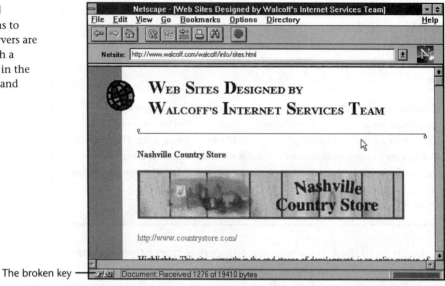

The broken key ──

Fig. 32.22
A connection to a
secure server is
marked with a
solid key in the
lower-left corner, a
blue bar under-
neath the location
line, and the
prefix https before
the site address.

──The blue bar

The key ──

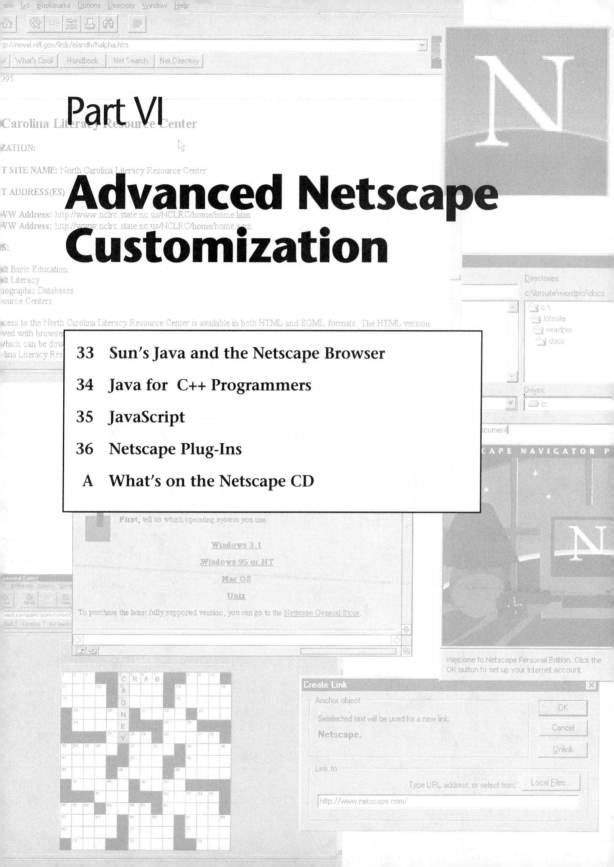

Part VI

Advanced Netscape Customization

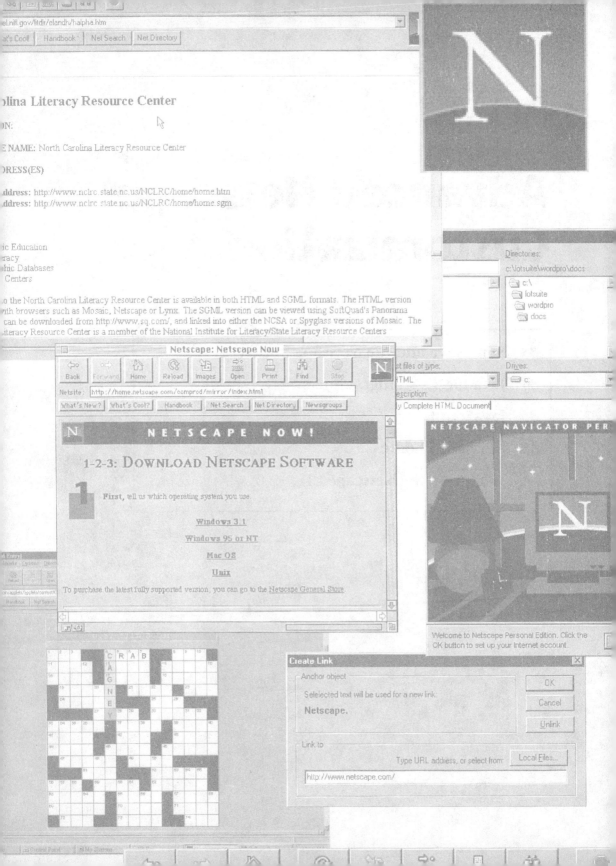

CHAPTER 33

Sun's Java and the Netscape Browser

Java is a new programming language created by Sun Microsystems, and has created a lot more excitement than new programming languages usually generate. Programmers are excited about Java because the language supports many useful features, such as an object-oriented structure, intuitive multi-threading, and built-in network support. The language also avoids many of the pitfalls of C++. Where C++ forces the programmer to keep track of the memory that he uses, a Java programmer doesn't need to worry about using memory reserved for the system or not freeing up memory appropriately.

Java programmers don't need to worry about how memory is utilized because of how a Java program is run. Java is a semi-compiled language. When you program in a compiled language like C++, the compiler takes your source code and creates a file that is ready for the system to execute. A Java compiler doesn't work this way. Instead, it creates a file that contains *bytecodes*. This file is then handed to an interpreter that sits on your computer. That interpreter executes the program. The interpreter keeps track of how memory is used, and can let the programmer know if something has gone wrong. This is different from an errant C++ program, which simply stops, sometimes after crashing the system. Because of this, it is much harder to debug C++ programs than programs written in Java.

But these advantages aren't the only reasons that Java is generating so much excitement. Its semi-compiled nature allows the language to be architecture neutral, which means that you can compile your Java program once and it is ready to run on many different platforms. But the real brilliance of Java is that it is designed with distributed systems in mind. Part of this is the built-in networking support. The more important part is a Java program can be transferred across the Internet to your computer and the interpreter can make sure that it doesn't do anything bad to the system.

But you are probably asking, "Why does this interest me, a Netscape 2.0 user?" The reason that it should is that Netscape 2.0 has a Java interpreter built in, which means that instead of just downloading pictures, sound, and text, Netscape 2.0 can download small programs called *Applets*, which are then run on your computer. These Applets, which are written in Java, can display animations, allow you to play games, or get stock prices from a remote computer. Whatever these Applets do, you don't have to worry about them crashing your system, spreading a virus, or wiping out your hard drive.

In this chapter, you learn:

- What a Java Applet is
- How Java Applets are changing the Web
- How Java works in Netscape
- What people have been designing Java Applets to do
- Where to find a wealth of online Java resources

Why Java Is Waking Up the Internet

In the Spring of 1995, Sun Microsystems released a Web browser called HotJava. This Web browser was written in a new programming language called Java. This language was originally intended to handle such tasks as interactive television and coordination of household appliances. The explosion of the Web in 1994 revealed the real opportunity for Java, and work on the Web browser commenced.

Though this Web browser was rough around the edges, it could do some things no other Web browser at that time could. With this Web browser, a user could see animation, play games, and even view a ticker tape of their up-to-date stock prices. Almost immediately after its release, Netscape decided to license HotJava's technology and incorporate it into its browsers. Netscape's incorporation of this technology into Netscape 2.0 makes this technology available to a much wider audience then before. This wider audience, along with the capabilities that Java provides, is revolutionizing the Web.

What Is a Java Applet?

Netscape 2.0 can run *Java Applets*, which are small programs that are downloaded from a Web server. There isn't anything special about how it does this; it downloads a Java Applet in precisely the same manner as it downloads any file. Just as any browser displays an image as it is received, a Java-capable browser runs the Java Applet. When the Java Applet runs, it is much (but not exactly) like any other program that can run on your computer. It can take input from your keyboard, mouse, or even a remote computer. The output displays on your screen.

But there are differences between a Java Applet and the applications that sit on your desktop. You wouldn't want Netscape 2.0 to download a virus. At the same time, you wouldn't want to have to check every program that came down, because most programmers have no interest in harming your computer. Because of the way that the Java language is structured, you don't have to worry about a Java Applet harming your computer.

But this does mean that there have been some restrictions placed on Java Applets. In fact, a Java Applet knows next to nothing about your computer. It can't look or write to any file in your file system. It can use your computer's memory, but not directly. These restrictions on a Java Applet keep your computer safe from harm, and also protect your privacy.

How a Java Applet Is Different From the CGI Program

Anyone who has been around the Web for a while knows that programs can be run on the Web without Java. One of the reasons the Web, without Java, has become so popular is that the Web allows simple interaction across the Internet. It does this through the Common Gateway Interface (CGI). The CGI underlies electronic forms, imagemaps, and search engines. Basically, it runs a program that resides on the server. The program, called a *CGI program*, outputs a Web page, and that Web page is sent back to the client (see fig. 33.1).

The Common Gateway Interface puts the Web a step above other information protocols such as FTP and Gopher because it allows you to tell a remote computer to do things for you. It is great for information providers because they can let you do very specific tasks without having to give you, and the rest of the world, the run of their machines.

CGI programs are great for a lot of things. For instance, let's say that you are an officer of a club that is running a Web server. Through the use of a simple CGI program, you can give your members a way to keep their mailing addresses up to date. You can put an electronic form on your Web site, and if someone moves, she can just access that form and enter her new address. Then, the CGI program takes that information and updates the database.

However, there are many limitations of CGI programs that Applets overcome (see table 33.1).

Fig. 33.1
How programs are
transmitted over
the Web.

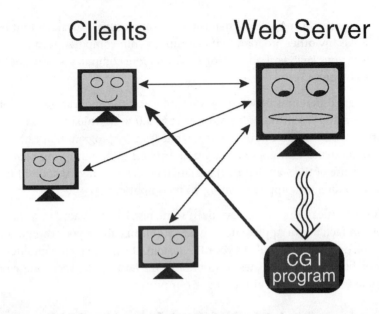

Table 33.1	Differences Between CGI Programs and Java Applets	
Property	**Java Applet**	**CGI Program**
Get information from remote computer	Yes	Yes
Computer that it runs on	Client	Server
How it handles input and output	Instantaneously across the Internet	Only after transmission

The limitations of CGI programs are outlined in table 33.1, but let's also look at something that has been done with both a CGI program and a Java Applet. Figure 33.2 shows a tic-tac-toe game that was done using a Java Applet. Tic-tac-toe also has been done many times using CGI programs, and looks a lot like this.

For both the CGI implementation and the Applet implementation, you simply click where you want the X to go.

First, let's look at how the CGI implementation handles the input. Your Web browser takes that information and transmits it to the Web server. The Web server runs the CGI program. The CGI program figures out the best response and writes a Web page indicating this. That page is then transmitted back across the Internet.

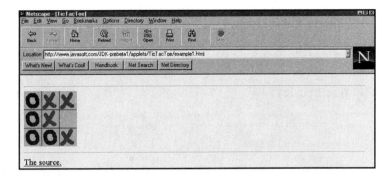

Fig. 33.2
Tic-tac-toe with a
Java Applet.

When tic-tac-toe is implemented using a Java Applet, the Java Applet figures out the best move. Because no communication takes place across the Internet, it is much faster.

Of course, for something as simple as tic-tac-toe, one could argue that speed isn't very important. But for something like Tetris, speed is important (see fig. 33.3). It would be a boring game of Tetris if you had to wait several seconds between each move of a piece. Because a Java Applet runs on your computer, it provides real-time animation. Also, when you interact with the Applet by clicking the mouse or pressing a key, the Applet knows about it immediately. A CGI program can only know after the data has been transmitted across the Internet.

There are many other examples of Web applications that are best done by an Applet. For instance, an Applet can ticker the current prices of your stocks across your screen. A virtual world can be downloaded in the form of an Applet, and if that virtual world is changed by someone else, your view of it is immediately updated.

Java Applets are faster because they don't have to transmit input and output across the Internet. They are also better than CGI programs for many applications because the server doesn't have to process anything. This was a big problem with Netscape's first attempt at animation and interactivity. This attempt was called *Server Push and Client Pull* and it was based on the Common Gateway Interface. After the page was loaded, a CGI program would hold the connection open and update the page as necessary. This allowed a Web page designer to make a page dynamic and interactive.

But Tetris, for example, would have two distinct disadvantages as a CGI program. First, playing the game is slower, because input and output still have to be transmitted across the Internet. Second, the increased load resulting from such rapid-fire contact slows down the server enough that other clients experience the delay, as we see in figure 33.4.

Fig. 33.3
Tetris with a Java
Applet.

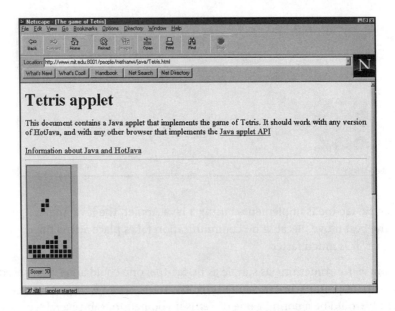

Fig 33.4
Interactivity
through the
Common Gateway
Interface.

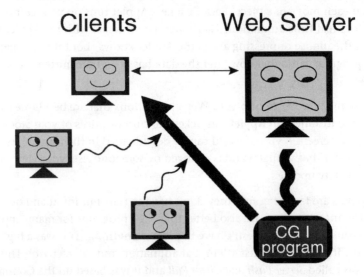

Because Server Push and Client Pull has such an ill effect on the server, many Web sites have banned their information providers from using it. This is a real shame because any machine powerful enough to run a graphical Web browser could easily be a Web server. The processing power of the client machine sits idle while a busy server handles the computation.

The use of Applets means that your machine can do processing that the server doesn't have to do, leaving the server to concentrate on its real

purpose: serving information. Even in cases where speed might not be cru-
cial, it is still better to use Java Applets for interactivity. The processing is
more evenly balanced, as shown in figure 33.5.

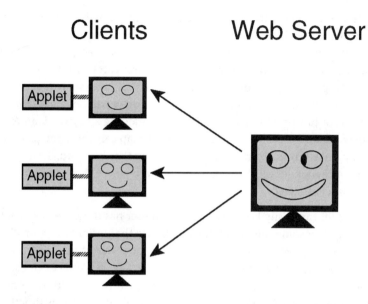

Clients   Web Server

Fig. 33.5
Processing
responsibilities
balanced with use
of Java Applets.

CGI Programs vs. Java Applets: When To Use What

If you are a Web page designer, you are probably wondering when a Java
Applet is appropriate and when a CGI program is. For two reasons, Applets do
not completely replace the Common Gateway Interface. First, not all Web
browsers are able to run Applets. Unless you can be guaranteed that the users
of your particular service are going to have a Java-enabled version of Netscape
or some other browser, you should consider providing an alternative version
of your service.

Second, if your program is using a central database, you should use a CGI
program. For example, a search engine should function as a CGI program.
Advanced search engines, such as WAIS, Lycos, and Harvest, maintain a database of keywords. Instead of directly searching Web pages for some keyword,
a CGI program simply looks in the database. An Applet couldn't act as a
search engine nearly as well because it would have to traverse the network
looking for some keyword.

In the search engine example, the database is only read. Since an Applet isn't
allowed to write to any file system, you can't use an Applet to modify a database, either. If you want visitors to your Web site to fill out a survey, you
would probably want to use a CGI program.

Unless you are dealing with a central store of information, you should consider using Java Applets. They reduce the load on the Web server and allow more interactivity. They also make more dynamic Web pages.

Remember, Java Applets and CGI programs are not mutually exclusive. Let's look back at the search engine example. We definitely don't want an Applet to search the entire Web when a CGI program can just do a quick lookup in its database. But by writing an Applet that communicates with the CGI program, we can provide superior interactivity. The CGI program can generate the raw results of the search, while the Applet provides an advanced interface. Instead of just providing a list of pages containing a keyword, an Applet can display a map for each of those pages. That map can show the pages that are directly linked from a certain page containing that keyword. Then, you can focus your energies on those parts of the Web where the information you want is most centralized.

Also, an Applet can easily keep track of what a user has done. Let's go back to the example of someone modifying a database that resides on your Web server. If you want people to be able to make a lot of modifications, you have to assume that they are going to make some mistakes. An Applet can easily keep track of what they have done and correct any mistakes with the press of a button. However, a CGI program has a hard time providing this functionality, since it is responsible for answering many users. It is quite difficult for a CGI program to keep track of who has done what, and even more difficult for it to provide an intuitive interface.

Let's expand this example a bit. Let's say that there are many databases on different machines that need to be manipulated by some user. An Applet can make it appear that all of them are the same. When the user wants information from a certain one, the Applet figures out which CGI program to connect to. This is much more intuitive and less time consuming than forcing the user to link directly to the CGI program. Still, the Applet can provide interactive features like an Undo key.

How Java Allows the Web to Evolve Itself

Java allows Applet writers to build on the Web's current infrastructure. If there is some capability that a Web browser doesn't have, a Java Applet can often be written to give the Web browser that capability. Such possible capabilities include interactive features that you expect from your normal desktop applications and the ability to understand new protocols. The Applet writer doesn't have to write an entire Web browser. This is important, because it is hard to expect the entire Internet to adapt to a new way of doing things, even if it is a great idea.

If a new way of compressing video data were to be invented, the inventors wouldn't have to convince everyone that it was great. Instead, they could just write an Applet that utilizes their new method. They wouldn't have to distribute software that everyone would then have to install on their computers. They wouldn't have to wait for Web browser makers to adopt their technology. The Applet could simply be downloaded at the same time the data is. If they decide to add a feature, they could just do it, and their improved software would be available instantly.

Java allows the Web to become a programming platform. Without Java, new network programs have to be developed from the ground up. Before, if you wanted to develop an Internet-wide conferencing system, you had to develop an application that would run on the user's desktop. Your users would have to acquire the software and install it themselves. With a Java-ized Web, you would simply write an Applet and put it on your Web site. Anyone with a Java-enabled browser, such as Netscape 2.0, would have whatever level of access to the software that you allow. Your distribution costs drop to nothing. Also, the development would be easier because the Java language was designed for distributed network computing.

This is what makes Java, in the words of Mark Andresseen, "as revolutionary as the Web itself." Given a Web server, anyone who can write a Web page can add information to the Web. With Java, any programmer can add to the Web's very infrastructure. The Web will not grow only in terms of content. It now has the capability of evolving itself. Instead of your bank or travel agent merely having information online, the future will see you being able to do all your banking and booking an entire trip from your computer. The Applets that you will use will have interfaces of equal or better quality then any other application on your desktop. Plus, you won't have to download them and install them on your computer; they will be instantly downloaded when you access the particular Web site.

What Java Can Do Beyond the Web

It is important to know that Java is not just a part of the Web. It is a complete, object-oriented, programming language designed to overcome some of the limitations of C++.

Right now, Applets as we know them can only run in some Web browsers. But Applets aren't bound just to Web browsers. Any application that sits on your desktop can be upgraded to connect to the Web and make use of special Applets.

Imagine that your spreadsheet program can deal with special Applets. One of these special Java Applets can talk to a server sitting on Wall Street. When the price of one of your stocks changes, the server tells the Java Applet, and the Java Applet updates your spreadsheet automatically.

Now your formulas that deal with stock prices always deal with live data. They deal with live data because when you open up your spreadsheet, it downloads this Applet that puts the appropriate stock prices into the places they are supposed to be. No longer do you have to look up the prices and enter them into your spreadsheet. They are already there, and they are current. When you take your report to your meeting, the data is as current as when you printed it out.

Still, this isn't the end of what Java can do for the Internet and the programming world. You may or may not turn your computer off when you leave for home. Could you be persuaded to leave your computer on all night if it could help solve some massive problem, like global warming?

Consider the following scenario: a central computer checks with your computer at some appointed time, a few hours after you go home. If it isn't busy, it sends an Applet across the Internet. Your computer runs that Applet all night. When you come in the next morning and press a key, your computer sends the Applet back across the Internet to the central "problem server." The problem server takes the data that has been crunched and incorporates it into a database. With the help of your computer and thousands of others, the problem is eventually solved. Better yet, the research institution working on this problem didn't have to go buy several supercomputers to solve it. And you were able to help solve a problem like global warming by simply going home.

The thrust of these examples is based on a simple fact: there is a lot of information and a lot of processing power on the millions of computers all over the world. What Java does is allow computers to access and deal with all of that information safely. There is no reason that you should have to manually insert data into a program when it is available on the Internet. Your computer is capable of getting the data and inserting it. Along the same lines, there is no reason that your computer should sit idle when there are pressing problems to be solved. The use of Java in software cannot not only make the end user's life easier, it can bring all of the computers on the Internet into a true working community.

How Java Works in Netscape 2.0

Netscape 2.0 has the ability to run Java Applets. Because of how it is set up, a Java Applet knows next to nothing about your computer. This means that you don't have to worry about a Java Applet doing damage to your computer. But if you just want to see cool Applets, you don't need to know anything about it. If this is all you want to do, just read the following section, "How To Access Java Applets With Netscape 2.0," and start exploring.

Note

At press time, Netscape 2.0 could run Applets only on the following platforms:

- Windows 95
- Solaris
- SunOS
- Irix

How to Access Java Applets with Netscape 2.0

There is nothing complicated about accessing Applets with Netscape 2.0. After your browser is set up correctly, you don't need to configure anything to enable Java. To the user, an Applet is simply a part of a Web page, just as an image or text can be. In the case that a page contains an image, the browser takes care of getting that image and displaying it. With a Java-enabled browser, the same is true with Applets. When you access a Web page that has an Applet embedded in it, the browser fetches the code and takes care of running it.

Running an Applet is not hard. It takes no advanced planning or configuring. As long as your version of Netscape 2.0 is Java enabled, you can just point your Web browser at a page that contains the Applet you want. There is a list of Web sites at the end of this chapter that have Java Applet pages. As long as these Java pages don't tell you that your browser doesn't support Java, you are ready to start exploring the Java-ized Web.

> **Caution**
>
> Some Java Applets cannot be accessed by Netscape 2.0, even if your version supports Java Applet handling. This is because many Java Applets were written while Java was still being developed. Those Java Applets are not compatible with the current standard.

How Netscape Runs Java Applets

Now let's look at the technical issues involved in running an Applet. When Netscape encounters an HTML page with an APPLET tag, it retrieves the compiled Java classes from the remote server in the same way that it retrieves any other object. After the Applet has been downloaded across the network onto your machine, it is subjected to various security checks before it is actually loaded and run. These checks are performed by the *Java verifier*. After the code is checked, it is loaded into its own place in the Netscape's Applet runtime environment. This is done by the *Java class loader*. This loading is done in such a way that an Applet is kept separate from system resources and other Applets.

> **Note**
>
> In object-oriented languages, *classes* are the definitions of objects. When a programmer is writing his program, he writes a class. When the program is run, the computer takes that definition and creates an object.

Because Java code is platform independent, it must be interpreted, or translated, into instructions that your machine can understand. This translation is performed by the *Java interpreter*. The Java interpreter can be thought of as a special viewer application that allows Netscape 2.0 to run Applets inline.

This whole process disallows the Applet from harming your computer in any way. This is explained further in the next section on Java and safety, "Why Java Applets Won't Harm Your Computer."

Why Java Applets Won't Harm Your Computer

The idea of your machine executing code fragments downloaded from a public network most likely makes your stomach a bit uneasy. People often ask if a Java Applet could erase their files or propagate a virus into their computer. Luckily, safe execution was a major consideration from the very start of making Java.

The Java language, and the technology Netscape 2.0 uses to run Applets, provides many defenses against malicious Applets. These strict language security mechanisms, coupled with Netscape 2.0's watchful eye, create an environment in which code can be run on your machine with virtually no chance of it accessing your private data or starting a virus.

The Java Console Window

Many programmers write their Applets so that they print out messages while they are executing. Usually, this information helps the programmer see whether or not an Applet is encountering problems. In Netscape 2.0, the Java Console window provides a way for you to view the direct output of an Applet as it is running. Just select Show Java Console Window from the Options menu. The Java Console window pops up as shown in figure 33.6.

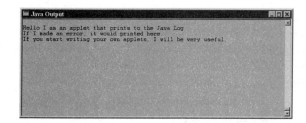

Fig. 33.6
The Java Console window.

Later, if you write your own Applets, this window is your way of keeping tabs on your Applet during the development process. If you need to, you can copy from this window and paste in another document.

The Four Layers of Defense

Java contains multiple layers of security, each serving to filter out harmful code. This section will provide you with a firm understanding of how Java's security layers serve to protect your machine. At the same time, this section will give you the security background necessary to program your own Applets.

The four layers of security built into Java and Netscape are as follows:

- The Java language and compiler
- Java bytecode verification and strong type information
- Java's class loader
- Restrictions on local file system and network access

Safety Layer One: The Java Language's Defenses

The first layer of safety in the Java language comes from its lack of the harmful language and compiler features that C and C++ both possess. Java does not allow the programmer to directly manipulate memory. C and C++ do allow direct manipulation of memory, which means that a careless programmer can manipulate memory that the system has reversed for its use. This is the usual cause for a system crash. A malicious programmer can also use this weakness to propagate a virus.

Let's focus on how the Java Applet interacts with Netscape 2.0 after it is downloaded. The fundamental line of defense is that Netscape 2.0 keeps the Java Applet from dealing with a specific memory address on your computer. Of course, a Java Applet does use your computer's memory. It is just that Netscape 2.0 won't let an Applet look at or write to a specific memory address. If the Applet needs to change something in that data, it hands its changes back to Netscape 2.0 (see fig. 33.7). Netscape 2.0 actually changes the data in memory.

Unlike C and C++, the structure of the Java language requires this interpreter. With a C or C++ program, the programmer might not be malicious or careless and maybe he used an advanced compiler that won't produce evil programs. You don't have to hope that a Java program won't harm your computer; the interpreter simply won't allow it. Because a Java program must access memory through the interpreter, that interpreter is in complete control. Netscape 2.0 acts as a firewall between a Java Applet and your computer. It does this by isolating the program from the rest of the system and acting as its guardian. By forcing a Java program to obey its guardian, the Java language itself keeps the program from misbehaving and harming your system.

Besides direct memory manipulation, the Java language also deals very carefully with casting. *Casting* allows a programmer to change one data type to another, even if this shouldn't be done. In C++, a programmer is able to cast a complex object to a much simpler type, like an array of bytes. Generally, doing this is an error and causes the program to crash. However, a malicious programmer can use this to change the object itself. He can overwrite the individual bytes that make up the object so that it does something that the language doesn't allow. The Java language only allows the programmer to cast between types when it makes sense to cast. It checks all attempts to cast very carefully, while C and C++ allow the programmer to cast between literally any two data types. Java's strong checking of casting closes the back door on the type of memory manipulation described earlier.

These are the ways that the Java language itself assures a certain degree of safety for all Java programs. But these features aren't enough to prevent an Applet from harming your computer. This layer is just the foundation for the other layers of safety in the Java environment. You will now see why this layer means very little without the support of the following layers.

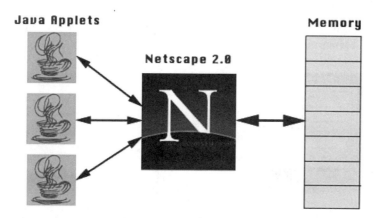

Java Applets

Netscape 2.0

Memory

Fig. 33.7
How a Java Applet
accesses memory.

Safety Layer Two: Making Sure the Applet Isn't Faking It

After a Java, C, or C++ program is written, the author compiles it. For C and C++, the compilation process produces an executable file. This file can be loaded into your computer's memory and run. Most programs on your desktop have been created through this process.

Java is a semi-compiled language, and its compilation process is different. When Java is compiled, the compiler produces platform independent machine instructions called *bytecodes*. These bytecodes are what Netscape retrieves from a remote server, and then executes on your machine (see fig. 33.8). Because a compiler can easily be altered to bypass the first level of security, these bytecodes must be subjected to strong tests before being executed on your machine.

The second layer of safety accomplishes this. When Netscape 2.0 downloads an Applet, the bytecode of that Applet is examined by the your browser's verifier.

The verifier subjects each code fragment to a sequence of tests before it is allowed to execute. It first looks to see that the bytecode has all of the information about the different data types that are going to be used. There is actually more of this type of information than strictly necessary. This excess of information helps the verifier analyze the rest of the bytecode.

It is possible for a malicious programmer to write a Java compiler that doesn't follow all the rules of the Java language. He could write it so that it produces code that tricks the compiler into harming your computer. The verifier ensures that no such code ever reaches the interpreter. It checks to make sure that the bytecode plays by the rules of the Java language, and protects the integrity of the interpreter.

Fig. 33.8
How Java Applets run.

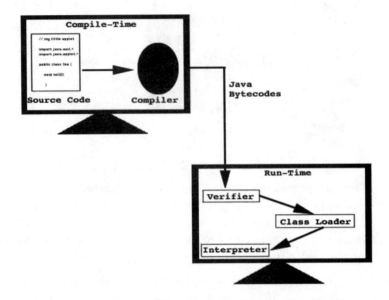

Safety Layer Three: Keeping an Applet Separate

The class loader offers Java's third line of defense. As independent pieces of code are loaded and executed, the class loader makes sure that different Applets can't interfere with each other. It also means that each and every Applet is completely separate from the Java objects already resident that it needs actually run. This means that an Applet can't go and replace parts of Netscape 2.0 needed to run Applets.

If it could replace these parts, all layers of safety could be undermined. All Applets depend on the interpreter to provide it with some of the basic constructs of the Java language. If the Applets aren't kept strictly separate, an Applet can override some of these basic constructs. By overriding these basic constructs, the Applet can violate the integrity of the Java language itself, and trick the interpreter into hurting your system.

Safety Layer Four: Protecting Your File System

The fourth level of defense against harmful Applets comes in the form of file system access protection. Applets are restricted from any access to the local file system, so they can neither read your files, overwrite your existing files, nor generate new ones. This not only protects your privacy, but also prevents your files from being corrupted or infected by viruses.

The interpreter protects your computer's safety by simply disallowing all Java language calls that deal with files. The Java language itself, being equivalent to C++, does have the ability to deal with a file system. But the interpreter in Netscape 2.0 won't allow Applets to have that capability. If an Applet tries to open a file, the interpreter just tells the Applet that the file system does not exist.

> **Note**
>
> The Java language ensures that a Java program can only affect your system in safe ways. Even if someone troubled himself to write a fake Java compiler, the verifier in Netscape 2.0 would figure it out and refuse to run the Applet. The class loader makes sure that Applets are kept separate from your system and other Applets. To top it all off, the interpreter doesn't even allow an Applet to access the file system. This means that an Applet only knows about the Netscape 2.0 Applet runtime environment, and can't access any part of your computer beyond that.

Including Java Applets in Web Pages: The APPLET Tag

Including an Applet in a Web document is accomplished via an extension to HTML called the APPLET tag. This tag, along with the PARAM tag, allows the Web page designer to include and configure executable content in documents. The general syntax for including an Applet in a Web page is as follows:

```
<APPLET CODEBASE=codebaseURL  CODE=appletFile.class WIDTH=pixels
HEIGHT=pixels>
<PARAM NAME=someAttributeName VALUE=1st_attributeValue>
<PARAM NAME=someOtherAttributeName VALUE=Nth_attributeValue>
{Alternate HTML displayed by non-java enabled browsers}
</APPLET>
```

The following are the definitions of the various tags:

- APPLET—Signifies that an Applet is to be included in the document.
- CODEBASE—The path, to the classes directory containing the Java code. If this field is omitted, then the CODEBASE is assumed to be the same as the document's URL.
- CODE—The name of the Applet to be included in your page. This file always ends in .class, which indicates that it is a compiled Java class. It should be noted that this variable is relative to the Applet's base URL and should not be given as absolute.

- ■ HEIGHT and WIDTH—The dimensions in units of pixels that the Applet takes up on your Web page.
- ■ PARAM—Used to pass a parameter to an Applet.
- ■ NAME—The name of the parameter. This name must be understood by the Applet.
- ■ VALUE—The value that corresponds to a given name. This is where you may enter your configurations.

As shown above, alternate HTML can be included between the open and close APPLET tags. This code is intended to be displayed if the person who accesses your page is not using a Java-enabled browser, such as Netscape 2.0. If Netscape 2.0 can't download the Java Applet, it shows the alternate HTML.

If the browser can run the Java Applet, then the alternate text is not shown. This feature comes in very handy when designing pages for an audience mixed between Java-enabled and non-Java-enabled browsers.

> **Tip**
>
> When including Applets in your Web pages, use alternate HTML inside the APPLET tag as a courtesy to people whose browsers are not Java-enabled.

The PARAM tag makes it possible for Web page designers to configure an Applet to their special needs. This feature allows Applets to be written as generalized tools that can be configured to work in many different situations. Someone who has no desire to learn all of the details of programming Applets can customize other people's Java Applets to fit his own needs. For example, a simple animation Applet can be told which sequence of images it should load and display. Because such an Applet can be configured, may people can run different animations using the same code. You can imagine that without the PARAM tag, using Java would become much more difficult for designers. If Applets were not configurable, in the case of the animation Applet, individual designers would each have to customize their own copy of the program.

Let's look now at a simple example which shows how to include a configurable Applet in a Web page. For simplicity, we will use the Blinking Text example from the Java Product Development Team. This Applet displays a text string in multiple colors and then blinks each word at random. It takes two parameters, lbl is the text string that is displayed and speed is the rate at which the text blinks.

To include this Applet in one of your Web pages, add this code:

```
<HR>
<APPLET
CODEBASE="http://www.javasoft.com/JDK-prebeta1/applets/Blink/"
CODE="Blink.class" WIDTH=300 HEIGHT=130>
<PARAM NAME=lbl VALUE="Configuring Applets is easy and very useful.
 with Netscape 2.0, we can make an applet do what WE WANT!">
<PARAM NAME=speed VALUE="4">
Sorry, you should be using Netscape 2.0. <BR>
Your browser is not Java enabled!!!!
</APPLET>
<HR>
```

Figure 33.9 shows what you should see when you load your page, if you are using Netscape 2.0.

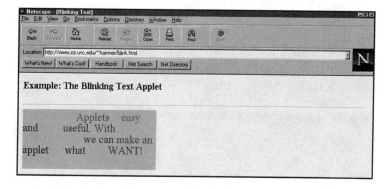

Fig. 33.9
Results of configuration.

In this example, the Blinking Text Applet is loaded from a remote site (**http://www.javasoft.com**, in this case). This shows that you are not obligated to download the Applet onto your own machine just to include it on a Web page. As always, when including someone else's work in your pages, you should make sure you have the permission of the author first.

Note

It is impossible to describe, generally, how Java Applets should be configured. It is totally up to the author of a Java Applet to decide how the Applet may be configured and to provide documentation for the Applet user.

Examples of Java Applets on the Internet

In the short time that Java has been alive, the World Wide Web has come to life with clever Java programs. Here are a few examples that show the kind of stuff that Java can do for the Web. Be sure to point Netscape 2.0 at the URLs to see them in action.

Entertainment and Games on the Web

Because so much of the Web is designed to entertain, it isn't surprising that people have been writing Applets to further the cause. Many Applets are designed to spice up Web pages. Probably the most common example is the use of Applets to embed animation into a Web page.

Many Applets let us play games over the Web. For example, Applets for mine sweeper and tic-tac-toe have been written. The Applet shown in figure 33.10 lets you fill in a crossword puzzle. It has a couple of advantages over the crossword puzzle in your daily newspaper. First, you don't have to strain to find the clue; you just click the mouse in the box. The clue appears at the top. Second, it gives you feedback. Incorrect responses are displayed in red, while correct ones are shown in black.

Fig. 33.10
Java crossword puzzle.

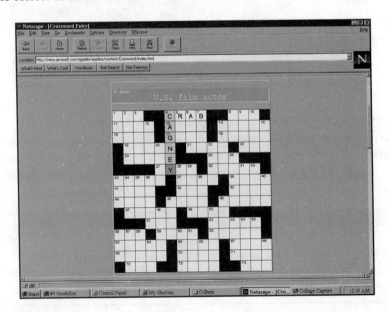

Crossword purists may not consider these improvements, but it is a good example of how Applets add interactivity to the Web.

Educational Java Applets

Java is providing new opportunities in education that were never before possible. Now an educator can write an Applet that demonstrates some complex subject. His demonstration can be interactive and instantly available to a worldwide audience.

A great example of the educational potential of Java is the Applet shown in figure 33.11.

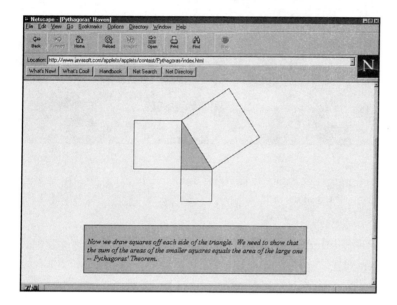

Fig. 33.11
Interactive mathematical proof.

This Applet walks us through the Pythagorean Theorem. In case you don't remember your geometry, the Pythagorean Theorem is the one that proves that the lengths of the sides of a right triangle are related.

Real World Business Applications

The ease with which Applets can deal with data on a remote computer makes them a good fit with the information needs of companies. Additionally, Applets can also provide a good interface to services provided by a company.

The example shown in figure 33.12 was created by the Java Product Development Team. For this particular demo, the stock prices are randomly generated by a remote server. They could just as easily come from a server that has the correct data. We can expect that a service providing real stock prices will be available soon from some enterprising Web site.

Fig. 33.12
Real time financial
portfolio.

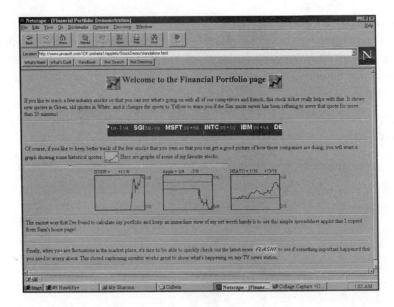

Many companies outside the software industry are exploring the usefulness of
Java. Some of these include:

- Dow Jones
- Internet Underground Music Archive
- NBC
- Random House

Where to Find More Info on Java

Sun maintains a complete set of documentation on Java at **http://
www.javasoft.com**. At this site, you can find everything from language
documentation to tutorials. Yahoo has a rather extensive index of pointers to
Java resources. You can find this listing at **http://www.yahoo.com/
Computers_and_Internet/Languages/Java**.

Finding Java Applets

If it is Java Applets you seek, then check out the Gamelan site at **http://
www.gamelan.com/**. This site acts as a registry of Applets. It contains
links to hundreds of Applets, all categorized by subject.

The Java Development Team also maintains their own listing of Applets
which can be found at **http://www.javasoft.com/Applets**.

Language References

The definitive overview of the Java language is the Java Language White Paper, written by the Java Development Team. It is at **http://www.javasoft.com/whitePaper/javawhitepaper_1.html**.

The Java Development Team also has an online overview of the security features inherent to Applets. It is available at **http://www.javasoft.com/1.0alpha3/doc/security/security.html**.

Newsgroups and Mailing Lists

For information specific about Java, you should regularly read the newsgroup comp.lang.java at **news:comp.lang.java**.

Sun Microsystems, the inventor of Java and Applets, also maintains a mailing list concerning Java. To subscribe, send mail to **majordomo@www.javasoft.com**, and enter **subscribe java-interest@www.javasoft.com** *<your email address>* in the body of the message. Replace <your email address> with your full Internet e-mail address.

Other Resources

J*** Notes, produced by Mentor Software Solutions, is a well-formatted, easy-to-read summary of the newsgroups and mailing lists pertaining to Java and Java Applets. Information is updated weekly and broken down into categories. You can find J*** Notes at **http://www.io.org/~mentor/JavaNotes.html**.

V

Netscape Customization

## CHAPTER 34

Java for C++ Programmers

Java is a new language and set of class libraries developed by Sun Microsystems. In its white paper on the language, Sun defines Java as "a simple, object-oriented, distributed, interpreted, robust, secure, architecture-neutral, portable, high-performance, multithreaded, and dynamic language." That's quite a definition! We'll look at exactly what Sun means by it in this chapter.

There is no way to cover every component of the Java language in one chapter. This chapter gives an introduction to the Java language and takes a look at its basic structure and classes.

In this chapter, you learn:

- Java fundamentals
- How Java differs from C and C++
- A basic Java program
- Java syntax
- Java's class library

The World According to Java

Until now, the various pages on the Web have been fairly static in their ability to interact with the user. With the current conventional Web tools, it's not easy to provide real-time interaction with a user without performing a lot of CPU processing on your Web server. For example, animation sequences require server push operations to send the new images out to the client browser program.

Another problem with the current paradigm is that you, the user—or your poor system administrator—has to keep up with all the different helper applications that you need to really use Netscape to its fullest. Now, how many of you have the latest versions of all your helper apps installed and configured?

Sun Microsystems raised the ante in the Web game when it introduced the Java language and the HotJava Web browser. The goal of Java is to provide a development language that is uniquely suited to developing Web applications. At the same time, Java gives you the ability to deliver both data content and a small application that manipulates the data to the client browser in real time. These small applications, known as *applets*, are downloaded to a user's computer and activated by his Web browser transparently whenever the user views a page that contains an applet. This keeps the promise of no longer needing to download and configure helper applications for all the different types of data that you want to view.

Java is uniquely suited for developing Web applications, and provides support for parallelism by supporting multithreading. Also, Java is a multi-platform language: any Java applet or application will run directly on any platform that supports the Java runtime system. We'll look at how this works later in the chapter.

Current Java Information

Since Java is a new language with lots of new features, it can be difficult to get current information on Java. As this book is being written, the Java Development Kit is in beta release from Sun Microsystems. It has gone through both an alpha and pre-beta incarnation stage. Supposedly, the methods for building applets and the API for the Java classes have been finalized—but be prepared for future changes just in case.

The best source for up-to-the-minute information on Java and the Java development tools is the Sun Microsystem Java Web site. It can be found on the Web at **http://java.sun.com/**. From this location, you can get the Java Development Kit (JDK), the documentation for the JDK in both HTML and PostScript format, all the documentation for programming the JDK API, and a whole series of lessons on learning to program in Java.

Java Language Features

Java was designed to be an object-oriented language similar to C++ to make it familiar to a large number of programmers. As you see later in the chapter, the syntax of Java is very similar to C++. Because Java is an object-oriented language, this chapter assumes that you are familiar with basic object-oriented concepts, such as classes and inheritance.

> **Note**
>
> In Java, the basic object-oriented programming element is the *class*. A class is a collection of related data members and functions, known as *methods*, that operate on that data. Everything in Java exists within a class—there are no global variables or global functions.

In developing Java, Sun chose to leave out several C++ language features. Specifically, Java does not support multiple inheritance, operator overloading, or extensive automatic coercion. Java also takes steps to make pointer operations much safer. Java's pointer model does not allow memory overwrites and data corruption. In fact, Java does not allow pointer arithmetic at all. It supports true arrays with bounds checking. You cannot change an integer to a pointer via a cast operator. In short, Java eliminates many of the confusing, often misused aspects of C++ and creates a smaller, easier to understand language.

Let's look at some of the new features that Java adds. The language has support for automatic garbage collection, so you no longer have to explicitly delete an object. Objects are automatically deleted whenever they are no longer needed. Java has extensive support for distributed applications. It has native support for the TCP/IP protocols, which allows programmers to easily work with objects as URLs.

Because Java was designed with native support for client/server applications, security is obviously an issue. Java has extensive security support to allow you to create tamper-free systems. Java uses a public-key encryption scheme to provide authentication, and its new pointer model makes it impossible to overwrite secure areas of memory.

If you look back to Sun's definition of Java, you are probably wondering about the architecture-neutral and portable part. Well, Java is really a bytecode-based interpreted language.

Bytecodes are essentially the components of a machine language. They are similar to the object files that you get when you compile a C++ program with your favorite compiler. However, the "machine" language that these bytecodes represent isn't a real machine at all. Bytecodes are really elements of a machine language for an imaginary machine.

By turning a Java program into bytecodes for an imaginary machine language, the bytecodes are not tied to any one computer hardware platform. In fact, they need a special interpreter program to convert them into actual machine instructions for the destination computer.

Why do it this way? A couple of different reasons. First, by not having the bytecodes represent an actual machine, the compiled Java file is not restricted to any one type of computer. Second, because the bytecode machine language is for an imaginary machine, the designers were able to avoid design problems that are specific to the various types of computers. They were able to design their machine language in a very efficient way, so that even though Java files must be run through an interpreter, they are still very efficient.

When a Java program is compiled, it creates a bytecode image that is interpreted by a Java runtime system. Because this bytecode image has nothing to do with the architecture that the Java program was built on, it will run on any platform that has a Java runtime environment. This means that you only have to write a Java program once—that one version is portable to any platform with the Java runtime environment!

In addition to being architecture-neutral, Java eliminates all platform-specific data types that have plagued C programmers for years. None of the primitive data types are architecture dependent. All of them have specified sizes and arithmetic operations. For example, a `float` is always an IEEE 754 32-bit floating point number—on any platform.

A common problem with object-oriented development is that when a company releases a new version of a library, all client software that uses that library will have to be recompiled and redistributed. Java was designed to allow classes to add new methods and instance variables with no effect on the client applications.

As you can see, Java truly is an object-oriented distributed language that solves a lot of problems with current object-oriented technology.

Java Development

In order to develop Java applets and applications, you need a copy of the Java Development Kit (JDK). At the time this book went to press, the JDK is in Beta release and is available on Windows 95 and NT and Sun Solaris 2.x platforms. A Macintosh port of the JDK is under development. You can get the JDK from the Sun Microsystems Java Web site at **http://java.sun.com/**.

The process of turning Java source code into compiled Java bytecodes is performed by the Java compiler, *javac*. To compile a Java program, write your code using your favorite text editor and save it in ASCII text format. The name of the file must have a .JAVA extension. Then, compile the file by typing

```
javac filename.java
```

where *filename.java* is the name of your Java source code file. For each class that is defined in your Java source file, the javac compiler generates a file named *classname.class* where *classname* is the name of the particular class. For complete details of the Java compilation process, see the online documentation for Java programmers at **http://java.sun.com/doc/ programmer.html**.

> **Note**
>
> Java places exactly one class in each bytecode compiled .class file.

After you have compiled your Java application into a .class file, you can run the file with the Java bytecode interpreter, which is, coincidentally, named java. To do this, you run the java command followed by the name of the .class file that has the main() method for your Java application. For example:

```
java myclass.class
```

This command would start the Java runtime environment and cause it to execute the file myclass.class.

Much of Java's functionality is encapsulated in pre-written collections of classes known as *packages*. These packages are provided with the Java development environment. Each of these packages contains several different classes that are related to a particular topic.

Table 34.1 lists the packages in the Java development library at the time this book was written. Packages prefixed with java are actual Java language classes. The other classes are HotJava classes, used in the development of Sun's HotJava browser.

Table 34.1   Java Packages in the Development Library

Package name	Description
java.lang	Basic language support classes
java.util	Utility classes such as encoders and decoders

(continues)

Table 34.1 Continued	
Package name	**Description**
java.io	Different types of I/O streams
java.awt	A platform-independent windowing system
java.awt.image	Class for handling images in the AWT windowing system
java.applet	Class for building applets to run within Web browsers
java.net	Support for TCP/IP networking

Hello World

We start our exploration of Java with an example that almost all good programming languages use—the Hello World program. In Java, there are two different types of programs: *applications* and *applets*. An application is designed to run directly in the Java runtime environment. An applet is designed to run as a component of a network browser, such as Netscape Navigator. Of the two, applications are a bit simpler in structure.

The concept of the "Java runtime environment" gets a bit fuzzy here. As you saw in the previous section, there is a stand-alone Java interpreter, java, that executes a bytecode-compiled file. This is how applications are executed. Applets, on the other hand, are designed to run within the context of a Web browser like Netscape. Applets require more complicated programming than applications because they are actually running within the context of another program. This other program, Netscape in this case, actually has a version of the Java interpreter embedded within it. This means that when Netscape executes a Java applet, it is actually acting as the Java runtime environment for the applet.

Here is the Java code for the Hello World application:

```
class HelloApp
{
        public static void main(String args[])
        {
                System.out.println("Hello World!");
        }
}
```

In Java, all functions and variables exist within a class object; there are no global functions or variables in a Java application. So, the first line of this sample application defines a class named HelloApp.

Inside `HelloApp`'s definition, there is one method called `main`. The `main` method is the method that is invoked when the application's execution is started in the Java runtime environment. Because you have to specify the class that you want to execute in the Java runtime environment, Java invokes the `main` method for that class.

The `main` method is declared to be `public static void`. The `public` keyword means that the `main` method is visible to all other classes outside this class. The `static` keyword indicates that `main` is a *static* method, which means that `main` is associated directly with the class `HelloApp` instead of with an instance of `HelloApp`. Without the `static` keyword, `main` would have been an *instance* method—a method that is associated with an instance of a class. We'll look at another example in a minute.

The next line of code in the `main` method appears to print the "Hello World" string as output. So what exactly is `System.out.println`? `System` refers to Java's `System` class. The word `out` is an instance variable in the `System` class, and `println` is one of `out`'s methods. Notice that we never declared an instance of the `System` class; we just called `out.println` directly. That is because `out` is a static variable of the `System` class. We can refer to it directly by just referring to the class itself.

Command Line Arguments

You'll notice that the arguments to `main` are different than they are in a regular C or C++ program. Instead of the traditional `argv` and `argc` arguments, Java gives you an array of strings that contains the command line arguments. This is not an array of pointers as it is under C and C++, but an array of real strings. You can get the length of the array with the `.length` function of the `String` class. For example, the length of the command line argument array is `args.length`.

Another major difference between Java and C++ is that the name of the application program is not passed in the command line argument array. The name of the application program is always the same as the class name where the `main` method is defined. So, while under C++, for example:

```
foo arg1 arg2
```

running the program foo with two arguments would make the first entry in the command line argument array "foo." While under Java:

```
java foo arg1 arg2
```

The word `java` invokes the runtime environment, and the word `foo` is the class that has `main` defined. Thus, the first argument in the command line arguments array, `args[0]`, is "arg1."

Introduction to Classes

Classes form the basic program component in Java. Every function and variable must be contained in a class. There are no global functions or variables supported by Java. Here is an example of a Java class declaration:

```
/** latitude and longitude of a location **/
public class Location
{
    int lat, long;   //latitude and longitude
    ...
}
```

This Java code segment declares a class named `Location`, which contains two instance variables that hold the latitude and longitude of some location.

> **Note**
>
> In this example, the ellipses (. . .) just means that there could be additional members or variables—we just didn't write them in the example.

You might have noticed that this class doesn't appear to have any parent class. In Java, all classes are subclasses of the class `Object`. So the above code sample is identical to:

```
/** latitude and longitude of a location **/
public class Location extends Object
{
    int lat, long;   //latitude and longitude
    ...
}
```

In this example, the `extends` keyword is used to indicate that the new class, `Location`, is a subclass of the class `Object`. In effect, it *extends* the `Object` class by adding new features. We'll look at this more in the next section.

Subclassing and Inheritance

A subclass is a class that is derived from another class. To create a subclass, you use the `extends` keyword. This allows a new class to be created that adds or changes functionality from its base class. Take our example of the `Location` class:

```
/** latitude and longitude of a location **/
public class Location
```

```
{
    int lat, long;    //latitude and longitude
    ...
}
```

Let's create a subclass of `Location` that knows how to print the location. So, we then have:

```
/** printable Location **/
public class PrintLocation extends Location
{
    void print()
    {
    ...
    }
}
```

This example simply creates a subclass of `Location` called `PrintLocation` and adds a `print` method.

Access Specifiers

C++ programmers will, by now, be wondering how Java supports class access specifiers. Java uses the `public`, `private`, and `protected` access specifiers like C++.

An access specifier states how visible an entity is during execution. In Java, these specifiers can be applied to a class, method, or variable. If an entity is declared `public`, it can be accessed from any class. If it is declared `private`, it can only be accessed from within the same class. A declaration of `protected` means that the variable can be accessed by the same class and any of its subclasses, but not by any external classes. If no access specifier is given, the entity is given `public` access within the package in which it is defined. We look at packages in a bit more detail later in the chapter.

Using `this` and `super`

Java provides two special variables to a class, which are known as `this` and `super`. The `this` variable is a reference to the current object. It is typically used when an object needs to pass a reference to itself to another method. For example:

```
/** latitude and longitude of a location **/
public class Location
{
    int lat, long;    //latitude and longitude
    ...
    void Plot(AnotherObject foo)
    {
        ...
        foo.DoSomething(this);
    }
}
```

In this example, the `Plot` method of the `Location` class calls the `DoSomething` method of `foo`, an object of class `AnotherObject`. `Location` passes a reference to itself, via the `this` variable, to `foo.DoSomething()`.

The `super` variable works the same way, except that it is a reference to a class's superclass. Remember that in Java there is no multiple inheritance, so there can be only one superclass for every class. In C++, there can be multiple superclasses, so there would be no way to know which class you are referring to with a `super` variable in C++.

Let's recap: In Java, the `Object` class is the ultimate superclass of all other classes. Each class can have, at most, one direct superclass, which can be referred to by the `super` keyword.

Constructors

A *constructor* is a special method that is used to initialize an object. It is indicated by being a method with the same name as the class itself and having no return value. A class can have more than one constructor, as long as they differ in the number or type of parameters. A constructor that takes no parameters is known as the *default* constructor. As in C++, a constructor is automatically called when an object is created.

You can call the constructor of a class's superclass by using the `super` special variable. You can explicitly place the call in your class's constructor. This is how you initialize the superclass's instance variables, for example. If you don't place an explicit call to a superclass constructor, Java will call the superclass's default constructor for you. Let's look at an example:

```
/** latitude and longitude of a location **/
public class Location
{
    int lat, long;   //latitude and longitude

    Location(int x, int y)    //constructor with 2 parameters
    {
        lat = x;
        long = y;
    }

    Location()              // default constructor
    {
        lat = 0;
        long = 0;
    }
}
/** printablelocation **/
public class PrintLocation extends Location
```

```
    {
        int foo;
        PrintLocation(int x, int y)
        {
            super(x,y);      // Calls Location(x,y)
            foo = 0;
        }
        PrintLocation()
        {
            foo=0;           // implicit call to Location()
        }
        void print()
        {
        ...
        }

    }
```

This example is a little bit more complicated than what you've seen before. We have expanded the PrintLocation class so that it subclasses the Location class. Both PrintLocation and Location each have two different constructors. If we create an instance of PrintLocation so that its default constructor is called, as in:

```
    blah = new PrintLocation();
```

the default constructor sets the foo instance variable of PrintLocation to be 0. Because there is no explicit call to PrintLocation's super class, Java calls the superclass's default constructor automatically.

On the other hand, if we create an instance of PrintLocation like this:

```
    blah = new PrintLocation(10,40);
```

the PrintLocation(x,y) constructor is called instead. This constructor makes a call to super(x,y), which calls PrintLocation's superclass constructor that takes two integer parameters. The default constructor of Location is not called in this case.

Comments, Operators, Types, and Identifiers

Now that you've seen how the basic class structure of Java works, it's time to look at some of the nuts and bolts of the language. You've already seen several of these components in the previous examples.

Types

Java supports five basic data *types*: integers, floating points, characters, booleans. You could argue that arrays are really a data type and should be discussed in this section. However, because arrays are also closely linked to Java classes, we will get to them in the next section.

Java supports four different sizes of integer data. All Java integers are signed. Unlike integers in other languages, none of the Java integer sizes are platform dependent. In Java, an 8-bit integer value is known as a *byte*, a 16-bit integer is a *short*, a 32-bit integer is an *int*, and a 64-bit integer is a *long*.

For floating point data types, Java supports both 32-bit single precision floating point and 64-bit double precision floating point. In order to preserve significant digits in floating point calculations, any operation that has at least one of its floating point operands as a double will give a result that is a double. Table 34.2 shows the numeric types in Java with their sizes.

Table 34.2 Sizes of the Java numeric data types		
Name	**Type**	**Size**
byte	integer	8 bits
short	integer	16 bits
int	integer	32 bits
long	integer	64 bits
float	floating point	32 bits
double	floating point	64 bits

The Java character set follows the Unicode standard character set. *Unicode* is an international character set standard that allows for direct support of non-Latin character sets, such as Chinese and Arabic. As such, all Java characters are 16-bit unsigned integers.

The boolean data type in Java denotes the result of logical boolean operations. This data type has two values: `true` and `false`.

> **Note**
>
> Booleans in Java, unlike C and C++, are not numbers. You cannot cast a boolean data type to be a number in Java.

Arrays

In some ways, Java *arrays* are similar to the arrays in C and C++, but there are very significant differences. Java uses arrays to replace pointer arithmetic. It is not possible to manipulate the pointer to an array and have it point somewhere else. Also, in Java, all arrays have bounds checking enabled, which prevents you from overwriting the end of your array and unintentionally creating self-modifying code!

> **Note**
>
> Under C++, you can do things like:
>
> ```
> int myarray[10];
> myarray[15] = 10;
> ```
>
> This code segment writes beyond the end of the allocated array and will probably crash your program. Java does not allow you to do this and will throw an exception if you try.

Java arrays are really classes, being a subclass of the Object class. As such, arrays are created explicitly with the new operator. For example,

```
int myint[] = new int[3];
```

creates an array of three integers named myint.

> **Note**
>
> Java arrays, like those in C and C++, are 0-based. This means that in an array of three integers, the elements will have subscripts: myint[0], myint[1], and myint[2].

Java does not allow explicit multidimensional arrays. Instead, you create arrays of arrays. For example,

```
int myint[][] = new int[3][5];
```

is used to simulate an integer array with dimensions 3 by 5.

Identifiers

An *identifier* is a symbolic indicator, such as a variable, that represents some value. In Java, identifiers must start with an underscore (_), a dollar sign ($), a character in the set "A" to "Z" inclusive, a character in the set "a" to "z" inclusive, or a Unicode character with a value greater than 00C0.

After the first character, the identifier can include digits and any character that is not reserved as a Unicode special character.

Operators

Java has a rich set of operators. You will find that they are very similar to operators in C++. Table 34.3 shows the order of precedence of operators in Java.

Table 34.3   Operator Order of Precedence from Highest to Lowest
Operators
. [] ()
++ −− ! ~ instanceof
* / %
+ -
<< >> >>>
< > <= >=
== !=
&
^
|
&&
||
?:
= op=
,

Integer Operations

When performing operations on integer values, if any element in the operation is a long the result will be a long. Table 34.4 lists the operations for integers.

Table 34.4 Operations for Integers	
Operator	**Definition**
-	Unary negation
~	Bitwise Compliment
++	Auto increment
−−	Auto decrement

Operator	Definition
+	Addition
-	Subtraction
*	Multiplication
/	Division
%	Modulus
<<	Shift left
>>	Shift right
>>>	Shift right with zero fill
&	Bitwise AND
¦	Bitwise OR
^	Bitwise XOR

Boolean Operations

Boolean, or logical, *operations*, work virtually identically to those in C. The bitwise logical operators &, |, and ^ force evaluation of both sides of a logical expression. You can shortcut the evaluation of the right side of the expression by using the && and || operators. Table 34.5 shows the boolean operations available under Java.

Table 34.5 Boolean Operations in Java

Operator	Definition
&	Bitwise AND. Forces evaluation of both sides of operation.
		Bitwise OR. Forces evaluation of both sides of operation.
^	Bitwise XOR. Forces evaluation of both sides of operation.
&&	Shortcut AND. Does not force evaluation of both sides of operation.
||	Shortcut OR. Does not force evaluation of both sides of operation.
!	Logical negation.
==	Logical equality.
!=	Logical inequality.
&=	Logical AND and assignment.
|=	Logical OR and assignment.
^=	Logical XOR and assignment.
?:	If-then-else ternary operator.

Comments

In Java, there are three different ways to specify a comment in a source file. You can use the original C syntax of /* */ to bracket your comments, in which all characters between the two comment indicators are ignored. You can also use the C++ style comments indicated by // . This causes Java to ignore all characters following the // to the end of the current line.

The third style of comments is indicated by bracketing text with the /** and **/ symbols. All text between these symbols is ignored. This style of comment should only be used immediately before a declaration. The comments between the /** and **/ symbols are used in automatically generated documentation and are taken to be a description of the immediately following code.

Literals

A *literal* is an entity that represents the actual value of an integer, boolean, string, floating point, or character value.

Integer Literals

For *integer literals*, Java supports literals in base-10 (decimal), base-8 (octal), or base-16 (hexadecimal). A decimal literal is a sequence of numbers without a leading 0. If a number has a leading 0 and only the digits 0 through 7, Java interprets it as an octal number. Hexadecimal numbers are prefixed by 0x and can include the digits 0 through 9 and the letters A through F.

Floating Point Literals

A *floating point literal* uses scientific notation to represent the number. It consists of a decimal integer, a decimal point, another decimal integer representing a fraction, the letter e or E, an integer exponent that may be signed, and a type suffix. Java supports both single and double precision floating point. A d or D character as the type suffix indicates a double precision floating point value. If the type suffix is an f, F, or is not specified, the number is a single precision floating point value.

To simplify things, here is an example:

```
2.0E14, 3.1e3f, 3.6e-6F          single precision

3.1e4D, 0.12E3d                  double precision
```

Character Literals

Java supports *character literals* by enclosing the character in single quotes. Like C and C++, Java also has support for a set of special, nongraphical characters. Table 34.6 shows the special characters that you can use in Java.

Table 34.6 Java Special Character Support	
Character	**Definition**
\b	Backspace
\f	Form feed
\n	Newline
\r	Carriage return
\t	Tab character
\ddd	Octal value
\xddd	Hexadecimal value
\udddd	Unicode value

In addition, you can represent the backslash, single quote, and double quote characters as character literals by prefixing the character with a backslash. So, a backslash literal is \ \, a single quote literal is \ ', and a double quote literal is \ ".

String Literals

A *string literal* is represented as a sequence of characters enclosed in double quotes. Every string literal is an instance of the String class. String literals can be continued as multiline strings by using a \ character as a continuation.

Boolean Literals

Of all the literals, booleans are the simplest. *Boolean literals* consist of two values, true and false.

Statements

Okay, you've fought your way through all that information about literals, operators, and identifiers. Now it's time to start learning how the various parts of Java work together.

Declarations

A *declaration* is an indicator to the Java compiler that you are going to use a data type. You are declaring that a certain variable is of a particular data type. For example:

```
int     i;
float myFloat;
```

are both declarations for simple data types. In this case, they declare variables of type int and float, respectively.

Declarations are also used to define variables that are class objects or arrays. In these cases, the declaration does not allocate any space for these objects. You must use the new operator to actually create an object. For example:

```
Location myLocation;
```

does not actually create an object of type Location. To do that, you would need to do:

```
Location myLocation;
myLocation = new Location();
```

Similarly,

```
int myInt[];
```

does not create an array of integers. To actually create the array, you would need to do:

```
int myInt[];
myInt = new int[10];
```

Java declarations can appear anywhere that statements can appear, and have a scope that is valid for the duration of the enclosing block. The enclosing block is denoted by the surrounding curly braces { and }.

Control Statements

Java gives you a variety of control structures to specify the flow of control through your program. Most of these are virtually identical to those found in C.

The conditional statement structure is identical to the if structure in C and C++. For example:

```
if (a==1)
{
    // do something
}
else
```

```
{
    // do something else
}
```

The Java multi-way conditional branch is the switch statement. As in C, you
switch on a variable and have a case entry for each possible value. There is
a default label that matches if none of the other case labels match. For
example:

```
switch(foo)
{
    case 1:
        break;      // do something;
    case 2:
        break;      // do something else;
    case 3:
        break;      // do something really strange;
    default:
        break;      // panic completely
}
```

Java supports three different looping structures, the syntax of which are identical to C. The Java for loop:

```
for (initial condition; while true; each iteration)
{
    // loop body
}
```

provides for loop indices, and looks like the following example:

```
for (i=0; i<5; i++)
{
    // do something over and over
}
```

The while loop has the following syntax:

```
while (boolean expression is true)
{
    // loop body
}
```

and looks like the following example when implemented:

```
while (i<6)
{
    i++;
}
```

The third loop structure is the do-while loop, which has the following syntax:

```
do
{
    // loop body
} while (boolean expression is true);
```

and looks like the following example when implemented:

```
do
{
i++;
} while (i<5);
```

> **Note**
>
> The primary difference between the `while` loop and the `do-while` loop is that in the `do-while` loop, the loop body is guaranteed to be executed at least once, since the test condition for the loop is at the beginning of a `while` loop and at the end of a `do-while` loop.

Java also supports the concept of labeled statements and labeled breaks. We saw the `break` statement in the example of the Java `switch` statement. The `break` statement breaks out of the immediately enclosing control structure. If a control structure is marked with a label, and a labeled break is used, control flow can break out of several levels of control structures at once. For example:

```
escape:
for (i=0; i<10; i++)
{
    for (j=5; j<20; j++)
    {
        ...
        break escape;
    }
}
```

The `break` statement in the above example causes the flow of control to break out of the labeled loop—in this case, the outer loop labeled `escape`.

To complete the Java control structures, the language includes the `continue` statement, which simply causes execution to continue when encountered, and the `return` statement, for returning from method calls.

Packages and Interfaces

Java includes two mechanisms for logically grouping and working with classes. These are the *interface* and the *package*.

Interfaces

An interface is a collection of method definitions without providing the method implementation. A class can implement an interface by providing method bodies for all the methods in the interface definition. Interfaces can be defined to be either public or private. All methods in an interface are public. Java uses interfaces to provide some of the features of multiple inheritance in C++.

The following code segment defines two interfaces:

```
public interface Test1
{
    Method1();
    Method2(int x);
}

public interface Test2
{
    Foo1(float myFloat);
}
```

A class can then choose to implement either or both of these interfaces. For example:

```
public class IntfExample implements Test1, Test2
{
    Method1()
    {
        ... // method body
    }
    Method2(int x)
    {
        ... // method body
    }
    Foo1(float myFloat)
    {
        ... // method body
    }
}
```

In this example, the class `IntfExample` implements both the `Test1` and `Test2` interfaces by providing method bodies for each method defined in the interface.

By using interfaces, you can specify an interface as a data type in a parameter list. This allows you to pass an object in the parameter list, as long as the object implements the specified interface. You don't have to know the exact class details of the object—only that it implements the interface. For example:

```
public class Blah
{
    void TestMethod(Test1 x)
    {
        ...
    }
}
```

In this example, the name of an interface, Test1, is used as a parameter type in the method TestMethod. This means that any object that implements the Test1 interface can be passed as a parameter.

Packages

A *package* is a Java construct that is used to manage the program namespace. It is a collection of classes and interfaces. Every class is contained in a package. If no package name is explicitly given, the class is contained in the default package. You may remember, from the earlier section on classes, that if a class does not give an access specifier to a method, it is considered public for its enclosing package.

To define a package for a compilation unit, you use the package statement. This statement must be the first statement in the file.

> **Note**
>
> A *compilation unit* is the basic compiled unit in Java. It is a file that contains one or more classes.

Sun's convention for Java packages is that they be named with period separated names. You should put the name of the organization that developed the package as the leftmost item in the package name.

The easiest way to use a class that is in another package is through the use of the import statement. With the import statement, you can import a specific class from a package, or you can import every public class at once.

Assume we have the package test.package that contains the classes Location and Mapper. If we want to use all the public classes from test.package in our current compilation unit, put the line

```
import test.package.*
```

at the top of your code, right after the statement defining your current package. The * character tells Java to import all the public classes in test.package. To import just one specific class, such as Location, use the following line instead:

```
import test.package.Location
```

You are now able to create and use objects of the Location class as if it were a local class.

Exception Handling

In order to manage runtime errors, Java supports runtime exception handling. When a statement causes some type of runtime error, it *throws* an exception. A special segment of code, called an *exception handler*, is said to *catch* the exception. Java has many different runtime exceptions defined. It is also possible to define your own exceptions and exception handlers.

Throwing Exceptions

You can define your own exceptions and exception handlers in order to cope with runtime error conditions in your code. In order to throw an exception, you must first define an exception class. The throw statement takes a class as a parameter. By convention, your custom-defined exception class should be a subclass of Exception. For example, we can define our own exception called PanicCompletely with the following very simple code segment:

```
class PanicCompletely extends Exception
{
}
```

Then, we can throw the exception when an error occurs in a class that is subject to a runtime error. For example:

```
class CausesErrors
{
    void Problem()
    {
        ...
        if (/* no error occured */)
        {
            // do nothing special
        }
        else /* we have error */
        {
            throw new PanicCompletely();
        }
    }
}
```

Now, when someone executes CausesErrors.Problem() and an error occurs, the PanicCompletely exception will be thrown.

Catching Exceptions

Throwing exceptions is only half the battle. In order for them to be effective, you must have an exception handler to catch the exception. To create an exception handler, we use the try-catch control structure.

To use `try-catch`, bracket the code that is likely to cause an exception with a `try` statement, and then put multiple `catch` statements below it, one for each exception that could be thrown. Let's look at an example:

```
try
{
    CausesErrors myClass = new CausesErrors();
    myClass.Problem();    // can throw a PanicCompletely exception
}
catch (PanicCompletely exc)
{
    // handle the PanicCompletely exception
}
catch (Exception exc)
{
    // handle any object of class Exception
}
catch (Object obj)
{
    // handle any improperly created exception
}
```

In the above code, there are three `catch` statements. The first one is for the `PanicCompletely` exception, which we know that `myClass.Problem()` can throw. The second `catch` statement catches all objects of class `Exception`. This should catch any other exceptions that we didn't explicitly write a `catch` statement for. The third `catch` statement catches all objects of type `Object`. If someone designed an exception that was not a subclass of `Exception`, it would be caught by this `catch` statement.

> **Note**
>
> Remember that all objects, even exceptions, are subclasses of the `Object` class.

Java also provides another keyword, `finally`, that is used to mark code in an exception handler that will get executed whether or not an exception occurs. If we add a `finally` statement to the previous example:

```
try
{
    CausesErrors myClass = new CausesErrors();
    myClass.Problem();    // can throw a PanicCompletely exception
}
catch (PanicCompletely exc)
{
    // handle the PanicCompletely exception
}
catch (Exception exc)
{
    // handle any object of class Exception
```

```
}
catch (Object obj)
{
    // handle any improperly created exception
}
finally
{
    // this always gets executed
}
```

The code in the `finally` block is always executed, no matter what exception is thrown by `myClass.Problem()` and even if no exception is thrown.

## CHAPTER 35

JavaScript

You already know that Web pages are written using the HyperText Markup Language, or HTML. You may also know that Netscape introduced a number of HTML extensions in the 1.*x* releases of Netscape Navigator. With the release of Navigator 2.0, Netscape has added a powerful new capability: JavaScript, a language that lets you write programs that Navigator executes when users load or browse your pages. This chapter teaches you how to use JavaScript to power up your Web pages.

In this chapter, you learn:

- What JavaScript is capable of doing
- How the programming elements of JavaScript are used, what they're for, and their relationship to Netscape and HTML
- The properties and uses of JavaScript objects, events, expressions, and operators
- Sample applications you can program using JavaScript

Introduction to JavaScript

> **Note**
>
> You've probably heard JavaScript called by its earlier-version name, LiveScript; at the time of this writing, most of JavaScript's capabilities are based on the functionality of LiveScript. As more and more HTML page designers and enterprise application developers develop scripts that define the behavior of objects to run on both clients and servers, you'll continue to see improvements and changes for the better in JavaScript. Just as Java (and any other software, for that matter) becomes better in response to its programmers' and developers' imaginations, so will JavaScript. If you're interested in following up on the latest revisions and additions, keep Netscape's home page (**http://home.netscape.com**) at the top of your bookmarks list.

JavaScript allows you to embed commands in an HTML page; when a Navigator user downloads the page, your JavaScript commands will be evaluated. These commands can be triggered when the user clicks on page items, manipulates gadgets and fields in an HTML form, or moves through the page history list.

Some computer languages are *compiled*; you run your program through a compiler, which performs a one-time translation of the human-readable program into a binary that the computer can execute. JavaScript is an *interpreted* language; the computer must evaluate the program every time it's run. You embed your JavaScript commands within an HTML page, and any browser that supports JavaScript can interpret the commands and act on them.

Currently, only Navigator 2.0 supports JavaScript, and other browser developers are taking a wait-and-see attitude. If JavaScript catches on, other browsers will probably support it. Because JavaScript is a relatively simple language, other manufacturers could write their own interpreters from scratch to create a Navigator-compatible engine.

Don't let all these programming terms frighten you off—JavaScript is powerful *and* simple. If you've ever programmed in dBase or Visual Basic, you'll find JavaScript easy to pick up. If not, don't worry; this chapter will have you JavaScripting in no time!

> **Note**
>
> Java offers a number of C++-like capabilities that were purposefully omitted from LiveScript. For example, you can only access the limited set of objects defined by the browser and its Java applets, and you can't extend those objects yourself. For more details on Java, see chapter 33, "Sun's Java and the Netscape Browser," and chapter 34, "Java for C++ Programmers."

Why Use a Scripting Language?

HTML provides a good deal of flexibility to page authors, but HTML by itself is static; once written, HTML documents can't interact with the user other than by presenting hyperlinks. Creative use of CGI scripts (which run on Web servers) have made it possible to create more interesting and effective interactive sites, but some applications really demand client-side scripting.

JavaScript was developed to provide page authors a way to write small scripts that would execute on the users' browsers instead of on the server. For example, an application that collects data from a form then POSTs it to the server can validate the data for completeness and correctness *before* sending it to the server. This can greatly improve the performance of the browsing session, since users don't have to send data to the server until it's been verified as correct. The following are some other potential applications for JavaScript:

- JavaScripts can verify forms for completeness, like a mailing list registration form that checks to make sure the user has entered a name and e-mail address before the form is posted.

- Pages can display content derived from information stored on the user's computer—without sending that data to the server. For example, a bank can embed JavaScript commands in their pages that look up account data from a Quicken file and display it as part of the bank's page.

- Because JavaScripts can modify settings for applets written in Java, page authors can control the size, appearance, and behavior of Navigator plug-ins, as well as other Java applets. A page that contains an embedded Director animation might use a JavaScript to set the Director plug-in's window size and position before triggering the animation.

What Can JavaScript Do?

JavaScript provides a rich set of built-in functions and commands. Your JavaScripts can display HTML in the browser, do math calculations (like figuring the sales tax or shipping for an order form), play sounds, open new URLs, and even click buttons in forms.

Tip

A *function* is just a small program that does something, and a *method* is a function that belongs to an object. For more lingo, see chapter 33, "Sun's Java and the Netscape Browser."

Code to perform these actions can be embedded in a page and executed when the page is loaded; you can also write *methods* that contain code that's triggered by events you specify. For example, you can write a JavaScript method that is called when the user clicks the Submit button of a form, or one that is activated when the user clicks a hyperlink on the active page.

JavaScript can also set the attributes, or *properties*, of Java applets running in the browser. This makes it easy for you to change the behavior of plug-ins or other objects without having to delve into their innards. For example, your JavaScript code could automatically start playing an embedded QuickTime or .AVI file when the user clicks a button.

What Does JavaScript Look Like?

JavaScript commands are embedded in your HTML documents, either directly or via a URL that tells the browser which scripts to load. Embedding JavaScript in your pages only requires one new HTML element: <SCRIPT>... </SCRIPT>.

The <SCRIPT> element takes two attributes: LANGUAGE, which specifies the scripting language to use when evaluating the script, and URL, which specifies a URL from which the script can be loaded. The LANGUAGE attribute is always required, unless the SRC attribute's URL specifies a language. LANGUAGE and SRC can both be used, too. Here are some examples:

```
<SCRIPT LANGUAGE="LiveScript">...</SCRIPT>
<SCRIPT SRC="http://www.fairgate.com/scripts/
common.LiveScript">...</SCRIPT>
<SCRIPT LANGUAGE="LiveScript" SRC="http://www.fairgate.com/scripts/
common">...</SCRIPT>
```

JavaScript itself resembles many other computer languages; if you're familiar with C, C++, Pascal, HyperTalk, Visual Basic, or dBase, you'll recognize the similarities. If not, don't worry; the following are some simple rules that will help you understand how the language is structured:

- JavaScript treats all letters as lowercase (except for quoted strings), so document.write and DOCUMENT.WRITE are the same.

- JavaScript is pretty flexible about statements. A single statement can cover multiple lines, and you can put multiple short statements on a single line—just make sure to add a semi-colon (;) at the end of each statement.

- Curly braces (the { and } characters) group statements into *blocks*; a block may be the body of a function or a section of code that gets executed in a loop or as part of a conditional test.

Figure 35.1 shows a small piece of JavaScript code embedded in an HTML page; the frontmost window shows the original HTML file, and the Navigator window shows its output.

JavaScript Programming Conventions

Even though JavaScript is a simple language, it's quite expressive. In this section, we'll cover a small number of simple rules and conventions that will ease your learning process and speed your JavaScripting.

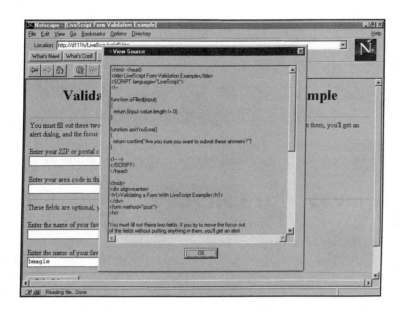

Fig. 35.1
The foremost window shows a small piece of JavaScript code embedded in simple HTML file; the Navigator window shows the result of loading that page (which executes the JavaScript).

Hiding Your Scripts

You'll probably be designing pages that may be seen by browsers that don't support JavaScript. To keep those browsers from interpreting your JavaScript commands as HTML—and displaying them—wrap your scripts like this:

```
<SCRIPT LANGUAGE="LiveScript">
<!-- This line opens an HTML comment
document.write("You can see this script's output, but not its
source.")
<!-- This line opens and closes a comment -->
</SCRIPT>
```

The opening <!-- comment causes browsers to disregard all text they encounter until they find a matching -->, so they won't display your script. You *do* have to be careful with the <SCRIPT> tag, though; if you put your <SCRIPT>...</SCRIPT> block *inside* the comments, Navigator will ignore it!

Comments

It's usually good practice to include comments in your programs to explain what they do; JavaScript is no exception. The JavaScript interpreter will ignore any text marked as a comment, so don't be shy about including them. There are two types of comments: single-line and multiple-line.

Single-line comments start with two slashes (//), and they're limited to one line. Multiple-line comments must start with /* on the first line, and end with */ on the last line. Here are a few quick examples:

```
// this is a legal comment
/ illegal -- comments start with two slashes
/*      Multiple-line comments can
        be spread across more than one line, as long as they end.
*/
/* illegal-- this comment doesn't have an end!
// this comment's OK, because extra slashes are ignored //
```

The JavaScript Language

JavaScript was designed to resemble Java, which in turn looks a lot like C and C++. The difference is that Java was built as a general-purpose object language, while JavaScript is intended to provide a quicker and simpler language for enhancing Web pages and servers. In this section, you learn the building blocks of JavaScript and how to combine them into legal JavaScript programs.

Using Identifiers

An *identifier* is just a unique name that JavaScript uses to identify a variable, method, or object in your program. As with other programming languages, JavaScript imposes some rules on what names you can use. All JavaScript names must start with a letter or the underscore character ("_"), and they can contain both upper- and lowercase letters and the digits 0–9. (Remember, JavaScript doesn't distinguish between cases, so UserName, userName, and USERNAME all refer to the same thing in a JavaScript program.)

JavaScript supports two different ways for you to represent values in your scripts: literals and variables. As their names imply, *literals* are fixed values that don't change while the script is executing, while *variables* hold data that can change at any time.

Literals and variables have several different types; the type is determined by the kind of data that the literal or variable contains. The following is a list of the types supported in JavaScript:

- *integers*, or positive whole numbers—Integer literals are made up of a sequence of digits only; integer variables can contain any whole-number value from 0 to more than 2 billion.

- *floating-point*, or numbers with fractional parts—10 is an integer, but 10.5 is a floating-point number. Floating-point literals can be positive or negative, and they can contain either positive or negative exponents (which are indicated by an e in the number.) For example, `3.14159265` is a floating-point literal, as is `6.02e24` (6.02×10^{24}, or Avogadro's number.)

- *strings*, or sequences of characters—Strings can represent words, phrases, or data, and they're set off by either double (") or single (') quotes. If you start a string with one type of quote, you must close it with the other.

- *Booleans*, or true or false values—Boolean literals can only have values of either `TRUE` or `FALSE`; other statements in the JavaScript language can return Boolean values.

Using Functions, Objects, and Properties

Before we go any further, let's talk about functions, objects, and properties. A *function* is just a piece of code that does something; it might play a sound, calculate an equation, or send a piece of e-mail. An *object* is a collection of data and functions that have been grouped together. The object's functions are called *methods*, and its data are called its *properties*. The JavaScript programs you write will have properties and methods, and they'll interact with objects provided by Navigator and its plug-ins (as well as any other Java applets you may supply to your users.)

> **Tip**
>
> A simple guideline: an object's properties are things it knows, and its methods are things it can do.

Using Built-In Objects and Functions

Individual JavaScript elements are objects; for example, string literals are string objects, and they have methods that you can use to do things like change their case. JavaScript also provides a set of useful objects to represent the Navigator browser, the currently displayed page, and other elements of the browsing session.

You access objects by specifying their name. For example, the active document object is named `document`. To use `document`'s properties or methods, you add a period and the name of the method or property you want. For example, `document.title` is the title property of the document object, and `"Navigator".length` would call the `length` member of the string object named "Navigator". Remember, literals are objects too!

Using Properties

Every object has properties—even literals. To access a property, just use the object name followed by a period and the property name. To get the length of a string object named `address`, you can write

```
address.length
```

and you'll get back an integer which equals the number of characters in the string. If the object you're using has properties that can be modified, you can change them in the same way. To set the `color` property of a `house` object, just write

```
house.color = "blue"
```

You can also add new properties to an object just by naming them. For example, let's say you define a class called `customer` for one of your pages. You can add new properties to the `customer` object like this:

```
customer.name = "Joe Smith"
customer.address = "123 Elm Street"
customer.zip = "90210"
```

Finally, it's important to know that an object's methods are just properties, so you can easily add new properties to an object by writing your own function and creating a new object property using your own function name. If you wanted to add a `Bill` method to your `customer` object, you could do so by writing a function named `BillCustomer` and setting the object's property like this:

```
customer.Bill = BillCustomer;
```

To call the new method, you'd just write

```
customer.Bill()
```

Array and Object Properties

JavaScript objects store their properties in an internal table that you can access in two ways. You've already seen the first way—just use the properties' name. The second way, *arrays*, allow you to access *all* of an object's properties in sequence. The following function prints out all the properties of the specified object:

```
function DumpProperties(obj, obj_name) {
    result = ""          // set the result string to blank
    for (i in obj)
        result += obj_name + "." + i + " = " + obj[i] + "\n"
    return result
}
```

You'll see this code again in the "Sample JavaScript Code" section, and we'll explain in detail what it does. For now, it's enough to know that there are two different, but related, ways to access an object's properties.

HTML Elements Have Properties, Too

Navigator provides properties for HTML forms *and* some types of form fields. JavaScript is especially valuable for writing scripts that check or change data in forms. Navigator's properties allow you to get and set the form elements' data, as well as specify actions to be taken when something happens to the form element (as when the user clicks in a text field, or moves to another field.) For more details on using HTML object properties, see the section, "HTML Objects and Events."

JavaScript and the Netscape Navigator

Now that you understand how JavaScript works, let's talk about how Navigator supports JavaScript.

When Scripts Get Executed

When you put JavaScript code in a page, Navigator evaluates the code as soon as it's encountered. As Navigator evaluates the code, it converts it into a more efficient internal format so it can be executed later. When you think about it, this is similar to how HTML is processed; browsers parse and display HTML as they encounter it in the page, not all at once.

However, functions don't get executed when they're evaluated; they just get stored for later use. You still have to explicitly call functions to make them work. Some functions are attached to objects, like buttons or text fields on forms, and they are called when some event happens on the button or field. You might also have functions that you want to execute during page evaluation; you can do this by putting a call to the function at the appropriate place in the page, like this:

```
<SCRIPT language="LiveScript">
<!--
myFunction()
<!-- -->
</SCRIPT>
```

Where to Put Your Scripts

You can put scripts anywhere within your HTML page, as long as they're surrounded with the <SCRIPT>...</SCRIPT> tag. Many JavaScript programmers choose to put functions that will be executed more than once into the <HEAD> element of their pages; this provides a convenient storage place. Since the <HEAD> element is at the beginning of the file, functions and JavaScript code that you put there will be evaluated before the rest of the document is loaded.

Sometimes, though, you have code that shouldn't be evaluated or executed until after all of the page's HTML has been parsed and displayed. An example is the DumpURL() function described in the "Programming Tutorial and Examples" section later in the chapter; it prints out all the URLs referenced in the page. If this function is evaluated before all the HTML on the page has been loaded, it'll miss some URLs, so the call to the function should come at the page's end.

Navigator Objects and Events

In addition to recognizing JavaScript when it's embedded inside a <SCRIPT>...</SCRIPT> tag, Netscape Navigator also exposes some objects (and their methods and properties) that you can use in your JavaScript programs. Also, Navigator can trigger methods you define when the user takes certain actions in the browser.

Browser Objects and Events

Many things that happen in a Navigator browsing session aren't related to items on the page, like buttons or HTML text. Instead, they're related to what's happening in the browser itself, like what page the user is viewing.

The location Object

Navigator exposes an object called location, which holds the current URL, including the hostname, path, CGI script arguments, and even the protocol. Table 35.1 shows the properties and methods of the location object.

Table 35.1 Navigator's location Object Contains Information on the Currently Displayed URL

Property	Type	What It Does
href	String	Contains the entire URL, including all the subparts; for example, http://home.netscape.com/comprod/products/navigator/version_2.0/script/script_info/lsnn.html
protocol	String	Contains the protocol field of the URL, including the first colon; for example, http:
host	String	Contains the hostname and port number; for example, home.netscape.com:80

Property	Type	What It Does
hostname	String	Contains only the hostname; for example, home.netscape.com
port	String	Contains the port, if specified; otherwise, it's blank.
path	String	Contains the path to the actual document; for example, comprod/products/navigator/version_2.0/script/script_info/1snn.html
hash	String	Contains any CGI arguments after the first "#" in the URL.
search	String	Contains any CGI arguments after the first "?" in the URL.
toString()	Method	Returns location.href; you can use this function to easily get the entire URL.
assign(x)	Method	Sets location.href to the value you specify.

The document Object

Navigator also exposes an object called document; as you might expect, this object exposes useful properties and methods of the active document. location only refers to the URL of the active document, but document refers to the document itself. Table 35.2 shows document's properties and methods.

> **Note**
>
> Because Navigator was still changing as this was written, Netscape may have defined additional properties in the document object. Please see their LiveScript documentation at **http://home.netscape.com/comprod/products/navigator/version_2.0/scripl/script_info/lsnn.html** for full details.

Table 35.2 Netscape's document Object Contains Information on the Currently Loaded and Displayed HTML Page

Property	Type	What It Does
title	String	Contains title of the current page, or "Untitled" if there's no title.
URL or Location	String	Contain the document's address (from its history stack entry); these two are synonyms.
last	Modified	Contains the page's last-modified date. String
forms[]	Array	Contains all the FORMs in the current page.

(continues)

Table 35.2 Continued		
Property	**Type**	**What It Does**
forms[].length	Integer	Contains the number of FORMs in the current page.
links[]	Array	Contains all HREF anchors in the current page
links[].length	Integer	Contains the number of HREF anchors in the current page.
write(x)	Method	Writes HTML to the current document, in the order in which the script occurs on the page.

The History Object

Navigator maintains a list of pages you've visited since running the program; this list is called the *history list*. Your JavaScript programs can move through pages in the list using the properties and functions shown in table 35.3.

Table 35.3 Netscape's History Object Contains Information on the Browser's History List		
Property	**Type**	**What it does**
previous, back	String	Contains the URL of the previous history stack entry (that is, the one before the active page.) These properties are synonyms.
next, forward	String	Contains the URL of the next history stack entry (that is, the one after the active page.) These properties are synonyms.
go(x)	Method	Goes forward x entries in the history stack if $x > 0$; else, goes backward x entries. x must be a number.
go(x)	Method	Goes to the newest history entry whose title or URL contains x as a substring; the string case doesn't matter. x must be a string.

The window Object

Navigator creates a window object for every document. Think of the window object as an actual Windows or Macintosh window, and the document object as the content that appears in the window. Navigator provides the following two methods for doing things in the window:

- alert(*string*) puts up an alert dialog box and displays the message specified in *string*. Users must dismiss the dialog box by clicking the OK button before Navigator will let them do anything else.

■ `confirm(string)` puts up a confirmation dialog box with two buttons (OK and Cancel) and displays the message specified in `string`. Users may dismiss the dialog box by clicking Cancel or OK; the `confirm` function returns TRUE when users click OK and FALSE if they click Cancel.

HTML Objects and Events

Navigator represents some individual HTML elements as objects, and these objects have properties and methods attached to them just like every other. You can use these objects to customize your pages' behavior by attaching JavaScript code to the appropriate methods.

Properties for Generic HTML Objects

The methods and properties in this section apply to several HTML tags; note that there are other methods and properties, discussed after the following table, for anchors and form elements. Table 35.4 shows the features that these generic HTML objects provide.

Table 35.4   These Properties and Methods Allow You to Control the Contents and Behavior of HTML Elements

Property	Type	What It Does
onFocus	Function	Called when the user moves the input focus to the field, either via the Tab key or a mouse click.
onBlur	Function	Called when the user moves the input focus out of this field.
onSelect	Function	Called when the user selects text in the field.
onChange	Function	Called only when the field loses focus and the user has modified its text; use this function to validate data in a field.
onSubmit	Function	Called when the user submits the form (if the form has a submit button).
onClick	Function	Called when the button is clicked.
focus()	Function	Call to move the input focus to the specified object.
blur()	Function	Call to move the input focus away from the specified object.
select()	Function	Call to select the specified object.
click()	Function	Call to click the specified object, which must be a button.
enable()	Function	Call to enable (un-gray) the specified object.
disable()	Function	Call to disable (gray out) the specified object.

Note that the `focus()`, `blur()`, `select()`, `click()`, `enable()`, and `disable()` functions are methods of objects; to call them, use the name of the object you want to affect. For example, to turn off the button named Search, you'd use `form.search.disable()`.

Properties for Anchor Objects
Hypertext anchors don't have all the properties listed above; they only have the `onFocus()`, `onBlur()`, and `onClick()` methods. You modify and set these methods just like others. Remember that no matter what code you attach, Navigator's still going to follow the clicked link—it will execute your code first, though.

Properties for Form Objects
Table 35.5 lists the properties exposed for HTML FORM elements; the section, "HTML Events," also presents several methods that you can override to call JavaScript routines when something happens to an object on the page.

Table 35.5   HTML Forms Themselves Have Special Properties That You Can Use in Your JavaScript Code

Property	Type	What It Does
name	String	Contains the value of the form's NAME attribute.
method	Integer	Contains the value of the form's METHOD attribute: 0 for GET or 1 for POST.
action	String	Contains the value of the form's ACTION attribute.
target	Window	Window targeted after submit for form response.
onSubmit()	Method	Called when the form is submitted; this method can't stop the submission, though.
submit()	Method	Any form element can force the form to be submitted by calling the form's submit() method.

Properties for Objects in a Form
One of the best places to use JavaScript is in forms, since you can write scripts that process, check, and perform calculations with the data the user enters. JavaScript provides a useful set of properties and methods for text INPUT elements and buttons.

You use INPUT elements in a form to let the user enter text data; JavaScript provides properties to get string objects that hold the element's contents, as well as methods for doing something when the user moves into or out of a field. Table 35.6 shows the properties and methods which are defined for text INPUT elements.

Table 35.6   These Properties and Methods Allow You to Control the Contents and Behavior of HTML INPUT Elements

Property	Type	What It Does
name	String	Contains the value of the element's NAME attribute.
value	String	Contains the field's contents.
default	Value String	The initial contents of the field; returns "" if blank.
onFocus	Method	Called when the user moves the input focus to the field, either via the Tab key or a mouse click.
onBlur	Method	Called when the user moves the input focus out of this field.
onSelect	Method	Called when the user selects text in the field.
onChange	Method	Called only when the field loses focus and the user has modified its text; use this function to validate data in a field.

Individual buttons and check boxes have properties, too; JavaScript provides properties to get string objects containing the buttons' data, as well as methods for doing something when the user selects or deselects a particular button. Table 35.7 shows the properties and methods that are defined for button elements.

Table 35.7   These Properties and Methods Allow You to Control the Contents and Behavior of HTML Button Elements

Property	Type	What It Does
name	String	Contains the value of the button's NAME attribute
value	String	Contains the VALUE attribute.
onClick	Method	Called when the button is pressed. The function's this method argument points to the button which was pressed.
click()	Method	Clicks a button and triggers whatever actions are attached to it.

Radio buttons are grouped so that only one button in a group can be selected at a time. Because all radio buttons in a group have the same name, JavaScript has a special property, `index`, for use in distinguishing radio buttons. Querying the `index` property returns a number, starting with 0 for the first button, indicating which button in the group was triggered.

For example, you might want to automatically put the user's cursor into the first text field in a form, instead of making the user manually click the field. If your first text field is named "UserName," you can put this

```
form.UserName.focus()
```

in your document's script to get the desired behavior.

Programming with JavaScript

As you've seen in the preceding sections, JavaScript has a lot to offer page authors. It's not as flexible as C or C++, but it's quick and simple. Most importantly, it's easily embedded in your WWW pages, so you can maximize their impact with a little JavaScript seasoning. This section covers the gritty details of JavaScript programming, including a detailed explanation of the language's features.

Expressions

An *expression* is anything that can be evaluated to get a single value. Expressions can contain string or numeric literals, variables, operators, and other expressions, and they can range from simple to quite complex. For example,

```
x = 7;
```

is an expression which uses the assignment operator (more on operators in the next section) to assign the result 7 to the variable x. By contrast,

```
(quitFlag == TRUE) & (formComplete == FALSE)
```

is a more complex expression whose final value depends on the values of the `quitFlag` and `formComplete` variables.

Operators

Operators do just what their name suggests: they operate on variables or literals. The items that an operator acts on are called its *operands*. Operators come in the two following types:

- *Unary* operators only require one operand, and the operator can come before or after the operand. The `--` operator, which subtracts one from the operand, is a good example. `--count` and `count--` will both subtract 1 from the variable `count`.

■ *Binary* operators need two operands. The four math operators you learned in elementary school (+ for addition, - for subtraction, * for multiplication, and / for division) are all binary operators, as is the = assignment operator we saw earlier.

Assignment Operators

Assignment operators take the result of an expression and assign it to a variable. JavaScript won't allow you to assign the result of an expression to a literal. One feature that JavaScript has that most other programming languages don't is that you can change a variable's type on-the-fly.

```
function TypeDemo()
{
  var pi = 3.14159265
  document.write("Pi is ", pi, "\n")
  pi = FALSE
  document.write("Pi is ", pi, "\n")
}
```

This short function first prints the (correct) value of *pi*. In most other languages, though, trying to set a floating-point variable to a Boolean value would either generate a compiler error or a runtime error. JavaScript and Java happily accept the change and print *pi*'s new value: FALSE.

The most common assignment operator, =, simply assigns the value of an expression's right side to its left side. In the example above, the variable x got the integer value 7 after the expression was evaluated. For convenience, JavaScript also defines some other operators that combine common math operations with assignment; they're shown in table 35.8.

Table 35.8 These Assignment Operators Provide a Shorthand Way to Do an Assignment and a Math Operation at the Same Time

Operator	What It Does	Two Equivalent Expressions
+=	Adds two values	x+=y and x=x+y
	adds two strings	string = string + "HTML" and string += "HTML"
-=	Subtracts two values	x-=y and x=x-y
*=	Multiples two values	a*=b and a=a*b
/=	Divides two values	e/=b and e=e/b

Math Operators

The previous sections gave you a sneak preview of the math operators that JavaScript furnishes. You can either combine math operations with assignments, as shown in Table 35.8, or use them individually. As you'd expect, the standard four math functions (addition, subtraction, multiplication, and division) work just as they do on an ordinary calculator.

The negation operator, -, is a unary operator that negates the sign of its operand. To use the negation operator, you must put the operator before the operand.

JavaScript also adds two useful binary operators: -- and ++, called, respectively, the *decrement* and *increment* operators. These two operators do two things; they modify the value of their operand, and return the new value. They also share a unique property: they can be used either before or after their operand. If you put the operator *after* the operand, JavaScript will return the operand's value, then modify it. If you take the opposite route and put the operator before the operand, JavaScript will modify it and return the modified value. The following short example might help clarify this seemingly odd behavior:

```
x = 7;  // start x as 7
a = --x;     // set x to x-1, and return the new x; a = 6
b = a++;     // set b to a, so b = 6, then add 1 to a; a = 7
x++;    // add one to x; ignore the returned value; a = 7 again
```

Comparison Operators

It's often necessary to compare the value of two expressions to see whether one is larger, smaller, or equal to another. JavaScript supplies several comparison operators that take two operands and return TRUE if the comparison's true, and FALSE if it's not. (Remember, you can use literals, variables, or expressions with operators that require expressions.) Table 35.9 shows the JavaScript comparison operators.

Table 35.9 These Comparison Operators Provide a Shorthand Way to Do an Assignment and a Math Operation at the Same Time

Operator	Read It As	Returns TRUE When:
==	Equals	The two operands are equal
!=	Does not equal	The two operands are unequal
<	Less than	The left operand is less than the right operand
<=	Less than or equal to	The left operand is less than or equal to the right operand
>	Greater than	The left operand is greater than the right operand
>=	Greater than or equal to	The left operand is greater than or equal to the right operand

It may be helpful to think of the comparison operators as questions; when you write

```
(x >= 10)
```

you're really saying, "Is the value of variable x greater than or equal to 10?"

Logical Operators

Comparison operators compare quantity or content for numeric and string expressions, but sometimes you need to test a logical value—like whether a comparison operator returned TRUE or FALSE. JavaScript's logical operators allow you to compare expressions that return logical values. The following are JavaScript's logical operators:

- &&, read as "and." The && operator returns TRUE if both its input expressions are true. If the first operand evaluates to FALSE, && returns FALSE immediately, without evaluating the second operand. Here's an example:

```
x = TRUE && TRUE;      // x is TRUE
x = FALSE && FALSE;    // x is FALSE
x = FALSE && TRUE;     // x is FALSE
```

- ¦¦, read as "or." This operator returns TRUE if *either* of its operands are true. If the first operand is true, ¦¦ returns true without evaluating the second operand. Here's an example:

```
x = TRUE ¦¦ TRUE;      // x is TRUE
x = FALSE ¦¦ TRUE;     // x is TRUE
x = FALSE ¦¦ FALSE;    // x is FALSE
```

- !, read as "not." This operator takes only one expression, and it returns the opposite of that expression, so !TRUE returns FALSE, and !FALSE returns TRUE.

Note that the "and" and "or" operators won't evaluate the second operand if the first operand provides enough information for the operator to return a value. This process, called *short-circuit evaluation*, can be significant when the second operand is a function call. For example,

```
keepGoing = (userCancelled == FALSE) && (theForm.Submit())
```

If userCancelled is TRUE, the second operand—which submits the active form—won't be called.

Controlling Your JavaScripts

Some scripts you write will be simple; they'll execute the same way every time, once per page. For example, if you add a JavaScript to play a sound when users visit your home page, it won't need to evaluate any conditions or do anything more than once. More sophisticated scripts might require that you take different actions under different circumstances; you might also want to repeat the execution of a block of code—perhaps by a set number of times, or as long as some condition is true. JavaScript provides constructs for controlling the execution flow of your script based on conditions, as well as repeating a sequence of operations.

Testing Conditions

JavaScript provides a single type of control statement for making decisions: the `if..else` statement. To make a decision, you supply an expression which evaluates to TRUE or FALSE; which code is executed depends on what your expression evaluates to.

The simplest form of `if..else` uses only the `if` part. If the specified condition is true, the code following the condition is executed; if not, it's skipped. For example, in this code fragment

```
if (document.lastModified.year < 1995)
document.write("Danger! This is a mighty old document.")
```

the message will only appear if the condition (that the document's Last Modified field says it was modified before 1995) is true. You can use any expression as the condition; since expressions can be nested and combined with the logical operators, your tests can be pretty sophisticated:

```
if ((document.lastModified.year >= 1995) &&
(document.lastModified.month >= 10))
document.write("This document is reasonably current.")
```

The `else` clause allows you to specify a set of statements to execute when the condition is FALSE.

Repeating Actions

If you want to repeat an action more than once, you're in luck! JavaScript provides two different loop constructs that you can use to repeat a set of operations.

The first, called a `for` loop, will execute a set of statements some number of times. You specify three expressions: an *initial* expression that sets the values of any variables you need to use, a *condition* that tells the loop how to see when it's done, and an *increment* expression that modifies any variables that need it. Here's a simple example:

```
for (count=0; count < 100; count++)
document.write("Count is ", count);
```

This loop will execute 100 times and print out a number each time. The initial expression sets our counter, *count*, to zero; the condition tests to see whether *count* is less than 100, and the increment expression increments count.

You can use several statements for any of these expressions, like this:

```
for (count=0, numFound = 0; (count < 100) && (numFound < 3);
count++)
if (someObject.found()) numFound++;
```

This loop will either loop 100 times or as many times as it takes to "find" three items—the loop condition terminates when count >= 100 or when numFound >= 3.

The second form of loop is the while loop. It executes statements as long as its condition is true. For example, you could rewrite the first for loop above like this:

```
count = 0
while (count < 100) {
   document.write("Count is ", count) }
```

Which form you prefer depends on what you're doing; for loops are useful when you want to perform an action a set number of times, and while loops are best when you want to keep doing something as long as a particular condition remains true.

JavaScript Reserved Words

JavaScript reserves some keywords for its own use. You may not define your own methods or properties with the same name as any of these keywords; if you do, the JavaScript interpreter will complain.

> **Tip**
>
> Some of these keywords are reserved for future use (hint: think Java!) JavaScript might allow you to use them, but your scripts may break in the future if you do.

abstract	double	instanceof	super
boolean	else	int	switch
break	extends	interface	synchronized
byte	false	long	this

byvalue	final	native	threadsafe
case	finally	new	throw
catch	float	null	transient
char	for	package	true
class	function	private	try
const	goto	protected	var
continue	if	public	void
default	implements	return	while
delete	import	short	with
do	in	static	

Command Reference

This section provides a quick reference to the JavaScript commands that are implemented in Navigator 2.0. The commands are listed in alphabetical order; many have examples. Before we dive in, here's what the formatting of these entries mean:

- All JavaScript keywords are in monospaced font.
- Words in *italics* represent user-defined names or statements.
- Any portions enclosed in square brackets ([and]) are optional.
- {statements} indicates a block of statements, which can consist of a single statement or multiple statements enclosed by curly braces.

break

The break statement terminates the current while or for loop and transfers program control to the statement following the terminated loop.

Syntax

    break

Example:

The following function scans the list of URLs in the current document and stops when it has seen all URLs or when it finds a URL that matches the input parameter searchName.

```
function findURL(searchName) {
    var i = 0;
    for (I=0; i < document.links.length; i++) {
        if (document.links[i] == searchName)
        {
```

```
            document.write(document.links[i])
            break;
        }
    }
```

continue

The continue statement stops executing the statements in a while or for loop, and skips to the next iteration of the loop. It doesn't stop the loop altogether like break statement; instead, in a while loop it jumps back to the condition, and in a for loop it jumps to the update expression.

Syntax

```
    continue
```

Example:

The following function prints the odd numbers between 1 and x; it has a continue statement that goes to the next iteration when i is even.

```
    function printOddNumbers(x) {
        var i = 0
        while (i < x)
        {
            i++;
            if ((i % 2) == 0      // the % operator divides & returns
    the remainder
                    continue
            else
            document.write(i, "\n")
        }
    }
```

for loop

A for loop consists of three optional expressions, enclosed in parentheses and separated by semicolons, followed by a block of statements executed in the loop. These parts do the following:

- The starting expression, *initial_expr*, is evaluated before the loop starts. It's most often used to initialize loop counter variables, and you're free to use the var keyword here to declare new variables.

- A *condition* is evaluated on each pass through the loop. If the condition evaluates to TRUE, the statements in the loop body are executed. You can leave the condition out, and it will always evaluate to TRUE. If you do this, make sure to use break in your loop when it's time to exit.

- An update expression, *update_expr*, is usually used to update or increment the counter variable or other variables used in the condition. This expression is optional; you can update variables as needed within the body of the loop if you prefer.

■ A block of statements are executed as long as the condition is TRUE. This block can have one or multiple statements in it.

Syntax

```
for ([initial_expr;] [condition;] [update_expr])
{
statements
}
```

Example:

This simple for statement prints out the numbers from 0 to 9. It starts by declaring the a loop counter variable, *i*, and initializing it to zero. As long as *i* is less than 9, the update expression will increment *i*, and the statements in the loop body will be executed.

```
for (var i = 0; i < 9; i++)
{
    document.write(i);
}
```

for...in

This is a special form of the for loop that iterates the variable *variable-name* over all the properties of the object named *object-name*. For each distinct property, it executes the statements in the loop body.

Syntax

```
for (var in obj)
{
statements
}
```

Example:

The following function takes as its arguments an object and the object's name. It then uses the for...in loop to iterate through all the object's properties; when done, it returns a string that lists the property names and their values.

```
function dump_props(obj, obj_name) {
    var result = ""
    for (i in obj)
        result += obj_name + "." + i + " = " + obj[i] + "\n"
    return result;
    }
```

function

The function statement declares a JavaScript function; the function may optionally accept one or more parameters. To return a value, the function must have a `return` statement that specifies the value to return. All parameters are passed to functions *by value*—the function gets the value of the parameter, but cannot change the original value in the caller.

Syntax

```
function name([param] [, param] [..., param])
{
statements
}
```

Example:

```
//This function returns TRUE if the active document has the title
//specified in the theString parameter and FALSE otherwise
function PageNameMatches(theString)
{
        return (document.title == theString)
}
```

if...else

The `if...else` statement is a conditional statement that executes the statements in *block1* if *condition* is TRUE. In the optional `else` clause, it executes the statements in *block2* if *condition* is FALSE. The blocks of statements may contain any JavaScript statements, including further nested `if` statements.

Syntax

```
if (condition) {
    statements
} [else {
    statements}]
```

Example:

```
if (Message.IsEncrypted()) {
    Message.Decrypt(SecretKey); }
else {
    Message.Display();
}
```

return

The `return` statement specifies the value to be returned by a function.

Syntax

```
return expression;
```

Example:

The following simple function returns the square of its argument, x, where x is any number.

```
function square( x ) {
    return x * x;
}
```

this

Use this to access methods or properties of an object within the object's methods. this always refers to the current object.

Syntax

```
this.property
```

Example:

If setSize is a method of the document object, then this refers to the specific object whose setSize method is called:

```
function setSize (x, y) {
        this.horizSize = x;
        this.vertSize = y;
}
```

This method will set the size for an object when called as follows:

```
document.setSize (640, 480);
```

var

The var statement declares a variable varname, optionally initializing it to have *value*. The variable name varname can be any JavaScript identifier, and *value* can be any legal expression (including literals).

Syntax

```
var varname [= value] [, var varname [= value] ] [..., var varname
[= value] ]
```

Example:

```
var num_hits = 0, var cust_no = 0;
```

while

The while statement contains a condition and a block of statements. while evaluates the condition; if *condition* is TRUE, it executes the statements in the loop body. It then re-evaluates *condition* and continues to execute the statement block as long as *condition* is TRUE. When *condition* evaluates to FALSE, execution continues with the next statement following the block.

Syntax

```
while (condition)
{
        statements
    }
```

Example:

The following simple `while` loop iterates until it finds a form in the current
document object whose name is "OrderForm," or until it runs out of forms in
the document.

```
x = 0;
while ((x < document.forms[].length) &&
        (document.forms[x].name != "OrderForm"))
{ x++; }
```

with

The `with` statement establishes *object* as the default object for the statements
in *block*. Any property references without an object are then assumed to be
for *object*.

Syntax

```
with object
{
statements
}
```

Example:

```
with document {
        write "Inside a with block, you don't need to specify the
object.";
        bgColor = gray;
}
```

Sample JavaScript Code

It can be difficult to pick up a new programming language from scratch—
even for experienced programmers. To make it easy for you to master Java-
Script, this section presents some examples of JavaScript code and functions
that you can use in your own pages. Each of them demonstrates a practical
concept.

Dumping an Object's Properties

In the section, "Array and Object Properties," you saw a small function,
`DumpProperties()`, that gets all the property names and their values. Let's look
at that function again now to see it in light of what you've learned.

```
function DumpProperties (obj, obj_name) {
    var result = ""      // set the result string to blank
     for (i in obj)
         result += obj_name + "." + i + " = " + obj[i] + "\n"
     return result
}
```

As all JavaScript functions should, this one starts by defining its variables using the var keyword; it supplies an initial value, too, which is a good habit to start. The meat of the function is the for...in loop, which iterates over all the properties of the specified object. For each property, the loop body collects the object name, the property name (provided by the loop counter in the for...in loop), and the property's value. We access the properties as an indexed array instead of by name, so we can get them all.

Note that this function doesn't print anything out. If you want to see its output, put it in a page (remember to surround it with <SCRIPT>...</SCRIPT>!), then at the page's bottom, use

```
document.writeln(DumpProperties(obj, objName))
```

where *obj* is the object of interest and *objName* is its name.

Building a Link Table

You might want to have a way to automatically generate a list of all the links in a page, perhaps to display them in a separate section at the end of the page, as shown in Figure 35.2. DumpURL(), shown in Listing 35.1 below, does just that; it prints out a nicely formatted numbered list showing the hostname of each link in the page.

> **Listing 35.1   DumpURL() displays a numbered list of all the URLs on a page.**

```
function DumpURL()
{
        // declare the variables we'll use
        var linkCount = document.links.length
        var result = ""

        // build our summary line
        result = "<hr>\nLink summary: this page has links to <b>" +
linkCount  + "</b> hosts<br>\n"
        result += "<ol>\n"

        // for each link in the document, print a list item with
its hostname
        for (i=0; i < linkCount ; i++)
            result += "<li> " + document.links[i].hostname + "\n"
```

```
            // add the closing HTML for our list
            result += "</ol><hr>\n"
            return result
}
```

This function starts by declaring the variables used in the function. JavaScript requires that you declare most variables before using them, and good programming practice dictates doing so even when JavaScript doesn't require it. Next, you build the summary line for your table by assigning a string literal full of HTML to the *result* variable. You use a `for` loop to iterate through all the links in the current document and add a list item for each to the *result* variable. When you finish, add the closing HTML for your list to *result* and return it.

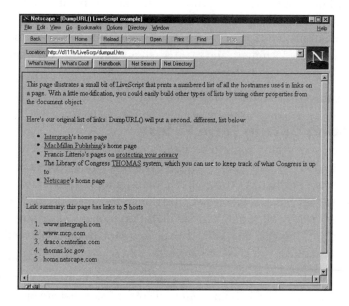

Fig. 35.2
The `DumpURL()` function adds a numbered list of all the links in a page at the end of the page.

Updating Data in Form Fields

There have been several mentions of the benefits of using JavaScript to check and modify data in HTML forms. Let's look at an example that dynamically updates the value of a text field based on the user's selection from one of several buttons.

To make this work, you need two pieces; the first is a simple bit of JavaScript that updates the `value` property of an object to whatever you pass in. Here's what it looks like:

```
function change(input, newValue)
{
        input.value = newValue
}
```

Then, each button you want to include needs to have its `onClick` method changed so that it calls your `change()` function. Here's a sample button definition:

```
<input type="button" value="Mac"
  onClick="change(this.form.display, 'Macintosh')">
```

When the button is clicked, JavaScript calls the `onClick` method, which happens to point to your function. The `this.form.display` object points to a text field named display; `this` refers to the active document, `form` refers to the form in the active document, and `display` refers to the form field named display.

Of course, this requires that you have a form INPUT gadget named display!

Validating Data in Form Fields

Often when you create a form to get data from the user, you need to check that data to see if it's correct and complete before sending mail, or making a database entry, or whatever you collected the data for. Without JavaScript, you have to POST the data and let a CGI script on the server decide if all the fields were correctly filled out. You can do better, though, by writing JavaScript functions that check the data in your form *on the client*; by the time the data gets posted, you know it's correct.

For this example, let's require that the user fill out two fields on our form: ZIP code and area code. We'll also present some other fields that are optional. First, you need a function that will return TRUE if there's something in a field, and FALSE if it's empty:

```
function isFilled(input)
{
  return (input.value.length != 0)
}
```

That's simple enough! For each field you want to make the user complete, you'll override its `onBlur()` method. `onBlur()` is triggered when the user moves the focus out of the specified field. Here's what your buttons look like:

```
<input name="ZIP" value=""
  onBlur="if (!isFilled(form.ZIP)) {
        alert('You must put your ZIP code in this field.');
        form.ZIP.focus() }">
```

When the user tries to move the focus out of the ZIP code button, the code attached to the `onBlur()` event is called. That code in turn checks to see if the field is complete; if not, it nags the user and puts the focus back into the ZIP field.

Of course, you could also implement a more gentle validation scheme by attaching a JavaScript to the form's submit button, like this:

```
<script language="LiveScript">
function areYouSure()
{
  return confirm("Are you sure you want to submit these answers?")
}
</script>
<input type=button name="doIt" value="Submit form"
  onClick="if (areYouSure()) this.form.submit();">
```

Figure 35.3 shows your finished page, including the politely worded dialog box that tells the user to go back and finish filling out the form.

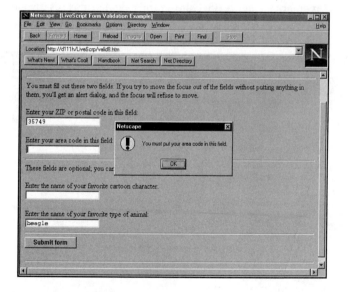

Fig. 35.3
The fields on this page are tied to JavaScript functions that keep the user from moving the input focus until the user supplies a value.

A Pseudo-Scientific Calculator

If you ask any engineer under a certain age what kind of calculator she used in college, the answer is likely to be "a Hewlett-Packard." HP calculators are somewhat different from ordinary calculators; you use *reverse Polish notation*, or RPN, to do calculations.

With a regular calculator, you put the operator in between operands. To add 3 and 7, you push 3, then the + key, then 7, then = to print the answer. With an RPN calculator, you put the operator *after* both operands! To add 3 and 7 on my HP-15C, I have to push 3, then Enter (which puts the first operand on the internal stack), then 7, then +, at which time I'd see the correct answer. This oddity takes a bit of getting used to, but it makes complex calculations go much faster, since intermediate results get saved on the stack.

Here's a simple RPN example. To compute $((1024 * 768) / 3.14159)^2$, you'd enter:

        1024, Enter, 768, *, 3.14159, /, x^2

to get the correct answer: 6.266475×10^{10}, or about 6.3 billion.

Netscape provides an RPN calculator as an example of JavaScript's expressive power. Let's take a detailed look at how it works. Listing 35.2 shows the JavaScript itself (note that these are really in the same file; we've just split them for convenience.) Figure 35.4 shows the calculator as it's displayed in Navigator.

Fig. 35.4
Navigator displays the RPN calculator as a table of buttons, with the accumulator (the answer) and the stack at the top.

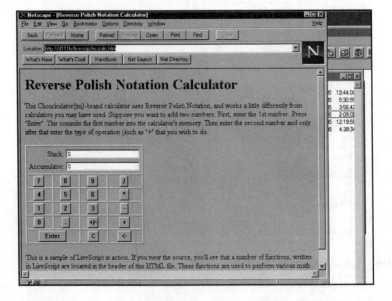

The HTML Page
Listing 35.2 shows the HTML for our calculator's page. For precise alignment, all the buttons are grouped into a table; the *accumulator* (where the answer's displayed) and the *stack* (where operands can be stored) are at the top.

Listing 35.2   The HTML definition for the RPN calculator example.

```
<table border="0">
<tr>
<td align=right>Stack:</td><td><input name="stack" value="0"></td>
</tr>
<tr>
<td align=right>Accumulator:</td><td><input name="display"
value="0"></td>
</tr>
</table>

</td>
</tr>

<tr align=center>
<td>
<input type="button" value=" 7 "
  onClick="addChar(this.form.display, '7')">
</td>
<td>
<input type="button" value=" 8 "
  onClick="addChar(this.form.display, '8')">
</td>
<td>
<input type="button" value=" 9 "
  onClick="addChar(this.form.display, '9')">
</td>
<td>
<input type="button" value=" / "
  onClick="divide(this.form)">
</td>
</tr>

<tr align=center>
<td>
<input type="button" value=" 4 "
  onClick="addChar(this.form.display, '4')">
</td>
<td>
<input type="button" value=" 5 "
  onClick="addChar(this.form.display, '5')">
</td>
<td>
<input type="button" value=" 6 "
  onClick="addChar(this.form.display, '6')">
</td>
<td>
<input type="button" value=" * "
  onClick="multiply(this.form)">
</td>
</tr>

<tr align=center>
<td>
```

(continued)

Listing 35.2   Continued

```html
<input type="button" value=" 1 "
  onClick="addChar(this.form.display, '1')">
</td>
<td>
<input type="button" value=" 2 "
  onClick="addChar(this.form.display, '2')">
</td>
<td>
<input type="button" value=" 3 "
  onClick="addChar(this.form.display, '3')">
</td>
<td>
<input type="button" value=" - "
  onClick="subtract(this.form)">
</td>
</tr>

<tr align=center>
<td>
<input type="button" value=" 0 "
  onClick="addChar(this.form.display, '0')">
</td>
<td>
<input type="button" value=" . "
  onClick="addChar(this.form.display, '.')">
</td>
<td>
<input type="button" value="+/-"
  onClick="changeSign(this.form.display)">
</td>
<td>
<input type="button" value=" + "
  onClick="add(this.form)">
</td>
</tr>


<tr align=center>
<td colspan="2">
<input type="button" value=" Enter " name="enter"
  onClick="pushStack(this.form)">
</td>
<td>
<input type="button" value=" C "
  onClick="this.form.display.value = 0 ">
</td>
<td>
<input type="button" value=" <- "
  onClick="deleteChar(this.form.display)">
</td>
</tr>

</table>
</form>
```

Notice that each button has an `onClick()` definition associated with it. The digits 0 through 9 all call the `addChar()` JavaScript function; the editing keys, C for clear and <- for backspace, call functions that change the value of the accumulator. The Enter key stores the current value on the stack, and the +/- button changes the accumulator's sign.

Of course, the operators themselves call JavaScript functions too; for example, the * button's definition calls the `Multiply()` function. The definitions aren't functions themselves; they include function calls (as for the digits) or individual statements (as in the "clear" key.)

The JavaScript

Of course, all these `onClick()` triggers need to have JavaScript routines to call! Listing 35.3 shows the JavaScript functions that implement the actual calculator.

Listing 35.3 The JavaScript code which makes the RPN calculator functional.

```
<script language="LiveScript">
<!-- hide this script tag's contents from old browsers

// keep track of whether we just computed display.value
var computed = false

function pushStack(form)
{
    form.stack.value = form.display.value
    form.display.value = 0
}

// Define a function to add a new character to the display
function addChar(input, character)
{
    // auto-push the stack if the last value was computed
    if(computed) {
        pushStack(input.form)
        computed = false
    }

    // make sure input.value is a string
    if(input.value == null || input.value == "0")
        input.value = character
    else
        input.value += character
}

function deleteChar(input)
{
    input.value = input.value.substring(0, input.value.length - 1)
```

(continued)

Listing 35.3   Continued

```
}

function add(form)
{
    form.display.value = (0 + form.stack.value) +
form.display.value
    computed = true
}

function subtract(form)
{
    form.display.value = form.stack.value - form.display.value
    computed = true
}

function multiply(form)
{
    form.display.value = form.stack.value * form.display.value
    computed = true
}

function divide(form)
{
    var divisor = 0 + form.display.value
    if(divisor == 0) {
        alert("Don't divide by zero, pal...");
        return
    }
    form.display.value = form.stack.value / divisor
    computed = true
}

function changeSign(input)
{
    // could use input.value = 0 - input.value, but let's show off
substring
    if(input.value.substring(0, 1) == "-")
        input.value = input.value.substring(1, input.value.length)
    else
        input.value = "-" + input.value
}
```

As you saw in the HTML listing above, every button is connected to some function. The addChar() and deleteChar() functions directly modify the contents of the form field named display—the accumulator—as do the operators (add(), subtract(), multiply(), and divide()).

This code shows off some subtle but cool benefits of JavaScript that would be difficult or impossible to do with CGI scripts. First, notice that the divide() function checks for division by zero and presents a warning dialog box to the user.

More importantly, in this example, all the processing is done on the client—imagine an application like an interactive tax form, where all the calculations are done on the browser and only the completed, verified data gets POSTed to the server.

A Note About LiveWire

At the time of this writing, Netscape has announced LiveWire and LiveWire Pro. These two products are intended for Web site providers who want to add JavaScript objects to their servers. Instead of embedding JavaScript in HTML pages and letting the client execute it, these products offer the tantalizing potential to put JavaScript scripts on the server and have them executed in response to client actions.

Unfortunately, the products, though announced, haven't been released, even in beta form, so we don't know exactly what they'll do or how they'll work. Netscape has publically talked about releasing the products sometime in the first quarter of 1996, so we'll have to see.

## CHAPTER 36

Netscape Plug-Ins

With the advent of plug-ins, Netscape 2.0 makes a quantum leap in the Web's possibilities. For the first time, the Web is able to come alive with animation, sophisticated interactivity, and video for a widespread audience, not just in high-tech development labs. Through plug-ins, Netscape users can integrate and access media standards created by other companies, helping to push the Web closer to the envisioned potential of being a truly live, truly real-time, truly interactive conduit to any computer in the world.

Most widely accepted cross-platform media formats are now supported by Netscape plug-ins—if they aren't, they soon will be. These include Macromedia Director, Adobe's Acrobat, and Apple's QuickTime. Netscape plug-ins are not limited to media support, but these are the plug-ins that are going to most radically impact the Web, and are the plug-ins this chapter focuses on.

In this chapter, you learn:

- What Netscape 2.0 plug-ins are
- What plug-ins mean for users, and for programmers
- What plug-ins are currently available, and how to install and use them
- What plug-ins are "coming soon" for Netscape 2.0

What Is a Netscape 2.0 Plug-In?

Plug-ins are feature add-ons designed to extend the capabilities of Netscape 2.0, much the way plug-ins extend the capabilities of other products such as Adobe PhotoShop. In more technical terms, plug-ins are dynamic code modules that exist as part of Netscape's Application Programming Interface (API) for extending and integrating third-party software into Netscape 2.0.

The creation of (and support for) plug-ins by Netscape is significant primarily because it allows other developers to seamlessly integrate their products into the Web via Netscape, without having to launch any external helper applications.

For Netscape users, plug-in support allows you to customize Netscape's interaction with third-party products and industry media standards. Netscape's plug-in API also attempts to address the concerns of programmers, providing a high degree of flexibility and cross-platform support to plug-in developers.

What Plug-Ins Mean for End Users

Because plug-ins are platform-specific, you must have a different version of each plug-in for every operating system you use, such as Windows or the Mac OS. Regardless of your platform, however, Netscape plug-ins should be functionally equivalent across all platforms.

> **Tip**
>
> Many plug-ins ship with the copy of Netscape you purchased, already designed for your platform. However, if you find other plug-ins that you want to either purchase and/or download from the Internet, make sure the plug-in is designed for your specific platform.

For most users, integrating plug-ins is transparent. They open up and become active whenever Netscape is opened. Furthermore, because most plug-ins are not activated unless you open up a Web page that initiates the plug-in, you may not even see the plug-in at work most of the time. For example, after you install the Shockwave for Macromedia Director plug-in, you will notice no difference in the way Netscape functions until you come across a Web page that features Shockwave.

Once a plug-in is installed on your machine and initiated by a Web page, it will manifest itself in three potential ways:

- Embedded
- Full-screen
- Hidden

An *embedded* plug-in appears as a visible, rectangular window integrated into a Web page. This window may not appear any different than a window created by a graphic, such as an embedded GIF or JPEG picture. The main difference between the previous windows supported by Netscape and those created by plug-ins is that plug-in windows can support a much wider range of interactivity and movement, and thereby remain live instead of static.

In addition to mouse clicks, embedded plug-ins may also read and take note of mouse location, mouse movement, keyboard input, and input from virtually any other input device. In this way, a plug-in can support the full range of user events required to produce sophisticated applications.

An example of an embedded plug-in might be an MPEG or QuickTime player, or the Shockwave for Macromedia Director player discussed later in this chapter (see fig. 36.1).

Fig. 36.1
Shockwave for Macromedia Director is an example of an embedded plug-in because it can seamlessly integrate a window within an HTML document.

A *full-screen* plug-in takes over the entire current Netscape window to display its own content. This is necessary when a Web page is designed to display data that is not supported by HTML. An example of this type of plug-in is the Adobe Acrobat viewer.

If you view an Acrobat page using the Netscape plug-in, it pulls up just like any other Web page, but it retains the look and functionality of an Acrobat document viewed in Adobe's stand-alone viewer. For instance, you might find an online manual for a product displayed on a Web site with Acrobat, and you'd be able to scroll, print, and interact with the page just as if it were being displayed by the stand-alone Acrobat Reader program.

A *hidden* plug-in doesn't have any visible elements, but works strictly behind the scenes to add some feature to Netscape that is otherwise not available. An example of a hidden plug-in might be a MIDI player or a decompression engine. A MIDI player plug-in could read MIDI data from a Web page whenever it's encountered, and automatically play it through your local hardware or software (such as QuickTime). Similarly, a decompression engine could function much the way it does on commercial online services, decompressing data in real time in the background, or saving decompression until the user logs off the Internet.

> **Tip**
>
> For more information on Netscape 2.0 plug-ins, point Netscape to **http://home.netscape.com/comprod/products/navigator/version_2.0/plugins/index.html**.

Regardless of which plug-ins you are using, and whether they are embedded, full-screen, or hidden, the rest of Netscape's user interface should remain relatively constant and available. So even if you have an Acrobat page displayed in Netscape's main window, you'll still be able to access Netscape's menus and navigational controls.

What Plug-Ins Mean for Programmers

For programmers, plug-ins offer the possibility of creating Netscape add-on products or using development plug-ins to create your own Internet-based applications. Creating a custom plug-in requires much more intensive background, experience, and testing than actually using a plug-in (such as Shockwave for Macromedia Director). If you are a developer, or are interested in creating a plug-in, the following discussion will be useful.

The current version of the plug-in Application Programming Interface (API) supports four broad areas of functionality. Plug-ins can:

■ Draw into and receive events from a native window element that is a part of the Netscape window hierarchy.

■ Obtain MIME data from the network via URLs.

■ Generate data for consumption by Netscape or other plug-ins.

■ Override and implement protocol handlers.

Netscape plug-ins are ideally suited to take advantage of platform-independent protocols, architectures, languages, and media types such as Java, VRML, and MPEG. While plug-ins should be functionally equivalent across platforms, they should also be complementary to platform-specific protocols and architectures, such as OLE 2.

> **Note**
>
> Netscape Corporation has a wealth of information online for programmers who want to create their own Netscape plug-ins. For starters, you can read the online documentation for the Plug-Ins SDK (Software Developers' Kit) for both Macintosh and Windows at **http://home.netscape.com/comprod/development_partners/ plugin_api/index.html**. You can also download the SDKs themselves from this page.

When the Netscape client is launched, it makes note of any plug-ins available, but does not load any into RAM. This way, a plug-in is only resident in memory when needed, although because many plug-ins may be in use at any one time, you still need to be aware of memory allocation. Plug-ins simply reside on disk until they are needed.

Integration of plug-ins with the Netscape client is quite elegant and flexible, allowing the programmer to make the most of asynchronous processes and multi-threaded data. To further this claim, Netscape makes note of plug-ins based upon the MIME type they support, since all plug-ins are associated with a MIME type not native to the Netscape client. Plug-ins may be associated with multiple MIME types, and Netscape may in turn create multiple instances of the same plug-in.

By allowing many instances of many plug-ins to be readily available, without taking up any RAM until just before the time they are needed, the user is able to seamlessly view a tremendous amount of varied data. A plug-in is deleted from RAM as soon as the user moves to another HTML page that does not require the plug-in.

At its most fundamental level, a plug-in can access a URL and retrieve MIME data just as a standard Netscape client. This data is streamed to the plug-in as it arrives from the network, making it possible to implement viewers and other interfaces that can progressively display information.

For instance, a plug-in may draw a simple frame and introductory graphic or text for the user to comprehend, while the bulk of the data is streaming off the network into Netscape's existing cache. All the same bandwidth considerations adhered to by good HTML authors need to be accounted for in plug-ins.

Of course, plug-ins can also be file-based, requiring a complete amount of data to be downloaded first before the plug-in can proceed. This type of architecture is not encouraged due to its potential user delays, but may prove necessary for some data-intensive plug-ins.

If more data is needed by a plug-in than can be supplied through a single data stream, multiple, simultaneous data streams may be requested by the plug-in, so long as the user's system supports this.

While a plug-in is active, if data is needed by another plug-in or Netscape, the plug-in can generate data itself for these purposes. Thus, plug-ins not only process data, but they also generate it. For example, a plug-in can be a data translator or filter.

Plug-ins are also provided a random access model of network data, via the proposed Byte Range extension to HTTP.

To embed a plug-in in an HTML document, you use the EMBED tag.

The Netscape page at **http://home.netscape.com/comprod/ development_partners/plugin_api/win_avi_sample.html** presents this example: If you were to compile and install the program they present, you'd get a plug-in that can serve as an AVI (Video for Windows) player. You initialize it from your HTML document with the EMBED tag and two parameters, "autostart" and "loop." The autostart parameter specifies whether the AVI movie starts playing right away or whether it waits for user input, and the "loop" parameter dictates whether playback repeats back to the beginning of the movie when the movie finishes. In this example, the EMBED tag in your HTML document might look like this if you wanted to display the AVI file "myavi.avi" in a 320 × 200 window:

```
<embed src=myavi.avi width=320 height=200 autostart=true loop=true>
```

In the example above, the EMBED tag serves as a command line for the plug-in, allowing you to pass different values as parameters. This tag also allows you to specify where in your HTML page the AVI window appears. Of course, you can create larger, even full-screen versions of this plug-in as well by implementing a full-screen plug-in that puts the AVI window in the center of the Netscape window.

Tip

To view actual C++ code for the sample AVI player plug-in discussed here, check out the "NPAVI32.DLL" page on the Netscape Web site at **http:// home.netscape.com/comprod/development_partners/plugin_api/ win_avi_sample.html**.

> **Note**
>
> While creating a plug-in is much easier to do than, say, writing a spreadsheet application, it still requires the talents of a professional programmer. Some third-party developers may soon offer visual programming tools or BASIC environments that provide plug-in templates, making the actual coding of plug-ins much less tedious. However, most plug-ins are, and will be, developed in sophisticated C++ environments, requiring thousands of lines of code.

The Shockwave Plug-In

Perhaps one of the most significant and awe-inspiring plug-ins supported directly by Netscape 2.0 is Shockwave for Macromedia Director, which allows you to view Director "movies" directly on a Web page. Director movies are created with Macromedia Director (don't confuse Director "movies" with other file types of the same name, such as QuickTime movies), a cross-platform multimedia authoring program that gives multimedia developers the ability to create fully interactive multimedia applications, or "titles." Because of its interactive integration of animation, bitmap, video, and sound media, and its playback compatibility with a variety of computer platforms including Windows, Mac OS, OS/2, and SGI, Director is now the most widely used multimedia authoring tool.

> **Note**
>
> Macromedia Director was originally designed as an animation tool, and when it added support for other media and interactive scripting several years ago, it blossomed into the multimedia authoring program designers craved. Director now supports all major types of multimedia and provides a sophisticated scripting language called Lingo.

Using Shockwave, a Director movie run over the Internet can support the same sort of features as a Director movie run off a CD-ROM, including animated sequences, sophisticated scripting of interactivity, user input of text right into the Director window (or "stage"), sound playback, and much more.

Shockwave for Director is not a new authoring environment, in and of itself. It's a collection of three distinct programs:

■ *Afterburner*, a post-processor application that compresses and converts standard Director movies by up to 60 percent for Internet playback. The Afterburner application doesn't alter the way a Director movie appears or behaves, but merely preps it for use on the Internet by compressing it and changing its file format. Users still create Director movies the same way they always have for other applications.

> **Tip**
>
> If you want to convert Director files for use with Shockwave, you can download Afterburner from **http://www.macromedia.com/Tools/ Shockwave/sdc/Dev/AftrbnDC.htm**.

■ *Shockwave player plug-in* (see fig. 36.2), which allows Web browsers such as Netscape 2.0 to play Director movies seamlessly within a Web page. This program is bundled with Netscape 2.0 and is ready to go as soon as you finish the installation procedure. Any Web page that contains a Director movie will automatically play in your Netscape Web browser in the manner prescribed by the Web page.

■ *Shockwave player helper application*, a program that works with any Web browser, but that only allows Director movies to appear in a separate window. This part of Shockwave is only used by Web browsers that don't support Netscape plug-ins or other Shockwave plug-in implementations created by Macromedia.

> **Tip**
>
> Macromedia maintains a treasure trove of pages to aid you in the creation of Director files for viewing with Shockwave on the World Wide Web. Check them out at **http:/ /www.macromedia.com/Tools/Shockwave/sdc/Dev/contents.htm**.

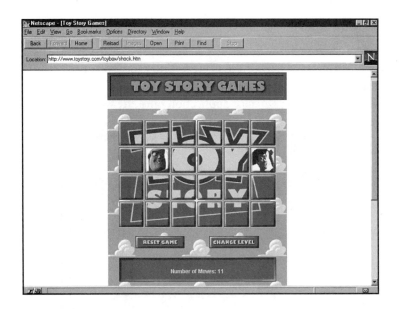

Fig. 36.2
The Shockwave plug-in for Netscape 2.0 plays interactive multimedia Director files inline in the Netscape window. These can range from simple animations to complex interactive games, like this "concentration" game from the Toy Story Web site.

Installing Shockwave

You can download Macintosh and Windows versions of Shockwave from Macromedia's Web site at **http://www.macromedia.com**. Follow the links from its home page to click and download the file using Netscape.

The Windows version is a self-extracting archive file. (The current version as this is written is named sw10b132.exe; it's just a little over 1MB in size.) Using Windows Explorer, you should create a new folder, and then drag the file you downloaded into it. Double-clicking the file in Explorer causes it to self-extract into several files. Make sure Netscape is not running—if it is, close the Netscape window before proceeding. Then double-click the Setup icon to run Shockwave's setup wizard, which installs the plug-in into Netscape for you.

> **Caution**
>
> Make sure you have the latest version of Netscape 2.0 properly installed before you install the Shockwave plug-in, or any other Netscape plug-in. They will not work with earlier versions of Netscape.

Running Shockwave

Like all plug-ins, once it's properly installed, Shockwave runs automatically whenever you encounter a file it can interpret. In Shockwave's case, this means Director files, which usually have a file name extension of .DCR,

.DXR, or .DIR (though you'll never see the file name unless you look for it—downloads are automatic).

When you encounter an embedded Director file, you'll see a "placeholder" in the Netscape window until Shockwave executes it (see fig. 36.3). This is then replaced by the running Director application once the whole file is in place.

Fig. 36.3
Netscape shows this placeholder pattern while a Director file loads.

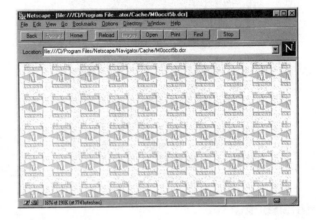

This means that Shockwave doesn't display Director files in real time. Of course, this makes sense because Director files are really interactive multimedia programs that must be run, not mere linear audio and video data streams like RealAudio or QuickTime files. You can't run a Director file before the whole thing is available, since user interaction might result in having to jump to some command near the end of the file. However, movies or audio files that have been embedded in Director files can, themselves be played in real time off the Web using Shockwave.

There are no controls or menus inherent in the Shockwave plug-in. However, many Director files incorporate interactive elements like menus, buttons, and so on. You'll have to trust the file's designer to explain them somewhere on the page or make them intuitive to use.

Macromedia's Web site at **http://www.macromedia.com** includes an entire online gallery full of sample Director files for you to view with Shockwave. They range from simple animations to full-fledged applications, like the Toy Story "Concentration" game shown in figure 36.2. Even a cur-

sory sampling of the files on Macromedia's site should give you a good idea
of the kind of revolutionary content that Shockwave and Macromedia Director are capable of bringing to the Web.

Caution

Because of the relatively rigid conditions under which Shockwave for Director must
operate, there are many special limitations for networked Director movies that do not
apply to standard Director movies. Most of these limitations are due to the fact that
the Director movie must be able to interact with the network and does not have the
luxury of working just within a local environment. For complete information on the
Director architectures, features, and Lingo commands and functions that do not work
with Shockwave, see Macromedia's Web site at **http://www.macromedia.com/
Tools/Shockwave/shock.html**.

Tip

For more information on Shockwave, check out Macromedia's Web site at **http://
www.macromedia.com/Tools/Shockwave/shock.html**. Here you'll find links
to Shockwave Plug-In FAQs, a "What is Director?" page, and the Shockwave for
Director discussion group.

The WebFX Plug-In

Another interesting plug-in is WebFX from Paper Software (see fig. 36.4). This
plug-in works under Windows 95, Windows 3.1, and Windows NT, and gives
you the ability to view embedded VRML data. WebFX is an elegant solution
for anyone interested in providing Web users with a three-dimensional image
or animation.

Virtual Reality Modeling Language is an emerging standard for network-based
3D graphics. Several popular 3D animation programs will now save files in
VRML format, allowing you to easily integrate such work into an HTML page.
WebFX supports multiple VRML windows within the same HTML page, so
you can have multiple 3D environments running at the same time. While
WebFX is fairly fast at rendering images to the screen, the more VRML windows open at once, the slower things are going to run.

◄ See "Using VRML," pg. 491

Some of the features supported by WebFX include:

- Fast and fully compliant VRML 1.0 viewing
- Support for 3D acceleration hardware such as Creative Labs' 3D Blaster
- IRC-based chatting with VRML avatars
- General purpose in-place VRML authoring
- Physics-based navigation with optional collision detection
- Support for common Open Inventor nodes
- Background rendering and parsing
- Multitasking support for viewing multiple worlds at once
- Support for .GIF, .BMP, .RAS, .RGB, and .JPG textures
- Object-oriented user interface with heads up display
- Extensions for collision detection, sound, and animated textures
- Light, camera, and object manipulation
- Multiple nested inlines
- Full GZIP support
- Support for Windows 95, NT, and 3.1, with Mac support coming soon

Fig. 36.4
WebFX lets you view, zoom, and maneuver around 3D VRML objects like this in the Netscape window.

Installing WebFX

You can download WebFX from Paper Inc.'s home page at **http://www.paperinc.com/**. (The current Windows 95 file as this is written is npwfx32d.exe, and it's 2.74MB.) This is a self-extracting archive file, so use Windows Explorer to create a new folder, and then drag the file you downloaded into it. Double-click the file in Explorer to self-extract it into several files. Make sure Netscape is not running—if it is, close the Netscape window before proceeding. Then double-click the Setup icon to run WebFX's setup wizard, which installs the plug-in into Netscape for you.

Running WebFX

WebFX runs automatically whenever Netscape encounters a VRML "world" file (which usually have the file name extension .WRL or .FLR). When this happens, Netscape displays the user interface shown in fig. 36.4.

Controls at the bottom of the screen let you choose to "walk" or "fly" around the 3D model, and pick a preset top, front, or side view. You hold and drag the left mouse button to move in and out and left and right; you hold and drag the right mouse button to spin the world around. Though fairly standard for a VRML viewer, if you're not used to it the user interface can be somewhat tricky. If you get things hopelessly mucked up, you can go back to where you started by selecting reset from the menu.

The right mouse button can also be clicked on the image to access a drop-down menu that duplicates some of the menu commands and adds a few of its own, like turning on or off the "heads-up display" that shows you information about the image you're viewing.

3D objects can also be links. If an object is also a link, its URL will be displayed at the top of the screen, and the mouse pointer will turn into a hand. The VRML language and a viewer like WebFX thus give you the closest thing yet to a sci-fi "cyberspace"-style interface.

Some of the applications you can view with the WebFX plug-in include collaborative virtual worlds, 3D chat rooms, 3D special effects to highlight certain areas of your Web page, virtual walkthroughs of pertinent buildings, and 3D games. Paper Software's Web site at **http://www.paperinc.com/** includes a page of dozens of links to some of the best VRML sites on the Web.

The VDOLive Plug-In

The VDOLive Plug-in for Netscape 2.0 enables inline Video for Windows (.AVI) clips to be included in HTML pages and played back in real time (see fig. 36.5). If you are operating over a slow connection, VDOLive will intelligently download a video file, skipping over enough information to retain real-time playback. While this can result in jerky playback (especially over a slow modem SLIP or PPP connection), it sure speeds up viewing video over the Web!

Fig. 36.5
VDOLive displays video files inline, and can deliver reasonable performance over even a very slow Internet connection.

Autostart, Stretch, Width, and Height options let HTML designers customize inline Web page video for just about any purpose.

Installing VDOLive

You can download the VDOLive plug-in from the VDOLive home page at **http://www.vdolive.com/newplug.htm**. The file (currently called vdoplug32.exe, and only 332KB small) is an executable setup program. Unlike the other plug-ins discussed in this chapter, you don't have to unarchive the VDOLive .EXE file. All you do is double-click it, and it sets up the VDOLive plug-in for you. Things just couldn't be much easier than that. (Other vendors should take a lesson!)

Running VDOLive

VDOLive files automatically play inline when you encounter them. Though not much technical documentation is currently available, a .VDO file is simply a single line of ASCII text, something like this:

```
vdo://URL/filename.avi
```

The only purpose of this file seems to be to let Netscape know that it wants to play a Video for Windows file through VDOLive. The plug-in then takes over, playing the audio and video streams inline in real time, rather than having to download them in their entirety before they can be played.

A single click in the VDOLive display window plays or stops the video, if the autoplay option has not been set by the page designer. If it has been set, the VDOLive file automatically plays when you load the page. (You can restart an autoplay video by clicking the Reload button on the Netscape toolbar.)

There is always a short "preload" of some setup data when you first load a page with a VDOLive video, and then the video and audio start to play. If there is too much data for your connection to handle, VDOLive will intelligently throw enough away to give you as respectable a live feed as possible while maintaining real-time playback. Once you get used to it, viewing VDOLive files over even a very slow Internet feed is not bad. And it's certainly better than waiting dozens of minutes for a video file to download before you see anything at all! While a VDOLive video plays, a status bar in the lower-right corner of the playback window shows you what percentage of the data in the file you're actually receiving (refer to fig. 36.5).

The VDOLive Web site at **http://www.vdolive.com/newplug.htm** has some sample VDOLive format videos you can watch online in real time.

The Acrobat and QuickTime Plug-Ins

There are two other very important plug-ins currently available for Netscape—Adobe has created a plug-in for displaying Adobe Acrobat portable document files, and Apple has developed a Netscape plug-in for viewing QuickTime movies. Both are being distributed by Netscape Corporation as part of their Power Pack CD-ROM for Netscape 2.0 ($54.95).

Complete information on Adobe Acrobat and Apple QuickTime can be found in chapters 19 and 22 of this book.

◀ See "Configuring Netscape for Video," pg. 469

◀ "Adobe Acrobat and Other Portable Document Formats," pg. 551

Other Netscape Plug-Ins

Netscape has announced that there are many other Netscape plug-ins in development. Table 36.1 lists the additional plug-ins that had been announced as of press time.

Table 36.1   Additional Announced Netscape 2.0 Plug-Ins

Company	Plug-In
Asymetrix	Player for Asymetrix multimedia products
Citrix Systems	WinFrame executes Windows applications over the Internet
DSP Group	TrueSpeech player for on-demand audio
Iconovex	AnchorPage automatically indexes and abstracts viewed Web pages
Integrated Data Systems	VRealm VRML viewer
Intervista	WorldView VRML viewer
Johnson-Grace	ART Player decodes *.ART compressed files; compatible with ART Press authoring tool
Kaleida	Kaleida Media Player for ScriptX authoring language
Microsystems Software	Cyber Patrol allows parents and teachers to restrict Internet access by time and URL
Novell	Envoy document viewer
Progressive Networks	RealAudio real-time audio player
RAD Technologies	RAD MediaViewer multimedia player for applications built in RAD PowerMedia
MediaViewer	WebSmart allows new applications to be loaded over the Internet
Sybase	Template Graphics Software (TGS) viewer for Open Inventor 2.x and VRML 1.0
White Pine	CU-SeeMe video conferencing
Xing	MPEG and LBR (low bitrate) audio and full-motion MPEG video

Caution

The principal challenge that multimedia developers need to keep in mind is the speed of the Internet. Most Web users today dial in with modems at speeds between 9600 bps and 28.8 kbps, and these speeds should prevail in the mass market for the next year or two. In addition to these relatively low connection speeds, because the Web is growing so quickly, many users encounter delays caused by unusual network congestion and poor connections at important servers. Many of the most popular Web sites also slow down considerably during peak usage times. And considering all these potential delays, a multimedia application still must deliver the greatest amount of multimedia without making the user wait so long that frustration takes hold.

What's on the Netscape CD

After reading this book you're probably wondering where you can get some of that great software mentioned throughout. Look no further than that shiny compact disc bound in the back of the book. It's the CD-ROM on which we've assembled a collection of shareware, freeware, and commercial software for your experimentation and enjoyment.

How to Use Netscape CD

The CD is set up as a virtual Web site and can be "surfed" like any other site. Using your Web browser, simply open and load the file *Net1.htm* that's found in the root directory. Treat the CD as if it's another Web site and look through the different pages to find descriptions of the software and click the active links to download it to your computer. When the original file has included no information about it, we've linked you to that file's Web site so you can get the information directly from the authors.

The majority of the programs are compressed files; either "zipped" or self-extracting types. The .ZIP files can be decompressed using WinZip, which you'll find on the CD (and, in fact, may be the very first program you choose to download). You can configure Netscape to use WinZip to extract the .ZIP files after downloading (see chapters 16 and 23 for instructions on configuring helpers and decompression). Copy the self-extracting files to your computer's drive and simply extract them by "running" them or double-clicking the file name.

Although a great deal of effort went into putting the latest version of software on this CD we've provided some "hotlinks," links that will take you out to an actual Web site where you can find updated and additional software.

Many of the programs on the CD are shareware, a concept that's not always understood.

The rights to the program are held by the authors who have allowed the program to be widely and freely distributed. This gives you the opportunity to try out the software before deciding to buy it. It also saves them the grief of trying to market their software.

If you like what you see and want to continue using the various shareware programs, you must register with the author as a user of the software. Registering will often (but not always) get you something in return, perhaps a password allowing you to continue using the program after its built-in expiration date, maybe a manual, possibly a full or uncrippled version, phone support, free updates, or any combination of these things. The price is usually reasonable and much, much less than many commercial programs that may not be as good. Meanwhile the authors can continue developing newer and better shareware. For full information about any shareware product be sure to read the text files and license agreements in the documentation that comes with it.

You'll find that some of the software on the disk isn't shareware but *freeware* or possibly *public domain* software. Freeware is software that requires no payment and may be used by anyone (but the author still retains the rights to the program and source code). Software upon which the author has given up all rights has been placed into the public domain, allowing anyone to use or modify it.

If there is any doubt as to the nature of any program please contact the author whose e-mail address is usually listed within the program's documentation.

Compression/Decompression Utilities

- ARJ
- BinHex
- Drag & Zip
- UUCode
- WinCode
- WinZip

E-mail

- Eudora Light
- Pegasus
- WinBiff

FTP/Archie

- FTP Icon Connection
- QVTNet
- Serv-U
- WFTP Daemon
- WS Archie
- WS-FTP

HTML Editors

- Hot Dog Standard
- HoTMetaL
- HTML Assistant
- HTMLed
- HTML NotePad
- HTML Writer
- LiveMarkup
- Webber
- Web Easy/Help
- Kenn Nesbitt's WebEdit

HTML Utilities

- Color Manipulation Device
- HTML Library
- Map This!
- WebForms
- WebMania

Internet Relay Chat

- PowWow
- Visual IRC
- WS-IRC

Internet Utilities

- BCGopher
- CRT
- Drag & File
- Finger
- FingerD
- F-Prot
- Here
- HGopher
- IP Manager
- NetTerm
- NetTools
- QVTNet
- Stiletto
- Trumpet Telnet
- Trumpet Winsock
- WinWais

UseNet Newsreaders

- NewsExpress
- Trumpet News

Viewers

- ACDSee
- Adobe Acrobat Reader
- ColorWiz
- Cool Edit

- Drag & View
- GraphX
- Lview Pro
- MidiGate
- MOD4Win
- MPEGPlay
- PolyView
- Paint Shop Pro
- QuickTime Player
- QuickTime VR Player
- Streamworks
- VuePrint
- WebImage
- WHAM
- WinECJ
- WinJPEG
- WPLANY

VRML

- Fountain

Web Utilities

- Indexer
- NetDate
- WebWatch

Index

checkbox objects (Web page forms), 909
HTML objects, 903, 907-908
JavaScript objects, 902, 921
objects (Web page forms), 908-910
Properties command (Item menu), 214
property sheets (Bookmark Properties General sheet), 212
protocols
ConfigPPP, 92
FTP, 23-24
MacTCP, 89-92
MIME (encoding), 367
NCP, 13
NNTP, 374
POP, 43
PPP, 48-49
Internet connections, 52-53, 73-74
Windows 95 support, 48
S-HTTP, 299
Secure Courier, 296
Shen, 299
SMTP, 43
SSL, 289-291
TCP/IP, 13, 37-41
UUCP, 25
proxies
applications, 98
servers, 277-278
PSD (Adobe Photoshop) graphics, 446
public domain CGI script code, 771-773
public key encryption
Commerce server, 823-827
Netscape implementations, 824-826
public keys, generating for Commerce server, 828-831

Q

Qualcomm (Eudora Web page), 354
Que Web site, 648

Quick Recipients (Eudora Light), addressing e-mail messages, 359-361
QuickTime movies, 477-478
converting to MPEG files, 487
playing with Acrobat Movie plug-in, 559
plug-ins, 947
QuickTime for Windows video drivers, 477-478
viewer applications, 478

R

RADIO attribute, <INPUT> HTML tags, 763
radio buttons (Web page forms), 763
RADIO type, <INPUT> HTML tag, 267
ray-tracing (Web page graphics), 790
reading
e-mail messages with Eudora Light, 362-366
newsgroups, 96, 374, 384-388
README.TXT file (Netscape), 71
RealAudio Player sound file helper application, 434-435
receiving
e-mail messages, 336-337
messages with public key encryption, 823-824
rect region types (imagemaps), 707
referencing imagemaps in HTML, 718-719
regional newsgroups, 373, 379
regional service providers, 47
regions (imagemaps), 707-710
registering
domain names, 46
home pages with Yahoo, 185
registration forms (Web pages), 257-258

Registration Wizard, configuring Netscape Personal Edition, 130-143
relative URL references, 150-151
renaming
bookmarks, 214-215
MIME file types for personal use, 409
repeating actions (JavaScripts), 914-915
replying
to e-mail messages, 336-337
preferences, 324
with Eudora Light, 363-364
to newsgroup articles, 386-388
REQUEST_METHOD environment variable (CGI scripts), 768
requesting digital certificates (public key encryption), 830-836
requests (Web servers), 256-257, 270-271
Requests For Comment, see RFCs
RESET attribute, <INPUT> HTML tags, 268, 764
resetting Web page forms, 764
resolution (Web page graphics), 791-792
resources (Netscape home page), 170-171
restoring SmartMarks catalogs from backups, 251
return statements (JavaScript), 919
reverse Polish notation (RPN) calculators, creating for Web pages with JavaScript, 925
RFCs (Requests For Comment), 8
Rich Text Format (RTF) files, 564
RIFF (Resource Interchange File Format) graphics, 446
ROT13 encoding, 386

X–Y–Z

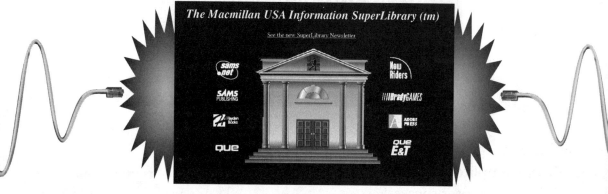

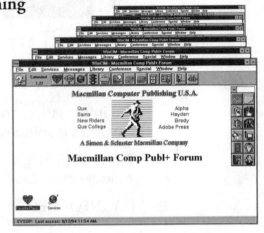

Complete and Return this Card
for a *FREE* Computer Book Catalog

Thank you for purchasing this book! You have purchased a superior computer book written expressly for your needs. To continue to provide the kind of up-to-date, pertinent coverage you've come to expect from us, we need to hear from you. Please take a minute to complete and return this self-addressed, postage-paid form. In return, we'll send you a free catalog of all our computer books on topics ranging from word processing to programming and the internet.

Mr. ☐   Mrs. ☐   Ms. ☐   Dr. ☐

Name (first) ☐☐☐☐☐☐☐☐☐☐☐☐ (M.I.) ☐ (last) ☐☐☐☐☐☐☐☐☐☐☐☐☐☐☐☐

Address ☐☐☐☐☐☐☐☐☐☐☐☐☐☐☐☐☐☐☐☐☐☐☐☐☐☐☐☐☐☐☐

☐☐☐☐☐☐☐☐☐☐☐☐☐☐☐☐☐☐☐☐☐☐☐☐☐☐☐☐☐☐☐

City ☐☐☐☐☐☐☐☐☐☐☐☐☐☐☐ State ☐☐ Zip ☐☐☐☐☐ ☐☐☐☐

Phone ☐☐☐ ☐☐☐ ☐☐☐☐ Fax ☐☐☐ ☐☐☐ ☐☐☐☐

Company Name ☐☐☐☐☐☐☐☐☐☐☐☐☐☐☐☐☐☐☐☐☐☐☐☐☐☐☐

E-mail address ☐☐☐☐☐☐☐☐☐☐☐☐☐☐☐☐☐☐☐☐☐☐☐☐☐☐

Please check at least (3) influencing factors for purchasing this book.

Front or back cover information on book ☐
Special approach to the content ☐
Completeness of content ☐
Author's reputation ☐
Publisher's reputation ☐
Book cover design or layout ☐
Index or table of contents of book ☐
Price of book ☐
Special effects, graphics, illustrations ☐
Other (Please specify): _____ ☐

How did you first learn about this book?

Saw in Macmillan Computer Publishing catalog ☐
Recommended by store personnel ☐
Saw the book on bookshelf at store ☐
Recommended by a friend ☐
Received advertisement in the mail ☐
Saw an advertisement in: _____ ☐
Read book review in: _____ ☐
Other (Please specify): _____ ☐

How many computer books have you purchased in the last six months?

This book only ☐   3 to 5 books ☐
Books ☐   More than 5 ☐

4. Where did you purchase this book?

Bookstore ☐
Computer Store ☐
Consumer Electronics Store ☐
Department Store ☐
Office Club ☐
Warehouse Club ☐
Mail Order ☐
Direct from Publisher ☐
Internet site ☐
Other (Please specify): _____ ☐

5. How long have you been using a computer?

☐ Less than 6 months   ☐ 6 months to a year
☐ 1 to 3 years   ☐ More than 3 years

6. What is your level of experience with personal computers and with the subject of this book?

	With PCs	With subject of book
New	☐	☐
Casual	☐	☐
Accomplished	☐	☐
Expert	☐	☐

Source Code ISBN: 0797-0612-1

Which of the following best describes your job title?

- ministrative Assistant ☐
- ordinator ☐
- nager/Supervisor ☐
- rector ☐
- e President ☐
- esident/CEO/COO ☐
- wyer/Doctor/Medical Professional ☐
- acher/Educator/Trainer ☐
- gineer/Technician ☐
- nsultant ☐
- t employed/Student/Retired ☐
- her (Please specify): _____ ☐

Which of the following best describes the area of the company your job title falls under?

- counting ☐
- gineering ☐
- anufacturing ☐
- erations ☐
- arketing ☐
- les ☐
- her (Please specify): _____ ☐

9. What is your age?

- Under 20 ☐
- 21-29 ☐
- 30-39 ☐
- '40-49 ☐
- 50-59 ☐
- 60-over ☐

10. Are you:

- Male ☐
- Female ☐

11. Which computer publications do you read regularly? (Please list)

_____
_____
_____
_____
_____
_____
_____
_____

mments: _____
_____
_____

Fold here and scotch-tape to ma

II'I'I'I'I''II'I'I'I'I''III''''II'I'I.I.

BUSINESS REPLY MAIL
FIRST-CLASS MAIL PERMIT NO. 9918 INDIANAPOLIS IN

POSTAGE WILL BE PAID BY THE ADDRESSEE

ATTN MARKETING
MACMILLAN COMPUTER PUBLISHING
MACMILLAN PUBLISHING USA
201 W 103RD ST
INDIANAPOLIS IN 46209-9042

NO POSTAGE
NECESSARY
IF MAILED
IN THE
UNITED STATES